Contents

Acknowledgements   vii
Preface to the first edition   ix
Preface to the revised edition   xvii
Introduction   xxi

PART ONE

THE STANDING ARMIES OF SCIENCE : AMERICA

Part One examines the growth of scientific medicine in America, its early battles with homoeopathy and the origins of the American Medical Association. It describes the interaction between government agencies, industry, science and health, then looks at the roles of three organisations. The American National Council Against Health Fraud is an extra-governmental agency which works with industry-connected government agencies like the Food and Drugs Administration. The American Council on Science and Health is an industry funded organisation which publishes pro-industry reports on health risks. The Committee for Scientific Investigation of Claims of the Paranormal (CSICOP), is a pro-industry group which lobbies for science and campaigns against alternative medicine.

Chapter 1   The American origins of scientific
medicine   3

Chapter 2   The beginning of the health
fraud movement   11

Chapter 3   The American National Council
Against Health Fraud   22

Chapter 4   Selling science and industry in America:
The American Council on Science and
Health   37

Chapter 5   The rational idea in a materialist world:
             Committee for Scientific
             Investigation of Claims of the
             Paranormal   48

PART TWO

THE INSURGENTS BEFORE 1989

Part Two looks at the early careers and work of a number of people from different disciplines involved in health care. They are all involved in innovative non-orthodox work, which has brought them under severe scrutiny and critical attack from those with vested interests in science, government or industry. Dr Jacques Benveniste is a French biologist, whose experiments with high dilution substances came under critical attack in 1988. Dr William Rea is an American pioneer in the field of illness created by toxic environments, work for which he has been frequently attacked. The British practitioners introduced in this part of the book were all attacked by the Campaign Against Health Fraud after it was set up in 1989. The detailed stories of these attacks continues in Part Five of the book.

Chapter 6   Dr Jacques Benveniste:
             The case of the missing energy   63

Chapter 7   Clinical Ecology:
             Stratagem for a poisoned world   74

Chapter 8   Dr William Rea:
             Clinical ecologist   89

Chapter 9   Dr Jean Monro:
             Clinical ecologist   99

Chapter 10   Bristol Cancer Help Centre   110

Chapter 11   Industrial food and
             nutritional medicine   132

Chapter 12   Dr Stephen Davies:
             Nutritional doctor   138

DIRTY MEDICINE

Science, big business and the assault
on natural health care

Slingshot Publications
1994

Dirty Medicine
© Martin J. Walker 1993

First published October 1993
Revised edition November 1994
Slingshot Publications
BM Box 8314
London WC1N 3XX

Keywords:
    Alternative and complementary medicine.
    Health-Fraud;
    Pharmaceutical Industry;
    Wellcome plc; AIDS; AZT

Typeset in 10pt Baskerville
By Sandra, Mike, Mona & John

ISBN 0 9519646 0 7

MARTIN J. WALKER

Martin J. Walker was born in 1947 and trained as a graphic designer. Over the last twenty years, he has written books and articles while working as an investigator and research worker. Dirty Medicine is his sixth book. His last book, 'With Extreme Prejudice: a study of police vigilantism in Manchester', was written following an investigation into the cases of two Manchester students who were harassed by the Greater Manchester Police. His other books include: with Geoff Coggan, 'Frightened for my life; an account of deaths in British prisons', published by Fontana. With Jim Coulter and Susan Miller, 'State of Siege; politics and policing in the coalfields. The miners strike 1984', published by Canary Press.

For
Elizabeth

Richard Henriques
and for the many people in this book,
who have had to put up with ridicule and professional
isolation as a consequence of their beliefs, most particularly those
British research workers, therapists, writers and activists who hold
dissident views about AIDS, HIV and AZT: Joan Shenton,
Michael Verney-Elliott, Brian Deer, Neville Hodgkinson,
Cass Mann, Jad Adams and the late Stuart
Marshall.

Chapter 13   Patrick Holford:
The Institute for Optimum Nutrition   147

Chapter 14   Belinda Barnes and Foresight:
Nutrition for two   152

Chapter 15   Robert Woodward and Rita Greer:
Larkhall   160

Chapter 16   AIDS: the plague that made millions.
Cass Mann, Stuart Marshall,
Positively Healthy, Alan
Beck and the Pink Paper   166

Photographs   Dr Jacques Benveniste / Dr Jean Monro
Pat Pilkington and Penny Brohn
Dr Stephen Davies / Patrick Holford
Belinda Barnes / Robert Woodward and
Rita Greer / Cass Mann.

PART THREE

THE STANDING ARMIES OF SCIENCE : BRITAIN

A campaign in defence of science, similar to that in America, has gone on in Britain for some time. Organisations with 'special relationship' links, have exchanged ideas about campaigning with American organisations. The Rationalist Press Association is one of the oldest English humanist organisations; it is linked to the American Humanist Association from which CSICOP grew. The British and Irish Skeptic was a magazine launched by U.K. Skeptics, a small pro-science group set up by the British branch of CSICOP. The last three chapters of this part look at British science and industry lobby groups, associated with food, pharmaceuticals and industrial science. Chapter 20 introduces the Wellcome Foundation and discusses the connection of this transatlantic pharmaceutical company with the health fraud movement and the British government.

Chapter 17   The Rationalist Press Association   189

Chapter 18   British and Irish Skeptics   197

Chapter 19   From the table to the grave:
              The British Nutrition Foundation   203

Chapter 20   Wellcome, Part One:
              A powerful concern   215

Chapter 21   The pollution of science   224

PART FOUR

THE BRITISH CAMPAIGN AGAINST HEALTH FRAUD

The British Campaign Against Health Fraud (CAHF) was launched early in 1989; it had links with many of the organisations already described. CAHF was set up by Caroline Richmond, a medical journalist, and drew together a number of doctors, practitioners and journalists who had often expressed views sympathetic to the pharmaceutical industry, the food industry or science. The one 'outsider' who was to speak in sympathy with the Campaign was Duncan Campbell, a left of centre investigative journalist. Chapter 28 analyses Campbell's changing perspective, which coincided with the beginning of the Concorde trials for the Wellcome AIDS drug AZT.

Chapter 22   Wellcome, Part Two:
              Developing and marketing AZT   239

Chapter 23   Wellcome, Part Three:
              AZT, the domestic market   248

Chapter 24   Caroline Richmond, Part One:
              The chemical agent   264

Chapter 25   Caroline Richmond, Part Two:
              The Richmond way   272

Chapter 26   The Campaign Against Health Fraud,
              Part One: Background
              and beginnings   280

Chapter 27   The Campaign Against Health Fraud,
              Part Two: Early targets   287

Chapter 28   Dr Vincent Marks:
              The company director   297

Chapter 29   Duncan Campbell:
              Sewers surveyed   307

Chapter 30   Professor Michael Baum:
              The trials of a cancer doctor   324

Chapter 31   The Campaign Against Health Fraud,
              Part Three: The players and the game
              1989 - 1991   334

PART FIVE

OVER THE TOP : BATTLES AND SKIRMISHES AFTER 1989

The last part of the book picks up the stories of the practitioners whose early careers and ways of working were examined in Part Two. After the setting up of the CAHF in 1989, all these people, together with a number of others, working mainly in the field of immunology, found themselves under constant attack, in the media and within professional organisations. By the use of a battery of prosecuting agencies and propaganda techniques a large group of practitioners and commentators were criminalised. There were substantial similarities between these attacks and the ones which were being carried out in America.

Photographs   Jabar Sultan/Philip Barker/
               Jad Adams/Dr Leslie Davis/Elizabeth Marsh
               Yves Delatte/Sandra Goodman/Dr Mumby.

Chapter 32   Wellcome, Part Four:
              Colonising the voluntary sector   355

Chapter 33   Fighting the invisible agenda   369

     • Jad Adams. Brian Deer.
      Cass Mann. Positively Healthy
      Alan Beck. The Pink Paper

Chapter 34   Trials of strength:
      Knocking out the opposition   406

     • Joan Shenton and Meditel

     • Dr Sharp, Jabar Sultan, Philip Barker

     • Dr Roger Chalmers, Dr Leslie Davis

     • Yves Delatte, Sandra Goodman,
      Monica Bryant

     • Elizabeth Marsh

Chapter 35   The assault on the
      Breakspear Hospital   507

     • Lorraine Hoskin. Dr Monro.

     • Lorraine Taylor. Liza Ensen.

     • Dr Freed. Dr Mumby

Chapter 36   Mugging the cancer patients   571

     • Bristol Cancer Help Centre

Chapter 37   Attacking healthy nutrition   608

     • Stephen Davies. Patrick Holford.
      Belinda Barnes. Rita Greer and
      Robert Woodward

Chapter 38   Conclusions   639

Chapter references   655
Bibliography   688
List of British and American self-help organisations 703
Index   718

ACKNOWLEDGEMENTS

The investigation which preceded this book was begun when I was contacted by Lorraine Hoskin, a young mother who was determined to find out who had tried to destroy the treatment being given to her daughter. This book would never have been written without her energy and fighting spirit. The writing of the book was sustained by the commitment, faith and support of a wide range of people whom I interviewed or endlessly discussed the book with: Frederica Colfox, Rita Greer, Sandra Goodman, George Lewith and Philip Barker, to name a few. Some of my old friends and new contacts helped with research and gave more time than money allowed: Tim Treuhertz, Sean Waterman, Isla Burke, Paul Clayton and John Ashton.

The period of the investigation was for me a stressful and occasionally frightening period; various people gave me the right kind of support at the right time, first and foremost Elizabeth, and particularly: Peter Chaple, Mike Peters and Tony Price. Two people deserve a special mention, because out of all those who helped me, they were inspirational. Without the ideas, the example and the strengths of Cass Mann and Stephen Davies, the book could not have been finished.

A book is never produced by a single person and this book more than most has been a collective endeavour. The cover to the book took two years to finalise because rather than trust to the considerable abilities of my friend Andy, I kept wanting to take control. I have to thank Ann greatly for the thorough and painstaking voluntary work which she did on the manuscript. She did so much work that sometimes I had to consider whether her name should go on the cover with mine. Sally Gold researched the list of alternative care organisations with such conscientiousness that I feared another book would grow out of it. Dr David Freed, John Ashton and Tim Treuhertz all gave sound editorial advice and support. Three people worked on typing the manuscript, Victoria Colfox, Becky Faith and Ann Webley. All were efficient and aided the progress of the book more than in the simple typing of the manuscript.

Lastly I have to thank all those who helped me with legal, business and financial advice. In the main these people would, I am sure, prefer to remain anonymous. I would however like to particularly thank Phillip Harrison whose two small seeds of help returned such a fine harvest of support for me.

Any mistakes which remain, and there are bound to be some, are entirely my responsibility.

Following the first printing of the book, I have many new people to thank for their commitment. It would be foolhardy to name all the people who have worked hard and conscientiously to see that the first issue was distributed. I must however acknowledge the help, consideration, practical work and commitment to the book shown by Richard Henriques who died in July 1994. His friendship and his wisdom will be missed.

Preface to the first edition

At home, on the evening of Friday June 21st 1991, I picked up the phone and heard a man ask if I were Mr Martin Walker. I asked who was speaking and the voice identified itself as Duncan Campbell – the investigative reporter who brought the Zircon affair to light. 'I understand that you have been carrying out an investigation on behalf of a number of doctors ...'

I hung up. Over the weekend which followed, I picked up the phone twelve times to hear Campbell's stony voice; each time I listened only long enough to get some idea of what he wanted before hanging up. I had, Campbell insisted, to do an interview 'on camera', to contact his research workers and explain myself. 'Who are you working for?' 'Who is paying you?' I had, said Campbell, set up in business as a private investigator in order to spread rumours and make peoples' lives a misery. This was all news to me.

Nearing the end of a year-long investigation into Campbell and his associates, I was all too aware of the portentous nature of these phone calls. On the following Monday afternoon, a well-respected firm of solicitors, whose partners I have occasionally worked for, received a two page fax from Campbell. The fax attempted to destroy my professional reputation; Campbell accused me of stealing documents from the offices of the New Statesman and Society, rifling through the dustbins of his friend and secretary of HealthWatch, Caroline Richmond, and making enquiries about peoples' sexual lives and drinking habits. Perhaps most revealing was the accusation that I had begun to investigate Campbell's own life and that of a 'prominent member of the General Medical Council'. The letter was rounded off with the threat that he would be writing about me in the New Statesman.

In the week following the fax, Campbell incessantly rang the offices of the solicitors, seeking information about me. He rang the senior partner at home, questioning him about a Broadcasting Complaints Commission hearing and one of his clients with whom I had worked. His researchers rang around medical journalists in London to find out whether I had talked to them. The same researchers rang doctors, with whom they imagined I was in contact. Campbell and his researchers spoke to a number of AIDS organisations, warning them about me, spreading rumours about me, and telling workers that I had intimidated and exploited people with AIDS.

On Thursday 27th June 1991, four days after Campbell sent the fax to the solicitors, a group of 'gay activists' demonstrated against Campbell outside the offices of the New Statesman and Society (NSS). These activists accused Campbell and the NSS of censoring health care alternatives for people with AIDS. Following the demonstration, Campbell spoke to a left-wing paper. He told a journalist on that paper that the demonstration outside the NSS offices was:

> *A fake campaign financed by wealthy doctors in private practice who are trying to sell phoney cures and quack remedies.*
>
> *One of the doctors is Jean Monro. She has made millions selling Allergy to the 20th Century. Another two doctors connected to the campaign are Dr Stephen Davies and Dr Alan Stewart, who run a luxury private laboratory off Harley Street, Biolab. Both of these doctors are members of the Cult of Scientology.*
>
> *The three doctors and others hired a private detective over the past six months to try to spread rumours about the sex, private life and alleged drug-industry connections of people who have exposed their malpractice.*
>
> *These people stand truth on its head ... These quacks around Dr Jean Monro exploit people with AIDS.* [1]

Each of these statements, and others made by Campbell to the paper, and to professional workers in the field of AIDS, together with statements made to journalists and doctors and in the fax to the solicitors, were untrue.

Since early 1989, Duncan Campbell and others linked to the Campaign Against Health Fraud (now called HealthWatch), Wellcome, and individuals within the 'AIDS industry' have conducted a crusade, termed by the American journalist John Lauritsen, 'gay McCarthyism'. [2] *This campaign was directed against critics or competitors of the Wellcome-produced drug Zidovudine (AZT) and more generally against those who opposed drug-dependent medicine.*

In the weeks following the phone calls from Campbell, I felt the campaign had become focused upon me. Its worrying effect lingered like a suppuration. There was apparently nothing I could do to stop or contain it. A number of things stood out in my mind as this period began. I checked back mentally on all the interviews that I had carried out with people who had been harassed and maligned by Campbell. For the first time I began to understand why his victims had been forced to move house, leave home, or had come near to breakdown. I too began to feel the deadening effect of the fear that had gripped those who had refused me interviews. Such people had referred to their periods of uninvited relations with Campbell as if they were times of tragedy: circumstances from which they had now recovered, but were still not strong enough to discuss.

I couldn't help but see the irony. This was the investigative journalist who had fought for years against the intrusive shadow of state surveillance.

In retrospect, I am glad that Campbell decided to harass me, if only briefly, and especially glad that he did so just as my investigation was coming to an end. He helped me to resolve a number of conflicts. Had it not been for the heady madness of the twelve phone calls and what followed, I might have lacked the complete identification with others whom Campbell had 'investigated'.

* * *

This book is the result of a two-year investigation. I was first asked to provide background material on the Campaign Against Health Fraud (CAHF) late in 1989. My report was finished in two months. I did not resume the investigation until I was approached a year later in November 1990, by a group of people who had been 'attacked' by the Campaign, which by then had changed its name to HealthWatch.

My first short investigation developed quickly from an examination of CAHF to cover a conflict which had divided the gay community in London. The conflict centred upon the right of people who were HIV antibody positive, or had AIDS, to choose their own treatment and be given the full information about the Wellcome-manufactured AIDS drug AZT. Those who had faith in the pharmaceutical companies and medical orthodoxy supported the prevailing medical research establishment in its propagation, testing and prescription of AZT. Others, wary of apparent medical altruism, and previous iatrogenic disasters, began to organise self-empowering treatment and therapy programmes. In the main, they did this by making information available on non-pharmaceutical treatments.

My first investigation showed that when a small number of gay men and alternative medical practitioners tried to minister to their own community, they were immediately labelled 'quacks'. AZT often appeared to be at the centre of these conflicts.

The conflicts around AZT and AIDS treatment were located within a much more extensive terrain of struggle involving alternative medicine, the processed food industry and the pharmaceutical companies. When I began to explore this wider landscape, keeping the Campaign Against Health Fraud firmly in sight, I found it difficult to orientate myself.

Why was a 'health-fraud' campaign aiming at health food products and progressive nutritionists? Why was a 'health-fraud' campaign attacking qualified doctors who, after years of orthodox practice, had made the decision to practise a non-pharmaceutical approach? Perhaps most confusing of all: should not a health-fraud campaign called HealthWatch be critical of the food industry and agribusiness over such things as additives and pesticides? Why was HealthWatch attacking those therapists and scientists who thought that the destabilisation of our natural environment was making us ill? Why was this particular 'health-fraud' campaign focusing on immunologists and those non-orthodox practitioners who might treat AIDS or cancer sufferers?

In this book, I have tried to answer some of these questions, although even I have to admit that the route to my conclusions seems on occasions tenuous. This is not due to any lack of intellectual rigour on my part, but more to do with the fact that my investigation only scratched the surface of a powerful and extensive underworld spawned by big business. It will be some time before we are able to understand fully and record in detail the present period of crisis and the shifts in paradigm which have thrown up the surveillance, sabotage, harassment and fraud which are increasingly becoming an everyday part of commercial competition.

In the last months of writing, three unrelated things affected me, forcing me to focus my mind more sharply on the importance of finishing the book.

On May 6th 1992 in the United States, the surgery and the laboratory of a well-respected nutritionist and doctor, Jonathan Wright, was raided by officers of the Federal Food and Drug Administration (FDA). The clinic was surrounded and then stormed by armed police officers. Clinic employees were made to raise their hands and stand against the wall, while officers pointed guns at them. Fourteen hours after the raid began, the FDA and accompanying police officers had stripped Dr Wright's laboratory and surgery of all its patient records, equipment, vitamin and mineral supplement preparations. [3]

Coincidentally, at around the same time, I received a call from a doctor and research scientist in Europe. Much of his work has concentrated upon chemical food additives and their effect upon the immune system. From 1986, he has been the victim of threats from an unknown source. An anonymous caller tried to lure him to a meeting in another country; when he checked the address with the country's embassy he found that it did not exist. Phone calls threatened his life and that of his partner. Anonymous letters to his local tax office falsely claimed that he had assets in Swiss accounts.

Again in May, I read Christopher Bird's book, which narrates the criminal trial, in Canada in 1989, of the renowned cancer scientist, Gaston Naessens. [4] In a re-run of the charges brought in the sixties against Dr Josef Issels, the German cancer doctor, Naessens was charged with having caused the death of a woman to whom he gave treatment. Like Issels, Naessens was exonerated. His acquittal did not however diminish the terror, suffering or social destruction which such a case brings. Bird's book and the case it describes address a matter of growing importance – the developing legal power of orthodox scientific medicine.

* * *

This book was difficult to structure because the investigation from which it grew covered many diverse areas of health practice. It is not a book with a simple or linear message. I have tried to create a narrative running from beginning to the end, but I realise that in places it is interrupted and is unlikely to engage the attention of many readers from start to finish.

The book is divided into five parts. Part One looks at the growth of scientific medicine and the history of health-fraud campaigns in America. It lays the basis for understanding the role of Rockefeller interests in defending orthodox medicine and scientific research.

Part Two examines in detail the early training and practices of some of the therapists who were 'attacked' by the health-fraud campaign in Britain. It follows their careers up until 1989. The story is taken up again in Part Five of the book which details attacks upon them after 1989.

Part Three looks at the British science lobby and its relationship to industry.

Part Four traces the historical conflict between orthodox and complementary medicine in Britain, and deals with the beginnings and growth of the London-based Campaign Against Health Fraud. It outlines the careers of the campaign's major activists. Included in this section is an analysis of the Wellcome Foundation and Trust with particular emphasis on the licensing, manufacture and sale of AZT.

Part Five picks up on the stories of those practitioners whose work was discussed in Part Two.

Given the relative complexity of the book, its large number of subjects and lack of continuous narrative, some readers may prefer to read sections separately.

I structured the book as I did, because I felt that the information was most accessible when presented in this way. I reasoned that readers would want to become familiar with the individuals and practitioners involved in alternative medicine before they read about the attacks mounted against them.

* * *

Words are often an inadequate means of communication. In this book, I have frequently found myself using terms which do not describe what I wish to say. Much of the underlying discourse in the book is about science. Often this is not however a pure or noble science but a corrupted science, one which serves profit rather than truth.

Scientific medicine does not always reflect the highest standards of medicine and is sometimes not at all scientific. On the other hand some of the research carried out into the basis of such things as homoeopathy and acupuncture has been high quality science.

Despite these contradictions, I have had to use the word science. I could have appended 'bad' to the word in some contexts or I could have called it pseudo-science, or something similar. I did not do this. Although it is not stated, on some occasions when I use the word science I am referring to a corrupted 'industrial science' or 'vested interest science'. I hope that people will be able to read between the lines.

The other concept which is referred to throughout the book is 'health fraud'. Naturally we are all against fraud of any kind, at the least it robs us of our expectations and at worst deprives us of our innocence. We might disagree about the prevalence of fraud in health care, but we are all against it.

While investigating and researching this book, I came across very little deliberate health fraud amongst alternative or complementary practitioners. Those practitioners who are not effective in their work are rarely fraudsters, more often they are naive but sincere individuals who would accept regulation if the matter were discussed. On the other hand, very real fraud in science, industry, business and research is increasing. In these areas, the intent of the fraudster is often blatantly criminal and their actions utterly unaccountable.

Part of this book is about the British Campaign Against Health Fraud and the American National Council Against Health Fraud. I hope that it will become clear to readers that I do not believe these organisations are using the term 'health fraud' in its generally accepted sense. If anything, those whom they tar with the brush of fraud are involved in nothing more than fair competition with orthodox medicine or medical research. Such organisations have however stolen the moral high ground, by incorporating 'against health fraud' in their titles.

One of the book's proof readers suggested that whenever the title 'Campaign Against Health Fraud' was used in the book, it should be prefixed by 'so-called' or 'self-styled'. This would have been impossibly clumsy. Instead, I have tried wherever possible to hyphenate 'health-fraud' and miss out the prefix 'anti' or 'against'. Where reference is made to the specific campaigns, readers will just have to bear in mind that I do not think that their titles befit their true aims.

There are two other circumstances where the casual use of words has proved difficult, both come from the lexicon of AIDSspeak. The most popular description of Wellcome's drug AZT is, an 'anti-AIDS drug'. I do not subscribe to the view that AZT is an anti-AIDS drug and feel that more probably it will prove to be an AIDS drug, so I have described it in this way.

The retrovirus HIV is usually spoken of in the same breath as the complex of illness which are called AIDS; people will say, 'HIV the AIDS virus', or of someone 'he was diagnosed HIV and then developed AIDS'. I think that the jury is still out on whether a virus known as HIV is causally related to AIDS. I am however certain that the condition called AIDS is not solely the product of a virus and therefore think that it is misleading to refer to HIV as *the* AIDS virus.

I have also tried hard to avoid suggesting that people have been diagnosed as having the HIV retro-virus, simply because no one is actually tested for the virus. Rather they are tested for the presence of antibodies to the virus. Because there is a body of opinion which says that if a person has antibodies then the virus itself is not a danger, I have made a point of saying that the test shows a person to be 'HIV antibody positive' rathert than 'HIV positive'.

In relation to AIDS, this semantic battleground is of great importance. There can be no doubt that certain people and institutions have created an enormously powerful construct in AIDS. This construct however often lacks scientific verification. As in war or under a totalitarian regime, language rather than verifiable facts has shaped our understanding of the illness.

Preface to the revised edition

Since the first printing of this book in October 1993, its distribution in Britain has faced considerable opposition. This opposition has come almost exclusively from the journalist Duncan Campbell. From the time of the book's post-publication launch, Campbell has campaigned ceaselessly, through his solicitors, Bindman and Co., and through his own enterprises to stop the book's distribution. He has sent long legal letters threatening anyone who distributed or wrote about the book with libel actions.[1] He threatened the Finnish printers of the first edition, WSOY, with a libel action: they immediately withdrew from any involvement in a second printing.

After writing a biased and defamatory account of a number of people whom I had defended in the book, in an *Observer* supplement,[2] Campbell threatened the paper when it printed replies refuting his article. The 'liberal' *Observer* was apparently so concerned that it paid Campbell an undisclosed sum thought to be in the region of £8,000, in an out of court settlement. Despite spreading rumours to the contrary, Campbell did not take any legal action against either myself or Slingshot Publications.

I had expected that *Dirty Medicine* would be marginalised, principally because it dealt in some detail with the Wellcome Foundation and the marketing of their drug AZT. There were however no attacks upon me or the book from any pharmaceutical companies or members of HealthWatch, the other organisation investigated in the book. Campbell's response to the book was peculiarly personal. Unable to cope with an open debate about his journalistic practices, he resorted to personal insults and outrageous accusations of moral opprobrium. With his outbursts, Campbell tried to reduce the book to that small part which is about him and reduced the discourse it contains to an unseemly personal squabble between two investigative writers.

I do not have, nor have I ever had, personal views about Duncan

Campbell; in writing *Dirty Medicine* I was most concerned to highlight
the historical struggle between natural and orthodox medicine and
chart the ascendancy of professional power within medicine. The
power of the drug companies and medical practitioners aligned with
high technology science, the desperate and disgusting scramble for
profits over diseased bodies and the consistent and corrupt assault
upon natural treatments, in Britain and America, are important
ingredients of a contemporary story. When Duncan Campbell is long
forgotten, future generations will still be having to make choices about
how to care for their health and whether or not they wish to be
subjugated to the totalitarian power of the medical establishment and
the drug monopolies.

The object of my book was from the beginning general and
political: it sought to defend those who had been unjustly attacked and
warn those whose choices were being eroded. Because it was never my
intention to become embroiled in a personal conflict with Duncan
Campbell, readers of this new edition of *Dirty Medicine* will find a
number of changes. Using Bindman's legal letter as a guide, I have
changed nearly all of the forty odd statements to which Campbell took
exception. I do not imagine for a moment that making these changes
will alter Campbell's response to the book, quite obviously he would
prefer that I had not written about him at all.

Looking back on the book now, a year after its publication, I realise
that it has serious faults. Like many others writing in this field, I find
now that I did not pay due respect to those who have written before
me. Since publishing the book, I have 'discovered' Hans Ruesch[3] and
the ground breaking work of Morris Bealle.[4] I was, at the time of the
first printing, acutely aware that I had failed to make clear the link
between Rockefeller medical philanthropy and the Rockefeller
interests in pharmaceuticals. Thanks to Bealle, I shall now be able
to rectify this in a much shorter, specifically American issue of the
book hopefully to be published in the spring of 1995.

In some ways I do not care that *Dirty Medicine* has been
marginalised. There is something very comforting about being in
the company of such fiercely independent investigative writers as
Ruesch and Bealle. For these are people of whom it can genuinely be
said that their thesis has not been corrupted by financial inducements
or the degenerative fast-track to intellectual stardom.

One of the reasons *Dirty Medicine* has been marginalised is that it reaches within that problematic area, deserted by most academics and respected journalists, belittlingly termed 'conspiracy theory'. I believe that theories of conspiracy are acceptable post-modern ways of recounting late twentieth century history. In fact, the large scale histories or sociologies of late twentieth century society, with its many secretive and competing power networks and its government against the people, could hardly be written up within any other framework. Unlike the citizens of earlier societies, we have very little information about power and we are consequently left to make assumptions. It would never cross my mind to wonder whether it was true that large multinational drug companies place individuals under surveillance, tap their phones or illegally enter their premises, set up front organisations or publish untruthful research data, for I know that such things have become common practice in a post-industrial free-market economy. To prove such things in a specific cause and effect manner is almost impossible; for this reason many people writing in this area work on the basis of assumptions which others unkindly call 'conspiracy theories'.

Inevitably, being called a 'conspiracist' makes one insecure. It is then always a relief when events prove you right. I was somewhat consoled when I heard recently that London's Metropolitan Police Complaints Investigation Bureau (CIB_2) has for some time been carrying out an investigation into the use by big-business and government departments of firms of private investigators. I understand that there have already been a number of arrests, including staff from British Telecom, police officers, civil servants and private investigators. Clearly those individuals I have written about, who suffered invasions of their privacy, had their mail intercepted, were fearful that their phones were tapped, or their property had been burgled, should make representations to CIB_2. They should also get together and press for an open, public, legal tribunal which will make public the names of the large companies involved in these illegal competitive strategies.

Following on from *Dirty Medicine*, I am about to begin researching a book about health and pollution. I should be glad to hear from anyone interested in publishing such a book and from those who would like to send funding, references, research material or accounts of personal case histories. There are pages at the back of the book outlining this next project.

Martin J. Walker
London, October 1994.

1. Letter from Bindman & Partners, Solicitors. 1 Euston Road, King's Cross, London NW1 2SA, to distributors of *Dirty Medicine*, February 1994. Copies obtainable from Slingshot Publications.
2. Campbell, Duncan. Health and Safety, Uncensored. *Observer* April 17 1994. Copies obtainable from Slingshot Publications.
3. Ruesch, Hans. *Naked Empress: The Great Medical Fraud*. CIVIS. 1986. Switzerland.
   Ruesch, Hans. *Slaughter of the Innocent*. Civitas 1991. USA.
4. Bealle, Morris A. *The Drug Story*. Columbia Publishing Company. 1949. Washington.
   Bealle, Morris A. *The House of Rockefeller*. Columbia Publishing Company. 1954. Washington.

Introduction

We live on the cusp of unbelievable change. The era of industrial production and the mass society which it created is coming to an end. The evolutionary necessity of the industrial revolution created enormous problems. The new means of production, the factories, belched out pollution and filled the air with chemical toxins. The noisy metal machines imposed upon their operatives the anonymity of yet another part of that machine.

Contemporary Western society is a product of that industrial revolution. The monumentally rewarding ideas which gave birth to it, concepts of rationalism and scientific enquiry which were to free the human body from its travail of work, were twinned with the debilitating effects of the new industry, effects which were inseparable from it. Nowhere was exempt from this maelstrom of the machine: from the depths of the sea to the bowels of the earth, to the planet's poles, the effluents of the new riches permeated everything.

The science which accompanied the industrial revolution was a science which grew from engineering, the making of metal machines. It was locked irrevocably into the understanding of industrial production. Science re-created a structure of knowledge which was itself based upon knowledge of the machine. The new science fought ceaselessly with the older and often religious ideologies through which people had previously understood their condition. From the beginning of the nineteenth century in Europe and America, the dominant ideology, of the most powerful groups, came to be based upon science.

Chemistry and medical science were intimately allied to the process of industrialisation. For the first time in the history of healing, medical practitioners divided up the body into its smallest functioning parts. With this came the separation of bodily functions from the life which those functions maintained. The whole ceased to be greater than the sum of the parts. This dissection of the body exorcised the being's inner self.

As the industrial revolution advanced, it was accompanied by the complete separation of objective science and the subjective consciousness of the scientist. Medical science and its teaching forbade, at the risk of exile, the involvement of the non-scientific mind of either the doctor or the patient in the mechanics of healing. It was to be as if one machine operated upon another.

The society which grew with the industrial revolution was a mass society. The individual of the eighteenth century was gradually displaced by the collective power of the nineteenth. In medicine particularly, the older individual-based art of healing, which depended upon the specific relationship between the healer and the sick individual, was crushed by machine-based medicine. It was not until Freud and psychoanalysis that medicine was confronted again with the idea that individuals might be essentially, if sensitively, different. By that time, however, it was too late for the mechanised world which science had created to divert its energies and cater for individually specific treatments. The pharmaceutical remedy had already been invented, and this was a remedy for the masses. The barbiturate paid no heed to the individual's history nor the idiosyncracy of their dreams. Like a hammer blow, it sent all into the same deep and unreasoning sleep.

The period of post-industrial production began in the latter part of this century. Like all new epochs, it came quietly at first, heralded by almost unnoticed changes in the means of production. Profit no longer needed the great machines of the industrial revolution. Their demise gave birth to cleaner machines, able to create even greater but less visible power.

A revolution in the method of production changes everything, even our ideas and our relationships. The change which is upon us now, from material power to invisible information-based power, is a vortex. It is passing over the globe leaving nothing unquestioned. The new post-industrial social relations affect all aspects of our lives. In the most conservative and power-based sciences the transition from the old physically based knowledge to the new more imaginative age has been hard won. The knowledge of the sciences which grew out of the industrial revolution consisted of immutable abstractions welded to social power. This power will not be transcended without a way of life coming to an end.

Those who hold this power will hang on like grim death.

PART ONE

The Standing Armies of Science: America

*Even the G-men of the F.B.I. were
touched by the image of the scientific investigator
who operates with a deadly detachment and laboratory
efficiency, and science came thus to be invoked by
Americans to preserve them from subversives
within as well as from enemies without.*

Max Lerner. America as a civilization.

*The Rockefellers own
more than half of the pharmaceutical
industry in America.*

Duncan Roads. Nexus New Times

Chapter One

The American Origins of Scientific Medicine

Powerful medical drugs easily destroy the historically rooted pattern that fits each culture to its poisons; they usually cause more damage than profit to health, and ultimately establish a new attitude in which the body is perceived as a machine run by mechanical and manipulating switches. [1]

There has been a continuous struggle between allopathy† and other kinds of medicine ever since allopathy began its ascendancy in America and Europe in the late eighteenth century. American medical orthodoxy throughout the first half of the nineteenth century consisted of homoeopathic and herbal practices used mainly by the rural population. The first homoeopaths came from Germany and settled in America in the 1820s. [2] Their medical practice spread quickly throughout the 1830s and 1840s.

Despite the fact that allopathic medicine practised many forms of treatment, such as bleeding, which were later found to have no scientific foundation, allopaths maintained a sublime confidence in their professional discipline. The insistence of homoeopaths that they could treat the whole person, and their assertion that they could deal with not only the physical but also the emotional and spiritual, left them open to accusations of religious mysticism. Allopathic physicians

---

† Allopathy is the name given to orthodox scientific medicine introduced in Europe following the Enlightenment. Allopathic treatment counters illness with a treatment which opposes the illness, in doing this it usurps the function of the body's own immune system. Homoeopathy, on the other hand, which is the opposite of allopathy, counters illness with a remedy which produces the same symptoms as the illness and so strengthens the body's own immune system. Allopathy has come to be the prevailing orthodox medical practice in America and Europe.

first began to dominate in the large urban areas in the middle of the century, and from their élite cosmopolitan position they waged a constant war against homoeopaths whom they labelled as 'quacks'. [3]

Those doctors who were brave enough to make public their practice of homoeopathy were expelled from the growing state medical societies. One of the arguments most frequently used by allopaths against homoeopaths was that they charged large amounts of money for treatment. On the whole at this time, salaries for allopathic physicians were low, and there was a need for them to develop some kind of strategy for wage protection. The criticism of homoeopaths would appear to have been part of such a strategy.

One way in which higher standards and therefore higher esteem could be introduced to the allopathic profession was by rationalisation. The National Medical Convention of 1847 brought the American Medical Association (AMA) into being. The AMA was to be the body most responsible for protecting and professionalising the status of allopathic doctors. Lurking behind many of the professional desires of the allopaths was their confident belief in the universal correctness of science. They were sure that the intellectual rigours of science, especially in medicine, would bring to an end previous 'irrational' and empiricist forms of healing.

From the beginning, the AMA was a tool of allopathic medicine, set up to defend its professional status. Morris Fishbein, the first Chairman of the AMA and editor of the AMA Journal, wrote two books which refuted homoeopathy and other forms of 'quackery'.†

The leading light in the formation of the American Medical Association in 1847 was Dr Nathan Smith Davis, who has been described as 'a bitter foe of homoeopathy'. [4] Davis joined the New York Medical Society's anti-quackery committee immediately after graduation and fought what he considered medical quackery throughout the rest of his life.

The AMA not only drew the allopathic profession together, it also shielded them from lay criticism or any attempt at public participation in health care and medicine. The first code of practice laid down by

---

† *Fads and Quackery in Healing: An analysis of the Foibles of the Healing Cults, with essays on various other peculiar notions in the health field*, in 1932. *The Medical Follies; An Analysis of the Foibles of Some Healing Cults, including Osteopathy, Homoeopathy, Chiropractic*, in 1925.

the AMA stated clearly that the patient's view was not to be entertained: 'The obedience of a patient to the prescriptions of his doctor should be prompt and implicit.' Another rule in the code of ethics warned that patients should not permit their 'own crude opinions' to influence attention to treatments given them by doctors. [5]

Attempts by the AMA to use its developing corporate power to curtail the influence of homoeopaths and any other non-allopathic practitioners began soon after the Association had been formed. In the early years it ordered all local medical societies to expel homoeopaths.

Although the reform of medical education and the rationalisation of the profession were two of the main objectives of the AMA from its inception, little was achieved until the first decades of the twentieth century.

Rockefeller : Patron of Scientific Medicine

> For the first quarter of the twentieth century the Rockefeller officers developed a definite strategy for their capital investment in medicine. The strategy sometimes supported and often opposed different interests in medicine, but such alliances and conflicts were never accidents on the part of the foundation. [6]

In the last quarter of the nineteenth century, 'scientific medicine' – the more rational aspect of allopathy aligned with fast developing scientific research technology – began to make headway in America. It was a concept which was taken up very quickly by both the allopathic professional élites and industry. This marriage of medicine and industry was particularly apt because in the practice of allopathy neither the mind, the emotions nor the soul, were involved in any degree as causal agents in illness or its treatment. Such reductionistic material theories of the person were a perfect adjunct to the material theories of engineering which had produced the wealth for the new industrial middle class.

As the AMA moved into the twentieth century, it sought and secured the backing of major industrial foundations which saw profit for themselves in the rapidly developing field of medical science. The profit which industry hoped to gain from medical science was not only financial nor just related to the advancement of mutually advantageous technology and chemistry. The greatest profits would come from an idea which was then merely a glimmer in the eye of industry. The welfare and the control of the human body and its processes were throughout the first half of the 20th century a matter of vital importance to industrialists. Before the development of sophisticated machinery, the human body was the essential link in the process of industrial production.

The most important patron of scientific medicine in America, and consequently throughout the world, in the twentieth century has been the Rockefeller family. John D. Rockefeller's millions came originally from his oil empire. By the end of the nineteenth century he was keen to offload some of his wealth into charitable and educational causes. When his money first intervened in the world of medicine, whatever his own personal intention, the result was the consolidation of the growing partnership of medicine and industry.

Rockefeller's money, and ultimately his Foundation, enabled a new generation of professional managers to modernise and rationalise the American medical model. The new model was one which leant heavily towards industry and biological research while utilising copious quantities of synthetic pharmaceuticals. This rationalisation was carried out in partnership with the AMA.

In 1892, John D. Rockefeller brought in Frederick T. Gates to manage his philanthropy. Gates quickly became not only manager of the philanthropic aspects of Rockefeller's fortune, but also his investment manager, in charge of all his interests outside of Standard Oil. [7]

It was Gates, and later Rockefeller's son, who from the turn of the century onwards were to determine the direction of Rockefeller philanthropy. After graduating, John Rockefeller Jnr. went to work with Gates. From that time, the independent administration of Rockefeller's money was gradually taken out of his hands. His individualistic and idiosyncratic philanthropy was replaced by a corporate plan based upon materialism and scientific development.

Rockefeller's original donations to the Baptist church and his lifelong belief in homoeopathy [8] were superseded by a concentration on science. He had argued that his philanthropy should deal equitably with homoeopathy but this view was vehemently opposed by Frederick T. Gates. Gates constantly pressed for Rockefeller's philanthropy to support a new age of 'scientific medicine'. 'We are in the interesting period of founding a great new science. Of that science you, perhaps more than any other single man, are entitled to be called the financial father.'[9]

In 1907, the AMA began to rationalise medical education. The Council on Medical Education, an AMA body, surveyed all schools, allopathic, homoeopathic and eclectic, and gave them a rating score. Because so many schools questioned their rating, the Council asked the Carnegie Endowment for the Advancement of Teaching to report on the matter. At this time Rockefeller interests already had considerable influence within the Carnegie Foundation. In 1908, Carnegie appointed Abraham Flexner who, accompanied by a member of the AMA, Dr N. P. Colwell, surveyed all the medical schools in America. This survey culminated in the Flexner Report. [10]†

The Flexner Report set an absolute standard for medical education in America, absolute because those schools which its on-going assessment found wanting were denied the right to award meaningful professional qualifications by state examining boards. By the end of the First World War, the number of medical schools in America had been reduced from 650 in the first decade of the century to 50. [12] Flexner's cuts, however, fell disproportionately on those colleges and schools which gave places to poorer whites, blacks or women. The Flexner Report advised the closure of all three of the women's medical schools, and all but two of those which catered solely for black people. Consequently, the effect of the Flexner Report was not only academic: disproportionate cuts meant that medical care for affected groups dropped drastically. [13]

Following the Flexner Report, Rockefeller joined with Carnegie to begin funding medical education. In doing so, the Foundation adopted the philosophy of the Flexner Report . Within a decade, the AMA had achieved total control over the administration of medical education, and had also found the necessary support for the scientific development of allopathic medicine.

---

† The links between the Carnegie Foundation and the Rockefeller empire are illustrated by the fact that Abraham Flexner's brother Simon was head of the Rockefeller Institute of Medical Research, while Abraham Flexner himself served for a number of years on Rockefeller's General Education Board. Another Flexner brother, Bernard, later became a founding member of the Council on Foreign Relations and a Trustee of the Rockefeller Foundation. [11]

Within a year following the report's publication, the General
Education Board entered the fray in earnest. By 1920, the GEB
had appropriated nearly $15 million for medical education and
by 1929 a total of more than $78 million. By 1938 contributions
from all foundations to medical schools exceeded $150 million. [14]

Rockefeller and Carnegie began immediately to shower
hundreds of millions of dollars on those better medical schools
that were vulnerable to control. Those that did not conform
were denied the funds and the prestige that came with those
funds, and were forced out of business. [15]

After the publication of the Flexner Report, the Carnegie Foundation
was pleased to be associated with the growing AMA, but by 1913
conflicts emerged when it became apparent that the AMA was using
the Flexner Report to pursue racist policies in medical education. The
Carnegie Foundation, like the Rockefeller Foundation, had previously
poured resources into black education of all kinds, believing that black
leaders should be educated. The AMA, however, operated a policy of
professional discrimination against black people, and was only finally
forced to admit them late in the 1950s.

The Flexner Report represented the beginning of industrial control
over medicine in America. Control over medical education ultimately
meant control of the content and direction of research. The Carnegie
and Rockefeller Foundations were by this time absolutely sure of
where they needed to take medicine. They wanted a highly scientific
medicine, based upon biological research and technology.

Since 1910, the foundations have 'invested' over a billion dollars
in the medical schools of America. Nearly half of the faculty
members now (1974) receive a portion of their income from
foundation 'research' grants, and over sixteen per cent of them
are entirely funded this way. [16]

As most of the major foundations which grew up in the first half of this
century were based upon the petro-chemical industry, financial
patronage for medicine primarily supported allopathic and pharmaceutical treatments. Other major foundations which subsidised, and
therefore had some control over, American medicine throughout the
twentieth century include the Ford Foundation (motor cars), the
Kellogg Foundation (cereals), the Commonwealth Fund (created by

Edward Harkness of Standard Oil), the Sloan Foundation (General Motors), and the Macy Foundation.

In 1915 the Rockefeller Institute was set up, intent upon rivalling the Pasteur Institute in France and the Koch Institute in Berlin. Both of these institutes were completely given over to the study of scientific medicine. In 1928, a single Rockefeller Foundation was established. It had five divisions and a new strategy of concentrating effort on the life sciences.

By the time of the Second World War, the Rockefeller business empire was co-operating with a large number of other pharmaceutical holding companies in a cartel arrangement which was headed by Rockefeller and the massive German chemical combine I.G Farben. [17]

Following the Second World War, the US Congress passed a number of public health statutes, which ushered in a weighty health care and research bureaucracy under the umbrella of the National Institutes of Health (NIH). As with many of the American federal bureaucracies, the NIH was closely aligned with big business. Between 1955 and 1968, its budget grew to over $1 billion. [18] Much of the money continued to be spent on the reductionist sciences like molecular biology.

> The effect of the lavish support of research in the 1950s and 1960s was to build up a cadre of highly specialised experts, grouped together in universities and medical schools, and the categorical institutes of the NIH, with a broad, long term relation to hospital-based, technologically intensive clinical medicine, practiced and made available within a system which perpetuated massive inequalities of access to health care. [19]

For over half a century the Rockefeller Foundation determined the direction and the content of medical research, without competition. Both before and after the Second World War, Rockefeller money washed around Europe, helping scientists to travel and hold conferences, providing equipment and laboratories for major European institutes after the war. [20]

From the beginning, the support of scientific medical research by industry meant that the responsibility for disease was placed within the internal biological structure of the individual organism. In terms of illness, at least, the individual became separated from their environment and the industrial process, both of which were inevitably seen by the large industrial foundations as benign. This view stood in sharp contrast to the older holistic view of medicine, which always tried to see the person within the context of their immediate environment. As industry developed in the twentieth century and the philanthropic foundations began to exert even more pressure on medicine and its practice, this conflict was to surface repeatedly.

Chapter Two

The Beginning of the Health Fraud Movement

Scientific matters can not possibly ever be decided upon in court. They can only be clarified by prolonged, faithful bona fide observations in friendly exchanges of opinion, never by litigation. [1]

Investigations against alternative practitioners follow a pattern of arrogance, dogmatism, deprivation of constitutional rights and a might-makes-right attitude. [2]

The United States Food and Drug Administration (FDA) is a nationwide regulatory and enforcement agency which has immense investigative, policing and prosecutorial powers. It was set up in 1938 to protect the American public against false medical and health claims and harmful products. Since its inception, it has tended to defend the interests of the large American food producing corporations, the pharmaceutical industry and medical orthodoxy. [3]

Before the Second World War, medicinal products did not have to be licensed in America. In 1937, at least 107 people died after taking 'elixir sulfanilamide', a drug which had been rushed into production without tests of any kind. [4] The Food, Drug and Cosmetic Act, which became law in June 1938, partially in response to this case, was a product of Roosevelt's New Deal administration. The New Deal, with its progressive if not socialistic intentions, heralded the beginning of a federal administration in a number of different domestic areas.

Senior staff of governmental agencies like the FDA have often come from liberal east coast backgrounds. They have been reformers with a left of centre view of economics and social administration. Such administrators had been waiting in the wings up until Roosevelt's presidential victory in 1932, working in the 'alternative government' of the large Rockefeller, Ford and Carnegie Foundations. Their modern views on social administration were also inevitably in favour of progressive scientific development.

The backgrounds of the new FDA administrators, like those who were to follow in other federal agencies, were close to the large industries which they were supposed to be regulating – the pharmaceutical, food and cosmetics sectors. It could be said that although these large monopolistic industries had 'allowed' the FDA to come into being they had little intention of allowing it to police their industries. There has always been a significant level of communication between officers and their client industries and, on leaving the FDA, high ranking career administrators have in the past been offered lucrative jobs in industry. Between 1959 and 1963, ten per cent of those who left the FDA went on to join companies that they had previously been regulating.[5] In 1960, a Senate investigation discovered that one of the FDA's top officials had been paid $287,000 by drug companies while in office.

In 1957, a Congressional investigation into drug pricing took place, it became known as the Kefauver Hearings.[6]† The investigation led to a structure of price regulation which was opposed by the drug companies. Then in 1962, following the first news of the Thalidomide horror,‡[7] Congress passed amendments to the Food and Drug Act, which ordered the implementation of drug effectiveness requirements by 1964. The amendments expanded the authority of the FDA and strengthened new drugs clearance procedures.

These additional laws empowered the FDA to make rulings and decisions about the effectiveness of any drug, medicine or food, regardless of its safety. As was pointed out at the time, effectiveness

† Estes Kefauver was an American Congressman and lawyer; elected to the House of Representatives in 1939, he served until his death in 1963. Kefauver was principally concerned with monopolies and the way in which they distorted the market. In 1957, he chaired a series of hearings into prices in the large monopoly industries in America; these became known as the Kefauver Hearings. The hearings which looked at the drug companies went on from December 1959, until the passage of the Kefauver-Harris legislation in October 1962.

‡ Thalidomide was a sedative for the sale of which, at the time it was manufactured in the late 1950s, there were no licensing regulations. It was widely sold in America and Europe with disastrous results. Pregnant women taking the drug gave birth to malformed children with truncated or missing limbs and a high mortality rate.

could only really be determined by clinical and scientific trials and not by the subjective views of administrators, some of whom had vested interests. The FDA were not to use their new powers against the pharmaceutical products which had caused them to be brought into force, or against processed food manufacturers, but against alternative remedies and non-pharmaceutical products. In 1966, for example, the powers were used to remove from sale throat lozenges which the FDA Commissioner considered 'ineffective'. [8]

Given that a large proportion of manufactured drugs were still not at that time proven or tested, the AMA and the pharmaceutical industry tried to distract attention from allopathic products by focusing upon non-orthodox remedies and treatments. Their main strategy of this distraction was a 'war against quackery'.

At the same time as legislating for the drug industry, and as if as a sop to pharmaceutical interests, the Food and Drug Administration moved against the manufacturers of vitamins and food supplements. In 1962, the FDA issued regulations which imposed a very low limit on potencies for vitamins, hoping to restrain their medical use. The National Health Federation, a particularly energetic lobby, campaigned from 1962 until 1976 against this regulation of vitamins and food supplements. [9]

It was not until after the amendments to the Food and Drug Act had been passed, that the American public began to understand just how far the FDA had moved from its original role in public protection.

> The Food and Drug Administration is charged by Congress with an onerous responsibility – that of protecting the nation's health. Instead of shouldering this heavy responsibility, we find the agency engaged in bizarre and juvenile games of cops and robbers. Instead of a guardian of the national health, we find an agency which is police orientated, chiefly concerned with prosecutions and convictions, totally indifferent to individuals' rights, and bent on using snooping gear to pry and to invade the citizen's right of privacy. [10]

The most energetic investigative and policing operations were saved for what the FDA frequently referred to as 'nutritional nonsense'. 'Nutritional nonsense' included any product or advice with which either the FDA, the AMA or their backers disagreed. As early as 1944, Lelord Kordel, a nutritionist who was mercilessly harassed by the

FDA, recalls being investigated by zealous FDA agents.

> When Gaylord Hauser, Paul Bragg, Edward McCollum and I,
> among others, preached the importance of natural whole grain
> bread – free of chemical preservatives – the dictocrats seemed to
> act as a gang to give us all the trouble possible. In their opinion
> we were quacks of the lowest order to suggest that it was harmful
> to eat devitalized, denatured, chemicalized, and highly preserved
> white bread. [11]

> My first encounter with George Daughters (FDA Agent) was in
> San Francisco in 1944. I was lecturing at the Woman's Club ... it
> was a time when FDA inspectors began harassing health food
> teachers. During the intermission I went into our supply room
> and found George Daughters holding my eight year old son on
> his lap and asking questions. 'How much money does your
> daddy earn? Does your daddy use these vitamins? Do you?
> Where do you go to school?' [12]

The FDA surreptitiously enlarged the area of its powers by working
with a number of other centralised US agencies. By joining with the
Inland Revenue Service, the Federal Trade Commission and the
Postal Service, the FDA was able to use its powers of investigation,
surveillance and policing on many different fronts.

Organisations used by pharmaceutical interests inside the FDA are
those which have a national reputation for assessing standards, such as
City Medical Boards, standards authorities and organisations like the
Better Business Bureau (BBB). In his book *The Dictocrats' Attack on Health
Foods and Vitamins*, Omar V. Garrison goes as far as to say that the BBB
is little more than 'an unofficial publicity bureau and aid to Food and
Drug Administration's enforcement arm'. The BBB has been
responsible for publishing the FDA view of pending court cases
against alternative medicial practitioners, vitamin and food supplement companies.

Other agencies which have supported the FDA from the beginning,
especially in their war against nutritional medicine, vitamins and food
supplements, are the US Department of Agriculture, the American
Nutrition Foundation (an organisation which is completely supported
by industry), and the American Dietetic Association, which is also
supported by industry. These last two groups are advocates of the
nutritional value of the 'average American diet': this mythical diet is

supposed to fulfil all the nutritional needs of all the population.

The message from the FDA is not only supportive of the 'average American diet', and favourable to the chemical companies, but also earnestly antagonistic to most popular modern writers on health and diet. It is heavily against vegetarianism and in favour of the meat industry. Most pointedly, in terms of powerful vested interests, the FDA has always supported the international sugar industry, while launching frequent assaults on honey and anyone who makes health claims for it. [13]

The campaign against Dr Carlton Fredericks, a nutritionist, began in 1949. During this campaign, the FDA used a wide range of strategies to put him out of business. These strategies included 'vilification by press release; slander by poison-pen letters to academic and civic organisations; intimidation of broadcast licensees; censorship of books; extra-legal annoyance of friends or supporters who held government jobs, and so on'. [14] FDA agents have in the past been responsible for arresting lecturers while they gave talks about vitamins and impounding and destroying books about vitamins and food supplements. There are many recorded cases of electronic surveillance being used against nutritionists by the FDA in America. [15]

In order to spread its message against health foods, vitamins, food supplements and alternative medicine, the FDA spends large amounts of money commissioning market research surveys and organising anti-quackery congresses. In 1964, when the second 'anti-quackery congress' was held, a representative of the Food Supplement Manufacturers and Distributors was specifically barred from being present. Writing in 1970, Garrison explains how the FDA-AMA representatives propagate their case at such meetings.

> Extreme and often absurd examples of medical charlatanism will be described in detail as being typical of the kind of fraud and deceit the FDA-AMA alliance is attacking. Once these villainous straw men are set up all the unorthodox researchers, healers, health food distributors and auto-therapists are identified with them. [16]

> There are emotive fulminations against 'bizarre therapies', unproven arthritis cures, unorthodox cancer treatments, new-fangled gadgets and radionic devices; against books which spread

'false ideas', 'unsupported theories', and 'information on health
subjects contrary to established scientific facts'. [17]

The assault upon alternative practitioners, which began in the early
sixties and continued through the seventies, focused particularly upon
vitamin supplements. Both vitamins and organic foods were seen as
aspects of a preventative health programme and in this sense they
represented a threat to purely symptomatically prescribed pharmaceutical remedies.

Throughout the sixties, the FDA tried to regulate the make-up of
vitamin supplements and curtail the consumer choice. The most
frequently used argument was that certain vitamins were dangerous if
taken in too high a dose. The most commonly cited were vitamins A
and D.

Measures which the Federal Trade Commission (FTC) tried to get
through Congress attempted to end any label reference to foods which
had not been chemically treated. In the late sixties the FTC attempted
to enact regulations which forbade any use of the terms 'health',
'health foods', 'natural', 'organic', or 'organically grown'. They tried to
end any comparative claims between non-processed and processed
foods, any descriptions of the nutritional value of, say, 'fresh orange
juice' as against an orange drink, or orange cordial. Fines for violations
of FTC rulings were set, in the original proposals, at $10,000 on every
day or occasion that the regulation was broken.

In 1973, Senator William Proxmire, a Democrat, proposed a 'Food
Supplements Amendment Act'. This was to be an amendment to the
Federal Food, Drug and Cosmetic Act: it guaranteed that people
could buy vitamins of any potency without a prescription from a
doctor. This bill was passed unanimously in 1976. The AMA and the
pharmaceutical interests put up massive opposition to the Bill between
1973 and 1976, but in the end opposition to it was seen clearly to be
flying in the face of consumer rights so that even those who
represented the Rockefeller interests found opposition difficult.

Rockefeller interests, in the form of the First Boston and Chase
Manhattan Bank, have always exerted considerable influence over the
New York Times. [18] The newspaper's press coverage of the Proxmire Bill
clearly showed its vested interests. When the Bill was announced in
1973, the paper ran a front page story, headed 'Disputed health lobby
is pressing for a bill to overturn any limits on sales of vitamins'. The

disputed health lobby was the National Health Federation. The article began:

> Thousands of food faddists, 142 Congressmen and a health lobby, which the Federal Government says has been linked to quackery, are backing an obscure bill that would allow Americans to obtain as many vitamins as they want. Yet the Food and Drug Administration, the American Medical Association and experts in pharmacology insist that massive doses of vitamins A and D can be harmful and indeed life threatening in extreme cases. Pending regulations would limit how much of a vitamin a person could buy without a prescription. [19]

The use by the FDA of other agencies in their war against vitamin users is well illustrated by the example of the Cardiac Society (CS), a non-profit making group of several hundred heart patients set up in the nineteen sixties. The group promoted a preventative health treatment based upon Vitamin E. When the CS started a buyer's group for Vitamin E, the FDA came down on them. The US Postal Service got a ruling against them, claiming that they were promoting a scheme to defraud. From that time, all mail addressed to the Society was intercepted and returned to sender with 'FRAUDULENT' stamped over the letter or package. This happened despite the fact that the Society's president was a judge and its honorary directors included another judge, a university president and the president of a telephone company.

The FDA has punitive powers which enable it to seek imprisonment for such offences as making false claims and mislabelling. A Mr V. Earl Irons went to prison for a year after the FDA accused him of making 'unscientific' claims that his food supplements were beneficial to health. In 1962, a Vermont grandmother was taken to court and her whole stock impounded by FDA agents after she sold yeast to pregnant women for nutritional purposes. Her crime was not that she sold the yeast but that she also gave out a leaflet which made health claims for the product.

The FDA has led the attacks on all of the alternative cancer treatments which have been developed outside governmental or Rockefeller auspices. In 1963, it conducted a prosecution against Dr Stevan Durovic who had produced Krebiozen, a non-toxic substance found to be useful in the treatment of cancer patients. The trial lasted 289 days, and the jury heard 288 witnesses. At the end of the hearing, the jury found the defendants not guilty of the 240 charges which the FDA had brought against them. Other anti-cancer therapies dismissed or undermined by the FDA since the Second World War include the Rand vaccine, laetrile and the Koch treatment.

In 1968, the US Postal Service were awarded greater powers to stop certain material going through the mails. By June 1969, they had used this power to ban at least six books on alternative health. Clinton R. Miller of the National Health Federation claimed that there were three more bans threatened.

In order to bring charges against manufacturers who *did not* make health claims on their products, the FDA ingeniously extended the definition of a label to include books or literature about products sold on the same premises as the product itself. In cases where it appears desperate to prosecute, it has gone even further. Lelord Kordel was charged by the FDA on one occasion after it said that false statements and claims appeared in booklets accompanying dietary food products. The products in question had been shipped in July of one year and the 'labels' sent eighteen months later.

In May 1968, the FDA launched public hearings on proposed new vitamin regulations. The examiner who chaired the hearings was asked to step down by lawyers representing the health food retailers because he had been personally chosen by the FDA. Witness after witness who gave evidence for the FDA told the hearing that they had worked for vested interests. One witness said that he had been approached by the pharmaceutical companies after it had become public that he would be giving evidence. Sidney Weissenberg, the FDA's Assistant Associate Commissioner for Compliance and the sole individual in America responsible at that time for making decisions about whether food supplement labelling was false or misleading, 'ranted on the witness stand against "food faddists", "quacks", "quackery", and "so-called health food stores" '. Weissenberg spent a total of 52 days on the stand. [20]

Although the American Medical Association and the Food and Drug Administration have always been the wellspring of the health-fraud movement in America, they are closely followed by front organisations for industry and public relations companies.

One cause and one document have become seminal in the historical understanding of the post-war anti-quackery movement. The cause was the war against chiropractic therapy† and the document a memorandum which revealed the part played by the AMA in this war.

In January 1971, H. Doyl Taylor, then head of the AMA Department of Investigation, sent a memo to the Board of Trustees. The memo was about the group of physicians who practised chiropractic therapy.

> Since the AMA board of trustees' decision at its meeting on November 2-3, 1963, to establish a Committee on Quackery, your committee has considered its prime mission to be, first the containment of chiropractic and, ultimately, the elimination of chiropractic. [21]‡

The AMA Committee on Quackery, set up in 1964, was the forerunner of all other organisational attempts to put alternative medical practices out of business. To propagandise their cause, the Committee adopted a language of derogatory terms which it used to describe the medical work of its competitors: 'unscientific cult', 'unproven method', 'health fraud', and 'quackery'. [22] They linked up with other groups which had a vested economic interest in supporting allopathic medicine, principally, the insurance companies, licensing boards, colleges and lobbyists. [23]

A year after setting up the Committee on Quackery, the AMA Board of Trustees set up a secret organisation entitled the Coordinating Conference on Health Information (CCHI), headed by H. Doyl Taylor. The group lasted ten years. It drew together official government agencies with the representatives of business

---

† The American chiropractic movement is the second largest health care group in America; its practice is similar to that of osteopathy and relies upon the manipulation of bones.

‡ In 1976, a number of chiropractors sued the AMA and others, charging them with conspiracy. Eleven years later, in 1987, they won their case and the AMA was found guilty of conspiring to destroy the profession of chiropractic. Throughout the decade of legal hearings, the AMA freely admitted that it did not have any knowledge of the content or quality of the courses used to teach chiropractic practitioners. [24]

organisations and Foundation-funded campaigning medical groups.

Sitting on the CCHI were the AMA and the American Cancer Society (ACS). The ACS, the leading cancer research body in America, has led a continuous war against all forms of alternative cancer treatment; it was set up and is funded primarily by Rockefeller interests. [25] Also on the CCHI were the American Pharmaceutical Association, the Council for Better Business Bureau (CBBB), and the Arthritis Foundation, another important research funding body which receives its funds from the pharmaceutical industry and restricts research into alternative forms of treatment. Combined with these organisations were three of the largest government agencies: the FDA, the US Postal Service and the Federal Trade Commission.

The title of the CCHI bestowed upon the health-fraud movement a more constructive image of a health care monitoring group. Nevertheless, it was the Coordinating Conference on Health Information which launched an all-out offensive against alternative and non-orthodox practitioners across the United States. The AMA and the CCHI were given help and support by the large Foundations in chasing and harrying victims. [26] The American Cancer Foundation was responsible for assessing likely targets, and gathering intelligence on alternative cancer treatment organisations.

Government agencies never made their presence at meetings, nor their part in the CCHI, a matter of public record. They avoided declaring government interests by not describing the group as a committee at which they would officially have had to record their presence. [27]

These agencies in their attacks upon small alternative practitioners rarely used the courts or the police. More often they utilised the regulatory power of professional bodies, the Federal Trade Commission, the Post Office Department, the Food and Drug Administration and the United States Public Health Service. They were approached by the large Foundations, and prompted to initiate policing actions against targeted people. [28]

> In many cases, people were arrested for selling, or sometimes giving away, booklets which advertised such innocuous health practices as taking vitamins! These distributors now found themselves under restraining orders from the Post Office, the Department of Justice and the Food and Drug Administration.

> Others who were distributing various salves, nostrums and other preparations, most of them based on herbal formulae, received heavy fines and prison sentences. In every case, all of the stocks of these practitioners, many of whom were elderly and impoverished, were seized and destroyed as 'dangerous substances'. It was never alleged that a single person had ever been injured, much less killed, by any of these preparations. [29]

Behind this smokescreen, the pharmaceutical companies continued to sell treatments which had not been tested, were not effective and in some cases caused terrible damage. One of the most energetic attacks from this conspiracy was fermented against those who advocated the anti-cancer treatment laetrile. The propaganda offensive against laetrile was carried out in concert with large-scale police operations, sometimes using SWAT teams. [30]

In 1974, the CCHI held its last minuted meeting and at more or less the same time, the AMA department of investigation was disbanded. Over the ten years of its existence, the CCHI had put together a massive data bank which had been used by various bodies to investigate and attack alternative health practitioners.

Chapter Three

The American National Council Against Health Fraud

The more the role of the practical physician becomes identical with that of the test mechanic or an agent of specialised surgery, the more exclusively he becomes someone that places orders with and represents the pharmaceutical industry [1]

In 1982, US Representative Claude Pepper introduced three Bills in the House of Representatives. The Bills were preceded by Committee hearings which came to be known as the Pepper Hearings. Each of the Pepper Bills argued for legislative codification of the aims and strategies of the defunct Coordinating Conference on Health Information (CCHI). One of the Bills called for a national clearing house for consumer health information. Another called for increased criminal penalties against 'quacks'. The third called for the formation of a Federal strike force inside the Department of Justice, to be used in the prosecution of 'quacks'. In 1984 all of the Pepper Bills fell at the committee stage.

The next appearance of the non-statutory health fraud movement coincided with the defeat of the Pepper Bills. In 1984, a meeting was held in Sacramento, California. For the first time after the disbanding of the CCHI, a public group was formed with the main object of fighting quackery. The meeting took place at the Department of Health and was organised by the recently-formed National Council Against Health Fraud (NCHF). The NCHF representative was the only one present who was not a government official. Those present included representatives from the FDA, the California Food and Drug Board, the Board of Medical Quality Assurance – a California State Board that has the power to revoke medical licences – the US Postal Service and the Federal Trade Commission. [2]

The object of the Sacramento meeting was to discuss strategies against health-fraud and to try to implement some of the ideas which had previously been discussed by both the CCHI and the Pepper Hearings. The two central strategies debated by the group had been in the air for almost twenty years: the institutionalisation of an investigative agency with a 'strike force', which could be used to police alternative practitioners and, secondly, the organisation of a database and clearing-house for health-fraud information. Such information was to be fed to government agencies by the emergent National Council Against Health Fraud.

At the first meeting, the NCHF gave a summary of the groups, individuals and practitioners whom they wanted to attack: health promoters, chiropractors and 'diploma mills which issue false degrees' [3]. The later history of the NCHF shows that these subjects were only the tip of the iceberg. Over the next five years, pronouncements by the NCHF listed a wide ranch of diagnostic aids, therapies and treatments which did not coincide with the views of allopathic practitioners. These ranged from individuals promoting nutritional supplements and vitamins to any form of treatment described as holistic, including homoeopathy, naturopathy, and faith healing. Diagnostic aids such as hair analysis and cytotoxic testing for food allergies and any alternative cancer therapies were listed for censure.

In the summer of 1985, there began a tide of health fraud articles directed against 'quackery'. This first propaganda offensive was followed by the first National Health Fraud Conference, held in September 1985 at the National Press Club in Washington. Organised by the FDA, the Federal Trade Commission and the US Postal Service, its venue gave a hint as to both its membership and its audience. Despite what the Council's leading advocates were to say later, the NCHF did not start because of consumer disquiet, endangered patients, or long-suffering victims of health fraud.

Surprisingly, it was the gay community who first began to seriously demonstrate against the National Council Against Health Fraud. For those who were HIV antibody positive, who had ARC (AIDS Related Complex) or AIDS in the mid and late eighties, the question of available treatment choices was anything but academic. The only treatment offered by orthodox medicine and sanctioned by the FDA, from 1987, was AZT, which the Wellcome Foundation claimed could extend the period of good health, between contracting the HIV virus and the development of full blown AIDS.

AIDS patients were the perfect people to challenge the NCHF because they were the very people NCHF claimed to be representing, vulnerable patients likely to be cheated by quacks. This was not, however, how many people with AIDS saw their position. They saw themselves as victims of a massive, uncaring medical monopoly, supported by the AMA, the FDA and the pharmaceutical companies. Some six years after the HIV virus had been isolated and AIDS identified as a complex illness, there was only one expensive chemotherapeutic treatment legally available. What is more, many people with AIDS were beginning to understand that whenever non-pharmaceutical treatments did become available, their promoters were quickly 'exposed' as 'quacks'. The organisations which were doing the exposing and so standing between AIDS subjects and possibly alternative treatments were the FDA, the NCHF and a wide range of interconnected medical science and pharmaceutical interests.

In September 1990, members of ACT-UP, a gay 'find a cure' group, demonstrated at the Kansas City National Conference on Health Fraud, sponsored by NCHF. The *Kansas City Star* quoted Jim Greenberg, who was HIV antibody positive and had been maintaining his health with acupuncture, Chinese herbal remedies and vitamin supplements: 'I am here to fight for my right to choose what treatments I take for my body.' [4]

ACT-UP activists in America had thought for some time that the NCHF was using its campaigning profile to draw public attention away from the fact that scientists had not found a cure for AIDS. They had concluded that the NCHF was allied with organised medicine and the pharmaceutical and insurance industries to deny patients unorthodox treatments for Acquired Immune Deficiency Syndrome and other diseases. [5]

The organiser of the Kansas City NCHF conference was Dr John Renner. Renner works in Kansas City where the NCHF resource centre is based and is a national figure in the 'quackbusting' movement. At the time of the conference, he claimed that he was not opposed to alternative medicine and was surprised to see that the demonstrators had allied themselves with 'questionable health groups'.

Such groups, he said, 'have a long history of promoting nonsense science and weird practices'. [6]

John Renner set up the Kansas City Committee on Health and Nutrition Fraud and Abuse in 1985 only a little while after the NCHF parent organisation was set up. All the funding organisations for Renner's group are ultimately linked to the $12 million (1983) Speas Foundation. The largest percentage of the Foundation's money is invested in drugs, chemicals and medical interests. These interests include Eli Lilly and Merck, as well as a number of other companies, all of which were involved in the FDA/PAC 'quackery' campaign. The Speas Foundation gets its money from the Speas company, a processed food manufacturer. [7]

Now promoted as an authoritative commentator on health issues, Renner, who trained as a psychiatrist, filed for bankruptcy in the early seventies, leaving creditors wanting for over a million dollars. [8] The Kansas City Group has been responsible for campaigns against a number of herbal and natural treatments, most particularly a series of preparations designed by Dr Kurt Donsbach under the label of Herbalife. The strategies used against Dr Donsbach were almost entirely covert. They included Fraud Unit investigators from the Sacramento Department of Health posing as Herbalife distributors.

John Renner is one of three or four major activists at the centre of the NCHF. The Council was founded, and is presided over, by William T. Jarvis, Professor of Health Education at Loma Linda (Calif.) University School of Medicine. Another prominent member is Stephen Barrett who organises the Lehigh Valley Committee Against Health Fraud and also runs the NCHF bookshop in Allentown.

In his book *The Great Medical Monopoly Wars*, P.J. Lisa suggests that the Pharmaceutical Advertising Council links up with the FDA to organise campaigns against 'quackery', and to promote articles in newspapers, television programmes and advertisements. He names the companies which supported these promotional strategies in the eighties as Lederle, Syntex and Hoffmann-LaRoche. Paul Chusid, a past President of Grey Advertising which handles both Syntex and Lederle accounts in America, told Lisa that many of the health fraud campaigns originated in his office.

Claims that NCHF is independent and consumer-orientated have been questioned by America's greatest consumer activist, Ralph

Nader. Such claims are also undermined by the fact that three of its major activists, Dr Victor Herbert, Stephen Barrett and William Jarvis, are also on the Scientific Advisory Board of the American Council on Science and Health. Founded in 1978, this organisation is funded solely by the large pharmaceutical and chemical companies, the AMA and industry-supported Foundations.†

The NCHF maintains working parties, which it calls 'Special Task Forces'. These are meant to issue literature and call upon speakers in specialised areas of medical fraud. However, pharmaceutically and medically induced illness (iatrogenesis), any kind of chemically-induced ill health, or any orthodox but exploitative practices do not appear as working party subjects. The principal Task Force areas are Acupuncture; AIDS Quackery; Broadcast Media Abuse; Diet and Behaviour; Dubious Cancer Care; Herbal Remedies; Supplement Abuse and Nutritional Diploma Mills.

The NCHF resources list for 1991 advertises over 500 articles, pamphlets and booklets, the subjects of which give a good guide to NCHF priorities. Articles attack acupuncture, alternative AIDS treatments, clinical ecology, alternative cancer treatments, herbal medicines, nutritional theories, holistic practices, naturopathy and general quackery. Although these articles come from a cross section of publications, a high proportion of them have been published in pro-NCHF publications such as the *FDA Consumer*, *Nutrition Forum*, and American Committee on Science and Health publications.

The NCHF bi-monthly *Newsletter* is a digest of press reports reminiscent of intelligence reports put out by government departments in the immediate post-war years. It details raids by FDA officers and police forces on alternative cancer therapists, doctors who have been struck off – 'Clinical Ecologist MD Loses License' – and details of what NCHF claims to be dangerous alternative practices – 'Insight into the Macrobiotic Diet Sham', 'NCHF considers macrobiotics to be very dangerous because of needless deaths that have occurred due to applying its philosophy to cancer care.'[9]

The *Newsletter* has frequent dismissive allusions to books which support ecology and natural health treatments, 'Society to be Plagued

† See Chapter Four.

by Crank Ecology Books.' [10] The leading figures of the Council appear to have a prodigious output of books and magazine articles, especially in a wide range of popular magazines. Apart from its *Newsletter*, the NCHF publishes little under its own imprint, but works closely with the American Council on Science and Health publication, *Priorities and Issues in Nutrition* and with the Consumers' Union.†

The contradictions in the theoretical and campaigning constructs of 'quackbusters' are often transparent, simply because they are clearly straining to combat a phantom. For example, one of their central hypotheses is that most of those involved in 'natural medicine' are involved in a profitable business – this, in a society which is based upon the ethic of private enterprise, a society in which the smallest pharmaceutical companies turn over £40 million a year.

In 1980, Victor Herbert, the doyen of health fraud activists in the United States, published a collection of his writings entitled *Nutrition Cultism: Facts and Fiction*. [11] Herbert cut his teeth on laetrile (B17), a treatment for cancer synthesised in the 1940s from apricot kernels by Ernest T. Krebs, a biochemist. The foreword to this book, written by Stephen Barrett MD, is a good example of phantom chasing.

> The quack tries to boost his image by attacking science. Doctors, he tells us, are 'butchers' and 'poisoners' ... Scientific farmers, he says, are 'poisoners' and 'polluters' ... Government agencies, he says, instead of protecting us, are 'conspiring' with organised medicine and the food industry. And anyone who speaks out against quackery is accused of being part of that conspiracy ... To promote 'organic' food, he [the quack] lumps all additives into one class and attacks them as poisonous ... He [the quack] doesn't mention how natural toxicants are prevented or destroyed by modern food technology. Nor does he let on that many additives are naturally occurring substances ... While warning against preservatives, he is careful not to mention that an ounce of Swiss cheese, which you might eat in a sandwich,

† The Consumers' Union is a non-profit making, New York organisation, set up in 1936, just two years before the FDA. In its early beginnings it was a Rockefeller initiative, having a similar view of product regulation to the FDA. There is an international Consumers' Union network of which the British Consumers' Association is a part. These organisations are mainly independent of the American industry-influenced Union.

contains the amount of calcium propionate used to preserve two
loaves of bread ... Sugar has been subjected to particularly
vicious attack, being (falsely) blamed for most of the world's
ailments. [12]

The intellectual orientation of such pieces is quite different from the
scientific arguments which are suggested against alternative therapies and
'quack doctors'. A subtle shift of emphasis means that the 'case evidence'
of quackery is no longer under discussion. Instead, we are pulled into an
abstract discourse about ideology. The Quack referred to here is no
longer the 'hole in the wall' unqualified or struck-off medic who dupes the
elderly by selling them an unproven cancer cure. He or she is now
someone spreading criminal rumours about the dangers of additives and
sugar. Quacks are here defined as those who spread despondency and
lower morale by criticising capitalism. Using such criteria, criminalisation
has extended to a great cohort of ill-defined people who question the
nutritional and toxic status of modern processed food.

By the end of the 1980s, this semantic medical criminalisation was
leaching into ever-wider areas. In a development which has taken
place in other fields, Elizabeth Whelan of the American Council on
Science and Health coined the expression 'food terrorists', a term
which does not apply to those who destroy the nutritional value of
food or adulterate it, nor to those who create and sustain grain
mountains or butter mountains in deserts of world hunger but to those
who criticise the food industry.

The NCHF attempts to 'criminalise' those who suggest that
industry is responsible for an unhealthy lifestyle. William T. Jarvis,
describing the various groups who fell victim to 'quackery', had this to
say at a 1989 National Health Fraud Conference in Kansas City.

Lastly are those with antagonistic attitudes, people who believe
that the food supply is depleted and contaminated or that
physicians are butchers. [13]

Those described here are the paranoid 'subversives' in the war
taking place around health in America. These are the wrong-minded,
a major group who fall prey to charlatans and tricksters. Yet such a
grouping contains those who have every right and reason to believe in
alternative life-styles and frames of philosophical reference, including
the use of complementary medicine.

Kafka Comes to New York : The Case of Warren Levin

'Victor Herbert is the epitome of everything bad in American medicine politics today'. [14]

The campaigns waged by the National Council Against Health Fraud are campaigns of attrition: continuous complaints to professional bodies and regulatory authorities which erode the enemy's stability and plausibility. The NCHF ensure that they use any forum within which they have friends to prosecute their campaigns against individual doctors or therapists practising eclectic medicine.†

Warren M. Levin had been a holistic, mainly nutritional, family practitioner for twenty years before he was forced to stop practising and become a full time defendant in 1980. It was then that his professional and personal reputation was brought into question by what was originally an anonymous complaint made to the Office for Professional Medical Conduct (OPMC) of the New York State Department of Health.

Warren Levin's nightmare began when he was sent a subpoena ordering him to appear at the OPMC offices with the records of three specifically-named patients. Levin had not seen the patients in question since 1976 when they left his practice, apparently happy with their treatment.

When Levin tried to find out what the charges against him were, he was told that the State had 'inquisitorial powers' in such cases. He was also told that he didn't need a lawyer. Fortunately, Levin got himself a lawyer who tried to quash the subpoena. Levin believed, wrongly as it transpired, that the fact that he could not know what he was charged with, or by whom he was charged, was unconstitutional. The initial assessment of costs from his lawyer was $1,500.

The first legal wrangle over the anonymity of the complainant and ownership of the patient records took six years to resolve. By then the

---

† Many of the physicians who practise non-orthodox medicine in America have received an orthodox training. Rarely do they practise only single alternatives, such as homoeopathy or acupuncture. For this reason, the term eclectic is often used by Americans to describe a physician who uses a variety of alternatives or complementary practices.

various court appearances had cost Warren Levin some $50,000. In September of 1986, Levin turned over the three patient records, but it was not until June 1989 that he heard back from New York State Administration – some thirteen years after his last dealings with the patients in question.

The next communication from the New York State Administration to arrive at Levin's surgery contained hundreds of pages which listed almost 150 charges. These charges cited most forms of treatment that Levin had used in his practice. Prior to this action against Levin by the OPMC, other physicians had usually only been charged on a small number of counts, necessary to force them back into line with mainstream orthodox practice. Levin describes his feelings when he saw the final charges as being like 'a kick in the stomach'.

> I was accused of negligence and incompetence, and as if to emphasise it, gross negligence and gross incompetence, and finally fraud. Simply because I was testing patients for nutritional deficiencies and using orthomolecular† principles in my practice. [15]‡

When he received the list of charges, four new cases had been added to the 'indictment'; these were the cases of patients whom Levin had treated in the early 1980s. He recognised them because there had been hearings as to whether the medical insurance companies should compensate the patients for their treatments. Each of these enquiries had been instigated by the insurance companies who said that Levin's testing of patients for their 'nutritional state' and his treatment of them with vitamins and nutrition, did not qualify as routine or necessary treatment, and was therefore not covered. In each of these cases, the 'peer review committees' had found in favour of the insurance companies. Not only that, but they had apparently found Levin's form of medicine 'so dangerous' that they had gone on to report the cases to

---

† Orthomolecular is a word coined by Professor Linus Pauling in 1968. It means a form of treatment which is given without introducing foreign substances into the patient's body: that is to say, using molecules which are found naturally in a healthy body .

‡ Unless otherwise stated all quotes are either from Warren Levin himself or from the official transcipt of the hearing cited by Levin in his campaign tape recording 'PANIC'.

the Office of Professional Medical Conduct.

After a thirteen-year lapse in framing the charges, Levin was given only ten days to respond. The case began on September 18th 1989.

*   *   *

When the hearing began, Warren Levin found out who was giving evidence against him. The prosecution were bringing only one witness, the notorious 'quackbuster' and anti-health fraud activist Dr Victor Herbert. As the prosecution began, Herbert was asked if he had any prejudice against Dr Levin, he replied, 'I have no prejudice with relation to Warren Levin.' Five years previously, however, at the Claude Pepper Anti-Quackery Congressional Hearings, Herbert had named Levin along with a number of other doctors allegedly involved in health fraud. Herbert had stated that '[he] uses a wide range of questionable diagnostic tests and therapies, including chelation, in his New York practice.'†

Victor Herbert is an MD and an attorney who works at a Veterans' Administration hospital where he treats AIDS patients. He speaks constantly of the need for, and the importance of, science and double blind studies. As well as appearing before the Pepper Hearings, Herbert, who rose to prominence in the early eighties, testified before the 'New York State Assembly Republican Task Force on Health Fraud and the Elderly', held in 1985. There he had also read Levin's name into the record, as a fraudulent practitioner. Out of line with most other thinkers in the field, even orthodox doctors, Herbert opposes the need for vitamin supplements for elderly patients.

The list of Herbert's attainments and experience is extensive. In an inventory of his expertise, prepared for the Veterans' Administration, he asserted that he had expert knowledge of Great Britain, Yugoslavia, Southeast Asian countries, India, Near Eastern countries, North African countries, Mexico, Brazil and other Central or South American countries. Asked a few simple general knowledge questions

---

† Chelation therapy involves the use of a chemical which removes from the body minerals, some desirable, some toxic, and improves circulation in some people who have hardening of the arteries (arteriosclerosis): that is, people who are at risk of heart-attack and stroke.

on these countries at the OPMC Hearings, to test his knowledge as an expert witness, he got a number of the answers wrong.

Victor Herbert's curriculum vitae is an awesome document consisting of over 50 typed pages. It lists two degrees, and membership of 22 medical and legal professional societies, nine editorial boards and fourteen consultancies, with over 600 scientific publications. His articles and papers are listed as 'publications either in books or peer review journals'. Some of the articles, however, appear in such magazines as *Ms* Magazine and *Woman's World*.

Victor Herbert is a typical anti-health fraud activist. A member of both the NCHF and the ACSH, he has been responsible for instigating prosecutions against vitamin and mineral supplement suppliers and vitamin companies. He took one such action against a major supplier of Evening Primrose Oil. He was a key-note speaker at the annual meeting in Kansas of the NCHF, and is frequently interviewed as a leading light in the organisation. Like his colleague, Stephen Barrett, Herbert has been a major contributor to *Consumer Reports* which frequently attacks alternative medicine.

Herbert has refuted expert physicians on the importance of nutrition in mental illness and commented negatively on the use of vitamin C, and other vitamins. Although there is no evidence that Herbert receives any remuneration from the food or drug industry, his campaigns and his pronouncements reflect on-going support for, and deep involvment with, the processed food, pharmaceutical and medical insurance companies. On one occasion at least, like Elizabeth Whelan of the American Council on Science and Health, he has spoken in support of the nutritional quality of McDonald's hamburgers. [16.]

He was called as the expert witness by Blue Shield, the medical insurance company, in their defence against a suit by a New York holistic physician who had been denied payments. He has also been a star speaker at the Annual Meeting of the Association of Life Insurance Medical Directors of America. At their ninety third Annual Meeting he spoke on 'How to recognise questionable diagnostic tests and therapies.'

Like many of the prominent personalities in the anti-health fraud movement, Herbert is highly litigious. He does not however only believe in settling things in court. In May 1987, while giving a talk on

'Protecting the consumer from health fraud: medical and legal issues', he leapt from the rostrum, climbed over seats and after a physical fracas, took a tape recorder from a member of the audience.

The row occurred at a seminar organised to discuss the First Amendment at the Old Capitol Senate Chamber. Ironically, the seminar was part of the celebration of the bicentennial year of the US Constitution entitled, 'Does the First Amendment Protect Commercial Speech?'. Herbert was using the opportunity of the meeting to attack the work of Dr Lawrence Burton, a doctor of zoology, working with cancer and AIDS patients.†

Herbert cited Burton's Immuno-Augmentative Therapy as an example of fraud and when he saw the President of its Patients' Association, Frank Wiewel, tape-recording his talk, he accused him of theft of intellectual property. Herbert repeatedly interrupted Wiewel with the aid of the microphone, as he attempted to offer his opinion on the therapy. 'That's a lie. That's a big, fat lie', Herbert shouted, 'Don't you know that that's a lie?' [17]

Following the tape-recording incident, Frank Wiewel took a criminal action against Herbert for assault. Although he won his case in the lower court, the decision was later overturned on appeal.

Herbert also became involved in a major row with the National Academy of Science over the 10th edition of Recommended Dietary Guidelines, [18] which he said should not include information about vitamins and cancer.

* * *

On the second day of Victor Herbert's testimony at Warren Levin's OPMC hearing, Levin's lawyer, Robert Harris, asked Herbert if he was the person who had made the complaints against his client. Despite the fact that Herbert was the only expert witness and there appeared to be a causal link between Herbert's anti-health fraud campaign and Levin's position before the tribunal, Herbert refused to answer.

When Herbert refused to answer the question for the second time,

† Dr Lawrence Burton had to move his clinic to the Bahamas following frequent attacks from the anti-health fraud lobby. Dr Burton has advocated and used Immuno-Augmentative Therapy (IAT) for cancer and AIDS patients.

Judge Storch, sitting on the tribunal to guide the lay members on points of law, advised that Herbert be dismissed as a witness. In the legal argument which followed, the prosecuting lawyer, employed by the State of New York, let it be known that his instructions had been to direct the witness not to answer the question. This admission further confused Herbert's relationship, as an independent expert witness. Was Herbert the complainant, the prosecutor or an independent witness? Levin's lawyer called Herbert's relationship with the prosecution 'incestuous'.

When, having been instructed to answer by Judge Storch, Herbert again refused, the judge advised the panel to dismiss the case. In any fair system, that would have been the end of the matter, but in February 1990, the decision was reviewed by Dr David Axelrod, the OPMC Commissioner for the State of New York. The Commissioner is an unelected political appointee and not a lawyer. Axelrod reversed the order discharging Herbert as a witness and returned the case before the same panel and the same judge. He ruled: 'The Public Health Law prevents the disclosure of the identity of the complainant in a professional medical conduct proceeding.'

Throughout the cross-examination of Herbert, Robert Harris managed to cast doubt upon Herbert's suitability as a witness. As an example of his specialised knowledge in nutrition, Herbert claimed to have been accepted onto the American Board of Nutrition (BON) in 1967. Warren's lawyer, however, established that Herbert did not take an examination for the Board, as he said he had. He had actually been excused the exam by the BON, 'By general acclaim of the examiners, without having had to take any examination whatsoever'. By the time Herbert had finished giving evidence, Warren Levin had incurred expenses of almost $100,000.

Counsellor Harris frequently made the point during the hearings that the case was 'a test of the right of a physician to practice according to the point of view and the philosophy of a minority group of physicians'. The prosecution, he said, was 'depriving patients of their prerogative to choose what type of medical care they wish to pursue'. The prosecutor denied that any such hidden agenda existed.

At the end of their case, the prosecution subpoenaed four more patient records. Each subpoena increased Levin's legal fees. The State produced a woman who testified about treatments which Dr Levin had prescribed for her now deceased husband and her teenage daughter, who was still alive but was not called to testify.

The witness claimed that Levin had refused to fill out a diagnosis on her husband's insurance form, had billed her daughter twice for one procedure and charged *her* for a short conversation.

Two other cases produced by the State were both from the early 1980s. In relation to one complainant, Levin was charged with having diagnosed a chronic candida related complex.† Herbert and his colleagues in the NCHF consistently claim that this condition is extremely rare. The prosecution claimed that not only had Levin diagnosed an almost non-existent illness, but he had prescribed Nystatin, a drug which Herbert said was dangerous and only to be prescribed in the most serious cases of immune deficiency, such as AIDS.

Levin's defence against all the charges was essentially a defence of the many 'natural' practices with which he had treated people over the last twenty years. The expert witnesses whom he called were ones who could demonstrate that his practices were sound and proven, while casting doubt upon Victor Herbert's plausibility.

Professor Linus Pauling, a man with 48 honorary PhD degrees and the only person to have been awarded two Nobel prizes, was Levin's most esteemed witness. Pauling began his evidence for Levin before the OPMC on August 22nd 1990, when he said of Herbert:

> I have known him for about 21 years now, I don't think that he is a scientist. It seems to me he has little understanding of science, and little ability in that field.

> You know that he [Victor Herbert] is not a scientist, he doesn't know how to assess evidence. I don't think that he knows much about bio-statistics. He just says that he refuses to look at the evidence. When I have sent him my analysis of 14 controlled

---

† Candida albicans is a yeast/fungal infection, better known as Thrush, which can affect the mouth and vagina. A significant number of doctors have become increasingly aware of the role of Candida albicans as a cause of chronic ill-health and treat patients with diet and preparations with anti-Candida activity. It is one of the most common opportunist infections which occur in AIDS Related Complex (ARC) cases. Since the mid-eighties orthodox practitioners in Britain and America have frequently denied the prevalence of the infection outside of AIDS cases.

trials, he just refuses to look at it. He continues to make false statements about vitamin C and cancer and vitamins in general.

If you can believe what he says he believes, there is no doubt that his beliefs aren't based upon the evidence. They are based upon some sort of bias, some sort of other activating influence.

Based on the statement of the charges, and my understanding of the tests that Dr Levin carried out and the treatments that he prescribed, I formed the opinion that he [Warren Levin] was a good sound, orthomolecular physician. [19]

Victor Herbert and his anti-health fraud colleagues frequently state that their beliefs are based upon scientific principles. Linus Pauling, perhaps the most notable biologist in the Western world, clearly considers that Herbert's claims to a knowledge of science are ill-founded and in a telling phrase he suggests that Herbert's views are 'based upon some sort of bias, *some sort of other activating influence*'.

The OPMC tribunal against Warren Levin changed the orientation of professional medical prosecutions in a number of subtle ways.† Tribunals of this kind in both Britain and America have in the past relied almost entirely upon lay complainants coming forward.

There are good reasons why tribunals which hear cases of complaints, rather than internal disciplinary hearings, should depend upon independent, lay complainants. If they do not, such tribunals can become investigative and prosecuting agencies which are vulnerable to exploitation by vested interests. The prosecution of Warren Levin turned the principle of complainant tribunals on its head. His prosecution was manifestly not directed by lay complainants, and witnesses were sought to bolster the prosecution. Such procedures open the door to a multitude of corrupt practices and possible miscarriages of justice.

---

† At the time of writing, six years after the initial charges were laid, the OPMC tribunal has not delivered its reserved verdict on Warren Levin's professional position.

Chapter Four

Selling Science and Industry in America

By the mid-1970s, working through a variety of trade associations, domestic and international think-tanks, universities, policy institutes, planning agencies, foundations, and select offices of the Executive branch, highly mobilised business élites had forged a counter-attack. This counter-attack disparaged what was called the 'antiscience' movement and proclaimed a new age of reason while remystifying reality. [1]

Many of the Foundations which had funded science after the Second World War, such as Ford and Rockefeller, were by the mid-seventies considered by the Right to have gone to liberal seed. For the Rockefeller financial interests in particular the seventies and early eighties were difficult times. While they needed to stay in control of economic policies and defend the old industrial order, their philosophy was steeped in a tradition of overtly egalitarian partnership projects between industry, government and academia. The young Turks then emerging on the Right had on the other hand, a philosophy of élitism and class confrontation. It was a combative New Right, which was more than happy to have a head-on conflict with anybody who expressed liberal or left of centre views.

It was the view of the New Right ideologues that to appease social democracy or liberalism, even superficially, was ultimately to appease the communists. They believed that it was through the door left open by social democracy that the far Left came to the seat of government. [2] The political and financial mandarins who came of age in the mid-seventies refused to support projects which shaved off at the edges into liberalism. They were outspokenly proud of being Right.

Amongst other patrons, the New Right found Richard Scaife and Joseph Coors; Coors had himself been looking for New Right groups that he could finance in 1971.† Both men were virulently anti-socialist conservatives, who hated what they considered to be the liberal drift of Republicanism. Their money was new, hard industrial money, not money from the farming interests of the older American families nor money which mixed with the liberally dominated Foundations like Rockefeller, Ford or Carnegie.

Scaife, Coors and other New Right funders spawned lobby groups and organisations which bombarded the American people and the Administration with New Right philosophy.‡ Shredded into this plethora of economic and political policy groups, were groups whose aims were more centrally involved in affecting the hearts and minds of the American people.

If the money men were disillusioned with liberalism, they could have been no more so than the business men. Angry at the Rockefeller-influenced 'social democratic', regulating policies of the Carter Administration, American multi-national business pushed for more power within the Administration. This was particularly the case when it came to science and technology. Both the New Right and the older liberal foundations poured money into advisory bodies which ensured that the Administration supported industrial science. Inside a decade, American science turned from an academic discipline with only a secondary application to industry, to a highly competitive and key element of the military industrial complex.

The first signs of the re-emergence of science, and its tendency to

---

†Richard Scaife married into the Mellon family, which had contacts in British and US intelligence. Joseph Coors inherited a fortune based on beer. Coors began his funding by supporting organisations fighting legal battles over public interest issues. In 1973, together with the architect of the American New Right, Paul Weyrich, he set up the Heritage Foundation which was to inform, subsidise and help organise many of Reagan's domestic and foreign policy adventures. Around the same time that Coors set up the Heritage Foundation, Scaife bought Kern House Enterprises, a CIA shell-company. Within Kern, he set up Forum World Features which became one of the most influential CIA news agencies of the seventies.

‡Such groups included: the National Humanities Center, the German Marshall Fund, the Center for Strategic and International Studies at Georgetown University, the Foundation for Research in Economics and Education, the International Institute for Economic Research, the National Legal Center for the Public Interest, Americans for Effective Law Enforcement.

determine congressional policy on behalf of business, came at the end of the seventies. The message at that time was that the growth of bureaucracy could be cured by 'rationalising' government. In effect, this meant taking a more objective view of the needs of industry. Greater rationalism in the structure of government also meant greater rationalism in the philosophy espoused by government. From the late seventies there was to be an all-out assault upon those movements which were seen as subjective, emotional, or unscientific.

> Widespread democratic challenge to traditional science policy is lumped directly with what are claimed to be anti-science and anti-technology movements. Popular criticism of a particular type of rationality – that which underlies production for profit and for military purposes – is purposefully confused with a critique of reason in general. Any dissident can thus be dismissed as, by definition, irrational and unreasonable. [3]

To reshape the public perception of science, the authority of science first had to be restored. Personal experience and popular perceptions had to be challenged. The experiential message of campaigning pressure groups and the subjectivity of unorthodox life styles had to be eroded. In relation to health and welfare, a new area of bowdlerised science was to take the place of proper scientific enquiry. The new philosophy was called 'risk management and evaluation'. This 'scientific' discipline, introduced a new relativity. The Chemical Manufacturers Association for example hired the J. Walter Thompson advertising agency to put together a $5 million media blitz with the message that risk was part of life itself.

The naturalness of chemical pollution was also a major theme at Dow, whose ads included the message that 'the chemicals we make are no different from the ones God makes ... There is an essential unity between chemicals created by God and chemicals created by humans.' [4]

Whereas the old question had been 'is this substance harmful?', a question which had often been repeatedly answered with a simple 'Yes', the new questions became: 'If this substance is harmful, is it very harmful? Can we live with it? Is it any more harmful than another substance which we used before?' Answers to such questions were complex. The new generation of industry-subsidised scientists was however well-equipped to answer them.

What industry liquidated from the equation on safety, when the new philosophy of risk management was introduced, was the view of the affected, non-scientific individual. With the new profile for science, any thoughts of those deleteriously affected by chemical processes having a say was discounted. These people became the casualties of the new 'risk' equation. They were the inevitable few who were damaged in the course of progress. If we accepted risk factors, then we had to accept a certain level of damage. Not only was the critical voice of those who were affected liquidated, but those individuals were stigmatised and made responsible for their own illnesses. Not only did the minority suffer under a policy of justifiable risk, they were also made to appear peculiarly vulnerable to that risk through some fault of their own.

> All but the technically initiated are excluded from the debate from the onset, forced to become spectators rather than participants in the central political struggles of the day. Once restricted to the de-politicized realms of 'objective analysis', policy evaluation neutralizes passions and abandons principles. In the alchemy of the experts, horrible 'bads' are magically transformed into relative 'goods', 'wrongs' into 'rights'. [5]

The mid-seventies saw the birth not only of the New Right but also of a new cynicism. The philosophy of designer science was one which declared itself capable of weighing up the value between one life and another, and capable of wiping out, if need be, those groups on the periphery who, as a consequence of their own inadequacy, made claims to being damaged by high technology. Believers in the new cynicism were determined to strip the developed world of irrationality.

Although the slogan on the cover of the Burroughs Wellcome Fund Annual Report for 1989 read *'The Magic of Medicine'*, the newly-defined science of the late seventies and eighties was actually determined to divest the world generally and medicine in particular of any hint of magic.

This period also saw a growing privatisation of science. The interests of academic science were subordinated to work for profit rather than for national, or community goals. Idealism was stripped away. Much of this was achieved by big business colonising previously state-funded academic organisations in both Britain and America. Industry moved onto the university campus in a big way. Education, in the field of science, became not so much a matter of equipping the individual to develop abilities, nor even educating the individual to aid the wider community, but subsidising the individual so that they could, at some future date, profit the private corporation. Throughout this transition the integrity of science suffered.

A series of scientific organisations, which had all but collapsed in both Britain and America, were re-activated in the seventies. In America the structures and organisations which had been dismantled during the Nixon era were re-instated by the Carter Administration. In 1976, the Office of Science and Technology Policy was reinstated. This Office had a close relationship with the Office of Management and Budget, which was used to ensure more than adequate funding for science and industrial research and development. However, such links went further because the two Offices worked actively to ensure that other Offices did not get budgets. They attempted, for instance, 'to remove health effects research from the Environmental Protection Agency'. [6]

Institutions outside the Executive which had fallen into disuse were re-financed. Journals and professional societies were re-awakened to a new and more powerful idea of science, its great future and its superiority as a philosophical and methodological approach to life.

The American Council on Science and Health

> *Journalists who blindly quote 'experts' without illuminating their agenda are simply adding another layer of fog to an already confusing debate.* [7]

The American Council on Science and Health (ACSH) is one of two major organisations which support the American National Council Against Health Fraud. As its title implies, ACSH puts the emphasis on the scientific objectivity of its advice and information. Set up in 1978, in the modern tradition of the 'think-tank', the Council made it an early objective to publish position papers on a wide range of products and substances and their effect upon health. Equally, from the beginning, ACSH did its best to obscure the link between its papers and the organisation's sponsors.

Setting up a consumer organisation which does not immediately receive money from vested interests, with the long-term strategy of bringing in such money at a later date, is good thinking. The reputation of a 'clean' organisation will continue for some time to overlap with an organisation which has begun to receive 'dirty' money.

ACSH was in existence for two years before it declared money which it received from industry. The organisation was pump-primed by the Sarah Scaife Foundation with a grant of $125,000. This grant came at a time when the New Right was in the ascendancy and conservative industrial causes were looking round for organisations and people to champion their cause. Two years after ACSH was set up, Reagan became President and the causes of the Right were taken into the Administration. The Sarah Scaife Foundation money was heavily based upon Gulf Stock, [8] which had funded a large number of campaigning right-wing groups in the second half of the seventies.

Following a policy decision in September 1980 that there should be no restriction on accepting industry money, Elizabeth Whelan, the organisation's founder and executive director, said:

> We realise that the people who criticised us for [our] funding [base] were criticising us no matter how clean we tried to be. We went to the Scaife Foundation. The Scaife Foundation is as clean as I could ever possibly imagine, people keep telling me about how they own Gulf Oil stock ... well, so does practically everyone else these days ... But they have no association with food chemicals ... they're a very wealthy American family. If that isn't accepted as clean then I realise that they would accept nothing as clean. So [I said] the hell with it ... just take money anywhere, and that's what we're doing. [9]

By May 1st 1981, ACSH reported that it had received donations from 111 corporations. Of these, 27 had a potential interest in food, drugs, air pollution regulation, or chemicals. [10] Since that time, the link between the funding and the work of ACSH has become bold and obvious.

ACSH is funded by many of the largest chemical companies such as: American Cyanamid, Amoco Foundation, Dow Chemicals of Canada, Hooker Chemical and Plastics Corp., Mobil Foundation,

Monsanto Fund, and the Shell Companies Foundation. ACSH has published two cancer reports, both of which exonerate chemicals. The President of Dow Chemicals is a foundation trustee of the Rollin Gerstacker Foundation from which ACSH has received payments of over $75,000. [11]

ACSH has presented work funded by paper companies and timber concerns which use vast quantities of herbicides. The organisation receives money from all the industrial sectors which contribute to the production of chemically-treated foodstuffs. It receives money from most of the largest companies involved in chemical production from the raw materials to the production and distribution of refined chemicals. While receiving money from firms like International Flavors and Fragrances Inc., and McCormick and Co., both producers of artificial flavourings and colourings, ACSH published a report which denied that the ingestion of food colouring agents leads to hyperactive behaviour in children.

In respect of sweeteners, ACSH takes money from the sugar companies, the synthetic sweetening companies and those soft drinks companies which are the world's largest sugar consumers. ACSH receives money from the Coca-Cola Co., the Holly Sugar Co., the National Soft Drink Association, and the Pepsico Foundation. Amongst processed food companies, ACSH receives money from: the Campbell Soup Fund, Heinz USA, Hershey Foods Corp., Kellogg Co., and the Universal Foods Foundation. [10]

Amongst medical and pharmaceutical interests, ACSH is funded by the Alliance of American Insurers, the Burroughs Wellcome Fund, Ciba-Geigy and Pfizer, as well as the AMA.

Elizabeth Whelan is a combative career woman in her late forties who bears comparison with the most dedicated anti-health fraud activists. She has a doctorate in Public Health from Harvard, where she studied under Professor Frederick Stare. [12]

The chemical and pharmaceutical companies often make public the view that the press is responsible for false perceptions about toxins and risk. One of Whelan's arguments is that the media are responsible for running scare stories. ACSH is there to right the balance, Whelan says, by providing conservative scientific information to the press. The origins of such scientific opinions are, however, rarely made clear and Whelan's views have been quoted in many prestigious articles without

ACSH's funding sources being mentioned.

Whelan claims that there are 200 scientists affiliated to the group and that the findings of ACSH are 'scientific' because they have been 'peer reviewed' by experts. Often such scientists are paid consultants for industry. While funded by Coca-Cola, ACSH has defended saccharin, praised fast food while supported by Burger King, and defended the use of hormone treatment for cows while financed by the National Dairy Council and American Meat Institute.

Both Whelan personally and ACSH corporately defend fast food, claiming there is insufficient evidence of any relationship between diet and disease. 'The assignment of foods to the evil categories of junk is very arbitrary. The gorgeous cheeseburger contains ingredients from all of the Basic Four Food Groups, but if you eat it in a fast food restaurant, some people will regard it as junk.' [13]

ACSH campaigned for Alar, while receiving a grant of at least $25,000 from the Uniroyal Chemical Company who manufacture it. When Whelan wrote an article defending Red Dye No. 3 for *USA Today*, she was introduced only as a 'guest columnist'. [14]

How deeply the views of ACSH are accepted as those of a genuine consumer organisation can be gauged by the fact that in 1989 Elizabeth Whelan got the veteran independent American reporter, Walter Cronkite, to narrate a film *Big Fears, Little Risks*. The film was an exercise in bias, only featuring commentators who believed that industrial carcinogens present 'only a negligible contribution to the cancer toll in this country'. [15] Whelan herself featured in the film described as 'one of a growing number of scientists who fear that overstating the risk of environmental chemicals is actually threatening the health of Americans'. [16] Cronkite, who was paid $25,000, admitted later that 'he did not do his homework properly'; he apparently knew nothing of ACSH's corporate funding. [17]

Elizabeth Whelan is an able propagandist. From the start she and her backers have understood the need for a dynamic new language which sells chemical products while criminalising those who speak out against them. She is credited with having coined such expressions as 'toxic terrorist' and 'self-appointed environmentalists'. She refers to the research work of Greens and clinical ecologists as 'voodoo statistics'.

Whelan argues that 'there are far more natural cancer causing substances than man-made ones'; that the link between high fat, high cholesterol diets and disease is greatly exaggerated. She minimises the risk of single low doses of a wide range of toxic substances, from asbestos to caffeine, and Agent Orange to PCBs. [18]

A founder member of the ACSH board is the old-school nutrition campaigner, Dr Frederick Stare. Former head of the Nutrition Department at the Harvard School of Public Health, Stare has associated himself with many campaigns against vitamins and food supplements. Over the years he has been actively involved with the FDA and the precursor groups to the National Council Against Health Fraud. Both Whelan and another Board member, Dr Robert Olson, were pupils of Dr Stare at Harvard.

Stare created the Harvard Nutrition Department himself in 1942 and built it up largely by attracting huge grants and gifts from food companies like General Foods, Borden and Kellogg. He is a board member of one large can company and has received extensive grants for his work from food processing companies. In 1960 the nutritional laboratories at Harvard received over a million dollars from the General Foods Corporation. [19] Between 1971 and 1974, the food industry provided about $2 million dollars to Harvard for nutritional research; the money came from the Sugar Association, Coca-Cola and Kellogg amongst others. [20] Professor Stare has developed his own Foundation which also supports ACSH.

Many of the biggest corporations which have funded Frederick Stare and the ACSH are part of the Rockefeller interest group.† General Foods, for example, which has donated large amounts of money to both the Harvard Nutritional Laboratories and ACSH, has a large percentage of Rockefeller directors on its board. In 1969, when General Foods was Fortune ranked 46th, six out of fifteen of its directors were Rockefeller Group directors. [21]

For its critical report on ACSH entitled *Voodoo Science, Twisted Consumerism*, published in 1983, the Center for Science in the Public Interest (CSIPI) approached eight well-regarded scientists to review ACSH reports which covered topics in their specialist areas. Almost

---

†Corporations are locked into the Rockefeller group in a variety of ways, some being owned directly by Rockefeller-owned financial institutions, while others are owned in part through stock by other Rockefeller companies. Another way of having a controlling interest is to have a predominance of Rockefeller-influenced directors.

without exception, the scientists concluded that the ACSH reports were biased and unscientific with many serious omissions of fact. [22]

- **On cancer:** the ACSH report had failed to discuss the possible involvement of industrial production and products in human cancer. The discussion in the paper on diet and cancer was termed 'inadequate'.

- **On heart disease:** the ACSH report demanded the highest level of proof in relation to the high-fat diet being a contributory cause of heart disease while readily accepting without the same level of proof that smoking and obesity were causal factors. The scientist who reviewed this paper found numerous errors and misrepresentations, some so severe, he labelled them 'astounding', 'stunning' and 'unscientific'.

- **On 2,4,5-T pesticide:** the ACSH report failed to mention contemporary studies carried out in Sweden which indicated increased rates of cancer amongst workers exposed to phenoxy herbicides. The company which produces 2,4,5-T is one of the major ACSH funders. ACSH claimed in this report that 'any substance' will cause birth defects if it is used in large enough quantities. [23]

The reviews commissioned by the Center also draw attention to an attitude which is common in many of the ACSH reports. The reports on 'Saccharin', '2,4,5-T', 'Caffeine' and 'Diet and heart disease', all argue that animal testing is not a valid guide to the effect of substances on humans. This suggestion throws into question the whole of accepted scientific method, for it is said that the only value of testing substances on animals is to gauge the risk to humans. The ACSH reports are forced to adopt what is from a scientific point of view an illogical position in order to avoid discussing scientific evidence, which often shows damage to animal subjects during trials.

Perhaps more serious even than the conflict over scientific practice is the unanswered question posed by the CSIPI in relation to the source of some of of the material published in the ACSH papers. There are hints in the CSIPI reviews that not all ACSH papers have been written wholly by their stated authors. In a number of the papers, 'position statements' and 'summary conclusions' come to quite different assessments from those suggested by the bulk of the report.

> This would have been a relatively good report if it did not
> contain the 'position statement' ... this work has been shackled
> with a political statement, prominently featured, which flagrantly
> contradicts the careful, objective tone of the report itself ... the
> body of the report is intended to provide readers with an
> objective, balanced assessment ... but the position statement
> seems designed to reassure readers there is nothing to be
> concerned about.

> The report's major problem is its 'position statement', the
> summarizing few paragraphs which is all most readers will
> pursue. From all I can tell, the position statement was written by
> someone other than the report's author ...

> It is almost as if the 'conclusion' paragraphs were written by
> someone other than the author of the [literature] review, since it
> is difficult to see any connection between the two in this case. [24]

Once again with ACSH, as with the NCHF and other important
organisations linked to the anti-health fraud movement, although
science is espoused, what is produced is a bastard progeny, a
consequence of an illicit liaison between large corporations, career
academics and journalists.

In 1986, Elizabeth Whelan came to England on a tour financed by
the Sugar Bureau. For a week she campaigned on behalf of sugar and
did a series of interviews with the gullible British media. During this
tour, Whelan claimed that there was no link between sugar and poor
health: 'There's no proof that sugar adversely affects behaviour, causes
cravings or obesity, or is associated with diabetes or heart disease.' [25]
Whelan blamed the adverse publicity for sugar on 'food faddists' and
'food extremists'.

1985 and 1986 were the years in which the campaigns in support of
industrial food and pharmaceuticals were brought to Britain. There
was a brief gestation period while forces grouped, before the British
'Council' Against Health Fraud was inaugurated.

Chapter Five

The Rational Idea in a Materialist World

Now, what I want is, Facts. Teach these boys and girls nothing but Facts. Facts alone are wanted in life. Plant nothing else. You can only form the minds of reasoning animals upon Facts. [1]

Although they were operating in the name of science, theirs was not in any traditional sense a 'scientific' enterprise but an ideological, political, or even — to the extent that the humanist agenda was being served — theological one. [2]

The other influential organisation which is affiliated, along with ASCH, to the American National Council Against Health Fraud (NCHF) is the esoterically named Committee for Scientific Investigation of Claims of the Paranormal (CSICOP). At first sight it is hard to see how an American socialist organisation, which in the 1930s set out to attack religion and promote humanism, could by the 1980s be involved in a series of attacks upon alternative medical practitioners, in Europe.

Paul Kurtz, the founder of the Committee for Scientific Investigation of Claims of the Paranormal, is a philosophy lecturer and writer at New York University. A prominent humanist, Kurtz was originally a member of the American Humanist Association and is now the leading member in a group of breakaway humanist organisations.

Kurtz's philosophical position owes much to the American pragmatists and the American humanists. Pragmatism became the final retreat for those Americans who had flirted with communism in the thirties and forties, ditching it as the Cold War set in. It is a philosophy which encompasses the most humanistic elements of social organisation and civil rights without actually challenging the industrial and productive power of capitalism which creates inequality and infringes those rights.

Politically Kurtz is a social democrat, part of that post-war American non-communist Left which was so relentlessly courted by the CIA in the fifties, sixties and seventies.† Kurtz was influenced by Sidney Hook, a leading American Liberal and free-thinker. [3] Hook was prominent amongst the American post-war intellectuals who were used by the CIA to propagate liberalism in Europe. He was a founder member of the Congress for Cultural Freedom and the American Congress for Cultural Freedom,‡ both of which were anti-communist groups, funded covertly by the CIA through the large American Foundations like Ford and Rockefeller. [4]

The American Humanist Association (AHA), which Kurtz joined in the fifties, was formed in 1933. A materialist organisation, it was broadly based on beliefs in atheism, socialism, free thinking and individualism. By the late fifties, the AHA was an influential organisation on the periphery of American philosophical and cultural life. It was particularly influential amongst intellectuals in east coast cities like New York.

In 1967, Kurtz became editor of the AHA journal the *Humanist* and during the early seventies this journal was considered by some humanists to be the best free-thought paper in the English speaking world. [5] Kurtz managed to recruit distinguised academic contributors and raise funds from wealthy individuals and foundations. [6]

While editor of the *Humanist,* in 1970, Kurtz set up Prometheus Books, a publishing company which was to become the leading free-thought publisher in the United States. In 1975, Kurtz demonstrated

†From the nineteen fifties onwards, the American Government, funnelling money through its administrative agencies, tried to re-define the political and cultural hegemony of Europe. The CIA conduited money to artists, magazines, newspapers, party leaders, community workers and sociologists, in an attempt to nurture influential organisations which would turn people, especially in Europe and the Third World, against communism.

‡ The Congress For Cultural Freedom (CCF) was founded in 1950. It was an avidly anti-communist organisation. After its first Congress in West Berlin, it organised conferences all over the world. Many of its prominent members were secular free-thinkers and humanists who were philosophically left of centre. The CCF was dissolved in 1967 when the CIA funding of it and its many journals was made public.

a departure from the previously conservative image of the AHA. Apparently concerned about a revival of astrology in the United States, he sent a letter to leading European and American scientists asking them to put their names to a manifesto entitled 'Objections to Astrology'. [7] He collected the signatures of 186 scientists.

The manifesto and the radical new departure upon which Kurtz had taken the AHA, began a series of schisms in the organisation. After drawing up and publishing the document, Kurtz led a breakaway group out of the American Humanists. This group called itself the Committee for Scientific Investigation of Claims of the Paranormal (CSICOP).

When Kurtz left the AHA, he took with him the Foundations and their money, a number of scientists attached to the AHA and his mentor Sidney Hook. He kept his publishing company, Prometheus, the success of which appeared outstanding, despite its short and esoteric list of books offered at very low cover prices.

It was evident from the beginning that the new group set up by Kurtz was to be radically different from the old AHA. Out went the overt association with the rather spartan humanist tradition, even further out went any identification with the non-communist Left, to be replaced by a zippy and popularist, highly influential pro-science organisation. The tone of the new organisation was slightly marred, some thought, by its dogmatism and incipient authoritarianism. Kurtz clearly wanted his new organisation to be more than a talk-shop; it wasn't so much going to debate the issues, as spread the word and tell its followers what they should believe.

Soon after launching CSICOP,† Kurtz held a press conference in New York to announce a campaign to purge the media of occultist leanings. He pledged that CSICOP would try to ensure that no TV programme dealing with parascience would go out unvetted by the appropriate authorities, that was, CSICOP.

---

† The co-chairman of CSICOP with Professor Paul Kurtz was Professor Marcello Truzzi, a sociologist from Eastern Michigan University. The best known American members were: Isaac Asimov, scientist and science fiction writer; L. Sprague de Camp, another science fiction writer; Martin Gardner, philosopher and scientific journalist; Professor W.V. Quine, philosopher at Harvard; James Randi, magician and showman; Professor Carl Sagan, astronomer at Cornell University; Professor B. F. Skinner, behavioural psychologist at Harvard University.

The new organisation began a journal, the *Zetetic*, which ran for a year before being replaced in 1978 by the *Skeptical Inquirer*. During its first years, CSICOP was riven by disputes. Some of the scientists who had come into the fold found the organisation too authoritarian. 'Statements contradicting borderline, folk or pseudoscience that appear to have an authoritarian tone can do more harm than good'[8] said Carl Sagan, a scientist who nevertheless stayed in CSICOP. Others suspected that CSICOP was not a genuine scientific organisation. They saw that it was not likely to carry out or sponsor any serious scientific work and appeared to be concerned only with ridiculing or 'debunking' the work of others.

The zealous McCarthyite style of CSICOP was illustrated soon after its inception in 1976, when Marcello Truzzi was 'denounced' for being 'soft' on CSICOP targets. Truzzi consequently resigned.[9] In 1976 Kurtz set up CSICOP's first piece of combative 'research' to disprove the work of Michel Gauquelin, a French psychologist,† whose work had shown that those born under certain configurations of Mars had certain types of personality. Unfortunately for Kurtz and CSICOP, a replication of Gauquelin's research also replicated his results. Faced with a damage limitation exercise, Kurtz and his colleagues wrote up the results of their research in the *Humanist* as if they had actually disproved Gauquelin's results.[10]

This jokey but cynical style was to be a hallmark of any 'scientific' work which followed. Studies were never conducted with regard to correct scientific procedures, and results which did not give the conclusion which CSICOP wanted were simply changed and re-presented. To those at the centre of CSICOP, privy to the organisation's funding and long-term aims, such exercises must have seemed hugely entertaining. For the serious scientists, spiritualists and healers, who were the subject of these japes, the costs were personally, professionally and financially extremely damaging.‡

† Gauquelin carried out his work in the 1950s. He worked out the position of the planets at the birth of 576 members of the Académie de Medécine. He found that, against a control group, they had been born most commonly under a rising Mars and Saturn.

‡ Uri Geller has spent years locked into a personal and financially costly action against James Randi. Geller is suing Randi, after Randi accused him of fraud. Following the action, Randi was forced to resign from CSICOP, so that Geller could not sue the organisation.

At least one prominent member of CSICOP, Dennis Rawlins, was alarmed by the attempt to cover up the results of the alternative Gauquelin research and continued to enquire into the matter, eventually writing up the whole story in *FATE* magazine. Accompanying the story in *FATE*, an editorial said 'They call themselves the Committee for Scientific Investigation of Claims of the Paranormal, in fact they are a group of would-be debunkers who bungled their major investigation, falsified the results, covered up their errors, and gave the boot to a colleague who threatened to tell the truth.' [11]

When the major focus of CSICOP's attacks became psychic research, people speculated about links with the intelligence services. In the nineteen sixties, the CIA and the KGB were deeply committed to psychic research and the possibility of using aspects of it in weapons systems and to prime covert agents to carry out assassinations.[12] Some writers speculated CSICOP was a policing organisation funded by the CIA to censor extra-governmental research which overlapped with intelligence work.

As CSICOP became more settled, its structure did resemble that of organisations chosen and set up in the fifties and sixties by the Foundations and the CIA to mask their operations. One or two central characters handled the administrative and organisational work, while the organisation was made to appear bigger than it was by the use of public relations, including the ability to place articles in journals or papers from all corners of the world.

One technique used frequently by CIA funded groups in the fifties, was to list large numbers of advisers and associates, so raising the profile and plausibility of the organisation. Just like the two hundred scientific advisors named by ACSH, CSICOP listed philosophers, scientists, writers and magicians as committed participants in their organisation. Such a strategy is very like that used by the Congress for Cultural Freedom by which a small low budget operation is given international intellectual authority.

* * *

The most aggressive public performer from CSICOP has always been the ex-magician, James Randi. Randi's methods for debunking 'non-scientific' practitioners are not new, but based upon the methods of Harry Houdini, the famous magician and escapologist. In 1924, *Scientific American* 'offered a prize of $5,000 to anyone who could demonstrate supernormal physical phenomena to a committee of its choosing'. Besides Houdini, the committee was composed of several Harvard and MIT professors.[13] Early in 1926, Houdini went to Washington to enlist the aid of President Coolidge in his campaign 'to abolish the criminal practice of spirit mediums and other charlatans who rob and cheat grief-stricken people with alleged messages'. [14]

In 1980, Randi was involved in another intervention in scientific research which went seriously wrong. Randi sent two young men whom he later claimed he had trained to cheat, as volunteer subjects to the MacDonnell Laboratories for Psychical Research. Randi's intention was to make fun of and cast doubt upon the research at the Laboratories by showing that a study was badly designed and the results could have been produced by fraudulent means.

When the sorcerer's apprentices went to the MacDonnell Laboratory, however, they found that under the controlled conditions they were unable to cheat. Despite the failure of his intervention, Randi held a press conference at which he claimed the researchers had allowed themselves to be duped. The hoax received massive and sympathetic publicity in a number of newspapers and on radio and television.[15]

CSICOP's campaign in support of science has run parallel with its campaigns against groups which maintain belief systems at odds with science. For many years in the seventies and the eighties, CSICOP spent its energy attacking Scientology. Later it moved on to small, especially Eastern, religious movements. Any spiritual group which believes in a deity and particularly if it has come to America from another culture, is described in derogatory terms as a 'cult'. Such groups are rarely tackled on a philosophical level, but are usually seen as politically subversive.

> There is always the danger that that once irrationality grows, it
> will spill over into other areas of society. There is no guarantee
> that a society so infected by unreason will be resistant to even the
> most virulent programmes of the dangerous sects. [16]

CSICOP campaigned hard in the early years against what it saw as the misrepresentation of science and the propagation of irrational ideas in the media. On November 8th 1977, Kurtz wrote to the Chairman of the Federal Communications Commission to lodge a formal complaint about a 90 minute 'special' NBC television had broadcast. 'Exploring the Unknown' dealt in a positive fashion with various psychic claims. CSICOP lawyers claimed that the programme showed bias and was not a 'fair' portrayal of the subject. The complaint was rejected. At around the same time another CSICOP official, magician Milbourne Christopher, claimed that some 200 people had killed themselves as a result of believing horoscopes published in the press or after believing palm readings. No supporting evidence was reported.[17]

Throughout the late seventies and the early eighties, CSICOP continued its campaign on a number of fronts. It made inroads into the scientific journals and associations, campaigning within them to push out research which did not conform with mainstream science. In the late 1970s, CSICOP ran a campaign to get the Parapsychological Association thrown out of the American Association for the Advancement of Science to which it had been admitted in 1969.

Certain elements in science, especially those close to the US Government, pushed CSICOP as a much-needed scientific policing organisation. *Science* and *Scientific American* published articles on its behalf; *Scientific American* supporting CSICOP against *FATE* magazine, allowed CSICOP to say: 'Who will guard the truth? The answer is CSICOP will!'[18]

Some working scientists have observed that the defence of CSICOP and its inordinate influence appear to be directed by hidden forces. Reviewing C.E.M. Hansel's book on ESP, the psychiatrist Ian Stevenson remarked:

> I know of no other branch of science past or present, other than parapsychology, where innuendos and accusations of fraud are allowed to appear in print and go unpunished unless the charges are substantiated. No one would think of accusing me of fraud for my work in conventional psychiatry, but obviously I lose this immunity when I work in parapsychology. Why?[19]

Others have seen CSICOP's strategies as an unwarranted intrusion into the scientific community by a group of unaccountable outsiders.

Writing to the *Times Higher Education Supplement*, Harry Collins made the point that science did not need 'a scientific vigilante organisation ... Science can and must police itself, without the help of self-appointed outsiders who, even when acting in all good faith, threaten its professional and political integrity'. [20]

CSICOP's major success has been in the popular media, appearing on TV shows, radio programmes and publishing articles in popular magazines and journals. CSICOP's 'viewpoint dominates the treatment of paranormal claims in nearly all élite, opinion-shaping publications, including *Science*, the *New York Review of Books*, and *Time* magazine, and in mass-circulation periodicals such as *Reader's Digest* and *Parade*'. [21] CSICOP claims that its own journal the *Skeptical Inquirer* now has 30,000 subscribers. To consolidate its links with the media, CSICOP endows an annual 'Responsibility in Media' award, to the editor, reporter or writer who most effectively represents the CSICOP view.

Although it was hard to see where CSICOP was coming from in its early years, by the late nineteen eighties its direction and perspectives were clearer. In 1986, James Randi received a grant of $272,000 from the MacArthur Foundation to see him through five years of hoaxes and attacks upon all matters spiritual, psychic or holistically medical. [22] The MacArthur Foundation, which was set up in 1978, is now worth over $3 billion. The Foundation interlocks with the Rockefeller Foundation, the Carnegie Foundation for International Peace and the U.S. Government's science programme.† As well as giving money liberally to the arts, black community projects and academics, it has given large grants to foreign policy researchers studying communism and such subjects as health claims and unproven alternative medicines.‡ [25]

† The MacArthur Foundation has on its selective board of directors, Professor Murray Gell-Mann, Professor of Theoretical Physics at California Institute of Technology and also a committee member of CSICOP; Jerome B. Wiesner, President of and Professor at the Massachusetts Institute of Technology; previously head of science and technology policy in the Kennedy administration, he once was said to have 'accumulated and exercised more visible and invisible power than any scientist in the peacetime history of America'; [23] Elizabeth J. McCormack, a member of the Rockefeller Family and Associates. [24]

‡ In 1990 the Foundation gave $30 million in grants to its Programme on Peace and International Cooperation. Amongst many grants, it gave nearly half a million dollars to the London based International Institute for Strategic Studies, an Institute set up with American money after the Second World War. It also gave over $7 million to the Social Science Research Council in New York to pursue research into International Peace and Security.

CSICOP and Medicine

By the end of the 1980s, there was rarely any serious debate about religion within CSICOP. There were still a good number of articles in the journals about ghosts, UFOs and the paranormal. CSICOP made the most of fashionable idiocies as they came and went, including sightings of little green men from Mars, and the odd account of abductions by extra-terrestrials. It is doubtful though whether anyone was fooled into thinking that a European and North American-wide organisation existed purely for the purpose of debunking these or other more reasonable claims.

The CSICOP journal included the occasional article about the lack of science education, but by far the most serious departure from the simple atheistic origins of the group was a new and determined focus on 'anti-health fraud'. CSICOP activists stated the case with clarity at the Fourth Conference of European Skeptics, in August 1990. According to the *Skeptical Inquirer,* the Conference was organised by CSICOP and SKEPP, a newly formed Flemish group, in Brussels.†
The Conference, held on the campus of the Free University of Brussels, brought together some 120 delegates from 20 nations, including fourteen European countries.‡

> Of special concern in this session was the popularity among Europeans of alternative health cures, such as holistic medicine and homoeopathy. In our view [Paul Kurtz reporting], adequate scientific verification has not been made to support these fields. The European Skeptics at our meeting agreed that many of these practices can be dangerous to the public health. Unfortunately, government and health professionals are hesitant to criticise questionable therapies because of the economic and political power of their advocates. [26]

It is difficult to imagine how even a 'philosopher' could make such an allegation. The most establishment-minded social scientists and economists agree that many of the most powerful groups in Western society are those linked to the petro-chemical industry. How could

† Studiekving voor Kritische Evalvtie van Pseudowetenschop en het Paranormal.

‡ The similarity of this type of large and expensive conference with those held by the CIA-funded Congress for Cultural Freedom in the 1950s should not pass unnoticed.

practitioners of alternative health care have social or economic power?

> Lars Jepson of Denmark described the situation in his country. He said that although the Danes have a tradition of rationalism and enlightenment, the New Age has recently made considerable inroads on the public consciousness. He focused on the use of homoeopathy and other 'natural medicines' and also took issue with the government's endorsement of dowsing. Alain Mey, representative from France, deplored the sale of homoeopathic medicines in most pharmacies in his country. [27]

> James Randi highlighted some of his investigations of the paranormal. Afterwards, Randi was asked about his recent criticism of a homoeopathy experiment conducted at a French laboratory (by Jacques Benveniste). His investigation was done in cooperation with the British science magazine *Nature*, quite independent of CSICOP. [28]

> Of special interest was the paper given by Dr A. Gertler, head of the skeptics group in Rossdorf, Germany (formerly East Germany). Gertler discussed the dangers of alternative medicine to the public health.

> Some important practical results came out of the Brussels conference. Much of this is consistent with the new mood in Europe as the unification of the continent approaches. Efforts are being made to coordinate political, economic, scientific, and cultural activities in time for 'Europe 1992'. [29]

An organisation set up to challenge religion and mysticism appeared by 1990 to be more concerned about the role of alternative medicine in a united Europe. An age of economic recession, cut-backs, high technology and high production costs to the pharmaceutical industry had brought about a radical change of tack. CSICOP was no longer as concerned with esoteric ideas but was 'debunking' health care treatments used by 40% of the French population (homoeopathy) and to which 30% of British general practitioners would consider referring their patients (various alternative treatments). [30]

Following the CSICOP conference in Belgium, Kurtz issued a press release through Reuters, giving journalists information about the conference.

> The new Belgian group said that it aims to investigate claims that

are incompatible with present scientific knowledge and to warn
the public about practices that could harm them. Wim Betz,
Professor of Medicine at the Free University of Brussels, said he
was particularly concerned about medical quackery. 'In twenty
years of practice, I've heard dramatic stories of people, faced
with dying of cancer, selling their houses and giving their money
to quacks', he said, 'The relatives are so ashamed that they don't
want to talk about it'. [31]

Such stories and the language are identical to those which were to
flood the British media during 1989 and 1990.

CSICOP have always put the case for scientific methodology even
if they refuse to practise it themselves. 'It is our view that when a field
has rigorous peer review and journals providing adequate critical
evaluation, there is little need for CSICOP to play a role.' They have
not, however, turned the cold gaze of scientific methodology on
alternative medicine. Nowhere is their poverty of scientific method
more clearly demonstrated than in relation to alternative and
complementary medicine. Here there are no references cited, no
scientific work commissioned; there is only propaganda and hot air.

Homoeopathy comes in for continuous attack from the major
CSICOP activists. They have assigned to it the most derogatory label
in the CSICOP lexicon, naming it a 'cult'. By traducing something as
a cult, they inevitably pronounce its followers as 'mindless' and
without rational individual will. In the Summer 1989 issue of *Skeptical
Inquirer*, James Randi stated:

> I certainly agree with Gardner's designation of homoeopathy as
> a 'cult'. It meets many of the criteria, including the invention of
> attitudes or statements on the part of those who oppose its
> notions and claims (sic). [32]

By the end of the 1980s, CSICOP had waded into the deeper end of
the health-fraud movement and was giving away tit-bits about its
involvement with the FDA and Rockefeller interests. The major
Rockefeller health industry interest in America is in cancer research,
which is funded and controlled by the American Cancer Society.
When unreferenced articles began to appear in the *Skeptical Inquirer*
about worthless cancer 'cures' such as macrobiotic diets, the use of
vitamins and food supplements, visualisation, spiritual and faith

healing and immune therapy, links between CSICOP and the pharmaceutical industry became clearer.

> Of special concern is the immense popularity of 'holistic' medicine and alternative forms of therapy. Dr Bernie Siegel, in his best-selling book *Love, Medicine, and Miracles*, claims that his patients can will away their cancer, although the lion's share of his evidence is anecdotal. [33]

This is a good example of CSICOP propaganda. As we have not read the book ourselves, we do not know whether Dr Siegel treated his cancer patients within a multi-disciplinary framework, nor do we know the number of patients Dr Siegel is suggesting helped their prognosis by will. On top of all this, we have to understand that, as Kurtz does not have a training in medicine, it is possible he knows nothing about the subject.

When CSICOP members begin railing against cancer cures, we know where they are coming from, because we have traversed this ground already, looking at the history of the health-fraud movement. When this part of their hidden agenda comes into view, it is more possible to understand why William Jarvis and Stephen Barrett, prominent activists in the movement, have linked up with CSICOP and why CSICOP is affiliated to the National Council Against Health Fraud.

While the NCHF puts forward the view that 'food faddists', allergy doctors, holistic medical practitioners, and clinical ecologists are all fundamentally involved in scams which fleece a vulnerable public of their hard-earned cash, CSICOP's case is slightly more complex. They promote the view that not only are vulnerable people being parted from their cash, but that people are being philosophically duped: they are thinking wrong thoughts!

PART TWO

The Insurgents Before 1989

Like a man in solitary confinement, he
found the other theory, the one he wasn't supposed to
have, becoming unreal because there was no one to discuss it with,
or because to entertain it only deepened his feelings of
being locked up alone inside his head.

Paul Ferris. The detective.

Develop your legitimate strangeness.

René Char.

Chapter Six

Dr Jacques Benveniste:
The Case of the Missing Energy

*French biology has been 'Cocacolonized'. If you come to France
with your dog, you have to tell the dog to bark in English or
American. If as well you put a sign on his head, which says
'scientist', he will be met with respect everywhere he goes.* [1]

In 1988, the reputation of Doctor Jacques Benveniste, one of France's
leading biologists, was almost destroyed. His work was internationally
labelled as fraudulent and he was held up to ridicule. He nearly lost his
post with INSERM, the French national medical research institution.

Five years later, news has not travelled fast enough nor reached the
furthest corners with sufficient intensity, to inform many people that
what was said about Benveniste and his research into the effects of
homoeopathic dilutions consisted mainly of innuendo and propaganda.

Jacques Benveniste is a well-respected French scientist. He will tell
you that he is an immunologist, and that is all he is; this though is to
undervalue him. He is an entertaining and charismatic man who has a
considerable history as a medical research scientist. He is committed to
one of the most exciting areas of biological research: the communication between cells, especially the cells which make up the human
immune system. He has devoted his life to trying to discover the
pathways between a select group of cells which are activated when
foreign substances enter the human body. He has a good track record,
but like many immunologists who have strayed from orthodox
pharmaceutical research and become involved with alternatives, he
feels that the American, British and French scientific establishments
have deprived him of deserved accolades.

After training as a doctor and working with cancer patients for twenty years, Benveniste began research into allergic conditions. On this subject he speaks with the common bitterness which many allergists feel about their governments and the orthodox medical establishment.

> I set up a group to research allergy inside INSERM, but this is the only group which is researching at a basic level problems which affect 15% of the population. At the same time, one billion francs are spent on pharmaceuticals for allergy each year.† [2]

The amount of money which the population spends on pharmaceutical preparations for allergy would be irrelevant if such preparations helped to resolve the problem. Benveniste believes, as do many others both inside and outside orthodox medicine, that drug solutions to allergy do nothing more than alleviate a minority of the symptoms; moreover Benveniste believes that chemicals generally take an increasing toll on health, creating more immune system illnesses. 'There has been practically no progress in the treatment of asthma and more generally in the management of allergy, in twenty years. Despite all the Nobel prizes given for work in this area, more people die today of asthma than did twenty years ago.'

Benveniste's research into allergy has taken him deep into the mechanisms which create such responses. Understanding that the smallest amount of a substance affects the organism – 'a person can enter a room two days after a cat has left it and still suffer an allergic response' – led Benveniste to research how homoeopathic dilutions‡ appear to have a real and material effect upon immune system cells called basophils. He was subsidised in this work by a company which produced homoeopathic remedies.

Benveniste's lack of commitment to the pharmaceutical companies and his implacable commitment to what he believes should be the French position in international science have frequently brought him

† Unless otherwise stated all quotes in this chapter are taken from the author's interviews with Jacques Benveniste.

‡ Homoeopathic remedies are usually diluted to a high degree. On occasions, the dilution is so great that orthodox scientists say that the original substance cannot be detected in the solution.

into conflict with the international medical research establishment. Throughout these conflicts he has made a name for himself as a scientist who will fight his corner.

He sees himself now isolated to some extent because of this consistent opposition.

> When there was a large conference on allergy in the beginning of the eighties in Britain, I sent a public letter to everyone. The French government sent no French scientists of international renown. I was at that time leading the most productive French allergy research group and I was not even invited. There were 0.3% French people in the programme, with 65% Anglo-American.

As the biggest drug companies moved into immunology and the kudos and money attached to finding cures for asthma and allergy grew, so did the anger and resentment against Jacques Benveniste. He found that his discoveries were often deprecated by the scientific establishment and he was not recognised for them. 'I was known previously, in 1972, for the discovery of a small molecule It is called the "platelet activating factor" (PAF). This discovery went against the grain of main-stream medical research.'

Benveniste puts his isolation partly down to the facts that he is French, and that he has not worked closely with a major pharmaceutical company.

> For example, in asthma research, during the seventies, medical research workers promoted very heavily in papers all over the place, that leukotrienes† were the molecules that did the job. There was enormous interest from the drug companies, who all wanted to get involved. Ten years later, it is clear that leukotrienes have only a modest importance in asthma treatment. We are still waiting for real progress to be made.

Benveniste feels that throughout the eighties he was excluded and isolated from the discussions around his own work and discoveries. He was excluded from committees and scientific seminars and conferences.

---

† Leukotrienes are highly-inflammatory substances which are derived from essential fatty acid metabolism and have been shown to be present in high quantities in the wind-pipes of asthmatics and in the skin of people with inflammatory skin conditions.

While other medical scientists have worked on histamine and helped the drug companies generate huge profits from 'me-too' (copy-cat drugs which have not been researched but copied by the producing company) anti-histamines, Benveniste's independence has led him to be considered a trouble maker and a maverick.

*   *   *

On June 30th 1988, *Nature*, Britain's top scientific journal, published a paper authored by thirteen scientists, including Jacques Benveniste of Paris Sud University. The paper, entitled 'Human basophil degranulation triggered by very dilute antiserum against IgE ', was the result of a five-year study which showed that, even in great dilutions, aqueous solutions of antibodies retained biological activity which was not present in plain water. [3]

This paper in *Nature* was, however, no ordinary scientific publication. It was accompanied by a most unusual editorial written by John Maddox, the journal's editor. [4] It was prudent, Maddox said, 'to ask more carefully than usual whether Benveniste's observations may be correct'. According to Maddox, the conclusions of the paper struck at the roots of two centuries of observation and rationalization of physical phenomena. Using the most irrational language, Maddox wrote that 'there can be no justification at this stage to use Benveniste's conclusions for the malign purposes to which they might be put'.

Benveniste had designed his experiments in 1982, and began work in 1983. The salaries of the large INSERM team which he heads – the INSERM unit for immunopharmacology and allergy (INSERM U200) at Clamart, Paris – are paid by the French Government. Practically all the medical research in France comes under the control of INSERM, which is roughly equivalent to the British Medical Research Council.

As Benveniste's work involved homoeopathic preparations, he received help from a small homoeopathic company, LHF, which in 1987 was bought up by the biggest – though still very small in pharmaceutical terms – French homoeopathic company, Boiron. While he was working for Boiron, Benveniste was also working on contracts for mainstream pharmaceutical companies. In 1989, two other homoeopathic companies took over from Boiron, one French,

Dolisos, and the other, Homint, half-German and half-Dutch.

The first problem that Benveniste encountered with his work came in 1985, when interim results were leaked and then taken up in a full-page article in *Le Monde*. Following the *Le Monde* article, Benveniste was invited onto a popular TV discussion show, where he found himself being heavily attacked. Although he had no means of knowing it, this attack was the first skirmish in a war declared upon him by a then unknown enemy. Like a guerilla army, this enemy did not wear a uniform, and fought covertly.

Benveniste's antagonist on the television programme, a scientist, did most damage when he asked Benveniste 'in front of the cameras, while the whole of France watched', if he knew what a 'control' was?[†] The question itself was so rudimentary and therefore so damning that, Benveniste says, it left him without a voice. The question stripped him of his experience, his advanced knowledge in the field and his status as an internationally renowned scientist. Benveniste was not able within the parameters of the discussion to outline his expert experience. 'I had already published four papers in *Nature* and over 200 scientific articles, two of which are called "citation classics" by the Philadelphia Institute for Scientific Information, and there I was being asked in front of millions of lay people whether I knew what a control was.'

It was during that programme that Benveniste realised that he was going to meet some hard opposition to his work. More than anything, he was amazed by the vehemence of the argument used against him. Being a reasonable man and an intellectual, he had expected a debate, not the kind of anger which was now hurled at him. He felt, he says, like a European intellectual who, on visiting a Muslim country, had denied the existence of God. It was as if the opposition wanted to kill him. To Benveniste, this attitude was antipathetic to science or to any kind of intellectual discourse.

> I was completely overcome because for me it is not worth dying
> for ideas. I can not understand that scientific data is important
> enough for everyone to get on their feet and start a bloody war.

[†] In research, a control group is one which is not experimented upon, but which is exactly similar in composition to that subjected to the experimental intervention. Most scientists consider the control to be one of the essential components of correct research method.

Benveniste submitted the results of his research in a paper to *Nature* in 1986. At the same time he submitted papers to the *British Journal of Clinical Pharmacology* and the *European Journal of Pharmacology*. Both the latter articles were eventually accepted and published in 1988 and 1987. [5] In these two journals, Benveniste's work was treated as conventional research. There were a few questions before publication about the way the statistics were handled.

Benveniste got no answer from *Nature* until a year after he had submitted the paper. A more usual delay might be two or three months. The next communication from *Nature* was a demand that he should arrange for the work upon which the paper was based to be reproduced in other laboratories before publication. To Benveniste, this demand went against the grain of any scientific research. Such a principle, if it were put into effect universally, would make the whole scientific process unworkable. 'Which scientists are going to give their unpublished data to other scientists to check?'

It began to dawn on Benveniste that someone was 'having him on', not with any sense of humour but with quiet derisory intent. Believing that he had become involved against his will in a struggle not only to preserve his own good name, but to defend the objective basis of scientific research, Benveniste agreed to the demand. He found two laboratories, one in Israel and one in Canada, which willingly replicated his work and his results. A team from Italy also replicated the work, doing eight experiments, of which they were happy with seven. All the results were then sent to *Nature* in the summer of 1987, with the revised paper signed by all the scientists who had carried out the work. Benveniste heaved a sigh of relief. As far as he was concerned, the matter was over: he could return to his research.

In the first quarter of 1988, John Maddox faxed Benveniste with a peer review of the first paper he had submitted eighteen months previously. This was the first time Benveniste had seen this review, and its two pages of comments struck him as a joke. Some were simply stupid while others were now outdated.† However, for the record, Benveniste provided a three-page reply. With the review, Maddox

---

† Benveniste was to find that the reviewer was Walter Stewart, from the US National Institutes of Health, one of the men who were later to arrive at his laboratory as part of the inspection team assembled by Maddox.

asked for other explanations, which were also sent. Then, on June 15th 1988, Benveniste received another alarming fax which told him that the paper would be published with an editorial reservation *only* if he agreed to a team visiting his lab to monitor his work. Sick of the whole dilemma, but completely sure of his scientific work, Benveniste accepted.

Why should he have been alarmed? He imagined that the team would check the laboratory books and see that his experiment had been carried out properly. After all, that was the internationally recognised manner for dealing with such situations. In retrospect Benveniste asks how he 'could have anticipated that, rather than examine the protocols and the record books, the team which was sent to France would ask to do the experiments themselves?' For that was exactly what the self-appointed investigators wished to do: replicate Benveniste's research in *his* laboratory.

If Jacques Benveniste had expected the investigators to be top-flight scientists, he was disappointed. James Randi was a leading member of the Committee for Scientific Investigation of Claims of the Paranormal (CSICOP). An ex-performing magician, Randi had dedicated the last twenty years of his life to attacking the work of scientists in the area of psychic research. Although Benveniste did not know it at the time, Randi was an implacable opponent of homoeopathy.

The second member of the visitation was Walter Stewart, a man who worked in the National Institutes of Health, at Bethesda, the hub of the government-funded US medical research establishment. John Maddox described Stewart as a man 'chiefly concerned ... in studies of errors and inconsistencies in the scientific literature and with the subject of misconduct in science'.

John Maddox, who was himself the third member of the team, was in no sense independent. Though held in high regard by the scientific community, he had for a long time been opposed to research which conflicted with the accepted scientific orthodoxy. From the early eighties he had been linked to the British offshoot of CSICOP, which was called CSICP. In 1984 he had called for the burning of a book by Dr Rupert Sheldrake which proposed the existence of a 'morpho-genetic memory field'. [6]

Benveniste was especially embarrassed by Maddox's presence in his laboratories. Here was a man whom he knew as an honourable scientist, acting in opposition to all scientific principles. Benveniste says of his visit:

> I had in my lab one of the men with the highest position in science, John Maddox. I was in the position of a man who meets the Pope and the Pope asks for his wallet, what was I to do? It is not easy to say no.

Having agreed to the visit, Benveniste turned over his laboratory, his records and his staff to assist the three strangers in their replication of his work. Unskilled in the particular area of work, unfamiliar with the lab and insistent upon much gratuitous ballyhoo, the visitors made a terrible mess. James Randi frequently made light of the proceedings by playing childish pranks.

> Randi introduced a bit of theatre into the proceedings when he wrote down the code that could identify the true samples from the controls, and put it in an envelope which he stuck to the ceiling. It was a ruse to see whether anyone would attempt to tamper with it during the night. [7]

* * *

The research having been carried out, the results, which conflicted with those Benveniste arrived at, were published in *Nature* four weeks later. [8] Headed 'High Dilution Experiments a Delusion', the article claimed that Jacques Benveniste had been guilty of 'delusion' and 'hoaxing'. The learned opinion of the team after three weeks' research, was that Benveniste had got it all wrong. 'There is no substantial basis for the claim that anti-IgE at high dilution (by factors as great as 10^{120}) retains its biological effectiveness, and that the hypothesis that water can be imprinted with the memory of past solutes is as unnecessary as it is fanciful ... The claims of Benveniste *et al* are not to be believed.' [9]

Nature gave considerable publicity to the report of their 'independent' investigators. And the idea that Benveniste's work was fraudulent was picked up by a number of newspapers and journals. One of the British 'quality' newspapers, the *Guardian*, followed the 'independent investigation' with an article by Peter Newark which claimed that the original paper was 'so bizarre that anyone could have spotted the problems ... it was a piece of outrageous research. But we were not hoaxed'. [10]

By the end of the visit, Benveniste knew that Randi was a member of CSICOP and with a thought about previous cases, and the way in which CSICOP's pranks had led to major career damage, he reacted angrily for the first time. His response in *Nature* was published alongside the results of the team.[11] In this article, Benveniste gave details of the absurd behaviour of the 'investigators', while they had been in his lab; he concluded: 'I now believe this kind of inquiry must immediately be stopped throughout the world. Salem witchhunts or McCarthy-like prosecutions will kill science. Science flourishes only in freedom. We must not let, at any price, fear, blackmail, anonymous accusation, libel and deceit nest in our labs.'[12]

Benveniste's work on the biological activity of high dilution substances was not the first in this area. The number of fifty previous studies was quoted by Denis MacEoin in the *Journal of Alternative and Complementary Medicine*.[13] What Maddox and CSICOP were banking on was that the scientific establishment and the lay public would come to immediate and uneducated conclusions on the basis of their unscientific investigation.

* * *

For Benveniste the experience has been one of learning. In the last five years he has turned from being a relatively naive and perhaps academic scientist into someone desperately involved in the reality of the struggle between science and industrial vested interests. Even so, like other previous victims, Benveniste knows little more about the men who tried to destroy his career and his reputation than he did at the time.

As a consequence of the attack, he began gathering information about CSICOP and its connection to the European rationalist movement.† Like others before him, he cannot understand how the original ideas of rationalism have become subverted, so that they now

---

† Rationalism is a philosophical current which grew out of the European revolutions of the seventeenth and eighteenth centuries. Its arguments support reason, logic and scientific enquiry while opposing superstition, religion and magic.

stand for censorship and irrationality. Benveniste considers himself a rationalist and has always been in sympathy with the ideas of the rationalist movement. He does not however agree with the way in which CSICOP and the rationalists express their views, 'were it not for the conservative and authoritarian attitudes of CSICOP and the rationalists (in France, L'Union Rationaliste) I would belong to them.'

The modern movement of European rationalism is evangelical in its support for multinational pharmaceutical companies, in particular, and for science, in the service of the military industrial complex in general. Benveniste sees now that CSICOP and the rationalists represent the older and most conservative of capitalism's science-based industries.

> Even if these people are defending industry rather than science, they are clearly stupid, because if we are right our discoveries will ultimately augment any possible intervention in the market by the pharmaceutical companies.

Benveniste puts the matter in a rudimentary economic context, posing it as the old problem for capitalism and conservative ideology; 'it is the problem of the stage-coach manufacturers, are they going to turn into car manufacturers or not?' He points out that if a wide range of modern scientists are right in their evaluation of what he calls 'the new science', then the companies which are now acting defensively will inevitably disappear, while others with more imagination will take their place.

Benveniste has found few platforms from which he has been able to express the injustice which he feels has been done to him. CSICOP and James Randi, on the other hand, have continued publicising the case of Jacques Benveniste's 'fraudulent' work. On Wednesday 17th July 1991, Granada Television screened the first in a series of programmes hosted by James Randi, 'psychic investigator'. [14] Designed to debunk and refute all things 'non-scientific', the programmes lacked method or substance. Randi, who was himself presented by the press as a New Age character, was only a medium success, coming across as a humourless and rather wooden entertainer.

Some of the many interviews with Randi at the time of these programmes mentioned his accusations against Benveniste, while none

of them attempted to put Benveniste's point of view. A book, authored
by James Randi, and published to coincide with the programmes, [15]
mentioned on its first introductory page Randi's role in exposing
scientific frauds, one case being that of Jacques Benveniste.

> The scientific world was understandably sceptical. John
> Maddox, editor of Nature, took the bold (sic) decision to
> publish Benveniste's results, on the understanding that he could
> later send in a three man team of 'ghost busters', including
> Randi, to monitor the experiment. [16]

* * *

When Jacques Benveniste's reputation was 'attacked' in early 1988,
some of his friends and many who were not his friends, pointed out
that he was, after all, no stranger to controversy and might himself be
partially to blame for his own victimisation. What no one was able to
do in 1988, however, was to see the 'attack' upon Benveniste as one of
a number, rooted in a plan of campaign against allergists,
immunologists and those working in allied fields. As they developed,
these attacks could be seen to be focused upon those whose work
touched upon research into and treatment for illnesses of the immune
system.

Chapter Seven

Clinical Ecology: Stratagem for a Poisoned World

It was a town of machinery and tall chimneys out of which interminable serpents of smoke trailed themselves for ever and ever and never got uncoiled. It had a black canal in it and a river that ran purple with ill-smelling dye ... [1]

The development of clinical ecology – the study of illness created by our surrounding environment† – has been little different from the development of any social idea despite being a matter of health and therefore one of some urgency. New social forces and their actors create feelings of passion and commitment, both for and against. New ideas are disputed by those with both altruistic and mercenary motives. Progress, however, is like the statues which Michelangelo described as trapped within his blocks of marble: it will eventually be released.

The philosophy and practice of what is generically called clinical ecology assumes that the mechanical and chemical processes of the industrial revolution, the electrical and the nuclear age, have all had a deleterious effect upon the health of individuals and societies. This idea has met with more resistance than perhaps any other non-ideological philosophy. The basic demand of clinical ecology is in fact a radical one: that the industrial means of production be reorganised to suit the health of the whole of society.

---

† Clinical ecology is the diagnosis and treatment of illnesses caused by environmental factors. The discipline has come under such heavy attack in America that practitioners in Britain recently dropped the title 'clinical ecology' and substituted environmental medicine. For the purpose of this chapter, however, which is mainly historical, I have continued to refer to the field as 'clinical ecology'.

The initially observed links between illness and industrialisation were fairly straightforward. The city of Salford, which abutts Manchester in Lancashire, used to have the highest rate of bronchitis in the world. Such health problems appeared relatively easy to resolve. There was a direct causal link between the smoke from Salford's many domestic and industrial chimneys and the lung disease. Over time, industrial processes changed, pressured and cajoled by campaigns and new laws, and aided by the change from fossil fuel to electricity. Decades after the problem was recognised, Manchester got 'clean' air.

Following the Second World War a movement of doctors and therapists grew up. They were mainly rooted in the fields of allergy and immunology, principally because it was these disciplines that dealt with the effect of ingested alien substances on the human being. These practitioners considered that singular illnesses such as bronchitis and pneumoconiosis and chronic complaints caused by inhaled pollen, dust and mites were only the tip of a submerged iceberg of illness caused by environmental factors.

The major body of twentieth century illnesses and their pathogens, it was thought, lay hidden beneath the surface of a general miasma of poor, but not necessarily ill, health. The movement which grew with these theories differed from previous medical movements in the way that its practitioners placed the emphasis upon a preventive approach to sustaining good health.

Clinical ecologists began to consider that a great many of the illnesses associated with a generally falling standard of health, from allergy to alopecia, migraine to eczema, from arthritis to stomach ulcers and including such serious illnesses as cancer, may be linked to the substances which we ingest voluntarily and involuntarily.

These doctors and therapists began to redraw the boundaries of 'the environment', until it included anything from the food taken by the pregnant mother, to the quality of the air at its furthest reaches. Consequently, clinical ecology developed as an internally diverse movement, which contained, amongst many practitioners, nutritionists, surgeons, allergists and paediatricians. They had however one central message in common: what was taken into the body by a number of means inevitably affected the balance of its internal ecology, and particularly its immune system.

That such ideas would meet with the most aggressive and

determined resistance was inevitable. After two centuries of industrial development, there were those whose very lives, wealth and family heritage rested upon the science of productive industry. The power and identity of a whole class were vested in products as diverse as petrol and animal feed, products which clinical ecologists claimed were causing an erosion of health.

Clinical ecologists have been at the forefront of many significant contemporary battles over health, such issues as the dangers of lead in petrol and passive smoking. The part they have played has, however, been 'hidden from history' principally because they are insurgents struggling against an accepted and prevailing power which tends to record only its own history.

For many clinical ecologists, the chemical treatments of the pharmaceutical industry are yet one more aspect of a toxic environment. Allopathic medicine has taught us to see the many diseases of the twentieth century as diverse and not necessarily related to life-style or environmental causes. Allopathic medicine has also taught us that the symptoms of each illness may be treated separately. It has developed many site-specific chemicals to treat these symptoms and has tended to ignore the whole person and their environment.

It is now becoming clear that we ignore the whole person at our peril. At the heart of the human eco-system is the immune system, a self-regulating mechanism which protects the body from invasion. The human immune system is under attack as never before, as our bodies manifest a series of new and debilitating illnesses in addition to an increased incidence of old ones.

A Short History of Allergy Medicine

Unlike the history of 'scientific' medicine, which has developed principally in relation to the piece by piece discovery of human biology, the history of clinical ecology has relied much more upon the ad hoc subjective experiences of its practitioners.

The earliest discoveries about antigens entering the human body uninvited and creating allergic responses, focused mainly on food. François Magendie first created allergic symptoms in animals in 1839. He found that animals sensitised to egg white by injections died suddenly after a later injection. [2]

Dr Charles Blackley, who practised in Manchester in the 1870s, had hay fever. He covered slides with a sticky substance, left them outside and found that his symptoms were invariably at their worst on the days when the most pollen stuck to the slides. [3] He later scratched a tiny amount of pollen into his skin and found that it produced a red weal; when he tried this test on a number of his patients, the weal only came up on those who suffered from hay fever.

The first doctors to use injections of allergens — the substances which create allergic reactions — were Drs Noon and Freeman of St Mary's Hospital in London. In 1911 they found that injections of pollen temporarily cured those who suffered from the allergy. [4]

Dr Carl Prausnitz and Dr Heinz Kustner were allergic to different substances. Kustner suffered from an allergy to fish, the briefest taste of which would make his mouth swell. In 1921, these doctors injected themselves with small amounts of each other's blood and showed that sensitivity to particular substances could be passed from one person to another through blood serum. [5]

As early as 1925, when Dr Erwin Pulay published a book on eczema and urticaria, [6] doctors were making diagnoses of allergic responses in sensitised subjects, not only to foods, but to chemicals placed on the skin.

> A lady consulted me regarding a long standing and painfully irritating eczema which had spread all over her body. When she first called, her eyes, ears and face were inflamed, the skin disfigured all over by scratches, and the patient felt her unpleasant condition acutely. Her eczema was diagnosed by the specialists as being of the nervous type, and its cause asserted to be unhappiness in her married life.
>
> The conspicuous discolouration of the skin and the state of the finger nails allowed me to diagnose immediately that the eczema was due to nothing else than naphthalene, and investigations bore out this conclusion. It had originated as follows: the patient had rolled up three Persian rugs and strewn them with naphthalene. When she put naphthalene in her clothing during spring-cleaning, she was immediately attacked by severe inflammation of the skin. The carpets had sensitised her skin and she had become allergic to naphthalene. [7]

Even from this example, it can be seen that from the beginning allopathic specialists were prepared to diagnose psychiatric and emotional causes for allergic responses, rather than carry out proper scientific investigations. Scientific proof of environmental illness has always been difficult. The human body with its infinitely complex and individualistic metabolism refuses to be generally classified. Apart from the most extreme invasions, which are likely to trigger similar responses in many people, ingested antigens affect people differently. The preconditions for an allergic response may vary from a fault in the body's metabolic pathways, of which six thousand have been recorded, to a previous, specifically induced, compromise of the immune system.

Between 1900 and 1930, a number of doctors observed and recorded allergic responses amongst themselves and their patients, particularly to high protein substances such as egg and milk. In 1921, Dr William Duke reported cases in which eggs, milk and wheat produced severe stomach upsets.

From the first recognition of allergy, doctors were in two minds about its meaning in relation to treatment. In the early part of the century, doctors restricted their search for antigens to a narrow field of common substances. They also restricted the symptomatic picture presented by allergy sufferers, to weals, swellings, itching and runny noses.

One of the first clinical ecologists, a British psychiatrist, Francis Hare, went much further. In 1905 he published *The Food Factor in Disease*.[8] His research showed that far from being a simple equation between food and allergic response, allergy was a complex matter, sometimes dependent upon state of mind, which could result in degenerative diseases. Hare suggested that migraine, bronchitis, asthma, eczema, gastrointestinal disturbances, epilepsy, angina, high blood pressure, gout, arthritis and a number of other conditions were almost wholly the result of an intolerance to sugar and starch. Hare was not taken seriously by his contemporaries.

Dr Albert Rowe translated a French work by two Paris doctors, *L'Anaphylaxie Alimentaire*,[9] in which they recorded all the available accounts of illnesses caused by food in France. Following this translation, Rowe began work with his own patients on their allergies. It was Rowe who first used systematic skin injections of allergens to produce reactions. He found such tests, however, to be ultimately unreliable and began to work on elimination diets.

Rowe's work was influential and his techniques were quoted as being good treatments for migraine, asthma, eczema, hives, chronic catarrh, persistent indigestion, ulcers of all kinds, period pains and a condition of tiredness known in the 1930s as 'allergic toxaemia, characterised by fatigue, nervousness, mental confusion and an aching of the body'.[10] Rowe was still practising in the early nineteen sixties in California, where he introduced a new generation of students and doctors from Europe and America to clinical ecology.

Dr Arthur Coca, a Professor at Cornell in the 1930s, was a founder of the *Journal of Immunology*. He researched a number of allergic responses to ingested substances. Many of these produced no outward signs, but did speed up the pulse, making the sufferer feel slightly unwell. His theories were not well received by the orthodox medical establishment. In one of his books, he complained:

> The reason for it [the skepticism] is that the medical profession is again faced with scientific findings and their consequences that are so far out of line with settled concepts as apparently to represent the impossible. [11]

In the late thirties, Dr Herbert Rinkel, then practising as an allergist, himself had a severe allergic response. For years previously Dr Rinkel had suffered from recurrent fatigues, headaches and a distressing runny nose. After reading work by Rowe, Rinkel wondered if he were allergic. Suspecting that he was allergic to eggs, he ate six raw eggs at once. When they produced no reaction he thought that he had made a wrong diagnosis. Some years later, still suffering from chronic health problems, Rinkel decided to eliminate eggs completely from his diet. His symptoms began to fall away. But on his sixth eggless day, his birthday, he took a bite of angel-food cake, containing egg, and crashed to the floor in a dead faint.

The experience led Rinkel to understand that some patients who showed symptoms of allergy might be ingesting a number of foods regularly and not know that they were causing an allergic response. He coined the phrase 'masked allergy'.

In 1944, Dr Rinkel met a young doctor called Theron G. Randolph. Randolph was later to become one of the pioneers of American clinical ecology. After taking case histories of his apparently healthy students and nursing staff at the Northwestern University near Chicago, he came to the conclusion that two thirds of them had a history of food allergy. Randolph began to think that food allergy was also involved in alcoholism, and different forms of mental illness.

It was the careful detective work of Randolph which gave clinical ecologists their first real understanding of the fact that many chemicals, other than those occurring in foods, could cause illness akin to allergy. After four years' work, Randolph diagnosed a particular patient as being sensitive to petroleum exhaust fumes.

One conclusion reached before the Second World War about allergic responses was that they were person-specific. Different people are allergic to different allergens at different times. For this reason, it has always been easy for orthodox practitioners to suggest that such individually experienced symptoms do not have a scientifically measurable organic base.

The specificity of sensitisation to 'everyday' substances has presented particular problems to diagnostic practitioners, not least because patients themselves and observers will often be sceptical about a diagnosis for which they cannot see clear material causal reasons.

Over the last twenty years, a major schism has developed between those doctors who are willing to accept only food intolerance as a classic cause of allergy, and those who have developed the work of the early clinical ecologists.

The major difference between the groups is that for the orthodox allergists, the patient's response is a transitory disorder, caused when a substance which acts as an antigen enters the body. This discomfort passes when the antigen has left the body and the cells have stopped breaking down. Clinical ecologists, however, are convinced that many chemical antigens, though they may cause a primary allergic response, are not dispelled from the body but stay as continual irritants to the immune system, often lodged in fatty tissue. The illnesses which are consequent upon this toxic storage and the toll which it takes on the immune system, can be long-term. They also believe that once a person is sensitised to a substance, future exposure can lead to dangerous and debilitating illness.

Clinical Ecology and Chemicals

The decades which followed the Second World War brought a new consciousness about the environmental causes of illness.† This was partly as a consequence of the invention and use of the atomic bomb, and partly as a consequence of the continuing development of chemical weapons. Following the Second World War there was almost constant weapons testing which involved the releasing of radioactive matter into the atmosphere. The nineteen fifties and sixties were decades of anxiety, when minds were continually preoccupied with the effects of strontium 90 and atomic fall-out. This concentration led to a greater public education about the nature of the food chain than has probably occurred before or since.

The post-war generation was taught to worry not just about nuclear 'fall-out' in the abstract, but about its presence in milk, in water and, inevitably, in the vegetables which grew in the soil.

> Strontium 90, released through nuclear explosions into the air, comes to earth in rain or drifts down as fallout, lodges in soil, enters into the grass or corn or wheat grown there, and in time, takes up its abode in the bones of a human being, there to remain until death. [12]

By the early sixties there existed serious concern about the effect upon foods from chemicals which were either used in their cultivation or production. Pesticides have been used from the early nineteenth century. [13] The substances which were common in these preparations were lime and copper sulphate, lead arsenate, mercury and arsenic. The first synthetic pesticide was DDT, made from chlorinated hydrocarbons. It was discovered by a Swiss chemist in the 1930s and called a 'wide spectrum' pesticide because it killed everything.

The development and manufacture of nerve gases, which paralysed the nervous system, which began in earnest after the First World War, had immediate consequences for agriculture. Following the Second World War, the main ingredients in nerve gases, organophosphorous compounds, were used as pesticides. Organophosphorous (OP) compounds soon began to take the place of DDT. They had certain

† The Clean Air Act was passed in 1956.

advantages over chlorinated hydrocarbons, one being that they degraded more quickly. However, it was to take over forty years to fully understand the cost of OP in terms of human illness.

Production of synthetic pesticides in America after the Second World War went from 124,259,000 pounds in 1947 to 637,666,000 pounds in 1960. [14] From the very beginning of the use of these substances, illnesses were recorded in direct relation to their use. Those cases recorded were, however, usually the most extreme cases; thousands of cases of disease which involved all the classic signs of chemical sensitivity went unnoticed by doctors and patients who presented with symptoms which appeared little different from 'flu or nervous exhaustion.

Awareness of the unhealthy effects of pesticides was felt first in those countries which had developed intensive farming techniques, such as America, Canada, Australia and New Zealand. Within twenty years of the Second World War, over two hundred chemicals were being manufactured mainly to aid farmers 'in killing insects, weeds, rodents, and other organisms described in the modern vernacular as "pests"'. [15]†

The initial use of pesticides in the fifties and sixties killed thousands of birds, wild animals and insects. DDT was banned in the USA in 1971. In Britain, although 'voluntarily' banned from 1974, it was not finally removed from the market until 1984 even though it has been banned for nearly twenty years. The residue of DDT, called DDE, can still be traced in products in those countries where it was used on a massive scale.

In her book *The Silent Spring*, published in 1962, Rachel Carson quotes extensively from patients who became severely ill as a consequence of exposure to pesticides and insecticides.

> One case history concerned a housewife who abhorred spiders. In mid-August she had gone into her basement with an aerosol spray containing DDT and petroleum distillate. She sprayed the entire basement thoroughly, under the stairs, in the fruit cupboards and in all the protected areas around ceiling and

† There are some 2,500 named products listed in the 1988 Pesticides Manual issued by the MAFF Health and Safety Executive.

rafters. As she finished the spraying she began to feel quite ill with nausea and extreme anxiety and nervousness. Within the next few days she felt better, however, and apparently not suspecting the cause of her difficulties, she repeated the entire process in September, running through two more cycles of spraying, falling ill, recovering temporarily, spraying again. After the third use of the aerosol new symptoms developed: fever, pain in the joints and general malaise, acute phlebitis in one leg. When examined by Dr Hargraves she was found to be suffering from acute leukaemia. She died within the following month. [16]

Other compounds very similar in structure to chlorinated hydrocarbons used in the fifties and sixties, were polychlorinated biphenyls (PCBs). Their toxicity was first noted in 1919 and it was estimated that by 1939 six human deaths had occurred as a result of industrial operations with these chemicals. [17]

The environmental problems associated with PCBs only became apparent after research into chlorinated hydrocarbons. PCBs enter the food chain, usually through fresh water or marine fish, which have been contaminated with industrial effluents.

Once substances like DDT, PCBs or OPs enter the food chain, they can be found in a wide range of produce eaten by human beings, from butter to fish, and from egg yolk to vegetables. Certain organophosphates will be commonly found in grain and therefore in animal feedstuff and bread.

America's war against the Vietnamese led to the development of more effective herbicides, which were used to defoliate whole areas of Vietnamese countryside by indiscriminate spraying. The most prevalent of these auxin herbicides are 2,4,5-T and 2,4-D; the former contains dioxin, an impurity produced during the manufacturing process. Dioxin is one of the most deadly toxic substances known to man. [18]

The eventual toxic effects on individuals of pesticides, herbicides and insecticides relate in part to other aspects of the individual's health status. Much scientific work done on the toxicity of pesticides takes into account the effect of what is termed 'the normal dose', while failing to take into account the sizeable proportion of the population who are especially vulnerable: pregnant woman, the elderly, the sick or the very young. Perhaps most importantly, little longitudinal research has been done into the accumulated storage levels of a multiplicity of such toxic substances in the human body.

From the 1950s, pesticides played a substantial part in what has euphemistically come to be called 'animal welfare'. Generally, animal welfare means keeping animals in good short-term condition before they are slaughtered. Most animals reared for meat are nowadays arbitrarily given regular doses of antibiotics, the residues of which are passed on to the consumers. Cattle and sheep are sprayed continually with chemicals to keep them sterile and free from smaller insects and bacteria. Whatever the cumulative effect upon the inner biology of the animals, the workers who have to douse them are prone to chronic illnesses. In 1990 it was estimated by campaigners that as many as 2,500 farmers could be suffering side-effects from the use of organophosphorous sheep dips. [19]

> Of the 3-4,000 people who have registered with us after suffering from the effects of pesticides, more than 2,500 are directly attributable to contact with sheep-dip. Organo-phosphorous compounds are designed to kill, whether it be insects by ... fly spray or humans through the inhalation of nerve gas. [20]

Many farmers cannot understand why doctors and the MAFF have refused for decades to recognise the symptomatic picture presented by those who have been adversely affected by sheep dip.

> Three years ago, I first passed out after using sheep dip. Doctors and specialists could not get to the bottom of it even after giving me every kind of test, even a brain scan. Only by chance did I link it all to sheep dip. I have thirteen of the nineteen possible side effects which can come from being in contact with sheep dip. Exposure to sheep dip has done my nerves irreparable damage. There are farmers who feel they are going crackers because no one will recognise their symptoms. Doctors are amongst those who send sufferers away with no explanation for their dire symptoms. [21]

Sheep dip is a mixture of antibiotics and pesticides which protect sheep from scab, fleas, ticks, and mites. Every year the National Rivers Authority (NRA) has to warn farmers about the dangers of sheep dip leaking into the water course, either directly, or as a consequence of sheep running through rivers after being dipped. Sheep dip is described by the NRA as a 'powerful pollutant'. Its constituent chemicals can kill fish and present a threat to drinking water supplies.†

Contamination of ground water by agricultural chemicals of all types has become a serious environmental concern. This concern has moved on from nitrates in fertilizers to include substances which are used above ground. *A survey of levels of pesticide residue in England and Wales* revealed levels above the Maximum Admissible Concentration for any single pesticide in 298 water supplies. [22]

A recent British Medical Association report, *Pesticides, Chemicals and Health*, [23] groups the deleterious effects to health of pesticides into five categories: toxicity which has the ability to cause cancer, to damage genetic material, to damage the foetus, to create allergy and affect the immune system and, finally, to affect the nervous system.

It was estimated by the World Health Organisation in 1986 that there were between 800,000 and 1,500,000 cases of unintentional pesticide poisoning worldwide, leading to between 3,000 and 28,000 deaths. [24]

There is a continuing increase in the amounts of chemicals used in farming and the acreage which this use covers.

> In the three years between 1974 and 1977, the area of cereals sprayed with aphicides increased 19 times. Between 1979 and 1982, the area of crops treated with insecticides doubled, while the area treated with fungicides more than doubled. BAA [British Agrochemicals Association] figures from 1979 to 1982 for the five major crops grown in Britain (cereals, potatoes, oilseed rape, sugar beet and peas) show a 29% increase in the area sprayed with herbicides, a 37% increase for insecticides and a 106% increase for fungicides. Yet the actual cropped area only increased by 4%. [25]

Controls on pesticides in Britain first began to be introduced in the 1950s, when the Gower Committee recommended that protective clothing should be used by all farm workers using toxic chemicals. The Gower Committee was followed by the Working Party on

† In July 1992, MAFF decided that the dipping of sheep against sheep scab was no longer compulsory, so bringing to an end one of the biggest post-war scams perpetrated by the chemical industry. For decades the production of sheep dip had been a licence to print money.

Precautionary Measures against Toxic Chemicals used in Agriculture. This last Committee suggested statutory controls on the sale and use of pesticides. MAFF, however, rejected any such controls as 'an unwarranted interference with the freedom of commercial concerns'. Statutory controls did not come into being until 1986. [26]

Despite frequent demands by environmentalists and farmers, MAFF and other statutory organisations, heavily influenced by vested interests, have dragged their feet over the issues of pesticides and such things as sheep dip. As late as 1989, various environmental bodies, together with trades unions, were still trying to squeeze statutory concessions out of MAFF.

A joint group called for increased resources to be put into the testing and approval and monitoring of pesticides. The group called upon the Agriculture Minister for 'a completion by 1992 of reviews for all (some 120) "older" pesticides, a hundred new Health and Safety Executive Inspectors in the field and a more frequent and thorough programme of pesticide residue monitoring in foods and a national pesticide incident monitoring scheme'. According to the MAFF, it would take at least a decade to review the older pesticides, which at present are reviewed at the rate of two or three a year with a waiting time which is 'indefinable'. [27]

One recent debate showed clearly the way in which science serves the most convenient master. Despite propaganda by chemical companies and campaigning 'anti-health fraud' groups, in 1989 the US Environmental Protection Agency (EPA) banned the use of Alar (daminozide), a pesticide spray used on apples. The Agency found specifically that a carcinogen was produced when apples treated with Alar were heated and 'an inescapable and direct correlation' between the use of Alar and the 'development of life-threatening tumors'. [28]

In January 1989, the UK Advisory Committee on Pesticides (ACP) reported that 'there is no risk to consumers' from apples sprayed with Alar. The Chairman of the ACP, Professor Colin Berry, claimed that the different findings by the EPA and the ACP were the result of using different models. Uniroyal, the principal UK manufacturer of Alar, halted sales of the chemical for food applications following the EPA decision to ban the spray in America. The British government, however, continued to pursue a laissez-faire policy with respect to statutory constraints. 'The continued use of Alar is a commercial matter for those who make and use it. The [ACP] has concluded that the safety factors are so great, even where there is extreme consumption, there is no risk to health.' [29]

Despite the increased use of pesticides, insecticides and herbicides in Britain and America and regardless of well-documented research into their cumulative effect on the human system, especially the immune system, the AMA and the BMA have both failed to develop any diagnostic strategy or treatment programmes.

In developed countries, people are exposed to chemicals in the air they breathe, the water they drink, the food they eat, the drugs they take, and in many of the products they handle each day. People come into contact with chemicals of one kind or another in both their work and their domestic circumstances. Between 1965 and 1978 over 4 million distinct chemical compounds were reported in the scientific literature, approximately 6,000 per week. Of these, about 55% are now used in commercial production. An unknown proportion of these chemicals however cause cancer, birth defects, or other human ills, as well as causing damage to plants and animals. Having accepted the proliferation of chemicals without much control in the past, societies now face the expensive and complex tasks of identifying those that are dangerous and then deciding what to do about them. [30]

Although many of the chemicals found in the home which cause sensitivity are those which one might expect to be toxic, other substances often go unnoticed. There is a well-documented relationship between chemical sensitivity, perfumes, scented toiletries, newsprint, commercial paints, domestic gas and exhaust fumes.

Clinical ecologists have begun to understand that many different chemicals, ingested in only small amounts on an everyday level, can have an immuno-compromising effect. Just like foods, they can create masked symptoms during prolonged periods of contact and can result in recurring illness on sporadic or low dose contact, years after the initial sensitisation.

Increasingly, doctors working in this field are concluding that the immune system has a load threshold which, once reached, will precipitate a variety of other symptoms in response to toxicity. Such a threshold is not fixed but can be lowered by stress, infections, lack of sleep, lack of exercise or exposure to chemical substances. According to this theory, a whole series of factors and toxins, experienced over a period of time, can gradually destabilise the individual's immune system. When there is a critical imbalance and the immune system is no longer capable of responding, a variety of illnesses can occur.

People who are sensitive to this wide range of chemicals may often not consider themselves ill, or may even have learned to cope with a variety of low-level chronic complaints such as eczema, migraine and rhinitis. The high level of masking of sensitivities, and the low level of presentation or recording of them, have led some doctors to suggest that the number of undiagnosed chemically-sensitive people could have been massively underestimated.

Chapter Eight

Dr William Rea: Clinical Ecologist

> *The deterioration of our natural environment has been accompanied by a corresponding increase in the health problems of the individual ... the industrialised countries are plagued by the chronic and degenerative diseases appropriately called diseases of civilization.* [1]

Those who are deeply involved in the journey to a new age rarely have time to stop and ask whether others understand. Their new vision is usually clearer to them than are their explanations to others. They are carried through their lives, often naively, on the energy that their work provides; they become to some extent estranged.

Dr William Rea, now in his sixties, is one of the most experienced of the first generation clinical ecologists in America. His career has developed almost in tandem with the careers of great practitioners like his countryman Theron Randolph. Now, with Randolph, Rea is one of only two American surgeons to run a hospital based upon the principle of the diagnosis and treatment of environmental illness. The unaccountable development of American capitalism has strewn medical problems of national proportions in its wake. Dr Rea is in the forefront of the battle between industry and the ever more toxic environment. Consequently, over the last decade and a half, his name has been vilified, his hospital and his practices attacked and insurance cover withdrawn from his patients.

*   *   *

I met Professor William Rea in the Robens Institute of Health and Safety at Surrey University after his appointment to the Chair of Environmental Medicine. Thin and relaxed, Dr Rea tipped himself back on his chair.† His southern accent was slow and his attitude informal; he was wearing cowboy boots. It was not at all what I had expected from a thoracic surgeon and the pioneer of a new medical movement.

First impressions can be deceptive. When I listened to what Dr Rea said, there was nothing laid back about the concepts he described. His conversation exhibited a vigorous commitment to a new medical paradigm.

Dr Rea is the kind of populist the British establishment is incapable of producing. Despite being a highly trained professional, he appears an ordinary man who cares deeply for people and their health. In an English context, he appears free from pre-conceived notions of class and vested interest, willing to take people as he finds them.

I travelled back with Dr Rea on a train to London after our meeting at Surrey University. Inevitably, we talked about allergies. As we talked, the train began to fill with schoolchildren and people returning from work. An Asian schoolboy about twelve years old, whose demeanour gave the impression that he had lived at least four times the number of his natural years, threw himself into the seat next to me, facing Dr Rea.

I began to notice from the corner of my eye, a look of incredulity on the boy's face as he picked up bits of our conversation. I felt embarrassed: Dr Rea was after all 'a world expert'.

Quite suddenly, and with perfect confidence, the boy interrupted us.

'I couldn't help listening to what you've been saying', he said to Dr Rea.

'I've got a lot of allergies which have caused me real problems.'

The boy began to recount a list of adverse reactions to different foods. His was a classic case. He was, he said, concerned that if he eliminated more and more foods from his diet, he would end up eating less and less.

Without visible change of pace, Dr Rea diverted his conversation from me to the boy, happy to converse with someone who had direct personal experience. The boy began expounding well-considered theories about allergy.

After a while Rea lighted on one of his comments with a chuckle and said, in his southern drawl:

'Hey, and what would you say if someone said to you that all this was in your

---

† Dr Rea was appointed to the Chair in Environmental Medicine, after being proposed by members of the Environmental Medicine Foundation, whose idea it was to begin degree-level courses in clinical ecology. Following his appointment at Surrey University, there was much opposition and argument, stemming mainly from research workers and academics who were linked to the chemical and pharmaceutical industry.

mind?'

'I'd say that they were crazy' said the boy, 'I know that what I experience is real and it is related to food. One doctor told me it was because I had small faults in my metabolism.'

I sat back and listened. There didn't seem much that I could contribute. I smiled when Dr Rea made the kind of unexpected comment that marks his populist attitude.

'One of the ideas that I have utilised myself is to switch the food base of meals. Just for a time try slightly rarer things like moose and possum.'

The boy responded with a nod, as if he knew just the place to get both moose and possum.

* * *

Like many others involved in clinical ecology, Dr Rea arrived at his position through painful personal experience. In the early seventies, he was working as a cardiothoracic surgeon when he began to have attacks of dizziness and suffer 'flu-like' symptoms.

The problems got worse until on several occasions he had difficulty standing up in the operating theatre. After initial ineffective professional advice, he saw a physician who diagnosed an ecological illness. The diagnosis not only led to his recovery, but to changes in his life's work. He became deeply involved in the idea of clinical ecology.

Dr Rea had been told by his physician that he suffered from a number of allergies and that he was sensitive to certain chemicals present in the operating theatre. He read all the authorities which were available at that time [2] and having healed himself, he began to specialise in the treatment of patients who suffered similar illnesses.

If the diagnosis of chemical sensitivity was difficult to define in the mid nineteen seventies, the treatments which Dr Rea began to work on are still today regarded with scepticism. As with all revolutions, those who espouse them begin by living in ghettos, because only there, in small safe spaces, can they put theory and practice together.

> Now, I have an ecologically sound home, a good office and a good unit. The operating rooms are pretty good and I never wear clothes that aren't all cotton, and aren't all washable, and I rarely eat out. I have a big extractor fan over the cooking range, we have no gas, everything is electric. I take care of myself very well and when we travel we take our own water and food. I still

> take injections for the allergies, food shots and also pollen, dust
> and mould shots and terpenes, every four days. I eat once a day
> and rotate the foods over a two weeks period. [3]

William Rea sees in his patients the same confused helplessness that he
had experienced himself. By 1975, he was dealing with patients whose
cardiac problems were often left unaffected by surgery or drugs.

> I treated a thirty-seven year old mortician. He had been a
> mortician all his life and his father before him. He had
> hardening of the arteries and heart pain. They did a bypass on
> him because they found on coronary angiogram that he did have
> narrowing of the arteries. But he went on having chest pain and
> arrhythmia. He came to me, about a year after the bypass
> operation. We placed him in the unit, fasted him, and took him
> off all his medicines and in five days, he was totally clear so we
> went ahead and challenged† him on beef which reproduced all
> his symptoms. His challenge with formaldehyde also reproduced
> it and then the story came out that as a child he slept over the
> embalming area of his father's mortuary. We could see that he
> had had plenty of years of sensitizing substances. [4]

The ideas of William Rea are not new: they are part of the foundations
of classical immunology, but as clinical ecology began to establish
itself, it came into conflict with its closest body of similar knowledge –
allergy medicine. The allergy doctors were on the whole conservative.
They restricted their enquiries into allergy to a few well-known effects
of specific foods. Sometimes they restricted the field so severely as to
suggest that only the smallest number of substances created allergy and
these only in children.

Conventional allergy specialists walked a tightrope of conflicting
interests, for they were often grant-aided by pharmaceutical and
agrochemical companies. To this industry-dominated school, the
newer and more extensive ideas of environmental medicine, which
discerned dangers in the air we breathe, the energy by which we light
our world and the water we drink, represented a real threat to
established learning.

---

† 'Insult' and 'challenge' are two words which describe the purposeful or accidental
introduction of an antigen into the body.

The first American organisation to represent doctors practising the diagnosis and treatment of allergy was the American College of Allergy. Its founders and most of its early members were surgeons like William Rea. They had a broad approach to the field of allergy diagnosis and treatment. However, it was not long before another group, the American Academy of Allergy (AAA), representing the interests of the pharmaceutical companies, was in the ascendancy.

Many of the original attacks upon environmental medicine came from the AAA and factions with which it was aligned within the American Medical Association. The AAA was composed almost entirely of academics who had little contact with patients and contempt for the ideas and practices of the American College of Allergy. Research undertaken by members of the AAA was almost exclusively funded by drug companies. There developed an antipathy between members of the AAA and the College of Allergy, so much in fact, that AAA members were aware that they could lose valuable funding if they co-operated or even entered into dialogue with the College of Allergy.

When old medical ideas were expressed as clinical ecology, the representatives of industry conspired to portray them as at best 'unscientific' and at worst mystical or irrational. Ideas which had been accepted for years in relation to a variety of accidental toxins were hotly disputed when the toxins were by-products of profitable economic systems.

> It's quite clear that if you take something into your body it has to be disposed of in one of three ways, it can either be utilised, spit out, or compartmentalised. With each 'insult', some of the substance is stored in the body, and it gets to the point where tissue injury has been so continuous that that part of the body is damaged. The immune system is overworking, having to deploy its forces at all the different sites where this material is stored. And it is not simply the immune system, it is also the non-immune detoxification system; the liver, and other organs. [5]†

The diagnostic theories of William Rea and those of other clinical

---

† This quote and others which follow are taken from interviews with Dr Rea carried out by the author.

ecologists depart from those of the more conservative allergists and
toxicologists in two major ways. Firstly, Rea says that it is the
continuous accumulation of damaging substances which cannot be
excreted by the body which leads eventually to degenerative disease.
Secondly, he and other clinical ecologists consider it fundamental that
the diversity of such damaging substances is wide ranging, and made
even more so when initial substances are combined with individual-
specific metabolic and nutritional deficiencies.

* * *

It was not until the late seventies that William Rea realised that
industry was hostile to his work. A medical training does not best equip
people for political or legal struggles. When the doctor, who wishes
above all else to heal, becomes drawn into damaging litigious battles,
valuable time which could be spent with patients goes to waste.

> In about 1982, 1983, we got a lot of letters from major insurance
> firms which claimed that the American Academy of Allergy said
> that we were using experimental, unproven, and unscientific
> treatments, therefore they weren't going to pay. I filed a suit
> against them.

> We went to court with several of our patients whose hospital bills
> had not been paid. The judge said at the first hearing that no
> one had been hurt in Texas, so the hearing had to be moved to
> Milwaukee in the same area as the headquarters of the AAA.
> This was a great distance and I was unable to get involved going
> up and down there. The judge said that every case could be filed
> individually and this was done. Eventually everyone of them got
> paid, they were all paid before the case went to trial, so there is
> no public record and no precedents were set.

It is impossible to separate the general context of politics and
economics from the attacks against clinical ecology. It is clear that as
the economic recession began to bite in the late seventies, medical
insurance companies were desperately trying to cut back on pay-
outs.

> From 1974 when I started the unit to 1982, when the economic
> crunch began, every insurance company paid. Then with the

economic crunch, we suddenly became experimental. Reagan came in in 1980. It was very difficult during this time to separate out the action which was taken against environmental practitioners from that which was taken against orthodox practitioners. However, they did at first single out everyone they thought was on the periphery. Now, in the present period, we are no worse off than anyone else because they too have been hit.

Inevitably, it was being undermined by the insurance companies which had the most serious effect upon Rea's work. Had they been successful, his patient referrals would have dried up. The more politically motivated attacks, though linked to the economic situation, also had an internal dynamic of their own, one which was deeply rooted in the need for industrial science to control the field of medicine and dispute the scientific credentials of non-chemical therapists.

In the late seventies, one particular insurance company claimed that Dr Rea's work was 'experimental' and he should therefore seek certification from the AMA dominated County Medical Society. The company insisted that the treatments used should be peer-reviewed and if they were found not to be experimental, the company promised to pay claims. Dr Rea went to a hearing, taking with him accepted specialists in the field. Following the hearing the Medical Society wrote to say that although the treatment might be controversial, it was not experimental. The insurance company paid up.

* * *

The American political lens is a distorting lens, which does not clarify apparently simple issues of class and nationality, such as those to be found at the heart of British politics. Because medicine is almost completely controlled by the multi-national drug companies, the natural distortion of American politics is, in the case of medicine, even more confused. The biggest drug companies will side with and support socialised medicine over private practice, simply because government contracts give assured and stable profits without the threat of competition. As a conservative, William Rea analyses the attacks upon him and his hospital as possibly being mediated by liberals, who favour what he calls 'socialist' solutions to medical care. At the head of this movement, in his view, are the Rockefeller Trilateralists.†

> It was when Carter came to power that we began to get all the
> attacks. Some of his administration had a 'socialist' mentality.
> We had always been free to do almost anything in medicine until
> that time. Then they started to regulate medicine from
> Washington. We actually have the biggest 'communist' state in
> the world — meaning that it is the most highly regulated and
> bureaucratised. We have a bigger veterans administration system
> than most of the socialist countries. It is centrally funded by
> Washington D.C. Once you become a physician for them, unless
> you commit mass murder you stay with them for life. It is so big
> that it can't be administered.

Behind the administration and regulation of medicine in America, Dr
Rea sees the dead hand of the FDA, a government agency which he
suggests is run by business. Officers of the FDA, Rea says, are 'bought
and offered positions with business in exchange for them acting
favourably to that company'. The FDA, he says, will do anything for a
price and this includes ignoring the results of clinical trials and
falsifying research material.

The conflicts which have beset Dr Rea are not easily understood
even by those who are involved. Why is a free enterprise conservative
being attacked by large liberal leaning corporations? Why, if Dr Rea is
a rationalist and a believer in a scientific approach to medicine, is he
being attacked by scientists?

The issue of science and 'pseudo-science'‡ has from the beginning
confused Dr Rea. Like Dr Jacques Benveniste and others, he considers
that what the other side calls science does not conform with easily
understood historical precepts. Increasingly, 'science' appears to be
only that discipline which brings in profit and which humours the
military industrial complex.

---

† The Trilateral Commission was set up by Nelson Rockefeller in 1974. Its purpose was
to create a world economy which would operate across all national boundaries. Its
members were influential leaders of multi-nationals and serving ministers in the
European, American and Japanese governments. See Chapter Twenty.

‡ The term pseudo-science is used by CSICOP members to describe scientific work
done by people opposed to industrially based science and the pharamaceutical
companies.

In the early eighties, Dr Rea's work began to be rejected by journals which had previously accepted it. Papers were returned as 'unscientific'. Rea gave the first article which was turned down to a colleague at the University of Texas at Dallas for assessment. It was taken back to the University research committee and reviewed for scientific credibility. 'They told me that scientifically it was O.K. and that I had been "had" politically.'

The doctor, more than most professionals, is dependent upon the public's often conservative perception of his work. The clinical ecologist is hit hard by censorship or biased popular journalism which taints him or her with quackery. Such a stigma is easy to acquire but almost impossible to shake off. The doctor who is fighting big business is fighting in the dark, never completely sure which parties constitute the enemy. The strategies of the other side are often underhand and destructive. A good doctor profits little from considering a similar offensive against the chemical companies.

> By 1982 or 1983, it was evident to me that 'the other side' had a dossier on me, because they were reading into various trial transcripts information about my work over a period of time.

> We always had good articles in newspapers, or at least they were not destructive. Then in about 1988 we had 'a number done on us'. A television group called 'Inside Edition', came into the hospital bringing a bogus patient with them. I gave them a 45 minute interview and they had the run of the clinic. One of them had a hidden microphone. Their television programme said that I was a Guru. Out of the forty-five minute interview, they picked only negative aspects. The producer called me up two days before the programme and said he wanted to check things with me. He told me that I wasn't going to like the programme, I told him that it was a free country and he had the capacity to help or hurt people with his programme, I told him that it was up to his conscience as to whether or not he was honest, he swore at me and hung up.

William Rea is an honest and straightforward man who believes in an open approach to his hospital and his practice. Like Dr Jacques Benveniste he is ironically bemused by the short-sightedness with which the major US companies have responded to environmental medicine.

Clinical ecology or environmental medicine would not do away
with drugs, because it has a different aim from orthodox
medicine. The real crux of clinical ecology is prevention. That
doesn't mean that if a person gets cancer you are going to do
away with a variety of drugs or surgery. By then, the horse is
already out the barn, it's been going on for twenty or thirty years
in your body already.

As in many pioneers, there is an evangelical aspect to Dr Rea; he has a
passionate belief in the ideas of the new movement. He is convinced
that environmental medicine is the medicine of the future, and that its
theoretical precepts represent a great advance in the history of
medicine. This commitment can sometimes blind him to the more
pervasive economic influences of American society.

If there was the thrust for clinical ecology which you have at the
moment for chemical medicine, we can't say what would
happen. It might be that a whole series of diseases are stopped.

The political contradictions which Dr Rea is faced with and which are
implicit in his work are illustrated by the following story. In 1978 he
was appointed to the Scientific Advisory Board of the Environmental
Protection Agency, a liberal orientated government agency. His advice
and that of fifteen other experts was sought over houses built above a
stream of toxic waste near Niagara Falls. There was only one objection
to Rea's appointment. It came from Victor Herbert of the National
Council Against Health Fraud.

Chapter Nine

Dr Jean Monro:
Clinical Ecologist

> *Like lambs to the slaughter*
> *They're drinking the water*
> *And breathing the air.* [1]

In February 1981, Sheila Rossall, a young woman pop singer, flew to the United States to get treatment for a condition that the media were calling 'total allergy syndrome'. At the time of her flight out of Britain, following unsuccessful NHS treatment, Rossall weighed five stone twelve pounds and was close to death. She had said of her National Health treatment 'When I go into hospital they certainly do not understand my condition, and make me feel a lot worse into the bargain.' [2]

'Total allergy syndrome' was a deceptive and inexact description of Sheila Rossall's illness. It suggested that her condition was absolute, one in which from the beginning to the end, a massive number of substances create an allergic reponse. Leading clinical ecologists explain the condition differently. Their model describes the immune system as a container able to hold a large number of toxic insults before it finally overflows and becomes ineffective in protecting its host.

At the time Sheila Rossall was coming back from America, twenty-four year old Amanda Strang was reportedly suffering from the same illness. Unlike Sheila, who had been ill since childhood, Amanda became ill in her early twenties. Previously she had been a fit and healthy young woman, a keen sportswoman who swam for Middlesex County. Throughout her childhood, however, she suffered from minor allergic responses, hay fever, asthma and allergic conjunctivitis.

Again, in Amanda's case, the NHS had no answer. Doctors found themselves standing by while her isolated and weakened condition left her almost completely dependent upon charity and the care of her family. [3]

The condition from which Sheila Rossall and Amanda Strang suffered was the condition which clinical ecologists had warned of for many years. With public recognition of the condition, came the first acceptance that it was possible for damage to the immune system to cause general illnesses which were much more serious than previously diagnosed substance-specific allergies. There was however still a great deal of scepticism, and some journalists found it more convenient to label Rossall and Strang as suffering from psychiatric illnesses. Such a 'pop' diagnosis was even easier when the victims were women.

The attitude of conventional scientists and immunologists to extreme circumstances of immune system breakdown, even before the advent of AIDS, was interesting. In the main they did not believe that damaging substances were stored in the body and could lead, sometimes in conjunction with emotional crisis or in the wake of a viral illness, to an almost complete and degenerative debilitation of the immune system.

Sheila Rossall had done the rounds of the facilities which the National Health Service made available in the late seventies for someone suffering from an officially unrecognised illness. Avoiding any deeper analysis of her condition, many doctors and media commentators likened the condition to that of anorexia nervosa, a condition suffered by young women who deny themselves food. Evident in many of the news programmes about Sheila Rossall was the desire to see the illness as something for which Rossall herself was responsible: a condition she could allieviate if only she were to 'get a grip' on herself.

In America, Sheila Rossall was a patient at the special environmental unit set up by Dr Rea at Brookhaven Hospital in Dallas. After six months' treatment in the unit, she weighed eight stone and was able to go to California to convalesce. Her treatment, however, had not been without cost. When she left the hospital she was £19,000 in debt. What is more, she was in continuous danger of collapse, if at any time she was brought into contact with any of the many chemical substances which exhausted her immune system.

By 1982, Sheila Rossall had become a transatlantic medical

embarrassment. Despite work by American friends and campaigners, insufficient money had been raised to see her through her convalescence. It was clear that Britain would have to accept her back, even if this meant admitting she might die because the NHS did not recognise her illness. A spokesman for the Department of Health said:

> Doctors are not agreed whether or not there is in fact a condition
> of total allergy. Certainly if a consultant thought it necessary he
> could recommend suitable treatment for such a condition. [4]

This was the language of medical diplomacy spoken by a civil servant who probably knew that there was no consultant in the country who would diagnose this kind of immune system break-down. The cost of treating more than one case of such an illness would be prohibitive for the National Health Service or the medical insurance companies.

Late in 1982, a Foreign Office civil servant phoned Dr Jean Monro, a leading British expert on chemical sensitivity and a friend of Dr William Rea. Although Dr Monro had not met nor treated Sheila Rossall, the Foreign Office asked her if she would go to America and oversee Rossall's flight back to this country in environmentally controlled conditions.

* * *

Dr Jean Monro is one of the foremost practitioners of environmental medicine in Britain and a writer on migraine and food allergy. [5] Since 1985 she has run the Breakspear Hospital, one of only a few specialised private hospitals in Britain for the diagnosis and treatment of allergy and chemical sensitivity. The road to the Breakspear Hospital was hard and financially rocky.

Dr Monro has had more than her fair share of personal difficulties. Her two sons were born with coeliac disease, an intolerance to wheat or any of its products. Her husband, who had multiple sclerosis (MS) for many years, died in February 1990 from cancer. Coping with these arduous personal problems while tending her career has turned her into a fighter. Her feminine, and sometimes apparently vulnerable, exterior harbours a cast-iron determination to fight for her patients and her special area of medicine.

From the time that they were born, both Jean Monro's sons failed to thrive. Her first-born son in particular was very ill before she found that he had coeliac disease. Like many others who have had to face up to serious illness in themselves or their loved ones, Jean Monro embarked upon a process of learning which was to equip her with information the NHS could not provide.

> I began to read about diets and food sensitivity. At that time, I couldn't get any help at all from the National Health Service. In fact, the Institute of Child Health began to suggest that I was a neurotic mother and that I should see a psychiatrist. Here were two children with constant diarrhoea and they were telling me that it was something I was thinking. It was at this time, that I first began to have worries about my own profession. [6]†

Dr Monro began to use elimination diets with her sons, starting with two foods and adding to them one new food a week. It took a year of hard and methodical work to resolve an effective diet and from that point onwards both her sons began to thrive. During the process of working out the diets, Dr Monro found that her sons were sensitive to all milk products and all grains, including rice.

> I took the information I had gained while doing this work with my children to an expert in coeliac disease. He said that the chances of this happening – the combination of intolerance to dairy products and all grains – were millions to one. I had documented the information very clearly. I knew then that my profession was not going to take this information on board.

In 1968, with others, Dr Monro started the Coeliac Association, a classic self-help organisation. It would be easy to understand if Dr Monro's experience in caring for her two sons had turned her against orthodox medicine and the National Health Service. It did not and she continued to work in General Hospitals. Even when her husband was diagnosed as having multiple sclerosis, and it was evident that the NHS had no treatment programme, she continued to believe in a state-supported health service.

---

† This quote and those which follow, unless otherwise stated, are taken from interviews between the author and Dr Monro.

> My husband had been very depressed at times, but when he was
> on the same diet that had been worked out for my sons, his
> mood changed completely. We 'managed' his illness by diet for
> the next twenty five years. Despite the multiple sclerosis, he was
> driving a car up until two months before he died.

In the sixties, Dr Monro came into contact with American research
which confirmed her own ideas and also inspired many people
working in the field of nutrition and illness at that time. She began to
consider the links between nutrition and mental illness and became a
medical advisor to both Sanity and the Schizophrenia Association.

By the late sixties, Dr Monro had reached sub-consultant grade.
She sensed that her chosen area of work won her few friends. In fact,
because she worked on the nutritional context of illness, an area which
does not necessitate the use of pharmaceuticals, her work was not
taken seriously.

In 1974, she was seconded by her Regional Health Authority to the
National Hospital for Nervous Diseases to work two days a week. She
continued to work there in an honorary capacity for the next ten
years, researching fatty acids and multiple sclerosis.

It was not until 1980 that Dr Monro decided that she could achieve
no more in her particular field while working inside the NHS. She was
becoming a specialist in allergic responses to food but there was only
the most limited comprehension of this field within the NHS. She left
the National Health Service while continuing to do unpaid research
into the food causes of migraine at the National Hospital. She began
working partly from home and then from a succession of different
private hospitals.

While in private practice and developing her ideas and treatments
for allergy and food-related illness, Dr Monro was influenced by the
work of American clinical ecologists. In 1979, at a seminar organised
by Dr Richard Mackarness at the Royal College of Physicians, she met
Dr Rea.

Through the American practitioners, Dr Monro was introduced to
skin testing techniques which diagnose sensitivity to foods. In 1980 she
began practising skin testing and in 1981 travelled to the States to
attend a seminar given by Dr Joseph Miller at the Miller Center for
Allergy. Dr Miller had developed a diagnostic method and treatment
which came to be called 'provocation neutralisation'. Dr Monro began

to work with this technique.

In 1982, Dr Rea, Dr Theron Randolph and Dr Doris Rapp, the world leaders in clinical ecology, gave a series of lectures in Germany. From Germany, they contacted Dr Monro to ask if she could organise meetings in England. The American doctors stayed in England for a week, addressing meetings in some of the major teaching hospitals and one public meeting at the Central London Baptist Church in Bloomsbury which was attended by over 900 people.

In 1983, some years before AIDS made T lymphocyte function famous as a measure of immune efficiency,† Dr Monro began working with Professor Hobbs at the Westminster Hospital. The object of this classic immunological work was to show how the T lymphocyte function was suppressed in many patients who were exposed to damaging chemicals or viruses, an idea which was to become more popular and fully realised in the late eighties.

> There is considerable evidence to show that toxic chemicals can
> suppress or stimulate the immune system. For example, DDT
> can suppress the degranulation of MAST cells. [7]

The paper which described Dr Monro's work on immuno-suppressing chemicals was not published until 1989. [8] This work, combined with her previous work on the immuno-compromising effects of certain foods and toxic chemicals became increasingly relevant to the AIDS debate throughout the second half of the eighties. By then it was becoming clear that some people diagnosed as HIV antibody positive succumbed very quickly to AIDS, while others managed to live relatively healthy lives for extended periods.‡ The issue of immuno-suppressing chemicals was to become a specific focus for some scientists looking at the history and origins of AIDS.

---

† The measurement of T lymphocyte cells has become the standard orthodox measurement in cases of HIV antibody positive diagnosis. A normal quantity of such cells can be up to and over 1,500 cells per cubic millimetre. 500 is a fair cell count, but below this, as the number of the cells falls, so the patient's immune response is seen to be less and less effective. The clinical definition of asymptomatic HIV infection, according to US and British mainstream doctors, is around 400 and below 200 with accompanying opportunist infections a person is considered by them to have AIDS.

‡ The longest survival period for an HIV antibody positive AIDS case in Britain is around 13 years.

Dr Monro has always combined a commitment to clinical practice with an aggressive desire to push forward the frontiers of education about environmental medicine. To this end, in 1983, she helped to found and became the medical advisor to the Environmental Medicine Foundation (EMF),† set up to educate people about environmental illness and its treatment.

The primary goal of the EMF, a charity, was to get a university Chair in Environmental Medicine. A number of different universities and hospitals were approached before the Foundation finally settled, in 1987, on the Robens Institute for Occupational Health and Safety at Surrey University. The Foundation had always had Dr William Rea in mind to take the Chair and, in 1988, the EMF and Surrey University agreed upon his appointment.

Dr Monro was never that happy as a practising outpatient specialist. Particularly in clinical ecology, once patients leave the confines of the surgery, they become prey to an uncontrolled toxic environment. She wanted to establish a working environment similar to that created by Dr Rea in America. In a hospital with a controlled environment she would be able to do more consistent work with her most serious cases. In 1987, she raised a mortgage on a building at Abbots Langley in Hertfordshire which she turned into the Breakspear Hospital for the diagnosis and treatment of allergy and environmental illness.

> My previous work with allergy patients had shown me that in the setting of the general hospital a patient was prone to many allergens in the ambient environment. The control of diet, an important aspect of diagnosis and treatment, is also more difficult within an ordinary general hospital.

> Beds and residential care are important for those patients who only find a doctor when their illness is advanced. Such patients may have travelled considerable distances. In order to receive properly controlled environmental treatment, a patient will need to be kept separate from all those things which could be contributing to their illness.

† The Environmental Medicine Foundation is a charity which supports education and research on environmental and medical issues and distributes information on environmental illness to both victims of illness and professionals.

Setting up a private hospital was a considerable undertaking and Jean Monro had to re-mortgage her home and take out a large loan to renovate the new building and equip it as a hospital. She knew that in all probability she would be unable to pay back the mortgage on the building within her lifetime.

The move to a fully equipped environmental hospital which tried to be free from chemical toxins, and within which a number of de-sensitising and detoxification programmes could take place, massively changed the position of Dr Monro's work within the broader context of medicine. With the establishment of the Breakspear Hospital, she was sending out clear signals that she believed this area of medicine to be vital to the future of health care.

Chemical sensitivity, which can arise following an accident with chemicals at work, as well as with constant and long-term contact, needs new and diverse treatments. In acute cases following industrial accidents, clinical ecologists have begun to develop new programmes to detoxify the body. In America, medical management programmes have included organic food, spring water and control of environmental pollution, aerobic exercise, the use of polyunsaturated fats, Niacin and low-heat saunas.

People who attended Breakspear were often at the end of a frustrating trail from one NHS doctor to another; more often than not their whole life was in crisis because their illness had resulted in the breakdown of relationships, or unemployment. The condition of patients who suffered sensitivity from such things as pesticide exposure may well have deteriorated over a period when their general practitioners failed to diagnose the cause of the illness. Patients came to Dr Monro some in states of paralysis, or so weak that they were able to stay awake only for short periods during the day. Such patients needed bed care of a kind which National Health hospitals were unable or unprepared to provide.

> I was particularly determined to run a hospital because I believed that the treatment of chemical sensitivity and the practice of environmental medicine could most safely take place in a hospital setting. I also felt that discharging some of the patients straight after their tests was inadvisable. This was particularly the case with patients who had driven to their treatment.

> The kind of patient who comes to Breakspear is often suffering
> more severe symptoms and illnesses than the patient who will,
> for example, go to a community-based general practitioner who
> practises complementary medicine. Our patients have frequently
> passed through the hands of many practitioners.

The advent of the Breakspear Hospital created problems in relation to
the insurance companies. In Britain, patients undergoing hospital
treatment have to be supervised by a consultant and such a consultant
has to be someone recognised by the insurance companies. It is this
consultant who sends an assessment of treatment to the patient's
insurance company, who in turn decide whether or not to pay out.

Dr Monro had not become a consultant and, if she was not to lose
control over her own treatments, she had to bring in consultants who
were sympathetic to her work. This in itself was a difficult task. For
Breakspear consultants then to convince insurance company advisors
was even more difficult. Such advisors were almost always trained in
the drug-orientated world of orthodox medicine and were much
quicker to believe that an allergic patient was suffering from a
psychiatric illness which did not merit an insurance payment.

* * *

Committed as she was to working on behalf of the new medicine, and
concerned as she always had been to do the best by her patients, Jean
Monro never thought to look over her shoulder, or to take cognizance
of the opposition to her work. She was aware that the older school of
allergists, their practices restricted by vested interest, were always
murmuring, but she never considered that they might actually be
plotting her downfall.

In the winter of 1986, Dr Monro saw an advertisement in the
newspaper, placed by Caroline Richmond, a medical journalist, and
Dr David Pearson, an NHS allergy specialist; the advertisement
sought to contact people who knew that they did not have allergies
even though they had been diagnosed. Such people were asked to
come forward and appear on a Granada television programme.

One of Dr Monro's patients, seeing the evidently destructive bent
of such a programme, contacted Granada to say that she had been
diagnosed as having allergies and she was quite certain that she did

actually have them. The programme makers asked both Dr Monro and her patient to appear.

> Caroline Richmond, David Pearson, and a doctor called Tim
> David were all in the front of the audience. Dr Miriam Stoppard,
> who gives popular advice on health matters, was hosting the
> programme. There was a panel and an audience. The
> programme set out to show that people who had been
> diagnosed as having allergies either didn't have a problem, or
> had another undiagnosed problem. The point was to 'debunk'
> the whole idea of allergy.

In a Manchester hotel following the filming of the programme, Dr Monro was drawn into her first conflict with Caroline Richmond.

> After the programme we went back to the hotel and Caroline
> Richmond was at the bar. We got into conversation. I said 'I feel
> strongly about a variety of environmental issues.' She said 'I
> don't know why, it's completely ridiculous, there isn't an
> environmental problem now, with the Clean Air Act there is
> no pollution in London.' I replied that there were other
> problems, like acid rain which we hadn't known before. I was
> very surprised at her attitude and her response: she began taking
> notes of what I was saying and said, 'I'll use this against you one
> day.' I said, 'What do you mean?' She said 'Well you talked
> about acid rain, how could that affect someone's health?' I said,
> 'It would be very foolish to assume that such things did not affect
> people.' She asked me what the formula for acid rain was. I told
> her and sent her references the next day.

Jean Monro was not to know that in Caroline Richmond, she was talking to someone who was to spend the next five or six years attacking clinical ecology. With that one conversation with Caroline Richmond, Dr Monro placed herself on an extensive list of individuals involved in alternative or 'natural' medicine who would eventually be 'attacked'. In 1987, not long after the Granada programme, Caroline Richmond fired her first shot at Dr Monro when she sent a complaint, in the form of an affidavit, to the General Medical Council (GMC). Richmond based her complaint that Dr Monro was advertising, on a sympathetic newspaper article accompanied by a photograph of Dr Monro. [9] The GMC did not uphold the complaint. It was however an ominous sign.

By May 1987, Bill Rea had been introduced to the Robens Institute and he and Dr Monro were beginning to map out courses in environmental medicine for doctors and postgraduate medical students. Unknown to either Professor Rea or Dr Monro, the management team of the Robens was heavily weighted on the side of the chemical and pharmaceutical companies. By 1987, through a series of networks, both Dr Rea and Dr Monro were becoming known as serious commentators on the ill-health caused by industrial chemicals.

The first organised opposition to Dr Monro's work became evident in 1987. In 1985, she had been joined at the Breakspear by Dr James Ussher who had previously been with the Private Patients Plan medical insurance company (PPP). Dr Ussher's successor at PPP, Dr R. H. McNeilly, showed himself to be very antagonistic to the work of the Breakspear Hospital. From 1987 onwards, Dr Monro received frequent correspondence from Dr McNeilly who made it clear that he did not agree with the treatments offered at her hospital.

Dr McNeilly also refused recognition to Dr Ussher, claiming that he was not competent to care for people with allergic illnesses. When Dr Monro put forward another consultant physician, Dr Frank Binks, he too was rejected by PPP. McNeilly insisted that both these doctors had experience only with geriatric medicine, despite the fact that they were consultants in general medicine. In 1988, PPP withdrew recognition, for the purposes of insuring patients with allergic conditions, from both Drs Ussher and Binks. Despite a time-lapse of almost ten years, Dr Monro was beginning to run into the same problems in the pursuit of clinical ecology that William Rea had experienced in America.

Chapter Ten

Bristol Cancer Help Centre: Waving Goodbye to the Cancer Industry Gently?

A legal review of the prosecutorial cases brought by the medical establishment against patients, physicians, nutritional manufacturers and distributors, clearly reveals that the main issue in most of these cases has been the single therapeutic theme of immune enhancement. Natural methods of immune enhancement are an extreme threat to the cancer chemotherapy advocates. [1]

The history of cancer research and care is two histories. On the one hand, there is the history of the 'official' cancer research industry and on the other there is the history of alternative care and research. The official history is that of an ever expanding bureaucracy, which like cancer itself, grows unchecked. The history of alternatives, on the other hand, is a diverse history of pioneers who have often died unknown except to their patients. Increasingly it is a history of medical criminalisation.

Within the canons of alternative cancer care and research, different therapies are often referred to by the names of their practitioners: Max Gerson, Josef Issels, Wilhelm Reich, Dr Carl and Stephanie Simonton, Harry Hoxsey. The histories of such practitioners and their therapies are, on the whole, not public; they have been buried. To speak their name in the company of orthodoxy is to invite excommunication.

Each of the practitioners who make up the history of alternative cancer care has been systematically relegated to the criminal margins by a highly competitive medical establishment. Dr Wilhelm Reich a pupil of Freud and one of the leading psycho-analysts of his day, died while serving a prison sentence in America after being charged by the

FDA with fraud.[2] Dr Max Gerson became a medical outlaw in Mexico when he found that there was no room in America for his clinic or his ideas.[3] Dr Josef Issels, who set up a clinic in Bavaria in the 1950s, was sentenced to a year's suspended imprisonment for fraud and manslaughter in 1963.[4]

The history of 'official' cancer research is the history of the struggle for the domination of bourgeois life science. It is also a history of failure. Not only do the deaths from many cancers go on rising in Britain and America, but deaths in Britain for some cancers remain higher than in any other country in the world.[5] The incidence of breast cancer in England, for example, is almost three times as high as that in any other country. Advances made by the cancer research industry, at a cost of millions, over the last fifty years, have at best been minimal and at worst a huge waste of money.

The approaches of official and alternative cancer care are at odds with each other. Despite placatory remarks by established physicians, there can in reality be no reconciliation between them. Official cancer research, like all official medical research, is based upon the science of the cell. Alternative cancer treatment is based upon the whole person and their life condition and is most particularly concerned with prevention.

Official cancer care uses a limited number of techniques to destroy tumours, either cytotoxic drugs, surgery or radiation and sometimes a combination of all three. Orthodox cancer treatment is a short-sighted half-measure, which pays little heed to the patient's life before or after the emergence of the tumour. For alternative cancer therapy, getting rid of the tumour is only one battle in a war. Most alternative treatment programmes suggest a life programme, which is preventative and often subversive to the modern industrial way of life.

Many of the post-war alternative cancer practitioners have believed in an immunological approach to cancer. At the heart of these ideas is the belief that the health and efficiency of the human organism depends upon the health and strength of the immune system. To make the immune system strong, life should be lived as naturally as possible. Organically grown produce should be eaten, often raw, and all processed foods, except the most simply processed, avoided. As many non-nutritional chemicals become lodged in the body and are a continual drain on the immune system, their ingestion should be avoided and various regimes adopted to regularly de-toxify the body.

Amongst contemporary exponents of alternative treatments, theories lean heavily towards the idea that the mind can be used to affect, or 'have power over' the body. Many of these beliefs hark back to ancient times and non-European cultures.

The orthodox cancer establishment is fundamentally threatened by concepts of cancer treatment which have more to do with the patient's mind, will or soul, than the physical body. The might of the cancer research industry is geared not to the discovery of new ways to treat and care for cancer sufferers but to the discovery and patenting of high technology instruments of diagnosis and new cytotoxic drugs.

* * *

Penny Brohn is one of the founders of the Bristol Cancer Help Centre: she is also a woman with cancer. The illness has shaped the course of her life and, as in so many other cases, her own suffering led her to go out into the world and help others. What is principally important about Penny Brohn's work is not that she has established new regimes, treatments or therapies for people suffering from cancer, but that she has made alternative and complementary forms of cancer therapy accessible to a large number of people, especially women.

> I had cancer diagnosed in 1979. Existing support systems were pretty inadequate at that time. The hospitals gave you treatment for your physical illness, but it stopped at that. There were, and still are, a lot of emotional and psychological difficulties involved in having a disease for which there is not a definite cure. [6]

Not long after she first had cancer, Penny Brohn, depressed by the attitude of her National Health doctors, went out to Josef Issels' clinic in Bavaria. She describes Issels as an extraordinary man, a man 'years ahead of his time'. It was in Bavaria that she became acquainted with the idea of holistic cancer treatment.

Penny Brohn's stay in Issels' Clinic placed her firmly in the camp of believers in alternative cancer care. When she returned to England, she brought with her all the hope and new optimism which the treatment at Issels' Clinic had gifted her. Throughout her stay in

Bavaria, Penny Brohn was aware of the terrible difficulties Dr Issels had in setting up and maintaining his clinic.

Ironically, while Brohn brought back to England new strategies of cancer care which she had learned during her treatment, she returned without the knowledge she would need to fight similar struggles to those Issels was forced to fight in Germany. Lessons about self defence and resistance are the hardest to pass on, and no doubt Josef Issels saw himself first as a healer and not a tutor in medical guerilla warfare.

Josef Issels

> Pressure is put on him in a hundred different ways. The medical press cannot find room to print his advertisements for doctors. Medical journals reject his articles. Foreign specialists who visit Rottach Egern and depart full of excitement, suddenly, for no explicable reason, lose enthusiasm and withdraw support. [7]

Even in his twenties, working as a surgeon in Dusseldorf, Josef Issels was shocked by the damage that cancer surgery did to people: 'Why has so much to be taken away when there was so little cancer?' [8] It was not long before he became doubtful about the curative nature of scientific medicine: 'I realised the limits of the science and was shaken. I decided that I must look for new ways of helping the sick.' [9] On holiday from the hospital where he qualified, Issels worked for a rural general practitioner. It was then that he began to understand that the emotional, psychological environment and the history of the patient were all important to their illness and particularly their treatment and he began to develop a holistic idea of medicine.

By the time that he set up his own general practice at the age of thirty one in München-Gladbach, Issels had come to the conclusion that every case was different and each individual's illness was predicated upon its own specific background: 'It is clear that each treatment must also be highly individual.'[10] During the Second World War, having refused to join the Nazi party, Issels worked as a doctor on the Western and Eastern fronts, all the time reading and learning about homoeopathy.

In 1951, Issels met Dr Max Gerson and was influenced by his ideas about treating cancer with diet.† In the same year, he set up a clinic in Rottach-Egern, thirty miles south of Munich in the Bavarian Alps. The clinic was financed by one of his cancer patients, the director of a large shipping line.

From the beginning, treatment at the clinic was based upon the idea of the 'whole person'. Issels was by this time a specialist in immunology and believed that all treatments should help strengthen the immune system. He also believed that the patient's will played a part in the treatment. He exhorted patients to exercise by walking up the mountains which surrounded the clinic.

Rather than use pharmaceuticals, Issels treated his patients with homoeopathic and herbal remedies, insisting upon a well-balanced and carefully controlled diet. Organic fruit and vegetables were grown without the use of chemical fertilizers. The diet had little meat in it and specifically no pork. Smoking was not allowed, nor were tea, coffee, or spirits. No drinking at all was allowed with meals.

Like Gerson, Issels believed in the regular detoxification of the system using coffee enemas. He also developed a fever therapy, in which patients suffered an induced fever, the idea being to strengthen the immune system by replenishing the white blood cells.

To give the immune system every opportunity to combat growing cancer cells, other sites of infection which the patient experienced were treated. This could mean that bad teeth and damaged tonsils were removed. [12]

Issels' clinic at Rottach-Egern had 130 beds, and accepted resident patients for short periods. In the main, the patients who arrived at the clinic were those whom orthodox practitioners had given up on, often terminal cases. Issels' independently agreed research recorded a 17 per cent success rate in people who had come to the clinic as terminal cases. Success was measured by a complete regression of tumours and a return to health by the patient.

---

† Throughout the forties and early fifties, Dr Max Gerson, practising in New York, was in turn vilified and ignored by the orthodox medical establishment. Especially vociferous against him were the Rockefeller-backed cancer research organisations and the pharmaceutical companies. Gerson's success was plain to see for anyone who took the trouble to look at his cases. [11] The attacks upon Gerson, often promoted by industry, concentrated mainly upon his diet therapy.

* * *

On September 15th 1960, Issels was arrested on charges of fraud and manslaughter. To support the charges of fraud, it was claimed that he had promised cures to terminally ill patients and their families. The manslaughter charges related to three patients whom the state prosecutors maintained *would have lived longer* had they received orthodox treatments.

The charges and the ensuing trial led to a five-year closure of the Rottach-Egern clinic. For periods prior to the trial, in 1961, Issels was imprisoned. His first trial lasted 42 days. Found guilty, he was sentenced to a one-year suspended prison sentence and struck off the medical register. It took two years for the case to come before the appeal court, where it was ruled that the lower court had been wrongly directed. A further two years passed before the case was listed again in the lower courts. In 1964, the lower court ruled that the prosecution had no case. They found that: 'Dr Issels is a serious man, a competent doctor who fights for the lives of his patients, who takes his work most seriously.' [13]

In this last hearing, it was shown that the three dead patients had of their own volition refused to have surgery for their cancer. It was also conceded that Issels had never misled anyone about the chances of a complete cure. When Issels' clinic re-opened, after his acquittal, it attracted patients from across Europe, especially from Britain. Often those who were unable to pay were treated free of charge.

In the early sixties, an Englishman Peter Newton-Fenbow, then twenty-one, had been diagnosed as having terminal cancer. In the coming years, he fought hard both against his cancer and on behalf of Dr Josef Issels. Newton-Fenbow's case had come to the attention of Issels after a BBC film 'Living with Death'. Issels had written to the BBC to contact Newton-Fenbow suggesting that he travel to Germany.

In his book, *A Time to Heal*, Newton-Fenbow explains how the BBC acted on the letter from Dr Issels.

> The BBC had sent the letter on to my surgeon as a matter of corporation policy. My surgeon had replied (to the BBC) saying that he would not allow me to be treated by Dr Issels as the latter could not do me any good. [14]

Neither Newton-Fenbow's surgeon nor the BBC informed him of the letter from Dr Issels, and he had to wait some months before a reporter from a German newspaper brought the matter to his attention. When he heard of the offer in 1967, Newton-Fenbow and his wife Wendy immediately made arrangements to stay in Issels' clinic. Issels refused to charge him the full rate for his treatment and Wendy was allowed to stay without charge.

Towards the end of his stay at the clinic, Newton-Fenbow began campaigning in support of Issels and the treatment which he believed had led to a considerable regression of his cancer. While at the clinic, Newton-Fenbow was approached by one of the major German television channels and persuaded to discuss his case on television.

It had not occurred to Newton-Fenbow that the forces ranged against Issels were powerful enough to distort any programme in which he took part.

> When it was finally screened ... the programme had certainly been very expertly edited. It showed part of the BBC 'Living with Death' film ... then shots of Wendy and me window shopping in Rottach-Egern. Then followed the recorded interview ... the interview had been so drastically edited that it consisted of little more than the question: 'Would you consider yourself cured?' and my reply: 'Of course not!' ... the programme was merely being used as a peg upon which to hang a blatant attack against Dr Issels. Immediately after the distorted interview there appeared the press spokesman for the Bavarian Chamber of Doctors. He condemned Dr Issels as a fraud and a charlatan. The interviewer asked him about my (cure) case. 'That is quite simple' he replied 'if he has improved since arriving in Germany then he has never had cancer.' [15]

Newton-Fenbow found that many of the German papers on the morning following the programme carried front page stories about Issels and medical fraud. The articles were based upon a statement given out by the Bavarian Chamber of Doctors, the German equivalent of a branch of the British Medical Association.

Newton-Fenbow felt so strongly about the underhand opposition to Dr Issels that, together with other patients, he set up a small committee which was named the Committee Against Tyranny in Medicine. In their first press statement the Committee demanded that the Chamber of Doctors substantiate the claims which they were making against Dr Issels.

> Many doctors in Germany must feel extremely alarmed at the present smear campaign being mounted by certain members of their *Arztekammer*. This is 'McCarthyism', in which no one dare speak out for fear of falling victim to these same techniques. [16]

Returning to England, Newton-Fenbow continued his campaign in support of Issels' treatments and tried to get BBC television interested in a programme. High level opposition soon became apparent; 'they [BBC staff] were told by quite high authority, that Issels was a charlatan and a quack.' [17] Newton-Fenbow and Gordon Thomas, who was to become the director of the BBC programme, travelled back to Bavaria to do research. They also persuaded an English cancer doctor, Professor John Anderson, to go out to the clinic. Anderson came back full of optimism about doing research into Issels' techniques.

The film was finally made in January 1970. When it was finished, however, the BBC insisted that it was viewed by a variety of orthodox cancer doctors. Two of these doctors, including Dr Anderson, were of the opinion that Issels' work should be the subject of more research. Other more influential members of the panel felt that quite enough had been heard of Issels. The film was shelved.

On July 25th, the *Amsterdam Telegraaf* carried an exposé of the behind-the-scenes banning of the film, headlined 'Great Battle Over BBC Film'. The *Observer* followed with a story, [18] in which the BBC maintained that everything was going well. 'Aubrey Singer, head of the BBC-TV Features Group said: "The film is in the final stages of editing. No transmission date has yet been fixed".' The film had actually been finished eight months previously.

In the heated debate which followed the *Observer* article, it was said that Dr Issels was still under suspicion of criminal charges and nothing should be done by the BBC to elevate him in public esteem. Reference was also made to the Cancer Act, which stated that no claim to a cure for cancer could be made in the media. It transpired later that Michael Latham, the producer of the film, had actually been instructed by his

seniors in the BBC to destroy the film negative and all the prints.
Fortunately he did not do this. [19]†

On November 3rd 1970, a drastically edited version of the film
entitled 'Go Climb a Mountain' was shown on television. Despite the
evident scepticism the film conveyed, and the barrage of criticism from
orthodox practitioners which followed its screening, the film provoked
renewed interest in Issels' work. Lillian Board, a young British athelete,
already very ill with cancer, was sent to the clinic on money raised by
her family and well-wishers.

In the months following the film, the cancer research industry
made a number of complaints. According to their representatives, the
film had looked too favourably upon Dr Issels. The BMA complained
about the film, as did Sir David Smithers, the Government's adviser
on cancer, and his colleague Professor Hamilton-Fairley. Smithers had
apparently tried to stop the showing of the film because, although he
had not observed them at first hand, he considered Issels' treatments
'worthless'.‡

It was unfortunate for Dr Issels that the case of Lillian Board so
captured the nation's imagination when she set off for Bavaria. On her
death in December 1970, it was easy for Issels' detractors to suggest
that she might not have died had she continued with her conventional

† The Cancer Act was passed in 1939; although some parts of it are still on the statute
book, the majority has been incorporated in more recent Acts such as the 1946 National
Health Act and the 1968 Medicines Act. Although brought in ostensibly to 'further the
provision for the treatment of cancer', it contained punitive clauses aimed at non-
orthodox practitioners. Section 4 (1) stated 'No person shall take any part in the
publication of any advertisement (a) containing an offer to treat any person for cancer, or
to prescribe any remedy therefor, or to give any advice in connection with the treatment
thereof (outside hospitals or qualified doctors).' Section (8) threw the net very wide on its
description of an advertisement: 'includes any notice circular, label, wrapper or other
document, and any announcement made orally or by any means of reproducing or
transmitting sounds'. Contravention of the Act was punishable in the Crown Court with
up to 2 years' imprisonment or a fine of up to £1,000.

‡ Sir David Smithers is now Emeritus Professor of Radiotherapy at the University of
London and Vice-Chairman of the Council of the Cancer Research Campaign. At the
time he went to Bavaria, Smithers was Director of the Radiotherapy Department of the
Royal Marsden Hospital and the Institute of Cancer Research in London. Professor
Gordon Hamilton-Fairley worked at St Bartholomew's Hospital, where he was a mentor
of Professor Tim McElwain, who was up until his death in 1990 a member of the
Campaign Against Health Fraud. In 1975, Hamilton-Fairley was killed when an IRA
bomb, meant for his next-door neighbour Hugh Frazer MP, blew up his car.

treatment.†

The apparent inability of Issels to help Board gave the cancer research industry, the BMA and pharmaceutical vested interests the chance that they had been waiting for. On January 25th 1971 the Co-ordinating Committee for Cancer Research (CCCR) sent a team of orthodox doctors to Bavaria. The CCCR was composed of representatives from the Medical Research Council, the Imperial Cancer Research Fund and the Cancer Research Campaign. It was presided over at that time by Lord Rosenheim, President of the Royal College of Physicians. Rosenheim claimed 'the team is going only because of public pressure'. In fact there had been no public pressure, though there might well have been had more people known that the trip was likely to cost some £10,000. [20.]

When Issels heard that a British team was to examine his work he said: 'I will welcome the team, but I hope that they will send somebody who knows about immunotherapy, not just orthodox doctors who know only about surgical and radiotherapy cancer treatments.' Issels imagined that the team of British scientists would be 'tough but fair'. He saw the announcement as a possible final recognition of his work and joyfully told his staff that he was 'confident British specialists would make a favourable report'. 'At last,' he said, 'the world is getting to know about our work'. [21]

The research team which arrived in Bavaria on January 25th 1971, was led by Professor Smithers, accompanied by his colleague Professor Hamilton-Fairley, Dr Harris from the Department of Environmental Carcinogenesis at the Imperial Cancer Research Fund laboratories, Dr Medvei who had previously been the Principal Medical Officer at the Treasury and Dame Albertine Winner, Deputy Chief Medical Officer at the Department of Health and Deputy Medical Director of St Christopher's Hospice, London.

On their return to England, the team were quick to prepare their report, which was published by HMSO within two months.‡ The

---

† Years later, Issels spoke warmly to Penny Brohn about Lillian Board, saying that he admired her courage and fighting spirit. Issels had continued to treat her free of charge when her funds were depleted.

‡ The HMSO report was published under the auspices of Keith Joseph, at that time the Social Services Secretary.

report was a broad but vague indictment of Issels' therapies and research practices. Massive publicity accompanied its publication. The headline of a *Sunday Times* article published a week before the report came out, summed up the report: 'British cancer men attack Issels'. [22]

> A team of five British medical specialists has firmly rejected some
> of the spectacular claims of success in the treatment of advanced
> cancer attributed to the controversial Dr Josef Issels.

The report was not theoretically a Government report, nor even a Government-sponsored report. It had not been sanctioned by Parliament, nor any Government committee; it had however been financed by the Medical Research Council, which receives its money directly from the Government. Had the report been published under the names of the research doctors who went to Bavaria, they would all have been open to legal actions, a possibility avoided by providing them with Crown immunity.

The visiting experts found it hard to distort the doctor-patient relationship which existed at the Ringberg Clinic, or to paint Dr Issels as a quack. They had to admit that he developed a good relationship with his patients which even involved him telling them about their illness – the very thought of such a thing must have struck terror into the hearts of the visiting physicians.

> The doctor-patient relationship here is very remarkable. Dr
> Issels and his patients become partners in a venture to try and
> save the patient's life. He tells them everything, including the
> sites of the primary and secondary tumours, promises nothing
> but offers with confidence to do his best. The patients respond
> and appear to be inspired and impressed with it all. They take
> their own temperatures and pulses, chart their own fluid intake
> and output and assess vomit and are responsible for fluid
> replacement. There was no doubt about their feeling for Dr
> Issels, amounting to devotion at times. [23]

Disputing Dr Issels' results, the visitors argued that many of the patients whom Issels had treated probably did not have secondary cancers, but were suffering from the effects of previous treatments:

> In other words, in our view Dr Issels has been treating a number
> of patients suffering from irradiation oedema, necrosis and
> fibrosis on the basis that they had tumour recurrence and we are

of the opinion that these form quite a high proportion of his 'successes'. [24]

Accounting in this way for the serious illnesses suffered by many of Dr Issels' patients, the report was forced to make some interesting comments on orthodox medicine:

> Dr Issels received some patients who have been shockingly mishandled medically as well as psychologically. Some of his patients seem to us to have been grossly over-treated by drugs or radiation, the treatment having been continued or repeated only to make matters worse when reactions had been mistaken for signs of tumour activity. His supportive regime, without cytotoxic drugs for the first week in most cases, allows time for partial recovery from some of these therapeutic disasters. [25]

Despite the report claiming that Dr Issels' records were not kept in a way that easily led to comparisons between his case management and previous orthodox treatments, it concluded that his principal treatments were ineffective.

> Dr Issels' main treatment regime has no effect on tumour growth. He aims to put each patient in the best possible condition to combat his (sic) disease, which is admirable; but there is no evidence from our examination of the patients and their notes that it makes a significant contribution to their survival. [26]

According to the report, Issels was not a charlatan, just a misguided foreign gentleman who was very kind to his patients.

> We are convinced that Dr Issels believes implicitly in the treatment he gives. We think he does a great deal to help most of his patients. We sadly think, however, that he is misguided in his beliefs and that the treatment peculiar to his clinic is ineffective. [27]

The British doctors could find little wrong with Issels' clinic, and the report contented itself with vague and offhand dismissals of his work. Dr Issels' statistics, for example, recording the length of survival of patients were invalid according to the team because they were not compared with a like sample of patients who had been treated with purely orthodox treatments. Issels was also criticised for *not taking all the patients that came to him*, regardless of whether they could afford the treatment or not.

The paucity of the scientific and philosophical arguments contained in the report did not escape those who felt strongly that orthodox medicine had contributed little to cancer care.

> The sum of the team's arguments that Dr Issels' cures are not really cures boils down to this – 'we cannot accept the cures because cancer is incurable' ... I hope readers will not have missed the logical imperfection in the team's reasoning, which is that no statistical analysis of the results could be made, and yet they were able to conclude that the treatment did not work. [28]

Dr Smithers, publicising the report to the press, gave away a little more than the report: 'I do not think that you will find better treatment for cancer than we have in this country within the National Health Service.'

Following the publication of the report, Issels felt justifiable anger; he accused the British team of 'dismissing his twenty-one years work, on the basis of a three and a half day visit to his clinic'. [29]

The publication of the report temporarily reduced the number of patients attending the Bavarian clinic and caused Issels an estimated loss of £150,000. Although within a year there were again long waiting lists, the HMSO report put in train a sequence of events which was to close Issels' clinic.

In October 1972, Lord Shawcross, in a comment obviously related to cancer care, suggested the setting up of a committee to censor medical news and prevent the raising of false hopes and fears. Such a committee for lowering hope and eradicating panic had a peculiar ring of 1984 to it.† Shawcross made his suggestion at the Royal Society of Medicine, where he was supported by Sir Ronald Tunbridge, Chairman of the BMA's Board of Science. Tunbridge informed the conference that 'the instant reporting which might be acceptable for sports items was unacceptable in the health field'.

---

† Lord Shawcross, who had been an Attorney General in a Labour Government, had interests in the Rockefeller complex, being a special adviser to the Morgan Guaranty Trust of New York since 1965. He also had interests in the processed food and pharmaceutical industries, having been a director of Shell, Rank Hovis McDougall and Upjohn.

Despite Lord Shawcross, journalists, relatives and patients still reported on the amazing regression of tumours at the Ringberg Clinic. Eight year old David Towse had gone to the Clinic after British doctors had given up on him in 1970. By the time he got there his cancer had spread from his neck to his brain and his legs. By 1973, however, the tumours had regressed completely and David was back in England playing football for his school. David's mother, Ann Towse, wrote to the Social Services Secretary, Sir Keith Joseph, in defence of Dr Issels. Joseph wrote back: 'The best proved treatment for cancer is, in fact, available at National Health Service hospitals and will continue to be available for David at any time.' Mrs Towse told the *Daily Telegraph* that in 1970 David's consultant had told her that they could not treat David any more. [30] David Towse was not the only person for whom, 'the best treatment for cancer on the NHS' was not sufficient; in 1973 cancer killed nearly 120,000 people in Britain.

Reporting for the *Daily Express*, James Wilkinson spoke to three British patients at the clinic, all of whom said that British doctors had simply given up on them when their cancer was diagnosed. [31]

In April 1972, David Emery, Lillian Board's fiancé at the time of her death, revisited the clinic and spoke to Issels for the *Sunday Mirror*. In this interview Issels pointed out that British doctors were now refusing to continue the prescription of drugs, which he believed was important to the continued well-being of his patients after they left the clinic. The cousin of journalist Kenneth Allsop was also refused prescribed drugs from British doctors for four months after returning from Issels' clinic.

Gordon Thomas, the producer of the BBC programme 'Go Climb a Mountain', had since the programme been working on a book about Issels called *Issels, the biography of a doctor*. The book was due to be published by Hodder and Stoughton in June 1973. At the last minute it was withdrawn. Hodder and Stoughton announced that they were postponing publication of the book after the BBC complained to the publishers that there had been a violation of copyright.

The real reason was probably different. In the book Thomas describes his struggle to get the film on television. It transpired that the BBC had canvassed extensive medical opinion before they were willing to screen the film. The person who most strongly objected to the film was Mr Aubrey Singer, then Head of TV Features, and someone particularly interested in promoting science programmes. The book detailed the 'considerable internal opposition to the showing of the film'. [32.]

In order to avoid a legal confrontation with the BBC, Hodder and Stoughton published first in America. Two years passed before Hodder were able to publish in England, [33] by which time Issels had been forced to close his clinic in Bavaria. Thomas was certain that there had been a conspiracy to stop the publication of his book: ' I feel sure that the medical establishment has brought pressure to bear on certain people within the BBC. There has been a "cover up" done on the whole question of Dr Issels and his techniques. Certain people cannot face the possibility that they might be wrong.' [34]

In July 1973, Dr Issels announced that he would be closing his clinic that October. A spokesman for the clinic said: 'opposition over the past months reached an extent against which Dr Issels is powerless'. [35] Issels told the *Daily Telegraph* that the BBC had prepared another film which was very critical of him and he had to get a London solicitor to act for him. 'Wasting time on legal squabbles did not leave enough time for my patients.' [36.]

The decision to close the clinic had been taken reluctantly by Issels, 'under the pressure of external influences and sabotage inside the clinic'. He claimed that there had been a 'conspiracy' and a 'systematic campaign' to shut his clinic down.

Since Issels' difficulties began in the seventies, he had lost twenty members of staff, including four doctors from a complement of ten. In 1973, the clinic had 115 beds but only 88 patients. When Issels tried to recruit more staff, the orthodox medical bodies did everything possible to stop people applying for jobs. The administration of the clinic had become prey to a whole range of dirty tricks. Callers using false names and titles rang the clinic to get the names and telephone numbers of staff, who were then harassed. At every opportunity Issels was labelled a 'quack'. Medicines sent by post from the clinic to some 400 outpatients were taken from parcels and propaganda notes about quackery substituted.

Issels blamed many of his staff who had been bought off by orthodox medicine. 'Betrayal and conspiracy by some members of his staff, half of whom finally sided with orthodox medical critics in condemning his cancer treatment, had led to his decision to close the clinic.' [37.]

No doubt Dr Issels felt isolated in Germany as these attacks upon him and his practice mounted. Powerful forces were also at work in Britain to cut off his support. On August 5th, the *Sunday Telegraph* carried a long story quoting an unnamed 'leading British scientist', and 'one time sympathiser of Issels'. The scientist claimed that any attempt he had made to research Issels' treatments had been sabotaged by the denial of grants. He had returned to orthodox medicine.

In September, Dr Smithers, the leader of the Co-ordinating Committee for Cancer Research team which had been to Bavaria, made clear his feelings about the closure of the clinic. He told the press that he 'shed no tears'. In fact, the clinic wasn't completely defeated; Issels closed it at the end of 1973 but re-opened it nearby in 1976. For three years he ran a smaller but equally successful clinic, until in 1979 he had to close the residential building and continue only with outpatients.

The Bristol Cancer Help Centre

When Penny Brohn returned to England and began discussing cancer treatment with the friends who had visited her in Bavaria, it was clear that Josef Issels' work had had an effect not just upon her but also upon her visitors. In 1980, Penny, her friends Pat Pilkington and Dr Alec Forbes – at that time a consultant physician at Plymouth General Hospital – set up a small self-help group for cancer sufferers. Penny Brohn brought to the group all her personal experience of fighting cancer with alternative therapies, and her experience of fighting her orthodox doctors.

The beginnings were small, with six people attending one meeting a week. The demand was evident, people wanted a system of support and advice away from the hospitals and the alienating professionalism of orthodox doctors. Influenced by Issels and Gerson, the discussion in the early meetings centred upon the relationship between cancer and nutrition and the possible relationship between cancer and vitamin deficiencies.

From the beginning, the Bristol Centre worked on the assumption that if the onset of cancer could be related to deficiencies in diet then there was some point, even when people had cancer, in trying to redress such deficiencies. Another focus of the group's discussion was the relationship between stress and cancer. Teaching stress control was obviously something which a small self-help group could do, and they began to work with relaxation techniques and meditation. The group became familiar with the work of the Simontons in America. They encouraged cancer patients to do 'creative visualisation' or 'imaging'. Counsellors joined the group, so that people could talk about what was troubling them. Healing, involving the laying-on-of-hands was also included in the programme. In the early eighties, when Penny Brohn, Pat Pilkington and Alec Forbes began working, such ideas seemed revolutionary.

* * *

Ironically, it was a series of BBC television programmes which were responsible for transforming the BCHC from a small self-help group, into a nationally recognised organisation. In 1983, the BBC screened a set of six programmes which took a close look at the Bristol Centre and other alternative forms of cancer treatment. The programmes, remarkable for their honesty, were probably the only independent review of alternative cancer treatment ever to be broadcast in Britain.

The six programmes were made by the 'Forty Minutes' documentary team who had spent nine months following the lives of six patients. Following the screening of the programmes Roger Mills, the executive producer, discussed the problems involved in making films about cancer for the BBC. 'Within the BBC, to some, simply to publish information about a radical alternative to orthodox medicine and to enumerate its successes seems to imply a criticism of orthodox medicine and its multi-million pound research programme.' [38]

Mills says that he was pressured into making the same points in every episode, points which defended the pharmaceutical companies and orthodox medicine. He had to make it clear, for example, in every programme that there was no proof the Bristol philosophy 'worked'. He was told to take extreme care in pointing out that attendance at Bristol was not a substitute for orthodox medicine, but a complement. During work on the programme Mills found that damaging rumours were being spread beyond the BBC. One doctor informed the film team that Dr Alec Forbes, the Centre's medical adviser and an orthodox consultant physician for twenty years, had been struck off the Medical Register: this was not true. Another doctor told them that BCHC was purely a commercial organisation being run for financial gain: in fact at this time the services at Bristol were free to attenders.†

The biggest bombshell came just before the programmes were to be transmitted. Just as they had done with 'Go Climb a Mountain', the BBC insisted that the programmes should be followed by a discussion programme. They were also to insist that a question mark should be added to the title of the films, thereby disputing the objectivity of the statement, 'A Gentle Way With Cancer'.‡

In the discussion programme, the anger and antagonism between orthodox and alternative cancer therapies were evident. On one side, speaking for orthodox medicine, were ranged, Walter Bodmer the Director of Research at the Imperial Cancer Research Fund (ICRF), Professor Ian McColl,†† and Professor Tim McElwain from the Institute of Cancer Research and the Royal Marsden Hospital. On the other side speaking in favour of an alternative approach, were Brenda Kidman the author of the book, *A Gentle Way With Cancer*, [39] and Dr Dick Richards. For some reason which was not made clear, an empty chair took the place of the third spokesperson on the side of alternative cancer care.

The discussion came to no resolutions. The supporters of orthodoxy suggested that there was no evidence to support claims

† Such rumours are similar to those which surfaced in 1990. They show the very real continuity which exists in the tactics of the anti-health fraud lobby.

‡ Perhaps the most bizarre of the pre-transmission demands was the demand made by Aubrey Singer of one of the programme producers that Penny Brohn produce written evidence that she had actually had cancer in the first place. The producer was able to produce a letter from Penny's doctor outlining her case and her diagnosis.

†† Professor of Surgery at the University of London at the United Medical Schools of Guy's and St Thomas' Hospitals since 1971. Research Fellow at Harvard Medical School, Johns Hopkins Hospital 1976. Medical Advisor to BBC Television 1976. President of the Mildmay Mission Hospital. Later to become Lord Ian McColl after being ennobled by Margaret Thatcher.

made in the films by practitioners at Bristol. Dr Dick Richards talked about the immune system and how therapies had to enhance the capacity of the immune system to help people overcome illness.† At the core of the discussion, however, was a gauntlet thrown down by the orthodox practitioners, a challenge to conduct formal research into claims about alternative cancer treatments.

Feeling confident after the programmes, Penny Brohn's husband approached the discussion panelists to suggest that they themselves might like to conduct the research into the Centre's work. The Centre felt that they had nothing to lose from having their work evaluated scientifically; such research might in fact lend authority to their practices. The Centre, however, had no money for the project.

By 1985, the Bristol Cancer Help Centre had agreed to a research project which would measure the efficacy of the therapies used at Bristol. All three doctors who had appeared in the discussion programme which followed 'A Gentle Way With Cancer?' were to play a part in the research. It was Lord McColl who promoted the research, while the cost was agreed by Walter Bodmer at the ICRF and supported by the Cancer Research Campaign (CRC). One of the study's main participants was to be Professor Tim McElwain.

Following the BBC programmes, the Bristol Cancer Help Centre went from strength to strength. It grew quickly, buying an extensive and beautifully situated old building in Clifton, Bristol, which was converted into a peaceful residential care centre.‡ The ideas which guided the Centre also developed. Penny Brohn was in her element setting up the Centre and driving it forward. She was seeing a dream come true. Within sight of realisation, at Bristol, was that spiritually

---

† Dr Dick Richards was a vehement opponent of orthodox cancer treatment. In 1982, he wrote *The topic of cancer: When the killing has to stop.* [40] The first chapter began with the words 'Considered in the broadest terms, orthodox cancer treatment today is a failure and a disgrace'. The book outlined histories of alternative cancer therapists. In October 1983, only months after the television programmes had been screened, Dr Richards was arrested in America after allegedly paying a Dr Bennett £2,000 to arrange the 'disappearance' of Richards' London partner Dr Peter Stephan. At his trial in Los Angeles in 1984, the prosecution claimed that Richards had also offered Bennett the US patent for an anti-herpes treatment developed by Stephan. Dr Richards was found guilty and sentenced to 4 years' imprisonment. Throughout the case Dr Richards protested his innocence.

‡ Grove House was opened by Prince Charles in July 1983.

supportive environment, which she had not found until she travelled to Bavaria.

The responsibility people assume when they offer treatment of any kind is a profound responsibility. To those who set up the Bristol Cancer Help Centre, the continued re-appraisal of this responsibility was crucial.†

> We had come across sufficient case studies of people who had made recoveries, using what they considered to be 'complementary therapies', that we felt quite justified in saying to patients, 'Well look, this is what they did, you might want to try it.' We were getting people then whose lives were being measured in months and weeks, and some of them are alive and well today.

In the main, they found that the majority of people who came to them were already undergoing conventional treatment. They were, however, given little assurance that such treatment would work, and often it had severe side effects. There were as well those people whom orthodox medicine had simply given up on.

> They had had conventional treatment and the cancer had recurred and they had now been told, 'There is nothing that we can do for you.' More recently, not so much at the beginning, we have been coming across a noticeable group of people, who have had a cancer diagnosed *for which there is no known treatment*. They have absolutely *nothing* offered to them.

From the beginning Bristol was used as a centre for complementary therapies. There were, however, a small number of attenders who were completely opposed to orthodox medicine. Penny Brohn knew all about the fear that a rejection of orthodox medicine can create: she had refused to have a mastectomy.

> Although I have never ever recommended to anyone that they should refuse conventional treatment, if they did *we would support them*. I think that this has annoyed a lot of orthodox practitioners.

Ironically it was Alec Forbes, after forty years work inside the National

---

† Unless otherwise stated all the following quotes are from interviews between Penny Brohn and the author.

Health Service, who was most vituperative about the terrible damage inflicted by orthodox medicine. There was a continuous debate about whether the approach at Bristol should be uncompromising or whether they should work alongside conventional practitioners. When the debate was not expressed openly, it was internalised. Workers at Bristol constantly suffered the insecurity which comes with being a fringe organisation in a hostile environment.

By the late eighties the early evangelical style had softened. Books like *The Bristol Programme*, written by Penny Brohn in 1987, bear witness to a much gentler style of therapy and a less acerbic radicalism. If the rhetoric had changed, the basic ideas and therapies had not. These still suggested that, by utilising mental and spiritual energy, people were able to influence their physical body.

No one attending the Bristol Centre had to continue the therapies if they created pressure and conflict. By the late eighties, after ten years in existence, counselling and stress control therapies were still available along with visualisation, meditation and healing. New therapies had been added to the programme such as music therapy, art therapy and massage.

The one aspect of therapy which had been consistently reviewed was the emphasis on diet. In the early years, attitudes to diet based upon Gerson's work had been stark and workers at the Centre began to find that people felt guilty if they could not keep up with it. This tended to induce in people a sense of failure which in turn added to their disempowerment.

Consequently, in the mid-eighties, the attitude to nutrition at the Centre changed.

> What we tried to do was to respond to what the patient was telling us. If a patient came and said, 'I have read about the grape cure', or 'I have read about the Gerson therapy, and I want to do it, what do you think?' then, we would help them with that. We served a vegan diet, which was a whole-food diet, organically grown, with no animal products at all.

The Bristol Cancer Help Centre had a conventional and scientific attitude to processed food, maintaining, for example, that sugar represented 'empty calories'. The Centre still adhered to Gerson's philosophy that the food which is most nutritional is the food which has been least processed. However, in those cases where patients had had such treatments as radiotherapy to the stomach and fibre was not recommended, individual regimes were worked out.

Gerson's ideas are still very important to Penny Brohn who believes that the consumption of chemicals has a serious effect upon the immune system and the individual's ability to fight cancer.

> You should just check out mentally what has actually happened to this food since it was picked; has it been frozen, has it been processed, has it been dried – read the side of the packet, the more it sounds like a chemistry kit and the less it sounds like food, the more you should try and get back to the natural product.

While the Bristol Centre developed, there were those in orthodox medicine looking for an opportunity to destroy it. Despite the 'live and let live' attitude which appeared to characterise the relationship between the Centre and medical orthodoxy, commercial and ideological competition lay just beneath the surface.

None of the Centre's founder members could have known that their challenge to have orthodox doctors and scientists carry out research on their work was like a time bomb ticking away behind the scenes.

Chapter Eleven

Industrial Food and Nutritional Medicine

> *Most people are convinced that boiled vegetables and a little fruit will be enough to give them all the vitamins they need but a mixture of foods of this kind has little or no effect on the vitamin content of the body; not only will the vegetables in nine cases out of ten be wrongly cooked, but those small quantities of vitamin food which are generally considered sufficient are far too small to be beneficial.* [1]

The relevance of nutrition to health has been known since the Enlightenment. Before industrialisation and processed food manufacture, it was commonplace for doctors to treat conditions with dietary controls or supplements. In the 1740s a naval surgeon, James Lind, gave fresh fruit to the sailors he treated and cured their scurvy. In 1753, he wrote 'A treatise of the scurvy', describing this new method of nutritional treatment.

At the end of the nineteenth century, a Dutch doctor, Christian van Eijkman, traced the cause of the fatal disease beri-beri to a diet of polished rice. When van Eijkman experimented, he found that by feeding patients rice bran, the part of the plant which had been stripped off to make polished rice, he was able to bring about an almost immediate cure. When Eijkman presented the results of his work, the medical establishment rejected them.

With such discoveries, made during the eighteenth and nineteenth centuries, the illnesses associated with gross nutritional deficiencies were cured. As the industrial revolution and mechanised agriculture developed in the nineteenth century, scientists began to understand the more complex make-up of food. They identified the relationship of trace elements and minerals to human health and towards the end of the nineteenth century came the discovery of some of the most important elements, such as iron, copper and zinc. The first vitamins were also identified at the turn of the century.

What science was not able to do until much later in the twentieth century was to describe the interaction of vitamins, minerals and other elements in their journey through the human body. The development of knowledge about nutrition has grown with the development of the technology used to assess increasingly small parts of biological material. Only in the last ten to fifteen years has the effect on human health of the more esoteric elements like vanadium, cobalt, and nickel been identified.

During the nineteen twenties and thirties, great strides were made by science in identifying vitamins and minerals and relating these elements to human health and nutrition. During this period, a divergence became evident between the producers of industrially processed food and those who followed the scientific evaluation of nutrition. Vegetarianism and veganism began to grow in the decades before the war, and the National Association of Health Stores was founded in 1931. A 'school' of nutritional medicine began to develop, but, even in the nineteen thirties, those who followed the scientific paradigm of nutrition were isolated and their ideas ridiculed.

A number of doctors and therapists had begun to base their practice solely on the regulation of diet. Dr Max Gerson treated cancer with cleansing diets based on fruit and vegetables, from which tea, coffee, sugar and refined carbohydrates were sternly excluded. Dr Max Bircher-Benner cured patients of a variety of illnesses with a regime based on raw fruit and vegetables. [2]

Progressive ideas about food and nutrition proved useful to the government as Britain went into the Second World War. The need for soldiers to be fit sharpened the minds of industrialists and politicians. For the first and last time, during and just after the war a national food policy was adopted by a British government. The British diet immediately after the Second World War was a nutritious diet which had at its centre the brown loaf and fresh vegetables grown during the 'Dig for Victory' campaign. High protein produce, such as milk, butter, eggs and cheese, was rationed as was sugar. The diet was, coincidentally, relatively rich in fibre, low in meats, fats and refined flour.

By the end of the Second World War, the food and nutrition progressives had carved out a place for themselves in both science and popular dietary advice. Views on 'live foods' and natural non-processed fruit and vegetables enjoyed a brief ascendancy lingering in the mainstream for a couple of years after the war, until industry got back into its stride. In this period, a number of influential figures had an impact on mainstream thinking: scientists and popular writers such as Sir Robert McCarrison, Sir John Boyd Orr, Barbara Cartland, Gaylord Hauser, Leon Cordell, Max Bircher-Benner, and Dr Thomas Allinson.

Soon after the war, the food industry resumed its long courtship with the chemical industry and from the late nineteen fifties onwards, it was downhill all the way for the British diet. The end of the war left the economy with a glut of chemicals and a wide range of new industrialised processes. With the sudden growth of the processed food industry and the greater dependence of the medical profession on pharmaceuticals, there came a divergence between those nutritionists who pursued a scientific theory of nutrition, and the food manufacturers, who no longer knew nor cared about nutritional content.

By the mid-sixties in America, old ideas about wholefoods and the high quality nutritional status of vegetables and fruits were being revitalised by the 'health food' revolution. Representatives of the chemical and pharmaceutical industries tried to ensure, however, that those who believed in the 'health food' concept did not link concepts of nutrition with those of disease.

What industry was trying to contain, and what it is still trying to contain, is preventative medicine; those doctors and therapists who believe in the practice of nutritional medicine lay down rules for life, not single treatments. Such rules for life have usually implied a basic antagonism to the industrial and chemical empire.

The Old and New Schools of Nutrition

Today there are two schools of nutrition, the 'old' and the 'new'. Almost all the 'old school' nutritionists are linked to the processed food industry and represent vested interests. Although such people claim to be guided by science, their theoretical position consists of highly generalised assumptions. At the centre of these assumptions is the 'balanced diet'.

Because industrial production is production for the masses, the nutritional arguments of the old school are not individual-specific. At the heart of old school nutrition is the idea that we are all the same, regardless of environment, health at birth, occupation or early experience of illness. The old school of nutrition assumes that we all need roughly the same amount of nutrients daily for our bodies to function with the same efficiency.

The old school looks at nutritional elements in isolation, generally unconcerned with the biological processes which occur once a substance has entered the body. Were they to enter this terrain, they would be forced to face *relative* questions about the bio-availability of different vitamins, metals and minerals. The old school are absolutists, concerned with general trends and absolute quantities.

Many nutritional scientists and doctors of the new school, despite having diverse philosophies, agree upon one thing: industrialised processed food is food stripped of its nutritional integrity. And perhaps more complex than this, once the pre-industrial nutritional 'balance' is overturned, by man's intervention, it cannot be simply recreated by adding synthetic vitamins.

Whereas the old school looks at singular nutrients and their effect, the new school has a more holistic approach, looking at the reverberations of that one nutrient throughout the whole being. More than this, the new school nutritionists will be feeding data into the equation relating to such things as environment, smoking, drinking and stress.

Because of modern technology, the nutritionist is now able to have a more detailed understanding of the make-up of the body and the complex interaction which takes place between elements within it. It is now possible, by testing body fluids and blood, to examine the various quantities of vitamins and minerals present in the body. It is also possible to discuss what is termed 'nutritional status'.

Rather than relying upon generalised considerations such as Recommended Daily Allowance (RDA) levels, new school nutritionists draw upon information which shows that many nutrients, in amounts considerably higher than RDA levels, have positive or beneficial effects in certain states of ill health.

Specific nutritional circumstances identified by the new school of
nutritionists, demonstrate just how individual people are. The person
who works at a painstaking or stress-producing job, or the person who
internalises emotional conflict, will inevitably burn up different
nutritional fuel from the person who is of a calmer temperament or
in more relaxed employment. The stressed person will need advising
upon a different vitamin balance from the calmer person.

Chemical toxins, whether they arrive in the body through the
ingestion of food, or through the absorption of ambient environmental
substances or even an excessive use of particular vitamins, minerals, or
drugs, all draw upon and to some extent counteract the body's
nutritional balance. This is simply demonstrated by the examples of
tea and coffee. It has been shown that heavy consumption of either of
these, and the caffeine they contain, can reduce the bio-availability of
B1 (Thiamine) by as much as 60%.[3] Continuous B1 deficiency, like all
important vitamin or mineral deficiencies, can lead eventually to
degenerative disease.

> When people have a vitamin B1 deficiency they become tired,
> nervous ... They have a general malaise, aches and pains,
> particularly at night. This progresses to a kind of tingling in the
> legs, the feet, then it goes on to cardiovascular disturbances. [4]

Caffeine affects other vitamins and minerals in the body; it destroys or
depletes potassium, calcium, zinc, magnesium, vitamins A and C. It
can have an adverse effect upon the 'nervous system, the heart, the
pancreas and the adrenal glands – and it is a factor in as many as two
dozen degenerative diseases'. [5]

It is evident from this that a 'balanced' diet for a person drinking
large amounts of tea or coffee is different from a 'balanced diet' for the
person who drinks neither. Alcohol and sugar are other 'taken for
granted' foods which have an effect upon vitamin and mineral
absorption, de-stabilising an otherwise 'balanced' diet.

The new school nutritionist has moved on far beyond the simple
slogans of the old school and is now in a position to understand much
more about the catalytic effect of a wide range of vitamins and
minerals. Given the complex state of our present knowledge, anodyne
advice about 'square meals' and balanced diets is about as useful as
passing a hacksaw to a micro-surgeon.

Doctors and Nutritional Medicine

Because we are, on the whole, what we eat, there are some doctors of the new school of nutrition who maintain that one of the very first tests which a doctor should carry out on patients is to measure their nutritional status. Those doctors who do not assess the nutritional status of their patients rarely take it into account during diagnosis.

The training of orthodox doctors has consistently failed to take nutrition into account. Even when dealing with food-based problems such as allergy and intolerance, many orthodox doctors steer their way carefully through any discussion of nutrition. Some doctors would not consider it a part of their role to give patients authoritative advice on the consumption of certain foods. These same doctors tend to avoid making judgements about nutrition. The idea of nutritional treatment conflicts with their training and the culture of modern medicine which has been largely shaped by pharmaceutical interests.

The avoidance by orthodox practitioners of nutrition has meant that nutritional practice and advice have been relegated to a sub-professional area of health care which tends to be populated by more malleable, often female, ancillary workers: an area which tends to be dominated and controlled by the processed food, chemical and pharmaceutical companies.

Increasingly, general practitioners have been de-skilled in the 'healing arts'. Gradually, they are losing any understanding of the biological effects of the drugs which they prescribe and the foodstuffs and chemicals which their patients consume. In a world in which doctors become detached from the basic skills of healing, issues of nutrition tend to be approached in only the crudest terms.

Chapter Twelve

Dr Stephen Davies: Nutritional Doctor

I had no idea what it was, but I did know that the whole theoretical matrix upon which orthodox medical care was based was fundamentally flawed. [1]

By the end of his first month in clinical practice, Dr Stephen Davies knew he was not happy with it. Twenty years later, he looks back on two experiences which explain this lack of affinity with orthodox medicine. Reviewing the first experience, which happened while he was working in a large London teaching hospital, he draws out two themes: that some orthodox doctors did not care for their patients in anything which might be vaguely termed a psychological manner and that even those doctors who did care seemed to be oblivious to the fact that medicine is as much about alleviating symptoms as looking for cures.

> I was late for the first ward round that I made. Just as I arrived, the entourage of Consultant, Senior Registrar, Registrar, two Senior House Officers, two Housemen, the Senior Nursing Sister, three Staff Nurses, two Junior Nurses, and six Medical Students plus a couple of hangers on, were moving away from a bed. The woman was lying there in tears. I said 'What's the matter?' She said, 'They were talking about cancer and this and that.' I said, 'This is a teaching round, they probably mentioned lots of different conditions which had absolutely nothing to do with your illness. Don't worry, dear.' I was desperately trying to reassure her, I patched her up emotionally, as best I could and turned to the next bed, again, just as the entourage left another distraught patient in their wake. I thought, this is nuts. That experience, at the very beginning of my career, coloured my perception of what medicine was about.

Four or five days after my first ward round, I was with a lovely
physician, a rheumatologist; he was kind, caring and conscien-
tious. We were sitting with him in the outpatients clinic. He said,
'The next patient has been a patient of mine for 25 years.' Bells
rang. I thought, something is wrong here if the man has been a
patient for 25 years. In came a man in his early forties, a nurse
holding him up under each arm-pit, and with a Zimmer frame.
He had had juvenile rheumatoid arthritis and it had continued
throughout his adult life. I thought then: there has to be some
error in that doctor's underlying approach to medicine. [2]†

Since those days as a trainee doctor, Stephen Davies has
revolutionised the way in which he conceives of and practises
medicine. Like all those who bring about change, he has had to carve
out a very personal direction, a course which led up many false paths
and unproductive avenues. Now, in his forties, Davies is well
established as a nutritional doctor who has built one of the most
effective biological laboratories in the country.

At university, I didn't know what I wanted to do. I only knew
that I wanted to do something that was 'people-related' and I
knew that I wanted to do something to help people. All the time,
at my first hospital, I was on the verge of dropping out of
medicine. Even then I saw that there was so much destructive-
ness in medicine, that I did not feel comfortable being a party to.

Part of Davies' thinking is situated in the late sixties and early
seventies, a period when everything was being questioned, and
disciplinary boundaries broken down. There is, in the history of his
search, that kind of self-inquisition that is illustrated in the books of
Hermann Hesse. There is also science. Davies is a rigorous scientist
and his laboratory provides the hard diagnostic information which
enhances his eclectic, creative and personal approach to medicine.

From the beginning I had come to terms with the idea that just
because something was established it didn't mean to say it was
right. It's a matter of being eclectic. I got involved in Scientology
for a period, in the early seventies, simply because I thought that

† Unless otherwise stated, all the quotes in this chapter come from interviews between
Stephen Davies and the author.

there might be something in there of value.

After graduating and failing to find a niche for himself in orthodox medicine, Davies took what was to turn out to be the most important step of his medical career. He went to live and work in a poor community on the north east coast of Canada. He planned a six month visit, but stayed for eighteen months. He was one of three doctors at a hospital in the south of Newfoundland, giving hospital care to a population of ten thousand.

> I saw a disease pattern which was completely different from that which I had seen in England. The people came from more or less the same genetic stock as the people I had seen in practice in England, so it was more than probable that their different medical condition had been affected environmentally.

In the extremes of poverty, in areas where industrial food production, in this case fish canning, has laid waste natural communities and their cultures, medical lessons are sometimes easier to learn.

> It was a fishing community with a great deal of unemployment. The town was dominated by a fish plant where they froze the fish. The illnesses I saw were those associated with very poor communities, for example, a six year old child, having to have a complete upper and lower dental extraction because all the teeth were brown and eroded.

> There was a great deal of depression and a lot of high blood pressure amongst young men and young women. A lot of cardio-vascular disease, a lot of young deaths, miscarriages and still-births. In 2,500 people, I saw an enormous amount of congenital malformations, the kind of cases that I would just not see in general practice in England.

Davies concluded that diet was of major importance in shaping the pattern of illness which he saw. His observation of this community gave him a foundation upon which to build his future medical practice.

> The people's diet was basically frozen food, no fresh fruit, no fresh vegetables, white bread, Coca-cola and ice cream. There was a vast amount of drinking, Newfoundland has a very high intake of alcohol. They were also eating a lot of salted fish, which had very few vitamins left in it.

Solutions offered by the doctor who worked in the town before Davies arrived had mainly been dependent upon the prescription of drugs. Davies began to treat the community with vitamins and nutritional advice. In his first six months, using vitamin B complex, he took more than 300 dependent people off psychotropic drugs prescribed by the previous doctor. He had only one treatment failure, and none of those who came off drugs went back on during the eighteen months he was there.

Arriving back in England in 1977, Davies set about his quest through books and discussions with other doctors for an eclectic medical model. In the beginning, working from home, learning as it were from his patients, he charged £2 an hour. The charge was, he says, just a way of making the statement 'that there was a formal exchange going on'. He did not, however, ditch his allopathic training completely.

> Even now, I still use all my orthodox learning. I use it in relation to pathological diagnosis, biochemical diagnosis and patient examination. I employ all the diagnostic techniques that I learnt at medical school and since. The fundamental difference in the way I practise is that I do not have a blind adherence to drug therapy.

Like many pioneers, Stephen Davies wanted to set up some kind of institutional network which would support and further the ideas, research and clinical work which he was doing. The only real forum available at the time for nutritional practitioners was the British Society for Allergy and Environmental Medicine, which allowed Davies only 15 minutes a year at its conference and, at that time, had no interest in placing nutritional medicine on its agenda. In 1984, together with other doctors, he set up the British Society of Nutritional Medicine.† The Society produces the *Journal of Nutritional Medicine*.

In 1984, following a bequest from his recently deceased dentist father, Stephen Davies set up Biolab Medical Unit, with the help of a biochemist. Having a clinic and laboratory was to enable him to have control over testing and measuring the samples taken from his

---

† In 1993, the BSNM merged with the British Society for Allergy and Environmental Medicine.

patients. Setting up the laboratory was a costly exercise, although it enabled him to work more cheaply and efficiently than if he were still having the tests done outside the practice.

> I started Biolab in 1984. At the time I was booked up 5 months ahead with patients. I looked high and low for someone who was willing to measure vitamins and minerals in my patients. Everyone I asked said, 'Yes, we'll do that for a minimum 40 samples a week.' I couldn't guarantee that, as it might not have been indicated on that many of my patients.

As in many other of Davies' ideas, the emphasis in Biolab is on developing practices and services which can be accessible to people who do not have the capital or the resources which he has.

> Biolab looks for trace element deficiencies and toxic element excesses, using atomic absorption spectrophotometry. One of the main research thrusts is the development of biochemical tests which can be performed in a routine biochemistry lab, without any specific expertise or high technology equipment. These are low tech, low expertise tests which give very similar results to the high tech tests. We have developed a number of them.

> We also provide free technical write-ups for doctors who are using Biolab. They can take these straight to their local NHS biochemistry department. They explain the protocol, the exact tests and the way to interpret results. These enable any interested biochemists at the local district hospital to tee up the facilities for the tests without requirement for any new equipment or expertise.

It was not until the early eighties that Stephen Davies became aware that there were people who were opposed to his medical practice. In 1982, he responded forcefully to an article by Dr Vincent Marks, a biochemist, in *Doctor*.[3] The article was about hypoglycaemia – low blood sugar. At that time, and since then, Vincent Marks was representing the sugar industry. Some might think that such vested interests might preclude any doctor from passing medical opinions on sugar and illness.†

---

† Vincent Marks has also been the chairman of the MRC Committee on Diabetes, despite the fact that excessive sugar intake which stimulates insulin secretion is a major cause of hypoglycaemia.

Although there were general and consistent rumblings against nutritional medicine and the setting up of the British Society of Nutritional Medicine, it was not until 1988 that the first public shots were fired at Stephen Davies. On May 22nd 1988, the *Observer* published an article by Annabel Ferriman. [4] At the time this article was published, it did not occur to Davies or his colleagues that it represented the view of an organised opposition.

The article was an 'Open File' item headlined, 'The Great Minerals Gold Mine' and sub-headed, 'Annabel Ferriman diagnoses the supplements kick'. The article was a mish-mash of prejudice and misinformation. *Observer* journalists sent an unsolicited sample of hair for analysis to Larkhall Laboratories, a firm which sub-contracts its hair-mineral analysis† to Biolab. It was said in the article that the journalists had sent two samples of hair from different sides of one person's head, in two separate envelopes. The results which they got back were different on many counts.

> The *Observer* took the results to Dr Stephen Davies, Medical Director of Biolab and a specialist in nutritional medicine, *who practises in luxurious premises above his laboratories close to Harley Street.* [Italics added] [5]

A whole half of the article deals with the apparent discrepancy between the two results. However, the article does not explain that there had been considerable dialogue between Stephen Davies and the *Observer* prior to publication. When Stephen Davies was asked for his opinion on the discrepancies in the hair-mineral analysis, he asked the journalists to explain how they had taken the sample. They admitted that they had taken the sample incorrectly, without concern for either the part of the hair, or the part of the head the sample came from. Biolab instructions for hair samples make it clear that hair has to be taken from the back of the head, cut as near to the scalp as possible, and preferably from a good quarter inch square.

---

† Hair is very rich in minerals, which once in the hair stay there for long periods. Hair analysis is a valid measure for toxic elements such as lead and cadmium; in certain circumstances, it is considered *the* test. It is good for looking at the overall picture of mineral nutriture, whether or not diet is adequate or absorption is adequate or inadequate. It is exceptionally good for assessing levels of lead, mercury, arsenic, aluminium and cadmium.

Annabel Ferriman and her colleague whose hair had been used arrived at Biolab at half eight one morning and sprung their story on me. We checked the internal quality control for the two days in question and it was impeccable. I asked them how they had taken the hair and they told me that they had taken it half way up the hair; there was a proximal sample for one and a distal sample for the other. There was a three month difference in the life of these two samples, three months of exposure to everything in the environment. This is why we insist upon the hair being taken from as close to the scalp as possible.

Confident of the scientific accuracy of hair samples analysed at Biolab, Stephen Davies offered the journalists 10 free sample analyses from the same head and said that they could compare any two of those samples, and then write their story. The journalists refused to take up the offer.

When they refused the offer, Stephen Davies sought an injunction in the High Court, to postpone the publication of the article for a week. 'I wanted the judge to tell them that they had to get their sampling procedures correct.' The judge, however, said that if he had got the journalists to hold the article, he would have been infringing the freedom of the press. He also made the point that Stephen Davies would later have recourse to libel law.

When I realised that we were being attacked I felt very protective of Biolab, its staff and all the patients who were benefiting from the kind of care that we are able to give. I felt how dare they distort the truth in an attack upon a form of medicine that can be so effective, and which attempts to help patients at the same time as reducing the risk of the patients falling foul of the side effects of potent and potentially toxic pharmaceutical drugs.

The half of the article which did not deal with hair analysis argued against there being any conceivable value in taking vitamins and mineral supplements. There are extensive quotes taken from Professor John Garrow and Isobel Cole-Hamilton, both of whom are old school nutritionists, antagonistic to the use of vitamins and mineral supplements.

Lurking behind this apparently investigative report on hair-mineral analysis is the much more serious covert content of the article, which attempts to expose nutritional medicine as quackery. John Garrow says:

> So far as minerals are concerned, I do not know of any evidence
> that there is any benefit to the population of taking supplements.
> I would be surprised if there were. [6]

The fact that Professor Garrow's research has been funded by Rank
(previously Rank, Hovis McDougall), one of the largest processed food
manufacturers, is not mentioned in the article. Dr Davies, the subject
of the attack and a doctor with twenty years' experience in the
treatment of nutritional deficiencies, is not asked for his opinion. Isobel
Cole-Hamilton, who is not even a doctor, is quoted as saying:

> If people were eating a healthy diet with plenty of fruit,
> vegetables, lean meat, potatoes and bread, particularly whole-
> meal bread, they would be getting all the zinc, iron, vitamins and
> other minerals they need. [7]

The new school of nutritional doctors and practitioners has good
scientifically based arguments with which to counter this statement but
they were not put forward in the article. The article ends with a quote
from the *Drug and Therapeutics Bulletin*:

> Books distributed by health food stores suggest that many people
> lack zinc and that this may explain problems ranging from brittle
> nails, acne, and premenstrual tension to alopecia and impotence.
> These sweeping claims......are unsubstantiated. [8]

Such 'sweeping claims', which are never particularised, could well be
unsubstantiated, as indeed is the pedigree of the *Drug and Therapeutics
Bulletin*. The *Drug and Therapeutics Bulletin* is published by the
Consumers' Association, but was until recently produced and
circulated with help from the Department of Health. It is now
distributed by a private company. Although a reforming 'paper' it is
most definitely steeped in the tradition of pharmaceutical therapy and
is sent to general practitioners giving details of new products. It is
hardly surprising that it takes the side of pharmaceutical companies
and orthodox practitioners on the use of supplements.

The last paragraph of the article really helps us to understand the
underlying view of the article's authors. The anti-vitamin lobby in
America has a tired joke about Americans having the most expensive
urine in the world, because of the vitamins they consume but do not

metabolise. Like all bad jokes about national identity, it can be quickly turned round to reflect on people of other nations. Annabel Ferriman deflects it onto the British.

> Since many of the minerals and vitamins that we consume but cannot use are excreted in our urine, doctors believe that Britain could soon have the most expensive urine in the world. [9]

Someone should have told Annabel Ferriman one of the first principles of economics: that for something to be expensive, it must have an exchange value. Perhaps Annabel Ferriman knew someone in the market for used urine, or had the *Observer* taken it all?

From the point of view of Stephen Davies, a hard working doctor seeing many patients with a variety of illnesses, the article was damaging to his practice because it upset patients and impugned the integrity of the scientists working at Biolab. It also caused Davies himself considerable upset because it questioned his professionalism. No one was to know at the time that the article was only a first shot fired by powerful covert vested interest.

Chapter Thirteen

Patrick Holford:
The Institute for Optimum Nutrition

*I went to one of the major universities to be interviewed for a
Master's Degree in nutrition. I was interviewed by a senior
member of staff, I told him about the work of Dr Carl Pfeiffer
and Dr Linus Pauling. He sat there with his coffee, sugar and
Alka-Seltzer, looked at me and said, 'A load of rubbish, vitamins
can't do any of that.' I asked what they did in the Nutrition
Department and he took me to a room full of big white rats and
told me, 'We feed them until they are obese. I'm trying to develop
a way to make them thin.' I knew then that I couldn't survive
there.* [1]

Patrick Holford makes no excuses for having New Age ideas. The
influence of the East is all around his small south London home. He
has been particularly influenced by the attitudes of Eastern religion to
food and the body. He runs one of the only institutes in the private
sector which give an education and training in nutrition.

> From about the age of 14, I got involved in different
> consciousness-raising groups. At the age of fifteen, my two
> heroes were Jung and Hesse and I read whatever I could. I also
> went to the States and did various courses over there. I finally
> decided to study psychology at York University, which turned
> out to be science-based experimental psychology, psychophar-
> macology and brain biochemistry!

> I was also sponsoring transpersonal consciousness-raising groups
> in York. I had always been a member of the consciousness
> movement, an extremely vocal one. My first book, *The Whole
> Health Manual*, [2] came out in 1981. It talked about the mind,
> body and spirit; it sold 10,000 copies in the first year. I was often
> in the press, and the media. In 1983, it was re-published by

Thorsons. [3]†

As with Stephen Davies, the years between university and his first serious work venture, the Institute for Optimum Nutrition (ION), were years in which Holford began coming to terms with the scientific parameters of his previously mystical philosophy.

In 1983, he helped found the Nutrition Association, and for the first year he was the Chairman, working with Geoffrey Cannon, one of Britain's most respected writers on food. Cannon and Holford didn't, however, see eye to eye. Patrick Holford says now that 'Cannon was convinced that nutritional fine tuning should all be done with food and that supplements were bad news.' In 1984, Holford set up and became the director of ION. Within three years, the organisation was in deep financial trouble and went into liquidation.

Undaunted, he set the organisation up again in 1987. The main focus of ION is now on training practitioners, on two-year courses. It also has a clinic for one-to-one consultation. As well as carrying out research, it holds courses and meetings for the general public. It has been a difficult organisation to run, dependent on a continuous flow of students for its courses. Since 1984, the Institute has had around 80 students go through the process of training.

> ION promotes the concept of optimum nutrition, that is, how to be as healthy as you can through good nutrition. We want to create a shift in the public consciousness away from the idea that as long as you eat a well-balanced diet, you get all the vitamins you need, and towards the idea that optimum nutrition is a dynamic process and many illnesses are the result of faulty nutrition.

* * *

Patrick Holford did not start out wedded to the idea of vitamins and mineral supplements. When at university he realised that nutrition was central to health, he organised a meeting 'Beyond Nutrition', and

† Unless otherwise stated, the quotes in the section from Patrick Holford come from interviews with the author.

invited a representative from a vitamin company.

> I found it quite extraordinary. They said that if you change your diet and take vitamin and mineral supplements, it makes a lot of difference to your health and well-being. I was always willing to test new ideas, so I thought I would give it a try.

> I had appalling acne, I had migraines at least once a month if not every other week, I didn't know it but my energy level was very low. After I changed my nutrition, the effects were astonishing. I lost a stone in weight very rapidly and never put it on again, my energy shot up, my number of hours sleeping went down, my skin cleared up and my headaches went. I was eating no wheat and virtually no meat, lots of fruit and vegetables, mainly raw, and a few vitamins and mineral supplements.

Like many others in the field of nutrition, Holford was influenced by work on nutrition in America. He began to read work on schizophrenia and nutrients. Much of this work with nutritional programmes achieved better results in the treatment of various mental conditions than did drug treatments or psychotherapy.

He read the work of Dr Abram Hoffer [4] and Dr Humphry Osmond,[5] then later came under the influence of Dr Carl Pfeiffer.[6] It was Pfeiffer's work which really impressed him.

> He was involved in studying the effect of chemicals and nutrients on the brain for something like fifty years. By his fifties he was treating mental dysfunction, mainly schizophrenia, with nutrients. He set up a private charity called the Brain Bio Center in the early seventies.

Like many of those whose time has not yet arrived, Patrick Holford has become used to being isolated and marginalised and used to the continual rebuke that he is a crank. Having accepted that the prevalent social view is not his view, he has developed a certain insecurity that can look like diffidence.

> I don't really mind what people think about nutrition or how they live their own lives, but my job, I know, is to make what information I have available to those who wish to listen and to pursue it.

* * *

Despite the fact that, after leaving university, Patrick Holford went to work in America with some of the eminent nutritionists whose work he had read, he still felt the need for a formal education in nutrition. In a world which was utterly in conflict with his ideas, acceptance proved elusive.

His first disappointment was an interview at Queen Elizabeth College, University of London, in 1982. It left him dispirited and pessimistic at his chances of finding a place where he could pursue nutrition without having to accommodate vested interests. In 1985, he began to consider the possibility again, eventually choosing to do an MPhil at Surrey University. It was a decision which he was to regret bitterly.

> In 1985 I made enquiries to do research into the clinical significance of hair mineral analysis. I had become very interested in trace elements such as zinc and manganese. I applied to do this at Surrey University, in the Human Nutrition Department, which comes under the control of the Biochemistry Department.

At the time when Holford applied to do his research, Professor Dickerson held the Chair in Nutrition at Surrey. Holford found him sympathetic and supportive. He was able to work with a company that had an atomic absorption spectrophotometer, a comple expensive piece of equipment which analyses and me   es the mineral content of hair.

Professor Dickerson arranged for Holford to do   external collaborative MPhil. He began work on this in 1985.   problems began when the laboratory he was working with was s ddenly sold and its operations moved to Hull. Soon after that,   financial difficulties set in at ION; he neither had the time nor the equ ..icn. do his research. He took a year off, postponing the research until he was better equipped to do it. At about that time, Professor Dickerson retired and Professor Vincent Marks took over as head of the Biochemistry Department.

Patrick Holford knew of Vincent Marks and his views on nutrition. Derek Bryce-Smith, an expert at that time on lead in petrol, and one of ION's medical and scientific consultants when the Institute was formed, was of Marks' generation and able to tell Holford what interests Marks represented. At the time Marks became head of the Biochemistry Department at Surrey, apart from publicising sugar for the sugar industry [7] he was involved in the development of melatonin, a pharmaceutical solution to jet lag.

> Almost as soon as Marks took over, he wrote me a letter, the long and the short of which was that I had a few weeks to come up with a thesis which included experimental data, following which would be a live examination. I wrote back and told Marks about the difficulties I had had, and that I was thin on experimental data because I had little access to analytical equipment. My protest had little effect. The deadline for the exam was delayed a few weeks but not long. I scrambled to get my thesis together and submit it, knowing that it wasn't in the form that I would have liked it to have been.

Holford's verbal examination, his 'viva', took place before Dr Trevor Delves from Southampton. Delves was a colleague of Marks. Holford found out later that Delves was opposed to alternative health therapies and such things as hair mineral analysis. Delves chose to examine Holford mainly on the principles of atomic physics and the practicalities of the method of analysis, while Holford's work had been almost entirely about the nutritional implications of the results of hair mineral analysis. Holford was failed.

It was a year later when he found out from other people in the Department that Trevor Delves had a history of antagonism to, as Holford puts it, 'the kind of people who have the kind of ideas which I have'.

Soon after this failure, Holford was offered a place in the Chemistry Department, working under Dr Neil Ward, a lecturer who was particularly interested in hair mineral analysis. By 1989 Holford had re-established the Institute for Optimum Nutrition, this time with stronger foundations. He got over his personal difficulties of two years before and put the failure of his MPhil down to experience. He was beginning to enjoy his work again.

Chapter Fourteen

Nutrition for Two:
Belinda Barnes and Foresight

Organisations like Foresight grow like a tree, they don't just start on one day. The learning has been a very gradual progression. [1]

Even many of the most conservative old school nutritionists agree that there are certain categories of people who may need their diet supplemented with vitamins. In the past, one of these categories has been pregnant women. Many doctors and therapists now believe that the health and nutritional status not only of the pregnant woman, but of both prospective parents for some time prior to conception, affect both the chances of conception and the health of any new-born child.

The relatively recent understanding of the various ways in which the actions and nutritional status of the future parents affect the health of a child has led to a growth of practice in the field of pre-conceptual care. Allopathic medicine and orthodox doctors, though they may consider the more obvious agents of pre-conceptual damage, such as smoking and drinking, rarely consider the nutritional status of possible parents.

For those doctors and practitioners who use nutritional status as a guide to health, pre-conceptual care is one of the most important areas of work. Dealing with the health of couples who wish to conceive is dealing with the very foundation of life. If we are what we eat, for a period of nine months at least, so are our children. It is the circumstances of conception and the medical history of the two parents which will to a great extent lay the foundations for the life-long health complexes of the child.

All the nutritional deficiencies and the chemical toxicities which affect the adult have an effect upon foetal development. Cigarette smoking, consumption of alcohol and chemical interventions such as the contraceptive pill have an effect on the nutritional status of the adult and therefore the baby.

Work by Professor Michael Crawford of the Institute of Brain Chemistry and Human Nutrition, in London, has shown that poor nutritional status of the mother can result in low birth weight and small head circumference. Small head circumference can mean also that there are disorders in brain development, ranging from brain damage to poor learning ability. [2] Professor Crawford believes that 'between eight and ten per cent of the population fail to reach their full genetic potential because of poor nutritional status.' [3]

Professor Crawford's last study of 500 babies in Hackney, a low income inner-city area of London, showed that 96% of low birthweight babies (below 5lb 8oz) involved in the study were born to mothers having inferior diets.

Factors which are likely to affect congenital malformations of the foetus are deficiencies of protein, amino acid, essential fatty acid and an inadequate carbohydrate intake. Vitamin deficiencies, especially of B1 and B2, folic acid and vitamin A, can also tend to produce congenital abnormalities, as can mineral deficiencies of, for example, zinc and manganese. [4]

Many orthodox doctors have a one-dimensional view of pre-conceptual nutrition. It has, for example, been common until recently for doctors to automatically prescribe an iron supplement to pregnant women. Research now shows, however, that this supplement is likely to inhibit the absorption of zinc. As British and American women tend to have a poor zinc intake, the prescription of such supplements could be counter-productive.

Because orthodox medical practices are drug-dependent, there are inevitable difficulties in trying to convince orthodox doctors that pre-conceptual care is an important issue. This, however, is the task that Belinda Barnes, the founder of Foresight (The Association for the Promotion of Pre-Conceptual Care) set herself some years ago.

At least now she is able to say that orthodox medical science is catching up with her. She and the doctors who work with Foresight have been giving nutritional advice to pregnant women and providing medical help to couples who have difficulty in conceiving or have frequent miscarriages, for over a decade.

Mrs Barnes is of a long tradition of exceptional and informed British amateurs. She has extended her own education through extensive reading, correspondence and frequent meetings with experts. She has the amateur's determination to prise information from professionals and then put it to use in the public domain. She has no faith in the mystique of professional opinions nor any regard for the hallowed institutions of academia. She believes first and foremost in information for the people.

Like others in the field of pre-conceptual care, Belinda Barnes found herself committed to the subject following her own bad experience with child health and orthodox medicine.

> My first son had coeliac disease. It took a long time to get that diagnosed. We nearly lost him. We had a number of poor interventions in his case and I suppose that it was at that time that I began to query conventional medicine. [5]†

> Then my daughter was born with a tumour on the spinal cord; this partially paralysed her. For a long time I couldn't get any doctor to agree that there was anything wrong with her. It wasn't until she was 19 months that they agreed there was something seriously wrong. This experience again gave me an insight into the limitations of the orthodox medical profession.

> My son had a lot of problems as a consequence of his coeliac disease. I now know that these were deficiency illnesses, he had eczema, bad dyslexia and hyperactivity.

Belinda Barnes learnt serious lessons from the birth of her three children. After her third child started school, she began trying to help others by dispensing the dietary information she had learnt while treating her first son's coeliac disease.

> We lived near one of the Cheshire Homes, we used to go up there and take fruit and things; one day after reading an article by Roger McDougal, the playwright who overcame his own MS, I suggested that I could help them to produce a gluten free diet for the people who had Multiple Sclerosis. There was a lot of opposition and negativity about it.

> We did finally start a gluten free diet and Roger McDougal

---

† All quotes unless otherwise stated come from interviews by the author with Belinda Barnes.

advised vitamin and mineral supplements. After a while we
found a doctor who was willing to prescribe them. We then
began to circulate the diet, firstly to the other Cheshire Homes.
Many of the people who had only MS improved a great deal on
the gluten free diet. This was around 1973.

The need for nutritional advice for coeliac disease was evident, but just
as Dr Jean Monro had found, Belinda Barnes began to suffer the
irrational hostility of some orthodox doctors. Within weeks of
distributing dietary advice on MS, she and her colleagues were
getting 250 letters a week and interest from the local newspapers.
Then a doctor reported them to the General Medical Council because
they had given advice to 'his' patient. Barnes says whimsically: 'I
suppose he considered us quacks.'

By the mid-seventies, Mrs Barnes was getting more deeply involved
in learning about nutrition. She was corresponding with people,
meeting experts privately and at conferences, and she was reading
voraciously. Looking back, she points out that organisations like
Foresight do not just suddenly appear, ready made. They have a long
and rickety gestation, particularly when powerful interests like the
orthodox medical profession resist them.

In 1990, twelve years after starting Foresight, Belinda Barnes wrote
Planning for a healthy baby: essential reading for all future parents, with Suzanne
Gail Bradley. [6] This book managed to do something which the whole
of orthodox medicine had been unable to do, about a subject as simple
and as popular as pregnancy and pre-conceptual care. The book maps
out the steps that possible parents may take prior to conception to
ensure the optimum health of their child.

In the introduction to the book Belinda Barnes explains how a
friendly and inquisitive letter to an American doctor, whose paper she
had read in the *Journal of Orthomolecular Psychiatry*, set her off on the
serious quest for knowledge about nutrition.

> Dr Elizabeth Lodge-Rees flew into Heathrow one memorable
> dawn: 'I've got arms the length of an orang-utan, honey, from
> carting all those darned books in my hand-luggage – I've nearly
> dislocated both shoulders!' The hand-luggage contained educa-
> tion for life! Amongst those 'darned books' were Dr Weston
> Price's epic *Nutrition and Physical Degeneration*, [7] the works of that

brilliant and witty nutritionist Dr Roger Williams, [8] Wilfred
Shute on Vitamin E, [9] Linus Pauling on Vitamin C [10], Carl
Pfeiffer on trace minerals, [11] and Adelle Davis. [12] Despite having
Beth as a house guest, I read until 4.30am that night.

Belinda Barnes' enthusiasm to turn her knowledge into practical help
for people made her many friends and throughout the seventies she
met and read about an increasing number of people who were
beginning to do work on deficiencies and toxicity.

> I met Professor Sir Humphry Osmond's sister Dorothy and then
> got to know him by letter. He was working in the USA with
> vitamins and minerals and the effect which they have on people's
> mental efficiency or difficulty.

> I was in touch with people in America and Canada where
> different people were working on different things, like Oberleas
> and Caldwell on zinc, [13] and David Horrobin, [14] and Lucille
> Hurley. [15]

When Elizabeth Lodge-Rees next came to stay, she and Belinda
Barnes tried to organise meetings with orthodox doctors and hold a
press conference about nutrition. By that time, medical science and its
industrial backers were moving into pharmacology and genetics. They
met only indifference from most of the doctors they contacted.

Mrs Barnes was, however, beginning to meet the people who would
form the supportive structure of Foresight – the doctors and scientific
analysts on whom Foresight would depend to formulate programmes.
She was in touch with the Schizophrenia Association of Great Britain
and on the committee of Sanity, the organisation to which Dr Jean
Monro was a Medical Adviser.

By the late seventies she became convinced that the majority of
early child health problems were the consequence of vitamin and
mineral deficiencies or a high intake of toxic metals and pesticides. She
met Professor Derek Bryce Smith who was working on the damaging
effects of lead in petrol.

As her commitment grew, Mrs Barnes began to notice that certain
areas of her work were, for one reason or another, being suppressed.
She interprets this now as the product of professional jealousy. In
America, Elizabeth Lodge-Rees, who was using hair analysis and
working on vitamin and mineral deficiencies, was also having a hard

time. Belinda Barnes found that so much of the original work in the field of nutrition, like that done by Pfeiffer on zinc, was quickly relegated to a sub-culture of alternative health practice. Barnes saw also that Dr Jean Monro, with whom she was now working, found it very difficult to get her work published in journals. Dr Ellen Grant, who was doing extensive scientific work on the deleterious effects of the birth control pill, [16] was being shunted to the margins of science and medicine.

Nutritional advice for future parents was considered 'cranky' by most doctors. Belinda Barnes, despite being an amateur, has, however, a more rigorous and intellectual attitude than many orthodox professionals.

> The history of nutritional medicine is real history, the history of a real movement which has gained knowledge since the 1930s. It is a scientifically serious movement, one which is documented in scientific and medical research papers. We are not talking about some quack treatment which a few cranks have tried.

* * *

Foresight doctors and advisers now have a continual and growing case-load. Patients are referred from a wide variety of sources, some from midwives and health visitors because they have had miscarriages, while increasingly others come via their general practitioner.

The problems that the pregnant mother and the pre-conceptual parents face in the nineties are perhaps more serious and yet more submerged than those faced in previous decades. Foresight's under-standing of pre-conceptual care has developed in tandem with the most recent threats to babies and mothers; at the same time their views have developed a more public conflict with the chemical and pharmaceutical companies.

> Because of pesticide residues in food, there are now many more allergic conditions amongst children and children are getting them even sooner. The situation is deteriorating all the time. We now know for instance that pesticides reduce the bio-availability of magnesium. The number of children born with complaints like eczema, epilepsy and asthma is increasing all the time,

seemingly in relation to the increased use of chemicals in the environment. Miscarriages, malformations and cot death are also increasing.

In relation to chemical solutions to these problems, there is a kind of circular pattern. A chemical company may make a crop spray which gives people allergic, cold-type symptoms, and the same company will market an over-the-counter remedy for such illness.

In 1986, Foresight published a pocket-sized booklet, [17] 'designed for the handbag'. It listed all chemical food additives and colour coded them, so that they could be easily identified as those which might be dangerous (red), those about which there were conflicting views (orange) and finally those which appeared to have no adverse side effects (green). The gradual development of Foresight into this more combative area of nutritional advice, together with an emphasis on the problems caused to mothers and babies by pesticides, have taken them out of the 'interested amateur' category and thrown them into the thick of the battle with the chemical companies.

Also in 1986, well into its critique of pesticides and chemical additives in food, Foresight produced its own wholefood cookery book [18] and Belinda Barnes wrote *The Hyperactive Child*, [19] a book which has become a classic.

The cynicism of many orthodox doctors and a lack of patient participation made it more or less inevitable that Foresight would be pushed to the margins. However valuable its work, Foresight is part of an underclass of health organisations. Access to media is restricted, and there are few windows in the prevalent medical ideology through which it can voice its opinions. By the early eighties, Foresight and Belinda Barnes had met up with the large number of individuals and organisations that have been forced by the orthodox monopoly to inhabit that same extensive underclass of health theorists and clinicians.

Professor John Dickerson, Professor of Human Nutrition at the University of Surrey and Dr Neil Ward, a leading figure in metal-to-metal interaction in the body, were both advising Foresight about toxic metals and nutrition. Dr Jean Monro was acting as a medical adviser to Foresight, and Belinda Barnes was attending the seminars which Dr Monro regularly organised at the Breakspear Hospital. At one of these seminars she met Professor William Rea.

By 1985, Mrs Barnes and Foresight had placed themselves in the very centre of the growing lobby on nutrition. Foresight had originally sent hair to America for hair mineral analysis, but in 1985 Dr Stephen Davies and Biolab began doing their analysis in London. By this time, thirty or forty nutritional doctors were working with would-be parents on a wide range of problems. Belinda Barnes was still a long way from her ultimate goal of getting pre-conceptual care integrated into the National Health Service, but at least Foresight had a regular following and appeared to have been accepted by many professionals in the field.

Chapter Fifteen

Larkhall:
A Small But Healthy Business

I knew of the reputation of the Quackbusters from friends in the USA who had been harassed by them. I was fearful of their methods and wondered if in the future I would be the subject of an attack. [1]

It was not until the late sixties that a number of large companies began to compete in the vitamin and supplement market. Until this time the development of the health food and natural therapy market from the nineteen thirties can be seen mainly as the growth of a scattered number of small, often family businesses based upon the personal and sometimes idiosyncratic experience of their founders. Whether they manufactured or sold mineral waters, herbal remedies, health foods or chemical tablets, these businesses were inevitably small because their customers were on the philosophical and cultural margins.

The advent of a youth movement in the late sixties which grew out of a generation not pressed by economic necessity directly from school to factory, radically changed views about personal health and well-being. Many of those who participated in this emancipation found themselves collectively part of what came to be called the Age of Aquarius, a New Age of consciousness, an apparently softer age which eschewed war, authoritarianism and forced industrial work, replacing them with communal living, the deification of nature and the exploration of an inner spiritual life.

It was on this tide of the New Age, as it broke into the seventies, that ideas about health foods, organic farming and vitamins became meaningful for a large number of people for the first time since the nineteen thirties. During this period, many of the idiosyncratic small family businesses began to experience a renaissance along with a burgeoning number of health food shops and therapists.

The small firms who continued to manufacture vitamins and supplements often also provided advice about health. Moving over these small producers like a dark cloud was a new highly capitalised pharmaceutical industry which had utilised the findings of life sciences research. The firms which made up this industry were large and often multi-national. Their interests lay in developing new chemical substances which were active against specific disease states and symptoms. Such substances had to be patent protected, monopoly exploited and sold to the rich socialised health services which had developed in most western countries. Companies advocating self-help, health through diet, vitamin and mineral supplements and natural therapies were from the beginning treated as enemies by the pharmaceutical companies and their medical handmaidens. This gathering conflict had little to do with science and a great deal to do with profit.

* * *

Larkhall Natural Health Ltd. has its roots in a health care company set up in 1894. In 1957 it was taken over by the ten year old tablet making company of G. O. Woodward. It operated originally from Larkhall Lane in Clapham, London. Its main factory is now near Putney Bridge. Larkhall is run by Robert Woodward PhD, a pharmacist and the son of the founder.

Larkhall produces the majority of its vitamins and supplements under the brand name of Cantassium, which came into being in the twenties. In the seventies, Cantassium began working on special diet products and called on Rita Greer, a nutritionist and popular writer on food and health, to assist with the development of these products.

Before she began writing on nutrition and cookery, Rita Greer had been a well-established jeweller and silversmith and then a successful painter. When she began working on nutrition with Dr Robert Woodward in the late seventies, it was particularly as a consequence of her personal experience. Rita Greer's husband, a jazz musician, had been diagnosed as suffering from multiple sclerosis. To manage his illness and care for him, she researched nutrition, concentrating especially on multiple exclusion diets and gluten-free foods.

Throughout the nineteen seventies and eighties, Rita Greer

published sixteen books, containing popular dietary advice for a variety of illnesses affected by foods. The emphasis in these books [2] is on helping people who have to manage their own illness or care for others. The books are based upon Greer's personal experience and research carried out at Larkhall. However, the focus is always on the reality of the condition suffered by both the carer and the patient. Her books deal with many nutritional issues which the National Health Service has generally chosen to avoid.

As well as writing, Rita Greer co-operated with Robert Woodward and his business in producing a range of products which could be depended upon to be free of certain substances. Between them, they developed a system of labelling which gives easily accessible information about foods and supplements which are free of fourteen different substances. With the labelling symbols designed by Greer, it can be seen at a glance whether foods or supplements have, amongst other things, a low sodium level, are cholesterol free, egg free, or free from artificial additives. Woodward and Greer began this product labelling in the late seventies; fifteen years later none of the major food companies seem inclined to take it up.

Rita Greer's seven gluten/wheat free products for coeliacs, TRUFREE, have been available on prescription from the National Health Service since the early eighties. Rita Greer even managed to produce grain free flours which are available for allergy sufferers.

The production of good, highly nutritious, genuine special foods for coeliacs did not make Woodward and Greer popular with the official organisations set up to help coeliacs.

> We discovered in the course of making up our special foods that the bulk of gluten free foods made for coeliacs at that time were in fact made from wheat starch, which contains a small amount of gluten; this fact was kept from patients and G.Ps. The production of our gluten free foods came in for a lot of criticism, mainly from the vested interests which then produced 'gluten free' food, that wasn't really gluten free at all, merely labelled as such.

> The Coeliac Trust – as separate from the Society which has patient meetings – gets its money from the 'white diet', semi-pharmaceutical interests. They pay for a lot of research and thereby keep out a lot of competition. We were never allowed

into meetings or conferences and if we were invited by mistake the people who had invited us were reprimanded. TRUFREE was never allowed advertising space in Coeliac Society literature and Rita Greer's books written especially for coeliacs were never reviewed. It was the bakery interests which were behind the other brands of gluten free products. They felt that it was important to preserve their image as producer of something which was always healthy – bread. It was not acceptable to make it public that wheat products could be deadly for some people. [3]

The food producers expect consumers to take it for granted that their products can do nothing but good for those who consume them. Just like the drug companies, they work hard to minimise the information on illnesses caused by particular products. The sugar industry argues that sugar, even in large amounts, has few if any deleterious effects, [4] while the dairy industry minimises the number of people affected by allergy to milk and its by-products.

By the end of the seventies, Woodward and Greer had placed themselves firmly on the 'other side' from one of the world's biggest processed food groups, the producers of food containing wheat and grain. By the beginning of the eighties, the non-allergenic and gluten/wheat free nature of Cantassium products had become their most important asset, a production principle that other firms found difficult to develop.

> Our approach throughout the eighties was, I think, different from many other vitamin and mineral producers, because we placed the emphasis on the idea of a non-allergic, gluten/wheat free and artificial additive-free product. [5]

Woodward and Greer had a serious commitment to health and they were continuously developing ideas in this area. Larkhall began advertising a professional testing service for people who were allergic to foods. These tests, which include hair mineral analysis and allergy testing, gave people an idea about which foods might be adversely affecting them and which minerals and food supplements might be used if those foods were cut out.

One way and another, throughout the eighties, Woodward and Greer were in co-operation with many of the other people working in the field of dietary approaches to disease management. Their philosophy, like that of Patrick Holford, Jean Monro, Stephen Davies and Belinda Barnes, was scientific.

> Our consistent approach has always been that a good diet and
> vitamins are major contributors to good health, and we have
> been outspoken about this. The food industry does not do a very
> good job, even with the adding of vitamins to food products like
> cornflakes. With artificial vitamins, you may need something in
> the region of five or six times the RDA [Recommended Daily
> Allowance] to ensure that the right amount gets through to the
> body at all. The problem of nutrient malabsorption is generally
> ignored. [6]

The feuds which began over the development and sale of gluten-free
foods by Cantassium simmered throughout the eighties, with the food
industry and its representatives taking every opportunity to criticise
both Woodward and Greer. The Coeliac Society was in the forefront
of these criticisms, and alongside them, the British Nutrition
Foundation (BNF). Robert Woodward came into conflict with
Professor Arnold Bender, an academic and old school nutritionist,
on more than one occasion in the mid-eighties when Bender was
representing the BNF.

In 1985, Cantassium participated in a trial of vitamin supplements which set out to test whether or not they could raise IQ levels.
The research was started by Gwilym Roberts, a science master at
Darland High School in Wales. This first trial managed to raise IQ
levels in some pupils by up to six points. The results were virtually
ignored. [7]

Following those first trials, Larkhall worked on a bigger study
lasting nine months, with Dr David Benton, a psychologist at
Swansea University who, prior to his involvement in the second
Darland trial, was sceptical about any link between vitamins and IQ.
The results of the Benton study, which took place at the same school,
showed that amongst those who took the vitamin and mineral
mixture, the IQs of some children went up by up to nine points
compared with no rise at all amongst those who were taking a
placebo. [8] IQ was measured on a standard non-verbal intelligence
test. This trial attracted a great deal of attention when the BBC
programme 'QED' reported its results, together with the results of
similar work carried out in America.

Rita Greer and Robert Woodward were both pleased with the

project, its scientific conduct and the implications for education, nutrition and intelligence. Neither of them could have foreseen that within a short time, the results of this work would lead to them being harassed, threatened, charged with criminal offences and brought to court.

Chapter Sixteen

AIDS:
The Plague That Made Millions

When a woman was lying in a corner of her hut with a very high temperature, she was described to me as being dead which no doubt meant that they had given her up for lost. [1]

Like AIDS itself, our understanding of it has grown with incredible slowness, nudging itself into our consciousness like a half-remembered nightmare. At first, society was a publicly unwilling host, almost refusing to believe the disease or its prognosis. It was, though, the perfect illness for the years of Thatcher and Reagan; it built upon our separation from each other, bolstering their ideology of individualism, pushing us back into the confinement of controllable private space. Not since the lawless and plague-ridden years of the seventeenth and eighteenth centuries have people been so untrusting of the everyday intercourse of human relationships.

Whether or not AIDS was the product of some vast existential conspiracy, no one could have designed a better antidote to the frenetic coming together, communality and intimate sharing which had been the hallmark of the post-sixties period. It was an antidote of staggering efficiency.

As with the history of all classic plagues, there were warnings of sorts, omens which we failed to understand. Throughout the seventies, gay men were paying a high price for their liberation. Their freedom brought them medical and social chaos, drug taking and an ultimately restrictive promiscuity. In the late seventies and early eighties in New York and San Francisco, gay men were turning to their doctors in larger numbers with hepatitis B, syphilis and gonorrhoea. Many of them used incessant courses of antibiotics in attempts to rid themselves of such infections.

Though then unnamed, AIDS became a definable syndrome in America in 1980. In that year a small number of physicians, especially those who had worked in the heartland of the gay community, realised that the men who came to them with a variety of conditions, often involving the herpes virus, cytomegalovirus, swollen lymph nodes, fevers and anaemia, were suffering from a new mix of illnesses. The first patients presented with a range of infections, most particularly a rare pneumonia, *Pneumocystis carinii* pneumonia (PCP), which had previously been found in children with leukaemia after chemotherapy had suppressed their immune system.

Also present in a number of early patients was Kaposi's sarcoma, a cancer which was even rarer than PCP; it often developed on the foot or lower leg, spreading in purple blots covered with lesions. It was a cancer previously only seen in older men, particularly of Italian or Jewish descent. In America before AIDS, no one died from Kaposi's sarcoma, but now in these early patients, the course and intensity of the disease seemed to be speeded up.

In July 1982, AIDS (Acquired Immune Deficiency Syndrome) received its name and the AIDS epidemic officially began. From the beginning, there were diverse views about its origins and cause. Such theories divided naturally into two major categories. The virus which caused AIDS was a wholly new virus or one which had been around for many years and recently developed a virulent strain amongst a vulnerable population. Amongst those who suggested that AIDS was a new virus, there was speculation as to where it had come from, many plumped for the idea that it was the product of either biological warfare experimentation or a rogue vaccine. Amongst those who thought that AIDS was caused by an old virus, some took the side of clinical ecology, declaring that as well as a primary virus, co-factors such as chemical toxins were weakening the immune system and preparing the terrain for the virus to inhabit.

In a complex twentieth century society there are many different stages between the recognition of an illness and its treatment. What begins as a subjective experience for the patient is seized upon by doctors and scientists and used as a vehicle for the pursuit of glittering prizes and corporate profits.

The responsibility for investigating and treating AIDS was quickly taken out of the hands of doctors and activists committed to the gay community and turned over to governments and a high-tech, pharmaceutically-orientated 'health industry'. In America, this meant the intervention of the National Institutes of Health (NIH) and the cancer research agencies, massive Federal organisations which worked hand in glove with industry.

To disempower the community, to alienate it from its own discourse about a devastating illness was to do exactly what AIDS did to the body's immune system. The gay community was left defenceless and weakened by its inability to work for itself. AIDS was hijacked and appropriated by government, scientists and big business, [2]† and from that point, those who suffered AIDS became simply pawns in a much larger industrial and political game plan.

* * *

The progress of Acquired Immune Deficiency Syndrome is not regular or uniform in every case. What is the same in every case is that the sufferer's immune system has become damaged, or, in the language which has grown up in the wake of AIDS, 'compromised'. The immune system is a complex mechanism, which firstly seeks out alien substances entering the body, analyses them and then with miraculous precision creates an antibody which neutralises them before finally discharging the debris.

In those who develop AIDS, the immune process has been so impaired that the body is left vulnerable to any marauding alien germ or virus. Many scientists claim this is because the HIV virus chooses particularly to infiltrate immune system cells. Others, who argue for a co-factorial cause of immune system depletion, or do not agree with

---

† What happened to the work of Dr Joseph Sonnabend is a good example of the appropriation by the 'AIDS Establishment' of work done in the community. Sonnabend is a doctor and research scientist, one of the men who discovered interferon, who has worked unceasingly with AIDS patients at community level. His research has been responsible for a number of breakthroughs, especially in relation to opportunist infections. In 1983, Sonnabend began a journal, *AIDS Research*, which was open to a wide range of views about the origins of AIDS and its treatment. In 1986, after ten issues, the publisher was persuaded to fire Sonnabend and nearly all the editorial board. The journal's name was changed to *AIDS Research and Human Retroviruses* and the new editorial board which included Dr Robert Gallo was dominated by government, military and corporate scientists. [3]

the HIV virus theory, point to many of the other immuno-compromising agents, such as drugs and chemicals† which may so damage the immune system that the door is left open for a virus, or other compromising agents. Those who put forward the proposition of co-factors argue that it is the terrain – that is to say the environment of the body – which could be as important as a virus.

The similarity between cases of extreme chemical sensitivity, ME and a number of debilitating post-viral syndromes, is an increasingly important aspect of the argument for those who believe in co-factors.

Despite the divergence of opinion, between the HIV virus and not the virus‡ and the virus alone and virus plus co-factors schools, it is clear that as AIDS occurs when the immune system is depleted, its treatment and its containment also have to do with the treatment of the immune system.

With AIDS, the immunologist came of age. Prior to AIDS, the work of the immunologist was conservative work under control. It was always work on the futuristic boundary of medicine but before AIDS the immune system appeared to be understood. The immunologist looked at the way in which the body defended itself. It had been established for many years that when the body was run down, either physically tired or emotionally drained, then the immune system was affected. If the body and the mind were healthy and energised, then so was the immune system. In fact, less mechanistically than this, it was possible to say that the mind, the body and the immune system were clearly interrelated.

From the beginning of AIDS, orthodox medical observers have held that the level of T lymphocyte helper cells is a measure of the progress of HIV and AIDS. They have adopted the following rule of thumb: when the level of these cells begins to slip below a count of 400, the immune system could be in a depleted state, below 200 the

---

† Chemicals which deplete the immune system and which have been mentioned in relation to AIDS as co-factorial elements are: Dioxin, various pesticides and Poppers (a recreational drug used by gay men) as well as prescribed drugs like antibiotics and illegal leisure drugs like cocaine and heroin.

‡ There are those strongly of the opinion that as the HIV virus remains inactive for long periods, the only sign of its passing being the HIV antibody, it cannot be unequivocally stated that it is an HIV virus which causes AIDS. [4]

body's resistance is likely to give way to opportunist infections; at a count in single figures, the person is in danger of dying.†

* * *

The gay community affected by AIDS did everything it could to confound the divisions and isolation engendered by the illness. As well as driving many people apart it brought some together, with a new focus. If gay men were isolated and circumscribed before AIDS, the onset of the illness forced a fierce sense of enquiry and care upon some parts of the community. In America, the AIDS world divided into first and third, not that there could be any difference in the specificity of death, but there was the greatest gulf between those who, on contracting the disease, lived it out according to the 'official' game plan, and those who bravely stuck to the *ad hoc* rules developing in a new community.

Such a new community was not willing to simply lie down and die on the instructions of a paternalistic medical establishment who pushed pills and other panaceas on a wing and a prayer. Just as the women's movement had done for women ten years previously, and as some cancer patients had always done, some gay men developed a spirit of enquiry about their own bodies and their own health. Some within the gay community crawled from beneath the heavy oppression of conventional medical wisdom and began to explore age-old propositions of healing.

* * *

Cass Mann: Lights on the Road

> People have to wake up to the fact that everything is political,
> and that our lives and our consciousness are controlled by a
> handful of people. [5]

In the early days of Cass Mann's conversion to medical politics, it

---

† These figures are per cubic millimetre of blood, they are expressed in scientific papers as 400 mm^3. For easy understanding they are represented here, and in other parts of the book as a single barometer figure.

would not have occurred to him that he was a heretic. In those days, his ideas appeared to be in tune with the times. Four years later, it is easy to see how his unorthodox intellectual independence and determination to pursue the truth have pushed him to the side-lines and marginalised him. Cass Mann is something of a showman and, regardless of his increasingly principled stand, he still clings to the accoutrements of a performing gay life-style.

Born in India, of an Indian father and a British-Tibetan mother, Mann came to England in 1964 with thoughts of becoming a doctor. His hopes faded however when he was faced with the intransigent attitudes of the English medical establishment.

> At one interview I was told that if I wanted to be a doctor, I would have to drop 'all the crazy ideas that people in the East have about such things as acupuncture, homoeopathy, and herbalism'. My family had always treated themselves homoeopathically. [5]

His first serious work was a long way from medicine, in the gay clubs of London's West End. He began working at the Embassy Club in 1979, and continued until it closed in 1984. The Embassy Club was not entirely for gay men; it was a West End night club where people could dance, talk or eat. Unlike the Embassy, Heaven, the next club that Mann worked in, was only for gay men. He was employed as Promotions Manager and PA to the General Manager and on some evenings he acted as a DJ. He enjoyed working in the clubs but now thinks of the period as a fallow one.

When he worked in the clubs Mann was not at all political. Political issues, he says, weren't drawn to his attention. From the time he woke to the time that he went to sleep, he lived club life: a life on a different plane from the everyday world of minor and major political decisions, like an actor who only glimpsed the real life audience in a shadowy and separate form across the footlights.

Now, some years later, one of Mann's most vehement criticisms of the gay world is that even in these days of politicised sexuality, gay culture is based more on entertainment than politics. He laughs at the way in which, despite casting his vote when necessary for Labour, he used to distance himself from politics.

> We had the launch of the SDP at the Embassy Club. I thought
> that was as political as I was going to get. After that, I thought,
> 'that's my politics for the year.'[6]†

After Heaven, again at a loose end, Mann became Marketing
Manager for New World Cassettes, a company which marketed
relaxation and meditation tapes. He had been interested in New Age
ideas for some time, had practised meditation and had always been
cynical about western medicine and science. Everything went well
with New World until Cass got involved on the side of the artists,
against the management, in a dispute over their contracts and royalty
payments.

   This intervention led to Cass being asked to resign. He took a form
of retributory direct action against the Company, which, though it
seemed justified at the time, he has since bitterly regretted. He
describes what he did as 'one of the dumbest things I have ever done'.

> I had a stock of cassettes which I took round with me to different
> shops. Like a jerk, I didn't return my stock to the Company. I
> was in a fury at the time because they owed me money and I
> didn't like being asked to leave. I sold the stock to one of their
> competitors; the day came when the competitors were at a music
> fair with a stall next to New World, selling their cassettes at half
> price. I was arrested and charged with theft. I pleaded guilty in
> the Magistrate's Court. During a five-minute hearing, the court
> said that whether or not I had a right to keep the cassettes I did
> not have the right to sell them on to another firm. I was fined
> £200, plus £25 costs, and had to reimburse New World
> Cassettes for £1,811.25 worth of tapes.

Although this incident would come back to haunt Mann, he now
looks back on it as being seminal in his political development. Being
arrested in an early morning raid on his flat by three detectives was a
moment of enlightenment which led him to ask himself where his life
was going.

   His arrest was the first and smallest part of a change in
consciousness through which Mann was to travel over the coming

---

† Unless otherwise stated all quotes from Cass Mann come from interviews with the
author.

years. A more controlled sign of changing times and consciousness was reflected in his attitude to his sexuality. It was in the London of 1984 and 1985 that fear of AIDS came to be a prominent motif in the lives of gay men. Between 1984 and 1987, three people with whom Mann had worked in the clubs, each of them with a history of heavy drug use, died of AIDS.

Cass Mann's personal response to AIDS was very different from that of his gay friends. In 1979, he had made a mysterious resolution.

> Sometimes you go through a day and suddenly you remember a dream you had, you have forgotten it because you didn't wake up remembering it. Something happened to me very early on, in 1979, that I didn't remember until many years later. An idea began to grow in my mind, which was not entirely clear, but was about the fact that everything in relation to health and disease was going to change, and AIDS was going to be the focus of this change. In 1979, for absolutely no reason at all, I stopped having sex. From a situation where I was fucking with say 300 men a year, I stopped completely, it absolutely ended, with no desire on my part to end it, and I have not had sex since. I did not do it because I believed in celibacy, I feel strongly that celibacy as a consequence of repression is ugly and against life. If there was a rational reason for this negation, it wasn't obvious and must have taken place at a very deep level of my subconscious. From the time that I stopped sex, I began to develop other aspects of my creativity.

Cass Mann says now, perhaps with the aid of hindsight, that the way in which gay men were having sex had to change: 'I felt that I had a message to give to other gay men, principally that the ways we were having sex were not nurturing us, they were actually going to kill us.'

If this appears to suggest that Cass Mann was a kind of visionary, this is not the impression he gives in conversation. In his more recently politicised frame of mind, a change in response to the way gay men were having sex was a matter of common sense. In the previous paradigm of gay sexual relationships, he saw all the old exploitative and power-based attitudes.

> The ways that we were having sex would have killed us anyway. We were having sex within a paradigm which suggested that to be old or ugly meant you had to commit suicide, if not physically

> then certainly emotionally. People were having sex with ten or
> twenty people a month, they didn't even want to know their
> names, they didn't care about them. We were consuming
> ridiculous amounts of drugs. All of this was working against any
> kind of consciousness.

Mann's time of change was to end with him immersed in the politics of
AIDS. With celibacy came a new definition of his sexual identity. No
longer simply a gay man, he was able to explore and utilise both the
masculine and feminine aspects of his nature. He began to recognise
that the idea of an androgynous identity is one which harks back to
ancient healers and forms of healing.

It is one thing to embark upon a new internal life and quite another
to get others to go through the same change. Most of the people to
whom he spoke about his changing consciousness knew and
understood what he was saying but found it impossible to follow.
He learned one of the first lessons of politics very quickly: 'I could
strike a match for them but I couldn't keep it alight.'

* * *

By 1987, Cass Mann had begun working with AIDS patients and
people diagnosed HIV antibody positive. Alpha Healers, a healing
group he set up, practised a range of therapies with hospitalised AIDS
patients, using hands-on healing, meditation, visualisation and
imagery.

In February 1987, Mann met David Reichenberg, a baroque oboe
soloist who had been principal oboist for the English Concert.
Reichenberg was also a man with AIDS who had advanced Kaposi's
sarcoma. They met by chance at a meeting and from that day
developed a very special relationship. They worked together daily for
at least three hours, until Reichenberg's death in June 1987.

It took a peculiar transforming incident to push Cass Mann over
the edge from personal care into political action. Shortly after David
Reichenberg's death, Mann got on a bus near Euston Station and sat
at the back on the lower deck. A young man got on; his appearance
was that of some contemporary gay men – checked shirt, jeans and a
moustache. He sat next to Mann, and then turned to him offering him
a leaflet: 'It's very important you read this. It will transform your life.'

Mann did not take him seriously; he nodded and smiled 'Oh, yes, fine'.

Later that night in David's flat, he read the A3 poster-like sheet and found it earth-shattering. In a series of referenced and erudite articles, the broadsheet discussed a number of ideas: that HIV might not be the cause of AIDS; that HIV could be a bio-engineered illness. There was also information in the document about the medical cartel which had for years blocked alternative treatments for cancer and was now gearing up to profit from AIDS. It talked about experiments on laboratory animals. It even discussed the fact that lots of gay men took recreational immunosuppressing drugs which orthodox practitioners did not discourage, even after patients had been diagnosed HIV antibody positive.

Reading the document laid the foundation for the thinking and the reading which Mann was to do over the coming years. He next read *AIDS and Syphilis: the Hidden Link* [7] and, from that time, began to change his working practice. He turned the work of the healing group upside down, using the group as a forum to discuss issues from the leaflet and the book and generate new ideas about self-empowerment. Gradually Cass Mann became deeply immersed in reading, researching and discussing the scientific research available on AIDS.

* * *

As AIDS began to take its toll, a group of gay men including Mann, Stuart Marshall,† and Duncan Campbell decided that they would organise a street-based research and information group similar to those set up in America. In 1988 they were involved in setting up the Community Research Organisation (CRO) which discussed both orthodox and alternative AIDS treatments.

After just four meetings the CRO collapsed. At that time neither Cass Mann nor Stuart Marshall realised that they had stepped onto a minefield. From the first meeting, the organisation was infiltrated by people loyal to the pharmaceutical companies. At one meeting, apparently acting on behalf of a drug company, a doctor announced

† Stuart Marshall was, until his death in May 1993, Britain's longest surviving HIV antibody positive person. He had survived with HIV antibodies for thirteen years.

that he could offer the organisation £25,000, to fund an administrator. There would, he said, be 'no strings attached'. Mann was amazed that a National Health doctor, who was meant to be independent of the drugs companies, could offer a small voluntary sector organisation £25,000 on behalf of a pharmaceutical company. The grant was declined.

Following the collapse of Community Research, both Cass Mann and Stuart Marshall determined to set up another grass roots organisation which could make contact with people who were HIV positive or had AIDS and give them a message of hope. Since Stuart Marshall had found that he was HIV antibody positive, he had steered himself away from pharmaceuticals and the burgeoning AIDS industry. In 1987, Mann and Marshall together with Dietmar Bollet and Simon Martin set up Positively Healthy. Martin had an enviable reputation in alternative health, being at the time Editor of *Here's Health* magazine, one of the founders of the *Journal of Alternative and Complementary Medicine* and co-author of the best selling book on the holistic approach to AIDS, *A World Without AIDS.* [8]

Both Stuart Marshall and Cass Mann had a fiery determination which, as time went on, they were going to need. They both felt angry about the logjam in information and research on AIDS treatment. It was their contention that in the early days 'more people were dying of misinformation than were dying of AIDS.' What made them most angry was the fact that gay men had stood by and watched the orthodox medical establishment walk into their community and colonise both the sufferers and the illness. Both men saw a real need for a cultural and political organisation which would not only treat and advise people with AIDS, but work with them and their friends discussing the difference between orthodox medicine and the alternatives. There was also a real need for a positive self-empowering philosophy which took people away from the focus of chemical therapies – the inevitability of death after being diagnosed HIV antibody positive – and placed them within supportive caring and life enhancing groups.

Mann says now that his work with Positively Healthy is not about

† Dietmar Bolle died in 1992.

AIDS but about self-empowerment.

> My work is about how to stay alive if your life isn't working. I am
> trying to get people to wake up and in that process of waking up,
> AIDS gets handled. AIDS is not the basis of my work, if AIDS
> wasn't around, there would still be cancer.

Like the many doctors and therapists who have fallen out with the
drug-dependent medical establishment in the past, Cass Mann places
a great emphasis on the individual's own will to survive.

> All the people I have worked with who have died of AIDS have
> died because their reasons for being alive were not strong
> enough. It's got nothing to do with the medicines you take, or
> the holistic remedies. My work is getting people to celebrate: to
> stop them from being attendants at their own funeral.

People were dying of loneliness and fear, as much as they were dying
of opportunist infections, Mann maintains. He saw that amongst many
gay men there was a great deal of Judeo-Christian guilt, which made
some AIDS sufferers relieved that the tortuous decisions of life were
being taken from them. Mann equates the condition of gay men who
test HIV antibody positive to the condition of those women who have
cancer for the first time. Those who have bought the story that cancer
inevitably kills often cannot see beyond that, or break away from the
damaging aspects of a self-destructive life-style. 'To break away',
Mann says, 'takes enormous strength.'

Cass Mann was, and still is, angry at the gay community itself. It is,
he says, a community based upon weaknesses rather than strengths.
He sees a community which has modelled itself upon 'glamorous
victims', those whose destiny it is to suffer and be persecuted both by
themselves and others because of their difference and vulnerability,
figures like Marilyn Monroe, James Dean and Judy Garland. So many
gay men are in Mann's opinion trapped in 'victim consciousness'.

> When a culture discloses its totems, it reveals its agenda. Gay
> men have become frivolous entertainment queens, self-parody-
> ing creatures of the night, which is not what we should be. Gay
> men have no culture within which to locate themselves. It's our
> consciousness which is going to kill us, not AIDS.

With the continuation of the AIDS holocaust, Cass Mann's fury at the

AIDS industry and the medical establishment mounted. He became convinced that the only way to survive AIDS was to live a life apart from the AIDS organisations. These organisations and the whole superstructure which has grown around them, he saw as genocidal, 'working to shove people through the crematorium'. The practice of allopathic medicine in the institutions of our major cities, he maintains, is programming people to die. Those who are vulnerable to AIDS, or for that matter cancer, must, he thinks, question the whole paradigm.

> The only ones who stand any chance of surviving are those who take part in the new paradigm. It's just like cancer, no one speaks about the cases that have survived by working beyond the present medical paradigm. Everyone knows that cancer can be treated by numerous different kinds of alternative treatments, but within the present medical treatment paradigm, they are killing people.

The Practice of Positively Healthy

> People ought to have the information which makes them doubt. But many people just turn off rather than consider this information. People are so frightened, so sick, they have been through so much loss, that they can't cope with the uncertainty that unconventional ideas generate. Psychologically I can understand this but in the long term politically, it's very dangerous. [9]

Positively Healthy began by holding monthly workshops, to which guest speakers were invited. As much information about HIV and AIDS as could be researched from different sources was presented. The meetings, discussions and guest speakers were combative and challenging. Positively Healthy disputed that everyone who was HIV antibody positive inevitably got AIDS and that such people inevitably died. They were proud of the fact that they worked only with statistics and verifiable information taken from the best scientific sources.

Positively Healthy was from the start a political organisation; its weekend workshops produced politicised discourses. They put people in touch with each other and they gave shape to a body of resistance against the medical establishment's singular belief in a specific pharmaceutical remedy. The workshops also taught simple health-enhancing techniques, like meditation, and generated information about diet and vitamins. The health ideas which the groups generated were eclectic.

As well as the workshops, Positively Healthy organised public meetings and day-long seminars. At these a homoeopath or a nutritionist might speak. By the beginning of 1989, they had started a bullish magazine, also called *Positively Healthy,* which was very much in the tradition of the early American AIDS activists.

Positively Healthy was a resistance organisation; with strength and considerable courage, it pitted itself against the growing tidal wave of money, propaganda and marketing which was beginning to sweep down on the gay community and its AIDS organisations.

It wasn't long before it became evident that Positively Healthy would simply not be allowed to exist. There was to be no freedom of choice in health care for those who were HIV antibody positive or had AIDS. Gay people who got involved in supporting and defending their own communities by helping people with AIDS walked straight into a 'fire-field'; neither their sincerity nor their kindness was any defence.

> Dietary advice, our advocacy of vitamins and supplements, and our position on AZT, these issues have been the problems throughout. The AIDS establishment is totally permeated with pharmaceutical money. [10]

Within no time, Positively Healthy was assailed by difficulties which undermined its very existence. In April 1988, the organisation was told that its adverts and articles were not wanted in the *Pink Paper,* the only national paper for gay people. Slowly it began to dawn on Cass Mann and Stuart Marshall that behind the scenes a few individuals were waging a campaign against them.

One of the prominent behind-the-scenes critics of Positively Healthy was Duncan Campbell. Although Cass Mann had heard that it was Campbell who had persuaded the editors and owners of the *Pink Paper* against Positively Healthy adverts, neither he nor Stuart Marshall knew him.

In June 1988, Duncan Campbell moved into public view. Cass Mann remembers vividly the occasion when he first came face to face with Campbell and saw the personal nature of Campbell's antagonism to him and Positively Healthy.

Evan Jones was a gay man who had been involved in Positively Healthy from its inception. Positively Healthy created a travelling photographic exhibition, entitled 'Victim to Victor', around the last year of his life. When Jones died of AIDS, a wake was held in his house and the photographic exhibition arranged around the walls of one room.

At the wake, Cass Mann was told that Campbell was making disparaging remarks about the photographs. One of them showed Jones reading pieces from the *New York Native*† about AZT. The photograph was titled: 'Evan chose not to take AZT because of its unacceptable toxicity.'

> I was walking round and looking at the photographs and I noticed this person commenting about some of them. I wondered what he was doing. As I wandered up to hear what he was saying, he turned to me and said, 'Who is this Guru, this charismatic Guru character that Evan was so dedicated to?' meaning me. 'I can't imagine', I said ironically, 'he must be a right rip-off merchant, you know what these Gurus are like.'

Looking back on that moment of meeting Campbell, Mann thinks that Campbell must have kept an agenda from that time: Positively Healthy plus charismatic guru, alternative medicine and dietary advice equals anti-rational orthodox treatment. In June 1988, the problems were only just beginning.

The Pink Paper and Alan Beck

> Of all the people who have had HIV and gone on to develop AIDS, one of those whom I was closest to was my friend who lived here in this house. I was cleaning up the mess, the vomit and talking him out of suicide all the time. He had been put on full-strength AZT. I was both dealing with the politics of all this

† The *New York Native* is a New York gay paper, which through its columns by John Lauritsen has carried out a ceaseless criticism of the FDA, Burroughs Wellcome and AZT.

and living it day by day. Mainly I was trying to persuade him into alternative therapies which he always refused. [11]

The *Pink Paper* is Britain's major national gay newspaper. It has an odd history. In the summer of 1987, a couple of months after Wellcome had been given a licence to market AZT in Britain, two doctors, one of whom worked for Ciba Geigy, the other his partner, floated the idea of a gay newspaper. The people who took part in the initial meetings which formulated its policy were members of the gay and lesbian left. They included Duncan Campbell who had not yet 'come out' as gay.

The first issue of the *Pink Paper* came out in November 1987. It was a relatively dull affair which managed to steer well clear of the most important debate concerning gay men at that time: AIDS and its treatment. By the end of 1988, the paper was running into financial difficulties and against the wishes of both founders it was bought out by Kelvin Sollis, a north London gay businessman. The response of the old guard to the buy-out was emotional and destructive. All the papers, files and correspondence in the *Pink Paper* offices were destroyed. No information about its early financing or its relationship with commercial concerns survived.

Alan Beck, a drama lecturer at the University of Kent, joined the new *Pink Paper* in February 1988, becoming its senior writer responsible for the weekly editorial. In contrast to Cass Mann, Alan Beck had for a long time been steeped in the politics of the gay movement. He was a die-hard political campaigner for the rights of gay men, an organiser and an activist.

When Alan Beck talks about the gay community, he speaks with a voice from the street. He is also light years away from the ideas and activities of the high profile media-friendly respectable gays whom he sees as inhabiting a rarified and still quiescent area of gay life, a world which often protects the anonymity of its members. Beck would organise and agitate for gay rights at work or in housing in much the same way as other grass-roots political organisers have fought for other civil rights. He respects socialist activists and campaigners like Peter Tatchell, rather than members of the essentially liberal gay intelligentsia like Duncan Campbell.

Like others of his generation, Alan Beck was radically affected by the sixties. From that time, he can count three decades of struggle, and discuss milestones, victories and set-backs. His view of the late sixties and early seventies is still optimistic and he chooses to highlight the good things which grew out of that period. Like the film maker Derek Jarman, [12] Beck emphasises the communality of the period and the social ideas it generated. Rather than stress the finally destructive promiscuity, he points to the organising, the networking, the spread of gay rights groups and the development of a politically conscious gay movement, which is no longer London centred.

> The Lesbian and Gay movement has been much more located in the community and through different classes, than, say, the urban bourgeois-dominated women's movement. The seventies wasn't solely a time of promiscuity, it was a time of growing political sophistication.

This coming together and organising prepared the gay community for the world with AIDS. Parts of the community had been learning about mutual support and education in health matters during the outbreak of hepatitis which came before HIV.

> It meant that in the AIDS pandemic of the eighties, we were able to give each other mutual support. Those of us who had been through previous struggles had learnt a lot and we were able to relate it to new generations of gay men who were coming into the arena of AIDS.

In the summer of 1988, Alan Beck became aware that a confidential document attacking Cass Mann had been circulated by Duncan Campbell. The document was written to workers at OXAIDS, an AIDS support organisation which was organising a conference on AIDS in Oxford. OXAIDS had asked Cass Mann if he would run a Positively Healthy workshop at the conference. At that time Alan Beck did not personally know Cass Mann or Stuart Marshall. This confidential document, and Alan Beck's later defence of Cass Mann, was to drag the *Pink Paper* into a costly legal action and make a High Court defendant of Alan Beck.

Pat Pilkington and Penny Brohn

Dr. Jacques Benveniste (left)

Dr. Jean Monroe (standing)

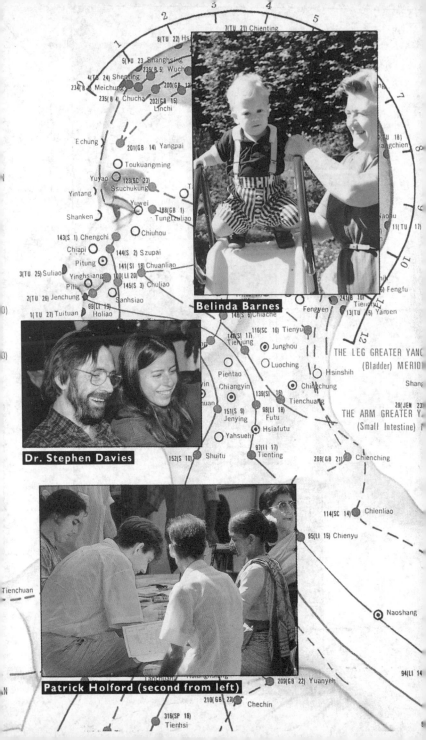

Belinda Barnes

Dr. Stephen Davies

Patrick Holford (second from left)

Rita Greer

Cass Mann (centre)

Robert Woodward PhD.

PART THREE

The Standing Armies of Science: Britain

As the result of the political situation and the frightful, not to say diabolical, triumphs of science, we are shaken by secret shudders and dark forebodings.

C. G. Jung. Memories, dreams, reflections.

Chapter Seventeen

The Rationalist Press Association

In science I missed the factor of meaning. [1]

The Rationalist Press Association (RPA), the oldest British rationalist organisation, was set up in 1899. Its primary objective was to publish books, provide educational material about the philosophy of humanism and to defend freedom of thought. After the Second World War, the RPA became one of the main theoretical forums of British rationalism. It held seminars, lectures and conferences and published the *New Humanist*. In the late twentieth century the philosophy still has echoes of radical free thought within it, but such attitudes are now at odds with the social stature of its senior members who are, in the main, establishment-minded conservatives.

From its inception, the RPA owned a publishing company which published books under two imprints, The Thinker's Digest and The Thinker's Book Club. In the late 1950s the RPA had 3,500 members and assets of around £100,000, most of which came not from the sale of their books and journals, but from gifts and bequests.

In 1961, the RPA affiliated to the International Humanist and Ethical Union (IHEU). In 1963 the Rational Press Association and the IHEU, both of which had charitable status and so were unable to campaign, came together to sponsor a national body called the British Humanist Association.

The British Humanist Association (BHA) became a campaigning body which despite being an 'all party' organisation, attracted to its cause a number of prominent activists and parliamentarians of the Left. It published a newsletter giving information about its various campaigns which were often left of centre issues.

The BHA itself was originally granted charitable status, even though it was a campaigning organisation. In 1965, however, the

Ethical Union lost its charitable status and consequently so did the BHA. The RPA had to stop funding the BHA when it lost charitable status, and in 1971 the RPA also lost its charitable status.

By the seventies, the BHA and the RPA, both losing members, had become virtually the same small organisation sharing the same President, Hermann Bondi, a cosmologist. In the late eighties, the RPA left its offices in Islington and moved in with the BHA in offices in the centre of London.

There had, since the Second World War, been a distinctly special relationship between the American Humanist Association and the British rationalist and humanist movement. The nature of this special relationship, especially in the fields of science and détente, seems to have mirrored the desires and the direction of powerful groups close to the American administration. By the early seventies, the rationalists and the humanists in America and Britain no longer bore any relationship to the atheistic radicals who had populated the organisations in their early years. Although still involved in a struggle for a non-theistic society, their anti-religious views happily mirrored those of ascending high technology capitalism.

The President of the RPA throughout the seventies was Lord Ritchie-Calder, a great populariser of British science. Calder spent the war years in the Political Warfare Executive, part of the Foreign and Colonial Office. Following the war, he worked as a journalist, as Science Editor on the *News Chronicle*, and then on the editorial staff of the *New Statesman* from 1945 to 1958.

The Vice President of the RPA at the same time was Professor Anthony Garrard Newton Flew, who was a Lecturer in Philosophy at Reading University from 1973. Throughout the seventies, Professor Flew was close to a number of right wing and liberal organisations, some of which were said to be CIA-funded. A radical right wing conservative, he has frequently written in the *Salisbury Review*, a policy journal of the radical Right. Flew was also the first Chairman of the far right international organisation, Western Goals.

Associate members and honorary associate members of the RPA were often well-regarded philosophers, men of letters, or scientists. In the fifties, members and associates were distinct as a group of progressive and scientifically-minded professionals at the height of their careers. Often these people held slightly left of centre or liberal views as well as having strong feelings about the irrelevance of religion. The names of Russell, Haldane, Boyd Orr, Crossman, Baroness Wootton and Fred Hoyle are all on the list of associate members during this period. By the late sixties and early seventies, however, the RPA was coming under considerable influence from America, and intellectuals were being replaced by career scientists and academics who more often than not had links with industry-funded bodies.

In 1970, Paul Kurtz, then a leading member of the American Humanist Association, became an editorial advisor to the RPA journal *Question*. In 1972, despite being short of money, and continually in a crisis over staff, the RPA launched a major new journal, the *New Humanist*. Within no time, this journal extended to fifty pages and was published bi-monthly. It had an A4 format and was priced at fifty pence. It carried no advertising and ran a large number of relatively limited articles on subjects which interested humanists and particularly those humanists who wanted to debunk paranormal experience. The Association first tried to sell the magazine to the public via paper stalls and shops. Not surprisingly, as it was full of apparently weighty intellectual discourses, it was a failure and quickly returned to being a subscription journal.

The American Cyrus S. Eaton was another even more surprising Honorary Associate of the RPA from 1966 onwards. Eaton had once been secretary to John Rockefeller, and was still in the post-war years dispensing Foundation money to causes which aided the American way of life. Eaton set up the 'Pugwash' Conferences, which superficially appeared to be the meeting of scientists from East and West who wanted to avert nuclear war. Many of these scientists had studied at the college set up by Flexner on his return to America after his Rhodes Scholarship at All Souls College, Oxford.

Paul Kurtz, who set up CSICOP after leaving the American Humanist Association in 1976, also became an Honorary Associate of the RPA in the late seventies. He had for a few years previously been an editorial adviser to the RPA journal. In 1982, four years after Kurtz became an Honorary Associate, together with Professor Anthony Flew, he suddenly became joint Vice-Chairman. In the year that Paul Kurtz became a Vice Chairman, the RPA had a its biggest financial surplus since the end of the Second World War.

One of the most committed of the British humanists was Hermann Bondi, who as well as being a Honorary Associate of RPA in the late seventies had been Director General of the European Space Research Organisation and Chief Scientific Advisor to the Ministry of Defence. Bondi was later to become Advisor to the Department of Energy. His position in the humanist movement clearly illustrates how an obscure liberal philosophical group, which resembles a gentleman's club, could have access to immense Anglo-American influence in the realm of natural and life sciences and science policy.

When Paul Kurtz set up Prometheus Books, the publishing company which began publishing humanist titles, he bought a number of moribund titles from the RPA which appeared to help put Pemberton, the RPA publishing house, in credit. By the time that Kurtz published the *Humanist Manifesto II* in 1973, a document which was signed by nearly 300 people in America and in Europe, arguments about religion had taken second place, especially in the American humanist movement, to confirmatory discourses about science. In 1976, Kurtz left the American Humanist Association to form the Committee for Scientific Investigation of Claims of the Paranormal (CSICOP).

Following the establishment of CSICOP in America, a British section of the Committee was also set up. [2] British members, however, did not like the term CSICOP† and so called themselves CSICP. The British section reflected the more laconic British character and did not appear to set about its task with the same alacrity as its American parent organisation.

The CSICP Committee consisted predominantly of RPA members: Dr E. J. Dingwall, a psychic researcher; Dr Bernard Dixon, at that time Editor of the *New Scientist;* Dr Christopher Evans, a scientific writer, broadcaster and psychologist; Professor Anthony Flew; Christopher Macy, a member of the RPA, Editor of *Psychology Today;* and Nicholas Walter, at that time Editor of the *New Humanist.*

Throughout the late seventies and the eighties, under the leadership of Paul Kurtz, the BHA and the RPA were linked to the American Humanist Association, and then further to other European

† The term PSI-COP could mean the policing of the paranormal or, if written as PSYCOP, could be a post-war intelligence term meaning 'psychological operation'.

Associations through the International Human and Ethical Union. Through CSICP, the BHA has friendly relations with CSICOP, as well as with members of the other organisation that Paul Kurtz founded in the late seventies, the Council for Democratic and Secular Humanism (CODESH).

* * *

The scientific McCarthyism so ably practised by CSICOP against Jacques Benveniste and others in the nineteen eighties emanated from those who had left the AHA and then set up CSICOP in 1976. Gone was the old style classical debate, rigorous in its intellectual and philosophical questing, to be replaced by 'debunking' or professional character assassination. This new style was not based on academic integrity or scientific method. Its tools were cynicism, ridicule and fraudulent exposition.

One of the first British scientists to be targeted by the new CSICOP style as it was practised in Britain, was Professor John Taylor of London University. In the early seventies, Taylor was considered to be a brilliant physicist and holder of one of the most prestigious Chairs in Mathematics in the country. A scientist who had worked in particle physics, he was asked by the BBC to argue the case against Uri Geller on television. When he met Geller, however, Taylor found himself convinced of his sincerity.

> One clear observation of Geller in action had an overpowering effect upon me. I felt as if the whole framework with which I viewed the world had suddenly been destroyed. I seemed very naked and vulnerable, surrounded by a hostile and incomprehensible universe. [3]

Taylor later carried out a series of very public experiments in which other untrained people bent metal objects at a distance. To those masterminding the war for scientific correctness, this was a terrible betrayal, for Taylor was himself a scientist. Relentless international pressure was put on him to conform and renege on his interest in Geller. *Nature* ran a debunking article on Taylor's 'bending effects' with children. [4] Within a few years he had recanted completely his belief in Geller. [5]

In his book, *The Hidden Power,* Brian Inglis calls this phenomenon of learned men coming to unpopular conclusions about the paranormal and then backing down 'Festinger's Syndrome'. He says:

> The frequency with which scientists who have accepted PSI on the strength of a demonstration and have later backed down suggests that the emotional conflict caused by the departure from what has been a lifetime assumption, and the relief at being able to return to it, has been powerfully reinforced by the realisation that to break ranks is to court ridicule. [6]

The Annual Conference of the RPA in 1975 was held at Churchill College, Cambridge. The programme over three days included lectures on 'A Philosophical View of Normality' by Professor Anthony Flew and two sessions on 'Current research in paranormal phenomena', one by Professor John Taylor. Reports of this Conference, in the November 1975 issue of the *New Humanist,* gave a good idea of the preoccupations of the Rational Press Association in the mid-seventies.

Professor Taylor was clearly at odds with the emerging new style cynicism. In the discussion which followed his talk, he stood out against the CSICOP-style gimmicks which the RPA was beginning to adopt.

> When the issue of fraud by experimenters and deception by subjects was raised again, and when Professor Taylor discounted the usefulness of conjurors taking part in such research because they are not scientists but 'professional deceivers', Nicolas Walter commented that he felt that Professor Taylor had been 'less than honest' in his presentation of the evidence by 'blinding us with science' and excluding the most likely explanation for the results he was getting, and that it was wrong to exclude conjurers who were best qualified for investigating such phenomena. Professor Taylor rejected this criticism with some heat, and asked people to re-read his book. [7]

Professor Taylor responded to the comment that he was being 'less than honest' by saying that he found the accusation 'disgusting', 'shocking' and 'insulting'. It was an indication of the kind of accusation and language which would come to be used in future 'scientific' debates. The assertion that Taylor had blinded his audience with science is odd, but this again is one which would be repeated.

Increasingly, members of CSICOP and British rationalists were coming not from a background of science themselves, but were philosophy lecturers, writers, sociologists and psychologists. Although this group was committed to the cause of state-sponsored industrial science, they were not in favour of rigorous scientific method. They were becoming essentially an anti-intellectual and anti-scientific rump of rationalism.

At the 1975 RPA Conference, there were a number of papers on parapsychology and a talk given by a conjurer, David Berglas, who was a contemporary of James Randi.

> A scientist is not qualified to investigate the phenomenon of a man like Geller or myself. There is just no way a scientist can investigate us, because this is our profession. I've been in this business for nearly thirty years now, and I've been subjected to so-called investigations by scientists all over the world, but so far nobody has found out either how I do it, or even why I do it.

In truth there is no realm of dialogue between a scientist and a magician, for while a magician might wish to learn about science, no proper scientist, except one with a leisure-time interest, would wish to examine a magician's tricks; it is axiomatic that they are tricks and it would simply be a waste of time to analyse how they are done.

The RPA had for a long time organised conferences on 'Science and the Paranormal', but the debate which CSICOP engendered in America pushed this kind of debate into a new, more public arena. The *New Humanist* of the late seventies and early eighties was publishing articles which, increasingly, had less to do with ethics or religion and more to do with the kind of 'safe' areas that CSICOP had colonised. The preoccupations and language of these articles are evidence of their American origin. They were to become the stock-in-trade subjects of CSICOP and all the groups which it influenced.

The focus was on popular subjects which could be outlined and then 'debunked' with large brush strokes and a noticeable lack of intellectual enquiry. The preoccupations of the rationalists, CSICP and CSICOP were to remain roughly the same over the next ten years.

As early as 1978, the New Age was being ridiculed by the rationalists. By the late seventies articles on religious cults,

Transcendental Meditation, Scientology and Hare Krishna had appeared in the *New Humanist*. The tone of these articles tended to be illiberal, authoritarian and peppered with scientific paternalism.

In the early eighties, the *New Humanist* carried a number of articles on the New Age. These articles give shape to many of the arguments which the Campaign Against Health Fraud would later use. Of cults the journal said:

> One can only say that the cults appear to be as successful as ever in trapping naïve idealists disenchanted with high technology materialism. Those attracted to the cults, apart from being utterly desperate, are often educated, upper middle-class and with enough money to pay the necessary costs of membership (some cults demand several thousand pounds in advance). The less rich or less educated tend to gather in looser groupings about Glastonbury and other supposedly sacred centres. [8]

During this period, for the first time, medical science began to work its way into the pages of the rationalist journal. As it did, the RPA moved from an abstract philosophical position to one which represented the establishment view at the very heart of industrial science. The views expressed in the *New Humanist* in the late seventies and early eighties would, however, be considered decidedly 'wet' compared with the vitriolic attacks upon alternative life styles and complementary medicine which were to follow.

Chapter Eighteen

British and Irish Skeptics

It should be observed that Scepticism as a philosophy is not merely doubt, but what might be called dogmatic doubt ... Sceptics, of course, deny that they assert the impossibility of knowledge dogmatically, but their denials are not very convincing. [1]

In January 1987, CSICOP brought its operation to Britain when it launched the *British and Irish Skeptic*, a bi-monthly magazine published in Dublin. The magazine was financed by CSICP, the British section of CSICOP [2] and according to its publishers was sent out to nearly 500 UK and Irish subscribers and ex-subscribers of the *Skeptical Inquirer*, CSICOP's American journal. Forty copies were sent to America 'to be distributed to the other national and regional skeptics' groups'. [3]

Such figures and costings must be viewed sceptically. Even the most rudimentary magazines cost money to produce and a constant commitment to distribute. It is highly improbable that the UK *Skeptic* could have broken even. Like the *New Humanist*, it was a magazine which carried no advertising and had no easily identifiable readership.

The first editor of the *British and Irish Skeptic* was Wendy Grossman, described in future issues as 'Editor of the *British and Irish Skeptic* and a folk singer'. Little information about any of the contributors or editorial personel was given in this or future issues, making it impossible to place them in the context of any academic, scientific or intellectual debate. Grossman, who was educated at Cornell University, has more recently written on micro-technology, [4] a subject which does not rest easily with her noted vocation as a 'folk singer', but does however show her commitment to industrial science.

The most important person on the Editorial Board of the first magazine was Toby Howard, who later moved to Manchester and

presided over the setting up of UK Skeptics and the journal's change
of name.† Other members of the Editorial Board were Peter O'Hara
and Karl Sabbagh, a journalist and film maker, who also appears on
CSICOP's list of Scientific and Technical Consultants. Sabbagh was
also the director of the Merck Sharp and Dohme Foundation, an
academic front set up by the drug company of the same name.

In December 1987, the first organising meeting of Manchester
Skeptics took place and from then onwards the Manchester
Committee became the strongest in Britain. The meeting was
organised at Friends' Meeting House by Toby Howard and Martin
Bridgstock, a lecturer in sociology. The meeting hosted visiting
speakers from South Devon and London. [5]

Manchester became the centre of CSICOP operations and the city
which James Randi and Paul Kurtz usually visit when in Britain. In
1990, the title of 'British & Irish' was dropped and the English group
became UK Skeptics, its magazine the *Skeptic*.

From the beginning, the health-fraud strategy was a considered
aspect of CSICOP's activities in Britain. As time went by, it became
clear that the same relationship which CSICOP had to the American
National Council Against Health Fraud was to be replicated in Britain.
Caroline Richmond, who was to call the first steering committee
meeting of what was at first called the British Council Against Health
Fraud, was from the beginning associated with the *British and Irish Skeptic*.
Early in 1988, nine months before she called the first meeting of CAHF,
Richmond was being reported in the *British and Irish Skeptic (B&IS)*.

> *The Times* and a few other papers reported that writer Caroline
> Richmond had written a spoof on the arguments against food
> additives and sent it to an organisation called 'Action Against
> Allergy'. The report, purportedly issued by the Dye Related
> Allergies Bureau (DRAB), said, amongst other things, that:
> 'Clothes are brighter than ever before, which accounts for the
> epidemic of obesity, malaise, flatulence, irritability, lethargy,
> indigestion, headache, dyspepsia, tiredness, and constipation'. [6]

Why would there be an inevitable coincidence of opinion between

---

† The Irish committee consisted of Chairman, Peter O'Hara; Frank Chambers; Michael
Farragher; Jacqueline Helm and Johanne Powell.

those who felt sceptical about flying saucers, space abduction and parapsychology, and those who might feel sceptical about allergy and the dangers of chemical additives? After all, allergic response to modern chemical manufacturing processes, like response to food additives, is fairly common ground between a good many allopathic doctors, scientists and nutritionists.

In the June 1989 issue, Nick Beard, another founder member of the Campaign Against Health Fraud, writing his second article in the journal, wrote a long piece on the inauguration of the CAHF. Just as CSICOP is an associate organisation of the American Council Against Health Fraud, so the Campaign Against Health Fraud (even after its name changed to HealthWatch) was advertised on the first inside page of the *B&IS*, as an affiliated organisation of the UK Skeptics.

* * *

The articles in the *B&IS* were, even in those first issues, peculiarly outdated. There was an incessant preoccupation with Uri Geller, and the reality of the Loch Ness monster. The *British and Irish Skeptic*, in those first few issues, advertised itself as 'investigating the Paranormal: UFOs, abductions, ghosts, faith healing, moving statues, weeping statues, metal bending, mediums'.

Nowhere did they list alternative medicine. This did not stop them publishing a major article in their third issue, on the BMA report on alternative therapies. This article, on a report which had actually been published a full year previously, disclosed an odd aspect of *B&IS*, revealing its links with orthodox medicine, the BMA and the AMA and inevitably, through these organisations, the pharmaceutical companies.

CSICOP had also carried an article on this BMA report in its journal, the *Skeptical Inquirer*.[7] The article, written by one of the UK Skeptics, Lewis Jones, uses all the key phrases and symbolic words which were to reappear again and again in the work of the CAHF. The article included a full page which detailed the damage which might be caused by the use of alternative remedies.

> A misconceived therapy can not only fail but can also cause damage. Instances of this are scattered through the British Medical Association Report like a recurring alarm bell ... In

Britain, the drinking of herbal tea has been known to lead to
deaths from fulminant hepatic fever. Acupuncture needles have
been found combined with kidney stones and have had to be
surgically removed from the chest and the abdomen. Acupuncture is yet another all-too-possible way of transmitting the AIDS
virus.

The review of the BMA report ends with a quote which had
previously appeared in the *Lancet*[8] from Petr Skrabanek, a CSICOP
member, 'medicine is defenceless against the travesties of reason
thrown up by irrational healing methods, because it lacks criteria for
the demarcation of the absurd.' The *Inquirer* article on the BMA report
is followed by one on Quackery by Congressman Claude Pepper, who
at that time, two years after the 1985 Pepper hearings, was Chairman
of the House Select Committee on Health and Long-Term Care and
Chairman of the House Rules Committee. In the *Inquirer* article,
Pepper suggests a number of legal and administrative measures which
could be taken to protect people against 'quacks'. 'To strengthen
medical practice statutes so that the practice of medicine without a
licence would be classified as a felony' and 'To adopt statutes
establishing criminal statutes for quackery.'

Articles such as these in the CSICOP journal and that of the UK
Skeptics, and the continual shuffling of ideas in defence of science and
orthodox medicine backwards and forwards across the Atlantic,
reinforce the supposition that all these ventures were in touch with one
another on some level.

Throughout 1987 and 1988, those who were to become the
Council Against Health Fraud expressed views about alternative
medicine through the pages of the *British and Irish Skeptic*. The 1987
CSICOP conference, held in Pasadena, California, in April
'highlighted a complementary aspect of the committee's [CSICOP's]
work – the promotion of science as the best approach to obtaining
knowledge about the world'.[9]

One session discussed medical controversies. As with other
discussions about 'quackery' begun by Skeptics, both in the United
States and in Britain, the debate quickly moved off the specific – which
in this case was a paper about chiropractic, the prime enemy of the
AMA – and on to the general. The general discussion was peppered
with remarkable insights such as 'quacks are recognised by, amongst

other things, their attacks on medicine.' [10]

Attacks upon religion, in the tradition of the humanist movement, increasingly became peripheral to the Skeptics' message. Only religious groups on the very fringe were attacked, especially if they put forward views about diet and healing. There was no philosophical discourse about the nature of religion itself, no criticism either of the Catholic Church, the Church of England or the Mormons and no comments upon the wealthy Evangelical churches. In the January/February 1990 issue of *B&IS*, Wendy Grossman contributed an article about Transcendental Meditation.

The November/December issue of the *Skeptic* carried an article about Scientology, by John Clarke: 'Scientology: What is it? Does it work? Is there anything worthwhile behind the cult image?' Scientology is still the *bête noir* of CSICOP followers. To them it represents all the classic aspects of a 'cult' and demonstrates the dangers of 'brainwashing' by pseudo science.

The most common kind of attack on health treatment choices in the *B&IS* and later in the *Skeptic* is the most general attack, unsupported by evidence. Diets of all kinds which take people away from their consumption of processed foods are always described as a confidence trick, though evidence is rarely supplied. There is a depressing uniformity about so many of the longer articles in both the *Skeptical Inquirer,* the *New Humanist,* the *British and Irish Skeptic* and the *Skeptic.* Most of the articles lack creativity and appear as if they have been computed from a databank.

The January/February 1988 issue of *B&IS* carries an article by Michael Heap, Principal Clinical Psychologist at Middlewood Hospital, Sheffield, and a Lecturer in Psychology at Sheffield University. In 'pro-forma' articles of this type, the observer walks round an alternative medicine exhibition or a New Age festival and makes a series of sceptical observations. In Heap's article, a slight deviation from the norm, he recounts attending an Alternative Medicine Exhibition *three years* previously. He recalls the day well, he says:

> And here we have another clue. All these alternative therapies promise you so much more than conventional medicine. 'Open the windows of your mind'. 'Develop latent talents and gifts' 'Move through life with ease' ...

Well, I picked up a pamphlet by the Natural Medicines Society entitled 'The Threat to Natural Medicines'. The pamphlet voices the Society's disapproval of government intentions to make NATURAL medicine subject to the same scrutiny for safety and efficiency as ... I suppose you could say ... UNNATURAL medicines. Medicines which are NATURAL, it is argued, have been proved to be harmless and efficacious by their usage over the centuries.

... to recognise how fortunate we in the West are to be able to even contemplate such luxuries as the alternative medicine industry offers us, and how in reality most of our ailments and complaints are as nothing compared to the daily suffering and misery of many of our fellow beings.

Heap's last point is interesting, for if he is serious, it applies not to alternative medicine, but much more obviously to the major part of expenditure on pharmaceuticals and such things as heart transplant operations. Again, it is a good example of how arguments disfigured by covert interests turn reality upon its head. Is there an 'alternative medicine industry'? If there is, how does it compare with the pharmaceutical industry? Are people in the underdeveloped world poorer because we use natural medicine? Might not poverty in the underdeveloped world be a consequence of unbridled industrial, scientific and technological development in the developed world? In whose interest would it be to suggest that an interest in natural medicine impoverishes the Third World?

Do the pharmaceutical companies not make even greater profits by dumping harmful drugs on the underdeveloped countries so helping to disrupt hundreds of years of natural medical practice?

This particular article, however, raises much more serious questions about the *British and Irish Skeptic* than it does about medicine. Are we really meant to believe that Heap remembered the details of all the conversations which he had at the Exhibition of Alternative Medicine three years previously? It might occur to some people that there was a considerable advantage in writing about an exhibition which was held three years ago, in that nothing which was said in the article can be seriously questioned.

Chapter Nineteen

From the Table to the Grave: The British Nutrition Foundation

> *In the drug business, the Drug Institute is the over-all association ... The food interests are similarly organised. These associations not only oppose the enactment of laws which limit dishonesty, but work consistently to prevent the rigorous enforcement of the inadequate laws which are enacted.* [1]

Thousands of synthetic chemicals now revolve endlessly within the food chain. Many of them leave residues in passing through the human body. Uninvited chemicals are introduced at every stage of food manufacturing. Feed-stuffs made from the remnants of dead animals are rife with damaging organisms which, when transferred to their host, lead to such illnesses as salmonellosis and BSE. [2] Animals and crops take in pesticide residues from grass or hay, nitrates from fertilizers, and even de-icing chemicals from the wings of aeroplanes have now found their way into the water supply.

In processed foods, and especially in 'luxury entertainments', such as sweets, cakes, chocolates and soft drinks, a great array of chemicals are added to make items more palatable and to extend their shelf-life. It becomes increasingly difficult to understand what we are eating and the effect it will ultimately have on our bodies and minds.

Food production and consumption in the modern world have nothing to do with nutrition or health. Like all capitalist production, food production aims for the highest number of manufactured units at the lowest cost and the maximum profit. We have radically departed from the path of simple nutritious food and strayed into a world where we take into our system, as if in a dream, a wide range of toxic substances which play no part in constructing a healthy body.

The chemical companies, the pharmaceutical companies, agribusiness, the processed food industry, the water supply companies and the health care sectors represent a global market for chemicals. Firms which are a part of this market tend to have the same marketing strategies, the same friends – and the same enemies.

* * *

Aware of the unhealthy relationship between chemicals, food and human health, the food processing industry and the chemical industry have, since the Second World War, made a determined attempt to ensure that they intervene in medicine, dietetics and nutrition. Powerful vested interests have tried to ensure that the public does not make links between food and health. Large companies like Coca-Cola, one of the biggest consumers of sugar in the world, [3] work hard at promoting a healthy, innocent image for their drinks. Food has to be good for you. Even if the product is a synthetic chemical manufactured by a paint company, such as an artificial sweetener, its marketing lever is that it is good for health.

The two major organisations which deal with food in Britain are the government department, the Ministry of Agriculture Fisheries and Food (MAFF), and a charity which receives large government grants and is closely linked to MAFF.† The British Nutrition Foundation (BNF) was set up in 1967 and is related to its American counterpart, the Nutrition Foundation of the United States. From 1967, and up until the mid-1980s, the BNF controlled most 'official' information about nutrition, which passed either to the public through the news media, or to parliament via the various Ministry-related food committees.

Both government and charitable organisations are supported by and in turn support British and American industrial interests in food production. Between them and a myriad of satellite committees and institutions, these two organisations control nearly all public information about food and health. [4]

Present subscribers to, and supporters of, the BNF include all the

---

† The BNF began receiving a MAFF grant in 1990: £20,000 annually for five years to fund elements of its programme.

major names in multi-national food production, such as British Sugar, Heinz, Kellogg, McDonalds, Nestlé, NutraSweet and Proctor and Gamble. But perhaps even more worrying than these sponsors, is the sponsorship by such chemical and pharmaceutical companies as: Boots, Imperial Chemical Industries, Roche, SmithKline Beecham and Unilever.

Of the nine major manufacturers who are represented on MAFF food committees, eight of them are also sponsors of the BNF. Nearly all MAFF committees on food and health have on them a representative from one of BNF's main backers, the food and chemical company Unilever. [5]

The British Nutrition Foundation claims to be completely independent of influence from any vested interest and puts great store upon this idea in its Annual Reports.

> Journalists, researchers, programme planners and others involved with the mass media have continued to make use of the Foundation as a dependable, balanced, reference point about nutrition and associated matters. [6]

> The BNF is an impartial scientific organisation which sets out to provide reliable information and scientifically based advice on nutrition and related health matters. [7]

Apart from writing reports and using their spokespeople to give statements to the media, the BNF staff also service a number of committees. For example David Conning, who became Director General in 1986, has serviced such groups as the Apple and Pear Research Council, the Food Safety Committee and the Training of Nutritionists Review Group at the Institute of Biology. The Science Director, Dr Margaret Ashwell, has been Principal of the Good Housekeeping Institute, which tests food industry products on behalf of consumers and advises the MAFF Food Advisory Committee. As with other establishment bodies, like the British Association for the Advancement of Science, the BNF has a highly influential member-ship which overlaps with the majority of government agencies and committees dealing with food.

A small and closely knit group of men and women often:

> perform, interchangeably, all three roles of expert, industrialist and policy maker. Most of these people see no conflict of interest

and believe they can carry out all three jobs with integrity and independence. [8]

Expert advisers who inhabit this small world are nowadays rarely independent academics; whether they be food scientists, doctors or biochemical research scientists, they have usually become experts on behalf of particular industrial interests. They are linked with such interests, either by working within them, receiving grants from them or being approached by public relations companies who pay them retainers. [9]

The BNF is also connected to all the influential committees and research councils which between them control the flow of information about health and food to government. With the Agricultural and Food Research Council (AFRC) and the Medical Research Council (MRC), the BNF set up the Human Nutrition Research Forum bringing together the MRC, AFRC, the DoH and MAFF, with representatives from industry.

* * *

The British Nutrition Foundation has no greater pedigree of independence than the American Council on Science and Health. And, like that body, it entertains a regular circuit of 'experts' whose attitude to health tends to be governed by their continuing receipt of research funding from the food industry. The area of food and health is a covert war area; while promoting a harmonious sense of co-operation, doctors and food manufacturers are increasingly locked into a savage but undeclared war in which the food industry, particularly, uses every means at its disposal to eliminate critical opposition.

The BNF has considerable influence within the more conservative enclaves of the BMA and the RCP (Royal College of Physicians) and the Department of Health. Sir Douglas Black, for example, who was Chairman of the BNF in 1989 and 1990, was Ex-Chief Scientist for the DHSS from 1973-1977; President of the Royal College of Physicians from 1978-1983; President of the BMA 1984-1985 and Chairman of the BMA Board of Science and Education from 1985 onwards. Consequently, Sir Douglas presided over the BMA Science and Education Committee which reported on Alternative Therapies. [10] Throughout 1983 and 1984, Black was a member of the joint RCP/BNF Food Intolerance Committee which reported on Food Intolerance and Food Aversion. [11]

Food Intolerance and Food Aversion (FIFA) was published in 1984 by the Royal College of Physicians and the British Nutrition Foundation. An understanding of this report adds important information to our understanding of the forces which were coalescing against alternative medicine in the mid-eighties. *FIFA* is a conservative document subtitled, 'Fact and Fiction'. Crudely paraphrased, its argument goes something like this: 'Yes, some people are allergic to a few classically allergenic foods, and it certainly is true that a few additives are not nutritious but many people who have been told they have an allergy, or worse still a number of allergies, are either confused or misled. There is a good case for saying that many people who think they have allergies are suffering from psychiatric conditions. Finally, if you think you have an allergy there is no point in turning to alternative medicine, nor should you consult a doctor who practises nutritional medicine or specialises in allergy diagnosis, on the whole these people are quacks.'

Following the publication of the report, a popular paperback version of it was written by Dr Juliet Gray, who had herself been the secretary to the Joint Committee that produced the official report. Dr Gray had previously been the Science Director at the British Nutrition Foundation from 1981 to 1984, and a member of the National Advisory Committee on Nutritional Education from 1979 to 1984. At the time she wrote *Food Intolerance*, Dr Gray was also a consultant to McDonalds the hamburger chain, and responsible for writing *'Good Food, Nutrition and McDonalds'*. [12] In 1985, when Dr Gray was nutritional advisor to Sutcliffe Catering, their pamphlet *Eat Fit* made this statement in defence of additives: 'There has been no case so far when an additive has proved dangerous.'†

Convenience foods, pharmaceuticals, food dyes and additives as well as a range of processed foods, all came under scrutiny by the committee, who had to make a professional decision as to whether any

† In November 1984, Dr Gray was appointed a lecturer in the Biochemistry Department of Surrey University: Vincent Marks is the head of this Department. See Chapter Twenty Eight.

of these things might be responsible for allergies or serious toxicity.

Professor Maurice Lessof, one of the committee members, wrote a short preface for the paperback book; at the time of the committee he was Professor of Medicine at the University of London. Over the previous ten years he had received funding for research from the International Sugar Research Foundation (1975 – 1982), Beecham (1975 – 1982), Imperial Group (1975 – 1982), the pharmaceutical firm Pfizer (1975 – 1976), Reckitt & Colman (1975 – 1976), Unilever (1981 – 1982) and Miles Laboratories, a company which manufactures food dyes and additives. [13]

The paperback version of the report by Dr Juliet Gray pits the solid and well-tested advice of the medical profession against the fashions and fads of quacks and charlatans.

> Most people think that any reaction to food is some kind of allergy. The word has become quite fashionable – everyone who is anyone must have one. One could almost say that concern about reactions to food has reached epidemic proportions; there has been an eruption of coverage in the media, a rash of diet and recipe books (some sensible and others rather weird and wonderful) and a proliferation of self-help groups of all kinds.

> Our approach is that, while accepting that it is an important subject, we're certainly not going to encourage you to blame all your troubles on something you have eaten. [14]

The staggering condescension of the style is intended to make popular the expression of complex ideas. *Food Intolerance* is written in the classic 'white coat' style, its advice being reminiscent of that given by white coat 'medics' who spoke on television adverts in the 1950s and 1960s. One chapter of the book is headed 'Ingredients, Additives and Processing – Why Process Food?' This section is a gem of the conservative style, reasonably weighing up the conflicting views on health foods, additives, the concept of 'natural' and what we mean by the term 'processing'.

> Food has been processed for centuries. Virtually anything you do to food is a form of processing. The most obvious example is cooking.

> *Health food* can be a misleading and perhaps meaningless term,

which seems unfortunately to be here to stay. You cannot really call a food good, bad, healthy or unhealthy.

Fundamental to selling most health foods is the concept of naturalness – another pretty meaningless word in the context of food safety or nutrition.[15]

Dr Juliet Gray then employs what was later to become a typical propaganda technique of the Campaign Against Health Fraud: she moves from the general concept of 'natural' which amongst those who eat wholefoods is applied to a number of different foods, to specific vitamin supplements, offering no evidence that anyone has suggested that these were 'natural'.

Think of the stockroom of an average health food shop: it is sure to contain a lot of medicinal products. Many of them are about as 'natural' as four star petrol. You will also find vitamin supplements galore – often expensive, usually superfluous and sometimes dangerous. [16]

When the report looks at convenience foods, it actually makes out a case for frozen foods being more vitamin-retentive than fresh vegetables. What it does not address is the question of who is convenience food most convenient for? It is commonly argued by the food industry that convenience foods arrived because of changing patterns of women's work. Yet the whole history of capital intensive food processing is the story of the search for greater profits by food processing companies. The story of preservatives, additives, canning, colouring, freezing and packaging is the story of the economic development of production, exchange and consumption in the food industry. The sole criterion which guides this industry is profit.

The convenience of frozen products makes it easier for people to follow the kind of dietary advice usually offered nowadays. For example, we are advised to eat more dietary fibre and less fat: *frozen peas have plenty of fibre*. [17] (Italics added)

It is, however, the section on additives which leaves the chapter on processing most seriously open to question. The report upon which the book was based failed to make clear that research had linked additives to hyperactivity and migraine in children; it said, 'There is no good evidence to implicate intolerance to food additives in hyperactivity.' [18]

In the book, Dr Gray does mention in passing a reaction to additives
but plays it down.

> Reactions to additives ... do exist, but probably in very small
> numbers. Present estimates suggest around 0.03-0.15 per cent
> (between 3 and 15 people in every 10,000 in the general
> population). [19]

In a popularist book, it is easy to dodge reference to serious scientific
or academic work. Dr Gray fails to mention the work of Professor
Soothill, Professor Graham and colleagues at Great Ormond Street
children's hospital who, in 1983 and 1985, showed that many coal-tar
dyes and benzoates are a potential cause of hyperactivity and migraine
in children. [20] Dr Gray wrote:

> The evidence linking hyperactivity to diet is quite poor, although
> every now and again the media makes a song and dance about
> it. It's an idea we have imported from the USA.

The report, *Food Intolerance and Food Aversion*, disputes work done by
Feingold in America which suggests that additive-free diets can
actually stop hyperactivity in children. [21] To dispute Feingold, the
report draws upon research from the Nutrition Foundation of America
and the American Council on Science and Health, both organisations
which are heavily funded by the food processing and chemical
industries.

It is not simply in relation to the diagnosis of allergy that the RCP
and the BNF come into conflict with the new school nutritionists and
clinical ecologists. Dr Gray in her book lays the basis for future attacks
conducted by the Campaign Against Health Fraud, when she discusses
the treatment of allergy problems.

> Any epidemic there has been, has been in the publicity given to
> the issue [of food allergy]; the actual condition is still quite rare.
> In its wake, it has brought a number of people who purport to be
> able to cure allergies through the use of various kinds of diet.
> Such people have encouraged the view that many of the general
> ills and tribulations we all suffer in everyday life, particularly
> psychological problems such as depression, can be ascribed to
> 'hidden' allergies. And, along with that, there sometimes seems
> to be an assumption that keeping to an 'allergen free diet' (often
> based on 'natural' unprocessed foods) somehow implies a purer

and more wholesome way of life. This is one approach, but it is not supported by the weight of scientific and medical thinking. [22]

When Dr Gray moves on to discuss other ideas associated with nutritional medicine, she is dismissive.

Some claim that a rise in pulse rate is a strong indication of a reaction to food; some use the idea of allergy or intolerance as an underlying cause of diseases like multiple sclerosis and rheumatoid arthritis; some use diet as part of a form of therapy to be given to any patient who is not responding to other forms of treatment. None of these theories seem to warrant serious consideration, partly (but not only) because they are not based upon conventional science. [23]

For some reason, Dr Gray then takes the opportunity to have a go at 'quacks', warning patients against providing

... samples of blood or hair to laboratories, which, for a fee, send their reports, their interpretation and their advice. They pay no heed to the fact that a proper medical assessment might disclose (as it has done in some cases) illnesses that require a completely different and specific form of treatment. [24]

The real relationship between hair analysis, 'quackery' and nutritional medicine, probably escaped many readers.

* * *

Clearly the concerns of the BNF are the concerns of the chemical and processed food industries. Rarely, if ever, do they produce material which is critical of food production. In 1977 the BNF produced a booklet entitled *Why Additives? The Safety of Foods*, which argued the industry's position on the safe use of additives. In October 1989 the Annual Conference of the BNF debated 'How Safe is Our Food?', the answer was, of course, very safe!

When the British Nutrition Foundation was set up in 1967, it had the American organisation as a model. Its first and major sponsors were the sugar refiners Tate and Lyle and the flour millers then known as Rank. [25] The first Director-General of the BNF, Professor Alastair Frazer, was a pharmacologist. One of the first public acts of the BNF was to make a film in praise of sugar, supported and supervised by the Director-General.

Views and reports of the BNF are clearly and inevitably influenced by their industrial sponsors. Nowhere is this more clear than in the case of sugar. In 1987, Professor Ian Macdonald was Chairman of the BNF and at the same time, a frequent conference guest of the World Sugar Research Organisation. Responsible for giving lectures in this country and in Australia, Macdonald has been quoted as saying that 'sugar consumption could prolong life'. [26]

Professor Ian Macdonald illustrates well the links between industry, academia and the government. As Geoffrey Cannon explains in his book, *The Politics of Food*:

> Professor Ian Macdonald, for example, served on the FACC (Food Additives and Contaminants Committee) between 1977 and 1983, and thus on the panel that produced the Interim Report on colours and dyes, before becoming Chairman of the food industry-funded British Nutrition Foundation, a member of the BNF Task Force on Sugars and Syrups, and a member of the central Ministry of Agriculture Food Advisory Committee. [27]

As with other organisations of its kind, the BNF has a number of internal awards and bursaries sponsored by industry. In 1989, it introduced the 'BNF Prize' sponsored by British Sugar. Bursaries to help medical students are given by Nestlé through the BNF, while Heinz funds a cash prize for schoolchildren.

* * *

Indicative of the lack of objectivity in the British Nutrition Foundation and those organisations with which it works, is the way in which specialised or professional bodies are set up primarily with the food industry in mind. A good example of this is what happened following the publication of the joint Royal College of Physicians and British Nutrition Foundation Report on Food Intolerance and Food Aversion.

One of the Report's recommendations was to explore the feasibility of setting up a central databank for food composition to register products free of ingredients known to be responsible for intolerance. While this sounds like a good idea and one step towards a standard labelling system, which would enable the lay consumer to see at a glance if a product were likely to cause an allergic response, the recommendation goes on to say that only doctors and dieticians should have access to such a database.

This recommendation, by its very wording, begins to set the tone for the kind of project which eventually came to fruition. Why should only doctors and dieticians have access to such a databank? After all, thousands of ordinary people suffer from allergies and food intolerance; should they not have easy access to lists of chemicals in food which might damage their health?

The recommendation and its implementation were not turned over to an acceptable academic or policy making body, or even a government department. Responsibility for setting up the database fell to the Food and Drink Federation, the food and drink manufacturers' professional association. The Federation then set up a working party upon which sat representatives from the Leatherhead Food Research Association, a private consultancy organisation; the British Dietetic Association, the professional organisation of dieticians, which is predominantly supported by industry and some of the smaller pharmaceutical companies; the BNF; the RCP and the Institute of Food Research at Norwich, a 'hived off' government department: all organisations funded, supported by or linked to the food industry.

In 1987, the database came on stream. Its scope was limited and it did not approach even the most rudimentary scientific analysis of allergy-producing foods. It is a list of products under different headings which contain ingredients known to cause food intolerance or allergy. It is financially supported by the companies which contribute to it, and it is compiled from 'information voluntarily submitted by companies wishing to participate in the exercise'. Access to the databank is 'restricted to State Registered Dieticians and hospital physicians'.

Such a database is quite clearly more than useless to any one who needs to take charge of, or educate themselves about, their own illness. Because the monitoring is voluntary, and the information is given by the food industry, it is highly restricted in its coverage of foods and not the product of a serious research initiative.

* * *

In 1985, the Claude Pepper Bills failed in the US Congress and the American National Council Against Health Fraud was set up. From the beginning, it was intended that the American NCHF would be a 'special relationship' organisation, and plans were quickly put into effect to bring health-fraud campaigning to Britain.

It was in 1985 that Elizabeth Whelan, Director of ACSH, visited England for a series of talks which were supported by the sugar companies. [27] In March 1985 an article appeared in the *Guardian*, based on a chapter of a book to be published in 1986 by Cambridge University Press. The book was entitled, *Nutrition, Diet and Health* by Dr Michael J. Gibney, of Trinity College Dublin.

The article on the 'Futures' page was a digest of apparently pre-fabricated American material. Its only references were two books by Victor Herbert,† which appeared at the end of the article, as a suggestion for further reading. Nowhere in the article was any link between Dr Gibney and the sugar industry explained. [28]‡

The article makes clear the role which is expected of the British Nutrition Foundation in the coming battle against quackery and health fraud: a role which the BNF itself, in a typically reticent British manner, had not yet made public.

> Vigilance against quackery is a duty of the appropriate branch of science. In Britain, the organisation best equipped to deal with such matters is the British Nutrition Foundation. Individual readers in doubt should contact them.

Perhaps it was that the BNF did not take willingly to its new role, as a pawn of industrial science and the sugar industry. It was to be three years before the coalesced forces of food and pharmaceuticals would find, or create, an organisation which would willingly wage war against 'quackery': three years before a suitable individual could be found to activate such an organisation.

Despite this delay, there can be little doubt that the first bridge – a very rough bailey bridge – across the Atlantic, suitable for health-fraud traffic, was thrown up by the same transnational food and chemical companies which sponsored both ACSH in America and BNF in Britain.

---

† *Nutrition Cultism* and *Vitamins and Health Foods – The Great American Hustle.*

‡ Professor Michael Gibney has written for promotional publications produced by the Sugar Bureau.

Chapter Twenty

Wellcome, Part One:
A Powerful Concern

For gifts blind the eyes of the wise and pervert the words of the righteous. [1]

Over the last half century, medical education and research in Britain have been dominated by the interests of Wellcome and Rockefeller. In 1911, three years after his report had radically re-structured medical education in America, Abraham Flexner† travelled to Europe and wrote a second report on medical education.[2] He gave evidence before the Haldane Commission on the University of London. This Commission, which sat for two years between 1910 and 1912, formulated a new constitution for London University and recommended the reform of medical education in London.[3]

Following the recommendations in Flexner's European report, Rockefeller money began to pour into British medical research and education, re-shaping the foundation of medicine in Britain as it had in America. The major recipient of Rockefeller largesse was London's University College, followed by the University of Wales and Cambridge University.[4]

In 1921, Rockefeller created a new School of Hygiene and Tropical Medicine as part of London University. The School was set up after tripartite discussions between Rockefeller representatives, the British government and London University. Between 1922 and 1927, the Rockefeller Foundation donated approximately half a million pounds to the new School, which was formally opened in 1929, incorporating the older London School of Tropical Medicine.[5]

† See Chapter One.

Rockefeller influence and money in London linked the major London hospitals to London University, creating one of the largest medical teaching and research complexes in the world. University College, University College Hospital Medical School and University College Hospital were all drawn together and between 1920 and 1923 the University College Hospital Medical School received nearly one and quarter million pounds from the Rockefeller Foundation.

Rockefeller money was utilised to put into practice Flexner's ideas of 'units' which combined teaching, research and clinical practice in adjacent buildings. It was this re-structuring which radically changed the nature and the direction of medical research in Britain. By the end of the Second World War, University College, St Bartholomew's, St. Thomas', the London Hospital and St. Mary's all had 'units' which had been created and financed initially by American money and inevitably influenced by the Rockefeller view of scientific medicine.

Having set up the 'units', the Rockefeller Foundation set about staffing them. Scholarships enabled leading figures in the administration of medical research to spend time in America observing American medical research and teaching. The Medical Research Council was an organisation much used by Rockefeller administrators to tutor British scientists and medical administrators in the American way. By 1939, the Rockefeller Foundation had supported 131 British Fellows through the Medical Research Council, at a cost of some £65,000. [6] By 1950, there were former Fellows who had received Rockefeller money in 31 professorial chairs in British medical schools. Such fellows were inevitably favourably inclined towards scientific medicine and in many cases their work was linked to pharmaceutical companies.

It was not until the mid-thirties that British-based Foundations and Trusts began to take an interest in medical research and education. The first sizeable British-based intervention came from Lord Nuffield, who gave two million pounds for the development of clinical research at Oxford. Any initial private medical research funding in Britain was soon to be eclipsed when the Wellcome Trust came into being in 1936. Wellcome and Rockefeller interests came together first in the teaching about, and research into, tropical illness.

By the late fifties, the Wellcome Trust and the Rockefeller Foundation had established common policies in medical research and teaching. In the post-war years, overlapping personnel on their boards, and similar interests in scientific medicine led gradually to the Wellcome Trust taking responsibility for the parts of London University complex which had previously been funded by Rockefeller.

Wellcome

The Wellcome pharmaceutical company was founded in 1880 by two US pharmacists, Henry Wellcome and Silas Burroughs. The fact that both Burroughs and Wellcome were Americans inevitably dictated the nature of the Wellcome corporation. Now one of the most powerful of the British multinationals, the Wellcome Foundation is particularly powerful because its multinational axis is Anglo-American. The corporation has built upon and concretised many of the older political, cultural and social power structures which straddle the Atlantic.

The Wellcome group worldwide employs some 18,000 people. In Britain, the structure of the company is complex. The company which produces the pharmaceuticals is now called the Wellcome Foundation; its operations include production sites at Beckenham, Berkhamsted and Dartford, and a sales and technical enquiries centre at Crewe. The administrative offices of the Foundation are housed in Unicorn House, a characterless glass office building on London's Euston Road.

The Wellcome Trust is also situated in Euston Road, in a large Victorian building which has recently been refurbished as a life science centre. The Trust is the apex of Wellcome's operations, it is funded in part by the profit from the Foundation. There is a series of academic and administrative units, in London and other major British cities, either wholly or partly supported by the Wellcome Trust, the function of these units varying from research to teaching and charity administration.

The Wellcome Trust, set up as a charity on the death of Henry Wellcome in 1936,† is now one of the biggest medical research funders

---

† Henry Wellcome's will, made in 1932, shows an interesting connection between Wellcome and the most powerful élites in American society. Henry Wellcome nominated two Americans to handle the legal matters relating to his will and the continuing Wellcome empire. The men were John Foster Dulles and Allen Welsh Dulles who were at that time both lawyers with Sullivan and Cromwell, one of New York's most influential law firms and a cornerstone of the Rockefeller matrix. John Foster Dulles was later to become Secretary of State during the early period of the cold war, and Allen Dulles, Director of the CIA.

in Europe. Up until 1986 the Trust controlled 100% of the shares of the Wellcome drug producing company. In 1986, however, the Trust sold off just over 25% of Wellcome plc, floating 210,800,000 shares at 120p each. The Trust retained its majority holding of 74.5%, and the drug producing company changed its name to the Wellcome Foundation. In July 1992 there was a second share flotation when the Trust disposed of a further 288 million shares, so reducing its holding to 40%. This second flotation was the largest for a private company ever seen in Britain; it raised £2.3 billion for the Trust.†

Following the first share flotation in 1986, Wellcome went from strength to strength. Earnings per share rose from 7.8p in 1986 to 36.0p in 1992. Dividends rose from 2.11p in 1986 to 13.0p in 1992. Meanwhile shareholders' funds have substantially more than doubled during the same period. In 1986, the turnover for human healthcare was £843.3 million and for animal healthcare £162.1 million; by 1990 Wellcome had jettisoned its animal healthcare production and had a £1,669 million turnover from human healthcare production in 1992. Turnover has risen 75% in the last six years.[7]

Wellcome's major production centres are in the U.K. (£536.1 million in 1992) and the U.S.A. (£750.2 million in 1992). The majority of trading profits come from the same countries (U.K. £139.4 million, U.S.A. £262.1 million gross profit after subtracting R&D costs).[8] This is followed by sales in Asia which account for £43.3 million profit.[9]

In the mid-eighties, by far the largest proportion of Wellcome's British income was earned by sales of over the counter (OTC) cough and cold preparations, which accounted for an income of £142 million, almost £50 million more than the second highest sales group of products. In the main these OTC preparations are anti-histamines and steroids. By 1992, OTC products represented only 14% of sales, the majority of which are cough and cold treatments or topical anti-infectives.[10]

Dragged into the Twenty First Century

For years Wellcome was regarded as a qualitatively different type of company from other drug companies; its Trust and its links within the

---

† In retrospect this sale seems unnaturally well-timed, in the following eight months, Wellcome plc's share price fell by 13%, while the FT All-Share index rose by 20%.

British ruling élite gave it access to both academia and government on an unparalleled scale. With the changing economic climate of the eighties, however, even Wellcome found it difficult to keep up the front of a benign and philanthropic enterprise.

The sudden transition from a well-regarded, 'ethical' and academically orientated position to a more market orientated one was reflected in a number of comments made by the Foundation in 1985 and 1986. Although the UK makes up Wellcome's second largest market, in its 1985 Annual Report it lamented what it termed the UK's 'deteriorating environment for pharmaceutical companies' brought about by 'UK government restrictions on profitability.'

Wellcome went through almost continuous rationalisation during the nineteen eighties. This was probably precipitated by the move in the late seventies into the new and profitable area of genetic engineering and medical biotechnology, as well as by American pressure on the Foundation to become more market orientated. In 1982, the Company made a first move towards the area of biological research, setting up Wellcome Biotechnology.

In the mid-eighties, the company began to run down the more 'old fashioned' hygiene, medicine and animal healthcare side of its business. In 1989, it sold Coopers Animal Health, a company which it had set up in partnership with ICI in 1985 to produce organophosphate sheep dip.

The period of change, rationalisation and re-appraisal came to a head in 1990. In October of that year Wellcome announced its desire to sell its human vaccine production, which finally went to the small British firm Medeva plc. It also decided to sell off its subsidiary hygiene business, Calmic.

By the early 1990s, Wellcome had a leading position in anti-virals, particularly for herpes and HIV. Its two leading drugs were Zovirax, for herpes, which was bringing in after-tax earnings of £293 million,† and Retrovir (AZT) the after-tax earnings of which were around £120 million.‡ These two drugs were followed by

---

† Figures for 1990.
‡ Figures for 1990.

Wellcome's cough and cold preparations, which earned £148 million, and cardiovascular treatments − £79 million.

In the summer of 1990, Wellcome brought in a new boss, John Robb, from Beecham's. His philosophy was heavily market orientated. He pronounced that scientifically interesting projects were to take a back seat to those with commercial promise. He instigated a vigorous cost cutting programme, which included the loss of 40 head office jobs. At the same time, a new finance director was appointed, John Precious. Between them they launched a cost control programme, tightening capital expenditure controls, capping research and development spending and trying to improve efficiency.

The rewards for reorientating Wellcome in the market have been enormous. The highest paid director received a salary of £590,000 in 1992. Four other directors were paid more than £250,000. In addition, John Robb has been granted options over shares worth £1.3 million, and seven more of the twelve other directors have option packages worth £350,000. [11]

Wellcome's commercial development has been uniquely shaped by its 'special relationship' position with both the British and American government and business élites. More than any other Anglo-American company, Wellcome has pursued an economic policy overshadowed by this relationship, a policy principally shaped by Rockefeller financial and political interests.

Seventy years after the beginning of public philanthropic involvement of Rockefeller interests in medical research in Britain and America, Wellcome still represents one of their major British bases. Sir Oliver Franks, who died in 1992, was Chairman of the Wellcome Trust for almost twenty years between 1965 and 1982; he had an impeccable Rockefeller background. Originally a civil servant and then a banker, he was a Trustee of the Rhodes Trust between 1957 and 1973. From 1947, on its inception, until 1979, he was a Trustee and later Chairman of the Pilgrim Trust, an archetypal Anglo-American cultural and philanthropic organisation. From 1961 to 1970, almost concurrent with his time at the Wellcome Trust, he was a Trustee of the Rockefeller Foundation.

Lord Swann, who was until shortly before he died in 1990 a Wellcome Trustee, had passed through the higher echelons of academia before becoming the Director-General of the BBC. Lord

Swann was a member of the Ditchley Foundation, which organises meetings, conferences and seminars attended by defence and security experts from America and Britain.

Sir Alistair Frame, who became Chairman of the Wellcome Foundation in 1985, was previously the Director of Rio-Tinto-Zinc, one of the most committed Anglo-American corporations.

The history of Wellcome's alignment with the most powerful and long-established sectors of British and American power puts it in a unique position when dealing with governments. Unlike other pharmaceutical companies, the Wellcome complex plays a commanding role in the British industrial military complex.

The Trilateral Commission

Nowhere is the influence of the Anglo-American 'special relationship' more noticeable than in Wellcome's present involvement with the Trilateral Commission. The Commission, set up by David Rockefeller in the early seventies, has acted since then as a shadow world economic policy meeting. Made up of industrialists, academics and politicians, especially in the field of foreign policy, it has at its core a group of multinationals whose corporate management is determined to break down all boundaries to world capitalism and its trade. The Commission has discussed and resolved questions about the most important foreign policy initiatives of the last twenty years, usually decades before these questions entered the public domain.

Throughout the late eighties, Wellcome kept up its work behind the iron curtain. Pursuing trade exchanges and bases in communist countries, it opened up factories and marketing windows in Hungary, the Soviet Union and Romania. In March 1989, as a sign of philanthropic goodwill, Wellcome sent 75 tons of baby products worth £500,000 to Poland. In April 1990, it sent a smaller aid package worth £70,000.

The major push, however, to capture new markets was in Japan. Wellcome's move to the East began in the mid-eighties. In September 1990, Wellcome opened a £14 million laboratory and warehouse complex, following its successful combination with one of Japan's biggest pharmaceutical companies, to form Nippon-Wellcome.

In 1990, Wellcome set up a series of subsidiary firms in

Scandinavia. All these contemporary strategies, consolidation in Western Europe, integration and ascendancy in Eastern Europe, capitalising on the run-down communist economies, and development in Japan, are global strategies of the Rockefeller Trilateral Commission. The object of developing trade with Eastern Europe has been the ending of the cold war and the integration of economic and financial structures across Europe. Japan is the third staging post of the Trilateral Commission, which intends to integrate the Japanese markets with those of Europe and America.

The Crisis of Profit and Ethics

Few pharmaceutical companies have avoided the public backlash which comes with damaging or unpopular drugs: Wellcome is no exception. By the early seventies, Wellcome was involved in major market conflicts over drugs which were said to have adverse effects. In 1973, both Wellcome and Burroughs Wellcome were criticised over their antibacterial drug Septrin (United Kingdom) or Septra (United States) when a number of articles and papers appearing in America and in Canada suggested that other antibacterials were safer for certain conditions. [12] In the mid-eighties, Septrin became the most used antibacterial drug for the treatment of secondary infections in people who have HIV and ARC.

In the 1980s Wellcome marketed a whooping cough (pertussis) vaccine. As with AZT, it eventually managed to obtain a monopoly National Health franchise on the vaccine. Some critics were later to claim that Wellcome's vaccine was less safe than other products. In 1987, Wellcome went to court in defence of its vaccine.

Although not originally a party to the proceedings between baby Susan Loveday's parents and the general practitioner who had vaccinated Susan with the whooping cough vaccine, Wellcome stepped into the trial to cover the GP and fight allegations over the vaccine. During this trial, it was never an agreed matter of fact that the actual vaccine given to Susan Loveday was the one made by Wellcome.

After a five-month hearing, the judgement in the Loveday case was given in April 1988. The original allegation had been that the vaccine given to Susan Loveday had caused permanent brain damage. Lord

Justice Stuart-Smith ruled that there was insufficient evidence to prove that the pertussis vaccine could cause permanent brain damage.

In June 1992, the Irish Supreme Court found in favour of another claimant, Margaret Best who had sued Wellcome on behalf of her son Kenneth Best. Although aged twenty three, Kenneth had the mental age of a 12 month baby. Following a re-trial to determine compensation, Kenneth Best was awarded £2.75 million.

These relatively private tussles were, however, as nothing compared with the problems generated after 1987 by the licensing of AZT, Wellcome's AIDS drug. AIDS was to become the great medical battlefield of the twentieth century and the prizes for its treatment were great.

Chapter Twenty One

The Pollution of Science

The third Industrial Revolution will be knowledge-driven, science-driven and enterprise-driven. In this new world, we will need the Parliamentary and Scientific Committee as never before to bring together the scientists who open up the possibilities of the future, the men of enterprise who harness their discoveries and the legislators who must enable both to flourish for the betterment of the people. [1]

For the last half-century, industrialists and academics in the United States have fought an uncompromising battle to keep science in the forefront of public consciousness and, more importantly, before Congress and the Administration. Key campaigning organisations have ensured that, regardless of their social value, multi-million dollar scientific projects have gone ahead.

In an advanced capitalist society, science represents a cultural backbone. A vital aid in the struggle to lower labour costs, its continual advance assures growing profit for a smaller and smaller élite. Inevitably, a society driven by science does not develop evenly. It becomes so inequitable that, while only an élite understand the new developments, the majority grow daily more ignorant of the forces which shape the society in which they live. The benefits of 'big' science to the community are small; they go nowhere towards resolving the immense everyday problems suffered by increasingly impoverished populations, either in the metropolitan countries or the Third World. This is especially true of the life sciences and bio-technology which are increasingly shaping the patterns of life and death in advanced societies. The problems which beset post industrial societies cannot necessarily be solved by the application of science: they are often problems of alienation and community.

In America, certain organisations have come to the fore in the crusade to defend and re-generate science. They function within government, are attached to government or lobby government. Examples of such organisations are the Office of Science and Technology and the American Association for the Advancement of Science, with its flagship magazine *Science*.

The power of British science and scientists, like the power of other British élites, resides in a series of private clubs and amateur institutions which in turn are dominated by industrial interests. Such scientific groups, though less professional than their American counterparts, are just as successful but in a thoroughly British way. Although the re-evaluation of science did not appear clearly and publicly on the manifesto of the first Thatcher government in 1979, such a policy did have a natural home inside the ideology of the new Right.

While the attacks upon alternative, complementary and natural medicine have been clearly generated by the medical profession and the pharmaceutical industry, a whole other part of the pro-science and health-fraud strategy is endorsed by members of the industrial and scientific élite. Why should this be? Unlike the clinical practitioners, scientists do not at first glance have anything to lose from the proliferation of alternative or natural medicine. Looking more closely, however, it is clear that the ideology of science extends far beyond the small patch defended by doctors. The ideology of science is the dominant ideology of the late twentieth century. Its expression is shaping a whole class of professionals whose claim is to know more about the forces of life than anyone else.

The establishment of the Campaign Against Health Fraud (CAHF), in 1989, had as much to do with the need to defend science, particularly the biological life-sciences of the pharmaceutical companies, as it did with the need to defend the prevailing medical paradigm. As we shall see later, a belief in science was often only a cynical mask for many CAHF members. Unable to use science to prove their arguments, time and again they would fall back upon propaganda.

The industrial science establishment is a relatively small and incestuous group; the many committees and organisations which form it frequently exchange members to carry out different projects.

One of the largest grass roots science organisations in Britain is the

British Association for the Advancement of Science (BAAS). The Association is a nationwide group set up in the nineteenth century by men predominantly from the large industrial cities, as a forum for scientific ideas. Such a sense of exploratory amateurism has died out now that science inhabits the high risk, high profit world of industrial professionals. The BAAS, however, still propagates the idea of amateur scientific experiment, particularly amongst the young.

The largest industrial concerns see the BAAS as a fertile breeding ground for future industrial scientists; their funding also ensures opportunities for corporate advertising. Pharmaceutical companies which are corporate members of the BAAS include Wellcome, Glaxo, Boots and Beechams, while the other supporters represent some of the largest industrial interests in the country: 3M UK, Racal, Taylor Woodrow, British Nuclear Fuels, BP and Shell.

Unlike the American Association for the Advancement of Science (AAAS), which plays a significant role in lobbying for the science budget, the BAAS does not have a major magazine or newspaper. It does, however, appear to have some influence with *Nature* and the *New Scientist*.

In 1989, BAAS awarded ten media Fellowships, sponsored by industrial concerns. 'Fellows' were placed in a variety of media and print organisations. Amongst the sponsors were the Biochemical Society, CEGB, Esso and the Wellcome Trust. The BAAS is committed to linking scientists to the media. Over the last few years they have held a series of one-day conferences at which scientists get to know how the media work. Fellowships to Westminster are also sponsored through the BAAS, so that budding scientists, or graduates, can work with MPs and brief them on science issues.

The Council of the BAAS is made up of 15 individuals, usually nominated or appointed by a variety of bodies. In 1989, Sir Walter Bodmer was a Vice-President, having been appointed to the committee by another influential institution, the Royal Society.

The full title of the Royal Society is 'The Royal Society of London for Improving Natural Knowledge'. It was set up in the late seventeenth century and has since that time acted as a club for the aristocracy of science. Royal Fellows of the Society have included Prince Philip, the Prince of Wales, Queen Elizabeth the Queen Mother and in 1971, His Majesty Emperor Hirohito of Japan. Sir

Walter Bodmer was elected a Fellow of the Royal Society in 1974 and since that time he has played an active role in its affairs and committees.

The Committee on the Public Understanding of Science (COPUS) was set up in 1985, jointly by the Royal Society and the British Association for the Advancement of Science. The organisation finances a quarterly magazine called *SPA*. The first Chairman of COPUS, chosen from the Royal Society to serve until 1993, was Sir Walter Bodmer. In 1985, a Press Briefing Committee was set up by the Royal Society and the Association of British Science Writers. It was to consider topics for scientific press briefings and to oversee their organisation.

It is a small committee with only eight members and a Chairman. The first Chairman was Sir Walter Bodmer, who was chosen in 1985 and again in 1987. In 1987, Caroline Richmond, who two years later was to become founder of the Campaign Against Health Fraud, was elected onto this committee by the Association of British Science Writers. In 1991 the committee was enlarged with five members for each organisation, and Sir Walter Bodmer was replaced by Professor Lewis Wolpert.

Despite the fact that she was neither a clinician nor a practising scientist, Caroline Richmond had become accepted at the very centre of the scientific establishment. In August 1990, as part of her role on the Press Briefing Committee, she gave a press briefing on Chronic Fatigue Syndrome (known as ME). The briefing was chaired by Professor Anthony Clare of Trinity College Dublin.

One aspect of laboratory scientific work which links many scientists together is their defence of animal experimentation. The Research Defence Association (RDA) was set up at the turn of the century, to defend the rights of scientists to breed animals and experiment upon them.

The Association lists as its Vice-Presidents Sir Douglas Black, who headed both the RCP/BNF *Report on Food Intolerance* and the BMA *Alternative Therapy Report*; Sir Walter Bodmer; Sir William Paton; Sir Stanley Peart, a Trustee of the Wellcome Foundation; Sir John Vane, previously a long-standing research scientist for Wellcome and from 1989 a member of the Campaign Against Health Fraud.

Over the last decade the RDA has felt increasingly under siege from animal rights organisations and, as the tactics of such groups have become more militant, the RDA has expanded its organisation.

> We are adopting a mainly catalytic role and are trying, with some success, to enlist the help of those who are, or should be, our natural allies. Chief amongst these are scientists, especially those engaged in biomedical research, doctors and surgeons, paramedical staff, patients and patient associations and medical charities. [2]

Surprisingly, this quotation fails to mention the organisation's biggest supporters, the pharmaceutical companies. All new drugs and medical techniques are first tested on animals.

In 1990, the RDA in co-operation with the British Association for the Advancement of Science floated a *Declaration on Animals in Medical Research*. The declaration was launched at a BAAS conference chaired by Colin Blakemore, a committed advocate of the need for animal experimentation, Sir Walter Bodmer and Sir Denis Rooke, President of the BAAS.

Since the failure of the Ministry for Science and Industry in 1964, science and scientists in Britain have been left to their own devices. Without representation, the various Science Research Councils which receive money directly from the government have frequently had their grants cut. With less government money available for science, industry has stepped into the breach and academics and industrialists have ended up fighting the corner for science.

After the election of the second Conservative government under Margaret Thatcher in 1983, this situation began to change. Industry wanted some return for its championing of science, and it particularly wanted more money from government for research and development. Many of the science-orientated campaigning groups were re-invigorated in this period and a push began to create a more formal governmental control over science policy.

The oldest all-party science committee of both Houses of Parliament is the Parliamentary and Scientific Committee (P&SC). This was set up in 1939 to take over the functions of the Parliamentary Scientific Committee which was suspended at the outbreak of war. Addressing its fiftieth anniversary gathering in 1989, a long-standing and enthusiastic member of the committee, Margaret Thatcher, pointed out that the it had been, 'one of the very few [committees] that regularly brings science and industry together'. [3]

This all-party group consists of members of both Houses of Parliament and the European Parliament, representatives of scientific and technical institutions, industrial organisations, science-based companies, and academia. The aim of the group is to keep science on the public and parliamentary agenda. The Parliamentary and Scientific Committee is in some ways a misnomer, for the Committee is actually eight groupings, which include universities and industrial corporations, with a total of nearly six hundred members.

Not surprisingly, many of the individuals who champion science and industry and defend the ideology of science are parties to this seminal scientific committee. In 1987, Sir Hermann Bondi, the head of the British Humanist Association, was one of its Vice-Presidents. Sir Ian Lloyd, a member of the Parliamentary Science and Technology Foundation, which set up the Parliamentary Office of Science and Technology, was the President in 1990. Past Presidents include Earl Jellicoe and Lord Sherfield. Sir Walter Bodmer is a Vice-President and a member of the council, Sir Gerard Vaughan MP is Chairman and a member of the council, while Lord Kennet is an Honorary Secretary.

The Wellcome Trust and the Wellcome Foundation are represented, as are the Royal Pharmaceutical Society, the Society of the Chemical Industry and the World Sugar Research Organisation. The Royal College of Surgeons is represented by Sir Stanley Peart, a Wellcome Trustee, the Imperial Cancer Research Fund by Sir Walter Bodmer. The Institute of Food Technology is represented by Professor Arnold Bender, and the Biochemical Society by Professor Harold Baum, both Campaign Against Health Fraud members. The British Nutrition Foundation and the British Dietetic Association are both represented, as is the British Association for the Advancement of Science. The Association of Medical Research Charities, a Wellcome-administered umbrella organisation, has two representatives on the general committee.

In the last five years, the Committee has been addressed by, amongst others: Lord Sherfield; Professor David Conning, Director-General of the British Nutrition Foundation; Professor C. Gordon Smith, a Wellcome Trustee and Dean of the London School of Hygiene and Tropical Medicine, and Margaret Thatcher.

The establishment nature of the P&SC can be judged from two of the committee's visits made in 1990, one to the headquarters of NATO and SHAPE and the other to the Metropolitan Police Forensic Science Laboratory. The Guest of Honour at the 1991 Annual Luncheon of the P&SC was Dr John H. Gibbons, the Director of the Office of Technological Assessment (OTA), attached to the US Congress. Gibbons was full of praise for the P&SC, and especially for the newly set up Parliamentary Office of Science and Technology (POST), to which he pledged his support. Gibbons said that the OTA were:

> ... trying to wrestle with the intertwined issues, of economy, environment and security. Our work is increasingly engaged in trying to understand issues such as health, pollution, international trade, education research, national defence conversion and energy strategy in the framework of how each relates to the more fundamental issues of economy, security and environment. [4]

The Parliamentary and Scientific Committee sees a major part of its task to be providing MPs with 'authoritative' scientific information, regular summaries of science and technology matters in Parliament, and taking:

> ... Appropriate action through parliamentary channels wherever necessary to reinforce the views expressed by members on matters of public interest and legislation, especially for financing scientific and technological research, education and development, and to ensure that the proper regard is had for the scientific point of view. [5]

The 'regular summary of scientific and technological matters dealt with in Parliament' takes the form of the magazine *Science in Parliament*. Originally this was a typed transcript of parliamentary questions and debates. However, during the eighties it developed into a typeset magazine, which also carried copies of the speeches given to the P&SC. More recently, the magazine began to include feature articles by members of the committee and other prominent people in science, industry and Parliament.

Science in Parliament is published by an outside publisher, Westminster Publications. Recent issues have been sponsored by the

British Technology Group and some by Hoechst, the drug company. In the last years of the eighties, the connection with the pharmaceutical industry was even more overt: from 1985 to 1989, *Science in Parliament* was published by the Pharmaceutical Press, a division of the Royal Pharmaceutical Society of Great Britain.

Influential members of the P&SC lobbied increasingly in the eighties for a government-based organisation that would 'undertake an impartial assessment of the scientific and/or technological background of the many issues of policy which the members of both Houses are asked to address'. [6]

An appeal was made to Margaret Thatcher for government funding. She, however, turned down the request, suggesting that such an organisation would be more appropriately funded through private sources. The P&SC accepted her suggestion and the Parliamentary Science and Technology Information Foundation (PSTIF) was formed. Successful appeals for funds were made by Sir Ian Lloyd MP, Sir Gerard Vaughan MP, Sir Trevor Skeet MP and Lord Gregson, amongst others, and PSTIF was able to establish the Parliamentary Office of Science and Technology (POST) in April 1988. POST was granted charitable status shortly afterwards. [7]

POST is modelled on similar American-type organisations which lobby Congress on behalf of the industrial and military science budget. The most prestigious of these US organisations is the Office of Technology Assessment.

POST's aim is to 'provide parliamentarians from both Houses with information which will enlarge their understanding of the scientific and technological implications of issues likely to concern parliament'. [8]

The Trustees of the Parliamentary Science and Technology Information Foundation reflect a common link between liberal Anglo-American interests and the far Right. Lord Kennet is a social democrat, a Fabian and now an MEP. From 1981 to 1983, he was the SDP Chief Whip in the Lords. Lord Sherfield has an Anglo-American 'special relationship' background, having served as UK Ambassador to the USA from 1953-1963; he was Chairman of the Ditchley Foundation from 1962-1965 and continues to be one of its governors. Sir Ian Lloyd, who was chairman of POST from 1989 and the President of the Parliamentary and Scientific Committee, is a former member of the South African Board of Trade and Industry

(1952-1958). He is known for his hard Right support for South Africa and the world strategy against communism. Sir Gerard Vaughan was Margaret Thatcher's first Minister of Health from 1979-1982 and parliamentary member of the MRC from 1973-1976. As Chairman of the UK AIDS Foundation, he attracted controversy when he urged that AIDS screening should be carried out on UK visitors from black African countries.

One of the major contributors to the PSTIF is the Wellcome Trust. For the year 1990, the Wellcome Trust also financed a Wellcome Parliamentary Fellow, in the person of Dr Helen Kyle. Dr Kyle's salary was paid entirely by a Wellcome bursary; she spent her first year producing a report on Medical Research and the NHS. [9] The next Wellcome Fellow, in 1991, was Dr Peter Border who was concerned with biomedical research. As well as full-time Westminster Fellows, the British Association for the Advancement of Science administers a scheme which enables scientists to spend three months on secondment to POST. [10] COPUS, the joint Royal Society and British Association for the Advancement of Science committee, funded three fellowships for three-month periods, for people to work inside POST.

Like other advisory bodies to government sponsored by industry, POST appears to prioritise environmental issues such as drinking water quality, passive smoking and air pollution. In 1990 for example, POST prepared briefing documents for different parliamentary committees including the Environment Committee which was examining pollution and related matters. It is, however, inevitable that their advice on such matters is conservative. An examination of the interests of members on the board of POST reveals weighty interests in favour of the chemical industry and private medicine. W.E. Garrett MP is Chairman of the All Parliamentary Group for the Chemical Industry and Parliamentary Adviser for BAT Industries. Sir Gerard Vaughan MP is on the board of Private Medical Centres Plc and has links with American private health care interests. Sir Alastair Pilkington was until 1989 on the board of the Wellcome Foundation.

Amongst the major funders of POST – over £10,000 in contributions in the first year – are Esso, Ferranti, IBM, ICI, Plessey and the Wellcome Trust. Amongst other committed sponsors (donating over £2,000 in the first year) were British Telecom, Merck Sharp and Dohme, National Power, SmithKline Beecham, Trafalgar

House and United Biscuits. Other less conspicuous donors were the Wellcome Foundation, Boots, and British Nuclear Fuel. Two interesting contributors, breaking ranks from their previous apparently unaligned positions, are the BBC and the IBA. POST is now central to the role of the Parliamentary and Scientific Committee. In 1991 the PSC amended its aims and objectives in order to incorporate the role of POST. [11]

In Britain, independent advice and briefing systems for parliamentary committees are poor and MPs get little money to use on research. The system is very vulnerable to American-style research and strategy groups which are funded from outside parliament by vested industrial interests. POST is the first such organisation in England and the Wellcome Foundation ensured from the beginning that it was a senior partner in the enterprise.

By 1989, the Conservative government was becoming increasingly concerned about the power of POST as a lobby group. The cabinet and MPs looked with trepidation on the development of an all-powerful but privately funded group which had a similar brief to that of the US Congress's Office of Technological Assessment. In 1990, the government began discussions to take the nascent power away from POST and replace it with a ministerial government agency which would handle scientific and technological assessment.

Anyone who looked closely at the 'Office of Public Service and Science', set up in May 1992, under the ministerial guidance of William Waldegrave and headed by Sir Peter Kemp, might have been excused for wondering what the exact role of the department was. It seemed to throw together consumer help, the Citizen's Charter, technology assessment and science budgeting.

The basic components of the department can, however, be analysed. The Science Branch of the old Department of Education and Science was moved into the new Department: this meant that it was firmly rooted in science budgeting and would be responsible for chanelling money to the five Research Councils. On taking up his post, William Waldegrave told the *Independent* 'We need to show that the powers that be are on the side of rationality.' [12]

This was a very interesting remark, which encapsulated the philosophy of CSICOP and all the powerful American health-fraud organisations. If the 'powers that be' were on the side of rationality, and therefore industrial science, where did this leave the disgruntled or complaining and even irrational consumer? If they were to enforce the Citizen's Charter, many no doubt hoped, the powers that be would be on the side of 'the people'. As for the other part of the department's brief, to inform MPs and the public of scientific assessments for consumers, this sounds remarkably like the role which the US OTA ascribes to itself in relation to a wide range of alternative medical practices and treatments.†

The other organisation which over the last ten years has pressed the government to 'do the right thing' by science is the Foundation for Science and Technology (FST). Launched in the late seventies, it was intended as a link organisation between industry and the learned societies to promote and develop science and technology, and to lobby for better scientific training and education. The FST draws together many of the same people who are influential within the parliamentary scientific groups, large industrial corporations and the Research Councils.

The President of the Royal Society and the head of the British Association for the Advancement of Science are both members of the Council of the FST and the Vice-Presidents have included Sir Alastair Pilkington and Lord Sherfield. Earl Jellicoe, the head of the MRC AIDS directed programme, represents the MRC on its council. The FST is funded and supported by a large number of industrial organisations, including Unilever and ICI.

During the period following the licensing of AZT, Wellcome managed to make an intervention in government at an even higher level than Parliament. The Advisory Council on Science and Technology is the body which advises both the government and the civil service on matters of science. Its meetings are attended by the chief scientific adviser to the Cabinet Office and Departmental chief scientists and scientific advisers. In July 1989, Sir Alfred Shepperd, who was Chairman of Burroughs Wellcome and Chairman of the

---

† Over the last decade, the OTA carried out a historical and nationwide assessment of all non-orthodox cancer cures. Inevitably, it gave most of them the thumbs down. All the expert evidence for the report was taken from the very industrial and pharmaceutical experts who for years had been fuelling the campaign against alternative cancer treatments.

Wellcome Foundation until 1985, joined this body; his appointment ended in July 1992. Shepperd was the only representative on the Council during this time who came directly from a pharmaceutical company. His favour with the Conservative government was shown in 1989 when he was knighted in Margaret Thatcher's last honours list.

Serving on the Council over the same period, from 1989 to 1992, was Professor Roy Anderson. Anderson, who heads the Department of Pure and Applied Biology at London's Imperial College of Science, Technology and Medicine, is also a Wellcome Trustee. His position as a Trustee means that he is one of a handful of powerful men who control the Wellcome empire. Throughout the time of his term of office on the Council Professor Anderson was one of the most vociferous proselytisers for Wellcome's AZT.†

---

† Professor Anderson is married to Clare Baron one of the salaried workers in the office of the All Parliamentary Group on AIDS, which receives funding from Wellcome. See Chapter 32.

PART FOUR

The British Campaign Against Health Fraud

*Some people will always seek what
others may deem irrational and unscientific,
nonetheless, whatever our own beliefs, it is vital to
the most basic spirit of democracy that we
should respect such decisions*

Simon Watney.

Chapter Twenty Two

Wellcome, Part Two :
Developing and Marketing AZT,
The Global Market

> *The pharmaceutical industry is highly competitive. A drug may be subject to competition from alternative therapies during the period of patent protection.* [1]

In America and Europe the pharmaceutical industry, as well as being immensely profitable, is at the forefront of scientific research. This research no longer concentrates upon singular issues of human illness but has reached out, godlike, involved in a quest to establish the cause and the content of human life itself. The transplantation of organs will in the future appear to be a gross kind of engineering, once scientists have found ways of intervening in the human genetic structure.

It is not surprising that it is at this sharp end of scientific research and marketing, where so much is at stake, that the health-fraud movement is most virulent. A small number of pharmaceutical companies have played a major part in developing the health-fraud movement in both Britain and America. With the licensing of AZT in 1987, Wellcome plunged even deeper into a battle with the many alternative remedies which it was being suggested might help the immune system fight opportunist infections in AIDS cases.

With such vast amounts of money used to research, develop and capitalise new drugs, pharmaceutical companies cannot allow themselves the luxury of free market competition. A variety of protective business practices have developed in the industry, all of which have one end in view, that of undermining competition. If the production of pharmaceuticals is very costly, the strategy for getting them accepted and creating a critical vacuum around their use is even more so. From the initial stages of research, development and pre-licence marketing, the pharmaceutical manufacturers are involved in 'skewing' the system in order to gain market ascendancy for their products.

Exploiting their monopoly interests and cartel structures, a pharmaceutical company like Wellcome is able to dip in and out of a complex network which exists between doctors, their professional societies, chemical companies and most importantly government agencies and departments such as the Department of Health and the Ministry of Agriculture Fisheries and Food.

Coming to the Aids of Wellcome

When AIDS was first recognised as an illness in the early eighties, the scientists of the largest pharmaceutical companies began an obscene scramble to identify its cause and produce a treatment. They did not begin this search as an extension of clinical work but as a knee-jerk commercial reaction. A licensed treatment for a new internationally recognised illness, in a market where there were no competitive drugs, represented the grail of pharmaceutical manufacture.

In America, Burroughs Wellcome sent numerous samples of possible anti-viral substances to the National Institutes of Health. One of these samples appeared to have anti-viral properties *in vitro* (in a test tube). The drug was Retrovir, which became known colloquially as AZT.

AZT had been developed in the sixties for use on cancer patients. Trials then had shown the drug to be toxic and relatively ineffective at killing select cancer cells. It became an 'orphan' drug, one for which there were no easy development opportunities. Such drugs bring various financial incentives, such as tax reductions and assured seven-year licences, to any company which adopts them.

The development of a drug to the point at which it is licensed may take anything up to twelve years. Even after that time, there is no guarantee that the licensing authorities will give the drug a licence. After development, extensive research has to be carried out on the drug, in the form of placebo-controlled trials. Following preliminary tests on animals, 'Phase I' trials test for toxicity in humans. 'Phase II' trials, carried out on a much bigger sample, test for efficacy and longer-term adverse reactions.[2] The process of developing a pharmaceutical medicine is expensive: research and development prior to licensing can cost anything up to £150 million.

The Phase II, double blind placebo-controlled trial for AZT began at ten centres in America in February 1986. Two hundred and eighty-two patients with recently diagnosed AIDS or severe ARC (AIDS Related Complex) were entered in the trial. After a period when the average patient had been undergoing treatment for four months, the Data and Safety Monitoring Board called for a summary conclusion to the trial on finding that one AZT recipient against 19 placebo controls had died.[3]

There are good reasons why trials, like any other scientific projects, have to be continued to the end. In the case of the Phase II AZT trials, it transpired later that the apparently low death rate amongst those subjects being given AZT may well have occurred because these subjects were given frequent blood transfusions to offset the adverse effects which AZT produced.[4] With a treatment for such a complex illness, involving such an unstable group of trial subjects as those with ARC, it is clear that the most extensive and lengthy trials should have been carried out before there was any question of licensing. However, the Wellcome Foundation was given a licence for the production of AZT, on 3rd March 1987, within months of the American Phase II trials ending. The almost spontaneous and unregulated licensing of AZT as *the* 'anti-AIDS' drug would put back the licensing of other HIV treatments by many years.† Not only would the direction of research now be dictated by the search for anti-virals, but all other treatments would have to be subjected to trials and licensed in comparison to AZT.

† Even when ddl, produced by Myers Squibb, and ddC, produced by Roche, both anti-virals, where given licences in 1992 and 1993, it was only after they had been tested against AZT and on condition they were prescribed with AZT.

Marketing a Difficult Drug

> In just two and a half years, Burroughs Wellcome took Retrovir
> from the laboratory to the clinic and *demonstrated its clinical
> effectiveness in treating AIDS*, overcoming enormous development
> problems along the way. [5] (italics added)

Wellcome frequently suggested that in developing AZT in the US and
the UK its staff rose to a crisis and, winning through, produced a
miracle treatment for AIDS. 'Burroughs Wellcome people worked at a
frenzied pace – some calling it a war mentality – while the enemy
claimed more lives everyday.' [6]

Unlike many drugs, however, AZT came to Wellcome at a bargain-
basement price: research and development expenditure on the drug
was minimal, around £25 million. What is more, even Wellcome
could not claim that AZT had been developed as a designed solution
to the HIV virus. Initially it had simply been shown to have an anti-
viral effect *in vitro*.

The frightening nature of AIDS and public pressure spurred
Wellcome on to get AZT licensed at all costs. According to their own
sources, when the British Beckenham laboratories produced a 4,500
page dossier on AZT for submission to the world's regulatory
authorities, so imperative was the issue that these highly technical
dossiers, whatever their country of destination, were produced in
English, without a translation. [7]

Secret Corridors of the DoH

In Britain, all matters to do with the licensing and marketing of
medicines are overseen by the Medicines Control Agency (MCA), a
body which grew out of the reorganisation of the Medicines Division
of the Department of Health in April 1989. The MCA administers all
aspects of medicines and drugs, from advice to permanent officials of
the DoH to liaison with European bodies. Six statutory advisory
bodies, set up under Section 4 of the 1968 Medicines Act, service the
MCA.

The committees are: the Medicines Commission, the Committee
on the Safety of Medicines, the Veterinary Products Committee, the
British Pharmacopoeia Commission, the Committee on the Review of

Medicines and the Committee on Dental and Surgical Materials. Of these six committees, two are important with respect to human pharmaceuticals. The Medicines Commission is important because it advises the Minister of Health on matters relating to medicines, either on its own initiative or when asked. The Committee on the Safety of Medicines is the committee which grants product licences.

Appointments to the Medicines Commission are for a four-year period. The appointments are made by the Minister after consultation with a variety of organisations. Ministers choose people who will be able to tender expert advice on matters within their field. From 1985 to the end of 1989, one of the most prominent members of the Medicines Commission was Professor Trevor M. Jones, the Director of Research and Development at the Wellcome Foundation, perhaps the most important staff position in the whole Wellcome complex. From his position on the Medicines Commission, Professor Jones would have been in a position to advise the Minister of Health on all matters to do with AZT and any other medicines or therapies which came onto the market for the treatment of HIV.

Besides Professor Jones, out of a total Committee of twenty five, no less than five other members on the 1989 Medicines Commission had interests in or connections with Wellcome.

Out of twenty-one members of the Committee on the Safety of Medicines, only two had interests in the Wellcome Foundation. However, this Committee rarely works by a vote on a simple majority. Intense politicking goes on behind the scenes with the interests of different companies agreeing often on a *quid pro quo* basis.

As with all the work of the four committees, the licensing of AZT and the discussion surrounding it are secret. AZT for use against the HIV virus took only eight months to research, develop and license. The drug was 'fast tracked' (speeded) through the UK licensing system. When AZT was 'fast track' licensed in Britain it had not undergone any trials at all in the United Kingdom. The UK licence was granted four weeks *before* the FDA had 'fast tracked' it through the licensing process in the United States.

Whatever lay behind the 'fast track' licensing of AZT without lengthy clinical trials, political and industrial pressure could have been put on government departments to ensure that no other anti-HIV drugs were given fast track licences. After all, if Wellcome could get a

national franchise for a 'fast tracked' drug, what was to stop others
from doing the same?

The Licensing Bonanza

In December 1986, three months after the American Phase II trials
had been halted, Wellcome began submitting its data to regulatory
bodies for approval to market AZT. Within a couple of months,
almost the whole of Europe had followed the lead of Britain in
granting a licence to AZT.† 'Approvals were rapid. What normally
takes years, took months.' [8]

On the 20th of March the FDA granted a US licence. Reagan
rolled back the State for AZT. The Administration had, he said,
'unlocked the chains of regulation' to allow the drug government
approval in four months. By the middle of 1987, AZT was licensed for
use in 15 countries. By September 1987, within a year of the only
placebo blind trial being aborted, it was further licensed in Japan,
Germany, Spain, and Italy. By November 1987, AZT was licensed in
35 countries.

Between 1983 and 1987, during first flushes of the development
and marketing of AZT, Wellcome's turnover almost doubled from
£674 million to £1132 milllion.

In the middle of this season of licensing, Wellcome was conducting
what was probably the biggest world-wide press blitz that had ever
been carried out by a drug company in Britain. Licensing hearings in
European countries were preceded and followed by symposia
engineered to attract extensive press coverage. In September 1987,
a symposium was held in Paris to launch AZT; one hundred and
eighty doctors and journalists attended an all-expenses-paid meeting at
the Hotel Sofitel, Sèvres. A similar symposium followed the licensing
of AZT in Holland in the spring of 1987.

In November, Wellcome held a Retrovir seminar for the European
press; journalists from more than a dozen countries attended an all-
expenses-paid two-day junket at the Beckenham works in Kent. The

† Norway and France in March 1987, Holland in Spring 1987, Spain in June
1987.

Vice-President of research from Burroughs Wellcome in the US attended and explained the cancellation of the Phase II trials. Also in attendance were those representatives of the medical profession who were even at that early stage contributing to an objective scientific debate on AZT and its effects.

> Dr Charles Farthing, of St. Stephen's Hospital London, said that he thought it was logical to administer Retrovir (AZT) earlier ... The stronger the (patient's immune) system is, the better the patient's quality of life ... Dr Farthing said that St Stephen's had probably used more Retrovir than any other hospital in the U.K. There, they had found out that 'early benefits are quite dramatic'. [9]

Answering a question about serious side effects, only a year after clinical studies had begun, Farthing made it clear that he did not think that AZT had any serious adverse effects. 'I would call a serious side effect one which is irreversible. The only side effect we have observed with Retrovir – anaemia – is reversible.' Later trials however suggested that there could be other more debilitating side effects.

In the autumn of 1987, there were symposia in Naples, organised to cover the African continent, and in Ecuador, giving coverage of the Caribbean and Latin America. Wellcome chose the Naples conference, 'AIDS and associated cancers in Africa', to launch the 'new generation' of AIDS testing kits; there was after all a huge market in Africa. Dr Jonathan Mann, at that time with the World Health Organisation, addressed this conference. The Ecuador conference was transmitted by television across South America and the Caribbean. A video on Retrovir, *A Ray of Hope*, was broadcast. Both these conferences were organised by Abbott Laboratories in conjunction with Wellcome.

Over the next four years Wellcome worked to obtain the national franchise for AZT in as many countries as possible. Much of this marketing depended solely upon the unfinished Phase II trials done in America. Future American trials were to raise questions about the reaction of Black and Hispanic individuals to AZT. [10]

Wherever the AZT caravan was hosted, it brought to the fore physicians from important metropolitan centres like London and New York. These two or three-day selling junkets were paid for in every last detail by Wellcome, Burroughs Wellcome or one of the other drug companies which made up the Wellcome cartel group.† In December 1989 the AZT marketing operation went to Brasilia, where AZT had been licensed that summer. Wellcome had established laboratories in Brasilia, in partnership with ICI. Doctors attended from all over Latin America and the guest of honour was the Brazilian Minister of Health, Dr Guerra. Other guests were Dr David Hawkins from St Stephen's Hospital and Dr Tom Lissauer from St Mary's Hospital in Paddington.

Professor Paul Griffiths, from the Royal Free Hospital in Hampstead, and Dr Brian Gazzard, from the Westminster Hospital, both gave accounts of the beneficial treatment of HIV patients using AZT. On listening to the accolades which were poured on AZT by the doctors, Dr Guerra renewed his country's commitment to fight the spread of AIDS and treat AIDS patients. In its in-house journal, Wellcome expressed its pleasure at the Brazilian government's commitment.

> Dr Guerra also reaffirmed publicly at the time, his intention to allocate US$130 million for the management of AIDS, *with a substantial part of that to be spent on the purchase of Retrovir (AZT)*. [11] (italics added)

On March 5th 1990, AZT was launched in Mexico. At a one-day AIDS symposium, Dr Anne Johnson from the University College and Middlesex Hospitals talked about treatment with AZT. On the platform with her was Dr Margaret Fischl, one of the prime American advocates of AZT and one of the authors of the Phase II trial report.

The Kuwaitis succumbed quickly to AZT in the summer of 1990. During a key-note speech at a Kuwait symposium, Dr Jonathan Mann, who had by then left his job as Director of the WHO Global Programme on AIDS, said:

> At least sixty different drugs were currently being tested but the only one to prove effective so far was Wellcome's Zidovudine. [12]

This statement naturally carried considerable weight, coming from the ex-Director of the WHO Global Programme on AIDS. It is, however, ambiguous: what did Dr Mann mean by 'proved effective'?

---

† These were usually either Abbott Laboratories or ICI.

By March 1988, Wellcome had patent applications pending in 40 countries. AZT had taken the world by storm; meeting next to no critical opposition, it had the scientific and pharmaceutical community rising for standing ovation after standing ovation. Science and the pharmaceutical industry had been called upon in a crisis and had risen to the occasion. Science could rid the world of AIDS.

In Britain, Wellcome was awarded two out of its five Queen's Awards for Technological Achievement, for AIDS-related work, one for AZT in 1990, the other for the HIV testing kits. In Spain, AZT was given the 'Best Drug of the Year' award in 1987, only a matter of months after it had been licensed. The French pharmaceutical industry was to wait a little longer, until 1989, before bestowing upon AZT its Pythonesque Golden Pill (Pilule d'Or).

Chapter Twenty Three

Wellcome, Part Three :
Marketing AZT,
The Domestic Market

The medical profession is a manifestation in one particular sector of the control over the structure of class power which the university-trained élites have acquired. Only doctors 'know' what constitutes sickness, who is sick, and what shall be done to the sick and to those whom they consider at a special risk. [1]

Wellcome was so successful in marketing AZT primarily because it has immense social, political and medical influence in British society. This influence extends from the top to the bottom of society.

Wellcome is represented in different ways within the House of Commons. One of the lobby groups which satellite the Commons itself is the Parliamentary Office of Science and Technology (POST), which is modelled on the American Congressional Office of Technological Assessment (OTA).†

Wellcome also has an influential input into the All Party Parliamentary Group on AIDS (APGOA) which was, from its inception in 1986, a more or less typical all-party parliamentary group which hosted meetings and discussions with various 'experts' involved in AIDS research. [2] In October 1988, just as Wellcome and the Medical Research Council were beginning the Concorde trials‡

---

† See Chapter Twenty One, The Pollution of Science.

‡ The Concorde trials were to test the effect of AZT on HIV antibody positive but asymptomatic patients. The trials were to determine whether or not the administration of AZT could lengthen the period of time between the diagnosis of HIV and the onset of ARC. For further information see this Chapter below.

the APGOA received sudden and quite substantial funding.

This funding came in part from the Wellcome Foundation,† which in 1988 gave around £10,000. The windfall enabled the group to set up offices and staff them with researchers. In November 1988, APGOA began regular publication of the *Parliamentary Aids Digest*, a forty or fifty page journal published four or five times a year. Over the years this journal has grown into a considerable compendium, which along with the two research workers employed by the Group, ensured the presentation of information about AIDS and its treatment to all interested Members of Parliament. The information which reached MPs has, however, been weighted towards anti-virals.

From the time that Wellcome began sponsoring the APGOA, the doctors who wrote for the *Digest* and those who attended the all-party meetings were, in the main, doctors involved in the Concorde trials or some other grant-receiving project of Wellcome. In the year 1990-1991, for example, items began to appear in the *Digest* about quacks and quack remedies for AIDS. Books, organisations or individuals who argued that HIV was not the sole cause of AIDS and those critical of AZT were either criticised or not referred to. The interests of the Campaign Against Health Fraud and its members were uncritically relayed to Members of Parliament.‡

From November 1988 onwards the meetings of the All Parliamentary Group on AIDS were dominated by Wellcome-orientated speakers, and especially by Dr Anthony Pinching, one of the major spokesmen for AZT and Senior Lecturer in the Department

---

† Other major contributors to the APGOA are the London International Group, whose subsidiary, the London Rubber Co., produces condoms, and Roche Ltd. In later years Wellcome-supported funding organisations were also to donate money; in 1990–1991 CRUSAID, itself subsidised by Wellcome, made a donation of £5,000.

‡ Jad Adams' book, *The HIV Myth*, which argued that HIV is not the sole cause of AIDS, was criticised, and articles appeared on Yves DeLatte and germanium (See Chapters 32 and 33). The Annual Report for 1990 contains an overview of 1989-1990 which makes clear the APGOA attitude. 'On Channel 4 a programme called 'Dispatches' disputed whether human immuno deficiency virus (HIV) really caused AIDS and argued that in any case it was not infectious. *In (both) these cases the group co-ordinated a response to try and repair the damage done by misinformation of this kind.*' (Italics added).

of Immunology at St Mary's Hospital Medical School.†

The Parliamentary AIDS Group has acted as a venue for all the voluntary sector groups and research doctors funded by Wellcome, or involved in Wellcome research. Over the years, Members of Parliament and concerned doctors have listened to Nick Partridge and Frankie Lynch from the Terrence Higgins Trust, Caroline Guinness from Positively Women, Nick Banton from Frontliners, as well as leading doctors working on Concorde, the AZT trial.

The Healing AIDS/ARC Research Project (HARP), at Bastyr College, Seattle, Washington, is one of the only projects in the world which has treated a significant number of HIV patients with naturopathic remedies. The protocol for the study specifically excluded anyone then taking AZT. The project's preliminary findings have been that these remedies have increased T4 cell count while the frequency and severity of ARC symptoms have decreased. [3] In 1991, a representative of the HARP project came to London to give a talk to APGOA. Despite protestations from practitioners of alternative medicine who attended, the meeting appeared to be filibustered by Dr Pinching. It seemed that the APGOA did not want information about the project to reach the group.

The domination of the APGOA by Wellcome is particularly sinister; as well as having influence amongst government ministers, Wellcome has gained influence over much of the information circulating about AIDS and HIV within the House of Commons.

Doctoring the Doctors

After Wellcome had managed to sell AZT to the governments of Europe, Africa and Latin America, its next strategic targets were the general practitioners. In Britain the general practitioner is the gate-keeper not just for all health services but also for specific drugs. It is the GP who often decides which drugs are used and which are not.

---

† One other doctor at St Mary's played an important part in the marketing of AZT. Professor Peter Sever of the Department of Clinical Pharmacology in the Hospital Medical School was the doctor most involved in organising the medical meetings and presenting the pharmaceutical and clinical data on AIDS for Wellcome. The Professor of Medicine at St Mary's from 1956-1987 was Professor Sir Stanley Peart, a Wellcome Trustee.

Up to the point of licensing, the production of AZT had, according to Wellcome, cost in the region of £80 million. If by 1989, no other AIDS drugs had been licensed, it was believed that in 1987, Wellcome would make profits of more than £200 million. [4] Projections for 1992, in the absence of other drugs, put the Wellcome profits from AZT at around £400 million. Wellcome needed marketing strategies which ensured that doctors did not suggest or prescribe other treatments.

In order to market AZT successfully, Wellcome had to ensure not only that everyone thought that it was the only life-preserving drug on the market but also that its initial distribution was in the hands of a few highly specialised doctors. Wellcome wanted general practitioners, who were consulted by HIV antibody positive patients, to channel those patients into the large teaching hospitals and the 'sexually transmitted diseases' clinics which were staffed by Wellcome-sympathetic doctors. It would seem that Wellcome wanted to stop general practitioners from either treating patients themselves or referring them to community-based alternative practitioners.

* * *

One of the controls that Wellcome had in this situation was its monopoly franchise on HIV testing kits, manufactured by Wellcome Diagnostics and sold to the National Health Service. In America, Robert Gallo, the scientist at the National Institutes of Health who claimed to have isolated and identified the HIV virus,[†] also owned the patent on testing kits. Such tests earned Gallo $100,000 a year in royalties. [5]

In August 1984, Wellcome was approached by Dr Robin Weiss, the Executive Director of the Institute of Cancer Research (ICR) – a postgraduate Institute and part of London University.[‡] The Institute receives much of its money from private sources and from the Medical Research Council. Weiss had offered Wellcome his ideas about

---

† Gallo's discovery was followed by the grandest scientific row of the post war years, when Luc Montagnier of the Pasteur Institute accused Gallo of stealing the discovery from him. The dispute was finally resolved in high level negotiations between President Ronald Reagan and French Premier Jacques Chirac.

‡ See Chapter 34, on the Bristol Cancer Help Centre.

diagnostic testing kits and had then gone into business with them to produce these kits. In 1985, it was estimated that the British market for diagnostic kits was worth between £3 million and £4 million, and a world-wide market worth £180 million.

Following the production of the first testing kits, Wellcome Diagnostics entered into a long-term research and development agreement with the ICR and MHMS and began working closely with them on a next generation of kits. The scientist who worked on this project with Robin Weiss was his colleague at the ICR, Angus Dalgleish. [6]

Wellcozyme HIV Monoclonal, the second generation AIDS testing kit, was launched by Wellcome in autumn 1987, at a Naples symposium on 'AIDS and associated cancers in Africa'.† The kits depended upon the production of monoclonal antibodies used to mark the virus. Coincidentally, work, grant-aided by the MRC, on the production of monoclonal antibodies was carried out in late 1987 by Vincent Marks, the head of the Biochemistry Department at Surrey University.‡

By the beginning of 1992, there were some 20 companies capable of producing cheap, individual HIV antibody testing kits, which could be used either at home or in a doctor's surgery. [7] Why were home testing kits opposed? Was it because of a genuine paternalistic concern for those who may test positive? Or could it have been that the drug companies feared that self-testing might lead to self-medication?

In March 1992, the Department of Health banned the public sale of home testing kits in Britain. From April of that year, it became a criminal offence either to sell or advertise HIV testing kits and related services directly to the public.

*   *   *

† The first generation AIDS testing kits produced by Wellcome received the Queen's Award for Technological Achievement in May 1987. The test made £3 million in its first year.

‡ See Chapter 28, Vincent Marks : Company Director. The Surrey University department which Professor Marks heads has received over half a million pounds from Wellcome since 1985. Professor Marks became a founder member of the Campaign Against Health Fraud.

Wellcome could also bring influence to bear on doctors through the doctors' professional association, the BMA. When the Wellcome Institute for the History of Medicine moved out of the Wellcome Building on Euston Road during refurbishment, it moved straight into the BMA building in Tavistock Square. Also situated inside the BMA building was the Wellcome-administered Association of Medical Research Charities (AMRC). Through AMRC, Wellcome directs and controls some forty research charities, ensuring that the company is first to know about important research developments in different fields. [8]

As well as this arrangement over accommodation, the BMA also publishes one of Wellcome's academic journals. Given that Wellcome is one of Britain's largest pharmaceutical companies, able to produce as many journals as it wants, there must be a reason for this relationship. A journal on medical history published by the British Medical Association is perhaps more prestigious than a journal on the history of medicine published by a drug company, or a Trust associated with a drug company.† It is not known whether Wellcome pays the BMA for this service.

How could the BMA help Wellcome sell AZT? In 1987, the BMA set up the British Medical Association Foundation for AIDS. The Foundation was registered as a charity, and took offices with two staff members inside BMA House. In the early months of March 1988, Wellcome gave a covenant, amounting to £36,000 annually for four years and totalling £144,000, to the Foundation. This meant that at the very centre of the BMA, Wellcome had control of the information flow on AIDS and its treatment.

One of the most impressive campaigns of the BMA Foundation for AIDS occurred in 1988, when Wellcome helped fund a £150,000 educational package for GPs about HIV and AIDS. The package contained three videos. It was expected that Wellcome representatives, together with Calmic‡ sales representatives, would be showing the

† Another minor but interesting relationship between the BMA and Wellcome is that of Dr Stephen Lock. Dr Lock, a full time medical journalist, was editor of the BMJ between 1974 and 1991. On his retirement in 1991, he took up a position as an associate research worker at the Wellcome Institute.

‡ A Wellcome Foundation subsidiary company which makes hygiene products.

videos and promoting the free package in all 11,000 surgeries in Britain. The press launch for the package was held at BMA House. [9]

The Chairman of the BMA Foundation for AIDS is Dr John Marks, who is also Chairman of the Council of the BMA. Dr John Marks is the brother of Vincent Marks, a keen member of the Campaign Against Health Fraud and prominent member of the Medical Research Council.

Another member of the small Trustees body of the BMA Foundation for AIDS is Dr Brian Gazzard, consultant physician at Westminster and St Stephen's Hospitals.[10] Dr Gazzard is one of the Concorde trials doctors. Before his work with AZT, he had been involved in research into HIV and AIDS funded by the Wellcome Trust at the London School of Hygiene and Tropical Medicine.

* * *

The London hospital doctors who dealt with AIDS patients were the ones who controlled all the major research projects and the patient base. Since the first production of AZT, they were the very hub of the wheel from which everything radiated. If Wellcome could not dominate this crucial area, patients would go spinning off and inevitably come into contact with doctors and treatments outside the authority of the NHS. Such patients could end up taking treatments other than AZT.

The major London hospitals had to become centres of AZT use, rather than centres of broad or independent research into HIV or AIDS. Patients turning up for treatment would be automatically drafted into the trial and treated with AZT. For anyone diagnosed HIV antibody positive, the proposition would undoubtedly be appealing. For three years or so, patients would get the best free health care as well as a continual supply of a product which apparently had already proved itself to be destructive of the HIV virus.

Even in the 'worst case' scenario, where a patient was one of the sample to receive a placebo, there was still the three years free health care. For the doctors and Wellcome such a trial would ensure a large patient base which would become used to treatment by AZT, a drug which they or the National Health Service would have to pay for when the trial ended. A strictly controlled AZT trial would also ensure that a large group of patients did not experiment with other treatments.

In August 1988, the Medical Research Council published the detailed protocols for the Concorde trials. These trials were an Anglo-French venture, which set out to measure the effectiveness of AZT in delaying the onset of ARC and AIDS in subjects diagnosed as asymptomatic HIV antibody positive. The American Phase II trials had used AZT on subjects who had already developed ARC or AIDS. It had, however, always been Wellcome's view that as AZT could target the virus in the early stages of its replication; the earliest intervention possible after the discovery of HIV, when fewest cells were affected, was the most effective. Wellcome argued that in the initial stages of infection, when the subject's immune system was still strong and the virus thinly spread, AZT could be most effective in combating the virus. It also argued that a very high dose of AZT, 1,000 milligrams a day, should be given to all patients for maximum effect.

From the time Wellcome obtained its first licence which enabled it to supply AZT to those who had ARC or AIDS, it campaigned to obtain the licence which would allow it to supply to those who had no symptoms of AIDS but who had been diagnosed as HIV antibody positive. The Wellcome position was based upon the life history of the classic virus, which first infects the subject then proliferates within the body. From the first discovery of the HIV virus, there were those who did not believe that this virus was the single cause of AIDS, or that the process of becoming infected, or the duration of the development of the illness, were wholly attributable to the virus. Such people believed that co-factors probably played some part in all three circumstances. There were, as well, those who were adamant that the introduction of chemicals to the body, especially ones which actually destroyed the same cells that the infection itself was killing, was just such a co-factor.

The most cynical commentators suggested that Wellcome's campaign to extend the prescription of AZT to non-symptomatic subjects was not solely based upon scientific reasoning: it was also a good marketing ploy. Concorde was not the only AZT trial: in the USA, despite the drug already having been given a licence, by September 1987 Wellcome was planning studies involving over 6,000 patients, independent of the 5,000 patients already being prescribed the drug. [11]

With Concorde, the Wellcome Foundation achieved clinical

respectability for the argument that AZT should be prescribed at the earliest possible time. For a period of three years, one half of the two thousand trial population – one thousand in Britain and one thousand in France – would be given 250mg of AZT four times a day, while the other half would be given a similar-looking placebo.

The agreement which set up Concorde was between Wellcome, the Medical Research Council and the Department of Health. In order to give drug trials a patina of independence, they are usually agreed between a university or hospital and the company producing the drug. Because Concorde was such a large trial, using considerable Health Department facilities, and because the whole issue of trialing a drug for what appeared to be a terminal illness was an issue designed to create moral panic, the Department of Health was, from the beginning, deeply involved.

The Medical Research Council, like the other 'science' Research Councils, is solely funded by government. There is inevitably, therefore, a high degree of government interest in its programmes and strategies. Because of this interest, and the considerable involvement of the Department of Health, it would be accurate to say that the agreement for the Concorde trial was in fact a partnership between Wellcome and the British government. The matter of how the Concorde trial was run, its efficacy, its scientific conduct and its ultimate plausibility, became, from August 1988, the date that the detailed protocol [12] was finished, an affair of State. The British government was deeply committed to Wellcome and to AZT.

The Concorde trials which began in October 1988 seem odd by any standard. They began only a year after Wellcome had been granted a product licence, even though there had been insufficient research into the effect of AZT on those who had ARC or AIDS and regardless of the fact that no one knew what the possible long-term effects of taking the drug might be.

The Concorde trials commandeered the facilities of six of London's principal hospitals. They also threw up a cohort of London doctors who were to become the major figures in the treatment of AIDS, using AZT and other Wellcome products. From the beginning of the Concorde trials in October 1988, large numbers of HIV antibody positive patients reporting to their general practitioners in the London area and then attending hospital were approached by the cohort hospitals where, in the main, they were drafted into the Concorde trials or one of the many other research projects which used AZT.

In a truly ethical situation, no one supported by Wellcome or receiving money from them, would have been involved in the administration of the trials. Usually, pharmaceutical companies provide the drug for trial and then pay the hospital or the academic institution per head for the treatment of trial subjects. In Concorde, the MRC was paying this money on behalf of the pharmaceutical company; in other words, public money was being used to test a drug manufactured by a private company, using NHS facilities and staff.

Because this trial involved HIV and AIDS patients, there was another major ethical consideration involved. Any hospital doctor who is contracted to trial a drug by a pharmaceutical company is in danger of mixing two sets of patients. A doctor's primary ethical concern should be the health of the patient, a secondary concern might be testing a drug. Few doctors, considering the patient's health, would advise only one course of treatment, especially if that treatment is being experimentally tested.

This is, however, what came to occur with the treatment of over a thousand HIV and AIDS patients between 1988 and 1992. Many patients were not given information about the possible range of treatments, but were taken straight into the Concorde trials.

Detailed information was important, considering that by 1989 there had been reports of serious adverse effects upon patients; these included muscle wasting, serious anaemia, loss of white blood cells and impotence. Consequently, the American FDA decided that 1,000 mg a day, which up until then had been the normal dosage, was, in fact, an over prescription. They dropped the ceiling on its clinical prescription by a half, to 500 mg a day. In Britain and France, however, the clinicians involved in Concorde continued to give trial subjects 1,000 mg a day up to the completion of the trial in 1992. They argued that as the study was blinded, it would have been impossible to reduce the dosage without destroying the trial. Was it ethically correct to continue with the trial, once it had been suggested that at 1,000 mg a day there might possibly be a chance of serious adverse effects?

The problems and contradictions which surrounded the Concorde trial made it imperative for Wellcome, and for that matter the MRC, that neither the ethics nor the administration of the trial were publicly questioned. The Concorde trial was not, however, just another small trial where the drug company could easily control the clinicians.

The problem of controlling a loose-knit community of HIV antibody positive young men and women, who might easily turn to self-medication, other pharmaceutical company trials or alternative medicine, as they had done in United States, had to some extent been solved by the introduction of Concorde.† The most probable policy of any drug company would now be to ensure the loyalty of the doctors administering the trial and shelter them from scrutiny or criticism.

The first stage in Wellcome's strategy was to ensure control of published information following the trial. Although ending up with a weaker settlement than it had set out to achieve, Wellcome did manage to negotiate a clause in the protocols which gave it complete control over any final report for uses other than publication. Such a report would only have to be 'reviewed' by the INSERM/MRC committee. Any final publication had to be agreed between all parties. Ostensibly these two items gave Wellcome control over all draft reports and final reports for all official uses other than publication. [14]‡ As publication was the very last stage in the process and might never actually happen, all report writing was in effect in the hands of Wellcome, despite the massive financial input into the trials by the British government.

The second stage of Wellcome's strategy, after control of the Concorde report, was to ensure majority representation on the committees which administered the trial. This matter was not of

---

† Patients entering the trial had to have abstained from the use of any other immuno-enhancing treatments for up to three months prior to being accepted on the trial. [13] It was also Wellcome's policy to warn patients, in or out of the trial, that the use of any other medication in conjunction with AZT could have hazardous repercussions.

‡ 8.1 ... The final publication will require the approval of the MRC/INSERM Committee. No other publications, either in writing or verbally, will be made before the definitive manuscript has been agreed and accepted for publication ... 8.2. The Wellcome Research Laboratories will prepare a detailed report of the study *for internal use and for submission to regulatory authorities*. The draft report will be submitted to the MRC/INSERM Coordinating Committee for *review*. [15] (italics added)

course discussed in the protocols for the trial.

The Medical Research Council

Since its foundation, the MRC has been close to Wellcome. The alliance has inevitably been consolidated over recent years because the Wellcome Trust has become responsible for administering larger and larger amounts of philanthropic cash, in the same areas funded by the MRC. With government cuts in the eighties, Wellcome frequently protested as it saw itself increasingly stepping into the breach to support medical research. The gradual dominance of private finance in research was, however, a political as well as an economic trend and had the advantage that private interests were able to have access to research and results. By the late eighties, medical research in Britain was controlled by a partnership between Wellcome and the government. In such circumstances it was not difficult to ensure Wellcome interests on the MRC committees overseeing the Concorde trials.

The Medical Research Council Committee on AIDS is made up of a Chairman and eight members, the majority of whom manifest various links with industry, the ideological Right, and organisations within the Wellcome Foundation's sphere of influence. The Chairman of the Committee is Lord Jellicoe, who was at the time of Concorde also the Chairman of the MRC. He joined the MRC in 1982 and was its Chairman from 1986 until 1990. He was leader of the House of Lords from 1970-1973 and a member of the All-Party Group for the Chemical Industry. He is also Vice Chairman of the All Parliamentary Group on AIDS.

Lord Jellicoe is involved in all those things in which someone dedicated to medical research and health would be expected to be involved. From 1978 to 1983, he was Chairman of the of the Board of Directors of Tate and Lyle, Britain's biggest sugar company. He is now Chairman of Booker Tate, the confectionery conglomerate. [16]†

† The links between the MRC and the sugar industry occasionally surface as major and quite farcical rows. In March 1992, the MRC accepted money from the British Sugar Bureau to organise a conference and then draw up a research stategy against tooth decay. One doctor suggested it was 'like putting Dracula in charge of a blood bank'. See also 'MRC's association with Sugar Bureau', in the *BMJ*, 11 April 1992.

Lord Jellicoe's other link with food processing and pharmaceuticals was through his place, from 1985-1990, on the board of the Davy Corporation, a company which makes plant for the pharmaceutical and food processing industries. Lord Jellicoe is also involved with Rockefeller interests especially through his directorship of Morgan Crucible.

Sir Donald Acheson was on the General Medical Council and the MRC from 1984 to 1991, during the period that he was the Chief Medical Officer for the Department of Health. When he left the Department of Health, he took up a post at the London School of Hygiene and Tropical Medicine.

Sir Austin Bide was the Chief Executive at the drug company Glaxo from 1973 to 1980, he then became first the Chairman of the Board and in 1985 their Honorary President. He was a member of the MRC from 1986 to 1990, and a member of its AIDS committee from 1987 to 1990. Sir Austin has been Chairman of the right-wing Adam Smith Institute since 1986 and was a member of the council of the CBI for ten years from 1974 to 1985. He too has an interest in confectionery, having been a director of J Lyons & Co in the late seventies.

An interest in the promotion of processed food is the one thing which stands out in the career of Sir David Crouch, Conservative MP for Canterbury from 1966 to 1987. He too was a member of the Society of the Chemical Industry, and chairman of the All-Party Group for the Chemical Industry for almost twenty years, from 1970 to 1987. He was a director of the pharmaceutical company Pfizer Ltd, for over twenty years, from 1966 to 1987.†

Apart from his involvement with the pharmaceutical and chemical industries, Sir David's real interests are in public relations. Since 1964, he has been chairman of David Crouch & Co, marketing and PR consultants, whose clients include Beechams. He has also been a director of two other leading PR firms, in the field of processed food marketing: Burson Marsteller Ltd, of which he was a director from 1972 to 1983, handle many of the large processed food and

† When Wellcome began making AZT, in the mid-eighties, it had to use a substance synthesised by, and only available from, Pfizer, with whom it entered into an agreement.

pharmaceutical accounts, including an account for Wellcome.

In 1987, Sir David became a director of Kingsway PR, a company which again handled accounts for chemical and food companies, as well as the account of one of Wellcome's leading pharmaceutical products. In 1989, Kingsway Public Relations was taken over by Rowland Worldwide, a subsidiary of Saatchi and Saatchi. At that time, Sir David Crouch resigned from Kingsway Public Relations and became a director of Kingsway Rowland, [17] the company which has handled aspects of the PR account of AZT for Wellcome.

In January 1990, Sir David joined Westminster Communications Group (WCG), a public relations company. WCG processes, reports on and presents information from the Houses of Parliament. It also acts as a lobby organisation on behalf of a variety of clients, presenting views and ideas to individual Members of Parliament and parties. WCG has a particular interest in scientific matters, and two members of its Board, Chairman Keith Speed MP and director Sir Marcus Fox MP, are both members of the Parliamentary and Scientific Committee.

Professor C. N. Hales, another member of the MRC Committee on AIDS, now the Chairman of the Systems Board, is a specialist in diabetes in the Clinical Biochemistry Department of Addenbrookes Hospital, Cambridge. Much of his work has been funded by pharmaceutical companies or their fronts, including the Wellcome Trust, Eli Lilly Research Laboratories, Serono Labs UK Ltd and Bayer Diagnostics. [18]

Dr Joseph W.G. Smith has been the Director of the Public Health Laboratory Service since 1985 and a member of the MRC since 1989. He has chaired the Committee on Vaccination and Immunology Procedures since 1976. From 1960 to 1965 he was a Senior Lecturer at the London School of Hygiene and Tropical Medicine, and then in 1969 went to work directly for Wellcome, becoming Head of Bacteriology at their research laboratories. Following his work with Wellcome he went to the Radcliffe Infirmary Oxford, where he was a consultant microbiologist.

One of the most important MRC AIDS sub-committees is the AIDS Therapeutic Trials Committee, which oversees trials for AIDS. At least five members of this committee have received funding through the Wellcome Trust.

The Chairman of the Committee, since 1987, has been Professor
D. A. Warrell. He is Professor of Tropical Medicine and Infectious
Diseases at the Oxford University Nuffield Department of Clinical
Medicine in the Radcliffe Infirmary. From 1979 to 1986 he was the
Director of the Wellcome Trust Tropical Research Unit. [19] Much of
his work for Wellcome has been done in conjunction with the
Wellcome malaria programme in Kenya. [20] The majority of his work
at Oxford – mainly into malaria, but also into AIDS and rabies – has
been funded by the Wellcome Trust. Other work into malaria has
been funded by the WHO, and the Rockefeller Foundation. [21]

Dr Jeffrey Kenneth K. Aronson, working at the MRC Clinical
Pharmacology Unit in Oxford, was awarded a Wellcome Senior
Lectureship in 1986. [22] This made him Wellcome Lecturer at the
MRC Unit and University Department of Clinical Pharmacology at
the Radcliffe Infirmary, Oxford. Much of his research work has been
funded by the Wellcome Trust. [23]

Dr G. E. Griffin, who is head of the Communicable Diseases Unit
in St George's Hospital Medical School, is on two Wellcome Trust
Advisory Panels, in the areas of infection and immunity and tropical
medicines. [24] The panels allocate research funding. He is also a
Wellcome Trust Senior Lecturer. In the eighties a number of his
research projects were funded by the Wellcome Trust.

Dr T. E. A. Peto is a consultant physician in infectious diseases in
the Oxford University Nuffield Department of Medicine, at the
Radcliffe Infirmary. He is a former MRC and Wellcome Fellow of the
Department. From 1987 to 1990 he carried out research into malaria
that was funded by the Wellcome Trust.

As well as being a member of the Therapeutic Trials Committee,
Dr I. V. D. Weller is also the Chairman of the UK Working Party for
the Concorde 1 trial. At the Middlesex Hospital, where he is an
Honorary Consultant, he has administered the key cohort in the
Concorde trial as well as acting as physician to many of its subjects, in
the Department of Genito-urinary Medicine. While Weller was sitting
on the MRC AIDS committees and doing his work on the Concorde
trials, he was a Wellcome Trust Senior Lecturer in Infectious Diseases,
funded for this post throughout 1988 and 1989 by the Wellcome
Trust.

Dr A. J. Pinching from the Department of Immunology at St

Mary's Hospital Medical School, a hands-on AIDS doctor working on the Concorde trial, is also on this committee. It is not known whether Dr Pinching, despite being a vociferous supporter of AZT and defender of Concorde, is linked in any way to Wellcome. One of the Wellcome Trustees, Professor Stanley Peart, was until 1987, however, the Director of the Medical Unit at St Mary's Hospital Medical School, a senior academic position to that of Dr Pinching.

There are three committees which deal only with aspects of Concorde: the MRC/INSERM Joint Co-ordinating Committee for the Concorde 1 Trial, the MRC/INSERM Joint Data and Safety Monitoring Committee for the Concorde 1 Trial and the UK Working Party for the Concorde 1 Trial. Of these three committees, the first and the third are the most important. The first has twelve members, three of whom have their salaries paid by Wellcome. Two work for Wellcome Laboratories and the connections of the third, Dr I.V.D. Weller, are mentioned above.

The eight-member scientific committee overseeing the Concorde trials was made up of four French and four British scientists. One of the most prominent members of the British team was Professor Robin Weiss. While the Director of the Institute of Cancer Research, Weiss himself worked with Wellcome when he developed their HIV testing kit.†

The Wellcome influence on the MRC AIDS Committees is nothing short of spectacular and is reflective of a peculiar characteristic of the British liberal intelligentsia. How was one of the country's biggest drug companies able to camouflage its market intentions with such apparent academic involvement?

† See this Chapter above on testing kits and Chapter 28, on Professor Vincent Marks.

Chapter Twenty Four

Caroline Richmond, Part One:
The Chemical Agent

Most of the most effective promotion of food is done 'below the line',
by ways and means not meant to be obvious as advertising. [1]

Caroline Richmond is a journalist and a populist campaigner on
behalf of industrial science and medical research. After gaining a
degree in Zoology and working at University College Hospital in
London, she did a number of laboratory jobs including work at the
Medical Research Council Clinical Research Centre, in north
London. In the nineteen seventies she became a Chief Technician
at the Department of Therapeutics at the City Hospital in
Nottingham. The Department was set up in the early seventies to
carry out clinical and biochemical research on the effects of drugs. It
encouraged industrial connections and while Richmond was there
worked closely with both Boots and Fisons.†

Richmond's life changed direction in the mid-seventies when she
trained as a journalist with IPC then worked as a casual sub-editor for
the National Magazine Company. In April 1978 she went to the
United Trades Press (UTP) then in Bowling Green Lane. At this time
UTP was an independent company producing a large number of trade
magazines, all subsidised by advertising and sent free to companies.‡
Each magazine had a staff of three or four.

---

† By pure coincidence, the leading scientist at the Wellcome Foundation,
Dr Trevor Jones, also used to work in Nottingham, where he was a chemist for Boots
Pharmaceuticals.

‡ On one open-plan floor of the building in Bowling Green Lane, UTP produced
six or seven magazines with titles like: *Soap, Perfumery and Cosmetics, Dairy Industries, Food
Manufacturer, Flavouring and Ingredients*.

Caroline Richmond began work with *Medical Laboratory World*, first published in September 1977. The magazine was, and still is, run entirely on money from laboratory equipment and pharmaceutical industry advertising. By April 1978 she had become assistant editor.

The articles dispersed between the pages of adverts in MLW are jobbing articles written by hacks. From the beginning of her journalistic career, Richmond aimed slightly higher than her fellow contributors. In October 1978, she became the editor of the magazine and in December following a conference in Czechoslovakia, she wrote a double-page article, with accompanying pictures and diagrams, about calves given artificial hearts. By this time, she appears to have been committed to an orthodox medical view of the world which involved the acceptance of pharmaceuticals, placebo trials and animal experimentation.

In her article of December 1978, she is apparently in awe of the internationally renowned scientists. At the same time she steers well clear of any ethical issue implicit in animal experientation:

> Professor Vasken, performed his 42nd experimental transplant on a twelve week old calf, Filip ... When I saw him [Richmond uses this style for Filip the calf, which has been given an artificial heart] two days after the operation, Filip looked a great deal better than might have been expected. Crouched in his stall, he was drinking water out of a bowl. The compressed air supply entered his body through a small opening at the side of his heart and was secured by a harness. Apart from a urinary catheter, the only other pipe was a small oxygen tube to the right nostril ... Professor Kolff has kept calves alive for up to six months in Russia and the USA. [2]

In August 1979, Richmond resigned from MLW. The next day she tried to rescind the resignation, arguing that she was suffering from pre-menstrual tension. She failed to get her job back.

At this time, Richmond's main social connections were with those people who straddled the worlds of science, industry and journalism. In February 1979, she became a member of the Institute of Biology and began to make contacts with people in the British Association for the Advancement of Science and the British Association of Science Writers. She was also a supporter of the Research Defence Association, which argues in favour of animal experimentation.

From its early years Caroline Richmond was a member of the Medical Journalists Association. In her capacity as a medical journalist, she was able to use the many contacts she had made in the chemical and pharmaceutical industries and she argued the case of their professional organisations ably.

By 1984, Caroline Richmond was having short articles accepted by the *New Scientist*, which up until 1979 had been edited by one of her contacts, and member of CSICP, Bernard Dixon. The *New Scientist*, although not as aggressive as *Science*, the journal of the American Association for the Advancement of Science, is the main British journal besides *Nature* which defends establishment science against all comers. Her articles in the *New Scientist* were at that time often unsolicited letters of a humourous nature.† At the same time, she had begun to get short pieces in the British Medical Journal.

In 1985, Richmond registered for an MPhil in the Department of History and Philosophy of Science at London University, her subject being, 'The development of physiology teaching and research in London 1860-1920'. Her course was situated in the little known Unit of History of Medicine at University College.

London University is different from many traditional older universities in one respect. Since the beginning of the twentieth century, and increasingly after the First World War, the University has been mainly subsidised by two private industrial interests, first the Rockefeller Foundation and then the Wellcome Foundation and Trust. The postgraduate medical colleges of London University are presently and have historically been funded almost entirely by pharmaceutical companies and profit-making research done for such companies.

The Unit of History of Medicine (UHM) at London University is situated in the Department of Anatomy and Developmental Biology at University College, a Department which was primarily patronised by Rockefeller money in the years after the First World War. In 1988 it had only nine research students doing postgraduate courses, and 16

† During her time with Women in Media in the seventies, Richmond was allotted the task of monitoring the media for the use of sexist language, a job which she apparently relished and one which resulted in many slighting letters to the *New Scientist* and other journals.

course students who were taught and super

One reason for the lack of publicity abc
could be the fact that the Unit is not a Un
proper sense of the term, but an Acader
Institute. 'The fifth Academic Unit, at Ur
effectively coterminous with the Acader
Institute.'[3] It has only a 'skeleton' secretariat within the ~~~
while the academic staff of the Unit are employed directly by the
Wellcome Institute and in the year 1987–1988, six of the nine postgraduate students were either wholly paid for or grant-aided by
Wellcome. Richmond herself was grant-aided by Wellcome from 1986
to 1988.

The Wellcome involvement with London University, like the
Rockefeller involvement before it, is enormous. In the 1987–1988
academic year, Wellcome was the largest financial benefactor to
University College, giving £126,885 to the History of Medicine Unit
alone. During 1988, Wellcome set up a new course in conjunction
with London University: this was within the London Centre for the
History of Science, Technology and Medicine. For the first time, there
was co-operative organisation between Wellcome and London
University and the Middlesex Hospital, resulting in a recognised
medical MSc.

After she began to work in the Unit of the History of Medicine,
Caroline Richmond's journalism took off. Her articles, both trivial and
serious, usually supported industrial science, pharmaceuticals or the
chemical industry. They now began to appear in journals and
magazines. She was fêted by Wellcome with an office and a position as
a research officer at the Institute while she studied for her
postgraduate qualifications, a situation which did not apply to all
bursary students. The Wellcome Foundation and Trust opened the
doors to important social and professional contacts.

On December 12th 1985, a few months after beginning her MPhil,
Richmond attended a press conference at the House of Commons
held by the newly-formed Food Additives Campaign Team, (FACT).
FACT was subsidised by the Greater London Council and was an
attempt to provide a public service in relation to health and nutrition.

The FACT team consisted of Felicity Lawrence, Geoffrey Cannon
and his partner Caroline Walker, Melanie Miller and Dr Peter

d. The press conference was called to launch their publication
es – *Your Complete Survival Guide*.[4] As well as support and affiliation
n a large number of reputable organisations, the organisation had
ross party support in the Commons.

FACT considered its principal opposition came from the Ministry of Agriculture Fisheries and Food (MAFF), which had frequently used threats of the Official Secrets Act to stifle debate about the substances added to foods. Given the weight of 'reasonable opinion' against many food additives, it came as a shock to members of the Food Additives Campaign Team to read Caroline Richmond's report of their press conference, which was not only slighting in its tone – 'The press conference was great fun'[5] – but dismissive of both FACT and any adverse effect of food additives. She had, she said later, written the piece after being assured by MAFF 'that food additives are probably harmless, have been screened, and are continually being monitored by government scientists world wide'. The apparent naivety of this statement is astonishing.

From the time of the FACT conference, this superficial approach to health risk and the chemical industry became the hall-mark of Caroline Richmond's writing. Her piece in the *New Scientist* was, it could be said, against the grain of accepted opinion. It was almost a positive defence of additives. In March of 1986, she followed up her article in the *New Scientist* with a piece in the *British Medical Journal*. Throughout both these articles there appear a number of threads.

A summary of her arguments in the mid-eighties provides an understanding of her developing attitudes: hyperactive children and others who complain of being affected by chemicals, the arguments go, rarely have any kind of chemical-related condition. Children who are hyperactive sometimes have serious psychiatric disturbances. Parents of hyperactive children are often to blame for their children's condition because they allow them too much time in push-chairs and in front of the television. Self-help groups, organised by parents and concerned individuals, only make things worse, doctors and other professionals at state agencies like MAFF know best and parents should accept their views. The inquiring press is also to blame, because journalists often exploit the vulnerability of depressed people by whipping up scares about such things as allergies. Fringe concern, outside the main establishment opinion, about such things as additives usually comes from unreasonable people like 'health freaks'.

Richmond's article on additives stirred up considerable controversy amongst those who were campaigning against their use. One of those who wrote to the *New Scientist*, and later wished that he had written somewhere else, was the food and nutrition expert and member of FACT, Geoffrey Cannon. Cannon at that time was married to Caroline Walker, also a food expert, who died tragically in 1988. Cannon's debate with Richmond over additives provoked Richmond to round on Cannon at a Royal Society of Health conference in early 1986. Richmond drew attention to a recent newspaper picture of Caroline Walker, who was at the time very ill, suggesting that she was a poor advertisement for Cannon's ideas about nutrition and food.

Cannon fought this personal attack by writing a letter of complaint to Dr Arnold Bender, the Regius Professor of Nutrition at London University and the person who had asked Richmond to speak from the platform at the conference. In March 1986, Richmond was given space in the *BMJ* to have the last word and explain just how irrational people were who disagreed with the use of additives. [6]

During 1986 and 1987, when Richmond was not writing for the *New Scientist*, or the *BMJ*, she wrote for women's magazines, especially the National Magazine Company titles, *Company, Cosmopolitan* and *Harpers*, all magazines of the Hearst Corporation stable which was taken over by Rockefeller interests in the 1970s. She also wrote for the pharmaceutical subsidised trade medical papers such as *Doctor, General Practitioner,* and *Pulse.*

In December 1987, the *BMJ* again gave Richmond space to attack those who believed in alternative treatments and diagnostic techniques not accepted by orthodox medicine. In the issue of December 19, she was given over a page to describe a CSICOP style hoax which she played on a woman campaigning on behalf of allergy sufferers. [7]

When Mrs Amelia Hill of Action Against Allergy received the manifesto of a new allergy campaigning organisation, the Dye Related Allergies Bureau (DRAB), she advertised the organisation in her quarterly bulletin. A small number of allergy sufferers from different parts of the world wrote to DRAB asking for more information. These people did not receive a reply; in fact the address given to Hill and reproduced in her newsletter was the home address of Jane and Nicholas Maxwell, personal friends of Caroline Richmond.

As Richmond explained in a rather childish article in a later issue of the *BMJ*, it had all been a set-up to show how silly were those who thought that industrial or chemical processes caused allergies. 'I wrote the manifesto for the Dye Related Allergy Bureau (DRAB) as a spoof on the literature put out by those who wish to protect us from food additives, fluoridation in drinking water and the like.'[8]

FOUR COMPANY ARTICLES FOR *COMPANY*

FOOD FOR SPORT: This is one of Richmond's first 'health-fraud' articles in which she suggests that many of the health food store products, made by vitamin companies – vitamins C, E, B15 which claim to improve performance – fail to do so. The article is based on the findings of a Swedish Sports Council Committee. She claims that research carried out by vitamin producers was found to be unorthodox: 'The research didn't use placebos or double-blind techniques (where neither those handing out the products nor the people taking them know what they are)'.[9]

ANIMAL PASSIONS: In this article, a full page under the heading 'Free speech: our column for controversy', Richmond argues that animal experimentation is necessary and not 'wrong'. Leaning on her ten years medical research, she discusses the testing of drugs. 'With medicines, too, new products aren't tested if they are merely new formulations of products that have already been checked. But all medicines are required by law (the Medicines Act 1968) to be safe, effective and of high quality ... A potential new drug is based on research by physiologists who study how that particular disease makes the body malfunction and by chemists who design and then manufacture a molecule that should be effective against it. Next, it is tested on cells in a test tube – a technique developed to reduce the number of animals used. If it doesn't harm the cells, it is tested on rats and mice to see if it works, to check that the effective dose is not dangerous, and to see that it doesn't cause cancer, make genes mutate, or damage the unborn foetus'. The argument about science, vivisection and animal testing, is an argument which runs as a thread throughout the conflicts in which Richmond and later HealthWatch have been involved.[10]

HEALTHY THOUGHTS: Reviews a study by Dr Barrie Cassileth at the Pennsylvania Cancer Center which found that patients' attitudes had no effect on their illness. 'US physician Dr Marcia Angell thinks that we should take this message to heart, and discard the idea that people succumb to illness because they lack the fighting spirit or subconsciously wish to die.' Again, this is one of the central themes of the 'health-fraud' debate, especially in the field of cancer treatment. [11]

CAFFEINE CONFUSION: This article is simply an advertisement for the American chemical industry. You might have heard that de-caffeinated coffee contains residuals of methylene chloride and this can give you liver cancer, but don't worry, Caroline Richmond has found that: 'The US Food and Drug Administration gave hundreds of long-suffering mice the methylene chloride, the equivalent of 70-80 cups a day and they didn't get cancer'. Anyway, we are assured: 'In fact, coffee, with or without caffeine, is safe in moderation and two or three cups a day is fine'. [12] †

---

† Vincent Marks, whose health-fraud activities are discussed in Chapter Twenty Eight, is well ahead of Caroline Richmond in his assessment of a safe Recommended Daily Allowance for coffee. He suggests six or seven cups a day. [13]

Chapter Twenty Five

Caroline Richmond, Part Two: The Richmond Way

Adherence to a fixed idea is a barrier to perception and to learning and thus to knowledge. [1]

In articles written by Caroline Richmond prior to the setting up of the CAHF, she names a number of the individuals whom the organisation was to target in 1989. In 1987 she promoted the joint British Nutrition Foundation and Royal College of Physicians report on food intolerance. In *GP* in October of that year, she refers to the report as an 'authoritative document'; she takes the opportunity of the launch of the food-industry-compiled allergy database, recommended by the report, to attack those who, she says, mistakenly believe they have food allergies. The article is one of many which ridicule health food while arguing that modern processed foods do no damage.

> However, many adults who read bizarre books bought in health-food stores and elsewhere have often been persuaded that everyday annoyances such as bad memory, headaches and irascibility are caused by foods. They often stop eating certain foods and do not realise that any perceived improvement is almost certainly a placebo effect. [2]

For her 'expert' opinions in the article, Caroline Richmond draws on a variety of people who were, a year and a half later, to form the backbone of the Campaign Against Health Fraud. One of these is Dr David Pearson who pursues his often recorded view that most people who think that they are suffering from food allergy actually have a psychological problem: 'Most people who present themselves to allergy clinics believing they are suffering from food allergy are wrong.' [3]

Professor Maurice Lessof, the man who chaired the joint BNF/RCP committee, and whose research has often been subsidised by food and chemical companies, provides Richmond with a quote which turns clinical experience and good sense on its head: 'more problems are now caused by the improper use of diets than by food allergy'. [4]

Dr Tim David enlarges upon Richmond's argument that parents and not chemicals are mainly to blame.

> The relationship between azo dyes and so called 'hyper-activity' is almost certainly a myth, nurtured by health food magazines and newspaper articles. Manchester paediatric consultant Dr Tim David says that most parent-diagnosed 'hyperactive' children are not; they are simply more energetic than their parents would like. [5]

As in much of the thinking of the Campaign generally, and Caroline Richmond particularly, emphasis is placed upon the professional opinion and taken away from the patient, or in this case the parent. Inevitably, because such views grow from a desire to protect professional skills and product markets, they are paternalistic, mystifying and often undermine any control which lay people could have over their own bodies.

Summing up her arguments, Richmond suggests that a vicious circle is created by 'fringe practitioners using absurd tests', over-diagnosing and convincing people that they have illusory allergies. In turn these badly misled patients 'raise NHS bills even further by presenting themselves as allergy patients'.

Even before such arguments had been enshrined in ideology by the Campaign Against Health Fraud, they appeared disreputable and bizarre. In this article, Richmond's argument seems to be suggesting that the NHS has difficulty dealing with allergy patients who should not really present themselves. While this is actually a true reflection of the condition of many NHS doctors, such a response would seem to leave sufferers little alternative but to go to 'fringe' practitioners. As for raising NHS bills even further, it is well known that the greatest part of the NHS bill is paid at monopoly prices to drug companies and the manufacturers of 'high-tech' medical equipment. The charitable appeals are for brain scanners and dialysis machines, not leaflets on exclusion diets.

In February 1988, Richmond wrote again in *GP* about claims made on behalf of vitamin pills and IQ. [6] This preoccupation on the part of both orthodox medical practitioners and orthodox nutritionists was later to lead to a campaign against Larkhall Natural Health. In January 1988, BBC television screened a 'QED' programme [7] about the effect which vitamins had upon the ability of children to work, concentrate and solve non-verbal problems. [8] With little pretence to rationality or science, Caroline Richmond reviewed the programme in an article which was headed: 'Caroline Richmond exposes a study trying to show that vitamins raise the non-verbal intelligence of children'.

> The whole experiment was conceived by an elderly Welsh schoolmaster whose commitment to dietary supplements could be inferred when we saw him breakfasting on 13 vitamin pills, chased down with lecithin and kelp. [9]

A mix of prejudice and campaigning zeal shows through the article and we find the first reference to another organisation which was to be targetted in 1989, the Institute for Optimum Nutrition, run by Patrick Holford.

> The analyses were done by an organisation called the Institute for Optimum Nutrition. Neither the British Nutrition Foundation nor the Dunn Nutrition Laboratory at Cambridge could tell me who they were. [10]

For expert opinion, Richmond introduces us to another of her friends who was to play a prominent role in the Campaign Against Health Fraud, 'old school' nutritionist Professor Arnold Bender.

> Professor Arnold Bender, Emeritus Professor of Nutrition at King's College London, reckons the tablets used in the survey did not contain the RDAs [Recommended Daily Allowance] of many nutrients. [11]

The article is accompanied by classic 'vitamin overdose' scare stories which became common in the CAHF campaigns after 1989. The vitamin overdose story is a technique developed and expounded for years in America. Such apocryphal stories are rarely supported by references. Readers should bear in mind what the definition of an overdose is: simply an excessive dose.

> Arnold Bender warns: Although cases have been reported of
> overdose from every vitamin, it is A and D that are the most
> common. They, and iodine, start to become toxic at around ten
> times the recommended daily allowance. People are likely to
> think, 'if one tablet is good for my child's IQ, 10 tablets are
> better' – it is human nature ... The 600 cases of vitamin A
> poisoning in the literature are the tip of the iceberg, no one
> knows how many cases there really are. [12]

As well as targetting health-foods, vitamins and alternative therapists,
by 1988 Caroline Richmond was also propagandising for industry and
for MAFF. A June 1988 issue of *GP* is intended to ease public fears on
Bovine Somatotropin (BST), the hormone injected into cows to
promote milk production. [13]

In this article, Richmond uses the expression 'food terrorist' first
coined by Elizabeth Whelan, the founder of the American Council on
Science and Health: 'not surprisingly, the food terrorists have been
raising the alarm. There have been allegations that the hormone could
harm human health, produce unknown chemical residues in the milk,
and produce milk with up to 27 per cent more fat'.

Standing solidly against the 'food terrorists', Richmond comes
down in favour of the facts – that BST has been thoroughly tested and
passed by MAFF – and then dismisses objections to it. Again, there are
no references and no scientific data.

In October 1988, again in *GP*, Richmond returns to the matter of
vitamins and IQ. [14] Eight months after the 'QED' programme, she has
now learned the location of Patrick Holford's Institute for Optimum
Nutrition (ION), and she has startling news for her readers.

> GPs who were astonished that a BBC TV programme hyped up
> a vitamin tablet that supposedly increased children's IQs won't
> be surprised to learn that London's Institute for Optimum
> Nutrition, where some of the programme was filmed, is the back
> room of Health Stop, a suburban health food shop. [15]

Adequately demonstrated here is a classic propaganda ploy; by using
the untruthful description 'the back room of', Richmond transforms
ION from a small but reputable Institute into a disreputable 'hole in
the wall' practice. ION is, in fact, completely separate both structurally
and financially from the health food shop and comprises a main
meeting room with four or five auxiliary rooms which are used as

consulting rooms and a wash room.

> One wonders how the authors of the *Lancet* paper and the BBC
> crew visited the 'institute' without mentioning that it was behind
> a shop that sold vitamins. [16]

The chemical and pharmaceutical companies are only one part of a
tripartite grouping, all parts of which are defended by the orthodox
scientific community and industry alike. The two other parts consist of
the processed food companies and the orthodox medical practitioners.
As society has become more toxic, new symptomatic pictures begin to
emerge. Orthodox pharmaceutically-based medicine often has no
treatment for these conditions. In a consequent attempt to defend the
professional stature of doctors, the pharmaceutical industry and the
medical establishment claim increasingly that those who present with
these symptoms are either being conned by others or suffer themselves
from psychiatric conditions.

In the November 1988 issue of *GP*, [17] Caroline Richmond returns
to the theme that many people who visit their doctors do not have
physical symptoms, or at least do not have physical symptoms which
they recognise. The problems which she describes would, however, be
recognised by practitioners of environmental medicine.

> Patients who have physical symptoms with no organic cause
> (somatisers) have always been with us, but recent years have seen
> a new boom in media-publicised diseases that are not in the
> medical text books. First it was allergy to the twentieth century.
> Then it was food allergy. In the late 1980s it has been *Candida
> Albicans* sensitivity, hyperactivity (in children, but it is the mother
> who complains), severe premenstrual syndrome, myalgic
> encephalomyelitis, and vitamin and mineral deficiency. [18]

Richmond quotes research carried out at Toronto University into
patients who present with no physical symptoms and who adopt what
the article cynically refers to as 'diseases of the month'. 'Normal
people', it is pointed out, disregard the same symptoms or 'ascribe
them to tiredness, a bad day, ageing, stress, dietary indiscretion or a
passing minor infection'. It is only those who are 'chronic somatisers'
who 'embrace each newly-described disease of fashion as the answer to
their long-standing, multiple, undiagnosed complaints'. [19]

In this article, Richmond argues the case for those whom in the past she has called 'proper doctors', those who recognise only 'proper illnesses'. Such a conservative view throws a cordon around intellectual investigation of both illness and its treatment, leaving some chronic complaints such as asthma, eczema and psoriasis, and other more serious illnesses like cancer and AIDS, unexplained and sometimes untreated by the orthodox medical profession.

Dr Stewart, the Toronto psychiatric researcher quoted by Richmond in her article, suggests that patients who present with symptoms which have no apparent physical basis should be humoured. 'Each patient needs to be convinced that his or her symptoms are being taken seriously. A balance must be drawn between making the appropriate investigations while avoiding over-investigation.' Most effective, the psychiatrist maintains, is 'psychotherapy, with antidepressants if necessary, or tranquillisers'.

Whatever happens to such patients, they must not be sent to alternative practitioners. 'The GP is an ideal person to manage patients with *environmental hypersensitivity* as he or she can *reduce* repeated investigations and consultations with multiple specialists' (italics added).

One of the ghost illnesses which Richmond is determined has no organic base is myalgic encephalomyelitis (ME).† The reasons why Richmond and the CAHF targetted ME as a bogus illness, only promoted by quacks, are complex. ME is one of a wide range of complaints which appear to be related to a compromised immune system. Those who suffer from ME show classic signs which are also common to people affected by pesticides and other forms of chemical exposure. One theory is that ME is a post-viral condition which besets the sufferer following a viral illness which has depleted the immune system. Few orthodox practitioners will treat the immune system or give patients advice about it, and as chemical therapies may do further damage, many doctors prefer to ignore the illness.

Caroline Richmond wrote one of her many articles on ME in a May 1989 issue of the *BMJ*.[20] The article gives intellectual gloss to Richmond's belief that not only are there a series of non-organic

---

† Caroline Richmond's attitude to ME has brought her into conflict with HealthWatch member Charles Shepherd, himself an ME sufferer and author of an authoritative text on the illness.

illnesses which go through cyclical fashions, but that these illnesses also have historical counterparts. She gives symptomatic pictures for a series of illnesses which she says have no physical basis. Allergy is singled out:

> ... total allergy syndrome, and allergy to the twentieth century, which will soon be out of style, replaced by twenty first century disease. The attraction of allergy to the hypochondriac is its personal uniqueness: if I say I've got an allergy you can't say I haven't, whatever your private opinion may be. [21]

Following this article, the *BMJ* received 43 letters all expressing the same greater or lesser disgust with the inferences which Richmond drew. Two of the letters were printed.

> During the first world war infantrymen suffering from shell-shock and the total fatigue of coping with immeasurable levels of stress ... were considered to be suffering from neurosis or a form of hysteria ... they were considered to be trying to opt out of their duty ... many were court martialled and executed as cowards ... It is interesting that within little more than 70 years, and with the advance and development of psychology in medicine, patients with chronic health problems are often told that they are opting out or avoiding work and that they are suffering from personality disorders rather than organic illness ... People ... are virtually put on trial because they have presented with certain symptoms, and they must then try and justify that they are sane, that they are not trying to upset the state economy by giving up their jobs, and that they do not have shady and ulterior motives for being ill, or stand to gain by their illness. [22]

> ... this should not obscure the fact that ME is a serious illness in which immunological abnormalities such as deficiency of T cell subsets are increasingly being shown ... There is no doubt that ME sometimes behaves like multiple sclerosis, a disease which also has no specific diagnostic test. No one would dream of saying that patients with multiple sclerosis were suffering from 'the vapours' or a 'wandering womb'. [23]

Caroline Richmond returned to the question of allergy in a November issue of *Pulse*, another magazine which is financed through pharmaceutical company advertising. [24] The article, which pretends to be an authoritative account of milk allergy, is little more than a long interview with Dr Anne Ferguson of Western General Hospital and Edinburgh University, and again an advertisement for the Food Intolerance Data Bank.

Dr Ferguson is a gastroenterologist who was on the joint BNF/ RCP committee in 1984 which produced *Food Intolerance and Food Aversion*. Richmond does not say in the article that Dr Ferguson is an advisor to the Dairy Trades Federation and the Milk Marketing Board, because she knows as we do, that such patronage could not possibly affect Dr Ferguson's views. 'Cow's milk allergy, a disease almost exclusive to children under two, occurring in 2% of infants, is a common cause of damage to the small intestine mucosa....About 5 per cent of white British adults are lactose intolerant.'

It is not, however, the stated extent of intolerance to dairy products which is interesting in this article. What is stunning, is the manner in which Richmond, having sided with orthodox medicine to make out a minority case for food allergy – nowhere near large enough to damage the dairy industry – goes on to champion health food shops: 'lactose-reduced milk can be bought in health food shops'. We can only assume that Mrs Richmond was severely reprimanded by her friend Dr Arnold Bender, who opened his 1985 book *Health or Hoax* with the information that '75 per cent of the products sold in American health food shops are positively harmful, causing accelerating blindness, cancer, convulsions, heart palpitations, insulin shock and even death'. [25]

Anyone who was keeping track of the Richmond philosophy, and its industrial roots over 1987 and 1988, while she was working at the Wellcome Institute, grant-aided by the Wellcome Trust, might have speculated that she was being groomed for greater things.

Chapter Twenty Six

The Campaign Against Health Fraud, Part One: Background and Beginnings

The malignant spread of medicine turns mutual care and self-medication into misdemeanours or felonies. [1]

Covert propaganda operations are not new to British industry. In the years immediately after the Second World War, fearful of nationalisation by a victorious Labour Party, Conservatives and industrialists set up a number of clandestine organisations, to champion the cause of free enterprise. Aims for Industry, which later became Aims, was set up to fight the post-war Labour Party's plans for nationalisation. The Society for Individual Freedom, set up in part by the intelligence agencies drawing on industrial support, was an organisation which championed individualist political freedoms eroded by wartime constraints.

Organisations like the Economic League were set up to gather intelligence on trade unionists. In the mid-seventies, the National Association for Freedom, sponsored by big business and organised by individuals with backgrounds in the intelligence community, campaigned first to get Margaret Thatcher to lead the Conservative Party and then for monetarist policies.

The pharmaceutical industry, intimately related to the great oil and chemical conglomerates, has often been at the forefront of covert industrial subterfuge and propaganda. Those who controlled oil have often also been close to the centres of foreign policy.

Gulf Oil, founded by the Mellon family, was before the Second World War part of one of the largest chemical cartels in the history of modern capitalism. It was dominated by I.G. Farben, a group of

German chemical companies. [2] In the 1960s, the London offices of Gulf Oil, now known as Chevron, were based in an unobtrusive high-rise office building called Gulf House, just off Oxford Street. From that building in 1967, the Queen Anne Press produced *Medicine at Risk: The High Price of Cheap Drugs*, by F. H. Happold. [3] The only acknowledgment the author gives in the book's foreword is to the Association of the British Pharmaceutical Industry (APBI).

The book was published at a particularly sensitive time. The British Trades Union Congress was raising social and political questions about the pharmaceutical industry and in America the Kefauver hearings had recently enquired about price and monopoly practices. Only six years before, the international effects of thalidomide had dealt the image of the pharmaceutical industry its most devastating post-war blow.

The themes of *Medicine at Risk* are the themes of propaganda for the next two decades: themes which were to surface with a vengeance in the late 1980s.

> The thalidomide incident stimulated attacks by those who profess to despise 'orthodox medicine' and all its works. Before examining the fallacies behind the accusations of the politically-minded critics of the pharmaceutical industry, it is useful briefly to consider the views of the *cranks*.(italics added) [4]

The only person whom Happold designates a 'crank' is Brian Inglis: he then cursorally looks at two of his recent books. [5]

> In *Fringe Medicine*, he [Inglis] describes approvingly the main forms of unorthodox healing, from naturopathy ('natural' food etc. school) to acupuncture (pricking with fine needles as practised in China); from Yoga to auto-suggestion; and from Christian Science (faith healing) to radiesthesia (black boxes, dowsing and all). [6]

The book outlines industry's arguments against such forms of natural medicine.

> Throughout history, the sick have been exposed to quacks and confidence tricksters, and a great deal of money has changed hands, for spurious remedies and treatments which did more harm than good. [7]

Unwilling to look seriously at the efficacy of alternative medicine, the propagandist always turns instead to charges of financial exploitation, obscuring the fact that the pharmaceutical industry is one of the most profitable in the Western world.

Books like *Medicine at Risk* were foisted upon a relatively unsophisticated audience in the fifties and sixties. Its arguments are transparent but useful to explain the marketing strategies of the pharmaceutical companies in relation to alternative and complementary medicine. Twenty years after the inauguration of the NHS, *Medicine at Risk* supports the cosy relationships which socialised medicine introduced between general practitioners and the pharmaceutical industry.

> Many attacks upon the pharmaceutical industry must be clearly recognised as attacks on doctors. The small minority of medical men who have associated themselves with wholesale denunciation of the drug industry.....do not seem fully to realise that their views reflect on the competence and even integrity of their professional colleagues. [8]

This is another theme which re-emerges in the 1980s. In the scenario presented by *Medicine at Risk*, economic power, price and profit are not mentioned. An infallible medical science serves a universal mankind manufacturing drugs entirely to rid the world of ill health. Doctors, who are solely concerned with the health of their patients, live in a world free of cultural, personal or commercial pressures.

Another important symbolic battlefield is the medical press. This too exists in a perfect world concerned only with disseminating bias-free information about the most appropriate treatments.

> Doctors regard M.I.M.S. (Monthly Index of Medical Specialities), distributed free by Medical Publications Ltd, as one of the most useful guides for general practitioners. It lists all products by brand name, has a therapeutic and pharmacological index, cross referenced to detailed information on individual products, manufacturer, formulation, disease, indications, possible side-effects, dosage and price. It is entirely financed by manufacturers' advertisements.

> The medical journals, which in Britain have a high reputation, provide in particular a source of information and opinion on

> treatment and drug action mainly at consultant level and also act
> as media for the exchange of medical opinion. They, in turn, are
> partly dependent financially on manufacturers' advertisements.
> Thus, the main part of the £1.5m (1964) spent by the industry
> on journal advertising is in fact devoted to supporting *independent
> information services to doctors.* [9](italics added)

To suggest that the pharmaceutical companies finance the medical
press, via advertising, so as to support an 'independent information
service', gives new meaning to the word 'independent'.

The arguments put forward by Happold show that even in the mid-
sixties, it was difficult to separate doctors from the pharmaceutically-
orientated infrastructure, which had grown up, densely, around them.

The Contemporary Scene

It was evident, in the early years of the nineteen eighties, that there
was a growth of interest in alternative and complementary medicine. It
was an interest about which pharmaceutical companies were
becoming increasingly concerned.

In 1981, the Threshold Foundation, a body primarily interested in
complementary healing, published the results of a survey into the
status of complementary medicine in the United Kingdom. [10] The
survey, thoroughly researched, was a major contribution to the
understanding of the status and social position of a wide range of
complementary treatments in Britain.

Some results of the Threshold Foundation study gave the
pharmaceutical companies serious reason to be concerned. Findings
showed that increasing numbers of patients were turning to non-
orthodox practitioners and that in the year 1980 to 1981, the numbers
of such practitioners were increasing annually by around 11%. The
number of lay homoeopaths registered with a professional association,
for instance, had risen from 25 in 1978 to 120 in 1981. The number of
practising acupuncturists had doubled during the same period, rising
from 250 in 1978 to 500 in 1981.

Such figures had a relevance far beyond their simple arithmetic.
The growing number of complementary practitioners would not be
prescribing or advising the use of drugs. Perhaps more startling to the
pharmaceutical companies, as each discipline set up its own training

programme, the education of 'healers' and specialists would begin to change. The survey showed that already, by 1981, the rate of increase in complementary practitioners was nearly six times that of the annual increase in the number of doctors in the UK. [11]

In July 1983, the *BMJ* [12] carried an editorial which warned doctors to remain sceptical about alternative treatments until they had passed the supreme scientific test of the 'controlled trial'. More should be done, the editorial suggested, to carry out rigorous clinical trials for alternative treatments: 'Stricter standards should be required, however, by a doctor proposing himself (sic) to use alternative treatments. If the treatment he (sic) proposes using has not been validated by a clinical trial then he (sic) is in just the same position as a clinical pharmacologist with a new drug.'

In 1984, the Royal College of Physicians and the British Nutrition Foundation published *Food Intolerance and Food Aversion*, which brushed over alternative treatments in relation to allergy. In 1986 the Board of Science and Education of the BMA published a report on Alternative Therapy, [13] which was clearly the profession's answer to the Threshold report.

Alternative Therapy argues the case for the allopathic doctor against the alternatives. The report was overseen by Sir Douglas Black at a time when he was President of the BMA. The first thirty six pages discuss the history of medicine from the birth of man, very useful for first-form secondary school pupils, but not so useful for those interested in alternative therapies. The description of the alternative therapies themselves is twenty five pages long. A short historical description of each practice – homoeopathy gets three pages, herbalism gets one page, acupuncture two pages – is followed by eighteen pages of discussion and analysis.

These eighteen pages represent the tablets of stone upon which later and more acerbic critics of alternative medicine, campaigning in the late eighties, came to base their case. The discussion begins with a short discourse in praise of science and from that point onwards a fog of cynicism emanates from the pages.

> Inasmuch as scientific method lays such firm emphasis on observation, measurement and reproducibility, historically it has become inevitably and increasingly separate from doctrines embracing superstition, magic and the supernatural.

> Herein lies the first and most important difficulty that orthodox
> medical science has with alternative approaches. So many of
> them do not base their rationale on any theory which is
> consistent with natural laws as we now understand them. *It is
> simply not possible for example, for orthodox scientists to accept that a
> medicine so dilute that it may contain not so much as one molecule of the
> remedy in a given dose can have any pharmacological action.* [14] (italics
> added)

What is interesting about such reflections on 'science' is that they
expose some of its value-laden assumptions. If scientific method
emphasises observation, measurement and reproducibility, why can
we not use such method to appraise homoeopathy? The report as a
whole argued that modern medicine began with the enlightenment
and any medical treatment which cannot be explained is invalid.

The authors of *Alternative Therapy* considered it important to make
clear not only that many alternative treatments were in their opinion
non-scientific but also to point out the fact that a number of alternative
therapies are propagated by 'cults'. By discussing medicine within this
context, the report begins the process of the 'criminalisation' of
alternative practitioners, which the Campaign Against Health Fraud
was to take up in 1989.

> Our attention has been drawn by many people to the activities of
> what have become known as 'new religious movements', a term
> which is perhaps more acceptable and descriptive, if not more
> accurate, than 'religious cults and sects'.

> Our particular interest is in the fact that many of these 'religious'
> organisations make direct claims to be able to cure disease,
> including cancers and fractures ... There are now over 100
> groups operating in the UK in such a manner as to have come to
> the attention of FAIR (Family Action Information and Rescue),
> which was formed in 1976.

> Alternative therapies may be used by these groups to induce
> belief, thus strengthening the religious dimension (which can
> qualify for charitable status with resulting tax benefits). Illness
> may be proclaimed as being a 'punishment' for lack of faith or
> other misdemeanour.

> We believe that, subject to the necessity to maintain the principle

> of freedom of religion in this country, they [the cults] should be carefully and continuously monitored in order to ensure that they do not become a threat to the health and wellbeing of those who enter into association with them. [15]

The inclusion of these unreferenced and poorly explained paragraphs about 'new religious movements' and alternative therapies is gratuitous to any proper analysis of such therapies in an apparently serious work.

Another idea which enters the public domain with this report, is that many alternative therapies are actually bad for you. Never is the information about health damage caused by alternative medicine compared to the dangers implicit in pharmacological treatment, or surgical intervention. Rarely are references given for claims and never are these claims the result of scientific studies.

> The 365 traditional points in acupuncture, run near, some perilously so, to vital structures, and complications ranging from the minor to the serious *and the fatal* have been reported. The public should not be exposed to acupuncturists who have not been trained to understand the relationship between the acupuncture points and anatomical structures, and also the physiology of organ structure.

> The potential dangers of *local and systemic infection* following an invasive technique such as acupuncture are real and well documented. While strict asepsis and sterile needles are self-evident requirements, *we were led to believe it was an aim rather neglected in practice*. Yet *the transmission of infectious hepatitis* has been reported and the increasing incidence of AIDS virus infection makes *the possibility of transmission by contaminated needles a reality* (italics added). [16]

Chapter Twenty Seven

The Campaign Against Health Fraud, Part Two: Early Targets

Ordinary monopolies corner the market; radical monopolies disable people from doing or making things on their own. [1]

Caroline Richmond called the first meeting of what was to be called the Campaign Against Health Fraud in 1988. She had been laying the foundation for the group, gathering information and organising critical attacks upon clinical ecologists and allergy doctors, for at least two years previously.

The campaigns against allergy medicine in particular, and clinical ecology generally, had perhaps been strongest during the previous decade in the north of England. The pragmatism of industrial Protestantism is seemingly unwilling to accept ideas about the delicate interleaving of the mind and body, and the hard commercial instinct remains unconvinced by alien notions of industry being bad for the health.

In the mid-eighties, after going to work with Wellcome, Caroline Richmond consolidated her friendships with a variety of natural allies, most especially orthodox doctors working in the field of immunology. Her most enduring contacts were made with doctors and activists in the Manchester area, the city which was to become host to the UK Skeptics. Two doctors in particular, Dr Tim David and Dr David Pearson, joined Richmond in her campaign against the alternative treatment of allergy.

In 1982, Dr David Pearson returned from the United States, where he had been working in an occupational illness centre funded by the US public health department. His first stop was Manchester University where he had previously received his PhD. Now his area of research was classical food allergy. Dr Tim David also became prominent in the early eighties working as a paediatrician, with an interest in allergy, at Booth Hall Hospital in Manchester. Dr David's interest in allergy developed in the late seventies and grew from his work with the National Eczema Society, a group which even then was patronised by the oil and pharmaceutical companies.

Both David and Pearson felt particularly offended by the work and life style of Dr Keith Mumby. His practice, in the early eighties in Stockport then later in Stretford, on the edge of Manchester, used the 'provocation neutralisation' technique to diagnose and then treat allergies. Mumby, a writer as well as a doctor, had come late to environmental medicine, and when he did get involved, it was with great enthusiasm. He travelled frequently to America to train with Dr Joe Miller, the 'father' of provocation-neutralisation. By the mid-eighties Dr Mumby was at the centre of a small northern contingent of environmental practitioners.

Another doctor who had been attracted to environmental medicine and especially to food allergy treatment was Dr David Freed, at that time based in Prestwich near Manchester. Despite being a classically trained allergist and immunologist, Freed turned away from orthodox medicine and towards clinical ecology in the late seventies. He is a large, bearded man, whose avuncular nature disguises a clear, disciplined mind. It was during his postgraduate training at Manchester University that Dr Freed first met Dr Pearson. In the mid-eighties, Dr Freed was working with an allergy therapist and dietician, Anna Foster.

From the early eighties onwards, these northern practitioners were to become the subjects of a propaganda assault organised by Caroline Richmond and her two close friends.

While at Manchester University, Pearson carried out an investigation into people who said they suffered from food allergy; he later published the study.[2] Pearson and his psychiatrically trained colleagues took a small group of individuals who either maintained that they suffered from allergy, or had been diagnosed as so suffering. Each patient was challenged with capsules of food additives and chemicals. Only 5 out of the 35 patients produced reproducible symptoms in a double blind test. The researchers concluded that the remaining 30 patients were suffering from psychiatric complaints.

This single piece of research by Pearson was to form the basis for the next decade of campaigning against doctors working in the field of allergy. The singular work was also to form the basis of Caroline Richmond's later contentions that people who complained of allergic responses or chemical sensitivity were in fact psychologically ill.

By the mid-eighties, both Pearson and David had got themselves quoted in the papers denouncing 'private allergy clinics'. [3] Dr Freed, who was working with Anna Foster in one of the few private allergy clinics near Manchester, 'The North West Allergy Clinic', inevitably felt that such attacks by Pearson and David were personal attacks on him.

Even in those early days of the campaign against clinical ecology, the vested interests supporting orthodox allergy work were beginning to show. Tim David denounced Dr Freed to the General Medical Council, after his name appeared on a list of doctors supporting the Hyperactive Childrens' Support Group, which had begun campaigning against chemical food additives.

In November 1986, a large two-day conference of classical allergists and immunologists was held in London. The proceedings were to be published as a book on food allergy. [4] The conference was sponsored by a leading nutrition company, Wyeth Nutrition, and held at Regents College. About twelve doctors attended a critical seminar prior to the conference at the Royal College of Physicians, at which each paper and potential chapter was discussed.

Following the seminar, the doctors gave a series of talks to the full conference. The audience was an invited audience consisting mainly of paediatricians and GPs. One of those present who was not a clinician of any kind was Caroline Richmond. When Dr David Freed went up to the podium to read his paper on 'provocation neutralisation', Richmond came bustling from the audience with a tape recorder.

In the mid-eighties, Richmond was already developing the tactics and gathering the intelligence, which were to form the basis of her work for the Campaign Against Health Fraud. A year after the Swiss Cottage conference, in Autumn 1987, while working at the North West Allergy Clinic, David Freed received a phone call from Caroline Richmond. She introduced herself as a journalist and asked for his comments on an article which she had written about the clinic.

After it had been read to him, Freed thought Richmond's article:

> fairly scurrilous; a biased story about a patient who had fallen
> out with the clinic. Although there was nothing factually wrong
> with the article, the slant of it was antagonistic to environmental
> medicine. [5]

In the article, Richmond accused Anna Foster of making a false
diagnosis of the patient. Dr Freed, who had been present during the
consultation, knew that no mistake had been made. Freed was so
concerned about the style and the content of the article that he
immediately rang the Medical Protection Society, who in turn put
pressure on Richmond to withdraw her story. At the time, Freed
recalls, there were a number of heated exchanges between himself,
Foster and Richmond over the phone.

By the end of 1987, Dr Freed had a very clear idea that he was
considered by Caroline Richmond and her small group of campaigners
to be in the enemy camp. In 1988, after Anna Foster had set up a new
organisation in Bolton called 'Nutritional Medicine', she received
another call from Richmond. Richmond said she was working for the
Observer on an article about allergy. When it became apparent that Anna
Foster was not going to take part in an interview, Richmond used tactics
which were to become common in later campaigns. She rang Foster
frequently. The continual calls, as late as midnight, became so annoying
that Foster was forced to refer the matter to the Press Council.

The Beginning of the Campaign Against Health Fraud

The major players in the British health-fraud movement, Caroline
Richmond, Dr David Pearson, Dr Vincent Marks, Professor Michael
Baum and Dr Nick Beard, had been coming together since 1985.
They were all heavily involved in the defence of scientific medicine
and most of them had a connection, however tenuous, with the
Wellcome Foundation†. Each founder member also had contacts who

---

† As well as working in the Wellcome Institute, and receiving a Wellcome
bursary, Richmond acquired 250 Wellcome shares in December 1986. She held
these shares until they were sold in 1990.

would be drawn into the campaign and help in reporting information and publicising cases. One 'quackbuster', whose role in the organisation was to be shrouded in misinformation, was Duncan Campbell. Campbell was later to claim on a number of occasions that he had never been a member. There are, however, a number of references from the early days of the organisation which show clearly that he was involved.†

It was first decided to call the Campaign, the Council Against Health Fraud. [6] This is a clear indication that the British Campaign had links with the American Council.‡ In November 1988, Caroline Richmond organised the first steering committee meeting for what was to become the Campaign. The meeting was advertised in the newsletter of the Medical Journalists Association (MJA). The MJA, of which Richmond is a long-standing member, is supported by Ciba Geigy and a number of other pharmaceutical companies. Companies use the Association's newsletter to advertise meetings and conferences and 'freebies' at which they promote their drugs to journalists.

Following the meeting, Caroline Richmond sent round a circular to the press and interested parties. 'At a meeting on 1st November 1988, a group including doctors, journalists and a barrister decided to form the Council Against Health Fraud, an information and action service

---

† The Autumn 1989 CAHF Newsletter quotes a letter sent by Campbell to *Hospital Doctor*: 'I enthusiastically welcome the recent launch of CAHF. In the few weeks since they launched, I and others have already benefited immensely from their assistance in working to expose the many (other) charlatans who are preying on the vulnerable for commercial gain'. [7] Around the time that the Campaign was launched, Campbell had meetings with Caroline Richmond and Nick Beard. He was cited in the Campaign's newsletter as a member and attended ordinary Campaign meetings and closed Annual General Meetings at the Ciba Foundation and St Bartholemew's Hospital. [8] At around the same time that it became public that the Campaign was funded by the Wellcome Foundation, Campbell began to distance himself from the organising core of the Campaign, and later claimed that he had never been a member. For the purposes of this book, Duncan Campbell has been considered as an associate member of the Campaign Against Health Fraud. He added a great deal of authority to the Campaign's strategy and was instrumental in many of its critical attacks. He used information supplied to the Campaign and was happy to use its founder members as a rich source of quotes for his articles, without questioning their vested interests.

‡ The Campaign Against Health Fraud was listed in the Newsletter of the American Council as an associate organisation. [9]

against the growing tide of quackery.' At the bottom of this short advertisement Richmond gave her address, for contact purposes, as The Wellcome Institute, 183 Euston Road.† [10]

Between the first meeting and the official launch of the Campaign in May 1989, the steering committee met at the Ciba Foundation, [11] the academic front for the drug company Ciba Geigy. The Ciba Foundation has an information service, the Media Resources Service (MRS), which was to some extent already doing the kind of work, in defence of science, health and the pharmaceutical and chemical industries, that CAHF planned. The MRS put scientists and sympathetic journalists in touch with each other.

At least two patrons of the Service were known to Caroline Richmond. Professor Sir Hermann Bondi was influential within the British Humanist Association, and Sir Alastair Pilkington was at that time one of the principal directors of the Wellcome Foundation. Amongst MRS Steering Committee members were two people with whom Richmond had closer links, Sir Walter Bodmer‡ and Dr Bernard Dixon. Dixon was both a founder member of the Campaign Against Health Fraud and a member of CSICP, the British branch of CSICOP.

The Ciba Foundation also plays host to a number of other organisations with which Caroline Richmond and Sir Walter Bodmer are associated. These include the Wellcome-administered Association of Medical Research Charities and the Association of British Science Writers. The British Association for the Advancement of Science holds meetings there for its Media Fellows, as does the Medical Research Council.

During the gestation period of the Campaign Against Health Fraud, Caroline Richmond was involved with the magazine *UK*

---

† Richmond later claimed that she was not influenced by her employers and that the Campaign was not supported by Wellcome. She told a number of people that she had almost lost her job as a consequence of using the Wellcome address at the bottom of the leaflet. In an attempt to correct the blunder she later replaced the Wellcome address with a box number and her home telephone number.

‡ For Caroline Richmond's links with Sir Walter Bodmer in the British Association for the Advancement of Science see Chapter 22, The Pollution of Science.

Skeptic †, which had been set up in 1987 with money from CSICP. [12] On its inauguration, CAHF was advertised as a co-member of the UK Skeptics in the first page of their magazine *UK Skeptic*. The British branch of the CAHF had the same relationship to UK Skeptics, as the American Council Against Health Fraud had to CSICOP. The health fraud campaign was, as it were, the armed wing, while CSICOP and CSICP were made up of theorists.

From the first 1989 issue of the *UK Skeptic*, Caroline Richmond and Nicholas Beard had the space to outline the strategies and attacks organised by the CAHF. In the February 1989 issue, Nick Beard contributed an article about the need to put natural or alternative remedies through clinical trials. He used the article to consolidate the attack on Jacques Benveniste carried out the year before, by CSICOP member James Randi.

> Last year *Nature* published a paper which claimed to provide *in vitro* evidence for an effect which could have helped to explain homoeopathy – the start of the Benveniste fiasco. The research appeared to show that basophil degranulation (an immune response in white blood cells) continued to be triggered by solutions of an antigen even to concentrations of 10^{-120}. However, this was followed shortly afterwards by a damning report from a team of investigators who found serious errors in the research methods involved, invalidating the research. [13]

Using *UK Skeptic* and the CSICOP journal, both a long way from being 'peer-review' publications, health-fraud activists were able to publish unreferenced stories. Both magazines were able to continuously recycle 'debunking' stories years after actual allegations had been found wanting. John Maddox, the editor of *Nature*, also had great fun talking to UK Skeptics about Benveniste.

> Let me just tell you a bit about our visit to Paris, a year ago to investigate Dr Benveniste's claim that it was possible to take a biological reagent, put it in water, dilute the water virtually indefinitely and still find the biological activity in the solution. We took with us a conjurer, an exceedingly good one, James Randi. When we arrived in Paris we found Dr Benveniste was

† See Chapter 18.

not doing his experiments with his own hands but that somebody else was doing them for him in an exceedingly sloppy way. He was not actually taking proper account of the statistical controls that in those circumstances any first year undergraduate biologist would recognise to be necessary. [14]

The *UK Skeptic*, for which both Richmond and Beard wrote, and which was financed by CSICP, continued to report the attacks mounted by the Campaign Against Health Fraud throughout 1991 and 1992.†

The Campaign proper finally got off the ground at a press conference held on May 8th 1989, at the Royal Society of Medicine. The invitation briefly stated that the campaign organisers were 'worried about the growth of quackery, and false, pseudo-scientific claims'. [15] Coincidental with the launch of the CAHF was a CSICOP European conference also held in May near Munich, West Germany. The launch of CAHF was discussed, as was the general subject of 'fringe medicine'.

The press conference was chaired by Caroline Richmond and attended by 20 or so journalists, who were treated to speeches from Professor John Garrow, the TV and radio presenter Nick Ross and Professor Michael Baum. The 'Today' programme reported the Campaign's concern about 'private food allergy clinics' and hair analysis, while Vincent Marks managed to get himself on LBC, attacking 'worthless cancer treatments' which deterred people from having surgery.

The CAHF launch got publicity in the *BMJ* and was reported with some seriousness in some daily papers, particularly *The Times*.

> Last year, Caroline Richmond, a medical journalist and research scientist, decided that the public needed to be protected from 'unproven and worthless' treatment, and she decided to set up a British equivalent of the American National Council Against Health Fraud or 'Quackbusters'.
>
> The campaign aims at promoting assessments of new treatments

† In the 1991 January/February edition of *UK Skeptic*, there is a biased account of the flawed *Lancet* paper on Bristol Cancer Help Centre, and a one-sided account of the CAHF-engineered attack upon Dr Jean Monro.

and protecting consumers from fraudulent claims. It will act as an independent information service for journalists who want to comment on fraud in medicine, and it will also set up specific enquiries. [16]

'Carefully controlled trials' for new treatments sound very laudable, until it is remembered that Wellcome was then involved in the most prestigious, costly and contentious 'controlled trial' of any modern pharmaceutical product: the Concorde trials for AZT. Was it simply coincidence that the CAHF, an organisation set up to investigate quacks, was linked with Wellcome, and began its life at almost the same time as major trials of AZT were begun in Britain and France?

Reports of the launch of CAHF by Thompson Prentice, published in *The Times*, made little attempt to disguise links between CAHF and Wellcome. The article in which news of the launch appeared was an unadorned advertisement for AZT. Headed 'AIDS RESEARCH', the sub-heading 'Drugs May Protect Carriers' stretched across three columns. The news content of the article simply reiterated basic information about the Concorde trials. Set in the centre of this article in bolder type was a single paragraph article about the launch of CAHF.

For a self-styled independent organisation, the proximity of these articles, their intimacy even, was a little embarrassing. On the following day, Thompson Prentice went to town in promoting CAHF, when *The Times* ran a four by three inch column article bannered 'ANTI-FRAUD CAMPAIGN', as if the newspaper had adopted the campaign. Even in this article, which described the new organisation and its launch, Thompson Prentice could not resist placing information from Wellcome in close proximity.

The article was clever in its orientation: headlined 'Quacks risk women's lives', [17] it quoted mainly from Dr Michael Baum: 'A growing number of women are dying from breast cancer because they are putting themselves in the care of "quacks", rather than orthodox specialists.'

Baum went on to describe how women came to his surgery with little chance of survival after they have sought 'unproven alternative therapies ... I have a cluster of patients who have been convinced that homoeopathy and special diets will help them. In fact, their cancers go unchecked'.

Vincent Marks was quoted as stating: 'Bogus explanations for ill health bring the genuine concept of scientific medicine into disrepute.' CAHF was an organisation, the article said, 'of doctors and lay members who aim to protect the public from taking cures and untested medical treatments'.

Following the launch, Michael Baum gave an interview to the Journal of Alternative and Complementary Medicine. In this interview he at least made clear his views about alternative medicine. He did not believe, he said, 'that any system of alternative medicine had any basis in scientific fact'. [18]

After the launch, Steering Committee meetings continued to be held at the Ciba Foundation, the first being on the 15th of May. [19]

Chapter Twenty Eight

The Company Director: Dr Vincent Marks

Many children are suffering from 'muesli-belt malnutrition', which could cause stunted growth and weight loss. [1]

Vincent Marks, a sixty two year old medical doctor and Professor of Biochemistry, is the perfect professor for the end of the twentieth century: an age when intellectual endeavour has been turned into private property and the greatest accolades of learning are tucked away in bank accounts. On the returns of one of his companies, Professor Marks describes his occupation as that of 'company director'. Like that of many other university scientists, his road to the top of his profession has been strewn with garlands from chemical, pharmaceutical and processed food companies.

In 1985, as a member of the British Association of Clinical Biochemists, of which he was later to become President (1989–1991), [2] Marks received the Wellcome Award for Good Laboratory Practice. The prize, which consists of a cheque and a piece of engraved glass, was for 'a significant contribution to the quality of laboratory practice'. Between 1985 and 1990, the Department of Biochemistry which Marks heads at Surrey University received over half a million pounds in grants from Wellcome. [3]

Marks comes from an eminent medical family, his brother John Marks being the head of the General Council of the BMA. He is one of the most influential founder members of the Campaign Against Health Fraud; his presence on MAFF and MRC committees gave him access to powerful agencies which CAHF were able to use in its attacks upon natural medicine.

At Surrey University Marks has built up the Biochemistry Department, and the Department of Nutrition, by linking up the work of his staff colleagues with lucrative grant-funding from the large food processing, chemical and pharmaceutical companies. For his own research work, Marks is adept at choosing funding bodies and has become an influential and experienced grant receiver from many powerful sources. Over the last ten years, he has received major grants from such diverse sources as the Cancer Research Campaign, the pharmaceutical company Eli Lilly, the Institute of Food Research at Norwich (AFRC) and the American National Institutes of Health. He has attracted to the Department staff who have a good track record of working with industry; in November 1984, for example, Dr Juliet Gray† was appointed a Lecturer in the Department. [4]

Other large industrial concerns funding projects in the Biochemistry Department throughout the second half of the eighties were Ciba Geigy, [5] Sandoz Pharmaceuticals, [6] Unilever [7] and the Flour Milling and Baking Research Association. [8]

Marks has also attracted the major grant-aiding organisations in medical research. The Cancer Research Campaign, (CRC) which unlike the Imperial Cancer Research Fund does not have its own laboratories, has throughout the eighties developed a base at Surrey University where it uses the laboratory services of the Biochemistry Department. In 1988 the CRC gave the Department in excess of £50,000 for work on two research projects. [9]

In 1989, the Breast Cancer Biology Group was established within the Biochemistry Department at Surrey. The Group grew from the amalgamation of two laboratories, the Hormone Biochemistry Laboratory at Surrey and the Tissue Cell Relationships Laboratory, which had previously been a part of the Imperial Cancer Research Fund Laboratory in Lincoln's Inn Fields. The location of the new group at Surrey maximised contact with the surgical, histopathological and breast screening teams already established at the Royal Surrey Hospital, Guildford. [10] It meant also that Vincent Marks was to work closely with the two major British cancer charities.

One of Vincent Marks' closest colleagues at Surrey University, a

---

† See Chapter Nineteen : From the Table to the Grave.

man who has often represented the HealthWatch view on his behalf, [11] is Andrew Taylor. Taylor studies deficiencies and over-exposure to toxicity; he is a member of a number of Department of Health working groups. He works in the Robens Institute for Occupational Health and Safety, which is responsible for researching industrial, occupational and environmental health. The Robens Institute is completely dominated by chemical and pharmaceutical interests. In 1985, the Management Committee was chaired by the Research Director of ICI, Dr C. Reese, and included: the head of the Division of Toxicology and Environmental Protection at what was then the DHSS, Dr McGibbon; a BP executive; Sir Geoffrey Allen of Unilever; Sir William Paton, then Director of the Wellcome Institute for the History of Medicine and Wellcome Trust Trustee from 1983, and Dr J. Griffin, who had been head-hunted from the top job in the Department of Health, Medicines Division, by the Association of British Pharmaceutical Industries, of which he became Director. [12]

A Commercially Interesting Area

As well as being a founder member of the Campaign Against Health Fraud, Vincent Marks is an active spokesman for populist campaigns against health foods, and those who he insists make large profits from the sale of vitamins. Although he is usually presented as an independent scientist, he is himself involved in a number of private companies which depend for their survival upon private medicine and processed food companies.

During the nineteen eighties, Marks was the director of no less than eight companies,† most of which are involved in the measurement and analysis of biochemicals.

Marks set up Radio Immunoassay in 1986 with two other scientists and a publisher. The company, which was based in Cardiff and provided services for medical research laboratories, folded in 1987. Probus Biomedical was incorporated in 1986, to design and market biomedical diagnostic systems.

---

† Radio Immunoassay, Probus Biomedical, Guildhay Laboratory Services, Guildhay, Clifmar, The Food and Veterinary Laboratory Limited, Bio-Stat Diagnostics and Quatro Biosystems.

In 1982, Marks set up Guildhay Anti-Sera, in partnership with Surrey University, and Guildhay Laboratory Services with his wife Avril, to develop laboratory reagents and provide laboratory services. Clifmar Associates, set up in 1985, was again a joint enterprise with Surrey University, to research processes for purification and recovery by specific binding (extraction of materials by chemical separation).

Companies with which Vincent Marks has been associated have had varied success. Three of them are specifically located within the University of Surrey and their directors or share interests overlap with those of the University. One of these companies, Guildhay Anti-Sera, made a £17,500 loss in 1988, and in 1989 had to acquire a mortgage on its property in order to stay afloat.

One reason for the Guildhay losses is probably the fact that although the company is able to carry out research, it is not able to go into production. A good example of this grant-aided research work, which tends not to make a profit, is the research into monoclonal antibodies carried out by Vincent Marks under the auspices of Guildhay. In December 1987, Vincent Marks and a business partner in Guildhay Anti-Sera, Dr K. Tan of Surrey University, together with Professor R. Spier of the University's Microbiology Department†, were given a Medical Research Council grant of £109,025 to investigate *the production* of human monoclonal antibodies to HIV.

The research into monoclonal antibodies was carried out at Guildhay Anti-Sera and, in November 1988, the three scientists were given an additional £10,000 to complete the work. It is difficult to find any published papers on the results of this work: the author made enquiries of both the MRC and Professor Marks' colleagues, and neither were able to put their hands on any published material.

Coincidentally, the Wellcome Foundation must have been working on the same research, for in October 1990, it joined forces with the MRC to support a new Therapeutic Antibody Centre, in Cambridge. The Centre was set up to produce monoclonal antibodies, for use in different scientific and commercial circumstances, such as those of HIV antibody testing kits.

All the companies with which Marks is associated carry out

---

† Spier is also a director, with Marks, of Probus.

biochemical measurement or testing of some kind. They fall into two groups: those which do the research tend to make a loss, while those which produce the systems based upon the research do well.

A particular example is the Probus Quatro Robotic Sample Processor, designed in 1986 by Probus Biomedical, a company incorporated in 1986 by Vincent Marks. Probus received a SMART award from the Department of Trade and Industry in its first year, and the annual returns stated a desire to trade in the United States. Despite such early promise the company failed to thrive. In 1990, another company of which Marks is a director, Quatro Biosystems, a thriving company set up within the new light industry enclave of Manchester's Old Trafford Park area, produced the Quatro Robotic Sample Processor.

The most interesting of Vincent Marks' companies, in relation to his involvement in the Campaign Against Health Fraud and the attacks upon health foods and natural medicines, is the Food and Veterinary Laboratory Ltd (F&VL).† Set up in October 1986 with Vincent Marks as one of its first two directors, F&VL opened early in 1988. Clear indications that the company was close to MAFF and other government departments emerged when the laboratory was formally opened in April 1988 by Dr M.E. Knowles, then Head of the Food Science Division of MAFF.

The Food and Veterinary Laboratory tests a range of foodstuffs for the large food-producing companies and MAFF. In 1988, the company worked on computer graphics for the prediction of chemical toxicity, and a major contract was pending for chemical toxicity screening. [13]

During 1989, the company continued the development of an immuno-diagnostic product range and was one of the biggest suppliers of immuno-assay kits for the detection of anabolic hormone residues, which they exported to 17 countries. F&VL also produces large animal disease diagnostic kits, specifically a brucella antibody kit. [14]

During 1988, a collaborative review for environmental analysis (pesticide analysis) was undertaken with manufacturers of pesticides and those responsible for their monitoring and control. It was,

† In 1988, a subsidiary of Sari Holding Company.

however, decided to stay with disease diagnostics in the short-term. [15]

In the late eighties and early nineties, F&VL became involved in the analysis of chemicals used as colourants and in food packaging. This service was aimed specifically at, and carried out with, food producers. F&VL also began assessing and analysing pharmaceutical products. [16] In 1989, F&VL was asked by the Overseas Development Agency to undertake a consultancy in South Africa. [17]

Despite the fact that Vincent Marks was a member of such relevant committees as the joint MAFF and DoH 'Advisory Committee on Novel Foods and Processes', and even though F&VL appeared to have access to an expanding market, collaborating with government departments, chemical, pharmaceutical and processed food companies, in 1989 the company made a loss of £275,954. [18]

Vincent Marks and Sugar – Sweet as a Nut

Vincent Marks' ongoing links with the sugar industry have been well documented by both Geoffrey Cannon [19] and John Yudkin. [20] As well as being involved in the promotion of sugar, Vincent Marks is also a member of the MRC Committee on Diabetes and has written substantially about hypoglycaemia. Many doctors and research scientists who believe that sugar plays a major part in the development of diabetic illness consider that there is a conflict of interests involved in these two areas of work.†

Scientists who are paid retainers by food producers, or public relations firms which represent them, are left to their own devices as to how they may best pursue the interests of these companies. The Sugar Bureau publishes a number of booklets and occasional reports mainly for dieticians. The *C-H-O International Dialogue on Carbohydrates* is published by Advisa Medica on behalf of the Sugar Bureau. The second issue of the eight page advertising freebee, published in June 1990, [21] carried a letter from Vincent Marks flattering Michael Gibney, who wrote for *C-H-O* in April 1990. 'If you continue to publish articles of a standard similar to that by Michael Gibney, *C-H-O* will become compulsive reading to anyone with an interest in

† For other information on sugar and the MRC see Chapter Twenty Three.

nutrition.' Michael Gibney in turn was responsible for an article in the *Guardian* which introduced the British public to the work of the American Council Against Health Fraud, Victor Herbert and the role which the British Nutrition Foundation could play in defeating 'quackery'.†

Assay, Assay, Have You Heard the One About British Food ?

In 1991, Vincent Marks wrote a booklet for the Institute of Economic Affairs (IEA) entitled *Is British Food Bad For You?*[22] The IEA, in conjunction with the Adam Smith Institute, was responsible for floating many Thatcherite policies. It is a free market organisation of the 'monetarist Right', funded by, amongst others, the large agro-industrial organisations which tend to determine food policies with and for successive governments.

The choice of title for the booklet is interesting; the use of 'British' in the title immediately deflects the argument of most contemporary critics of processed food. Another less misleading title like '*Is Industrially Produced Food Bad For You?*' would have engendered quite a different debate. In fact the booklet does not actually apply itself to the issue of *British* food, except in a couple of cases where, by implication, Marks argues against himself: on BSE for instance, 'So far the occurrence of BSE in other countries has not been reported'.

The first twelve pages comprise an assault upon those who do not share Marks' views on industrially produced foodstuffs. In these pages he manages to touch upon all the favourite targets of the Campaign Against Health Fraud. Of those who feel uncomfortable with the involvement of industrially-funded science in food production, Marks says:

> These, mainly middle-class, scientifically ill-informed individuals feel more comfortable with things that are naively or exploitatively referred to as 'natural' – without understanding quite what that term means – than they are with products they perceive as being manufactured or synthetic. [23]‡

† See Chapter Nineteen : From the Table to the Grave.

‡ Unless otherwise stated all further quotes in this chapter are taken from *Is British Food Bad For You?*

Such scathing and irrational attitudes have no place in a serious text, especially from someone who purports to be a scientist. Marks however seems to enjoy this kind of populist harangue. As he moves from the scientifically specific to the pathologically general, his science turns to ideology.

> In its most blatant form, exploitation of the gullible is through the sale of worthless, if not actively harmful, nostrums, elixirs or medicines. These are often marketed as 'health foods' or 'Nutritional Supplements' in order to circumvent laws designed to protect the public from the sale of potentially harmful drugs and medicines. Many 'nutritional supplements' are sold at greatly inflated prices, compared with identical or frequently much purer products which are available from reputable chemical suppliers but which do not carry spurious or misleading labels. Two worthless 'food supplements' causing damage are 'organic germanium' – which was heavily promoted as an essential nutrient when it is not – and tryptophan.†

By page seven, still continuing his invective, Marks is firing off shots into the intellectual darkness, on such grand themes as integrity and patronage.

> Some of the most notorious of today's hucksters have the effrontery to accuse scientists whose work is of the highest ethical and internationally recognised standards, but of whom they disapprove, as being in the pocket of those who fund their research. The intention, is to make such workers appear unreliable and untrustworthy.

Again we are not provided with any references, so it is difficult to know to whom Marks is referring; perhaps he was thinking of Geoffrey Cannon. Although not a 'huckster', Cannon gave Marks and other

---

† For a discussion of the banning of L-Tryptophan and Germanium see Chapter 34 of this book, and Manders, Dean W. The Curious Continuing Ban of L-Tryptophan and the Serotonin Connection, in Morgenthaler, John and Fowkes, Steven. *Stop the F.D.A.* Manders draws attention to the fact that L-Tryptophan, despite having been used for years in the effective relief of depression, was banned only a few years after Prozac, a chemical anti-depressant which has a similar effect, was launched. It is estimated that by 1995 sales of Prozac will have topped $1 billion, despite repeated reports of serious, adverse side effects. Prozac is produced by Eli-Lilly.

'scientists' a good drubbing in *The Politics of Food*. Cannon meticulously recorded sources of research funding, in order to demonstrate clearly, not that funding necessarily compromises the integrity of the researcher, but something more simple. It is his thesis that when industry pulls the purse strings of research and guides political decision making, there can be a critical vacuum created around issues of food and health.

Many of those who oppose Vincent Marks and his populist claptrap do so because in the field of health he is one of the major architects of that critical vacuum which exists around the issues of power, industrial food production and health.

In *Is British Food Bad For You?*, Marks outlines the tactics of the 'other side', saying that they indulge in 'character assassination' which is 'an anathema to scientists and similarly reputable people. It is, however, commonplace among gutter journalists and others who work on the basis that if you throw enough mud, some of it will stick.' It would have been interesting to see a referenced example of a reputable scientist whose character has been assassinated by a gutter journalist working for the health food lobby!

One of the often repeated assertions of those who support the paradigm of pharmaceutical health care and industrially processed food, is that their work is open to peer review: 'A scientist's work is reviewed critically by his peers, that is by people who actually understand what he says, and if it cannot withstand their criticism and be reproduced by those who are competent to do so, it will be discarded along with his reputation.' Such assertions are references to a mainly illusory world, which may have existed in the halcyon days of science but in more cynical times has crumbled. Many scientists now fail to write up their results in papers. If they do, and results are commercially viable, such papers frequently do not see the academic light of day but are passed directly to project funders. Other papers are published by 'in house' journals edited by sympathetic and like-minded people and funded by the research patrons.

Before Marks gets to British food, on his way through allergy and vitamin and mineral supplements, he even finds space to tilt at one of Caroline Richmond's favourite subjects, 'chronic fatigue syndrome' or ME. His unreferenced and anecdotal comments about vitamins could have been culled from one of a thousand pulp productions written by health-fraud activists. Even when talking about allergy, he manages to cram in a derogatory remark about health foods: 'A recently well-publicised example was the near-death of someone who ate a vegeburger containing, unbeknown to him, peanuts, to which he knew he was allergic and ordinarily avoided like the plague.'

By using this example, Marks ingeniously turns the focus away from allergy and the possibility that peanuts specifically can cause anaphylactic shock, onto the apparently poor labelling practices of vegeburger producers. At the same time he makes the surreptitious point that vegeburgers can be more dangerous than hamburgers. It's all very clever, but like most propaganda once you have the key it fails to stand up to intellectual scrutiny.

The central thesis of the booklet, which defends coffee, sugar, beef and irradiated food – hardly major British products – employs commonplace arguments unsupported by references or any mention of critical research. As well as admitting that BSE has not yet been reported in any other country, Marks suggests that British poultry farming practices which produce salmonella are long overdue for review. He puts forward the idea of poultry screening, by 'modern analytical methods, for carriers of the infection'. Just exactly the kind of work which the Food and Veterinary Laboratory Limited was set up to take on.

Chapter Twenty Nine

Sewers Surveyed: Duncan Campbell

He bugged the office of an appointment panel at the New Statesman and Society when a new editor was being interviewed. He has the frequent notion that everyone is either plotting against him or trying to grab the credit for his undoubted success. It comes from a mixture of arrogance and insecurity. He is prone to long periods of sulking if things seem to go against him.[1]

Duncan Wilson Archibald Campbell is a scientist at heart. He was born in Glasgow in 1952; his parents were both academics. His father, who had a university Chair in Economics, and was a government economics adviser for Scotland, died in the mid-seventies. His mother is a mathematics lecturer, who during the war worked at the code and cipher service at Bletchley, the forerunner of the GCHQ. He has two sisters, one works as a Glasgow lawyer, the other in the City of London.

Duncan Campbell went from Dundee High School to Brasenose College, Oxford, where besides a degree in Physics, he picked up a criminal conviction for theft from the Post Office. In April 1972, when a second year undergraduate, he was fined £200 with £400 costs after admitting guilt to the first charges brought in this country for 'phone phreaking'.† He was charged on two counts of dishonestly making telephone calls with the intention of avoiding payment. One call was to Los Angeles and others to Melbourne and Moscow. He asked for five similar charges to be taken into consideration.

After Oxford, Campbell took a Master's Degree in Operational Research, at Sussex, then, after deciding against taking up a job in an

---

† Making free phone calls by electronic means.

Aldermaston laboratory, he flirted with technical magazines and a community newspaper. In 1974, prior to his initiation into the world of investigative journalism, he was happily designing sewer surveillance systems with a small industrial co-operative.

In 1976, not long after graduation, Campbell wrote his first seriously contentious article, with Mark Hosenball for *Time Out*, about the network of electronic surveillance stations centred on GCHQ at Cheltenham.[2] During Campbell's work for the article, he trekked across the country tracing the surveillance stations.

In early 1977, Mark Hosenball and Philip Agee†, both of whom had helped Campbell with his story, were deported. Then, a matter of days later, Campbell himself was arrested following a meeting with another *Time Out* journalist, Crispin Aubrey, and an ex-soldier, John Berry. Berry had been a Corporal in the Intelligence Corps, chiefly in Cyprus, before leaving the army in 1970 and becoming a social worker. All three men were charged under Section One of the Official Secrets Act.

What was to become known as the ABC trial (Aubrey, Berry and Campbell) began in 1978. Part way through the trial, the charges under Section One were dropped and replaced by lesser charges under Section Two. On being found guilty of this lesser charge, Campbell was given a conditional discharge for three years and ordered to pay £4,700 in costs.

The trial, to which the Left and the trade union movement rallied, precipitated Campbell into a politically prominent position as a left-wing investigative journalist. His writing prior to the trial, and for that matter afterwards, gave no real evidence that Campbell was sympathetic to the radical Left or the trade union and Labour movement. Today he is a committed supporter of the Labour Party, and a believer in what used to be called new realism. His transatlantic contacts are often part of the American Social Democratic network which has influenced the British Labour Party for decades.

The kudos bestowed upon Campbell by the ABC trial gave him entrée into a small clique of left-of-centre journalists; his politics,

---

† Philip Agee was an American who had left the CIA and then written an exposure of its work in Europe.

however, tended to be science-related. He rarely made contact with the beating heart of the socialist or working class movement, and chose in the main not to tackle traditional Left issues such as Ireland, the Miners' Strike and cases of injustice. Throughout the late seventies and early eighties he became a regular contributor to the *New Scientist*, the *Leveller* and the *New Statesman*.

The *New Statesman* had been an independently left of centre, or liberal, journal since the early twentieth century. Like many such journals, it has on occasions been through sloughs of despond, near bankruptcy and collapse. Its circulation dropped by over 50% between 1965 and 1980. In 1978, when the magazine was in dire straits, its management brought in the first of a long series of new editors.

In the late seventies and early eighties, Campbell covered a number of stories which attracted attention, including one which detailed the routine occurrence of police and intelligence telephone tapping. It was not until February 1984, however, that he was again thrown into the full glare of publicity. Whilst he was cycling in Islington, a loose front light caught in the wheel of his bike and he was catapulted over the handlebars.

While Campbell was taken to St Bartholemew's Hospital, his bicycle was taken into custody by Kings Cross police. When the police searched the bike's panniers, they found government documents marked 'restricted', and, suspecting a breach of the Official Secrets Act, they entered Campbell's flat and stayed for six hours. They were later to say that they had photocopied Campbell's contact book containing some nine hundred addresses.

In June 1986, contracted to BBC television for a series of six programmes on secrecy, Campbell interviewed Sir Ronald Mason, who had been Chief Scientific Adviser to the Ministry of Defence between 1977 and 1983. According to *The Times*, it was Mason who later alerted the government to the fact that Campbell knew about Zircon, a secretly-funded spy satellite. Campbell was to later expose the fact that the £500 million cost of Zircon had been illegally kept from Parliament.

Campbell finished working on the 'Secret Society' programmes in November 1986. Besides the Zircon issue, he had prepared programmes on computer data banks, emergency powers, radar systems, the Association of Chief Police Officers and the Cabinet

Office. In January 1987, the Zircon programme was banned by the government. The ban followed Special Branch raids on Campbell's home, the BBC offices in Glasgow and the *New Statesman* offices in London. At the end of January 1987, the *NS*, which was also carrying Campbell's stories, came to an agreement with the government that it would not publish any more material about Zircon. Between January 1987 and autumn 1988, when the Zircon programme was finally shown, Campbell toured the country showing the film privately to appreciative audiences.

The Secrets Case That Remained Secret

The actions of the police and the security services ensured that Campbell's programme about the Zircon spy satellite became lodged in the public mind as a *cause célèbre*. Its ban brought Campbell's recent career to a climax. Less well publicised, though, was a legal wrangle of quite a different nature which accompanied Campbell's programme on the Police National Computer.

All journalistic investigators tread a narrow line between exposing powerful wrongdoers and systems, and being in receipt of information from those who have helped them but are not entirely innocent. This is the case whether the subject under investigation is a criminal network or a government agency. No investigative reporter can do without sources and sometimes such sources are contaminated. When, however, the investigator begins to police his sources, handing information on to prosecuting agencies, he or she is in danger of becoming a policeman rather than a reporter.

In January 1989, seven men went on trial in Winchester Crown Court accused, under the Official Secrets Act, of misusing information on the Police National Computer. This trial, which was to last three weeks and end with all the defendants being found guilty, was the first of its kind in Britain. Unauthorised use of the PNC which was set up in 1974, or the disclosure of data from it to unauthorised persons, is covered by the Official Secrets Act and, since 1987, the Data Protection Act.

The defendants at Winchester, all of whom pleaded not guilty, were two police officers and five private detectives. The police officers were charged with breaking Section Two of the Official Secrets Act, by conspiring to obtain information about criminal records or vehicle ownership. The five private detectives were all charged with conspiracy to receive information in contravention of the Official Secrets Act.

According to Detective Chief Superintendent Arthur Mandry, one of the arresting officers, Campbell, at that time working at the BBC on his 'Secret Society' programmes, had set up a bogus company called MMS which had its own telephone number inside the BBC. The company had been set up with the sole purpose of obtaining information from the Police National Computer through private investigators.

Campbell's colleague, private investigator and journalist Gary Murray, tape-recorded a series of conversations with one private investigator, Stephen Bartlett, who claimed to be able to get information from the PNC. Murray claimed that Bartlett said:

> I give my contacts 20 criminal record checks a week. I have got half the police force in Basingstoke doing them for me.

Murray later gave evidence at trial, that in May and June 1986 he had rung Bartlett, posing as an investigator, and told him that his client, an employer in Glasgow, wanted criminal checks carried out on staff. Murray and Campbell, using the name Sinclair, set up a meeting in a Basingstoke hotel in June 1986. At the meeting, which Campbell filmed and recorded for his BBC programme, Campbell asked Bartlett to run the checks and gave him a £50 advance. Nigel Pascoe QC, defending Bartlett, said in his defence:

> Mr Duncan Campbell, working on the BBC series 'Secret Society', had encouraged a man just started in business to check criminal records.

At the trial, Murray defended his actions and those of Campbell (who did not appear) by saying that he had 'adopted a cover story like any MI5 or Special Branch officer who wishes to infiltrate an organisation'.

All the defendants were found guilty and given suspended sentences; Bartlett, whose defence had been that he was 'fitted up' by Campbell, received a six month jail sentence suspended for two years and was ordered to pay £500 costs.

This case must have caused Duncan Campbell some considerable worry as there was a slight possibility that he and Murray might be charged for conspiring with Bartlett to get information from the PNC.

The Winchester case is only important in that it highlights a method of working which, while it might be considered fair when used against lawbreakers, could be considered unprofessional when used against people such as doctors or other professionals targetted by a journalist for more political or subjective reasons.

Coming Out, AZT and Wellcome

'Margaret Thatcher is intolerant of alternative strands of opinion'. [3]

On November 16th 1987, Duncan Campbell was a guest of the Center for Investigative Reporting in California. He celebrated the Center's tenth anniversary by speaking and showing the Zircon film. He was also in America to cover AIDS issues for the *New Statesman*. Interviewed by the *San Francisco Bay Guardian*, he told them that he wanted to take the opportunity of his visit to San Francisco to 'come out'.

Those who had observed Campbell's previous career might have thought that he would quickly become a leading intellectual spokesperson for the gay community. Here was a man who could bring to the gay world the resources of an investigator and commentator previously used to fight the State. And were there not many facets of discrimination against gay men that might be fought, from discrimination in housing and education, the armed forces and the police, to inadequate representation in the media, and in 1987, one of the greatest issues of all, the discrimination which accompanied AIDS?

> His writing is about to take a new course and focus on Gay Rights. He'll be on Saturday's march protesting about clause 28, and is working on a story about the next Republican presidential campaign in the US utilising the AIDS issue to attack the gay community. [4]

History will show that Duncan Campbell failed to take sufficient care in analysing what discrimination against gay men really entailed. History might also show that Campbell failed to live up to his early promises to deliver a serious left-of-centre critique of the Reagan and Thatcherite philosophies which turned the phenomenon of AIDS to their ideological advantage.

In January 1988, Jad Adams, author and film maker, attended an international conference of health ministers in London. Adams, who was working with a small film production company called Meditel, had just finished work on a film for Channel 4, 'AIDS The Unheard Voices'; he was also finishing a book about HIV, *The HIV Myth*. Adams knew Campbell as a journalist and had been sympathetic to his work since being involved in the campaign organised on Campbell's behalf around the ABC trial. When Adams met Duncan at the conference, their conversation was amicable. Thinking that a debate about the HIV issue would be good to launch the book, and not knowing the direction of Campbell's recent thoughts on AIDS, Adams suggested that he took part in the debate.

In 1988 Campbell set up Stonewall, an organisation to raise money for the gay cause. He was also busy researching the issues around AIDS. In December Campbell and others set up the AIDS Charter, which like the earlier Charter 88 based at the *New Statesman and Society*, was a liberal consensus organisation, with a manifesto signed by a number of prominent people.

The results of Campbell's research into AIDS were worth waiting for. In June 1988, in his first major cover article in the *New Statesman and Society*, entitled 'The amazing AIDS Scam'[5] Campbell was highly critical of the drug companies and the AIDS treatments which they were offering. The article showed support for AL721, a natural product used at an early stage in America to stop the spread of the virus. It lambasted the drug companies, opportunists, and medical researchers aligned with drug companies[6] who were, the article suggested, exploiting the fears and vulnerabilities of those diagnosed HIV antibody positive. To many AIDS watchers it must have appeared fairly obvious that the 'medical researchers aligned with drug companies', to whom Campbell was referring, were the many doctors and scientists working in the major London hospitals on AZT. Then, in October 1988, at the same time as the five private detectives and the two police officers were being committed for trial, and in the same month that Caroline Richmond was holding a steering committee meeting to set up the Campaign Against Health Fraud, four months after the publication of the 'Amazing AIDS Scam' the Wellcome Foundation sued the *New Statesman*.

The libel action was brought by Wellcome over a September cover story alleging that Wellcome had declined to invest in developing safer vaccines for diphtheria and whooping cough. The article, by freelance journalist Ed Harriman, appeared on 23rd September under the cover headline 'Watch Out Fergie', and went on:

> If little Beatrice has her whooping cough jabs, they could trigger convulsions, brain damage or death. That is because the government make doctors use an old fashioned British vaccine, even though safer vaccines are made abroad. [7]

According to the writ, the *New Statesman* article had suggested Wellcome was guilty of improperly paying scientific experts to procure favourable evidence, improperly vetting studies written by government scientists, sacrificing concern for the safety of its products to the pursuit of profit and concocting a sham defence for its product. All of which sounds like a healthy and spirited attack by a serious investigative journal on one of Britain's most profitable multi-national drug companies.

Despite the evident seriousness with which the Wellcome Foundation began the action against the *New Statesman*, the matter was quickly settled out of court for a sum apparently close to £10,000. Ed Harriman, the author of the article, was upset over the settlement. He stood by his research, convinced that he had a case. He was particularly angry that a left-of-centre journal had capitulated so easily to a multi-national company.

* * *

Campbell 'came out' into a booming economy for the pharmaceutical companies and the medical research agencies. In 1987 Wellcome licensed AZT and then in 1988 began the Concorde trials. This world of high level medical research, with its political power blocs and its tentacles reaching into the major teaching hospitals, government agencies, voluntary organisations and the scientific milieu, was undoubtedly a tempting subject to a journalist who had previously sniped at the State. But here in this network, as in all powerful social situations, there also existed the seductive influences of fame and fortune. Here, in this area of science, were all the glittering prizes: the glory of being present at the reverse of the most serious disease in recent history, a chance to mingle with the gods on the brink of life-saving discoveries, science in the service of humanity.

In spite of his radical and antagonistic position towards pharmaceutical research in June 1987, by the spring of 1989 Campbell appeared to be both a supporter of AZT and writing in defence of those conducting the Concorde trials. In the six months between September 1988 and May 1989, the period in which the Campaign Against Health Fraud was being set up, something seemed to happen which changed Duncan Campbell's views about medical research, AIDS and the pharmaceutical companies. All his later writing suggests that he re-orientated himself and turned his talents loose on those who under other circumstances might have appeared to be his natural allies.

It is possible that Campbell simply changed his mind, from thinking that the drug companies were ripping off patients, to thinking that AZT presented the only feasible alternative to the ravages of AIDS, and the inevitable encroachment of charlatans.

When Campbell had written 'The Amazing AIDS Scam', [8] in June 1988, he had seemed quite certain of his position. The article is uncompromising in its stand against large pharmaceutical companies and the way in which the AIDS research industry was being organised. The lead paragraph in 20 point type goes straight for the jugular.

> As if AIDS weren't enough ... the big drugs companies are moving in for financial killings in the largest new pharmaceutical market in history. Duncan Campbell reports on the scramble for profits which leaves promising treatments out in the cold and creates disturbing alignments between leading researchers and the drugs industry. [9]

In his article Campbell avoids bearing down too heavily on Wellcome specifically. However, when he addresses the question of marketed treatments, it is clear to which company he is referring.

> Meanwhile, the fears and vulnerabilities of people who are HIV+ or have AIDS, are being exploited by drug companies and opportunists. Drug companies have kept the results of drugs trials confidential, have released information selectively, or have even delayed trials, in the interests of profitability. [10]

Campbell deals with the important issue of positive new drugs and their research being pushed onto the margins by products which already have a patent and a licence.

> The commercial importance of developing a new, and therefore patentable, drug which provides exclusive products, means that existing drugs and therapies which show potential for treating AIDS are not being researched; and other promising drugs or treatments are locked up and not used until the manufacturers can get patents or exclusive licensing sewn up. [11]

The article tackles the way in which research workers are aligned with the major drugs companies.

> Many medical researchers are demonstrably aligned through financial support with the drugs companies, whose efforts they are supposed to police. At the same time, red tape and lack of research funds or staff have delayed important drug trials for months or years. [12]

One of the only real alternatives to AZT in 1987, a substance that had a provable track record, was AL721. Since the beginning of AIDS treatment research, in America, AL721 has been considered a realistic treatment for HIV. [13] In the article Campbell states the case for AL721:

> One of many drugs that AIDS patients can't get because of commercial interests is AL721, a cheap and natural anti-viral agent made from substances as commonplace as egg yolks. It is believed to spoil the AIDS virus's ability to continue infecting human cells. [14]

Campbell suggests that as AL721 is made from natural substances, it should be marketed as a foodstuff, without the company who hold the patent needing a licence for its sale as a medicine. He describes the 'home industries' which were growing up to produce other versions of AL721 'So people with AIDS and their helpers, as well as rival companies have been busy at kitchen sinks and at labs, trying to imitate the secret mixture'. Campbell does not condemn this 'unofficial' manufacture of what he calls 'workalike' substances, but explains their production as an inevitable result of the high-powered commercial war going on over the heads of patients.

In 'The Amazing AIDS Scam' Campbell puts his finger on the very essence of the problems inherent in allowing private industry to develop and research treatments for epidemic-type social diseases:

> If a simple generic drug like Aspirin were to turn out to be the answer to AIDS, the pharmaceutical industry wouldn't want to know, or to test it. The industry is permanently biased towards making new drugs, even if they work no better, or even worse, than existing drugs. [15]

Dealing with AZT, Campbell makes a number of invalid statements, even so, this part of the article is replete with 'shock' 'horror' accusations against the pharmaceutical companies and their drugs. Campbell does not shrink from advertising the legal action taken against the US government agency, the National Institutes of Health (NIH), by National Gay Right Advocates, following the accusation of a $55,000 payment by Burroughs Wellcome to NIH to help the licence for AZT. [16]

Three years after 'The Amazing AIDS Scam' was written, a few tenacious activists in the gay community were still publicising its basic premises, with much more detailed evidence available to support the arguments, evidence which pointed to the fact that Duncan Campbell was right to be concerned about the monopoly practices of the pharmaceutical companies and commercially interested AIDS researchers. Wellcome did colonise the whole area of medical research into AIDS; they did commandeer the personnel and institutions in the voluntary sector and requisitioned most of the major public research facilities. Perhaps more importantly, an ongoing analysis of Wellcome's drug AZT has brutally dominated the intellectual and scientific debate about AIDS treatment, despite the fact that a growing criticism has produced increasing evidence that it goes no way to cure AIDS.

For Duncan Campbell, however, the reasoning of 'The Amazing Aids Scam', turned out to be an 'Amazing Flash in the Pan': by the middle of 1989 he had become Britain's most public proselytiser for the MRC and by default of a thorough analysis, Wellcome's work in the AIDS field.

Campbell, Big Business and AIDS

> While both parties [pharmacologists and people with AIDS] welcomed the dialogue, it was with quite different goals in mind. For the people with HIV and for the AIDS workers present, it was an opportunity to express unease about the trial and to express needs for information, medical monitoring and treatment options. For the medical profession, on the other hand, the seminar was seen as necessary to convince us of the need for the trial. [17]

The Concorde Trials of AZT began in the winter of 1988 and from the beginning they generated conflict. While some HIV positive individuals and AIDS workers simply wanted more say in how the trials were conducted, others had fundamental worries about the very nature of AZT.

On November 30th, a month after the Campaign Against Health Fraud held its first meeting, and the month following Wellcome's legal action against the *New Statesman*, Wellcome and the Medical Research Council held the first and last *open access* meeting about Concorde. The meeting took place at the Body Positive Centre in Earls Court. The object of the meeting, which was organised by the MRC, Body Positive and the Terrence Higgins Trust, was for the MRC and pharmacologists to put the case for the trials to HIV antibody positive sufferers and AIDS workers.

Meurig Horton, who later wrote about the meeting in *Bugs, drugs and placebos*, [18] says that as each objection to the way in which the trials were to be conducted was brought up, it was refuted and essentially dismissed by those who spoke for the trials.

Following the meeting, Campbell wrote a piece for the *New Scientist*, which had the meeting as its starting point. [19] The radical rhetoric and analysis of 'The Amazing Aids Scam' was gone, replaced by a dull and detailed consideration of the apparently tortuous problems facing those *who were to conduct* the Concorde trials.

In 'AIDS: patient power puts research on trial', the reader can sense in every line the new realism which Campbell was quietly embracing. Despite the radical inference of the title, the article is not actually about 'patient power': it is not even about patients, rather it is about how the MRC accepted compromise after compromise while negotiating the protocol of the Concorde trial with Wellcome. The theme of Campbell's article is as follows: fearful that Wellcome would not consult with the MRC and might finance and carry out the trials on its own, the MRC intervened, carved out an administrative role, and assured patients of fair play and continual critical surveillance of Wellcome.

What this compromised arrangement did was to commit the MRC, countless government grants and a large number of NHS doctors to the cause of Wellcome's pharmaceutical solution to AIDS. So it was that over the next two years, these doctors, salaried and trained by the tax-payer, would effectively work for a private pharmaceutical company, defending its unproven product.

> Clause 4 of the draft protocol's 'terms and conditions' requires every participating doctor to agree to 'obtain Wellcome's written consent before the publication of medical or scientific papers arising from [the trial]'. The protocol specifically forbade doctors to object if Wellcome refused permission to publish 'for the purpose of protecting an application for a patent'. [20]

While showing how Wellcome won a number of important victories during the writing of the protocols, Campbell paints the MRC as being worthy opponents of Wellcome, battling out each issue in the protocols on behalf of the taxpayer. In supporting the MRC, Campbell appeared to think that he was supporting a regulatory agency which was applying a brake to Wellcome's private interests: he showed no sign of having investigated the overlapping interests which permeate this field.

While a socialist would find it hard to support a multinational pharmaceutical company, a socialist and a scientist might certainly wish to support the MRC. A socialist might also feel compelled to support doctors working in the 'death wards' with AIDS patients, doctors who were not themselves responsible for the manufacture of the drug AZT. Few investigators would, however, have given uncritical support to either party if they knew of the hidden links between them and the very pharmaceutical company which had a licence to produce the only available NHS treatment for AIDS.

Campbell's 'patient power' article heralds the beginning of his identification with the MRC doctors working on the Concorde trials programme. From the time of his 'patient power' article Campbell was to sally forth in defence of MRC doctors whenever they needed help.

Far from 'patient power putting research on trial', many HIV antibody positive people must have felt that with the advent of Concorde they had been 'sold' to a private pharmaceutical concern for the purposes of experimentation.

The article broaches difficult moral dilemmas from the point of view of an élite of university trained doctors.

> Ian Weller, the consultant at the Middlesex Hospital who chairs the MRC's working party, said the trial presented a unique situation. 'With AIDS', he said, 'sharing information with patients has been absolutely critical to compliance [with a trial] ... it's inevitable in such a young population that they're going to be better informed'. [21]

Here, in this article, is the beginning and the end of the enigma about

Campbell's role in the field of AIDS. He is on the side of the professionals, the overworked doctors who have given their lives to ministering to AIDS patients. He sees such people as driven by altruism and the bourgeois quest for scientific discovery. Looking at Campbell's writing in class terms, it is clear that he identifies with the educated, science-trained middle class. He cannot side with the experiential view of the people with AIDS.

In Campbell's next AIDS article of January 1989, [22] he is committed to the AZT trials and the doctors who are runnning them.

> In a tightly-packed clinic in London's Fitzrovia, Dr Ian Weller and his colleagues chart every week the fate of 300 courageous young men involved in an epic tragedy. He has known most of the 300 personally, for almost six years. Since 1982 – when his hospital, the Middlesex, began preliminary studies on the nature of AIDS – they have become his acquaintances and friends. By the end of 1988, about 60 of these originally healthy young men had died. Most of the rest are ill. [23]

This is truly heroic prose, but it lacks identification with the real subjects of AIDS, those who suffer it. By the introduction of Dr Weller as a hero in the first paragraph, the reader is blinded to the nature of his role as a scientific doctor, and the treatment he is giving. Weller and his patients are all seen as passive victims, carried along by the tide. In fact Weller's role is determined by his training, pharmacological perspective, and the drugs company on whose behalf he is working. If heroic sentiment alone were needed to cure AIDS, none of the people mentioned in this paragraph would have died. Unfortunately AIDS and HIV need remedies, as many as possible. Dr Ian Weller, be he a good, indifferent or bad doctor, was, when this article was written, a Wellcome Fellow and chairman of the MRC working party on the Concorde trials.

If Campbell's identification with the MRC in particular, and doctors in general, was becoming clearer in the six months before March 1989, his ideas about AZT were in flux.

> The new approach is already being tried, successfully, by pioneer clinics in the United States and Europe. At the University of Amsterdam, researchers have found that the well known anti-

AIDS drug, AZT or zidovudine, appears to work better and
cause fewer side effects when given to people who *haven't* yet
developed AIDS. [24]

Missing from this article is the more sweeping analysis of the Amazing
AIDS Scam. Instead of adopting the scepticism felt by many in the gay
community who saw massive profits being made out of AIDS,
Campbell was beginning to be persuaded by the MRC and Wellcome
rationale for intervention with AZT.

One of the fundamental building blocks in this rationale is the
argument that AIDS is caused entirely by HIV infection and there are
no co-factors involved. This argument was then, and is now, essential
for the effective promotion and marketing of AZT and important in
the exclusion of other treatments. By January 1989, Duncan Campbell
seemed to have closed his deliberations on the subject of co-factors in
AIDS. His views seems to have been influenced principally by Dr Ian
Weller.

> It took several years of carnage before epidemiologists could say
> with assurance that no 'co-factor' or second cause was necessary
> to turn HIV infection into full blown AIDS. (If so, it could have
> been attacked in place of the complex and seemingly ineluctable
> HIV virus.) Even if other infections or poor general health *speed*
> progression to AIDS, they do not appear to be essential *ingredients*
> of the disease. Once this was known for sure, the fight to erect a
> safety net against AIDS could focus on the HIV virus alone. [25]

Throughout these months of what appeared to be a growing closeness
between Campbell and the medical personnel involved in the
Concorde trials, Campbell's writing still expresses some faint
commitment to the community of AIDS sufferers. It is not primary,
and it is rarely expansive, but some space is given to the development
of community treatments and alternatives.

It was not long, however, before Campbell's writing began to drift
away from the more general subject of AIDS and its orthodox
treatment, to what he seemed convinced were bogus treatments. Not
bogus pharmaceutical treatments, engineered by powerful companies,
making hundreds of millions of pounds profit, but those offered by
therapists and practitioners on the fringe. In the critical attacks which
were to follow throughout 1989, 1990 and 1991, the same guiding

influences of MRC doctors can be seen behind Campbell's campaign. Suddenly Campbell had friends in high places, and was privy to the inner circles of the medical profession.

Whether he realised it or not, by the spring of 1989, much of what Campbell wrote about and investigated helped Wellcome retain its monopoly control on AIDS treatment and hindered the development of a wider range of both alternative and orthodox treatment. He had been 'passed on' from the heroic doctors on the front line in the AIDS clinics, to the back seat doctors, who burrowed away inside the MRC promoting Wellcome's case and the cause of science. This they did principally through the Campaign Against Health Fraud and as soon as the organisation was officially launched, Duncan Campbell joined.

> I gladly joined CAHF when I heard about it in May – a long time after I'd already been exposing (orthodox) doctors and drug companies who'd taken patients for a ride. (The first quack I 'busted' was an orthodox practitioner who I alleged was cheating AIDS and cancer patients. He faced a GMC disciplinary hearing on November 23rd.) I think CAHF is an important new initiative to help us all to better healthcare. [26]

Chapter Thirty

Professor Michael Baum: The Trials of a Cancer Doctor

'No consideration was given to my personal circumstances, my possible wishes or my individuality'. [1]

'As a sick patient I am at my most vulnerable. I must have absolute trust in those doctors treating me'. [2]

Like Vincent Marks, Professor Michael Baum comes from a 'medical family'; not long after he had helped set up the Campaign Against Health Fraud, his brother Professor Harold Baum joined.[†] Both Harold and Michael are very successful in their chosen fields. Unlike his brother's, Professor Michael Baum's career has not however been free from controversy. In fact, at the very time that he was helping to found the Campaign Against Health Fraud, which intended to disseminate information about science and medicine and put the case for clinical trials, he was at the centre of a major controversy over the issue of 'informed consent'. Criticism of Professor Baum had first been raised in an *Observer* article by Adam Raphael. The article brought to light, in detail, for the first time, the case of Evelyn Thomas who had been unwittingly subjected to a randomised drug trial in 1982 at King's College Hospital. Her consultant had been Professor Michael Baum.

Conflicts between the patient's right to know and understand what is likely to happen to them, and the progress of medical science or the careers of surgeons, have been endemic to scientific medicine from its

---

[†] In 1986 Harold Baum and two other doctors were awarded a grant of over half a million pounds for the period 1986-7 by Wellcome. Harold Baum has also received funding from CRC, SERC, MRC, Nuffield, NATO, and Eisa Pharmaceuticals Ltd. Michael Baum has carried out most of his research work for the CRC and ICRF, but he has also received funding from ICI for work on Tamoxifen.

beginning. Such conflicts, although inherent in the everyday relationship between the physician and the patient, are brought into sharper focus in the circumstances of a drug trial. In the randomised and blinded trial, one group of patients are, unknown to themselves, given a non-effective treatment, a placebo, while others are given the treatment on trial.

At the heart of such conflicts is the single principle of 'informed consent'. A doctor who is completely open and honest with a patient, who gives the full information about the nature of the trial and the drug being used, before obtaining the consent of the patient, is unlikely to be criticised on ethical grounds. However, many doctors and scientists argue that to forewarn a patient about the exact nature of a trial is to reduce its scientific usefulness, increasing the chances of subjective responses distorting the outcome.

Drug trials are at the very heart of industrial medicine, and it is at this interface between the loyalty doctors feel to science and industry and the individual patient in need of care, that the most seminal medical conflicts emerge. Trials not only take place in hospitals but are also organised by general practitioners who can give unknowing patients new and unproven drugs. To organise drug testing in any other way would, according to orthodox doctors and scientists, involve bringing the individual's subjective response to illness into the relationship and erode the principles of science.

If patients were fully informed, there is a possibility they might refuse to take part in trials. Hard commercial considerations also come into the frame, some patients might take the view that medicine is not a philanthropic affair and by making themselves available for experimentation, they will in the long run help a drug company to make profit. This being the case, they might ask for payment commensurate with risk, or commensurate with the failure to be effectively treated. They might also ask for insurance contracts covering the eventuality of adverse effects or serious mishap. Such an eventuality would put the relationship of the doctor and the patient into a clearly different alignment than presently is the case; it would perhaps be a more honest relationship.

The pressure to introduce informed consent and to democratise drug trialing has inevitably opened up a market for agencies which recruit subjects for drug trials on a commercial basis. Governed entirely by commercial contracts, there is the possibility that the work of such trial centres and their recruiting agencies could exploit populations such as students, the unemployed, the low paid and captive populations such as prisoners. It has been estimated that in excess of 10,000 human volunteers were used for drug trials in 1988; they were paid fees of about £2million, by drug companies. [3]

Hospitals which opt out of the National Health Service could well consider making a proportion of their money by using their facilities and patients for drugs trials. In 1988, it was estimated that individual doctors and hospitals in Britain were paid sums 'ranging up to £100,000 to test new drugs on human volunteers'. [4]

Spurred on by two deaths in 1984, the Royal College of Physicians produced a report entitled *Research on Healthy Volunteers* in 1986.† They concluded specifically that large amounts of money should not be used as an inducement to get people to take part in trials and that all volunteers should be fully informed. The report, however, dealt only with 'healthy volunteers' and not with those people who turned to their doctor wanting treatment for an illness and later became the subject of a trial.

Many critics of scientific medicine believe that science and its needs should never take precedence over the rights of the sentient human being. They argue that one of the most fundamental human rights is the right not to be subjected unwittingly to experimentation. Another basic right is that, on turning to a doctor, a sick person should receive *the most proven, effective* and available treatment.

* * *

Evelyn Thomas (1932–89) came from a family of which four members had died of cancer; she herself was in her late fifties when she found out that she had cancer of the breast. After diagnosis, she went into King's College Hospital, one of London's most prestigious teaching hospitals, accepting the fact that she would have to have her left breast removed. The operation for the removal of a breast is called a mastectomy; one of the surgical alternatives to mastectomy is

† Deaths occurred during drug trials in May 1984 and July 1984. [5]

lumpectomy in which only the tumour and surrounding area is removed from the breast.

Shortly after her operation, Evelyn Thomas noticed that the woman in the bed next to her, who had been through a similar operation, was being treated with a different regime. While her neighbour had received counselling and been given useful information, the counsellor, she said, had 'avoided me, and a breast prosthesis was given to me by a male fitter more used to fitting artificial limbs'. It took Evelyn Thomas four years to find out that she had been included without her consent in a trial, and a little longer to find out the full details of the trial, the treatment she had been given and the treatment she had been denied.†

The randomised trials of which Evelyn Thomas had been a part were initiated in 1980 by the Cancer Research Campaign, under the auspices of Professor Michael Baum. They were titled the 'Collaborative trial for adjuvant systemic therapy in the management of early carcinoma of the breast'. Translated, this means simply that the trials were looking at supportive treatment following breast cancer surgery. Besides the granting and denial of counselling, two hormonal drug therapies, Tamoxifen and Cyclophosphamide, were given to the different trial groups.

The trials involved 2,230 women at thirty hospitals across the country between 1980 and 1985. None of the women involved in the trials were informed that they were subjects. The progress and condition of one group of women who were given the different treatments singly or in combination with or without the counselling, were compared with the condition and progress of another group who were given no adjunct treatments at all.

When Evelyn Thomas read about the results of the trial in 1986, it confirmed her suspicions that she had been part of a randomised trial. She was furious.

I placed absolute trust in those treating me and assumed our

---

† Evelyn Thomas claimed that besides the trial to which it transpired she was unknowingly subjected, she was also involved without her knowledge in a trial of surgical alternatives. However, although there had been at least one known mastectomy versus lumpectomy trial at Guy's Hospital, this trial had finished by 1982 when Evelyn Thomas was admitted to King's.

> relationship was based on openness and frankness. Actually patients at that time had their treatment determined by computer randomisation. My rights to have information and to choose, and my responsibility for my own body were denied. My trust was abused. [6]

Evelyn Thomas's anger was the anger of the just, and it was not to be placated by excuses later offered by doctors and others who sprang to defend the medical and scientific establishment. To further her argument, Evelyn Thomas quoted the Nuremburg Code, drawn up after Nazis had experimented on concentration camp inmates: 'the voluntary consent of the human subject is absolutely essential'.

The defence of those who had experimented on Evelyn Thomas without her consent was weak. King's College Hospital claimed that their Ethics Committee had originally stipulated that informed consent must be obtained. However, after a nurse counsellor pointed out that some patients became distressed when faced with the uncertainty of having to choose their treatment, informed consent was waived for all trial subjects who passed through the hospital. This explanation did not really tell the whole story. The trial administrators had been against allowing informed consent but had found themselves compelled to compromise with the Hospital Ethics Committee.

Following the compromise, the trial administrators arranged for women coming into King's for this serious and frightening treatment, to be asked *the night before their operation* for their consent to be included in the trial. The raising of this complex and worrying issue on the eve of an awesome operation threw most women into a state of immobility and confusion. The majority declined to be included in the trial. When the poor results of trial subject selection were brought to the attention of the Hospital Ethics Committee, they withdrew their demand for informed consent.

In the public debate which followed Evelyn Thomas's campaign, Professor Michael Baum, who headed the trial and was Thomas's consultant, failed to tackle the important issue and chose instead to take offence at the wording of Evelyn Thomas's complaint as it was presented in the *Observer*.

> Professor Baum said that he deeply resented Mrs Thomas's charges (that her trust had been abused) as he was one of the leading advocates of giving patients greater information. [7]

Only six years previously, Baum had entered his patients into the trial without obtaining their informed consent. In a long letter to the *Observer* the week following Adam Raphael's first article,[8] Baum claimed that, with hindsight, Evelyn Thomas was not *actually denied* any treatment, because after randomisation she had been one of the subjects given Tamoxifen.† He side-stepped the mention of counselling, which some would consider a vital aspect of recovery, and of which Evelyn Thomas was deprived.

In his attempts to defend himself, Professor Baum went through intellectual contortions, drawing attention to such facts as: 'Mrs Thomas was a victim of breast cancer, not of human experimentation.'[10] This was not denied. What was in question was Professor Baum's right to administer or withhold experimental treatments to patients *without* their consent. In the same letter to the *Observer*, Baum complained that the paper used a photograph of him which made him look like Mussolini. In a debate which touches upon mastectomy and its resultant problems for the patient's self image, such a remark might be judged vain in the extreme.

In his letter, Baum asks what he considers to be the seminal question of the debate: 'Was her [Evelyn Thomas's] treatment in any way compromised by my concern to improve the quality of cancer care for future generations of women?' Again, he evaded the central issue. While it is clearly within the authority of a physician to ruminate in the abstract about what may or may not be best for future generations, in the present it is the patient's choice of treatment, not the doctor's, which is primary. Many patients may not wish to make the same personal sacrifices as Professor Baum for the glory of medicine's future.

Also writing to the *Observer* in support of Michael Baum was Caroline Richmond. Richmond, who made clear her friendship with Baum, argued in favour of science and randomised clinical trials, while at the same time failing to address the matter of informed consent. 'I respect and admire Professor Michael Baum of King's College

---

† Another future member of the Campaign Against Health Fraud, the barrister and medical journalist Diana Brahams, makes the same irrelevant comment in the aftermath of the Evelyn Thomas case, saying that as it turned out, she got the 'preferred regime'.[9]

Hospital, and was disturbed by Adam Raphael's one-sided report last week.'[11] †

Richmond's letter was sent from the Wellcome Institute for the History of Medicine and was written in the same month that she called the first steering committee meeting of the Campaign Against Health Fraud, of which Baum was a member and which was to campaign, amongst other things, for randomised clinical trials.

When Evelyn Thomas found that she had been used as a guinea pig, she complained to the South East Thames Regional Health Authority. The complaint was dealt with by professional medical and health workers, whose system of complaints investigation makes the Police Complaints Authority look like something from the Magic Roundabout. Her case was reviewed by two assessors, a cancer specialist and a consultant surgeon. The cancer specialist who oversaw the complaint was a close colleague of Baum, and another future member of the Campaign Against Health Fraud, Professor Tim McElwain. Unsurprisingly, the professional review found that Evelyn Thomas had been treated in a correct and professional manner.

* * *

Regardless of what many doctors say in public, those like Michael Baum who are involved in and under pressure from the drugs industry, are secretive about drug trials and their accountability, or lack of it, to the patient. Doctors involved in drug trials see themselves as a beleaguered community.

Despite a number of deaths which have occurred as a consequence of uninformed trialing‡ throughout the eighties, attempts to change medical research methodology have not been completely successful.

Carolyn Faulder, a writer with a history of taking up women's issues, has been writing about breast cancer since 1977. In 1986, she

† In May 1992, Caroline Richmond reported a surgeon to the police and the Director of Public Prosecutions, after he performed a hysterectomy on her, without informed consent, during the course of a routine operation. [12]

‡ In 1982, an 84 year old widow died after having been involved in a secret randomised trial, in Birmingham. [13] In 1983, another trial patient died; the woman had been reluctant to take part in the trial. [14]

was the first person to publicise the case of Evelyn Thomas. The circumstances of Carolyn Faulder's involvement with the Evelyn Thomas case and the issue of informed consent are ironic.

In December 1980 Carolyn Faulder was invited by Professor Baum to sit on a Cancer Research Campaign committee, 'The Working Party on Breast Conservation', which serviced the 'Breast Cancer Trials Co-ordinating Sub-Committee'. Carolyn Faulder was invited, Michael Baum said in correspondence, as 'a member of the public to help us with our deliberations on "informed consent" '. [15]

The breast conservation working party was formally set up in 1981, to prepare the protocols for a further trial which measured the effectivity of mastectomy against lumpectomy similar to the one which had been carried out earlier at Guy's Hospital. The new trial was to take place at the Rayne Institute, the trial centre at King's College Hospital where Professor Baum was the consultant. It was due to begin in 1983.

Carolyn Faulder accepted the invitation to join the working party, thinking that she could make a real contribution to the debate about informed consent. Besides Professor Baum, the Working Party on Breast Conservation included some of the most influential heavy-weights of the cancer industry.†

Carolyn Faulder's time on the working party began well; she was treated courteously, and apparently included in the important discussions. Over the five years that she remained a member of the committee, however, she became increasingly uneasy about the reality of informed consent and her use to the committee. More than anything else, her involvement as a well-known woman writer and adviser appeared to fulfil a useful public relations role for the doctors, who did not appear that interested in changing their own ideas about the scientific method.

In 1983, at the time the new trial began at King's, Carolyn Faulder wrote an article entitled 'A Conspiracy of Silence'. [16] Before it was submitted, the article was shown to members of the working party, some of whom felt that it was 'too hard on members of the medical

† A number of these doctors were to appear in the late eighties aiding the Campaign Against Health Fraud to attack the Bristol Cancer Help Centre, in particular Dr Jeffrey Tobias and Dr Lesley Fallowfield. See Chapter Thirty Six.

profession'. Carolyn Faulder, seeing the consensus in the group turn against her, made it clear to the committee that it was her article, and though she was willing to 'soften' some of its points, she would not change its central theme.

After 1983, and the article, the feeling in the working party became hostile to her, with disagreements being expressed about her criticisms of doctors, both inside and outside the group. For her part, Carolyn Faulder had become so concerned about information coming to light during her ongoing research into informed consent, that she began work on a book.

When women were properly informed about the trial at King's, few of them wanted to take part in it. After just over a year, with only 160 women signed up for the trial, the administrators were forced to close it down. With the trial closed down, the working party also became imperilled because its sole job had been to work out protocols for the trial.

As far as Carolyn Faulder was concerned, the working party could not close down a minute too soon. By late 1984, some members of the working party had all but stopped speaking to her. In October, at a working party meeting, from which she was absent, Dr Jeffrey Tobias expressed considerable dissatisfaction with Carolyn Faulder's role on the committee. The minutes record him as saying: 'Although Ms. Carolyn Faulder had been recruited to the working party to introduce the subject [informed consent] to the National Press, it would seem that a disproportionate emphasis was now being placed on the issue.' [17]

When she saw these minutes, Carolyn Faulder was hurt and amazed; the comment had reduced her role on the working party to one of public relations. It crossed her mind that this may have been the role the group had in fact wanted her to perform. She re-read the letter from Professor Baum, in which it was unambiguously stated that she was invited onto the group so that she could give her advice and help about informed consent from the patient's point of view.

Before the working party was closed down in early 1985, Carolyn Faulder forced an apology and a retraction of the minuted remarks. The atmosphere had become so bad that she felt she was being deliberately ignored. Later that year, Carolyn Faulder's book *Whose body is it?* was published by Virago. [18]

In 1986, Carolyn Faulder was able to redress the balance in the case of Evelyn Thomas, by helping to get her case made public. Even then, it was not until 1988, six years after she was the subject of the trial, that her case was taken up by Adam Raphael and became a real issue of concern.

Chapter Thirty One

The Campaign Against Health Fraud, Part Three:
The Players and the Game, 1989–1991

> *Quackery is practiced not only by barkers at carnivals, but also by men with doctoral degrees who are members and officers of prestigious medical-scientific organizations and who are shielded from detection and criticism by such organizations, by public officials, and by governmental, corporate and organizational secrecy and public relations.* [1]

The Players

Those who represented the core of the Campaign Against Health Fraud at its formation in 1989 remained involved over the next two years; others pulled in on the fringe soon drifted away. On April 3rd 1989 at a Steering Committee meeting held at the Ciba Foundation, two joint presidents were elected: Dr Michael O'Donnell, broadcaster and former GP, editor of *GP* magazine, and television and radio presenter Nick Ross.

At that time, soon after the press launch, the leading Campaign activists were Dr Nick Beard; Dr Christopher Bass, a psychiatrist and committee member of the British Association for the Advancement of Science; Dr Simon Wessely; Professor Michael Baum and his brother Professor Harold Baum, Professor of Biochemistry at King's College Hospital; Diana Brahams, barrister and journalist; John Walford; Mark Pownall; Dr Iain Chalmers; Dr Vincent Marks and Duncan Campbell.

An initial statement from the Campaign about funding suggested that it was largely funded by individual subscriptions which stood at £12 per annum. The claim that individual members were paying for the Campaign was similar to that made by the American Council Against Health Fraud. It might strictly have been true, but as the majority of the early core activists had some financial connection with Wellcome, as well as other companies, or worked in projects funded by the pharmaceutical industry, the exact source of their corporate funds is relatively unimportant.†

Apart from Caroline Richmond's obvious connections with Wellcome, most other leading members also had links. Professor Michael Baum worked at the Royal Marsden Hospital which was joined to the Institute of Cancer Research where Dr Robin Weiss had developed testing kits with Wellcome. In 1990 at the same time as he took up a position at the Institute of Cancer Research, Michael Baum became clinical advisor to Breakthrough, a cancer charity which is raising money for a Breast Cancer Centre at the Royal Marsden Hospital. The Centre will be staffed by, amongst others, a team of eight Wellcome-funded scientists.[2] Michael Baum also ran the Tamoxifen trials in Britain throughout the 1980s for ICI. Wellcome and ICI had a number of joint projects, not least between 1985 and 1990, when they jointly owned Coopers Animal Health. Professor Harold Baum with two other medical scientists received a large grant from Wellcome in 1985. Dr Iain Chalmers was running the National Perinatal Epidemiology Unit, which was hugely subsidised by Wellcome.[3]‡ John Walford was the Grants Officer for the Multiple Sclerosis Society of Great Britain and Northern Ireland; this Society is a member of the Association of Medical Research Charities, an organisation administered by Wellcome.[4] The MS Society research is funded by a number of industrial interests including pharmaceutical companies.[5] Vincent Marks, biochemist and entrepreneur, heads the Department of Biochemistry at Surrey University which received nearly half a million pounds from Wellcome between 1985 and 1990.[6]

Given that considerable emphasis was later to be placed upon the

† In 1992, the minutes of the CAHF Annual General Meeting disclosed that in the year 1991-1992 the Campaign received a grant from the Wellcome Foundation. Other granting bodies included medical insurance companies and other pharmaceutical companies.

‡ In 1990, the Wellcome Foundation gave £186,182 and the Wellcome Trust gave £24,888, to the National Perinatal Epidemiology Unit.

idea of supporting the National Health Service and the general practitioner, the above members and those who were to follow were an odd collection. Just as the Campaign did not have any representation from patients, there were few hard-working general practitioners or people with clinical experience of everyday illness. Even more interestingly, few of the active members obtained their salary from working as medics of any kind; a large percentage of them were journalists or scientists of one kind or another. Caroline Richmond describes herself as a medical journalist; the two Presidents, Dr Michael O'Donnell and Nick Ross, were both journalists. When Dr Nick Beard met up with Richmond he had just finished working for Coopers and Lybrand and was on a course at Imperial College while also doing some free-lance journalism. Bernard Dixon was a writer and journalist. Later, Andrew Herxheimer from the *Drug and Therapeutics Bulletin* was to join. James Le Fanu, who joined later, though working as a doctor was also a free-lance journalist. In various articles, Duncan Campbell was to make much of the idea that those he attacked were at the centre of private medicine, and yet those he was working with were often supported by private interests.

As the campaign began to gather members, others with a Wellcome connection joined. Dr Jeremy Powell-Tuck, for example, had been a Wellcome Fellow and Sir John Vane, who joined with his wife Daphne Vane, had recently been one of the most senior scientists at the Wellcome Laboratories. A number of those who were to join the Campaign soon after its launch were associated with the processed food industry. John Garrow and Arnold Bender, whose wife became the membership secretary in May 1990, had both previously been grant-aided by large processed food concerns. [7]

By the time of the second Annual General Meeting in July 1990, at the Nutrition Department of St Bartholomew's Hospital, there were a few committed new members. One in particular, Professor Tim McElwain, must have seemed like a prestigious catch. McElwain was one of Britain's most renowned cancer doctors and a man who had been committed to orthodox cancer treatment for the whole of his working life.†

---

† See Chapter 36, for Professor McElwain's involvement in the survey of patients attending the Bristol Cancer Help Centre.

By the first months of 1990, the Campaign literature was quoting the names of those who although they had been associated with the campaign from the beginning had never been listed as members before: Dr David Pearson, the allergy specialist from Manchester, Duncan Campbell who had been involved from the beginning with Nick Beard, and a medical sociologist with a good reputation in the field of orthodox medicine, Dr Petr Skrabanek of Dublin University.

The Game

Within a couple of months of its launch, the Campaign Against Health Fraud had produced a newsletter. It was not as professional as its American counterpart[8] but it provided a good platform for the Campaign to promote attacks and debunking projects which it had initiated.

Caroline Richmond seemed most concerned that journalists got the proper view of health matters. To her, one of the principal aims of CAHF was to inform the media about treatments which did not reach an acceptable standard. 'The campaign will give journalists and everyone in the media concerned with health, access to an independent assessment of the many claims about health that are currently in circulation.'[9] Nick Ross, writing as the co-chairman, pursued a line common amongst American campaigners: that it is the elderly, the old and the ill who are exploited by health-fraud. Ross seemed to envisage the Campaign as an extension of the para-policing work which he did on the television programme 'Crimewatch', homing in on criminal fraud: 'it is a particularly offensive form of fraud when people pose as healers and exploit that desperate need for help by offering illusions of cure that can never be fulfilled.'[10]

The newsletter provided Campaigners with a forum where they could criticise what they saw as 'unscientific' ideas about health in the media. In the first newsletter, Caroline Richmond complains about the absurdity of suggesting that electricity has anything to do with illness; John Garrow complains about an article in the *Today* newspaper which talks about apricot kernels in the context of nutrition and Nick Beard complains about an item on reflexology in the *TV Times*.

The strong American flavour of the Campaign showed clearly in their choice of books they reviewed. Nick Beard reviewed a book published by Paul Kurtz and CSICOP's publishing company Prometheus, while Caroline Richmond reviewed an American Medical Association bibliography of health fraud.

In June 1989, Michael Baum gave an interview to the *Journal of Complementary and Alternative Medicine*. The article was entitled: 'Why I Will Bust Quacks'. [11] From his first utterances about the Campaign, Michael Baum, like other members, was 'economical with the truth' about its objectives. 'What the campaign is not, I must emphasise, is a clique of doctors, ganging up against alternative medicine. Alternative and complementary therapists would be welcome to join the campaign as long as they agreed with its aims.' In fact, the CAHF had from the beginning a practice of restricting membership to those who endorsed the use of pharmaceuticals. The few natural medical practitioners who tried to join were usually turned down, without any reason being given.

CAHF was formed, Baum claimed, 'for the specific purpose of protecting the public by highlighting examples of fraudulent practice and providing a panel of experts to independently assess health claims.† Recent years have seen a flood of explanations and promised cures for illness whose validity has never been tested; vitamins to increase intelligence, hair analysis which reveals vital missing minerals, diets that promise to counteract childhood hyperactivity or prevent cancer.' [12]

In three lines of this interview, Baum gave away a good portion of the game plan which CAHF activists had been working on for the previous year. The vitamins to increase intelligence alluded to the work of Larkhall Natural Health and Cantassium products. Hair analysis related to the work of Biolab and Stephen Davies and diets which promise to counteract childhood hyperactivity alluded to the work of Belinda Barnes on child hyperactivity. In fact, in each of these cases there were mountains of referenced work and scientific papers, none of which were ever alluded to by the Campaign.

---

† From the beginning CAHF was keen on 'assessing' claims for diagnostic techniques and treatments. As in the main they knew nothing about alternative and complementary medicine, and some like Caroline Richmond had no clinical experience, it is difficult to see from where they thought their authority in this judgemental capacity came.

By the time the first newsletter was published, it was evident how the Campaign were to go about prosecuting their complaints against non-pharmaceutical treatments. Apart from sundry bodies like the Advertising Standards Authority, they were to rely upon the investigators at MAFF and the Medicines Commission, inside the DoH. The Campaign even made overtures to the Department of Health, asking if they might be formally recognised as a prosecutorial agency by them.

It is not surprising that they expected such official bodies to prosecute their complaints; both MAFF and the DoH generally have a cosy relationship with industry and what might be called an intimate relationship with the pharmaceutical and agri-chemical business. In the second newsletter, Mark Pownall, writing about a 'MAFF crackdown on misleading nutritional claims', points out germanium as being 'clearly dangerous', a product which 'should be subject to the Medicines Act' as should 'promotional claims of other health enhancing properties of "health food" products'. [13] Clearly the CAHF had powerful friends in high places, because germanium was not simply made subject to the Medicines Act; a short time after the newsletter was written it was banned.†

At the Annual General Meeting of CAHF in 1990, members voiced concern that the organisation had been accused of being in the pay of the pharmaceutical industry (in particular the Wellcome Foundation). This was refuted and the minutes recorded that: 'There is no connection, nor has any money been received from any pharmaceutical company towards any of our activities.'

Some time was taken up at the Annual General Meeting discussing under what circumstances and from whom, the campaign might accept money. 'The Committee decided that money from any source, including the pharmaceutical industry, would be acceptable if it was given on a *hands off* basis and provided that no single interested party contributed more than 25% of CAHF's annual requirement.'

Nick Ross was apparently unhappy with the decision, believing that the pharmaceutical and food industries had the greatest interest in the survival of CAHF. He felt that such donations would be used against

† For the story of how germanium was banned see Chapter 34.

the Campaign. In the discussion which followed, Professor Vincent Marks, Professor John Garrow, Wally Bounds, Dr Iain Chalmers and Dr Jeremy Powell-Tuck all agreed that money could be taken from any source. Sir John Vane pointed out naively that anyone contributing would do so because they had *an interest* and this need not influence the behaviour of CAHF.

By the time of the second AGM in 1991, commitment appeared to be waning. While there had been over sixty members at the first AGM, only twenty-one were present at the second. The Campaign felt that it had been penalised when earlier in the year it had been refused charitable status because of its campaigning activities.

The meeting decided to change the name of the organisation from the Campaign Against Health Fraud to HealthWatch. The point of this cosmetic exercise was to make the organisation appear less combative and more charitable. It also placed HealthWatch in the context of a number of other groups, mainly set up by the police: Neighbourhood Watch, Homewatch, Carwatch. In the following year, 1991, though its campaigning zeal had not abated and it had done immense damage to a range of alternative and natural practitioners, it was granted charitable status.

The British Health Fraud Philosophy

The modern health fraud philosophy is extensive and complex, but not really a philosophy, more a series of *post hoc* defensive arguments for orthodox medicine. At the heart of these assumptions is a simple equation: anything which challenges the monopoly hold of the chemical companies on food production and pharmaceuticals, the professional status of doctors, or the ruling paradigms of industrial technology should be attacked.

Much is made by activists of the fact that the health-fraud philosophy is based upon science. In fact health-fraud arguments are rarely objective, let alone scientific. Quite the opposite, they are usually highly personalised and apparently given weight by unsupported assertions.

The spate of articles and interviews which appeared between the beginning of 1989 and the end of 1991 give a good idea of the Campaign's preoccupations and points of intervention. Many of its arguments have a patina of seductive popularism.

One article which plainly illustrates the way in which CAHF uses opportunities to attack complementary medicine is an article by Anne Wiltsher in the *New Statesman and Society* of July 7th 1989. [14] This article purports to be a look at the fortunes of complementary medicine as we approach new European regulations in 1992.

The article begins with a brief introduction which lampoons complementary medicine (the article is accompanied by one large and one small photograph of individuals undergoing acupuncture treatment; both pictures are visual jokes). It then briefly discusses the attitudes of the European powers towards complementary medicine, before launching into propaganda for the CAHF.

> CAHF wants to see testing by clinical trials of all health products and procedures and better regulation of practitioners to protect the public. [15]

CAHF has, the article says, the backing of the Advertising Standards Authority and the Consumers' Association.

> The latter has recently pointed out the dangers of creating fashionable herbal remedies from garden plants. For example, camomile which is often taken as tea is now thought to cause vomiting if taken in large doses. Comfrey is now linked with liver cancer in rats. [16]

Oddly enough, both these examples are given in the report on complementary medicines published by the BMA, three years ago in 1986.

The January 18th 1991 issue of *GP* carried an article by Dr Charles Shepherd, a long-standing member of the CAHF and a Clinical Adviser to the Media Resources Service of the CIBA Foundation. Entitled ' "Natural health" pills can be lethal', [17] a centre column sub-heading reads 'Many of the remedies can have bizarre and disturbing toxic effects'. It is one of the most climactic anti-vitamin articles ever published: a kind of 'Vita-disaster' article.

The piece is illustrated with a large picture of Barbara Cartland. The caption to the photograph reads 'Novelist Barbara Cartland: renowned for championing "natural health" pills'. As the heading states that 'natural health pills' can be lethal, one wonders why Barbara Cartland did not sue.

A good deal in Dr Shepherd's article reinforces the fact that *GP* magazine is subsidised by drug company advertising. 'Many of the new-age pills and potions in the alternative pharmacopoeia are drugs in all but name. But they masquerade as "nutritional supplements" in order to evade the strict rules on efficacy, safety and product promotion which the Medicines Act imposes on conventional drugs.' [18]

The article proceeds to attack all vitamin and mineral preparations without giving any supporting evidence for statements made about their damaging effects.

> Far from being natural and safe, remedies sold in health food shops, can have disturbing toxic effects. Aromatherapy can result in allergic reaction and burns to the skin. Selenium is toxic and excess zinc can depress the immune system. Excessive intake of both fat and water-soluble vitamins can result in severe toxic effects. Vitamin A accumulates to cause encephalopathy (swelling of the brain). Vitamin B3 can produce severe hepatoxicity (poisoning of the liver). Vitamin B6 causes peripheral neuritis (inflammation of the nerve ending) at daily doses above 200mgs: and vitamin C is known to increase the bioavailability of oestrogen, so converting a low-dose contraceptive pill into a high-dose one. [19]

On January 7th 1991, Derek Jameson interviewed Professor John Garrow, at that time Chairman of HealthWatch, on Radio 2. [20] The interview was mainly about vitamins. Professor Garrow put forward the HealthWatch line, saying firstly that vitamin supplements were of no medicinal use and secondly that some of them were positively damaging.

> My view and the view of HealthWatch is that if any material, whether it's vitamins or minerals or Royal Jelly or Ginseng, or whatever is sold to people making them believe that it's going to do something for their health, it should have a product licence, they have to show the Department of Health that they are safe and effective ... Lots of these things which are sold in health food shops – so-called health food shops – as if they were foods, really are being sold as medicines to make people healthier. [21]

Professor Garrow, like Professor Bender, has a consuming passion against health food and health food shops. Professor Garrow took advantage of the interview to make an acute point about them:

> people go into health food shops thinking that everything there is
> natural and is bound to do them good, often it won't do them
> good, usually it's a waste of money, sometimes it'll do them
> harm. [22]

The greatest fallacy promulgated in these bizarre discourses about
'health foods' and 'health food shops' is the idea that the production of
processed foods is tightly controlled, and free of any damaging
substances. Only recently have manufacturers had to describe contents
on packaging. Now that they do, it is with reluctance and often in
mystifying terms. None of the substances added to processed foods go
through trials, or are tested over time for adverse effects.

'Thames Action', the ITV access programme, reported on vitamin
supplements on November 23rd 1990. [23] The programme began by
explaining how much money the vitamin producers make. Vitamin
producers must be the only groups within the capitalist economy,
(apart from criminals such as drug dealers) constantly criticised for
making profits. When it comes to vitamins and 'health foods',
journalists and health fraud campaigners radically change their
ideological position, suddenly finding the profit motive morally
reprehensible. Drug company profits are never alluded to.

> Vitamin supplements are big business – we're all taking them –
> but are they just a waste of money and are they safe ... The
> vitamin industry is massive. Last year it's estimated that we
> consumed a record 133 million pounds worth of vitamins – that
> means we popped an astonishing 2,000 million pills. [24]

'Thames Action' used a viewer to comment on the issue during the
programme, while experts supplied specialised views. Viewer Shelley
Batheram talked about the things which it was claimed vitamins do;
holding up a book she said: 'This book lists some of the claims that
have been made about vitamins in the past. For example, vitamin D
keeps you young and beautiful, vitamin E boosts your sex drive and
potency, vitamin A is meant to stop you getting cancer, vitamin B6
retards ageing and prevents tooth decay, and vitamin C, as we all
know, stops you catching a cold.' [25]

The tone of the item is determined by these sceptically introduced,
unreferenced claims. Viv Taylor-Gee moved the item to its logical

conclusion, before interviewing the expert, Professor Vincent Marks. 'It's possible to overdose on nearly all vitamins especially if the vitamin supplement comes in megadoses.' [26] It is also possible to overdose on ice cream and even water, not to mention a large array of pharmaceuticals, especially in megadoses! Vincent Marks explains:

> We recently had a patient in the hospital where I work ... a woman who had been led to believe that by taking vitamin D and A she would be made to look young and beautiful. She took her vitamins in the form of halibut liver oil capsules and ... believing that if one was good, two must be better, in fact she took so many [she turned into a fish ... No?] that by the end of a relatively short period of time she had produced severe kidney damage and presented in the hospital as a case of kidney failure. [27]

Once again we are given a truncated, anecdotal case history which tells us next to nothing about the clinical condition of the woman involved. Could it be for instance that she was mentally ill? After all most people know that while an aspirin can stop a headache, it would not be advisable to take a whole bottle to combat a bad headache.

Vincent Marks' message is simple and asinine: vitamins are basically very dangerous in the hands of ignorant people. If you take large quantities of halibut liver oil capsules to make yourself beautiful you will end up with kidney failure. The programme did not make it clear that Vincent Marks was an active member of HealthWatch, or that he has spent most of his professional life persuading people that sugar does you no harm – even in megadoses.

This programme, like many others, failed to interview a doctor who works with vitamins and food supplements. The final word was given to Vincent Marks.

> I don't think that people believe that there are any risks associated with taking vitamins. They subscribe to the view that vitamins are good for you and therefore things which are good for you cannot do you any harm. But of course they are completely and utterly wrong. [28]

Thompson Prentice of *The Times* is not a member of HealthWatch, although he reported sympathetically on its propaganda from the organisation's inception. In September 1990 he reported on a BMA conference in Edinburgh. [29] The piece, snappily headlined: 'Cures for chronic fatigue disorders "may be dangerous"', begins 'Many thousands of people suffering from chronic fatigue disorders are being exploited by private practitioners peddling "hocus pocus" remedies that are unproven and may be dangerous, a leading specialist told a medical conference yesterday.'

If the leading expert, Professor Ariel Lant, produced any evidence for his assertions, it was not reported by Thompson Prentice. 'The devastating effects of chronic fatigue syndrome have produced a host of alleged treatments, many from the realms of alternative medicine.' Professor Lant called for scientific trials to evaluate remedies, while Prentice intoned gravely: 'Professor Lant's comments on the treatments amount to some of the strongest criticisms expressed in recent years on the response by doctors to various forms of chronic fatigue.'

Although Professor Lant made it clear that he did not agree with the Caroline Richmond school of thought that ME is a figment of the 'imagination of either the patient or the practitioner', he did agree with HealthWatch that quacks were operating in this area: 'Patients were offered analysis of samples of their hair and skin, others were having tests for non-existent allergies, and some were paying for preparations of primrose oil or pumpkin seeds ... The list is enormous. Some of the hocus pocus treatments are so bizarre as to be unbelievable, and *I believe some of them may be harmful.*'(italics added). [30]

Well, there we have the considered scientific view, people being tested for non-existent allergies, *paying for* evening primrose oil or pumpkin seeds, where will it all end? Thomson Prentice had got himself another big news story!

Bella is an inexpensive woman's magazine. On April 14th 1990, it carried a classic anti-health food article, 'Food For Thought: Health food is more popular than ever – but "natural" isn't always safe', by Andrew McKenna. [31] The full page article was accompanied by a small picture of a widely grinning Professor Arnold Bender, a large picture of a worried woman scrutinising a 'health food' product in a 'health food shop' and another small picture of a tub of organic germanium, which, says the caption, 'can kill in large doses'. The artwork was as 'pulp' as the message, a kind of True Health Fraud story, to be read in a slow exclamatory American accent, reminiscent of Broderick Crawford in 'Highway Patrol' or the introduction to the 'Streets of San Francisco'.

> Nurse Jessie Thompson felt stressed, so she bought some herbal relaxation pills from a health food shop. She took 30 pills – and suffered jaundice, kidney failure and such serious liver damage she spent 10 weeks in hospital. Jessie, 60, who was off work for a year in total, has now recovered. 'I thought herbal pills were safe because they're natural ... I was wrong.' [32]

This sounds like an interesting case, a little like the fish oil woman reported by Vincent Marks. A classic of its kind, it makes all kinds of unsupported statements, which are backed up by the 'expert', HealthWatch member Professor Arnold Bender.

Professor Bender has worked, throughout his life, for the processed food manufacturers. He was head of research at Farley Infant Foods, head of research at Bovril, and has received research funding from Cadbury Schweppes, Heinz and Kelloggs. [33] Off he sounds on the pages of *Bella*: 'There is no such thing as a health food – there is such a thing as a health food industry. No one food is good or bad for you. What counts is a varied, balanced diet. A lot of people are being misled.'

That is certainly true! Andrew McKenna takes up the story: 'It's recent health scares over the £600 million a year diet supplement and herbal remedy industries that have led to the most scathing criticisms ... In Britain, we spend £137 million a year on mineral and vitamin pills. In 1989 alone, sales of Tandem IQ vitamin packs rocketed from 1,000 a month to half a million, after trials at a Welsh school claimed that extra vitamins boosted pupils' IQ.' [34]

The article makes use of a Consumers' Association report on health foods, which it says concluded: 'If you were to eat only foods from a health food shop, you could be following a very unhealthy diet.' [35]

According to McKenna, the Consumers' Association report found that health food shops stocked some nuts prone to cancer-causing substances; kidney beans which if improperly cooked could cause severe gastroenteritis and diarrhoea; a dried fruit preservative which causes asthmatic attacks in a few people and muesli bars with a very high sugar content. [36]

What a condemnation of health food shops! The mind boggles, and just think, if they found these things in health food shops, what would they find in any of the major food retailers? Perhaps the most amazing thing about articles of this kind is that it makes one realise that the Medicines Act should cover the licensing of journalists, some of whom can of course seriously damage your health.

PART FIVE

Over the Top: Battles & Skirmishes After 1989

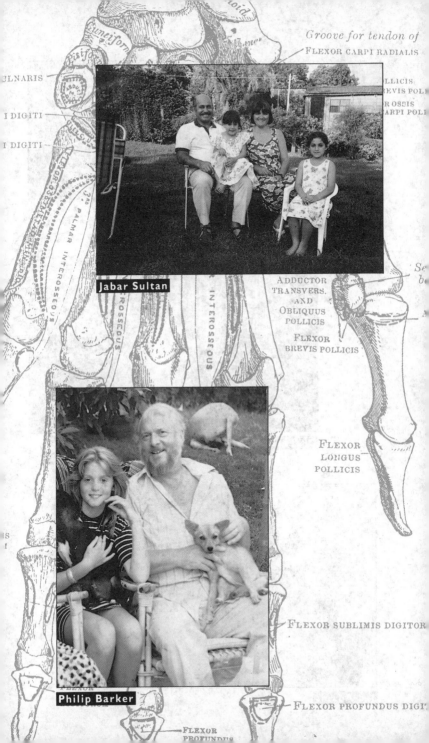

Jabar Sultan

Philip Barker

Elizabeth Marsh

Dr. Leslie Davis (left)

Jad Adams

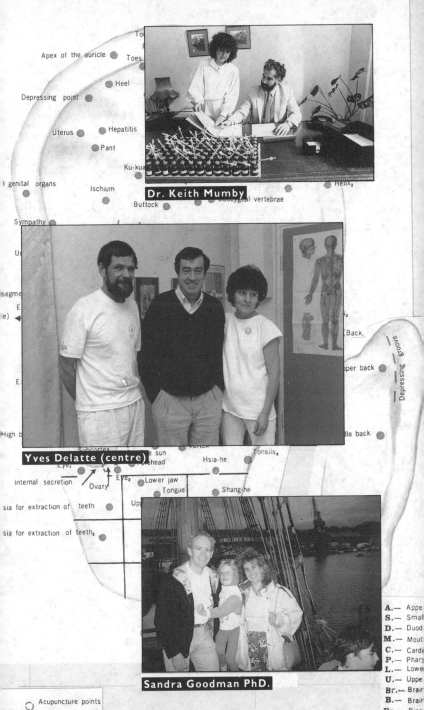

Chapter Thirty Two

Wellcome, Part Four :
Colonising the Voluntary Sector

Illness, a central concept of medicine, is not a matter of objective scientific fact. Instead, it is a term used to describe deviation from a notional norm ... If illness is a judgement, the practice of medicine can be understood in terms of power. He who makes the judgement wields the power. [1]

After a drug has been granted a licence, there is still competitive pressure from other manufacturers. The large sums invested in the research and development of most drugs mean that the product has to run the full course of its licence without competition in order to ensure maximum profits. The later years of the licence are the most important because it is only then, when research and development costs have been cleared, that the product begins to make a profit.

In the first twelve months of its licensed production, Wellcome did not make a profit on AZT. In fact the company made a loss. [2]† By 1992, five years on, AZT was more than paying for itself. Consumption of AZT in that year was estimated at 44.7 tonnes. Manufacturing cost per tonne had fallen from £6.6 million to £3 million. Research and development costs, though twice what they had been in 1987, at £12.6 million, were only half of the £24 million they were when costs had peaked in 1989 and 1990. [3] It was estimated in 1990 that by 1992 Wellcome could be making £335.7 million net profit from AZT. The years between 1988 and 1990 were clearly crucial years for Wellcome and the profitable acceptance of AZT.

---

† 0.9 tonnes of AZT were consumed in Britain in the first year of its production, 1987 to 1988. Its manufacturing cost per tonne at that time was £6.6 million; in the same year research and development costs totalled £6.4 million. Wellcome made only £10.4 million gross profit and no net profit.

The Wellcome Foundation knew from the beginning that AZT would not be an easy drug to market. There were two principal reasons for this. Firstly, few illnesses are community-specific and rarely do people with specific illnesses form cohesive communities unless compelled by social pressure. However, both these possibilities were on the cards with AIDS. Secondly, while cancer, for example, tends to strike an older and more conservative population, HIV had become a scourge of the young, and often marginalised, homosexual population. Would doctors be able to persuade these patients to trust to the apparent benefits of orthodox medicine as quietly as cancer patients had succumbed?

Rare contemporary examples of community-based illness, such as the site-specific aluminium pollution at Camelford, gave Wellcome a glimpse of how volatile and politically conscious a community assaulted by illness could become.

The marketing of a new pharmaceutical by specialised advertising and public relations companies begins long before it is granted a licence. For its marketing strategy on AZT the Wellcome Foundation employed the firm of Collier and Waring, an advertising agency which designed and presented everything from mail shots to doctors, to articles placed in the national press. A subsidiary of Collier and Waring, Colloquium, was employed to organise meetings, conferences and symposia. Colloquium had previously organised the presentation of Wellcome's largest selling anti-herpes drug Zovirax.†

The most important marketing job, that of publicising AZT and keeping it in the headlines, and if possible denigrating the opposition, was given to the public relations company Rowland Worldwide, à subsidiary of Saatchi and Saatchi. In 1986, Rowland took over an ailing PR company called Kingsway Public Relations, creating Kingsway Rowland. Kingsway had organised many campaigns for the processed food and chemical companies. One of its principal directors was Sir David Crouch, who while handling these campaigns had been appointed to the Medical Research Council's AIDS directed

† Colloquium contracted out some of the conference, meetings and presentation work to Mike Gibbs in Birmingham who worked closely with Dr Andrew Revell and Rosemary Hennings at Wellcome and Professor Peter Sever at St Mary's Hospital.

programme.† When Kingsway became Kingsway Rowland and was then taken into Rowland International, Crouch continued to be a consultant, until he moved on to the Westminster Communications Company.

The wider shores of public relations work are rarely revealed,‡ but, undoubtedly, Rowland would have been responsible for retaining many journalists and experts in the field of AIDS and sexually transmitted diseases, as well as those who might write or speak about clinical trials and the dangers of alternative medicines.

Each drug produced by Wellcome has a marketing team which works with advertising agencies and public relations companies organising the sales campaign. In the case of AZT, this team knew that their problems would proliferate as the marketing tendrils spread out to reach, first general practitioners and then gay society. In fact, Wellcome would have really liked to deal directly with the patient population and completely cut out possibly critical, medical professionals.

Experience in America had shown that there were doctors within the gay community who had worked with alternative therapies for years. These doctors had good contacts in the community and a number of them were from the start unsympathetic to AZT. There were alternative practitioners who might want to run trials with various treatments on HIV antibody positive patients, or even empower sufferers to research their own treatments. And at the very base of the AIDS pyramid, there existed the independence and free will of people with an inexplicable and apparently terminal disease.

AZT needed an aggressive marketing strategy. It needed maximum propaganda to counter accusations of profiteering which would inevitably be levelled at Wellcome. Most importantly, Wellcome needed a network of organisations which could ensure that people with AIDS came into contact with AZT; it also needed agents, possibly within the gay community itself, who could give intelligence reports and react against those who opposed the Wellcome line.

---

† See Chapter Twenty Three

‡ Public relations companies were implicated in the dirty tricks used by British Airways against Richard Branson's Virgin Airways. These dirty tricks were diverse, from approaching Virgin passengers with special offer BA tickets, to spreading rumours about the financial health of Virgin.

In 1990, three years after AZT had been licensed, and a year after the Campaign Against Health Fraud had been set up, market analysts Barclays de Zoete Wedd (BdZ) reported on the prospects and risks for the Wellcome Foundation in the production of AZT. [4] They detailed the profitability and pitfalls of AZT, both of which would increase with time.

According to BdZ, by 1990 the previously fluctuating and unstable market for AZT had stabilised, and with the 1989 decision of the American FDA to sanction the use of AZT for non-symptomatic HIV antibody positive subjects, the drug had reached a plateau of plausibility.

BdZ identified the destabilising factors which had been at work early in the drug's life in 1988 and 1989. These factors were: the possibility of the sudden obsolescence of Retrovir with a discovery of a 'cure' for AIDS; any word of debilitating toxicity; comment upon its questionable efficacy; possible rapid approval for competitors and, finally, a decline of the AIDS epidemic.

Reported neatly as these possibilities were, they did not reflect the 'street-reality' of fluctuating market forces in relation to AZT. Obviously, the scare which leads to a tailspin in share prices begins long before a new 'cure' is announced and months, if not years, before a licence is given to a competing product.

If we look at these market destabilisers more closely, they can be fleshed out. There could be no sudden 'cure' for AIDS within the boundaries of official pharmacology. It takes up to twelve years to develop, test and then gain a licence for a new drug. A 'cure' or a less toxic alternative to AZT might appear from the findings of alternative practitioners. Such a treatment programme might emerge quickly from any number of doctors working in the field of alternative medicine.

News of debilitating toxicity would obviously lead to shares plummeting. Such information could, though, be easily censored as long as most research related to AZT was sponsored and controlled by Wellcome and it was able to acquire a veto on any papers or published information. Obviously, in its own publications, Wellcome would make little reference to adverse side effects or toxicity. As we have seen, doctors like Dr Charles Farthing, who supported Wellcome and the use of AZT, felt able to say as early as September 1987, that the early benefits when patients started on AZT were 'quite dramatic', and that there were no serious adverse side effects. [5] There were though two other sources of 'idle talk' about side effects and toxicity: journalists and patients themselves. Such people might also be those who spread other market destabilising information – news of the lack of efficacy of AZT.

Possible licensing approval for a competitor company is again something which does not happen overnight. Wellcome was confident of controlling the apex of the system, with highly placed individuals, agreements with the DoH and influence inside the Committee on the Safety of Medicines. At the early stages of the journey to a licence, any competitor drug would have to go through trials. Trials were totally dependent upon the availability of cohorts of HIV antibody positive subjects. After 1988 and the beginning of the Anglo-French Concorde Trials, the majority of cohort subjects came under the control of Wellcome.

The final obstacle to profit analysed by BdZ was the possibility of a halt in the escalation of the AIDS epidemic. Official figures were the principal guide to this projection, and these were in the main collated by official sources, then re-presented in the press or via a populist interpretation through spokespersons for the voluntary agencies. Such sources promulgated three central themes throughout 1989 and 1990. Firstly, that the AIDS epidemic was an infinite spectre which would increase exponentially and consume Britain's population within decades. [6] The two secondary themes were ancillary but logically necessary if the first were believed: that death was the absolute and inevitable consequence of being HIV antibody positive and that AIDS in Europe was quickly transversing the boundaries of the homosexual population and beginning to infect the previously healthy heterosexual population at a similar unstoppable rate.

In Britain, during 1989 and 1990, all the theoretical arguments of the analysts which addressed the marketing obstacles for Wellcome and AZT, were fought out on the street. The social and political construction of the AIDS epidemic, the tenuous links between the HIV virus and AIDS, together with the questionable efficacy of the drug AZT, ensured that the marketing for the drug was one of the most hard fought in Britain.

The Voluntary Sector AIDS Organisations

Through the provision of zidovudine (Retrovir) the company has a high profile with the various HIV communities, but this is now no longer solely as manufacturers of an anti-HIV drug. [7]

People with AIDS have handed over their power to a pharmaceutical-medical cartel. [8]

Although the market for AZT was a highly volatile one which threatened to throw Wellcome into a sudden share price tailspin, the market did have one advantage for the company. With many new drugs, the drug company has first to persuade the general practitioner of the efficacy of the treatments. This is done by using marketing techniques which range from persuasive arguments to persuasive golfing holidays in the Caribbean. Because from the beginning AIDS had precipitated an organised community response, Wellcome was able to approach HIV antibody positive people and AIDS sufferers directly through the organisations which 'the community' had set up. All the persuasive methods normally reserved for the general practitioner were now brought to bear upon those who were HIV antibody positive, those with AIDS and their carers.

Between 1988 and 1992, the National Health Service and the Department of Health radically failed AIDS patients in Britain, letting them fall prey to Wellcome's monopoly power to press them into the experimental use of AZT. To captivate and colonise the patients, and their organisations, Wellcome used sophisticated marketing arguments and a seemingly endless stream of financial donations.

Wellcome's colonisation of the voluntary sector AIDS organisations was not a simple matter. It involved the subtle cultivation of philosophical and medical hegemony around the subject of AIDS and HIV. So covert and well organised was this infiltration and usurpation that large numbers of workers in the sector were completely oblivious of the fact that they were doing the bidding of Wellcome. A Wellcome-loyal position on HIV and AIDS meant that Wellcome and voluntary sector workers shared almost exactly the same scientific, political and cultural views. To some extent, the relationship was also based upon the creation of financial insecurity.

While the Wellcome Trust took care of the investment in AIDS research, the drug-producing Wellcome Foundation channelled finance and organisational support out into the community to the voluntary sector organisations. The Wellcome Foundation has a policy of philanthropic giving in and around the areas where it has offices and factories, so for example the London Borough of Camden has received donations for projects, as has the London Borough of Lewisham, which is home to Wellcome's Deptford works.

Wellcome's Community Relations Department organises apparently altruistic and non-profit-returning schemes, such as asking school teachers to take up placements inside the company and giving careers advice in schools. One major area of community interest is in the training of medical ancillary workers, for whom Wellcome has established a number of pre-entry NHS training courses.

Until 1989 the disbursement of funds and financial 'sweeteners' from Wellcome was carried out almost entirely through the Community Relations Department or through the Public Relations Department.† Either department might, in turn, use PR companies to approach beneficiaries. In 1989, however, the Wellcome Foundation senior management agreed the idea of a Corporate Donations Executive. This small group of people were to funnel money out of Wellcome to specific projects, mainly involved in AIDS work. The first staff appointee of this group was Ron Sutton, while the chair of the Committee went to Wellcome Foundation director, David Godfrey. [9]‡ At the first meeting of the Committee, money was allocated to, amongst other groups, Frontliners and the British Medical Students Trust.††

The sponsorship of and intervention in voluntary sector organisations by Wellcome was replicated in every country to which Wellcome exported AZT. Wellcome Australia sponsored three of the country's leading organisations concerned with AIDS, the New South Wales AIDS Trust, a major Melbourne teaching hospital and an AIDS unit

---

† The head of public relations in 1989 was Dr Martin Sherwood, the media relations manager was Clare Brown.

‡ On two occasions, while a director of Wellcome, Godfrey had been President of the Association of British Pharmaceutical Industries (ABPI).

††The Wellcome Foundation claims that in the year 1989-1990 it paid out £110,000 in donations to AIDS and HIV related groups and organisations. [10]

for education run by the Northern Territories Department of Health. [11]

In America, Burroughs Wellcome began financing organisations, as soon as AZT was licensed. It set up a department which did nothing other than organise meetings, contact community groups and co-operate with them on the publication of leaflets and booklets about HIV and AIDS. One of the most successful American strategies was the 'Town Hall meeting'. Community development workers from Burroughs Wellcome made contact with prominent people in a town or city and with them organised educational debates and question and answer sessions about HIV and AIDS. A speaker from Burroughs Wellcome was always present to answer questions about treatment alternatives and correct mistaken impressions.

A Persuasive Influence

The lengths to which Wellcome went in order to ensure that all available patients were channelled into AZT trials and that there was no overt criticism of AZT, are well illustrated by the case of Sally Smith.† Sally is a person who tested HIV antibody positive and was determined to help in an organisation which supported others who were HIV antibody positive or who had AIDS.

Sally joined an organisation called Positive Life (PL), which had been set up by people who were HIV antibody positive. It was a self-help group which differed radically from the prevailing groups which tended to be dominated by social workers and medics. The organisation was set up in 1986 and dealt almost exclusively with drug users. PL was a grass roots, unattached organisation which had a number of newly diagnosed HIV antibody positive people passing through it; because of this it quickly became a target for Wellcome intervention.

Sally went to work for Positive Life in 1991. Soon after joining, she was asked to write a number of articles on AZT. Doing research for these articles, she read that recent trials had shown AZT to be carcinogenic when given to rodents. Sally was nervous about writing

---

† Both the person's name and the organisation for which she worked have been changed in this account.

the articles, considering it a major responsibility. She worried that she might hurt people by suggesting that AZT was ineffective or toxic. She wrote as even-handedly as she could.

Not long after the articles came out, when Sally was off sick, the project co-ordinator rang her at home to say that Dr Susan Pearl, then head of the Health Education Authority AIDS programme, had contacted the project. Susan Pearl had read Sally's articles and thought that there might be a couple of inaccuracies.

A few days later when Sally was back at work, Susan Pearl rang again, telling her that she was on the board of CRUSAID, one of the largest voluntary sector funding agencies, which had in the past given PL money to publish posters. Now, Susan Pearl said, she was helping Wellcome to get to know more about what different organisations and workers in the voluntary sector wanted.

Susan Pearl was quite insistent that Sally meet with her and Rosemary Hennings, a media relations manager for Wellcome, who worked in the Public Relations Department.† It was Hennings' job to distribute information and answer marketing questions about AZT. Another of her roles was to arrange tours and visits to Wellcome's Beckenham works where AZT was manufactured.

The lunch at a wine bar was a peculiar occasion for Sally, who was not used to the blandishments of pharmaceutical companies. Over lunch no mention was made of the articles which Sally had written. Instead, Susan Pearl and Rosemary Hennings talked openly about the links between the AIDS community and Wellcome, and the problems of marketing AZT.

Soon after Sally had lunched with Susan Pearl and Rosemary Hennings, the co-ordinater of PL received a phone call from a public relations company telling them that a major pharmaceutical company wanted to offer funding to the organisation: the company was Wellcome. Positive Life did not accept the money.

Another sign of the intimacy voluntary sector organisations share with Wellcome is illustrated by one of Wellcome's advertising booklets for HIV antibody positive people: *Retrovir*. [12] This advertising booklet is

---

† Hennings had been one of the Wellcome staff working with Mike Gibbs to whom Colloquium sub-contracted some of its advertising and marketing PR on AZT.

made available on request from Wellcome directly to people who have been diagnosed as HIV antibody positive. The booklet takes for granted the fact that the reader has begun to take AZT. In the booklet Wellcome acknowledges the assistance in its preparation of doctors at St Stephen's Hospital, the Royal Free Hospital, the Middlesex and St Mary's Hospitals in London. The two voluntary sector organisations credited with help in its production are the Terrence Higgins Trust and Body Positive.

The Terrence Higgins Trust is mentioned twice in the 35 pages. In the centre of the booklet, across two pages, there is a list of support organisations, with phone numbers; these include those of the THT, Body Positive, Positively Women and Mainliners. The message of the advertising booklet is clearly that such organisations support and promote the use of AZT.

* * *

Voluntary sector organisations proliferated unbelievably after Wellcome got its licence for AZT in 1987. The central organisations at the top of the pyramid were not as 'voluntary' as they appeared, being closely linked, in one way or another, with the Department of Health or Wellcome and often both.

The Wellcome Foundation was quickly off the mark in supporting Britain's biggest AIDS organisation, the National AIDS Trust (NAT), donating £20,000 in 1989, a year after its inception. Such a donation inevitably entitled Wellcome to an interest on the Trustees Committee. †

The NAT was launched by Robert Maxwell, who placed Margaret Jay, now Baroness Jay, estranged wife of Peter Jay, as Director. Margaret Jay is also coincidentally related to Virginia Bottomley MP, the Secretary of State for Health, who has overseen the strategy against AIDS for the Conservative government. NAT distributes funds

---

† It was specified that half of the donation should go towards a fund then being set up to establish a mother and child unit at the Mildmay Mission Hospital in London. The Director of the Mildmay Mission Hospital is a Wellcome Trustee. The hospital is one at which AZT trials on mothers and babies diagnosed as HIV antibody positive have been carried out.

totalling £500,000 annually to organisations in the voluntary sector.

Although apparently an independent charity, NAT has close links with the Department of Health and is housed in one of its premises, London's Euston Tower. The Chairman of the NAT is Professor Michael Adler, who is the Consultant Physician and leading AIDS doctor at the Wellcome-funded Middlesex Hospital, the MRC trial centre for AZT and the data collection centre for the Concorde trials.

CRUSAID is the largest AIDS fund-raising organisation in the UK; founded in 1986, it has raised in excess of £4 million for AIDS related causes across Britain. The Wellcome Foundation quickly earned a strategic input into CRUISAID, when Dr Susan Pearl, head of the Health Education Authority AIDS programme, which worked closely with Wellcome, and Martin Sherwood, a man with the same name as the head of Wellcome's Public Relations Department, were placed on the management committee. With these loyal supporters playing a leading role in grant disbursement, Wellcome could ensure that money only went to AZT sympathetic organisations.

CRUSAID was left £500,000 in the will of Joseph Kobler, the hotel and food magnate. The money was used to build the Kobler Centre, a day care centre solely for AIDS patients using AZT, at St Stephen's Hospital.

Frontliners, a voluntary sector AIDS organisation, was one of the major beneficiaries of CRUSAID's grants from 1989 to 1991, before it was closed down amidst allegations of serious financial mismanagement.

Before Frontliners was closed down it had been responsible for a campaign against the AZT alternative AL721, telling those who sought advice from them that because AL721 was made from egg yolk it would cause salmonella poisoning. The group also warned against the use of AL721 on the grounds that it would raise the cholesterol count.

The largest and most influential voluntary sector advice and help organisation is the Terrence Higgins Trust. THT was set up early in the eighties, and was originally presided over by one of the country's most respected AIDS workers, Tony Whitehead. It was originally intended that the organisation would be an English version of the New York community initiative Gay Men's Health Crisis.

THT raises money in the gay community and also receives central government funding for its extensive programme of social and welfare support facilities, buddying, advice and help on financial problems and mortgages. In the late eighties, THT applied for 50% funding from Wellcome, which was immediately agreed. The gay user community responded with such fury that the Trust was forced to withdraw the application. Since that time, however, the organisation has remained Wellcome-influenced and very favourable to AZT.

Through their Helpline, THT advises most people in this country about AIDS and HIV antibody positive. From the inception of the organisation in 1983, the Helpline has been run by the Lesbian and Gay Medical Association (previously the Gay Medical Association). Many of the practising doctors in this organisation are funded by pharmaceutical companies. There is strict control, on the Helpline, over any advice about alternatives. THT does not discuss the use of AL721 with clients, despite the fact that it has been available on prescription.

The THT first took on salaried workers in 1985, and it was not until 1987 that the organisation became properly professional. The group originally had a sceptical view of AZT. This began to change around 1987, when Nick Partridge, who had joined the organisation in 1985, became the Press Officer.

In 1988, Nick Partridge, by then Chief Executive of the THT, went on an Australian tour, lecturing about the THT and the treatment policies which it supported. In 1992, he travelled to America, holding meetings and carrying out media interviews.

Throughout 1991 and 1992, articles appeared in Wellcome publicity material advertising the close relationship between THT and the Foundation. *Wellcome in the Community*, a glossy PR booklet, carried a two-page article with photographs, in its May 1992 issue, which extolled the virtues of the Trust.

The biggest scandal involving covert Wellcome funding and the THT involved the production in 1992 of four pamphlets, unashamedly designed to put forward the HIV hypothesis of AIDS and to point to AZT as being the only serious treatment contender. The four expensively produced brochures nowhere mentioned the fact that Wellcome is the manufacturer of AZT, nor were the adverse effects of the drug discussed.

The booklets were written by Dr Andrew Revell – the

communications manager within the marketing department at Wellcome – and then dispatched for comments to Nick Partridge at the THT and to Positively Women – the women only HIV/AIDS charity funded by Wellcome and the Health Education Authority.†

The viewing committee of THT, a body which historically appraises all publications which carry the THT logo, was bypassed by Nick Partridge on the issue of the booklets. The existence of the brochures was trumpeted in Wellcome's December 1991 'Journal', which stated that the booklets 'had been launched at a special World AIDS Day meeting of the All-Parliamentary Group on AIDS'. At the meeting, which was attended by the Secretary of State for Health, Virginia Bottomley, Nick Partridge said, 'Wellcome has provided very valuable support for these booklets which reflect our continuing shared commitment to explaining the often complex medical, scientific, social and personal issues raised by HIV in an open, honest and easily readable way'. A photograph accompanying the article showed Nick Partridge, 'flanked by Virginia Bottomley and Wellcome's communications manager Dr Andy Revell'. [13]

Nick Partridge was to further describe the brochures in THT's in-house newsletter *The Trust* in February 1992, as being 'a general public guide to AIDS – something very safe and orthodox'. He added, 'Ever since 1988, we've been in dialogue with Wellcome, although there was a great deal of reticence on both our parts about entering into a partnership, especially after Wellcome's experience with AIDS organisations in the United States'.

Simon Watney, an experienced and knowledgeable AIDS commentator, said of brochure number four, *HIV Infection and Its Treatment*, 'It entirely restricts discussion of treatment research to anti-virals, and only one type of anti-viral – the nucleoside analogues (i.e. AZT). This is especially regrettable in a publication which doesn't even mention treatment for opportunistic infections, let alone prophylactic drugs that can prevent the onset of clinical AIDS

† This was not the first time that Wellcome had produced information about AIDS in conjunction with either the NHS or the voluntary sector. Literature of a similar kind had already been produced by Wellcome working with the Middlesex Hospital. Dr Andrew Revell is responsible for producing the core HIV and AIDS literature disseminated by Wellcome; it is translated for countries overseas, or amended to suit their purposes by organisations in this country.

symptoms. These are hardly minor omissions, and they unfortunately strengthen the cumulative impression that the booklets are little more than a sophisticated form of advertising on the part of Wellcome Foundation'. He added, 'If you sup with the devil, take care to use a long spoon!'

With large amounts of Wellcome money and the influence which it bought shoring up the opinions and the organisations within the voluntary sector, it was not surprising that anyone who criticised AZT, or tried to get other trials off the ground, found themselves under attack. From the autumn of 1988 and throughout 1989 and 1990, the Wellcome Foundation built itself a towering and unassailable position from which to publicise and market AZT. Freed from many of the normal constraints of having to sell its product through the general practitioner, it created an influential power-base within the HIV and AIDS community.†

---

† Wellcome's objective, to gain sole medical power over, and direct company-to-patient, treatment advice to THT clients, was realised in 1993, when the THT set up a 'medical information service' with Wellcome. For this service, Wellcome planned to provide THT with, 'a series of medical updates for all staff and volunteers'. [14]

Chapter Thirty Three

Fighting the Invisible Agenda

This [book] is arrant and dangerous nonsense, there is no valid science in these claims, if people are foolish enough to believe this, then it will lead to more deaths. It causes distress in patients, they distrust doctors and they have nowhere to turn. They may refuse medication and they may refuse treatment. It makes me angry, I will have to spend hours arguing them out of this nonsense. It causes psychological and physical suffering. It is evil. [1]

In the majority of the confrontations between those associated with HealthWatch and those whom they criminalised as 'quacks', between September 1988 and September 1991, it is not the superficial arguments which are the most important. There is always a meta-language and it is this which is all-important.

While superficially the language of the health-fraud activists is clearly to do with morally reprehensible phenomena, such as charlatanism, criminal behaviour and quackery, the meta-language often relates to science and its predominant power within the belief system of advanced societies.

No confrontation within the whole of the health-fraud agenda forced the meta-language to the surface more clearly than the confrontation between those who have insisted that HIV was the sole cause of AIDS, and those who admitted to doubt, or suggested that co-factors were necessary for HIV to cause AIDS. Following on these two propositions were two more which became hotly contested. If HIV were the sole cause of AIDS, then AZT, which was said to destroy HIV, was the complete answer; if, however, there were co-factors, linked to life-style or other microbes, then another treatment or multiple treatments might be the answer.

Jad Adams and 'The HIV Myth'

When Jad Adams launched his book, *AIDS – The HIV Myth*,[2] at a meeting in the London School of Economics in April 1989, he had no idea that it would lead to one of the most painful periods of his professional life. He had no forewarning that Duncan Campbell was about to begin a crusade.

Adams expected a debate. He could see that he would inevitably be considered an AIDS 'dissident', because he questioned the stated certainties of the 'AIDS establishment'. He knew that some would find his book challenging; he had no idea that a handful of people would try to have it banned.

Adams did not get a debate; rather, he ran straight into a personal attack which for a short period damaged his professional reputation as a writer and journalist. It was as if a small group of conservative-minded academics and scientists had adopted the strategies of the pre-war race-track gangs.

After suggesting the public debate to Jad Adams, Duncan Campbell had vacillated about who should speak first. It was agreed that the Chair for the meeting should be Dr James Le Fanu, who was a member of the emergent Campaign Against Health Fraud, but a person who did not necessarily share Campbell's views about AIDS.

Eventually, Campbell decided to speak before Adams. His presentation, though, was not in the style of a debate; it was a hectoring harangue, for the most part personal rather than scientific or academic.

Campbell's case was conservative in the extreme. HIV causes AIDS: this, he said, was a fact. Campbell supported his declamations by saying that more than 18,000 papers had been published in the scientific literature, charting the mechanics of infection and the mechanics of disease spread. Once someone is infected by HIV, an acute phase is followed by the slow decline of the immune system and its function; this can take from one and a half to eleven or more years.

Campbell went on remorselessly. Loosely paraphrased, what he told the audience was: if you have AIDS you must have HIV and if you have HIV you will get AIDS. If you do not have HIV you will not get AIDS. Campbell's pursuit of scientific certainty was wiping away any possibility of hope or empowerment for anyone who had contracted HIV. It is the time between contracting the virus and full-blown AIDS which concerns many dissidents. If it were possible to know what co-factors were involved in the onset of AIDS, that is, in the immune system being completely compromised, it might be possible to 'manage' the illness, and keep it in an asymptomatic state. Campbell's message, that HIV led inexorably to AIDS, was bleak: it held out no possibility of scientific enquiry into whether or not co-factors precipitated AIDS. Campbell was basically telling people with HIV that there was nothing they could do to help themselves.

The anti-self-empowerment view, is a view not only of AIDS and HIV, but one held by many in the 'health-fraud' corner in relation to other illnesses. According to this argument, none of us have any alternative but to surrender our faith to the experience, knowledge and implicit 'goodness' of the medical profession. If they fail to restore your health, doctors, with their priest-like understanding of life and death, can counsel you during dying. Patients are all only as children, powerless to understand the inner workings of our being.

Implicit in this view is the mindless suspension of all critical faculties when considering the historical role of medical science and the peculiarly naive, even ignorant, social, psychological and spiritual views of its practitioners.

* * *

Campbell reduced Jad Adams' book to a small number of pages which dealt only with the subject of the causal role of HIV in AIDS. He did not address the surrounding arguments in the book which placed this theme in context. Campbell saved much of his contempt for the most obdurate AIDS heretic, Professor Peter Duesberg. But rather than tackle Duesberg's scientific arguments, he mounted a personal attack, accusing him, as he seemed to accuse everyone, of blocking the patients' path to AZT, the only treatment for AIDS.

Campbell seemed to assume as his starting point, that the motives of the AIDS heretics were reprehensible: a vindictive obstruction to the scientific understanding of AIDS. Duesberg in particular, said Campbell, fostered 'distrust amongst those who suffer from the disease and those attempting to understand it'. [3]

Campbell was scathing about Duesberg, an internationally

renowned scientist who had discovered the genetic 'map' by which
retroviruses like HIV are understood, 'What we have here in
Duesberg, is a mad ego-maniac. Nothing in this book is scientific.
Duesberg is capable of writing the most appalling crap'. [4]

For Jad Adams, Campbell had nothing but seething contempt. He
attacked the book, not on the grounds that the arguments could be
wrong and might be open to debate, but on the grounds that it had
been badly written by a stupid person.

> Nothing in this book makes any sense. It is, to be blunt,
> unmitigated clap-trap from beginning to end. Every key scientific
> statement in it is wrong, and provably wrong, and discoverably
> wrong. It's sloppy, it's self contradictory. [5]

Campbell felt that Adams had a reason for presenting such incorrect
information. Adams, Campbell said, believed that there existed a
conspiracy of the AIDS establishment. In fact Jad Adams did not
actually think that. He did share with others a profound unease about
the origins of AIDS and the manner in which the search for a cure had
quickly become the intellectual property of a few financially interested
parties, but he was a long way from being a conspiracy theorist.
Campbell himself, in his unnecessary refutation, made much of the
idea of conspiracy. It was as if he felt others might accuse him of being
a part of such a scenario.

> There isn't an AIDS establishment. There isn't a central
> conspiracy, an MI6 of AIDS networking. There are people
> getting on with the job, and there are to be frank, idiots like
> Duesberg, getting in the way, with no science to back them up. [6]

When it came to describing the damaging effect that the book was
going to have, Campbell drew upon the authoritative words of his
contacts on the Concorde trials – Dr Weller and Dr Farthing. Dr
Weller, a consultant at the Middlesex, said: 'Thank God, a lot of
patients knew this rubbish already.' Dr Farthing said the book was
'evil'.

* * *

At the LSE launch, Campbell used his tirade against the book to take
side-swipes at those who he believed were obstructing the Concorde

trials and the prescription of AZT. Throughout his presentation, Campbell made references to the case of Dr Sharp, the doctor whom he had 'exposed' for 'exploiting AIDS patients', the week before in the *New Statesman*.† [7] Campbell's spurious linking of Jad Adams, Cass Mann and Dr Sharp, none of whom were known to one other at the time, was a portent of the travails to come.

> I make these remarks with great seriousness, and I address them to everyone here, particularly I address them to you Cass Mann [turning and looking at Cass Mann on the front row] because you have taken on, in distributing the *Positively Healthy Bulletin*, the role of informing people who have to deal with this information. It behoves you, having heard this and hearing what is going to be said in reply, to make sure that you fairly, honestly, factually and accurately, distribute the information which you have gleaned from meetings like this. It is just as much an act of *evil quackery* as what Dr Sharp did to be peddling vitamin pills and mis-information to dying people, it doesn't matter whether you make a few pounds or a few thousand pounds [italics added]. [8]

By drawing Cass Mann into a debate on Jad Adams' book, Campbell showed that, even in early 1989, he believed in a conspiracy of charlatans and quacks, who were intent upon exploiting AIDS patients.

Whenever it comes to looking at human behaviour and people's belief systems, rather than the mechanisms of science, Campbell appears not to understand that others might disagree with him. He seems to make little attempt to understand why people might have views that differ from his own and he combines the certainty of science with a steadfast belief in his own entirely personal concept of righteousness. Seen from this dogmatic perspective, those who do not share his views are at best stupid, and at worst 'bad'.

Once Campbell moved off science into the area of personal behaviour, any vestige of rationality was thrown to the wind. Campbell knew that Cass Mann had held a Positively Healthy seminar in Newcastle, and he made an oblique reference to this during

† See Chapter Thirty Four.

the LSE debate. Cass Mann and Stuart Marshall were later to refer to
this anecdote as Campbell's 'Wuthering Heights scenario'.

> I know from my own experience of a man from Newcastle with
> AIDS, who precisely because this nonsense was fed into him, was
> found wandering on a moor dying of PCP, because he didn't
> want to go near a hospital, because this kind of nonsense led him
> to distrust those who are trying to save his life and his suffering. [9]

Because Campbell had a hidden agenda, winning a debate at the LSE
about Jad Adams' book was not a priority. In his defence of the
Concorde trials and the heroic work of Concorde doctors, Campbell
was to aim far higher than a small parochial victory; he wanted the
book withdrawn and pulped.

> I hope that Jad will take the phone numbers that I hand out right
> now, and [Macmillan, the publishers, will] do their homework
> tomorrow, I hope that they'll undertake to us, (sic) that if they
> find the facts to be wrong, as the scientists and doctors will tell
> them that they are, that the book will be withdrawn from sale,
> before it can do further harm, by putting out erroneous
> information. [10]

Who, one wonders, was Campbell referring to when he asked for an
undertaking to be given to 'us'; could it have been the Campaign
Against Health Fraud, or was it the cohort of friendly doctors working
on Concorde, or was it just a slip of the tongue?

After Campbell had spoken, a number of people asked questions. It
was Brian Deer, the man who was to become one of Campbell's high-
priority targets later in the year, who asked if either of the speakers had
travelled to a conference in Paris at Wellcome's expense.† The
question was answered in the negative by both speakers. Whatever the
purpose of the question, it must have occurred to Campbell then, that
the opposition which he was both creating and defining was not just
going to lie down and play dead. Even within the room at the LSE,
there was a growing sense that Campbell's attempt to censor treatment

---

† 'Whether either of the speakers have at any time, taken any financial support,
inducement, in the form of cash, or tickets for foreign travel, or hotel bookings
paid for, and specifically whether either of them have stayed at the King George
V hotel in Paris, in January, whether the bill was sent back to the Wellcome drug
company?'

options, would be met with serious and perhaps sustained opposition.

* * *

Campbell's assault upon Adams' book, beyond the arena of its launch at the LSE, was instructive as the first in a long line of covertly organised attacks. Campbell wrote a number of letters, and made a number of phone calls to Macmillan, the book's publishers, claiming that the book should be taken out of circulation. He wrote a damning attack on Jad Adams and his book, both in the *New Statesman* and the *New Scientist*, and circulated these prior to their publication to other magazines and journals such as *Nature*.

In retrospect it is clear that Campbell was involved, not simply in a scientific debate, but in a war. It is equally clear that there was more at stake than an opinion, even a fundamental opinion. It appeared that Campbell wanted Adams, his opinions and his book stopped.

AIDS – The HIV Myth had grown from a television programme which Adams had researched and produced for Meditel, a company run by medical journalist Joan Shenton. The programme, which was screened as 'AIDS – The Unheard Voices', was the first that Meditel was to put together arguing the case of the AIDS heretics in Britain and America. 'Unheard Voices', won the Royal Television Society Award for the best international current affairs documentary of 1987. Adams' book was itself highly praised by both the *Lancet* and *Nature*, the latter saying the book was 'meticulously researched'.

Regardless of how the rest of the world responded, Campbell continued an all-out assault upon the book. His most destructive attack took place in the *Pink Paper*. Despite the front page title, 'Making Money out of Myths', [11] the article says nothing about Adams having made money from his book. In this article, Campbell uses an old propaganda trick: he claimed in the first paragraph that there was a growing campaign against the book, a campaign which he said was having a telling effect.

> Pressure is mounting on publishers Macmillan to withdraw a new book about AIDS which is riddled with inaccuracies about the disease and which has been described by a leading AIDS expert as 'evil'.

In reality, there was no campaign, nor was there any pressure on Macmillan apart from Campbell's.

Following the crude mis-information distributed by Campbell, his arguments were laundered and made respectable, in the Parliamentary AIDS Digest (PAD). [12] This was to become a common pattern. While Campbell began attacks using misleading and outrageous claims, in purple prose, they were presented to Members of Parliament in more conservative and authoritative form in the Digest. The article about Adams' book argued that it contained 'dangerous inaccuracies'.

* * *

Jad Adams did not expect to find himself flung to the fringe following the publication of his book, but this is essentially what happened. The issue of AIDS was like an electric cable; those who grabbed hold of it did so at their cost. Adams, however, was a seasoned political campaigner, having cut his teeth as a young journalist on the campaign which got Campbell off official secrets charges in 1978, the ABC (Aubrey, Berry and Campbell) defence group.

Adams did not take legal action against Duncan Campbell, despite the fact that Campbell had woefully misrepresented him. He did, however, contribute an affidavit to the solicitors acting on behalf of the *Pink Paper*, which at a later date, Campbell was to sue for libel.† In this affidavit, Jad Adams makes crystal clear his analysis of Campbell's attack upon him, and what he believed to be its origins.

> Duncan Campbell's mode of operating was to claim falsely that I had expressed beliefs which I had not; and to attack me for not having done research which I genuinely had not, for as he knew, it was not germane to my work. He also mis-quoted me; put quotation marks around his own paraphrases of my ideas to make it seem I was being quoted and took individual words and phrases out of context so he could place his own, biased, interpretation on them.
>
> I believe the purpose of Campbell's attacks was to prevent the dissemination of information which questioned orthodox views

† See this Chapter below.

on the cause of AIDS and to stifle free debate about important issues surrounding AIDS. [13]

Brian Deer: Out in the Murdoch Press

The interest which Brian Deer had in AIDS differed from that of Jad Adams. In 1989, Deer, a gay journalist, was working for the *Sunday Times*. In the spring of that year, his attention was drawn to two articles by Duncan Campbell, one in the *New Statesman* and the other in *Capital Gay*. The *New Statesman* article was entitled, 'End of crisis comes into sight'. [14] Both articles were in Deer's opinion favourable to a pharmaceutical treatment-model response to AIDS. He began researching both articles and their background with a view to producing an article in the *Sunday Times* about AZT.

Deer was informed by contacts that subjects drafted into the Concorde trials were not being given all the information they needed to make an informed choice of treatment. He had also heard that some HIV antibody positive patients were being told that if they didn't take AZT they wouldn't get other treatment. It was a good story about a major drugs trial which was supported by many other referenced stories on other trials, going back beyond the Thalidomide scandal.

In April 1989, following the launch of Jad Adams' book, the *Sunday Times* published Deer's two stories about the Concorde trials.

Deer's first article 'Revealed: fatal flaws of drug that gave hope', [15] stands years later as one of the best pieces of investigative journalism on AZT. Drawing on FDA documents, and the work of Americans John Lauritsen and Dr Joseph Sonnabend, Deer drew attention to the aborted 1986 Phase II trial for AZT. He discussed the drug's cost and, more importantly, the serious adverse effects of the drug which appeared to affect large numbers of people. Deer pointed out for the first time, that while AZT might possibly give some AIDS patients a few more months of life, for others it seemed to hasten their demise. Deer was the only British journalist who saw clearly, in 1989, that the marketing strategy of Wellcome and Burroughs Wellcome involved tying-up as many available patients as possible.

> Despite the risks of AZT and its lack of efficacy, the American government is supporting twice as many drug trials and spending

four times as much money on AZT as on all other potential
AIDS treatments put together. [16]

'The implications for the development of new agents are
chilling,' said Dr Stephen Marcus, medical director of the Triton
Biosciences company in San Francisco. The patients are not
available. They are scooped up into clinical trials for AZT. Big
clinics and the top medical centres are extremely busy with AZT,
so they don't have the space and the staff to manage other
projects. [17]

Such an article might well have been the beginning of a major
campaign against AZT, and the influence which Wellcome was
wielding, if, that is, Deer had not been stopped and other journalists
had also taken up the story.

Deer's next article, 'Under pressure in an AIDS trial', [18] filled out
the skeleton of his remarks in the previous article, in relation to drug
testing in general and the Concorde trial in particular. Deer alleged
that doctors associated with the Concorde trial who gave patients AZT
were failing to give them full information about the drug and its
adverse effects. He also claimed that some doctors working on the trial
had made unproven claims for AZT and that, in some cases, patients
had been confronted by up to five doctors who had suggested to them
that they would not survive without the drug.

Neither article, however, recounted a facet of the AZT story which
to Deer had by then become the most important. Deer had found out
that Ian Weller, one of the central figures in the Concorde trials,
working from the Middlesex Hospital and the heroic doctor whom
Campbell had written about in 1988, was a Wellcome Fellow. He had
also found other connections between Wellcome, AZT and the
Concorde trials. As a gay man, Deer was angry that trials of the only
licensed drug used for AIDS patients seemed to be dominated by the
company which manufactured the drug.

As part of his research, Deer rang Dr Ian Weller, wanting to make
last minute checks on his piece. When he was told that he would not
be able to speak to Dr Weller, Deer tried to impress upon Weller's
secretary the importance of the article not coming out without Weller's
comments. Not long after what had turned into an argument with
Weller's secretary, Deer received two phone calls. The first was from
Martin Sherwood, the public relations manager at the Wellcome

Foundation. He wanted desperately to smooth over the situation, to explain everything, to put the matter in another perspective. Deer was not impressed.

The second phone call came in the early hours of the next morning, from Duncan Campbell. Campbell accused Deer of having threatened staff at the Academic Department of Genito-urinary Medicine at the Middlesex Hospital where Weller worked. Campbell had been told that Deer was trying to 'wreck' the Concorde trials. Deer, Campbell said, had it all wrong, the MRC doctors were the salt of the earth, the only people standing between the gay community and the pandemic. Deer could see no logic or reason in what Campbell was saying. After all, hadn't Campbell himself previously written a strong article, about medical research, drug companies and patients who got ripped off?

Whether it was logical or not, Deer had disturbed a hornet's nest. In the following months, Deer was thrown closer to Jad Adams, Cass Mann and the *Pink Paper*, into a group which was coming to contain the major AZT dissidents.†

Publicly the conflict between Campbell and Deer surfaced only in a small item in the *New Statesman* at the end of April. The article lumped Deer together with Dr James Sharp, then Campbell's 'enemy number one'. The article was entitled 'Discord over plans to 'wreck' drug study'.

> A journalist with the British newspaper, the *Sunday Times*, threatened to destroy a major scientific study of the anti-AIDS drug, zidovudine (formerly known as AZT), if he was not given the information he wanted. The journalist, Brian Deer, told staff at one of Britain's leading centres for the treatment of AIDS that, unless they collaborated with him, he would publish allegations that might destroy the Anglo-French 'Concorde' trial, which aims to find out if zidovudine can delay the onset of AIDS in people infected with HIV. [19]

† The effect of Deer's articles on some of the Wellcome directors can be judged by the fact that following the second article, some directors immediately dumped their Wellcome shares. Caroline Richmond's shares, which she had acquired in 1986, were also dumped a week after Deer's second AZT article.

Deer rang Dr Ian Weller, AIDS consultant at London's
Middlesex Hospital, early in March and directly accused him
of receiving funds from Wellcome. When Weller denied this,
Deer asked him to admit that 'this epidemic is a godsend to you'.
Weller has cared for hundreds of AIDS patients since the
epidemic began in Britain: a heart rending task. He says he was
'devastated' and hurt by Deer's 'onslaught' and 'felt like giving
up' his work on AIDS. [20]

Deer was to feature again in Campbell's *New Statesman* article,
'Positively Unhealthy' when Campbell targeted Positively Healthy and
Cass Mann. [21] In this article, having attacked Mann for charlatanism,
and lambasted him for his criticism of Concorde and AZT, Campbell
accused him of having 'assisted a *Sunday Times* journalist, Brian Deer,
in publicising damaging and inaccurate allegations about an important
Anglo-French trial of AZT, and attacking the reputation of AIDS
doctors.' Deer, Campbell said, had also tried to suggest that doctors
running the trial were in the pay of Wellcome, the manufacturers of
AZT.

All Deer's allegations, Campbell claimed, were 'without founda-
tion', yet the very doctor who had turned to Campbell to confront
Brian Deer, Dr Ian Weller, was at that time a senior lecturer for the
Wellcome Trust. [22]

To ensure that Deer's story never came out in any detail, Campbell
brought the most relentless private pressure to bear on him. As he did
with Jad Adams' editor at Macmillan, Campbell began to plague
Andrew Neil, the *Sunday Times* editor, with faxes, letters and late night
phone calls. In none of these communications did Duncan Campbell
present himself as a socialist in conflict with the right wing press. This
theme only surfaced later when socialists looking for an easy analysis of
the AIDS conflict, decided they had to disagree with Andrew Neil on
AIDS simply because he was the editor of Murdoch's *Sunday Times*.

In his long letters, Campbell accused Deer of being a front for
vitamin companies, of conspiring to damage the health of gay men
being treated because they were HIV antibody positive, and of being
an associate of quack doctors. This time, he had a companion in his
campaign, for Caroline Richmond also sent letters similar to
Campbell's to Andrew Neil.

As far as Andrew Neil was concerned, the conflict which had been thrust upon him, and which involved a journalist renowned for his acerbic personal confrontations, was tangential to the running of a major newspaper. Deer was called in for talks and interviews, and the *Sunday Times* solicitors were put to work looking for a hook on which to hang an action against Campbell. In the end, however, Campbell's campaign against Deer was conducted with such terrible acrimony and from behind the cover of his previous good name as an investigative journalist, that Neil took the most expedient course and asked Deer to apologise to Campbell.

The campaign which Campbell waged against Deer continued throughout 1989 and early 1990, and ended only when Deer was sent by the *Sunday Times* to work in America.

The War on Cass Mann and Positively Healthy

> I will decide the route that I will follow. I refuse to allow anyone,
> be they the pharmaceutical industry, doctors, political spokes-
> man or journalist, to tell me how I will live with AIDS. I will live
> and die on my terms. [23]

The March issue of *Positively Healthy News*, the journal which Cass Mann and Stuart Marshall had begun publishing in January 1989, led with a story about 'informed consent'. The article, entitled 'The trials of AZT', [24] cited a number of scientific trials of AZT, the results of which suggested that asymptomatic subjects suffered adverse reactions. A French study, reported in the *Lancet*, [25] which evaluated the use of AZT on 365 AIDS Related Complex (ARC) and AIDS patients, found that the benefits in 'extra life' were limited to a few months and AZT appeared to have a damaging effect on CD4 cells. A study at London's St Stephen's Hospital had reported [26] that AZT caused severe changes in bone marrow which were not easily reversed after ending administration of the drug. The report stated, '[the findings have] serious implications for the use of AZT in HIV antibody positive but symptom-free individuals'. An American study reported in January 1989 a case of jaundice following liver damage caused by AZT. Other London studies, reported in 1988 by Dr Pinching, suggested that AZT caused bone marrow toxicity with a serious reduction of both red and white blood cells, severe muscle wasting and a reduction in the platelets involved in blood clotting.

'The trials of AZT' went on to ask whether or not the information from these trials had been given to Concorde subjects. This was the line of enquiry which Brian Deer was to take up with his April articles in the *Sunday Times*. Apart from Positively Healthy, no other British AIDS organisation campaigned for all the facts about AZT to be disclosed. While most of the other organisations touted the interests of Wellcome, Positively Healthy argued vigorously in favour of a health programme of vitamins and food supplements, an organic diet and a complete abstinence from all kinds of chemical drugs, be they medical or 'recreational'.

In 1989, Positively Healthy had a case load of over 200 HIV antibody positive participants and was able to publish *Positively Healthy News*, with a £10,000 grant from the National AIDS Trust. Positively Healthy members went to workshops and seminars, organised activities together, received the journal and took part in the PH health programme. Nothing which PH suggested was mandatory. Participants in the organisation were allowed to take part in the regime which they felt was best for themselves; in the early days, some were actually taking AZT. There was every sign in the first months of 1989 that Positively Healthy would grow in influence.

The criticisms which Duncan Campbell had of Cass Mann were, however, to destroy the credibility which Positively Healthy had built. They were first aired at the launch of Jad Adams' book in April 1989 and continued to be expressed throughout the year, culminating in a highly personalised attack in the *New Statesman* on the 29th September. [27]

What made Positively Healthy different from many other organisations in the gay community, was the individual nature of Cass Mann and the other mainstay of the organisation, Stuart Marshall. When the attack upon them began, they didn't just go under or give up: they came back at Campbell with all the resources which they could muster.

There were two strands to the assault on Positively Healthy, the overt and the covert. Those who saw the public presentation of the conflict, saw only the published articles. Privately, Mann and Marshall endured a campaign which etched away at their confidence, their health, their self-esteem, and their social standing.

* * *

> Finding out that a confidential document had been sent round, I and the other people in Positively Healthy began to fight back against the information in that document. It was then that the real trouble began and we became targets of some unseen force. [28]

By April 1989, Duncan Campbell was expert in the techniques of journalistic campaigning. By circulating memoranda and letters and by telephone calls and a stream of faxes, Campbell began to get feedback from a variety of people about Cass Mann and Positively Healthy. Campbell began this investigation, as he began others, with no 'reasonable cause', no proven allegations against the subjects. Campbell was to admit late in 1989, that the Campaign Against Health Fraud 'passed information to him for his investigations'. [29] In fact, as in many of Campbell's campaigns, from the beginning leading members of HealthWatch were drawn in to make comment on Cass Mann and Positively Healthy.

A good example of how the web of HealthWatch 'experts' were used behind the scenes to aid Campbell's anti-personnel campaigns, is the involvement of Dr David Pearson at an early stage against Positively Healthy and Cass Mann. In April 1989, a Ms Rosson of the Department of Genito-Urinary Medicine at the Withington Hospital in Manchester sent a selection of material from Positively Healthy to David Pearson. In the letter which Pearson returned to Ms Rosson, [30] he carefully points out his qualifications for judging nutritional information. 'I am both a clinical immunologist and have an independent interest in several aspects of nutrition and health'. An 'independent interest' could be termed a 'private' or 'lay interest'. Abusing all principles of scientific discourse and without making clear that he was a member of what was then called the Council Against

Health Fraud, Pearson attacks the character of those working for Positively Healthy, apparently solely on the basis of Ms Rosson's letter and some literature she had included.

> I am extremely alarmed at the suggestion that you might base any advice to be given to patients in this District on the 'Positively Healthy' literature. [31]

> I am not certain if the authors of the above are cranks or crooks. Internal evidence (sic) gives strong cause for concern that they are the latter rather than a respectable voluntary organisation as you seem to believe. [32]

> The content of the the 'News' [Positively Healthy News, the Journal of Positively Healthy] is very similar to that of other dubious private operations, containing pseudo-scientific gobbledegook mixed with highly selective quotations from genuine authorities and others from (usually American) self promoting charlatans. [33]

Dr Pearson rounded off his letter with a simple piece of advice to keep everyone healthy, 'Enjoy a well-balanced orthodox diet', and the assertion that he was going to send copies of this material to the Council Against Health Fraud.

As well as using comments gathered from CAHF members, Duncan Campbell went about collecting information on Cass Mann from his friends and family. Mann's aunt and uncle, both elderly retired teachers, were phoned by Campbell from the *New Statesman*.

Not entirely understanding what Campbell's objective was, Mann's uncle spoke to him for forty minutes, and came away from the call concerned about his nephew's activities. Campbell left the *New Statesman* telephone number with Mann's uncle, just in case he wanted to give him any more information. To this day, Cass Mann does not know how Campbell obtained the phone number of his relatives who have a different name from his family name.

Campbell also rang Cass Mann's father, who was in poor health, telling him a number of unsavoury things about Cass. Right up until his death Mann's father was hurt by the allegations which were being made against his son.

Campbell also tried to sow division amongst Mann's close personal friends. Copies of Campbell's articles were sent, unattributed, not just to other papers and journals, but to a list of personal friends, relations and colleagues of Mann, including his father. The gay world, which makes up much of the AIDS community, proved to be a fertile ground for rumour-mongering.

Throughout 1989, coincidentally with the growing conflict between Campbell and Positively Healthy, both Cass Mann and Stuart Marshall became the subjects of constant harassment from unseen forces. Messages were left on Stuart Marshall's answerphone suggesting that his house would be burnt down, that accidents could happen to his car, unless he and Cass Mann withdrew their involvement in AIDS. Cass Mann began to get large numbers of calls on the PH answerphone, each time the caller would hang up after a period of silence; twenty or thirty calls blocked the tape. Both Marshall and Mann had the clear impression that their telephones were tapped.

Although this frenetic activity was going on behind the scenes, the attack upon Cass Mann and Positively Healthy did not become public until September 1989 when Duncan Campbell wrote 'Positively Unhealthy' in the *New Statesman*.[34] The months between April and September, the first four months of the official life of the Campaign Against Health Fraud, Campbell spent gathering information and then privately distributing critical material against Mann, Marshall and Positively Healthy.

* * *

OXAIDS is a small Oxford-based AIDS organisation, run by voluntary workers, dealing with the distribution of advice to people who tested HIV antibody positive and who had AIDS. In 1989 it fell to OXAIDS, essentially an educational organisation, to help administer a yearly conference entitled 'Promoting Our Health'.

OXAIDS was based in a one-room office in the Sexually Transmitted Diseases Department of the Radcliffe Infirmary, a major recipient of Wellcome Foundation and Trust money. There it came under the administrative control of the local Health Authority and was answerable within the hospital to the senior medical consultant.

Edward King volunteered to organise the 1989 conference. Working on the project in the first quarter of the year, he began inviting speakers. There were to be two sessions about treatment and research, and King had no hesitation in inviting both Cass Mann and Stuart Marshall to participate.

Body Positive, a CRUSAID-funded agency, suggested that Duncan Campbell speak at the conference on its behalf. Edward King contacted Campbell at the *New Statesman* offices, to sound him out; he was utterly unprepared for the reaction which his invitation received. Campbell told King that while he did not wish to attend himself, he would be interested to know whether there was to be any discussion of health-fraud at the conference. Campbell talked about the Campaign Against Health Fraud and then got on to the subject of Cass Mann, telling King that he had warned OXAIDS not to work with him.

Over the next few months an increasing number of calls were made to King at OXAIDS, by Campbell, in an attempt to stop Mann from speaking at the conference. OXAIDS stood its ground. Throughout June and July, pressure from Duncan Campbell mounted as he attempted to get OXAIDS to withdraw the invitation, then, a month before the conference was scheduled, Campbell circulated a confidential six-page memorandum on Positively Healthy. The document was sent to the major voluntary organisations which were to attend the conference: Terrence Higgins Trust, Frontliners, Body Positive, National AIDS Trust, Scottish AIDS Monitor and London Lighthouse.

All of the organisations to which the memorandum was circulated were supporters of the Concorde trials and AZT. All of them withheld from Positively Healthy and Cass Mann the fact that they had received the memorandum.

The 'Positively Healthy' memorandum, dated August 15th 1989, and sent out by Duncan Campbell from the *New Statesman* offices, is a sinister document. Its language is that of the most rabid 'Quackbuster', the allegations in it, unsubstantiated and written in the most fervent prose.

The document presents a good ground plan for the strategy which

Campbell was to use over the coming year. It reveals a number of his targets and unfolds the threadbare americanised Quackbuster philosophy which came to epitomise Campbell's writing.

It began with the allegation that Positively Healthy had 'vilified and abused doctors involved in the [Concorde] trials or the use of AZT'. With other themes, the idea that Cass Mann was about to wreck the Concorde trials which were backed by both the British and French governments, runs like a trickle of hysteria through the document. Positively Healthy, the document said, had persuaded people to take worthless 'quack' cures, particularly 'vitamin and mineral pills and supplements'. These 'treatments' were promoted for Cass Mann's personal gain.

The purpose of Positively Healthy, according to Campbell, was to gain 'power and prestige for its founder, Cass Mann'. Campbell says that PH got off the ground seriously in 1989 when it received 'substantial finance'. The question of where the money came from is left begging in order to make it appear vaguely sinister. With this new money, Campbell says Mann had made a 'belligerent and ugly attempt ... to destroy the current trial of the drug AZT on asymptomatic HIV patients'. Campbell also charged Mann with introducing a Concorde trial subject to Brian Deer.

Positively Healthy, Campbell says, advised people to eat macrobiotic diets and similar diets which a nutritionist from St Stephen's Hospital [one of the hospitals carrying out the Concorde trials] considered 'dangerous'. Campbell also claimed that Mann threatened a Frontliners worker who was critical of AL721. This is an interesting accusation, because Campbell himself had said in his article 'The AIDS Scam', that AL721 was one of the most serious casualties of the secret war which orthodox medical research workers were carrying on.

In this document, and later, Campbell was to make much of Cass Mann's contacts with a number of people who were involved in producing various alternative AIDS-related treatments. Positively Healthy seminars, Campbell said, had all been conducted by 'people with (to say the least) questionable skills, books, pills or powders to sell to psychologically vulnerable people'. In this way, Campbell claimed to link Cass Mann to a number of people who were, in his opinion, charlatans and quacks.

* * *

Annoyed that Edward King at OXAIDS had refused to be cowed and bar Cass Mann from the conference, Campbell wrote King a stern, 'private and confidential' letter, two weeks before the conference on August 27th.

> I was surprised and disturbed to be informed, when you telephoned me on Friday, that it was proposed to allow a contribution to your conference from the group 'Positively Healthy'. I had already taken steps to warn OXAIDS etc of the true nature of this organisation. I had supposed that by now you would be aware of the facts.
>
> ... PH has promoted a long string of crooks, idiots and quacks in their exploitation of PWA's [People With Aids], threatened and bullied doctors and patients, and done their utmost with dirty tricks to sabotage important medical trials. I and others are personally familiar with people who have lost their lives quickly or suffered more through Mann's relentless advocacy of worthless vitamin pills and dangerous quackery in places (sic) of such effective (sic) anti-Aids therapies as there are.
>
> He [a person with whom Campbell has discussed the matter] wishes to say to you, with me, that to include PH in any part of your conference, would in our view constitute a direct attack on the health of gay men ...

In an attempt to scare King into withdrawing Mann's invitation to the conference, Campbell told him that four days before the conference, 'national publicity will be given to a report on the promotion and sale of lethally poisonous germanium pills to PWAs'. Here Campbell is referring to the attack which he was to mount in the *New Statesman* on Monica Bryant.† Yet Campbell could show no relationship between germanium promotion and Cass Mann or Positively Healthy, let alone prove that germanium was a 'lethal poison'.

On August 30th, the Promoting Our Health Conference collective, wrote to Campbell informing him of their decision regarding PH. The collective, they said, having taken the advice of different groups did

† See Chapter Thirty Four.

not 'wish to censor voices that are controversial'.

As in the case of Jad Adams' book, Campbell had failed in his attempts to censor the oppositional view on HIV and AIDS treatment. By now, at least within the wider circles of gay debate about AIDS, people were catching on to Campbell's strategy.

The OXAIDS organised conference was held on September 11th 1989. Cass Mann and Stuart Marshall both spoke, but it was not until the end of the conference that both activists got to see the six-page memorandum. One recipient of the memorandum broke ranks and, taking Cass Mann to his home, showed it to him. Mann's first response on seeing the document, was to contact Stuart Weir, the editor of the *New Statesman and Society*, and question him about Campbell's allegations.

Returning from the conference, Mann went straight to the *Pink Paper*, which carried in its September 16 edition a front page story headed 'WITCH HUNT'. The article gave a fair airing to the views of both Positively Healthy and Duncan Campbell, but, for many readers, Campbell's frenzied language must have turned the balance of belief well over onto the side of Cass Mann.

> Campbell described Positively Healthy as 'a bunch of crooks, quacks and idiots'. When asked about the growing debate he said 'It is not a debate, I'm afraid. This is a tactic [by PH] to try and assert legitimacy. You don't debate whether it's right to put people in gas chambers or not. This is not a debate either'. He said that Cass Mann was 'implicated' in the article published the previous weekend in *Capital Gay* about germanium. When questioned on this, as no reference is to be found about Positively Healthy in the article, he said: 'I know! I'm being terribly kind to the B....d'. 'When you've got the degree of zealotry of this guru cult that Mann creates, it's actually much more important to get people away from the poison'. Campbell said, 'Mann is responsible with others for promoting germanium'. But Cass Mann told the *Pink Paper* that Positively Healthy had never promoted or sold germanium. [35]

The disclosure of the Campbell memorandum in the *Pink Paper*, within five days of the conference, signalled the beginning of internecine strife within the gay community. Their decision to stand by Mann's invitation meant that the OXAIDS workers who had disobeyed

Campbell themselves came under attack. Edward King came back from holiday following the conference to find that he was the centre of a raging row.

The OXAIDS Committee was in complete disarray, having been bombarded by Campbell with letters about Cass Mann, demanding that they took sides. The Chair of OXAIDS found himself subjected to continuous phone calls, letters at his home and faxes at work. By late September the Chair was at his wits' end.

Campbell tried to get the *Oxford Mail* interested in a story that OXAIDS staff had intimidated voluntary workers.

*   *   *

> This appears to have been a witch hunt conducted more in the
> manner of a *Sun* exposé than a piece of reputable journalism. [36]

Campbell published his *New Statesman* article, 'Positively Unhealthy', two weeks after the conference on September 29th. [37] The article was a reworking of the six-page memorandum. It was as if Campbell was forced to go public with the story following the disclosure to Cass Mann of the confidential memorandum. Certainly the *New Statesman* article was assembled quickly because instead of picturing Dr Michael Kirkman, named in the main photograph, the *New Statesman* pictured his chauffeur. The article begins with a comment on Cass Mann's clothes.

> It's [PH] run by Cass Mann, a self-acclaimed 'healer' who wears
> costumes reminiscent of seaside fortune tellers, and a large egg
> sized crystal around his neck. Mann has become a guru figure
> for a handful of patients and voluntary workers.

As in the memorandum, there were a number of unfounded tangential accusations against Mann, that he peddled vitamin pills at high prices to AIDS sufferers, for example. The central claim, though, was that he and others in Positively Healthy were, by unstated acts, planning to bring an end to the Concorde trials.

> Since January, he [Mann] has waged an intense campaign
> against doctors and orthodox medical treatments for AIDS –
> and especially against the use of the drug, AZT, the most
> efficacious treatment yet discovered.

The power of a handful of gay activists, objecting to AZT, is tiny
compared to the combined might of one of the world's largest drug
companies, the MRC and the British and French governments.
Campbell, however, was deadly serious, as were those whose interests
he ultimately, if unknowingly, served; the slightest threat to the
Concorde trials was a major threat to Wellcome and its share price.

The list of those people Campbell drew upon for his expert advice
in the article is instructive: he took a very personal and authoritative
quote from Michael Howard, the chief executive of Frontliners, which
was to shut down a year later following claims of financial
mismanagement.

As he had done in his six-page memorandum, Campbell calls up
the genies of HealthWatch. He links Mann with Yves Delatte,† whom
he calls a 'con-man' and Dr Kirkman of the BIAT company. On
BIAT, Campbell refers to the opinions of Professor Vincent Marks
and his colleague Andrew Taylor from the Robens Institute.

> Professor Vincent Marks, head of biochemistry at Surrey
> University, has carefully examined the data. BIAT, he says, is
> 'quackery', 'charlatanism', 'gobbledegook' ... being used to
> promote treatment where there is no indication whatsoever that
> treatment is required.

Using the invited opinion of Dr David Pearson obtained in April 1989,
Campbell says:

> Dr David Pearson, senior clinical immunologist at the University
> Hospital of South Manchester, had to intervene personally after
> Manchester Aids counsellors were persuaded to advise patients
> to follow Mann's immunutrition programme. 'Our dietician was
> horrified by what she read'. Pearson says 'It is psuedo-science
> and scaremongering nonsense which does more harm than
> good'.

---

† See Chapter Thirty Four.

It is important to remember that all Positively Healthy was suggesting to HIV antibody positive people, was that they take compound vitamin supplements and eat organic food which was preferably vegetarian. Such a regime would, Mann said, provide a balanced nutritional programme which in turn would strengthen the body's immune system. Stuart Marshall, who was HIV antibody positive and surviving well without recourse to any chemical therapies, was ideally placed to offer such advice. The protocol for the Concorde trial, however, stated that no immune-enhancing substances (such as vitamin supplements) should be taken by subjects for three months prior to their involvement on the trial. Campbell gives an example of the human damage which Mann's work has caused.

> [Dr Pearson's] fears appear to be confirmed by several cases we know of. For example a 26 year old man, who scrupulously followed every tenet of Mann's advice, has recently died six months after contracting AIDS.

Where is the science in such anecdotes? The case is not even reported by a doctor, but appears to involve a person Campbell came across. What does Campbell mean by the crucial expression 'contracting AIDS'? Campbell knew full well that in orthodox thinking, the patient is tested positive to HIV antibodies and might then be said to have contracted HIV infection; this then can progress to ARC, which is an AIDS Related Complex of infections, before finally developing into full-blown AIDS, clinically signalled by the complete breakdown of the immune system and the overcoming of the patient with different illnesses. At this last stage of AIDS no known orthodox treatment can save the patient's life. In fact, one study shows that while AZT might extend the period between HIV antibody positive knowledge to the onset of ARC, after the patient has developed ARC, death comes more quickly to those who take AZT, than it does to those who have not taken it. [38] Yet Campbell brings in another, this time unnamed, specialist who claims, 'six months is now an unusually short survival time for anyone with good access to the latest therapies' – poor data on which to base an accusation of manslaughter. All the while Campbell remains silent on the question of the 500 Concorde trial subjects, who, having been randomly given a placebo would be given *no treatment* at all for their HIV condition.

There is another anecdotal case history, again given by an unnamed specialist, which makes profoundly serious allegations against Cass Mann. 'A leading AIDS specialist in London also informed us of the harm done to a patient who was advised by Mann that "he should never have gone on AZT". The patient stopped taking AZT, took germanium instead and "went on to get AIDS".' The logic of this collage of quote and reportage is implied but not stated. Campbell is saying that if the patient had continued to take AZT he would not have developed AIDS. This is an interesting and utterly unsupportable claim, both in the particular and the general. Perhaps someone should have reminded Campbell of his own oft quoted advice, that it is a criminal offence to make an unsupported claim for a medicine. Even more deeply hidden, in this anecdote, is the germ of an idea that germanium contributed to the subject's death.

A whole page of the article attacked Brian Deer, claiming that Deer and Mann were partners in a conspiracy to destroy the Concorde trials.

* * *

As if his article in the *New Statesman* was insufficient to destroy the work of Cass Mann, Campbell proceeded to regale the gay community specifically with a four-page feature article in the London gay paper *Capital Gay*. [39] This article, published two weeks after the article in the *New Statesman*, was even more vitriolic than 'Positively Unhealthy'. It introduced more allegations, mainly along the same lines as previous ones.

The *Capital Gay* article, however, also made a radical departure from 'Positively Unhealthy': in it Campbell disclosed that Cass Mann had a conviction for theft. To make the crime appear more substantial, Campbell added fraud to theft and rolled the fine together with the costs which the court awarded against Mann, putting the fine in four figures. In fact, Mann had pleaded guilty to stealing music tapes from a previous employer and had been fined only £200. The idea of disclosing and publishing a gay man's criminal record consisting of one guilty plea, especially when that man was also a person of colour, struck many gay activists as beyond the pale. To some it was reminiscent of a time when blackmail was rife because

homosexual acts, even between consenting adults, were illegal. Alan
Beck described the publishing of the article as 'one of the most awful
things that happened, in this struggle, not just to Cass Mann but to all
gay people'.

In his *Capital Gay* article, Campbell also accused Mann of
promoting germanium, the mineral and food supplement which had
been taken by people without adverse affects for sixty years, but which
Campbell considered a poison. In fact, Mann had nothing to do with
germanium, or its promotion.

It was, however, the disclosure of the conviction for stealing the
tapes from his ex-employer which did the most damage, for now
Campbell was able to accuse Mann not simply and wrongly of being a
fraud, a quack and a charlatan, but also correctly of being a 'self-
confessed thief'. There were many in the gay community who wanted
to publish Campbell's own conviction for theft, but as was frequently
the case, they were too honourable to do this.

The most serious allegations made by Duncan Campbell against
Cass Mann, like his most serious allegations against Brian Deer,†
never reached the public domain, nor could they have, for Campbell
knew that he would have been instantly sued. In this strategy which
imparts the icing first in sensational news stories, leaving the cake to be
disclosed crumb by crumb over a long period, Campbell had the
perfect strategy for character assassination. While it was unlikely that
anyone would sue for libel with the first devastating article, it became
increasingly less likely that they would have the finance or the strength
of purpose to sue on subsequent occasions, as a string of allegations
followed.

A good example of this strategy can be found in the *New Statesman*'s
rebuttal of Cass Mann's complaint to the Press Council, made in 1990
and involving David Reichenberg, the musician to whom Cass Mann
had been very close. Throughout 1989, quite apart from any
published insinuations about Mann's possible criminal behaviour,

---

† One of the letters which Campbell wrote to the *Sunday Times* about Brian Deer
contained the accusation that Deer had recorded a conversation for journalistic
purposes with Tony Whitehead, [a founding Director of the Terrence Higgins
Trust and one of the most highly respected gay men in Britain] while they were in
bed together. The tapes, the letter said, had been forwarded to the *Pink Paper*. Tony
Whitehead later made it clear that there was no truth in this suggestion.

rumours were spread suggesting that Mann preyed on people with AIDS and then tried to claim their estates when they died. In 1990, Stuart Weir, then the editor of the *New Statesman and Society* and a close colleague and supporter of Campbell, wrote of Mann:

> He soon moved from Richmond into the flat of a dying Aids patient, a young musician, to whom he had presented himself as a healer. The patient died in June 1987. Mann, according to confidants at that time, attempted to retain possession of the dead man's flat and belongings for himself. He did not in fact leave the flat and return to Richmond before March 1988, eight months after the patient's death. [40]

It is difficult to think of a more heinous accusation than that of stealing the property of a dead AIDS sufferer after having pretended to heal him. Yet Weir placed this unevidenced suggestion in the public domain and in front of the Press Council. Shortly after having sight of the Press Council document, Cass Mann was able to obtain a letter from a firm of London solicitors, instructed on behalf of the late David Reichenberg's executors:

> These allegations are quite untrue and the position appears to be as follows ... prior to the death ... Mr Mann had not moved into Mr Reichenberg's flat ... Following the death in June of 1987 it was mutually agreed by Mr Reichenberg's parents and Mr Mann that Mr Mann should stay on and look after the flat until it was sold rather than leave it empty and vulnerable to squatters ... there was a long period between the death and the sale of the property due to problems in (a) finding a buyer and (b) exchanging contracts ... at no time did Mr Mann attempt to retain possession of Mr Reichenberg's flat or his belongings. [41]

If such enormously untruthful accusations, innuendo and rumour as those above were difficult to combat, how much more so were the smaller ones.

By the end of 1989, Duncan Campbell had established Cass Mann, in the eyes of the gay community, as a fraud, a charlatan and a criminal who preyed on people with AIDS. He had established Positively Healthy, an organisation made up mainly of gay men who were HIV antibody positive, and run, not by Mann alone, but by a group of people, a number of whom were HIV antibody positive, as a cult organisation created to promote the power and personality of Mann.

Of exceptional interest in the whole of this process was the fact that Campbell could not draw upon the verifiable evidence of a single witness who had been a long time participant in Positively Healthy, to aid his case. This is not surprising because in the main, those individuals who joined Positively Healthy after becoming HIV antibody positive were comforted, supported, and well advised by that organisation.

Cass Mann would not be able to drag off the mantle of criminality which Duncan Campbell had thrown over him. He was to spend three years fighting to re-assert his good name in the gay community and resolve his conflicts with all those organisations and individuals who for one reason or another had sided with Campbell. Although damaging Mann's name, Campbell failed utterly to quench his political spirit and it is due to him and a handful of others that much of the literature critical of AZT has reached the public domain in Britain. To have achieved this much is to have achieved a great deal.

The legacy of Campbell's attack upon Cass Mann is not simply the diminution of Mann's character and the esteem in which he was once held, for once the professional propagandist leaves the field, the jackals move in and the subject is vulnerable to attacks of a less literary kind.

> The night that the article came out in *Capital Gay*, a friend rang and asked if I'd seen it. It was a Thursday evening; I went into Earls Court and got a copy of the paper, then sat reading it on the station. A guy sauntered up to me, he was dressed like a typical gay man, a checked shirt, Levis and a leather jacket. He said:
>
> 'Oh, reading about yourself? You're Cass Mann aren't you? You killed my boy friend. You've caused havoc in the community and now you've been exposed.'
>
> A tube-train was just pulling in, the man grabbed me by the arm and tried to push me to the platform's edge. I held on to him for dear life, my fear gave me strength and I pushed him as hard as I could against the wall and then jumped onto the train. [42]

* * *

While other articles of Duncan Campbell on AIDS and medical fraud had picked on relatively isolated and vulnerable individuals, 'Positively

Unhealthy' struck at the heart of the gay community and the autonomous response of individual gay men to their illness. In asking gay men generally and those diagnosed HIV antibody positive in particular, to join him in criminalising Cass Mann, Campbell was drawing upon reserves of respect, affection and leadership, which he had not earned during his brief period of being 'out'.

Other activists and intellectuals had been immersed in the gay community for years, defending the rights of gay men and lesbian women, sometimes at the cost of their jobs and social contacts. Since the early eighties, such people had shouldered responsibility for the AIDS crisis, dumped on them by straight society. Campbell was not one of these people. He had 'come out', coincidentally, at the time the Concorde trials began. Prior to his 'coming out', little Campbell had ever done, said, or campaigned upon appeared to have been relevant to the oppression of gay men or lesbian women.

Within six months of coming out, Campbell expected to claim a position of intellectual and investigative leadership within the gay community. Not surprisingly, few shared his analysis that the movement was bereft of campaigning leadership. Certainly, many knew that they did not desire the moralistic and authoritarian style of 'straight' Left leadership that Campbell appeared to be offering. It was as if Campbell had carried with himself into the gay community, all the baggage of male heterosexual power complexes which he had utilised in his days of fighting the State with the 'straight' Left.

* * *

Cass Mann, the Pink Paper and Alan Beck

> The question you are always asked, is 'Why did Campbell do this to you, to them, to us all?' My first thought would have been, that it was as extraordinary as someone you had never seen before, coming up to you in the street and hitting you over the head. My answer now, with a great deal of hindsight, is that his actions relate to power and conspiracies. [43]

The *Pink Paper*, the only national paper for lesbians and gay men in Britain, is a potent symbol of an evolving and growing movement to defend the autonomous life style of gay men.

The paper was set up in November 1987, four months after Wellcome had obtained the licence for AZT, by two men, Steven Burn and Stephen Burton, referred to in the community as 'the two Stephens'. Both were community libertarians in their own way: Burn, a journalist, tended to the Left, while Burton, a doctor working for Ciba-Geigy, appeared more conservative.

Having worked his way up from the advertisement department, Steven Burn was, in the late eighties, the editor of *Capital Gay*. Both men felt that they could set up a better paper than *Capital Gay*, one which was more representative of the community. They began on a shoestring with a £15,000 business development loan, a couple of thousand pounds of their own money and £10,000 from other sources. Dr Stephen Burton left Ciba-Geigy and, while working on the paper, he continued to work as a consultant at a number of London hospitals, including the Kobler Centre, where he worked mainly with AIDS patients.

The two Stephens drew in a small group of journalists and activists who they believed would form the core of the new paper. From the second organisational meeting, both Duncan Campbell and Nick Partridge were considered a part of this group. Campbell was expected to be a regular columnist and the paper's investigative reporter.[44] Campbell stayed close to the two Stephens, and was to take their side later when the paper changed hands.

Working from a down-at-heel office in Islington, with the office staff paying themselves minimum wages and everything done on a shoestring, it was only weeks before the paper ran out of money. Kelvin Sollis, a young gay Islington entrepreneur, met the two Stephens at this time. Sollis gave them a £5,000 subsidy, as a gift. It proved insufficient to get the paper on its feet. When the two Stephens approached Sollis for more money, he asked for a part of the company.

Over the next three months, an acrimonious row developed between Sollis and the two Stephens over the new loan agreement; the two Stephens threatened to pull out of the paper, leaving Sollis to publish it. Before a negotiated decision could be reached, they published a leaflet accusing Sollis of wrecking the paper and then resigned. Before resigning, however, they trashed the offices of the *Pink*

Paper so thoroughly that no papers, records or equipment remained intact.

As an AIDS activist and a member of the gay community, Cass Mann had had contact with the *Pink Paper*, since its inception. Surprisingly, in its early days, the paper had steered clear of AIDS issues. Cass Mann had placed a number of half-page adverts for Positively Healthy workshops in the paper. Not surprisingly, as Campbell was associated with it, the *Pink Paper* came out against Jad Adams' book, early in 1988, and following that Campbell made his feelings known about the advertisements for Positively Healthy. Mann also offered the paper articles on AIDS issues and AZT which were not accepted. In the days following the resignation of the two Stephens, with Sollis desperate to get an issue out, Mann was asked for an article. Consequently, the very first issue of the new *Pink Paper*, owned by Sollis, carried an uncredited, critical article about the effect of AZT on T4 cell counts.

To anyone concerned about the marketing profile of AZT, the *Pink Paper* had become a loose cannon: a national gay paper, properly managed and financed, apparently willing to enter the fray candidly about AZT. With the Concorde trials just underway, the AZT marketing team at Wellcome must have looked aghast at that first issue of the new *Pink Paper*.

Long before Campbell began circulating his six-page secret memorandum, the *Pink Paper* was positioned in a war zone with respect to AIDS and AZT. The conflict between Campbell and the *Pink Paper* began to polarise when, under Kelvin Sollis's ownership, David Bridle became editor. Bridle had come up through BBC radio journalism and he saw the *Pink Paper* as a central forum for public discussion about AZT; he was as favourably inclined towards alternative medicine as Dr Stephen Burton had been opposed to it.

Soon after Cass Mann had seen the six-page secret memorandum, and shown it to the *Paper*, the *Paper* came to his defence, publishing the front-page article, entitled 'Witch Hunt'. [45] Campbell, however, was determined that there was to be no public debate about Mann, Positively Healthy, or his own provocative memorandum. As he had done frequently since the beginning of the year, one way or another, Campbell was going to do his best to ensure that opposition to his opinions did not become public.

In the first week of October, following the publication by the *New Statesman* of 'Positively Unhealthy', the *Pink Paper* published a second front page article, 'The Sick Statesman'. [46] It was a judicious response to Campbell's attack upon Cass Mann. Simon Watney, a writer and respected AIDS activist, put many of the issues at the centre of the row in perspective, articulating what many gay men must have been thinking.

> This appears to have been a witch hunt which has been conducted more in the manner of a *Sun* exposé than a piece of reputable journalism. It seems to me astonishingly one sided, that at a time when we've had all this hoo-ha about AZT, but no information about what might be important doses and so on, Duncan Campbell should be attacking a small, vulnerable organisation.

> Positively Healthy continues to play an important part in framing the sense of options open to people with AIDS. [47]

Within days of the *Pink Paper* article defending Cass Mann, Duncan Campbell and the *New Statesman* sued the paper for libel. And when, in the first week of November, the *Pink Paper* tried to comment in an editorial upon the libel action, Campbell and the *New Statesman*, together with their solicitor Bryan Raymond, went straight to the High Court where, losing at the first hearing, they obtained a gagging writ, after an Appeal.†

The four defendants named in the *New Statesman* action against the *Pink Paper*, were Alan Beck, whom Campbell accused of writing the 'Sick Statesman' article, the editor of the paper, David Bridle, Kelvin Sollis, the proprietor, and a woman named Allison who the *New Statesman* suggested was a co-editor.

On 9th October the *Pink Paper* wrote to Campbell offering him a 1,000 word article on page two of the paper. On the 23rd October,

---

† Campbell had been in pre-publication contact with the *Pink Paper*'s printers (the Socialist Workers' Party printers, East End Offset, who also print material for the government funded National AIDS Trust) and they had disclosed the editorial to him, even though the *Pink Paper* was in dispute with him. The issue of the *Pink Paper*, for the week ending November 11th, appeared with a half blank page and the caption: 'Editorial. This article has had to be withdrawn because of a High Court injunction issued on behalf of Duncan Campbell.'

through his solicitors, Bindman's, Campbell responded with demands that the *Paper* print a 1,000 word article by him on the front page, under his headline and with a guarantee that the paper contained no other articles about the Positively Healthy matter. The *Pink Paper* had also to pay Campbell's legal costs and make 'a substantial donation to an AIDS charity', chosen by Campbell, as 'a mark' of their regret.

The *Pink Paper* felt obliged to settle even though they did not consider that they had committed a defamation. An offer was made towards costs – paid in weekly instalments – and it was agreed that a response from Campbell would be printed on the front page. Campbell then demanded the mortgage on Alan Beck's home as collateral for the costs payment. The *Pink Paper* would not agree to this.

When Campbell sent his article for production on the front page of the *Paper*, the paper's lawyers found it highly libellous and defamatory of Cass Mann and Positively Healthy. The paper told Campbell that it could not print the article, whereupon the *New Statesman* continued with its action against the paper.

* * *

All these allegations made by the *New Statesman* against Alan Beck are nonsense. The letter they wrote is homophobic. All this is in the climate of Section 28 and you have got to realise that Alan is caught within an institution. There are only a handful of university lecturers 'out' in this country like Alan. [48]

For Alan Beck, the issue was a little more frightening than for those who were simply staff of the paper: the mortgage on his house was in jeopardy. When the *Pink Paper* published the 'Sick Statesman' article, Beck, who lived near the University of Kent in Canterbury, where he taught, was asked by the editor to send the article round to other newspapers. On the Saturday following the article's publication, Beck went into the University, to use their fax machine. He faxed four newspapers, giving his own telephone number so that journalists might contact him for comments.

The following Monday morning when Beck went into work at the University he found that a whole new procedure now governed the use of the fax machines. Within hours of copies of the article being sent to the four newspapers, Campbell had been in touch with the University administration, warning them that Beck had used their fax machine to issue libellous material.

Alan Beck is proud of being a university lecturer. He is a professional man who is good at his job. In the next few weeks all the fears and insecurities which inevitably affect homosexuals in a prejudiced world, rose to the surface of his life to haunt him. In the week following his use of the fax machine, he was summoned to a series of meetings with the University Vice-Chancellor and Registrar. They were uncomfortable and difficult meetings, at only one was Beck accompanied by his union representative.

Alan Beck found himself in a similar situation to that which Brian Deer had been in at the *Sunday Times*; there was however one difference. Whereas Andrew Neil had shown Deer the letters he had received, the University of Kent at Canterbury refused to disclose to Beck what Campbell had communicated to them. It wasn't until some time later that Alan Beck was able to find out exactly what Campbell had accused him of.

The extent of the allegations which Campbell had made to the University about Beck only slowly became clear. Campbell had fed the University administration what Beck later called 'a wonderful cocktail of allegations, which centred on the idea that I had brought young homosexual students to the *Pink Paper* offices'†. As Beck points out, there are a number of sub-suggestions; there was the suggestion that such students were under 21, and therefore people to whom Alan Beck was *in loco parentis*. Beck found out that in a series of phone calls, Campbell had also told the Registrar that he had got together a 'nest' of homosexual Kent graduates at the *Pink Paper*.

The wording of Campbell's letter to the Registrar at Kent gave the

---

† The exact wording of the principal letter was as follows: 'Following our conversation on Friday, I spoke on Monday to Messrs Steven Burn and Stephen Burton who were the joint founders of the *Pink Paper* and edited it from early 1988 until May 1989, when the paper was taken over by another. They informed me that Mr Beck was not (as I had previously understood) a salaried part-time employee of the paper. He was however, from the beginning a regular (paid) writer and a frequent attender at their offices ... Mr Burn adds that Beck would frequently bring with him to the *Pink Paper* offices young male homosexual UKC (University of Kent at Canterbury) students who were or had been under his tutelage and encourage Burn to employ them.' [49]

University the grounds to institute, if they wished, an enquiry about Beck's behaviour. It was the most serious matter which he had ever faced in his career as a university lecturer. Beck found it utterly unbelievable that he could be attacked in this way by another gay man on the political Left, because he had defended Cass Mann and involved himself in a debate. He saw Campbell's communications with the University as calculated to be discriminating against him as a gay man at work and also inviting the University to set up an enquiry and possibly involve the police.

> The worst thing which has happened to me beyond all the immediate inconvenience and fear, such as happens to any gay person in an institution, is the permanent long-term damage to any prospect of promotion.

> According to my tenure I can only be booted out for immoral conduct. I am a very professional lecturer and I have never had a relationship with any of my students, but the letters suggested that I had infringed the immorality clause in my contract. [50]

* * *

Throughout the last months of 1989 and all of 1990, people continued to come to the aid of Cass Mann and Positively Healthy. All were met with the same litigious attention and censorious resistance that had been visited upon Alan Beck and the *Pink Paper*.

One of the groups which sent Campbell a set of probing questions about his motives, was the London-based branch of ACT-UP, [51] the radical gay activists organisation which was begun originally in the United States by Larry Kramer.† Campbell's answer to their communication throws light upon what he was then claiming was his relationship with the Campaign Against Health Fraud.

> I am not in the 'Campaign Against Health Fraud', but I can tell you that it is precisely that – a campaign *against* Health Fraud [Campbell's emphasis]. I have looked into its origin and funding. It has no links whatsoever with any part of Wellcome. [52]

---

† The ACT-UP definition of themselves is: ACT-UP is a diverse, non-partisan group united in anger and committed to direct action to end the AIDS crisis.

While it is true that Campbell held no position on the committee of the CAHF, he was a participant in its inaugural months, at formal and informal meetings, with Caroline Richmond and Nick Beard. He continued throughout much of 1989 to be quoted on its list of members, and give interviews as a member; in 1991 he attended its Annual General Meeting, which was normally only open to members. For Campbell to say that the Campaign Against Health Fraud 'has no links whatsoever with any part of Wellcome', when Caroline Richmond, its initiator, was at that time a student on a Wellcome course and receiving a Wellcome bursary, was odd to say the least. The error was compounded by Campbell's desire to give the organisation a 'clean bill of health' after having 'looked into its origin and funding'.

In May 1990, following a debate in the Oxford Union on anti-homosexual discrimination – Campbell argued against it – Campbell was interviewed by Ivan Briscoe for *Cherwell*, the Oxford student union newspaper. [53] Ivan Briscoe's excellent, page-long, and mainly flattering portrait of Duncan Campbell, was not to Campbell's liking. In two short and not entirely critical paragraphs, Briscoe touched on the matter of Campbell's action against the *Pink Paper*, beginning 'In the eyes of many Gays and Lesbians he has overstepped the mark in his litigation against the *Pink Paper*, which has been issued with a writ as a result of criticising one of Campbell's articles in the *New Statesman* which had attacked an organisation called Positively Healthy'. Unfortunately, this simple interview with the complex Campbell had failed to alert the younger Briscoe to Campbell's inability to accept even the mildest form of criticism.

Following the article's publication, Campbell threatened the *Cherwell* editor and journalists with the possible loss of office and funds. According to Campbell, the article dealt with a political issue, the publication of which was in breach of their charter. *Cherwell* immediately published an apology. When Alan Beck tried to discuss the matter with the students who ran the small union newspaper, they 'were so frightened' that they would not even talk to him.

Following the 'Positively Unhealthy' article, two other critical articles were written. Both got their authors and editors into bad odour with Duncan Campbell. Tim Clark wrote in defence of Cass Mann and Positively Healthy in *Time Out*, and immediately lived to regret it.

Oppressed by an avalanche of phone calls, faxes and letters, demanding a right to reply, Clark finally left for France, and Campbell obtained his right of reply.

More lamentable than the capitulation of *Time Out*, which only allowed Campbell a letter, was the spineless forfeit of editorial freedom by that great bastion of liberal idealism, the *Guardian*. When Campbell heard that Nicholas de Jongh, a journalist then with the *Guardian*, was about to write a defence of Alan Beck and Positively Healthy, he began his common tactics. By isolating one particular editor, in this case Georgina Henry, and personally harassing her, Campbell managed to bring considerable censorious pressure to bear on de Jongh's article, which finally appeared, co-edited into insignificance by Campbell's intervention, in the *Guardian* of 11th June. [54]

In his bizarre quest to ensure that no one wrote about the Positively Healthy issue without his editorial approval, Campbell had papers delivered to the private address of Georgina Henry, late on the evening of a birthday party; she was not amused.

* * *

Campbell's action against the *Pink Paper* dragged on into 1992, when, in May of that year, rather than face the cost of fighting the matter out in front of a jury, the *Pink Paper* gave in. In allowing Campbell to win, the *Paper* relinquished its defence of the good name and the character of Cass Mann and Positively Healthy. Campbell was able not only to write yet another article, containing some of the rumours and untruthful innuendo which the whole battle was originally based upon, [55]† but was also able to ensure that the *Pink Paper* published an apology which castigated Cass Mann and claimed that the paper had been wrong to defend him.

---

† For example, amongst others things, the article brings up again the Reichenberg innuendo: 'Mann then became a "healer". After his first "patient" died of Aids, Mann moved into the man's north London flat, and stayed put for almost nine months.'

Chapter Thirty Four

Trials of Strength :
Knocking Out the Opposition

*The psychological tendency to resist new ideas ... gives widely held
beliefs a spurious validity irrespective of whether or not they are
founded on any real evidence.* [1]

Throughout the assault by Duncan Campbell upon Brian Deer, Jad
Adams, Cass Mann, Alan Beck and the *Pink Paper*, there was a
continual exchange of information between the voluntary organisations and their publications. The Terrence Higgins Trust was at the
centre of this exchange, seeming to be the leading voluntary agency
which set the moral and ethical standards for the community; usually
these standards reflected faith in AZT, and an intimacy with
Wellcome of which the community, had they been told about these
things, would not necessarily have approved.

Throughout 1989 and 1990, Campbell divided his commitment
between two roles. On the one hand, he came quickly to the defence
of doctors under attack as part of the Concorde trials, as if he were
committed to the defence of the MRC. At other times he did battle on
behalf of the voluntary sector AIDS organisations. Campbell's
relationship with the gay and AIDS community was odd. His role
of spokesman appeared to be one by self-appointment. He defended
science and the use of AZT, and thereby indirectly kept jumping to the
defence of the Wellcome Foundation.

In some strange and inexplicable manner, Duncan Campbell and
the Terrence Higgins Trust became the arbiters, censors and critics
not only of alternative treatments and trials, but also of critical views of
Wellcome's AZT.

The Meditel Story

> A controversial television documentary screened in Britain last year which claimed HIV was not the cause of AIDS, made people with HIV give up their medication, according to a survey carried out by a London clinic. [2]

Nowhere was this arbitrating role more profoundly illustrated than in relation to two television programmes about AIDS and its treatment, made by a company called Meditel.† In the critical assault mounted on these programmes can be observed the same attitude to censorship as was illustrated by Duncan Campbell over Jad Adams' book, Brian Deer's *Sunday Times* articles and Nicholas de Jongh's article in the *Guardian*.

In November 1987, Channel 4 broadcast an edition of 'Dispatches' entitled 'AIDS: The Unheard Voices'. The film was produced by Meditel, a small independent medical film-making company headed by Joan Shenton. Jad Adams had worked on this programme while completing his book *AIDS: The HIV Myth*. The film argued that HIV might not be the sole cause of AIDS and drew on the opinions and ideas of Professor Peter Duesberg, Professor of Molecular Biology at the University of California, Berkeley.

Over the five years prior to the film, Professor Duesberg had become an outspoken critic firstly of the idea that AIDS was caused solely by HIV, and then of AZT. As a consequence of his profile in this scientific debate, he had been ostracised by the world of orthodox medicine and medical science in America. Grants had been withdrawn and his position at his university jeopardised.

What criticism there was of 'Unheard Voices', was muted and took place predominantly outside the public arena. The programme was highly praised by a number of people. Still working on the same subject, and having gathered information on a worldwide basis, Meditel produced a second film, 'The AIDS Catch'; in 1990, this too was broadcast in the 'Dispatches' series. By this time, Joan Shenton and Meditel were wedded to the view that there was a critical vacuum

---

† These programmes, produced for the Channel 4 'Dispatches' series, were 'AIDS: The Unheard Voices' [3] and 'The AIDS Catch'. [4] A third programme was produced in March 1993, titled 'AIDS and Africa'. [5]

surrounding AZT, and that alternative theories of AIDS causation and treatment were being suppressed. They had effectively joined the growing AIDS resistance.

The second programme went further than the first in suggesting that AIDS might not be infectious and argued that rather than having one simple causation, it might be an amalgam of other previously known diseases. There was an immediate critical response to this programme. Three days after the showing of the film, Channel Four's 'Right to Reply' was devoted to it. The motivation for the critical standpoint taken by those who opposed the programme was not initially clear. After all, the film had simply offered another scientific view of a particular illness. Furthermore, there was nothing in the programme which could be said to be either morally damaging or patently untruthful.

And yet, by October 1990, the Terrence Higgins Trust had complained to the Broadcasting Complaints Commission (BCC), on behalf of Frontliners and Positively Women, both Wellcome-supported organisations, that the programme had unfairly treated the subject of AIDS. [6] In the hearing before the BCC, the Terrence Higgins Trust was represented by Duncan Campbell.

THT was not the only party to complain about the programme; in two days of hearings, the BCC also heard a complaint from the Wellcome Foundation. The motive for this complaint was somewhat more obvious: all the talk about AIDS not necessarily being caused by a single viral agent might deter patients from taking AZT.

> In addition, Wellcome complained that the programme had made damaging remarks about a product it manufactured – zidovudine or AZT – and, by implication, about the company itself. At the hearing, Wellcome's Chief Legal Adviser said that such irresponsible and alarmist comments might dissuade HIV patients from accepting treatment with AZT and so curtail their hope of survival. [7]

The way in which this complaint was worded suggests Wellcome held the view that programmes discussing alternative forms of treatment to AZT should not be broadcast. It also intimates that there should be a national media moratorium on criticism of AZT. This is exactly what Wellcome appeared to believe.

When the BCC reported in August 1991, it found in favour of the Terrence Higgins Trust, that 'The Aids Catch' had 'unfairly treated the subject of AIDS', and also in favour of the Wellcome Foundation, that three out of the four comments complained about had been unfair to Wellcome.

Meditel took 'The AIDS Catch' to the Edinburgh Festival, but when they tried to gain participation in the discussion following a showing of the programme, Joan Shenton found herself barracked, censored and organised against by a cohort of AZT supporters, which included Duncan Campbell. While Campbell spoke for forty five minutes, about the 'murderous' nature of the programme and the 'idiocy' of Professor Duesberg, Shenton was hustled off the platform after only five minutes.

In 1992 Meditel produced another programme, 'AZT – Cause for Concern'. Again shown in the Dispatches series, this was a full and damning analysis of AZT. Inevitably there was another BCC complaint.† The AZT lobby backed up the complaints to the BCC with other material and attitudes which ranged far beyond the idea of reasonable criticism. Julian Meldrum of the National AIDS Trust, the major Wellcome/DoH funded voluntary sector body, was quoted in the *New Scientist*, attacking the programme and supporting AZT: 'It was a lousy programme which gave a misleading account of zidovudine as a treatment ... the fact that it [AZT] prolongs lives is undeniable.'

Dr Brian Gazzard, one of the Concorde trial doctors treating people with HIV and AIDS, claimed that he and other doctors had carried out a survey of patients who had seen the programme. They concluded that because of the programme's negative comments about AZT 'as many as one in five HIV-positive viewers [may have] stopped taking Zidovudine'. [8]

The survey, which was not written up, peer reviewed, or published in a proper manner and seems to have been an anecdotal straw poll, asked questions of 60 men with HIV who attended St Stephen's Clinic

---

† In fact this time Meditel had gone much further than making a television programme: it had reported the Wellcome Foundation to the Medicines Control Agency and demanded that the company be prosecuted under the Medicines Act for advertising as a cure an unproven medication. Needless to say the Department of Health did not proceed with a prosecution, nor even an investigation.

in London. 'Of the 27 men who saw "AIDS – Cause for Concern", a third said that it had influenced their attitude to Zidovudine; six suspended their treatment permanently and three temporarily. Those not taking Zidovudine said that, having seen the programme, they were less likely to begin.' Dr Gazzard's startling conclusion drawn from this sociological 'quicky' was that there was 'the need for great caution in deciding whether or not a TV programme [of this kind] should be made'.

There we have in a nutshell the views of the prevailing powers in orthodox medicine: scientific or intellectual views critical of orthodox treatments and products should by censored from the public media. Following the BCC complaints, Joan Shenton and Meditel found themselves being pushed to the edge of the public debate. In attacking AZT, Meditel had volunteered for intellectual and scientific exile.

* * *

Dr Gazzard's survey was not the only time that AZT doctors had indulged in a bit of 'pop' sociology in support of AZT, at the same time as tending the sick, and trying to turn back the tide of AIDS. In 1990, Dr Anthony Pinching, while working with patients taking AZT, decided to carry out a trial of one of the more persistent alternative and natural remedies manufactured as an anti-HIV agent, AL721.

AL721 is a lipid compound derived entirely from natural substances. It was synthesised in the mid-eighties, and had already developed a good reputation by the time that AZT was licensed in 1987. With the licensing of AZT, however, all doors were shut for AL721, which was quickly proscribed in America by the FDA.

AL721 had undergone satisfactory Phase 1 toxicity trials and was considered safe enough to market as a food supplement. In the UK, Ethigen's AL721 was made available directly to people who were HIV antibody positive or had AIDS, under the Compassionate Use clause of the 1968 Medicines Act. Any GP was allowed to prescribe it using the standard FP 10 prescription pad. Hospital clinicians, however, who supported AZT, did their utmost to play down patient access to AL721.

Towards the end of 1989, Dr Anthony Pinching, then Consultant Immunologist at St Mary's Hospital, and member of the MRC AIDS

Therapeutic Trials Committee, organised his own 'trial' of AL721. Coincidentally, the 'trial' began at the same time that the gay community learned that AL721 was available on prescription.

Although a large number of people who were HIV positive expressed an interest in taking part in the trial, Dr Pinching managed to recruit only seven subjects. Half-way through the 'trial', stocks of AL721 ran out and the 'trial' would have been abandoned had it not been for the intervention of Positively Healthy who arranged for participants to receive further treatment.

At the end of the 'trial', which did not include a control group or a placebo arm, Dr Pinching published a short letter in the *Lancet*; [9] this represents all the published data. The letter discloses that all seven men on the 'trial' were severely ill with either ARC or AIDS, groups for whom AL721 was not designed. The manufacturers have always stated that it was only effective when taken at the earliest opportunity after an HIV antibody-positive diagnosis. Dr Pinching's trial claimed to prove that AL721 was ineffective, when compared with AZT.

The doctors who supported the 'trial' of AL721, were the ones who most vehemently defended AZT: Professor Donald Jeffries, Drs Pinching, Gazzard and Farthing. They were backed up and supported in further attacks upon AL721 by the Terrence Higgins Trust, Frontliners and Body Positive. The helplines for these charities all refused to advise callers of the existence of AL721 on NHS prescription, claiming that the St Mary's trial had buried the treatment once and for all.

It was not until 1991 and the publication of *Good Intentions* [10] by Robert Nussbaum, a senior writer for *Business Week*, that the full story of AL721's suppression in America was publicised. Subtitled '*How big business and the medical establishment are corrupting the fight against AIDS*', the book was a vindication of AL721 and charted its systematic suppression because of the marketing threat that it posed to AZT.

* * *

Consistently, during the last years of the eighties, doctors and others wanting to carry out trials with antiviral or AIDS therapies came to London. They came because London has for many years been considered a centre of excellence. Few who tried to set up trials, especially for natural remedies, had any idea of the organised opposition they would face.

Dr Howard Greenspan, the Medical Advisor to Advanced Biological Systems (ABS), an American medical company, travelled to London in 1990, to try to organise a base for trials of phytotherapeutics (treatment by plants) and herbal preparations. These treatments had been developed before the onset of AIDS by an American, Dr Roka. In 1990, the treatments were undergoing clinical trials in Jamaica with Dr Manley West, the Chair of the University of West Indies Department of Pharmacology.

ABS wanted to open an immunology clinic in Harley Street to treat those who were HIV antibody positive or had AIDS. Many of those who attended the clinic would be put on a trial for Dr Roka's anti-oxidant preparations which ABS had invested in. ABS intended the clinic to be a total immune support clinic, which would treat people with diet, exercise, meditation and psychological counselling, while developing social interaction and support groups.

In its desire to see how the land lay and to judge the climate for clinical trials in London, ABS had been in contact with a number of the voluntary agencies dealing with HIV antibody positive subjects in London. In December 1991 Greenspan wrote to Geoff Henning, the head of CRUSAID, telling him about how ABS intended to set up the proposed clinic.

Dr Greenspan was surprised to receive a return letter, not from Geoff Henning, but from Duncan Campbell. Campbell's letter was interrogatory. It demanded answers from Greenspan to a whole series of questions about Greenspan's personal and professional life, but mainly concentrated on the matter of the clinic which ABS wished to set up and the trials which they wanted to carry out.

Knowing the power which investigative journalists have, Dr Greenspan rang Campbell from America and answered as many of his questions as he could. Concluding the conversation, he asked Campbell's advice: what would be the best way to go about setting up trials in London? Campbell didn't hesitate, clinical trials could only be done in co-operation with AZT orientated doctors like Dr Pinching and Dr Gazzard.

Planning his next trip to Britain, Dr Greenspan arranged, through Geoff Henning, a meeting at the Terrence Higgins Trust with Nick

Partridge. When he arrived in London for the meeting in December 1991, Greenspan asked Henning why he had passed his letter on to Duncan Campbell. 'Oh,' said Henning, 'that's what Campbell does, he checks out people who want to do trials.'

The meeting in December 1991, at the THT, was a revelation to Dr Greenspan. He sensed as soon as he entered the room that the mood was antagonistic to him. 'As soon as you walk in and share a space with Nick Partridge you know what's going on. He is the most pompous person I have ever met in my life'. Before the meeting opened, and before Partridge had even spoken to Greenspan, he handed him a copy of an article about Dr Chalmers and Dr Davis,† both of whom had been struck off the General Medical Council Register after carrying out trials with HIV patients, using Ayurvedic medicine. Dr Greenspan could see clearly that Partridge, by handing him the article, was taking credit for having the two doctors struck off and issuing an unspoken warning to him.

The meeting was not a success. Nick Partridge appeared to have the same attitude as Duncan Campbell: anyone wishing to carry out trials in London should first approach either Dr Gazzard or Dr Pinching and seek their co-operation. Dr Greenspan went back to the States, from where he rang Gazzard, arranging a meeting with him for January 1992. Returning to London, he met with Dr Gazzard and had an amicable discussion about anti-oxidants and other non-orthodox subjects. Greenspan left feeling that it had been a good meeting, and that in all probability he could rely upon Dr Gazzard for help in the future.

Returning to America, Greenspan found that Dr Roka's natural treatments had suddenly become of great interest to the American medical establishment. Without any consultation, the National Institutes of Health, the body which had assumed primary responsibility for 'discovering' AZT, had decided to 'trial' the treatment. The NIH had done what Dr Pinching had done in London with AL721. It had carried out a quick test, pitting the treatment against large concentrated amounts of the virus. The man who carried out the 'trial' was one of those who had originally tested

† See this Chapter below.

AZT. 'It was' says Dr Greenspan, 'evident where his sympathies lay'.

It was while Dr Greenspan was at home in America that those he had met in Britain made their move to neutralise him. Not long after returning home, he received a phone call from a reporter on the *San Francisco Bay Times*. As soon as he answered the phone, he knew that the reporter was antagonistic and probably a friend of Duncan Campbell; both the questions and the tone were similar. Nevertheless, Dr Greenspan decided that it was important to talk, and for half an hour he explained the scientific basis for the treatment which ABS wanted to trial in London.

It was clear that the journalist had received his briefing from London, as he mentioned both Dr Gazzard and the Terrence Higgins Trust. Ten days after the phone interview, Dr Greenspan was amazed to read a scathing attack upon himself, extending over a whole page of the *San Francisco Bay Times*. [11] The harshest and most ill-founded criticisms were from Nick Partridge, who was moved to describe Dr Roka's treatments as 'a bunch of crap'. Mr Partridge does not have a scientific or a medical background.

The article quotes Partridge as describing Greenspan's presentation as 'slick' and 'leaving him [Partridge] and others uneasy'. According to Partridge, Dr Greenspan's 'application' for the right to trial a remedy in London, 'fell very much in line with [those of] others who have been trying to make a fast buck out of AIDS'. It was, said Partridge, 'a very dodgy sales pitch. We felt that we were dealing with another group of people misusing alternative treatments for their own financial gain'.

The article carried one quote from a doctor working with AZT, which suggested that one particular patient who had taken Dr Roka's treatments had later died. Dr Greenspan points out that the patient was in the last stages of AIDS anyway when he received the treatment. Dr Brian Gazzard, upon whom Dr Greenspan had placed some considerable hope, denied having had any contact with him.

The article in the *San Francisco Bay Times* [12] and the uninvited negative test by the NIH, together with the now publicly declared response of the leading London AIDS agency, the Terrence Higgins Trust, all but finished ABS's attempts to get trials of Dr Roka's anti-oxidant treatments off the ground in London. Ensuring that Americans did not continue with trials in Britain, was, however, logistically much easier than destroying the home-grown competition. And when the AIDS establishment came to deal with recalcitrant researchers and practitioners in Britain, it was forced to take more punitive action to halt attempts to treat HIV antibody positive patients with anything other than AZT.

Dr Sharp, Philip Barker and Jabar Sultan

When I first read Duncan Campbell's series of articles: 'Sharp practice', 'Positively Unhealthy', 'Let them eat shit' and 'Pretty poison', published in the New Statesman and Society in 1989, I was rocked on my heels by their power, and utterly convinced of their authority. As I had been employed in late 1990 primarily to look into the background of the World In Action programme 'The Allergy Business', I initially confined my investigation to this subject. After a relatively short time, I was convinced that the programme had 'framed' Dr Monro. I breathed a sigh of relief. Out of all the cases of exposed 'quackery', I had drawn the one case which was evidently unjust.

With a kind of terminal inevitability, however, I found myself drawn towards other victims of HealthWatch and their associates; they loomed like shadowy rocks in the course of the smooth path in and out of my investigation. I wondered how I might approach these other cases, for I was sure even before I talked to any of the subjects, simply on the basis of Duncan Campbell's writing, that I would not be sympathetic to them. People like Cass Mann and Monica Bryant, who apparently existed on the very fringes of New Age therapy, were clearly not my kind of people. Like Duncan Campbell I was a socialist and therefore believed in the regulation of medicine and health care, in order to safeguard the poor and the weak from charlatans and their criminal exploitation.

When I finally contacted Cass Mann, feeling that not to do so would be to avoid speaking to a major subject, he was a revelation: a clear thinking, sharp, politicised gay man who, as well as working therapeutically with HIV antibody positive people, was fighting the AIDS establishment in an almost single-handed attempt to make public scientific information about different AIDS therapies. Mann cared for and about people. He seemed to have a a genuinely altruistic sense of solidarity with other people. By the time I had researched Mann's case, spoken to Brian Deer and Jad Adams, I was convinced that Duncan Campbell had set out to criminalise him for reasons other than public interest, reasons which had nothing to do with care, justice, or socialised medicine.

With great reluctance, I began looking into the other cases which Campbell had marshalled against people involved in medicine or therapy. Over the next few months with a terrible hopelessness, it began to dawn on me that everything which Campbell had written was oddly off-centre, poorly researched and gravely biased.

After a year's investigation, I had still not seen Dr Sharp, Philip Barker, or Jabar Sultan, the three men written about by Campbell in his very first 'medical corruption article', 'Sharp practice'. Nor had I seen Monica Bryant, who had worked with probiotics and distributed germanium. She had been the subject of Campbell's 'Pretty poison' articles. Given what Campbell had written about these people, I could not bring myself to meet them. Exploiting the sick, with shady practices, made them social pariahs of the worst kind.

On the basis of Campbell's article, I had visions of Dr Sharp particularly, as something akin to a Nazi death camp doctor: a shady, evil man whose practice took place in the darkness of some distemper-flaking basement. Alternatively, I sometimes envisioned him as a futuristic con-man, within the neon cleanliness of an unregulated private hospital, carrying out bio-genetic research on dying AIDS patients. Jabar Sultan, Dr Sharp's colleague, described by Campbell as an 'Iraqi vet', was stained with the image of a foreigner who carried out experiments on animals while practising medicine. Philip Barker, the man who appeared to finance Sharp and Sultan, was portrayed by Campbell as the Mr Fix-it of the cabal. He was clearly a cold-hearted monetarist, who undoubtedly wore an expensive double-breasted suit and probably drove a Mercedes or a BMW.

As for Monica Bryant, who promoted the 'deadly poison' germanium and made up other potions in her kitchen to sell to sick and vulnerable people, the three witches in Macbeth, had they all been rolled into one, would still only have been her pale shadow. Yves DeLatte, another 'foreigner', who had sold bacteria from human faeces to AIDS sufferers, was clearly a diabolical criminal who, I was led to believe, was being pursued by the police of several continents.

When I did finally interview Monica Bryant, she put me in touch with Jabar Sultan and he in turn put me in touch with Philip Barker. These people, I was surprised to find, had not been in hiding. Far from it, Monica Bryant, Philip Barker and Jabar Sultan had all begun legal actions against Campbell, and were discussing their cases with others who felt abused by him.

Monica Bryant, now bankrupt, two years and three moves of house after the attacks upon her, was just finding the strength to fight back. Jabar Sultan, whom I *had expected to find living off the proceeds of his inhuman scientific experiments in a Mayfair penthouse, while mixing in his spare time with Iraqi arms dealers, turned out to be a committed, caring man, now unemployed and living in a south London terraced house with his wife and three small children.*

Whatever the complex ethical or moral context of Duncan Campbell's stories in the New Statesman, or for that matter of my investigation, there are two important matters which have to be kept in mind. Firstly, a good journalist like a good detective, while using emotion as a motivating aid, will try to avoid being guided by subjective or personal opinions. Secondly, the ultimate arbiter of serious right and wrong in our society is the judicial system, mainly the criminal and civil law. Most forms of aberrant behaviour are covered by the law, except some committed by the powerful. If, as a journalist or an investigator, you have a case against someone, it is always useful to ask if the case would stand up in a court of law, before you lay it out before the public.

* * *

In 1987, Dr James Sharp left London's King's College Hospital, where he had been a consultant haematologist for eighteen years, and with his wife set up Brownings Clinical Laboratories. Brownings was a laboratory service which hoped to make money from blood tests and measurements. Shortly after setting up Brownings, Dr Sharp employed Jabar Sultan as director of research.

Another part of Brownings was based at the private London Bridge Hospital, where Dr Sharp was doing clinical work with cancer patients, using an experimental process called Adoptive Immunotherapy (AI). In 1988, Dr Sharp decided to trial the use of AI on AIDS patients.

Dr Sharp had no business sense and by the middle of 1988 Brownings was in serious financial difficulties. In January 1989, the company, still run entirely by its two directors, employed Philip Barker as Managing Director to make the company profitable.

In April 1989, Duncan Campbell published 'Sharp practice', in the *New Statesman and Society*. The article's publication was preceded by a BBC 'Watchdog' television programme.[13] Both items told how Dr James Sharp, Mr Philip Barker and Mr Jabar Sultan had conspired together to defraud AIDS patients. More seriously, it contended that all the patients the trio had apparently dealt with had died. Both the programme and the article contained more than an insinuation that they had died as a consequence of the treatment given them by Dr Sharp.

Following Campbell's investigation, his article and television programme, Dr Sharp was called before the General Medical Council and struck off the medical register for life.

* * *

> 'It's not my problem' said Sultan – whose only qualification is to practise veterinary medicine in Iraq. He couldn't wait to get his hands on human guinea pigs on whom to try out his ideas. [14]

In 1980, Jabar Sultan received his MPhil in immunology from the University of London. Later he registered as a part-time PhD student in the Department of Haematology and became an Honorary Research Assistant in the Department of Medicine at King's College Medical School.

Jabar Sultan's PhD work involved research into Adoptive Immunotherapy. The object of the technique was to generate 'killer cells' *in vitro* in the blood of immuno-compromised subjects. When returned to the body, these immune-enhanced cells would attack infected or cancerous cells. AI had previously been developed principally in relation to the treatment of leukaemia.

Jabar Sultan's supervisor at King's College was Dr Sharp. In 1984, when Dr Sharp left King's College, Sultan was forced to to look for someone else to supervise his PhD. He moved to the Department of Medicine and began working under the supervision of Professor J. Anderson.

In 1985, Sultan published his first abstract, for an international conference on leukaemia in Holland. Later that year, he felt confirmed in his work, when Dr Rosenberg, an American researcher, published the results of his work with 'killer cells' in the *New England Journal of Medicine*. [15] In 1986, with others, he published in the journal *Clinical Rheumatology* a paper on rheumatoid arthritis, an illness of the immune system. [16]

When in the mid-eighties Jabar Sultan saw a television programme about a family of haemophiliacs who were HIV antibody positive, he felt he should use his knowledge of immunology to try to help AIDS patients. He began working on the protocol for an *in vitro* experiment with AI.

His premise at that early stage was that the immune system had to be activated in order to attack the virus. Little work had been done on this type of approach to AIDS. Those scientists who were of the opinion that 'the HIV virus' was directly responsible for AIDS held the opinion that stimulating the immune system whose cells the virus invaded, could also stimulate the virus. Later, Jabar Sultan was frequently told that the genetic material of the virus was more likely to bind to the genetic material of cells produced during the process of activating the immune system. If the immune system cells were to be stimulated to attack the virus, then this had to be done in the presence of a factor that also inhibited the virus from binding and replicating.

Jabar Sultan knew about AZT and in 1986 felt that in the absence of anything else, it would be a useful adjunct to AI therapy. Later he changed his mind, believing that it was probably more beneficial to try to use natural material to obstruct the replication of the virus. With others doing research in the same area, Sultan found out about a number of substances which appeared to interfere with the virus in proliferation or binding, including the soluble protein CD4, cyclosporin and dextran sulphate.

In late 1986, Jabar Sultan had worked out his first protocol for *in vitro* tests on immune cells. The new head of the medicine department, where he was continuing to write up his PhD, knew little about immunology and put Sultan in touch with Dr Anthony Pinching for advice. Dr Pinching was centrally involved in AIDS work and the use of AZT in particular.

> I went to see Dr Pinching at St Mary's Hospital. I showed him the protocol and had a talk with him. He had a completely negative approach. He said that it was a waste of time even doing the *in vitro* work. He said that the approach could not be of benefit to patients, and it would accelerate the disease, because I would be boosting the immune system, this in fact was what all the AZT doctors said to anyone who was working on a vaccine or in a similar way. [17]

Dr Pinching was very definite that Sultan's ideas and hypothesis were of no value. Sultan felt quite strongly that this was not the best way to deal with a postgraduate, working in the field of AIDS. It would have been enough to make many students give up.

Dr Anthony Pinching was later to say that Sultan on his first visit had seemed naive and ignorant about the biology of HIV and AIDS. It appears, however, that Dr Pinching did nothing to suggest ways in which Sultan might further his understanding of the subject. Nor did Dr Pinching offer any help on subsequent occasions when both Jabar Sultan and Dr Sharp went to see him.

Jabar Sultan knew that work similar to his own had been presented to AIDS conferences in France in 1986 and the transferring of white blood cells to AIDS patients had been reported in the *Lancet* in 1983. [18] Dr Pinching's lack of support prompted Jabar Sultan to seek further consultation about his work. In a meeting at the Public Health Laboratory at East Dulwich Hospital with a consultant virologist, Dr Sutherland, an AIDS expert, Dr McManus, and two other consultants in clinical immmunology, Sultan explained the AI protocols in the treatment of cancer and HIV infection. All the doctors at the meeting agreed to take part in carrying out pre-clinical experiments. In 1986, Jabar Sultan attended a conference in Florida to present his work on cancer. He found that in America there were at least six cancer research centres in the private sector offering similar AI treatment to terminal cancer patients.

Some time after his first visit to Dr Pinching, Jabar Sultan contacted his previous supervisor, Dr Sharp, who was now working at the London Bridge Hospital. He asked if there was any possibility of continuing his work on cancer patients at one of the hospitals where Sharp was a consultant. As a consequence of this renewed relationship and the discussions which followed, Dr Sharp decided to open an Adoptive Immunotherapy (AI) Unit at the London Bridge Hospital.

Money which Dr Sharp had obtained for Brownings enabled Jabar Sultan to build an advanced laboratory at the Hospital. There, Dr Sharp continued his treatment of cancer patients using AI. In the first months of 1988, Jabar Sultan and Dr Sharp decided that they were in a position to begin trial treatments, using AI, with AIDS patients.

Jabar Sultan was insistent that any such trial would have to be given to patients while they were resident in the Hospital and not simply attending consulting rooms. Jabar Sultan and Dr Sharp disagreed about this, principally because residence in the Hospital normally entailed considerable cost. Sultan insisted this was important because the treatment was experimental and if anything should happen to a patient, a fully-equipped intensive care unit should be accessible. Jabar Sultan won the argument. There was no argument over the next important matter, that any such trial treatments should be given to patients free.

Dr Sharp's first three AIDS patients came to him in September and October 1987. Two were referred to him by a consultant at the Newham General Hospital, both of these were male patients with ARC and neither of them were charged for the treatment. In 1989, both were still alive and their referring doctor was able to say that they had suffered no adverse results from the treatment. A third patient came over from America at this time for treatment.†

There was no reason why any of these first three patients should have harboured any ill-will towards Dr Sharp. The first two were both ARC patients and their prognosis was poor. Both had received their treatment free and neither of them appeared to have suffered any deleterious affects. In fact no one other than Duncan Campbell had ever suggested that adoptive immunotherapy had adverse reactions. In April 1989, Campbell was to quote one of these patients as saying:

> This Monday [three days before the publication of the article] 23 year old Johnny Matthews *rang me* to say that he had been one of the two (sic) 'guinea pigs'. (italics added) [19]

> He had suffered severe side effects from the treatment. He had not gained weight or seen the disappearance of thrush in his mouth ... In the months since Sharp had experimented on him, he had got worse; he had pneumonia and other progressive effects of HIV disease. [20]

---

† When Philip Barker found out that Duncan Campbell was producing a programme about the treatments, he contacted the patients. Contrary to what Campbell was to say, one London patient was relatively well, and happy with the treatment, the other was less well, but did not complain about the treatment. The American patient wrote to Barker:

> Since treatment in September 1988, administered under the supervision of Dr Sharp ... I am ... alive and well, and working regular hours ... My doctors here continue to monitor my blood profile bi-monthly, testing both T-cell counts and percentages ... These tests ... show a sustained condition, maintained by no other means of medication.

The suggestion in these two paragraphs is that Matthews' illness had got worse as a consequence of Dr Sharp's treatment; 'he had suffered *severe side effects*'. Campbell gave no evidence to support this claim, nor was it supported by Johnny Matthews' GP or the consultant from Newham General who first referred Matthews to Dr Sharp. Duncan Campbell had not seen these patients' medical notes, and did not produce any evidence on which to base the assertion that the treatment had worsened Matthews' clinical condition.

The minimal data from the trial of AI on the first three patients was presented by Jabar Sultan at an international conference in Japan and the abstract of this presentation was published in the *Journal of Immunopharmacology*.[21] When Sultan returned from Japan, Dr Sharp and he approached Dr Pinching once more and informed him of their observations. Pinching was, as he had seemed previously, implacably opposed to their work. Jabar Sultan was to say that Pinching was, if anything, even more definite than before. Dr Sharp wanted to publish a paper at that time, and asked for Dr Pinching's views; Pinching said that he would contact Sharp at a later date but never did.

The attention of the press was drawn to the abstract of the paper given by Sultan in Japan, and in December the *Daily Express* carried an article about the tests.[22] Jabar Sultan was not involved in this publicity. He even went so far as to ring the *Express* complaining that he was never consulted about the article and advised on the correction of errors. The article claimed that the AI treatment was killing the virus; this was not true and neither Sultan nor Sharp had ever claimed that to be the case. At best, the treatment was inhibiting the virus, and hopefully directing the immune-strengthened cells against the cells that harboured the virus. The *Express* article was picked up by a number of other papers, which published short articles.

Following the treatment of these first three patients, Dr Sharp and Jabar Sultan went to the General Medical Committee at the London Bridge Hospital to gain approval for the treatment of other AIDS patients. Dr Sharp was given both ethical and administrative approval by the Chairman of the LBH Medical Committee. The real and substantial problem relating to treating or trialing AIDS patients in 1988, was, however, access to such patients. Doctors treating AIDS with AZT had almost complete control over patient cohorts, in most cases from the time of their first HIV antibody positive test.

In March 1988, Sharp and Sultan met with Dr Pinching and again tried to elicit his help and support for their AI treatment. At this meeting, Dr Pinching made it plain that he did not want anything to do with the trials and would not tell any of his patients about the availability of AI. Dr Sharp and Jabar Sultan had better fortune when they met Dr Gazzard. He at least appeared sympathetic to the idea of using AI in AIDS cases.†

By the middle of 1988, Brownings was beginning to sink. Both men wanted to continue with the work, but money would increasingly become a problem. Dr Sharp told Jabar Sultan that if they were to conduct any more trials with AI and AIDS patients, they would have to get financial backing.

In December 1987, Sharp and Sultan had written to the MRC for evaluation of the use of AI in AIDS cases. The MRC replied that 'It was agreed that there would be interest in this method of treatment for AIDS patients and should you wish your proposal to be considered for MRC funding, you should proceed to submit a formal application for grant support.'

Eight months after their first letter to the MRC, in August 1988, Dr Sharp and Jabar Sultan made a formal application to the Medical Research Council, in the hope that it might fund a trial. Neither of them realised then that Dr Pinching was in fact at the centre of the MRC‡ therapeutic trials evaluation procedure, or for that matter that the MRC was involved with Wellcome, testing AZT.

In September 1988, Dr Pinching, as a member of the MRC AIDS Therapeutic Trials Committee, was asked to comment upon the application sent in by Dr Sharp and Jabar Sultan. At a meeting of the Committee and then later in writing, Dr Pinching reiterated his lack of faith in the work of Dr Sharp and Jabar Sultan and suggested that some of their proposed techniques might be hazardous.

When Dr Sharp and Jabar Sultan heard that backing would not be

---

† Dr Gazzard was later a signatory to a letter published in the *BMJ*, which described a variety of treatments which were being used with AIDS patients, AI was included on this list; this at least shows that Dr Gazzard was aware of some patients who were receiving the treatment. [23]

‡ See Chapter Twenty Three for Wellcome influence on the MRC AIDS Committee.

forthcoming from the MRC, they applied to the Wellcome Foundation asking whether it might fund a trial. An appointment was made for March 1989. Their thinking was straightforward: Wellcome was involved in trialing AZT, and concerned to find a cure for AIDS, perhaps it would be willing to give technical aid or financial help to trials of AI. They were both immensely naive.

On November 11th Jabar Sultan presented a paper at the autumn meeting of the British Society of Immunology (BSI), in Kensington Town Hall. The session he addressed dealt with AIDS and HIV infection. Sultan presented the three cases which Dr Sharp had treated with AI. Dr Pinching was later to describe Jabar Sultan's presentation as 'a long, rambling account, much of which was irrelevant or confused'. [24]†

Sultan presented two papers at the meeting; the second, on the use of AI to prevent or control graft rejection in human transplantation, was not mentioned later by either Duncan Campbell or Dr Pinching. In presenting Dr Sharp's three AIDS cases, Sultan made mention of AZT.

> I said at that meeting that the patients I had dealt with who had been on AZT had suffered serious cell damage. I said that I had been treating failed AZT patients, people who had failed on AZT over a period of two years. [25]

By December 1988, three months after the Concorde trial had begun and the first meeting of the Campaign Against Health Fraud had been held, a number of prominent people in the medical research establishment knew in detail about the work which Jabar Sultan and Dr Sharp had initiated and wished to continue with AIDS patients.

---

† A few days after the BBC 'Watchdog' programme had been broadcast, Jabar Sultan attended a leukopheresis conference in the United States. There he presented the same kind of paper that he had given at the BSI meeting a couple of months previously. Clinicians attending the American meeting seemed happy with Sultan's work and he was invited by the head of the scientific team of Boston University to present a paper there. Dr Seder from Boston wrote to Sultan after the meeting saying: 'I think your approach to autologous and allogeneic lymphocyte support of AIDS and ARC patients is a natural and important one, and indeed one which we have been considering for some time. The lack of side effects is encouraging, as are, of course, the clinical responses.'

* * *

While reporting on the first three patients and seeking funds to continue his work, Dr Sharp was approached by three more patients, two of whom he treated, one of whom turned out to be unsuitable for AI. Because Sharp was aware that Brownings was in a dire financial state, he made a unilateral decision, which was later to rebound on Jabar Sultan and Philip Barker, to charge these patients for their treatment. There can be little doubt that to charge such patients was wrong, primarily because Dr Sharp could not call on any evidence, other than the three original cases, that AI had beneficial effects in ARC cases.

Duncan Campbell suggested in 'Sharp practice' that Dr Sharp had made massive profits from experimenting with AIDS patients. Sharp was painted as a mercenary and callous man charging vulnerable people for a course of treatment which was ultimately to kill them.

Although Sharp billed two patients £5,000 each for a course of AI treatment, every effort was made to ensure that a variety of organisations funded the treatment. In the event, neither the patients nor their relatives actually paid any money to Brownings. If it was right to level charges against Dr Sharp, then it would also have been right to level the same charges against those doctors who were dispensing AZT. Wellcome was making millions from AZT, money which was indirectly being paid for treatment by the taxpayer. AZT was effectively 'unproven', and its recipients invariably died.

Dr Sharp's two new patients both had full-blown AIDS, which meant that they were near to death. Both had previously been given AZT for long periods, under NHS doctors. Inevitably some time after Dr Sharp treated them they died, as have most patients who have received AZT and all other forms of treatment. The patients did not die, as Campbell was later to imply, as a consequence of undergoing Dr Sharp's treatment. In fact, Jabar Sultan reported that both cases had shown some short-term improvement after the treatment. Even before the patients died, Sultan pronounced that in his opinion it was the AZT they had taken which had destroyed many of their non-infected cells.

When Duncan Campbell wrote his article in April 1989, he did not make it clear that the two patients whom Dr Sharp had treated at this time were patients at the end stage of their illness *who had already regularly taken AZT.* The implication of this omission is very serious because Campbell gives the impression that their deaths were hastened by the treatment which Dr Sharp gave them.

> When I pointed out to Sultan that all the Aids patients and most
> of the cancer patients he had experimented on, were now dead,
> he claimed 'that is not how you judge a protocol'. [26]

Campbell's statement was not true anyway: five HIV antibody positive – three ARC and two AIDS patients – had been treated by Dr Sharp. At the time of Campbell's article, three of these patients were still alive and had suffered no ill effects from their treatment. Campbell had on his own admission spoken to one of them only a few days prior to the article's publication.

Much more was omitted from Campbell's article than the fact that Dr Sharp's last two patients had been treated with AZT. Both patients were in fact resident in NHS hospitals at the time of their treatment, being treated under the consultancy of Dr Brian Gazzard. Dr Sharp and Jabar Sultan had looked for a doctor who, in order to offset costs, would agree to patients being treated in their hospital and be monitored by their own consultant.

In early August 1988, Dr Sharp and Jabar Sultan had a meeting with Dr Gazzard in the Endoscopy Unit at the Westminster Hospital. During that meeting they informed him that a female AIDS patient who had approached them wanted to be treated with AI. Dr Gazzard gave Dr Sharp and Jabar Sultan authority to view the patient's medical notes at St Stephen's Hospital with his registrar before they began treatment. Further, Dr Gazzard agreed to monitor the treatment of this patient and later another two AIDS patients who were given AI.

Three new patients finally approached Dr Sharp; all were being treated at St Stephen's Hospital, one of the main AZT trial hospitals. They all had full-blown AIDS. One patient was never given AI because he was found to be unsuitable for the treatment; he in fact was receiving another unproven treatment from Dr Gazzard, Interleukin 2.

Of the two new patients, one was very seriously ill; she had lost her memory and was unable to walk. She had a number of secondary infections and had received several blood transfusions; her CD4 cell count was very low. She had been given a month to live. The second patient was also in the advanced stages of AIDS and had proved to be allergic to AZT.

According to Jabar Sultan, both patients were clinically improved following their treatment. The CD4 count in both patients rose. The first patient began to remember more and started going out from the hospital for walks. Jabar Sultan remembers vividly the moment when she kissed her husband, and thanked him for donating his blood to her. Lesions on her back, caused by infection, began to heal and she gained weight. Despite this short term recovery, both patients were to die during the six month period between treatment and the publication of Campbell's article.

While co-operating with Dr Sharp on the management of these two patients, Dr Brian Gazzard appears not to have expressed any dissatisfaction with either the form or the content of the treatment, to Dr Sharp or his locum at that time, Dr Keel.

Nothing points more clearly to the conspiratorial nature of Campbell's attack upon Dr Sharp, Jabar Sultan and Philip Barker, than the fact that Dr Gazzard, a consultant using AZT, was not even mentioned as involved in treatment of the same patients. By the beginning of 1989, Dr Sharp and Jabar Sultan had been in continuous contact with the established AIDS doctors, the MRC and even Wellcome, for almost a year. If any of these doctors had doubts about the ethics of Dr Sharp, during this period, they were bound to report him to the General Medical Council. If they suspected that Dr Sharp was, as Campbell suggests he was, killing patients, they should have reported the matter to the police.

The decision to destroy the reputations of Dr Sharp, Jabar Sultan and Philip Barker, might of course have had nothing to do with the impropriety involved in setting out to charge two patients. It might have had more to do with the fact that AI looked like a possible alternative treatment to AZT and the fact that Jabar Sultan made public his belief that the AZT administered to two of the AIDS patients had badly damaged non-infected cells.

* * *

In a *Capital Gay* article, written by Duncan Campbell to accompany the BBC 'Watchdog' programme and his *New Statesman* article, Philip Barker is described as a 'Mayfair business man'. On other occasions, he was described by Campbell as the 'money man' and one of 'a bunch of greedy and unscrupulous charlatans'. While Sharp, Sultan and Barker were supposed to have conspired together, it was Barker about whom Campbell chose to be most vindictive: 'Even Sharp's behaviour was nothing to that of Philip Barker, the businessman in charge of Sharp's clinic'. [27]

Philip Barker is the kind of man whom you would want on your side. Passionately in favour of bringing people together, he is steeped in co-operative ideas, a caring man. Undoubtedly Duncan Campbell *would* have had Philip Barker on his side when he began investigating Dr Sharp's business, had he approached him. Philip Barker is a completely honest man.

Philip Barker was brought into contact with Dr Sharp through a neighbour. Dr Sharp, Barker's neighbour told him, was working with a new treatment which could be used for a variety of illnesses, perhaps even AIDS, unfortunately, his business was ailing and he needed help to raise capital.

Knowing nothing about AIDS or medicine, but having a profound belief in co-operative systems, Philip Barker's immediate response was to say that anyone who had found any therapy for AIDS should be working inside the National Health Service. His first thought was that money-raising for AIDS research and treatment should probably be done through a charity. Later he came to understand that medicine is not an altruistic business.

When Dr Sharp had told his accountant in 1986 that he wanted to leave the NHS and set up his own pathology lab, his accountant was able to put him in touch with one of his client companies, the Bergen Bank. Almost immediately, perhaps in retrospect rashly, the Bergen Bank was willing to put £1.2 million into Sharp's small family business.

Philip Barker first talked to Dr Sharp in December 1988 and became the managing director of Brownings on January 23rd 1989. By that time, Brownings was already in trouble; Dr Sharp had spent almost all the £1.2 million and what he hadn't spent personally had been swallowed up by company losses. Philip Barker did not know this; at the one board meeting which he attended prior to starting work, he was surprised to find that finance was not discussed.

On his first day in work, without an office in Brownings' Wimpole Street headquarters, Barker sat in the boardroom and went through all contracts, accounts and files, calling in each member of the staff asking for their reports and introducing himself.

At the end of the day, Barker was drained and depressed; the financial state of Brownings was atrocious. What Barker had been led to believe was a thriving, highly capitalised business, was actually an insolvent shell; creditors were threatening, as was the Inland Revenue. Barker rounded off his first day's work by writing a letter of resignation which he handed to Dr Sharp.

The massive investment from the Bergen Bank seemed to have thrown Sharp off the rails. He had spent lavishly, not only on building laboratories which were not being used, but on himself. He ate caviar almost every day, bought six company cars and spent a great deal of his time flying first class.

The auditor's report of the accounts in August 1988 was heavily qualified. In the first year Brownings lost £300,000, then over the following year, £900,000.

Barker was serious about his resignation. However, when he confronted Sharp with the reality of his massively failing business, Sharp seemed confident that the Bergen Bank would pour in more money. Barker told Sharp that he would stay if the Bergen Bank would immediately put another half a million pounds in; this Barker believed would be enough to enable him to turn the business round in the short term. The Bank agreed to put in only another £75,000.

Regaining the confidence of the Bergen Bank could only be done by Barker being honest with them. The Bank, one of the biggest in Norway, demanded weekly reports from Barker and continous information about whether or not he was pulling the business round.

When Philip Barker had been at Brownings for ten days, it occurred to him that Dr Sharp was not changing his attitudes. The man was his own worst enemy; he continued to spend, inspired by dream-like visions of worldwide expansion. Barker was finding Sharp to be a kind of Walter Mitty character; on occasions he could be insufferably arrogant, while on the other hand he gave willingly and amply of his time and skills to charitable work.

Despite his eccentricities, few people had anything critical to say about Dr Sharp's ability as a doctor. Most agreed that he was a good doctor. Some went as far as to defend his eccentricity as being unremarkable, even expected, in a top consultant. Barker noticed that the work appeared to get done.

Philip Barker took his responsibility as Managing Director of Brownings very seriously. He could see that, if Dr Sharp continued acting in the way he had been, his chance of turning the company round was slight. Two weeks after being employed as Managing Director, Philip Barker sacked Dr Sharp from being a salaried employee of the company and a member of its board. The choice was simple, Barker told Sharp: either he agreed to a demotion or Barker would get the Bank to close down the business. After detailed negotiations with the Bank, the solicitors and the accountants, in which Barker made sure of his legal position, he told Sharp that he would be retained as a consultant for 'the time being'. He was no longer a permanent employee and he would have to give up his position on the board. Sharp was furious; he tried unsuccessfully to hold on to his position on the board, and when he failed to regain control, he drifted into a slough of despond.

* * *

In the period that Barker was struggling with the business, Dr Sharp was working with patients at the London Bridge Hospital and Jabar Sultan was heading a small team of qualified laboratory technicians, working in a well-equipped laboratory at the LBH. The lab did the work necessary to support the Adoptive Immunotherapy treatment. A pathology laboratory in Wimpole Street was almost entirely concerned with blood testing and various assays, mainly for the doctors in the Harley Street area.

Philip Barker had come into Brownings two and a half years after it had been set up. When he had visited the Hospital and been shown round at the end of January, he had seen a modern and well-equipped laboratory. Barker had also seen that the AI Unit run by Dr Sharp was monitored by the local Area Health Authority and the Doctors' Committee, consisting of some 40 doctors. He was not a medical man but as far as he could see Sharp's work was professional.

The only patients who were in the AI ward during the time that Philip Barker was Managing Director of Brownings were cancer and leukaemia patients. Having talked to Dr Sharp and others, he knew that many of the patients who came to the AI ward were terminal patients, and consequently would die. Barker knew as well, that AI was a cancer treatment which was at a development stage and therefore 'experimental'. As far as Barker was concerned, however, Dr Sharp's work was being done under controlled and accountable conditions.

Philip Barker was even aware that the management of the hospital were so committed to Dr Sharp's immunotherapy treatment that they were trying to sell it to a number of other countries. In the first week that Barker began work, he lunched at the London Bridge Hospital with Dr Sharp and his locum, Dr Aileen Keel. Dr Keel was the consultant haematologist and director of pathology at the private Cromwell Hospital. Philip Barker had seen Aileen Keel's CV and knew that she was highly regarded; the fact that Dr Keel looked after Dr Sharp's immunotherapy patients gave him added confidence in the man's medical abilities.

* * *

On Philip Barker's fifth day at Brownings, Dr Sharp told him that he would be seeing an AIDS patient who had been referred by Dr Matthew Helbert. Dr Sharp did not know that Dr Helbert worked as an assistant with Dr Pinching at St Mary's Hospital, Paddington, nor that he was unlikely to refer patients and their medical records without the authority of a senior doctor. Sharp told Barker that the patient, called Peter Baker, had an early form of AIDS called ARC, and that the sooner he saw such AIDS patients the better, because AI treatment would be more successful the earlier it was used.

Dr Sharp met Peter Baker and then introduced him to Philip Barker after he said that he wished to proceed with the treatment and wanted an idea of the cost. Philip Barker had told Sharp that in future, he, Barker, would be responsible for all finances.

Barker felt sympathetic to Baker; he had never before met anyone whom he knew to have AIDS. Baker asked him about the treatment and whether he would get better. Barker told him that Dr Sharp was very able and that he should be optimistic. The treatment, as he understood it, would not harm him and it might well extend his life. Sharp had told Barker that the beauty of the treatment was that it could do no harm. It was a 'natural' therapy and once it took successfully, it could prolong a person's life for 10-15 years, even 'indefinitely'. That was the nature of AI, as Philip Barker understood it – it worked to restore the body's own immune system.

But Philip Barker was the new Managing Director of a laboratory services business and not a doctor. Without giving Peter Baker any medical advice, which he did not have, Barker tried to put him at ease. He even told Baker that he had only been the Managing Director for a few days. At Baker's request, Barker asked the accountant to draw up a proforma invoice for £5,088 – the standard charge for an initial course of treatment. This invoice was sent to Baker ten days later, with a covering letter referring Baker to a Dr Pearl, for further consultation and tests.

> Of course, we never heard from Baker again, he just disappeared off the scene. He never went to see Dr Pearl and when I tried to contact him a few weeks later, I found that he had given a false address. This did not worry me. I just assumed that he had decided not to take the treatment and, after all, he was being cared for by Dr Helbert at St Mary's. [28]

That was the last Dr Sharp or Philip Barker saw of Peter Baker. He did not go to see Dr Pearl. Neither he nor Dr Matthew Helbert had any further contact with Brownings. Helbert ignored calls. Later Campbell admitted in his *Capital Gay* article that Dr Helbert and Peter Baker had decided to set up Dr Sharp.

In *Capital Gay* Campbell wrote:

> Our investigation began early in January when leading AIDS expert Dr Matthew Helbert and prospective patient Peter Baker both became suspicious about the validity of Sharp's and Sultan's methods and the huge sums being charged. [29]

Campbell was later to make much of the conversation which had taken place between Philip Barker and Peter Baker. He accused Barker of pressurising Baker into accepting the treatment at massive cost. In fact Philip Barker had nothing to do with the clinical treatment of Peter Baker, and Dr Sharp understood only that the patient had been properly referred to him by Dr Helbert.

Within days of meeting Peter Baker, Philip Barker, concerned about Sharp's charges, had asked for an independent appraisal of the AI treatment which Dr Sharp was using. He had contacted the management of the London Bridge Hospital and discussed with them the need for an expert committee which would discuss ethical questions. A little later, in March, he had also put forward the idea that Dr Sharp should revert to the previous practice of not charging AIDS patients, and that charity sponsorship should be found for each patient receiving AI therapy as part of a trial.

*　*　*

On February 28th, some weeks after Peter Baker had attended the London Bridge Hospital, Dr Pinching met with Duncan Campbell for a four-hour evening meeting in his office at St Mary's Hospital. [30] Although Pinching claims to have known nothing about Dr Sharp charging patients, or any unethical behaviour, for some reason, he willingly discussed at great critical length with a journalist the work of another doctor who had previously tried to elicit his support. In fact, Jabar Sultan, apparently still hoping Dr Pinching would help him, phoned Pinching not long after Pinching had discussed his work with Campbell. Sultan wanted Pinching's advice on a new clinical collaborator. Dr Pinching did not mention his meeting with Campbell and passed Sultan on to Dr Gazzard.

The occasion of Jabar Sultan's telephone call to Dr Pinching, after he had recently had a four-hour meeting with Duncan Campbell, would surely, from a professional point of view, have been the correct time to inform Sultan, and through him Sharp, that they were both in serious trouble. After all, if what Dr Sharp was doing was so dangerous or so evil, there was a real need to stop new patients being treated. It appears, however, that Dr Pinching preferred to work with Duncan Campbell, than to approach the matter of Dr Sharp either through Jabar Sultan or the proper professional channels. Once Duncan Campbell had criminalised Dr Sharp on the pages of the *New Statesman*, putting an end to treatment of AIDS patients by Dr Sharp would be much easier.

*　*　*

On March 9th, Philip Barker saw a young man calling himself Wilson, who he believed was another AIDS patient. This man came accompanied by Duncan Campbell posing under the assumed name of Duncan Sinclair. The 'patient' was actually a gay friend of Campbell's whom he had brought down to London from Scotland. For this interview Campbell was wearing a concealed microphone. Outside the building a BBC van was secretly recording the overheard conversation.

What Campbell wanted to prove by his visit to Dr Sharp with a bogus patient is not entirely clear; it was evident by then that Dr Sharp was charging patients, because he had given bills to three patients, all of whom Campbell knew about.† On the day that Campbell and his bogus patient friend came for an interview to the LBH, Dr Sharp was out, which left the unfortunate Philip Barker to talk to them.

Again Barker was put in an invidious position; he told them a number of times he was not a doctor, despite being addressed as such by Campbell. Off the top of his head, he told them that there had been six AIDS patients treated so far, and that they were all alive. In fact, only five patients had been treated and two of them had since died. It was a serious error for Philip Barker to make; however, he had not been with Brownings when those patients had been treated, and he knew nothing about their cases or their treatments. As Managing Director of Brownings he had little to do with Sharp's work at the London Bridge Hospital. While Campbell and his friend were milking the interview for any apparently incriminating evidence they could get, Philip Barker, who should not even have been meeting with them, was simply wanting to get on with his work.

Later, on seeing the 'Watchdog' programme, Philip Barker was amazed that Campbell used less than twenty seconds from the sound recording of the meeting with him. Although this twenty seconds was represented as continuous speech, it had in fact been taken from four different parts of the tape edited together to give a false impression of the conversation.

Having seen Barker, Campbell and his bogus patient then made

† In fact no money at all was received at the Brownings' office for the first two patients who were invoiced, and the first patient whom Philip Barker saw, Peter Baker, did not intend accepting treatment .

arrangements to see Dr Sharp the next day at the LBH. This consultation with Sharp on the following day was entirely an attempt to entrap him. Later on in the 'Watchdog' programme and in the *New Statesman* article, Campbell was to radically misrepresent what had happened at the consultation.

One of Campbell's major selling points in his character assassination of Dr Sharp is that Sharp failed to even examine the patient who accompanied Campbell. Yet it is clear from the transcript of the secretly taped interview that Sharp intended to begin the treatment, the following day, with tests and measurements of the patient's health status. Dr Sharp gave the patient a competent case interview, but would inevitably have wanted to consult his previous medical records before beginning treatment. These records or a referral from a doctor did not actually exist. On the day of the interview, even before treatment began, the AI Unit Sister in charge invited the bogus patient to supply blood, so that they might begin the initial tests; he of course declined.

Despite the fact that Campbell later claimed that Dr Sharp was charging large amounts of money for an AIDS cure, it is clear from the transcript that Sharp does not, in fact would not, commit himself to talk about the therapy as a cure:

> Well, I think that we could hope to *make you better*. I could not undertake to give you, to guarantee a cure. [31]

Again, Dr Sharp is cautious even about short-term health benefits achieved by the treatment.

> I think that you might feel better within about 24 hours. But I cannot guarantee this sort of thing. [32]

*. * *

On 13th March, the Monday following his interview with the bogus patient and Duncan Campbell, Philip Barker, Dr Sharp and Jabar Sultan had a meeting at the Wellcome Foundation establishment in Beckenham. In the afternoon of that day Barker had another meeting with the director of the LBH and told him that he wanted to establish a committee to oversee Dr Sharp's work.

Barker had decided that a panel of a dozen consultants was needed, if the LBH was to continue with the AI Unit. He also felt instinctively that patients who were given immunotherapy should not be charged. He decided that the best way of inducing such patients into the hospital for the treatment was to bring the case before a panel, which could then help to identify charitable funds for their treatment.

A month previously, when Philip Barker had relegated Dr Sharp to the role of consultant, he had also put into operation checks on Dr Sharp's medical work. He contacted Dr Keel, Sharp's locum, and asked her to report on his work. He also asked Jabar Sultan to inform him of the progress of all the work which he was involved in. On the advice of Dr Keel, Barker wrote to a Professor Levinsky, asking for his professional opinion on AI.†

The day following Campbell's visit, Barker received a phone call from Professor Levinsky, who suggested that the AI treatment was possibly not as good as it could be, but more importantly, no patient should be charged for an unproven treatment. On the same day that Barker received this report on the AI treatment, Dr Keel came to him saying that Dr Sharp was having some kind of breakdown, principally as a consequence of his business and medical practice being all but closed down by Philip Barker. Dr Keel suggested that because of Sharp's collapse, and his instability, Brownings should completely sever relations with him.

On March 16th, Philip Barker wrote a letter to Sharp, stopping his consultancy and telling him not to treat any more patients. He put another consultant in charge of Dr Sharp's patients. Philip Barker did not take these decisions lightly, he even contacted the GMC to make sure that he had the right to stop Dr Sharp from treating patients.

From that time onwards, Barker took over all relations between Brownings and the LBH management. As a consequence of these changes, it became essential to contact the bogus patient that Duncan Campbell had brought with him, in order to inform him of treatment changes. Wilson had not turned up for his checks on 10th March. Dr Keel and Philip Barker decided to tell the patient that he should see

† Unbeknown to Philip Barker, Professor Levinsky was an adviser on AZT trials, a departmental recipient of Wellcome money at Great Ormond Street Hospital and on occasions a colleague of Dr Pinching. [33]

Dr Keel for a second consultation and that, if she decided he could still be treated, as part of a new policy, charitable funds would be identified to pay for this.

Barker phoned the number and wrote to the address which he had been given for the patient, and on March 19th he received a return call from the 'friend' Duncan Sinclair (Campbell). Somewhat nonplussed, Campbell accepted the offer of a free consultation on behalf of his patient friend. Having got a new name, that of Dr Keel, from Philip Barker, Campbell rang her and fixed up an appointment, with the clear intention of secretly tape recording her and then writing her into his ignoble conspiracy.

Unfortunately for Campbell's story, Aileen Keel turned out to be a well-qualified and charming doctor who had nothing but praise for Philip Barker and the way in which, within weeks, he had introduced major changes at Brownings. Unfortunately, Dr Keel pointed out, until these changes were properly introduced, Duncan's friend could not really be treated.

In just the same way that Dr Aileen Keel co-operated with Philip Barker, ultimately to the detriment of Dr Sharp, so did Jabar Sultan. It was primarily due to Sultan that Barker pushed for a committee who would review cases rather than leave it entirely to the doctor working on the AI unit.

Some three weeks before the 'Watchdog' programme and his *New Statesman* article, Duncan Campbell knew the truth about Philip Barker and the work which he had done at Brownings. Philip Barker had done a good job. Within two months of becoming Managing Director, he had put Brownings' affairs in order. All the staff at Brownings knew what he had done, even Coopers and Lybrand who were later called in to wind the Company up, paid tribute to Barker's work. Straying from his managerial function, he had even introduced a more ethical and stable approach to testing Adoptive Immunotherapy. Yet to satisfy some other agenda Duncan Campbell ignored these facts.

* * *

The attack upon Dr Sharp, Jabar Sultan and Philip Barker in the *New Statesman and Society* was perhaps the most spectacular of Campbell's attacks, second only in its force to 'Let them eat shit' the article about

Yves Delatte.† It was this first attack, appearing so well researched and competently written, which set the style for those which were to follow.

The style of 'Sharp practice' is post-industrial *Sun*. The article is littered with unattributed quotes and snatches of interview taken out of context, for example: 'One top consultant said: "I've never seen anything so appalling in my life – it was Micky Mouse stuff, it was unethical".' There is throughout the article a lack of relative or comparative material, confirming or contradictory quotes from the subjects. The article has similarities with the undistilled report of the prosecution case put in the first hour of a six-month court case. We are given only Campbell's absolutist moral view to use as a guide to such things as health care costs and practices. It is an utterly subjective piece of writing masquerading as an objectively researched overview. The holes left by missing facts are filled in with innuendo and even racism which make for good syntax, as in: 'an unscrupulous doctor and an Iraqi vet'.

Both the article and the 'Watchdog' programme were sensationalist in the worst possible manner. Both made great leaps of insinuation unsupported by evidence. Both frighten the audience, hitting hard at the mind's underbelly: young women dying of AIDS, young sick people deprived of those few extra days of life by toxic treatments, families selling all their possessions in the hope of a cure, powerful amoral men exploiting the sick. At the heart of the article are two motifs: firstly that of Dr Sharp as a contemporary Dr Death, spreading sickness through the back streets, with shady and unhygienic practices. Secondly the Dr Sharp who behaved more like a circus barker than a doctor, drawing in the patients with bold and embellished lies about cures.

There are elementally disturbing aspects of both the article and the accompanying 'Watchdog' programme. In the article, Campbell's case revolves around matters of money, leaving aside any discussion of Sharp's clinical practice.‡ As if believing that the scientific case would

---

† See this Chapter below.

‡ Since the downfall of Dr Sharp, Wellcome had begun trials on 350 patients with a combination of AZT and Interferon, using a technique similar to Sharp's AI therapy.

go away, Campbell used unattributed critical comments from doctors, mixed with unsupported accusations.

In this confusing metamorphosis between the science practised by Dr Sharp and Jabar Sultan and the accusations of their unethical financial behaviour, a terrible picture is created. As in many of Campbell's articles, the fact that science is not discussed is a serious omission, because it hides the fact that other doctors and specialists had been a party to Sharp's work. Campbell obscures the fact that there was a debate within the profession about Dr Sharp's treatment, particularly in relation to cancer patients. Knowing that Dr Sharp was not some mad Frankenstein practising in isolation raises questions about how Campbell came to alight upon this particular case of medical malpractice, and why such a blatant case was not disclosed by other doctors, through the proper professional channels.

The answers to these questions help us understand how the article came to be written, and lead us some way into the more important question of whose interests it serves. Readers of 'Sharp practice', would undoubtedly have seen the article in a different light, had they known, for instance, that Campbell was briefed on the case by Dr Anthony Pinching, the head of the MRC AIDS Therapeutic Trials Committee, a man who was himself involved in the Concorde trials, the prescription and testing of Wellcome's unproven drug AZT. The picture would change again, had the readers known that Professor Michael Baum, one of the founders of the Campaign Against Health Fraud, knew of Jabar Sultan's work and had previously invited him to deliver a lecture at King's College. The picture painted by Campbell would have become unrecognisable, had readers known that only a few weeks prior to publication, Jabar Sultan and Dr Sharp had been sitting in conference with senior Wellcome research staff, at their Beckenham laboratories, discussing possible co-operation on AIDS work.

*   *   *

No one I have spoken to has had anything bad to say of Dr Sharp's clinical practice. Months after Campbell's articles, the General Medical Council struck Dr Sharp off the Medical Register for life, after a short hearing to which Dr Sharp called no witnesses. The GMC got away with this, despite the fact that everything Sharp was supposed to have done wrong had been agreed, overseen and monitored by doctors dispensing AZT for the National Health Service. The case of Dr Sharp rests like a heavy stone in my mind, because it represents the final frontier of Campbell's aberrant moral outrage.

Dr Sharp's case, as Campbell recorded it, belied the need for any critical review, it was so clear and Dr Sharp so culpable. Now writing it up, it reminds me of other criminal cases, where men convicted of serious crimes have proclaimed their innocence to an impassive tribunal of blind, deaf and dumb judges who had, long before the tribunal sat, settled their findings.

Dr James Sharp was guilty of having charged two patients suffering from AIDS for an unproven AIDS treatment called Adoptive Immunotherapy. For this, his profession should have disciplined him. Unfortunately, the fact that Dr Sharp was dealing with AIDS patients, and the MRC, the British government and a great swath of the orthodox medical profession were promoting and testing a hundred million pound profit-earning Wellcome product, threw the whole matter off the rails into a wreck of conspiracy.

At the end of Campbell's investigation, and Dr Sharp's case, questions are left unanswered: questions about the role of orthodox doctors who advised their patients to use AZT, regardless of its effectivity or side-effects, their relationship with Campbell, and their honesty in dealing with other non-orthodox AIDS treatments which, in a professional capacity, they were asked to assess.

These important questions are sometimes obscured and often hidden by Campbell's use of covert investigative techniques. Because he never openly approached any of the major actors, and because there were no public references to give him information about his subjects, he got great chunks of the story wrong, and did immense damage to honest people. By working within a self-confirming intellectual vacuum, Campbell was able to stomp around in circles like a clever but immature child, ranting moral righteousness, without once articulating basic facts which would have put the case in a quite different light.

In his investigation into Dr Sharp and others, Campbell behaved like the very worst of police detectives. When the investigator is riding high on moral adrenalin, they care nothing for concepts of truth or justice. Campbell's absolute lack of care remade him in the mirror image of those stereotypical devils he convinced himself he was slaying.

Dr Leslie Davis and Dr Roger Chalmers

> *My work is primarily to provide clinical services to patients, including the use of methods of health promotion that are as yet unavailable on the National Health Service – although I believe that they should be. My clinical work is always adjunctive to the care received through a patient's NHS general practitioner and specialist advisors: I have not engaged in, or attempted to engage in, independent practice in relation to the treatment of AIDS, HIV infection, ARC, or indeed any other disorder.* [34]

> *In some respects ethical committees might actually be called unethical committees, because they have allowed doctors to put sick people into placebo controlled trials and thereby fail to treat them.* [35]

In July 1991, Doctors Roger Chalmers and Leslie Davis appeared before the Professional Conduct Committee of the General Medical Council (GMC). They were principally charged with having advertised traditional Indian Ayur-Vedic medicine and with having practised this medicine without adequate training. In October 1991, both doctors were struck off the Medical Register for life.

Davis and Chalmers, both highly qualified with excellent academic and clinical backgrounds, were at the time of the hearing in their late thirties. Both, as well, espoused the medical benefits of Maharishi Mahesh Yogi's Transcendental Meditation, taught in Britain under the auspices of a charity called the World Government of the Age of Enlightenment. They had left the National Health Service in the early eighties to begin the independent practice of the Indian life science Ayur-Ved.

Ayur-Ved is a generic term meaning literally knowledge of life, from Ayus (life) and Ved (knowledge). Its practitioners consider it the world's oldest science of life, having a recorded history of some 5,000 years. Its therapeutic approaches, which are integral to its overall understanding, focus mainly upon the prevention of illness. Meditation, diet and herbal treatments all have a part to play in this 'natural' health care system. Health is approached mainly from the point of view of consciousness, but also from the perspective of physiology, behaviour and environment. The Ayur-Vedic way of health is fundamentally holistic, its central axiom being the unity of mind and body and beyond the person, all aspects of life. Ayur-Ved would probably be described by western rationalists as a mystical philosophy, if not a religion.

In 1986, in common with many other practitioners, Doctor Davis began to take an interest in the treatment and management of HIV antibody positive patients and those with ARC and AIDS. Dr Chalmers had no special interest in the management of these patients. He placed his professional contact with such patients into perspective when he stated in an affidavit to the GMC, in 1990, that over the previous three years and four months he had been consulted by 2,099 different individuals for more than 5,000 consultations. Of those patients only four had been HIV antibody positive asymptomatics, and two had had AIDS. [36]

Dr Davis set up the Disease Free Society Trust in 1988, with the intention of treating AIDS patients with Ayur-Vedic medicine. Dr Chalmers agreed to act as a trustee. Within two years, both doctors had been reported to the General Medical Council, [37] principally, it appears, by Duncan Campbell acting on behalf of the Terrence Higgins Trust.

* * *

> I felt from the beginning that despite its undoubted advances there was a lack of authenticity in orthodox medicine, a lack of permanent benefit and integrity, a lack of getting to the basis of the problems, a sense of the solutions being artificial and contrived. I looked around for something more natural and effective. [38]

Dr Leslie Davis had a traditional British medical education. But he was frustrated by the incompleteness of the orthodox approach to health and became interested in non-pharmacological treatments, particularly Transcendental Meditation. He was particularly impressed by the scientific information about TM, and was happy to find that it required no particular religious belief or philosophical attitude.

After qualifying, first at Cambridge and then the Westminster Hospital in London, Davis worked for four years within the National Health Service, qualifying in 1982 as a Fellow of the Royal College of Surgeons. Reflecting now upon his desire to achieve this high qualification and the hard work it entailed, Davis says with wry humour: 'I thought that being a Fellow of the Royal College of Surgeons might stand me in good stead later. In restrospect, it didn't do me much good'. His training to such a high standard in orthodox medicine was not entirely a waste; Davis maintains that he gained skill in dealing with patients and a useful ability to evaluate and analyse scientific literature. He is still proud of his qualification as a surgeon.

Having become interested in Transcendental Meditation while at medical school, Davis and Chalmers, who had met on a TM course in the mid-seventies, became involved with the scientific institutes and universities founded by the Maharishi Mahesh Yogi. In 1982, both doctors decided to commit themselves full time to developing the medical applications of Transcendental Meditation and later Maharishi Ayur-Ved.

In 1982, Davis went to study for three years at the Maharishi Research University in Seelisberg, Switzerland. There he began his training in Maharishi Ayur-Ved. After finishing the course he went to continue his research at the Maharashi's University of Natural Law at Mentmore Towers, the centre for the Maharishi's organisation in Britain. Dr Davis was not given a wage for his work at Mentmore. He supported himself from savings and he raised money from well-wishers and sponsors for a variety of projects.

In 1985 Davis began seeing patients at Mentmore and in 1986 he did another four months further training in India in pulse diagnosis and herbal treatments. With his background in surgery he naturally took an interest in the treatment of more serious conditions like cancer, through Maharishi Ayur-Ved. Returning to Britain, he was affected by the grief and damage which AIDS was causing and, in 1987, became involved with AIDS patients for the first time. Doctors and healers in India who practised Ayur-Ved at the Maharishi Ayur-Vedic centre near Delhi, had been working on preparations and treatment programmes, made up of traditional herbal preparations, diet and TM, which they believed would help to manage the HIV antibody positive condition.

In 1987, the year that Wellcome received its licence for AZT, Davis approached the AIDS advice organisation Frontliners. Ron Macevoy, the then head of Frontliners, was interested in TM and the herbal preparations which Davis was using. He circulated his members about the availability of these preparations. A member of Frontliners used the herbal remedies for three weeks and reported that he felt very well. As a consequence of that case, Davis found himself treating two other members of Frontliners.†

Davis admits even now to having been sceptical himself about the treatments in 1987. After all, if HIV was the sole cause of AIDS, then the only real treatment was an anti-viral which destroyed or neutralised the HIV virus. Five years later, his confidence in the Ayur-Vedic preparations has been strengthened by clinical experience and by research showing that these treatments contain powerful anti-oxidants. His learning about AIDS has also led him to consider the fact that if there are co-factors involved in the onset of AIDS, then strengthening the immune response and the general health of the body is bound to help in the 'management' of HIV infection, if not in a cure for 'AIDS'.

On each occasion that Davis treated an AIDS patient, he adhered strictly to the rules, informing the patient's doctor of their treatment and progress. While Davis dealt with only three patients in London, in 1987, each of whom showed short-term benefits from the treatment, he received information about patients treated with Maharishi Ayur-Ved (MAV) in Holland and France. Collecting information about twelve cases, with two other doctors, Davis wrote them up as case histories.

Davis spent much of 1987, when he was not seeing patients, collecting and reviewing new data on AIDS. He realised that he would have to carry out a properly structured trial if Ayur-Vedic treatment was to be recognised. Between 1987 and 1989, Dr Leslie Davis approached a large number of orthodox specialists in the field, seeking support and guidance.

In November 1987, Davis telephoned Dr Anthony Pinching. One of Dr Pinching's patients had come to him enquiring about treatment and Dr Davis wished to ensure that he had Pinching's full co-

† Frontliners was to receive funds through CRUSAID in 1988 and 1989, and became a Wellcome-loyal organisation. In 1987 however this did not seem a relevant consideration for either Davis or Ron Macevoy. For details of Frontliners and CRUSAID and the Wellcome Foundation representation on the CRUSAID board, see Chapter Thirty Two.

operation before he began treatment. At that time, Dr Pinching apparently had no objections to the patient being treated with MAV. Pinching also agreed to look at a protocol for a trial of Ayur-Vedic treatment which Dr Davis was then working on.

Davis first sent Pinching a research protocol for an MAV trial in November 1987. Davis said in his letter to Pinching that he would 'appreciate the chance to discuss the steps required to get such a trial underway in London'. Pinching replied in December and from then on Davis and Pinching exchanged letters for well over a year. The exchange was interspersed with a number of meetings between the two. In December 1988, Davis was still writing to Pinching, seeking advice and help on new drafts of the protocols and help in 'training staff'.

Dr Pinching was quite specific with his advice to Dr Davis. He never said that there might be ethical problems, or that Dr Davis might find himself in trouble with the GMC. He did, however, suggest that he go to the voluntary sector organisations and obtain their help in drawing patients into the trial. Pinching told him that if patients came to him asking to receive Ayur-Vedic treatment, having heard about it through a voluntary sector organisation, he would be in a better position to support Dr Davis's research proposals. Despite Pinching's professional and seemingly constructive involvement over a long period with Davis, he appears to have been critical of the whole MAV treatment modality.

After seeing Dr Pinching for the first time, Dr Davis spoke to Dr Brian Gazzard at St Stephen's Hospital and tried to get him to support the research; he, however, was unenthusiastic. So sure was Davis about the ethical and professional acceptability of his work that he approached, amongst others, Professor Robin Weiss at the Institute of Cancer Research, the National AIDS Trust and Professor Peto at the ICR, for their help.† One professor advised Davis to take out an

---

† As in the cases of Sandra Goodman and Jabar Sultan, Dr Davis had no idea that a number of the people he approached had direct links with Wellcome and a commitment to the production of AZT. For the links between Wellcome and the National AIDS Trust see Chapter Thirty Two. For the links between Professor Robin Weiss and the Wellcome Foundation see Chapter Twenty Three. For the links between Wellcome and the Institute of Cancer Research see Chapter Thirty Six.

advertisement in a gay newspaper and undertake a small study of six patients.

Davis met with very little direct opposition from the orthodox doctors and research scientists he approached. Nor was he warned by anyone that he was heading for trouble. In fact there appeared, superficially at least, to be a tolerable equanimity about the advice that he was proffered. Professor Weiss, for example, despite his ongoing working relationship with the Wellcome Foundation, replied to Davis' letter which asked for guidance in these terms:

> 'Dr Davis ... I became very superficially familiar with Ayur-Vedic medicine when I worked in Kerala in 1961/62. The proposed study of the value of Ayur-Vedic herbal therapy and associated treatment modalities would appear to be a very thorough one, and I think it should be encouraged'.

Optimistic about the extent to which orthodox practitioners seemed willing to help in a trial, Davis approached St Thomas's Hospital, where doctors had been carrying out AZT trials with Wellcome. Although at first they were interested, when the doctors found out that Davis was outside the NHS, they wanted nothing more to do with him. This is despite the fact that this particular NHS hospital was 'lending' both its facilities and patients to a large private drug company for experimental purposes.

To Davis, collaboration with NHS doctors was important for a number of reasons. Firstly a trial done with NHS patients in NHS facilities would have more plausibility than one done independently. Secondly, he understood that any trial of Ayur-Vedic medicine and its protocols should really dovetail into other trials. Questions about other treatments in the case of opportunist infections and the avoidance of other medications while on the trial were far more likely to be resolved, within the more formal environment of the National Health Service than they would be working with a small voluntary cohort which was drifting between other agencies and treatments.

In 1988, Davis went back to Frontliners again and met with the director. At that time, Frontliners still had a section which dealt with alternative medicines. This group wanted to ask CRUSAID to pay for the Ayur-Vedic treatment, so making it easily available to anyone in their organisation. Despite such wildly optimistic ideas, as 1988 wore on, it was becoming clear to Davis that interest in alternative treatments was quickly waning. An antipathy towards independent non-orthodox practitioners was beginning to seep through the voluntary sector. This antipathy coincided with the start of the Concorde trials.

Having made little progress in his attempts to get practical help within the National Health Service, Davis helped establish the Disease Free Society Trust. Dr Chalmers, Dr Geoffrey Mead and Dr Geoffrey Clements, European Director of the TM programme, agreed to act as Trustees. One of the objects of the Trust was to support research into Ayur-Ved and AIDS. One sponsor gave £10,000 to help set up the Trust, and with other money the Trust came to be worth £15,000.

Using the Trust, Davis set up a surgery in January 1989 specifically to deal with AIDS patients. He also began a small research project, based at the surgery. From the beginning he had been advised by those he had written to, that the estimated cost of a study involving twenty patients would be in the region of £100,000.

He had continued to revise his protocols thoughout 1988 and the first month of 1989; he continued as well, to send these to a variety of people, for criticism and support. Copies were sent to Professor Donald Jeffries, Professor of Virology at St Bartholomew's Hospital, the Medical Research Council and Dr William Weir at the Royal Free Hospital. Dr Weir came closer than any of the other doctors contacted to playing a part in the trial. Having suggested that the Ayur-Vedic treatments should be tested for toxicity, and such tests having been incorporated in the study, Dr Weir agreed to act as an observer and attended a number of consultations.

Apart from a lack of money, there was one problem with the protocols and the trials which kept cropping up. The treatment which Davis wanted to test was multi-modular: as well as the prescription of herbal remedies, it included Transcendental Meditation, to lower stress levels, and an MAV diet suited to individual needs. It was pointed out by a number of advisors that they might have difficulty in separating out the cause and effect of the different aspects of the study.

Some purists also thought that it could be a problem that Davis would not allow a placebo control group because he considered it unethical to refuse treatment to patients. This perception of ethics was quite the opposite of that held by many orthodox medical investigators, who thought that a trial was only ethical if it included a randomised placebo control group the members of whom went untreated. This question was to be raised later during the GMC hearing.

In February 1989, having found some funding and sought as much professional help as was humanly possible, Dr Davis began the trial. It was originally intended that some twenty patients would be treated for a year, free of cost. In the end, however, patients were treated for a varying length of time, all less than the intended period. Money, assured from voluntary sector AIDS organisations to support the project, was not forthcoming and part-way into the trial, Davis found it necessary to ask patients if they could make contributions. Some patients continued to be treated free, one made an initial contribution of £100, one paid £160 a month, while two further patients agreed to pay £80 a month, half way through the study. The Trust was buying the made-up treatments from a company in Switzerland at about £180 to £200 a month.

There is no doubt that the trials did not go well and because Davis lacked finance he was forced to restrict the number of patients on the trial to six. The two matters which were later thrown at Davis during the GMC hearing were that he had not put his protocols to an ethical committee and that he made changes to the protocol during the trial.† Davis felt strongly on both these issues.

> The patients and the trial eventually merged into one another. In fact Pinching had said that when there was a conflict between a trial and treatment, you have to devolve into treatment. If the protocol says that the patient should only have treatment A but at some point in the trial it becomes apparent that they would benefit from treatment B, then you have to give them treatment B. That was the ethical thing to do. [39]

> I was criticised by the GMC for my attitude towards treatment and trials, but I always stuck to what I considered were good ethical principles; always putting the patient first. One of the tribunal said that it wasn't good research practice to begin with a protocol and then change it, but this is why research into

---

† Jabar Sultan had also been accused of changing the protocols of his trial and Bristol Cancer Help Centre had been accused of wrecking the study carried out by the ICR by refusing to allow a randomised placebo control group.

medical treatments sometimes is not 'ethical' and doesn't work like other types of research. [40]

To a great extent, you have to be led by the patient, some ARC and AIDS patients know a great deal about their illness, and no doctor or research scientist should necessarily imagine that they know better than the patient about the way they should be treated or whether they should be included in a trial. [41]

* * *

By 1989, alarm bells must have begun to sound within the Wellcome Foundation as yet another independent treatment organisation set up in central London began through the voluntary agencies to invite patients to use treatments other than AZT.

By the beginning of 1989, the reaction against natural medicine was gathering pace. Davis was starting work within a field which Wellcome was out to dominate, a field in which all non-pharmaceutical competition for AZT was to be eradicated. During the course of setting up the Trust, Davis met Dietmar Bolle, one of the early members of Positively Healthy. It was Bolle who first made him aware that behind the scenes the top level of both Frontliners and the Terrence Higgins Trust had become resolutely opposed to Ayur-Vedic treatments being given to AIDS patients. This was despite the fact that there was considerable interest from ordinary 'rank and file' members of both organisations. The very voluntary sector AIDS organisations which should have been cultivating a research bonanza were beginning to censor out non-pharmacological treatments.

The gathering antagonism towards alternative treatments did not initially bother Davis. He did not see it as an organised response and after all he was fairly used to scepticism, even ridicule. Dietmar Bolle continued to support him and wrote a favourable article for the *Body Positive Newsletter*. [42]

I have offered to support a clinical trial of the long-term effectiveness of a Maharishi Ayur-Veda therapeutic strategy in the management of HIV infection. This therapy is based on Ayur-Veda, the ardent health system of India, a natural and holistic approach. The trial programme is tailored to suit the needs and life-style of each individual, and aims to strengthen the body's natural immune system through the use of herbal preparations, special diet, meditation, and a variety of other therapeutic techniques.

Bolle reported favourably on the twelve case European trial report, which had found, 'increased weight and appetite, more energy, less fatigue, improved mental state and sense of well-being', and for those taking AZT at the same time, it had indicated some 'relief from its toxic effects'.

Davis spoke at an AIDS support group meeting in Slough in March 1989 and in the same month, the *Sunday Times* carried a serious article about the Ayur-Vedic treatment of AIDS. [43] The article centred mainly upon Dr Deepak Chopra, the most prominent theoretician of Ayur-Vedic medicine, who works in America. Chopra, who was previously chief of staff of the New England Memorial Hospital near Boston, had inspired the opening of a clinic in San Francisco dealing mainly with AIDS patients.

The *Sunday Times* article is responsible and straightforward, making it clear that with the holistic approach of Ayur-Ved, HIV antibody positive individuals might keep healthy and improve their T cell count. At the end, however, the article carried an advertisement for the clinical trials being carried out by Dr Davis of the Disease Free Society Trust. Eligibility for the trial, the advertisement stated, would involve 'agreement to give up taking AZT'. Davis was worried about this serious inaccuracy and wrote to the *Sunday Times* to correct the mistake.

* * *

While Leslie Davis had been working hard contacting as many experts as he could, strangers were trying to contact him. Duncan Campbell tried frequently and a Dr Dominik Wujastyk from the Wellcome Institute for the History of Medicine, also called his answering service. By the summer of 1989, Davis was refusing to return phone calls which came from anyone connected with Wellcome. He was convinced that he had been targeted by them and they were spreading misinformation about him.

The first time that Leslie Davis heard Duncan Campbell's name mentioned in relation to AIDS was in June 1989, and the first time he saw an article of his was in *Capital Gay* in October 1989. It was around this time that the difficulties really began and Dr Davis' life came under the same relentless pressure and harassment from Campbell that others had suffered.

As part of his attempt to contact the gay AIDS community through the AIDS voluntary organisations, Davis organised a seminar at London Lighthouse in November 1989. The seminar, similar to one which had already been held in Germany about Ayur-Vedic medicine and AIDS, was critical of the contemporary therapeutic approaches.

After a flyer was sent out to some 2,000 people on the Body Positive mailing list, advertising the seminar, the Trust received a phone call from Campbell. Campbell wanted to know what the seminar was all about; wasn't it just an advertising trick to sell Ayur-Vedic medicine? Davis did not have the right or the expertise, in Campbell's opinion, to organise such a seminar. Within days, the London Lighthouse cancelled the meeting on their premises. They were frightened, they said, of an article that a journalist was about to write. Next, Davis heard that the Terrence Higgins Trust would picket the seminar if it was held.

The seminar was finally held at the Institute of Complementary Medicine. One attending AIDS patient expressed anger at the fact that the Terrence Higgins Trust had considered forcing him to cross a picket line to attend a meeting about his own health. Following the seminar, Davis received a letter of complaint ostensibly from the Terrence Higgins Trust but most probably, he thought, written by Duncan Campbell. A further letter written in March 1990 was addressed to Dr Chalmers, although he had never had any contact with THT.

On February 9th 1990 a researcher from BBC Television's 'Pebble Mill', working on a programme about Ayur-Vedic medicine and AIDS, initiated by Campbell,† wrote to Dr Pinching asking him to

---

† Prior to an interview, the researcher for the programme, Abrin Hamid, told Dr Davis that Duncan Campbell was not involved. In fact Campbell was paid by the BBC for freelance research which was the basis of the programme. The programme series, 'Network East', one of the only ethnic series programmes for Indian viewers, was dropped in favour of the Indian historical melodrama, the 'Mahabharata', and Campbell's programme was not shown. Hamid also failed to tell Davis the real reason that she had requested herbal preparations from him. While it was suggested that they were for graphics, they were actually to be sent to the MRC for testing.

assess some of the claims made by Davis. In his later affidavit for the GMC hearing, Dr Pinching says that he was not approached directly by Campbell on this matter until around this time, when he met with Campbell to discuss Davis.

In August 1990, Campbell published his first serious attack upon Davis and Chalmers, in the *Independent on Sunday*. [44] In the article he quotes Pinching as saying that he 'could not see any evidence of substantial benefit' from the experiments.

At this time, Pinching had also discussed the dietary aspects of the MAV treatments with the dietician at St Mary's Hospital, Paddington, who then discussed the matter with officers in the food-industry-supported British Dietetic Association. The protocol which Davis had discussed with Pinching was for a multi-modular trial of which MAV dietary advice was a part. As a qualified doctor, Davis had always been adamant that any such diet should be individually suited to the health status of the patient. Despite all this, the British Dietetic Association issued a statement on International AIDS Day 1990, warning about the use of the 'MAV diet' by people with HIV, ARC or AIDS. The dietician at St Mary's was later to give evidence before the GMC hearing to the effect that the 'MAV diet' was dangerous for AIDS patients.† In fact there is no such thing as the 'MAV diet', as the GMC were later to hear. Dietary advice was given to each patient, according to their circumstances.

In September 1990, Campbell wrote 'Heaven on earth' for the *New Statesman and Society*. [45] This page-long article included a paragraph deriding Dr Davis and Dr Chalmers and their adherence to Ayur-Ved. Although the GMC hearing did not take place until June 1991, Campbell already had more information about the case against Davis and Chalmers than they had themselves. Campbell disclosed that both Chalmers and Davis were at that time being investigated by the GMC.

---

† Davis and Chalmers recommended a vegetarian diet and as far as was feasible they recommended the use of organically grown fruit and vegetables. There were also dietary guidelines based on the type of imbalance which was presented. Davis believed that AIDS was a multi-factorial condition; his advice to patients included avoiding as far as possible chemicals in food. Such advice would no doubt have triggered a similar response from orthodox doctors, dieticians and HealthWatch members as the dietary advice given by the Bristol Cancer Help Centre and other groups.

> Dr Chalmers and a colleague, Dr Leslie Davis, are currently
> being investigated by the General Medical Council following
> complaints by AIDS patients of serious professional misconduct.

* * *

> As far as AIDS is concerned, the orthodox view of research and
> drug trialing, is controversial and in some cases unethical, but it
> was by this orthodoxy that I was judged when I went before the
> GMC. [46]

Appearing before the Professional Conduct Committee of the General
Medical Council is perhaps one of the worst things which can happen
to a doctor, second only to being found guilty and being struck off.
Doctors are on the whole only brought before the Committee on
serious and substantial charges and only found guilty when there is
irrefutable evidence. Being struck off signals the end of years of
training and experience and shatters a professional career.

The complaint against Roger Chalmers and Leslie Davis to the
Professional Conduct Committee of the GMC was brought by
Duncan Campbell acting on behalf of the Terrence Higgins Trust.
The complaint was made at a time when the Chairman of the
Committee was Dr Michael O'Donnell, who was also the Chairman of
the Campaign Against Health Fraud.

As was to be expected, the witnesses for the prosecution were men
who believed unerringly in orthodox medicine. There were seven
main charges against both doctors, broken down into sub-charges.
Simply put, the substantive charges were these: that Davis and
Chalmers had treated AIDS patients without sufficient knowledge of
immunology; that they promoted, recommended and provided the
therapy Maharishi Ayur-Ved (MAV) without proper clinical trials and
without adequate qualifications in Ayur-Vedic medicine; that Davis
had promoted a seminar on MAV and AIDS and suggested in
literature that present therapeutic approaches to AIDS were
fundamentally wrong and that MAV could offer respite to or
improve the condition of those suffering from AIDS or HIV; that
they were involved in the production of a document advertising a press
conference which suggested that patients should stop using modern

medicine; that Davis failed to provide the doctor of a patient with details of what their medication contained. Despite Chalmers' virtual non-involvement in the management of AIDS through MAV, his charges were virtually the same as Davis's.

Even from the lay point of view, it is clear that in the case of Davis and Chalmers, we are not dealing with doctors who have broken the criminal law; they have not sexually assaulted patients nor prescribed poisonous or illegal substances. Only one of the charges related to a specific patient and it might be said that it was this charge which was the most substantial.

The patient concerned had died of AIDS some time before the hearing; however, his partner, who knew Duncan Campbell, appeared at the hearing as Mr X to give evidence on his behalf. Mr X's evidence was that after his friend had taken MAV herbal remedies for a couple of weeks, he had suffered stomach pains. He claimed that when the patient and his doctor spoke to Dr Davis, Davis was unable or unwilling to give the exact constituents of the MAV herbal medicine.

This charge, like the others, came nowhere near being logically or legally reasonable. The prosecution could only surmise and not prove that it was the herbal pills which caused the stomach pains. Nor could it be ascertained whether the patient's views before his death were as antagonistic to Davis and Chalmers as those of his partner. The partner's relationship with Duncan Campbell and the route by which he appeared as a witness before the hearing were not properly investigated and could have thrown doubt on the probity of his evidence.

However, by far the most serious injustice of the charge, was that no comparative evidence was brought before the tribunal to assess whether or not orthodox clinicians would in a single phone conversation be able to give a breakdown of any of the complex chemical remedies which they prescribe in large quantities to their patients. The fact that there have been reports of serious adverse effects from AZT, prescribed by doctors who would not know how to describe its make-up, or its pharmacological action, was never once put to the Council.

The evidence given against Davis and Chalmers by AIDS doctors Pinching and Gazzard, perhaps because they knew of the adverse effects of AZT, was extremely low key. Both doctors showed a reluctance to openly criticise Davis and Chalmers to the extent that it could be said that they left the complaint and its prosecution to Duncan Campbell and the Terrence Higgins Trust. Whether or not this was a façade for the purposes of professional etiquette, we do not know.

Naturally, having given Dr Davis consistent advice in respect of the MAV trial, Dr Pinching, in particular, could not reasonably make him out to be a quack or a charlatan, or even for that matter, a person who was ignorant about AIDS and HIV. In his statement to the GMC, Pinching affirmed:

> My overall impression of Dr. Davis was of a person wholly committed to the Ayur-Vedic approach to therapy and one who was apparently knowledgeable about it ... He showed considerable knowledge of AIDS and HIV, at least from a study of the literature. He was very responsive to constructive criticism and the amendments to the protocols I saw indicated a willingness to respond to at least some of my criticisms ... I was impressed by the overall integrity of his approach, even though I was always unconvinced of the benefits of the Ayur-Vedic treatment for AIDS. [47]

Dr Gazzard too had great respect for the abilities of both Davis and Chalmers, both of whom he had taught at Westminster Hospital.

In a court of law, or even a better educated legal tribunal than the GMC, few of the charges brought against Dr Davis and Dr Chalmers would have remained on the indictment. Many of them were essentially matters of opinion and prejudice rather than fact or precedent. The charge, for example, that neither Davis or Chalmers, who were both well-qualified doctors, one a Member of the Royal College of Physicians, the other a Fellow of the Royal College of Surgeons, had sufficient knowledge of immunology to treat patients for HIV management, ARC or AIDS, was utterly spurious.

As has been said often, ARC, particularly, is not one new illness but a number of older ones which occur together in the patient whose immune system is failing. While there are apparently no effective antivirals that destroy any virus which may cause this condition, there are many ways of giving a patient immune-enhancing remedies and of treating opportunist infections. To do either of these things, a doctor does not necessarily have to be a specialist in immunology.

The only charges which might have held water before a legally educated tribunal were those which accused Davis and Chalmers of making claims for unproven remedies. The claims, however, would have to have been such that they suggested that MAV therapy could cure AIDS. No evidence was presented that either doctor had at any time made such claims. What is more, neither doctor had treated any patients without corresponding with or contacting their consultant or general practitioner, seeking their agreement on the treatment they were to give the patient unless the patient did not agree to this.

Finally, it seemed never to occur to the tribunal, that it was certainly not the fault of Davis or Chalmers that their immune-enhancing treatments were not proven or disproven. Dr Davis had spent two exhaustive years trying to get a trial off the ground and those who were brought before the GMC to give evidence against him, were the very people who had obstructed this process.

During the hearing, great evidential weight was put on the herbal tablets prescribed by Davis and Chalmers, to the virtual exclusion of other aspects of the MAV therapy. Two of the tablets were tested at the Medicines Testing Laboratory of the Royal Pharmaceutical Society of Great Britain, on behalf of the GMC. This test was apparently to find out whether or not the tablets contained any microbiological bacilli, or organisms capable of causing infection. On testing, the micro-organism *Enterococcus faecium* was isolated from one of the tablets.

The GMC emerged from the hearing, in respect of this point in particular, as rank amateurs, condoning the breaking of a number of rules of forensic evidence. Absolutely no regard was paid to the 'continuity' of the exhibits from their finding to their analysis. Strict procedures governing the handling of exhibits in criminal cases heard before the courts, ensure that all exhibits are accounted for at every change of possession from the time that they come into the hands of the police to the time that they arrive at court, having been to the analyst. In the case of the two tablets, which presumably came from the patient who had died and were passed by his partner to Duncan Campbell and then to the solicitors for the GMC and from them to the Medicines Testing Laboratory (MTL), no record of their handling on this journey was presented to the GMC. Quite evidently with such gimcrack procedures, the microbiological findings were of no evidential value at all; any one of the people handling the tablets could have been responsible for their faecal contamination.

Perhaps less serious, given this laxity, was the fact that the analyst at the MTL had broken another cardinal rule enforced by more qualified tribunals and their investigating officers and plain scientists. The analyst had carried out what she referred to as 'a destructive test' on both tablets. That is to say that during her one test, she had used in dilution all the material of the two tablets, so being unable to carry out any control tests. More importantly, she left no material available for the defence to carry out the same tests had they so wished.

Although it is not possible to know what evidential weight was given to the finding of faecal material in, or on, the tablets prescribed by Dr Chalmers, there can be no doubt that as in the case of Yves Delatte, the power of such evidence was bound to be immensely prejudicial to the case of Davis and Chalmers. In the end, the charge that Davis and Chalmers had prescribed potentially harmful herbal tablets was dismissed.

It is, however, the more obtuse and legally indefensible charges which showed that the GMC hearing was a hearing in defence of orthodox medicine and the pharmaceutical companies, rather than patients. What are we to make of the charge that Davis and Chalmers had recommended that patients should 'stop using modern medicine' or that Davis participated in a seminar the literature for which claimed that 'the present therapeutic approach to the treatment of AIDS and HIV must be fundamentally wrong'. Do doctors not live in the same democracy as the rest of us? It appears not. Doctors, it appears, live under the authority of some strange industrial junta.

It was Duncan Campbell and Nick Partridge, giving evidence on behalf of the Terrence Higgins Trust, who added most weight to such charges. This after all was the only kind of evidence they could give: neither Campbell nor Partridge was a clinician of any kind and they would have been hard pressed to give serious scientific evidence. They were, however, the fulcrum of the prosecution case, because they together with Mr X were the complainants. What was their complaint?

Campbell gave evidence to the fact that a number of newspaper articles had appeared about Ayur-Vedic medicine; they were not ordinary newspaper articles, contended Campbell, but advertisements and promotions. There are two major difficulties with this line of argument. One is that the two main articles were written by reputable journalists, in reputable newspapers. [48] The second is that articles and television news items ceaselessly advertise orthodox pharmaceutical treatments and none of the doctors who prescribe these treatments are brought before the GMC.

The other main aspect of Campbell's complaint was to do with an issue of apparently great importance to both him and Nick Partridge. Campbell maintained that Davis had told patients to stop taking AZT. The basis for this unwritten charge seems to consist entirely of moral and personal prejudice and have nothing to do with the rules of the GMC or any formal ruling made by the GMC or any other tribunal. In matters of treatment for illnesses other than cancer or AIDS, it would seem fairly ordinary for a doctor to change a patient's therapy, or review it, particularly in the case of adverse reactions. In the case of cancer and AIDS, the medical establishment holds the opinion that only certain treatments are of value. Campbell and Partridge, despite their lack of training and clinical experience, appear to be convinced of the same arguments.

Throughout the hearing there was a great deal said about AZT, which is surprising, because the tribunal was hearing a case which should have stood independently about the use by Davis and Chalmers of Ayur-Vedic treatments. It was contended by counsel for the GMC, however, that the only proper treatment for the HIV infection or AIDS was an anti-viral. He was categorical about this. The MAV herbal treatment, it was said, showed no anti-viral qualities. Neither Davis nor Chalmers had ever suggested, to the public, that the remedies, or the other modalities in the programme acted purely by an anti-viral effect: their case from the beginning had been that AIDS probably had more than one causative factor.

> We make it clear in our literature that our view is that HIV is only part of the problem, and that the solution to HIV infection and indeed to any infectious disease does not lie primarily in

attacking the organism but in strengthening the whole person. [49]

This argument was an anathema to those 'experts' in the medical and pharmaceutical establishment who had from the beginning, like shoppers at a Harrods sale, rushed for the 'magic bullet' theory. The hypothesis that HIV and HIV alone was responsible for AIDS and that once a person had HIV they would inexorably die of AIDS, was the corner stone of AZT marketing. It established AZT as that magic bullet, even though it had not been tested against either a whole range of natural treatments, or a regime which took away the patient's immunosuppressant lifestyle habits.

The GMC hearing of the cases of Chalmers and Davis should have been independent. Instead it was unashamedly a defence of AZT. The GMC listened to hours of evidence which evinced the view that for anyone to dissuade a patient from taking AZT was criminal. Expert witnesses attested to the fact that AZT represented the 'gold standard' by which all other AIDS and HIV therapies must be measured. It was Mr Langdale, the prosecuting counsel for the GMC, who first introduced the notion of a 'gold standard'.

> AZT, which is the gold standard by which we work at the moment, although I accept that it has got toxicity problems, nevertheless that is our gold standard ... [50]

Langdale also explained to the hearing that there were two indices for a therapy, its concentration to produce a therapeutic effect and its concentration to produce a toxicological effect. In the case of AZT, he explained that both indices were much lower than, in this case, liquorice which according to the prosecution was one constituent of some Ayur-Vedic treatments dispensed by Davis and Chalmers. In relation to the toxicity of AZT as compared with the toxicity of liquorice, there seemed to be no doubt, liquorice could be highly toxic and cause terrible stomach pains, on the other hand AZT ... well, there were no actual studies to measure its toxicity. The toxicity of liquorice was common knowledge.

> Mr Langdale: Is there any way in which liquorice could cause severe stomach pains?
>
> Professor
> Paul Turner: Yes, of course. One knows from personal

experience that if you over-dose with
Pontefract cakes or liquorice you can get
diarrhoea. [51]†

The Ayur-Vedic preparations used by Davis and Chalmers, should,
this same expert agreed, have been measured rigorously as an anti-
viral against the 'gold standard' AZT.

Neither Davis nor Chalmers argued that patients should stop taking
AZT, even though Davis openly espoused the view that the long term
use of AZT would not ultimately be in his patients' best interests. He
argued only what they had been advised by Dr Anthony Pinching: [53]
anyone recruited onto a trial for MAV should preferably have taken
no other treatments for a substantial period prior to the trial.‡

> In the GMC hearing, Campbell claimed that I had stopped
> patients from taking AZT. In fact that was not true, my policy was
> that I wrote to their doctors and told their doctors that they should
> continue taking whatever other treatments they were taking. We
> did have a research protocol for the trial which was only for those
> people who were not taking AZT or other treatments. [54]

It was during cross-examination on this issue of whether or not Davis

---

† The exchanges between Mr Coonan, acting for Dr Davis, and Professor Turner,
Professor of Clinical Pharmacology in the University of London and Chairman
of the Committee on Toxicity at the Department of Health, were strained. Turner
claimed that the Ayur-Vedic tablets dispensed by Davis and Chalmers were more
toxic than AZT.

> Mr Coonan (Counsel for Davis): May I suggest this to you Professor
> Turner. In the ordinary box of Bassetts Liquorice All Sorts, for example,
> one is getting about, what, 290 mg of glycyrrhizic acid per 100 g of
> liquorice, is that right? Let us just assume that the same analyses apply,
> and I suggest that you are not going to get more than about 1.5 to 1.8 mg
> of acid which would produce on the basis of one of these tablets three
> times a day, about 115 mg of acid a week? Can you help us about an
> unsafe level for liquorice?

> Professor Turner : No, I would entirely agree that the cases that have
> been described have generally been in patients who have eaten large
> quantities of liquorice-containing confectionery, such as Pontefract cakes
> and black liquorice and I cannot give you a figure for the total quantities
> eaten. [52]

‡ This same rule, with respect to any therapy other than AZT, was laid down
clearly in the protocols for the Concorde trials.

had told patients that they must not take AZT, that Duncan Campbell found difficulty in substantiating the claims he had made in an original affidavit. During a telephone conversation with Davis, Campbell had roughly noted that in relation to one particular patient Davis gave his opinion about trial subjects and AZT. Campbell's notes, as read by Mr Coonan representing Davis, during his cross examination of Campbell, consisted of short bursts of dialogue: 'We should favour people who were not taking AZT' ... 'He [a patient] wouldn't qualify' ... 'We felt people should be off it for a certain length of time'. These contemporaneous notes had, according to the counsel, later been 'interpreted' and a new inference put upon them in Campbell's fifty one page sworn affidavit, made out for the GMC a year after the phone call.

Campbell's affidavit summarises the conversation with Davis about trial subjects being off AZT, in this manner: 'In other words, Dr Davis was saying, patients were only being offered free treatment or reduced cost treatment if they agreed to come off AZT, or if they had not been taking AZT in the first place'. Davis' counsel made a serious point when he put it to Campbell that the idea of re-writing contemporaneous rough notes into a formal affidavit a year after the conversation, was 'fraught with danger'. The multiple injustices of the criminal justice system which have surfaced over the last twenty years seem to have passed the GMC by. Its proceedings, though able to terminate the professional career of any doctor standing before it, are shot through with the faults and prejudices of a barrack-room mock trial.

Help for Davis on the issue of AZT came from the most unexpected quarter. In his affidavit for the Council, Dr Gazzard stated that in 1989 most doctors would have considered AZT a toxic drug:

> particularly as the standard dose was 1.2 gms a day ... It is true that many patients did stop therapy and felt much better as a result. Thus, although I would personally not have recommended cessation of AZT therapy to ill patients in 1989, I would believe that some competent doctors would have felt that such advice was reasonable. [55]

It seems incredible that the General Medical Council could accept the evidence of a lay witness like Campbell, over that of an experienced consultant like Dr Gazzard.

Perhaps the most bizarre charge faced by Davis and Chalmers was that neither doctor was properly qualified in Ayur-Vedic medicine. On what grounds did the General Medical Council consider that it was qualified to hear this issue? The whole tenor of the hearing from its first day was one of prejudice against the very plausibility of Ayur-Vedic medicine. Yet in order to prove that Davis and Chalmers were not properly qualified, the prosecution was forced to bring an expert in Ayur-Vedic medicine to testify.

The prosecution witness brought to give evidence that Chalmers and Davis were not qualified to practise Ayur-Vedic medicine was Dr Dominik Wujastyk. Surprisingly, Wujastyk was not a doctor of medicine but a PhD in Sanskrit and the Associate Curator of the South Asian Collections, at the Wellcome Institute for the History of Medicine. Wujastyk had tried to phone Dr Davis on a number of occasions over the year before the hearing.

Wujastyk worked in the same building and the same department as Caroline Richmond. It is almost beyond belief that the General Medical Council would call, as its main witness to testify to the Ayur-Vedic qualifications of two British doctors accused of treating AIDS patients, a man who worked for a Trust which was funded by the very company which produced the one licensed treatment available for AIDS: a museum curator and non-practitioner.

Mr Langdale, counsel for the GMC, was quick to put at rest any worries which the tribunal might appear to have about Dr Wujastyk's links with Wellcome.

Q.   I think we should make it clear – obviously since Wellcome is a well-known name – are you in any way connected with Wellcome plc or the Wellcome Foundation?
A.   Not at all. No. I am employed by the Wellcome Trust and that is a completely separate body. [56]

Having established to the satisfaction of the hearing that the Wellcome Trust has absolutely nothing to do with the Wellcome Foundation, apart, that is, from its being almost entirely dependent upon the Foundation's profits, Dr Wujastyk gave his evidence.

Dr Wujastyk's evidence was not, however, about the learning or abilities of Davis or Chalmers; in order to have established that, there would have had to have been some kind of test. The Council heard only that in India there were three standard accepted qualifications for Ayurvedic training: a Bachelor of Ayur-Vedic Medicine and Surgery (BAMS), a Doctor of Ayur-Vedic Medicine (MD Ayu) and a PhD in Ayur-Vedic research. Neither Dr Davis or Dr Chalmers had any of these qualifications.

The evidence of Dr Wujastyk about qualifications cut to the very heart of the case. Dr Chalmers and Dr Davis had in reality been put on trial by the General Medical Council, primarily because they had treated AIDS patients with remedies other than AZT, challenging in however small a way the multi-national power of the Wellcome Foundation. The fact that the two doctors were members of what the CAHF would call 'a cult', went towards making an excellent rationale for the prosecution. Like contaminated medicine, bizarre philosophies from the East are likely to be harbingers of evil quackery.

* * *

Those newspapers which reported on the GMC hearing did so in the manner of a criminal trial, that is, while they reported the opening speech for the prosecution they failed to report the defence. Even the quality papers embellished their reporting with emotive expressions, and homed in on the finding of *Enterococcus faecium* on the two tablets. *The Times*, the *Independent* and the *Daily Telegraph*[57] all had Davis and Chalmers 'peddling AIDS cures', and all three papers had them 'peddling' tablets which 'contained' faeces.

It was, however, the Terrence Higgins Trust and Nick Partridge in particular that continued to make capital out of the downfall of Davis and Chalmers for some period after the end of the case. On a tour of Canada, during which he gave a number of interviews sympathetic to AZT, Nick Partridge appeared on a CBC radio programme on May 17th 1992. Appearing with him on the programme was the founder and President of the American National Council Against Health Fraud, William Jarvis.

The distortion countenanced by the programme's presenter was a gross libel against Davis and Chalmers, but Nick Partridge made no attempt to correct him and appears happy to have embellished his remarks.

Presenter :   ... The case [of Davis and Chalmers before the
                   GMC] centred around a patient... who was treated
                   for AIDS with Transcendental Meditation and
                   Maharishi herbal medicines. He developed serious
                   diarrhoea and died.

In this fictionalised version of events, Davis and Chalmers are guilty of
the manslaughter of a patient. Partridge didn't appear to be happy with
this and introduced a greater liability into the discussion which would
have meant that Davis and Chalmers had murdered the patient.

Partridge   ... it was discovered that they [the tablets] included
                   faecal matter ... and I believe that the two doctors
                   knew that that was what it (sic) included. [58]

According to Partridge, he had been forced to take Davis and
Chalmers to the GMC because they had 'resolutely refused to follow
accepted medical and clinical practice'. Partridge after all 'knew' that
the MAV therapy was 'not going to do anyone any good'. Nick
Partridge must have made William Jarvis' day, when every other
Canadian and American AIDS organisation was laying into the
National Council Against Health Fraud on the grounds that it was
censoring treatments for those with HIV and AIDS, here was Nick
Partridge toeing the pharmaceutical line. Yes, coced Jarvis, 'being a
doctor is kind of like being an airline pilot, you carry the lives of
strangers in your hands'.

Another link with the National Council Against Health Fraud in
the case of Davis and Chalmers surfaced in an article in the *San
Francisco Bay Guardian* of December 18th 1991. This was the newspaper
which had carried Nick Partridge's reflections upon the anti-oxidant
herbal treatments which Howard Greenspan had unsuccessfully tried
to trial in London. The paper carried a long anti-cult story by Ric
Kahn [59] which gave details of the Davis and Chalmers GMC hearing.
The story included a quote from Dr John Renner, the Kansas City co-
chair of the National Council Against Health Fraud's AIDS Quackery
Task Force.

By far the most damaging article about Davis and Chalmers
appeared in the London *Evening Standard* on March 27th 1992. [60] This
article, although written by previously unknown investigative reporter

Keith Dovkants, had Duncan Campbell stamped between every line. The article claimed that Davis and Chalmers were 'sinister forces' behind the Maharishi's Natural Law Party which was at that time contesting seats in the British General Election. The article had Davis, 'late of Harley Street', 'selling miracle cures to AIDS patients', which made AIDS sufferers who turned to them 'feel unwell'. An unnamed member of the Terrence Higgins Trust is quoted saying: 'These men conned AIDS patients to make money'.

The real stories behind such tribunal hearings fade over time. The truth collapses as it is pressed into a shape which will fit the institutional convenience of the medical establishment. The enemies of truth ensure that the victims of their schemes are hauled before the world and the skeleton shaken at regular intervals to keep a distorted message strong in the mind of possible followers. Legal and regulatory infrastructures, scaffolded by ideology and propaganda, have immense power to assassinate and then bury reputations. From such an assassination and such a burial there is no resurrection, for even if the name is cleared, the stigma remains like a boulder blocking entry back into social life. The names of the guilty are expunged from the record and from institutional life.

The Great Germanium Scandal

Taken orally, organic germanium is highly safe. [61]

On the surface, the two women associated with the mineral germanium, Sandra Goodman and Monica Bryant, and the person principally responsible for the probiotic preparation 'Delta Te', Yves Delatte, had little to do with the chaotic post-AIDS gay community. By a chain of odd circumstances, however, all three came by separate routes to be concerned with AIDS treatments and ultimately to be attacked by Duncan Campbell.

The cases of Sandra Goodman, Monica Bryant and Yves Delatte are perhaps the clearest illustration that Campbell had a hidden agenda when he carried out his wide-ranging attacks in 1989. Goodman, Bryant and Delatte are, all three, intelligent and sincere people, individuals who would, had there been an opportunity, have gladly worked with National Health Service doctors in testing the various health products with which they were involved.

Campbell's articles in the *New Statesman and Society* [62] appeared to be very effective. The principal preparation that Monica Bryant and Sandra Goodman were working on was proscribed by the Department of Health. Monica Bryant, Yves Delatte and their respective companies were dragged before the Magistrate, and warehouse copies of Sandra Goodman's book on germanium were pulped. Looking back upon these three cases, within the context of the other attacks, it is obvious that there was only one reason for this flurry of heavy and repressive activity: to stop the production or trial of any experimental AIDS or HIV treatments during the time of the Concorde trials.

Sandra Goodman

Sandra Goodman PhD was never a member of the complementary medicine circuit. In the mid-eighties she was, and is now, a scientist. She did not know anything about germanium, until Monica Bryant asked her to make an appraisal of all the available literature on it.

Goodman is a short, gutsy Canadian with a soft but authoritative accent. By the time that I interviewed her in 1991, she was aware that she had detonated a considerable furore, first with her research and later with her book on germanium. [63] Even though she herself had suffered no personal repercussions, two years later she appeared vulnerable and concerned about speaking to me. The experience of having had her life mauled by Duncan Campbell had left her anxious about being interviewed. Initially, she insisted that I interview her in the presence of her partner and in full view of other workers at her workplace.

Sandra Goodman is a citizen of the United Kingdom and has a green card status for residence in the United States, gained because of her important scientific specialisation in an area where there were few qualified Americans. She has a science degree and a doctorate in molecular biology from McGill University, Montreal. She is justly proud of her educational achievements, which encompass fluency in three languages and an extensive education in the social sciences and maths. She has published widely in scientific journals.

Following her doctorate, on genetic manipulation in soyabean plants, Sandra Goodman got a job with the agricultural research unit of a large US corporation where for five years she worked to extend the work of her doctorate. In 1986 she came to Britain, and between 1988 and 1989 left again for the States where she took up a position as assistant director of research at one of only two accredited colleges of naturopathy in the United States, John Bastyr College.

Soon after arriving in London in 1986, looking for work as an independent researcher, Sandra Goodman met Monica Bryant. Some months later, Bryant contacted her to ask if she would evaluate a number of papers on germanium, a mineral which Monica Bryant was considering marketing in Britain. Goodman accepted the job and within a short time was engrossed in a mountain of material about germanium.

From the beginning, it was the immunological information that Goodman found fascinating. She read about how germanium modulated the immune system and how it had been used to fight cancer. Papers published in Japan showed precisely the effect which the mineral had upon the immune system. Although she had begun her work with a degree of cynicism, Goodman found that the results in many of the vast number of papers she reviewed were impressive and recorded by reputable scientists.

She reviewed papers which had been researched and written in America about the effect which germanium had upon T cells, the cells most affected, according to some orthodox doctors, by the HIV virus. Reading this work, she began considering whether there might be a role for germanium in the treatment of HIV or AIDS. Coming to the end of her work for Monica Bryant, she decided that even if she could not find funding for such work the information should be published. When she had finished her review, assessing the claims made for germanium, she began a search for someone who might help her publish a book.

Monica Bryant

Monica Bryant has committed most of her life to the field of human nutrition and health. As a child in Sweden, she witnessed the work of a number of health farms. Her training is eclectic. She has a BSc in Human Sciences from Sussex University. With others, she has brought to British nutrition the experience and the learning of the American field leaders, and an experience of Scandinavian and German approaches to biological medicine.

In Monica Bryant's ideas about health and nutrition there is a link between the relatively materialistic or orthomolecular work of the American nutritionists, like Dr Alexander Schauss, and the more ecologically and spiritually-inclined work of Scandinavian naturopaths. Monica Bryant is a self-effacing person, happy to work as a facilitator, introducing other peoples' work to new communities. On her own initiative, she was involved in work to improve prison nutrition and attended the first meeting at the House of Lords on this issue. In the mid-eighties she lectured in nutrition at the University of Sussex for four years.

In 1984, on a visit to Denmark, she learnt about probiotics, the use of beneficial lactic acid producing bacteria to maintain health. She found the idea of using the body's own bacterial ecosystem to regulate health more interesting than simply using vitamins and minerals. In February 1986 she published one of the first British articles on the use of probiotics for human health. [64]

Monica Bryant felt proud of the fact that she was a pioneer in bringing probiotics to Britain. This approach to health seemed timely when doctors were getting disillusioned with the adverse effects and over-use of antibiotics. Probiotics were a natural way to redress the imbalances created in the intestinal flora through the use of drugs and stressful lifestyle habits.

The use of lactic acid bacteria is common in many cultures throughout the world. The use of acidophilus has been known for many years, and 'live' yoghurt is considered helpful for thrush. In Europe, lacto-fermented foods are commonly used for their health-giving qualities.

Having met health practitioners in Sweden working with probiotics, Monica Bryant began to import into Britain an intestinal flora supplement called 'Probion'. This was based upon the two bacteria which make 'live' yoghurt; it was used extensively in Scandinavia and had been well researched by scientists. As the demand for 'Probion' grew in Britain, Monica Bryant expanded her small import agency by using an established distribution company.

In 1986, with her business just keeping afloat, Bryant was offered the agency, in Britain, for germanium. Germanium had not previously been marketed in Britain as it had in other European countries. Being a responsible person, Bryant felt the need to obtain a review by a scientist of all the information currently available about germanium. She found Sandra Goodman to do this.

Monica Bryant could see that germanium had a wide range of established uses: it had an oxygen-enhancing effect, and helped interferon production, as well as modulating the immune system in other ways. In 1986, she set up an agency called Symbiogenesis; a number of major companies acted as distributors for her. No claims were made for germanium and the information on the packets was kept to a few lines which Bryant had cleared with the Products Advertising Authority. By 1988, Symbiogenesis was handling probiotics and germanium. Then Monica Bryant developed her own probiotic product, giving it the trade name Symbion.

The supplier for the particular bacterial strain which Monica Bryant used in Symbion was a man called Yves Delatte. Delatte delivered the bacteria directly from the University of Dundee, where it had been made up. Looking back on the beginnings of her work with Delatte, even after the nightmare years following Campbell's attacks, Monica Bryant knows that she would never have worked with Delatte, had she not thought him a person of integrity with a professional commitment to his work.

Yves Delatte

Yves Delatte is a European, a man who has spent much of his life shuttling between France, Holland, Finland and Britain. He is widely educated, with a number of degrees, principally in biology. He speaks English with a little difficulty.

In 1979, Delatte was working with a French company, developing probiotics for use in animal welfare. He was working principally with mink which, because of constant inbreeding in captivity, have a weak immune system. In 1986, Delatte and his work were taken up by a Swedish company, Kemi Interessen, part of the Kema Nobel group. The company wanted to develop his ideas and work on probiotics, for use in animal welfare, again with mink.

His work with Kemi Interessen took Delatte to mink farms in Ireland and Scotland, and during this time he settled in England. He worked for only a year with Kemi Interessen, and left following disagreements about the direction which his research should take. This was a difficult time for Delatte, for as well as leaving his job, he had to stay for two months in a Finnish hospital with one of his daughters after she became seriously ill.

The Scandinavian medical tradition is deeply rooted in biological treatments like probiotics, so much so that Yves Delatte and his daughter's doctors thought nothing of giving his daughter lactic bacteria, with its immune-enhancing properties, to aid her recovery.

In 1987, after his daughter had recovered, Delatte came to England again, to tie up his work and his papers. During the first months of 1988, unsure about his future, he continued his research working alone, using probiotics with mink, dogs and horses. What he would have liked to do was set up a business and get his research on a firmer footing.

In the summer of 1988, he began to consider the possibility of using lactic bacteria for humans with immuno-suppressive illnesses. By that time Delatte had been using probiotics in animal welfare for a period of fifteen years, and had developed considerable knowledge.

Eventually, Delatte decided to try to make contact with HIV antibody positive patients who were willing to trial probiotic treatments. He was sure in his own mind of the benefits of such treatments. He also knew that with no cure for AIDS, probiotic treatments could at least help tackle a variety of AIDS related opportunist infections and illnesses.

In London, he talked to Dr Dorothy Brey, a researcher in the Department of Protozoology, at the London University School of Hygiene and Tropical Medicine. With Dr Brey, and mainly at her suggestion, Delatte patented his probiotic formula. Brey also introduced Delatte to his first AIDS patient, Michael Emblam.†️ Emblam had been diagnosed HIV antibody positive and prescribed AZT, but stopped taking it after suffering severe side-effects. Delatte

† This patient's name has been changed to protect his identity.

gave Emblam 10^{10} per gram, quantities of lactic bacteria, mixed with milk powder to bulk it out. Delatte was careful to ensure that Emblam first obtained the authority of his general practitioner before taking the treatment. The general practitioner soundly advised him that, at worst, the remedy would do him no harm. Within three weeks of his taking lactic bacteria, Emblam's T cell count had risen.

Happy with his treatment, Michael Emblam sent three other people to Delatte and so began a small cohort of people, who started to see him regularly and to whom he gave probiotic treatments. For the first few months of this work, Delatte charged no-one for the preparation. The substance was costing him about £800 a kilo and he was giving out three or four kilos a month.

In a second wave of individuals who went to see Delatte, was Michael Dreer,† an accountant whose partner had AIDS. Visiting Delatte at his friend's house which he used for business, Dreer was astounded at Delatte's lack of business organisation. As far as he was concerned, Delatte's incompetence as a business man was going to make the beneficial production and distribution of probiotics a failure and perhaps a disaster. Dreer persuaded Delatte to set up in business and produce a properly packaged product which could be distributed through doctors or alternative practitioners.

Up until the autumn of 1988, Delatte had been importing the basic constituent of his probiotic treatment from America. As part of the re-organisation of his business, Delatte approached the laboratories at Dundee University with the specifications for the bacteria. Dundee were happy to make up the preparation to Delatte's specification.‡

As the numbers of HIV antibody positive subjects seeing Delatte grew, he felt obliged to begin charging but disinclined to make a profit. For a month's course, of taking lactic bacteria every day, Delatte began to charge around £75, the cost price of the product. Other

---

† This man's name has been changed to protect his identity.

‡ At a later date, after Dundee University had divulged the details of Delatte's business to Campbell, they claimed that Delatte had told them the preparation was to be used on animals. Delatte maintains that he had made it clear from the beginning that he was preparing a human health product. Dundee also claimed that Delatte had called himself doctor. The correspondence shows, however, that Delatte never once used that title in any of his letters.

probiotics preparations, made by large companies and imported from Scandinavia, are sold in Britain at higher prices. It was at the time that Delatte's business became better organised, in the autumn of 1988, that he met Monica Bryant.

* * *

When Sandra Goodman had finished her review of the germanium literature, she began her book. In 1988, around the same time that the CAHF had its first meeting and the Concorde trials began, Thorsons published *Germanium: the health and life enhancer.* [65] This book perhaps more than anything else, led to the destruction of Monica Bryant's business and reputation.

Two sentences from the blurb on the back cover of the book, no doubt seemed like a red rag to the AZT marketing team at Wellcome: 'Sandra Goodman also looks into its [germanium's] possible use in the treatment of AIDS patients' ... 'She is currently involved in co-ordinating a double-blind trial with organic germanium for AIDS patients'.

Inside the book, in a section entitled 'Centres of Organic Germanium Research', Goodman listed Monica Bryant's International Institute of Symbiotic Studies, saying that it provided 'a focus for the compilation and dissemination of information, quality control, education and research into the use of organic germanium for various diseases including AIDS'.† In fact, Monica Bryant had never been involved with AIDS patients, nor recommended the use of germanium for HIV antibody positive people or ARC sufferers. These scattered pieces of information, however, must have provoked powerful people, who did not want Monica Bryant, or anyone, distributing information about research into AIDS and germanium – or any other substance, except AZT.

Work on her book had reinforced Sandra Goodman's conviction

---

† Monica Bryant's only contact with the AIDS patients was when, on odd occasions, she talked on the opportunist infections suffered by AIDS patients, especially fungal infections; in 1988, she gave a lecture on AIDS in Germany, called 'An ecological approach to AIDS', and on another occasion, 'AIDS; what are the real issues', at Rudolph Steiner House in London.

that trials for germanium in relation to HIV, ARC and AIDS were important and she began looking for funds and support. As a scientist who had tackled such research before, she began by contacting field leaders, in the hope that she might draw one of them into an agreement on research funding. She even hoped that she could find someone who would work with her on a research programme.

In April 1987, Goodman wrote to Dr Anthony Pinching; later, she wrote to the Medical Research Council and the Wellcome Foundation; she also had a meeting at the National AIDS Trust, who forwarded her research proposal to Dr Ian Weller at the Middlesex Hospital. Pinching wrote back, telling Goodman that facilities and time were stretched, and it was better to 'focus attention on a number of therapies'; he hoped, however, that she might find someone else to assess her 'novel ideas'. [66]

In June 1987, Monica Bryant found a company willing to put up enough germanium to support a trial. Sandra Goodman worked hard writing out the research proposal and protocols for such a trial. She managed to obtain the help and support of the director of a private clinic but she could not raise the research budget of £50,000. Becoming daily more frustrated that no one would help with her research, she eventually went to see Chris Patten MP, then wrote to the Department of Health and again to the Medical Research Council. She even contacted the Terrence Higgins Trust.

Any replies which Goodman received were negative. It was made clear that either there were not enough patients for clinical trials, or there was insufficient evidence to support the anti-viral or immuno-modulating effect of germanium, or it was just not a good idea. Goodman, however, was very persistent; she carried the idea around with her for another year, writing a variety of proposals [67] and publishing a number of papers. [68]

Goodman had no idea that her persistence was becoming a serious concern to a number of people. Unbeknown to her, research work had been going on for some time in Japan into the immuno-modulating effect of germanium. If Sandra Goodman were able to link up with scientists in other countries to carry out her trials, the results might pose a serious threat to AZT and the whole way in which HIV management therapies were viewed.

* * *

Yves Delatte, Monica Bryant and Sandra Goodman were all interested in the immune-enhancing properties of various supplements. None of them were looking to find or to sell a cure for AIDS. None of them actually saw AIDS in the way that the orthodox medical establishment defined it, as a disease spread by a single viral infection. In that all three of them thought it was valuable to work with immune-enhancement, even in 1988, they were, like others in this book, part of a minority heterodoxy. In 1988, Sandra Goodman wrote: [69]

> Acquired Immune Deficiency Syndrome (AIDS) is the result of the infection and subsequent devastation of immune system function. Originally, the Human Immunodeficiency Virus (HIV) had been described as the causative agent of AIDS; however, recent reports imply that AIDS may more accurately be described as a multifactorially caused condition, with genetic, constitutional and environmentally implicated factors. These factors may typically include past history with other viral (Epstein-Barr, Cytomegalovirus) and bacterial (Syphilis) infections, poor nutrition, drug abuse, and repeated antibiotic use. [70]

This view had ramifications which extended beyond the medical concerns relating to Sandra Goodman's research. For one thing, it held that preventative therapies were all-important, and that diet and lifestyle had to be taken into account in those who were HIV antibody positive. It also hinted at the idea that there might not be just one 'cure' for AIDS. If an illness had co-factorial origins, it might best respond to multiple integrated treatments. This view of AIDS inevitably extended the debate about health and the HIV antibody positive condition well beyond the chemotherapeutic 'solution' of AZT. It opened up health care options for people with HIV related conditions into multiple treatment choices, a debate which the AIDS establishment, industrial scientists and drug marketeers at Wellcome wanted to damp down.

The new year of 1989 began well for Yves Delatte. He had borrowed £20,000 from his bank and with Michael Dreer had registered a company, Whitecliffe Pharmaceuticals. This however did not make Delatte a businessman. He did not know, for example, that he could not trade as a pharmaceutical company unless he sold his products through retailing pharmacists. His lawyers didn't inform him of this until he had been using his new letterheaded paper for two months.

All of Delatte's first customers kept in touch with their general practitioners to be regularly tested for T cell counts and given physical check ups. Delatte found that the administration of probiotics often stopped the severe diarrhoea which could be one of the first signs of developing ARC. He made no claims for his brand of probiotics, which he had now labelled 'Delta Te', but he was convinced that even if it only stopped the diarrhoea, meaning that food was properly digested and nutrients made bio-available, he was doing something to help the seriously ill.

Contemplating his next move, Yves Delatte was keen on setting up a laboratory of some kind so that he might return to research and further develop his probiotic formula. He was still selling his product at cost price. Delatte had still not made much of an inroad into the gay community or its organisations. He was based at the north London clinic of a homoeopath contact and he gave circular letters to those that used his product. These information sheets, which suffered badly from Delatte's poor English, stressed the fact that those who had begun the treatment should stay the course, particularly because Whitecliffe Pharmaceuticals would collapse if he over-ordered the preparation. There was no 'hard sell', just an honest appraisal of his vulnerable economic position mixed with a sympathetic understanding of his clients' condition. Delatte never said he had a cure, quite the opposite: 'Unfortunately an immune system which has been distroyed (sic) for years, cannot be back on the track in a fortnight'. So as not to deprive people of hope, he added in one of his letters, 'although we are working on this'.

In Febuary 1989, an AIDS patient who had taken AZT but could not tolerate it, visited Delatte. The patient began to use Delta Te and told his physician, Dr Michael Connolly at St Stephen's Hospital, about it. St Stephen's was at that time one of the largest reception hospitals for the Concorde trials. Following the conversation with his patient, Dr Connolly, happy with the improved condition of his patient, agreed to meet Yves Delatte and discuss probiotics with him.

In his first letter to Dr Connolly, written when a cold prevented him attending a meeting, Yves Delatte discussed work which he had done in the previous year with mink suffering from Aleutian Disease (AD). He pointed out the similarities between AD and AIDS: 'A retrovirus, same losses of T cells, same way of transmission, and probably same causes; too much use of anti-biotics in the fur industry, feeds conserved with acids, feeds from scraps of the agro-industry. Hence, the mink are by definition immune depressed models (sic)'. [71] In the letter Delatte discusses the number of AIDS and ME sufferers he is presently treating, tells Dr Connolly that he has patented his probiotic formula and asks for a discussion at a later date, about 'more serious clinical trials'.

What is clear from Yves Delatte's contact with Dr Connolly, is what was also apparent about Dr Sharp and Jabar Sultan's contact with Drs Pinching and Gazzard and Drs Davis' and Chalmers' contact with Dr Pinching.[†] Delatte's approach is not that of a con-man, nothing is done covertly, he acts as a researcher and scientist seeking colleagues and stimulating debate. Nor is his approach that of a dangerous, exploitative, 'hole in the wall' practitioner, but one of a person openly interested in the whole clinical problem of AIDS and hopeful of offering help and support to sick people.

In May 1989, after a number of meetings, and an exchange of correspondence with Dr Connolly, Delatte says that Dr Connolly offered him possible access to 80 AIDS patients, with whom he could conduct a trial.[‡] Connolly stressed, however, that the matter would have to be agreed by the St Stephen's Ethical Committee. Optimistic about the possibility of authoritative work on probiotics, Delatte provided Connolly with a large quantity of documentation about Delta Te.

Yves Delatte was now feeling better about his future; he had what he calls a 'little business', which despite being a registered company, was not making any money. About six kilos of lactic bacteria were regularly passing through his hands, and he was engaged in discussions

---

† For the cases of Dr Sharp and Jabar Sultan, Dr Chalmers and Dr Davis see this Chapter above.

‡ In this correspondence, Delatte discusses the exact make-up of his product and the cost of it: 'It would be nice to start clinical trials as soon as possible, and if we could have at least more than 30 paying patients, the price of the bacteria would drop down from £150 to £100 per month.' [72]

with a supplement production company called 'Biocare' run by John Sterling.†

In May, however, Delatte began to notice that things were going wrong. He had no idea why, nor even if the matters were connected, but a series of things happened. Delatte had been staying with an elderly female friend of many years in Princes Risborough and had set up Whitecliffe Laboratories on her premises. The first thing that Delatte noticed was that his friend's phone was clearly being tampered with and he suspected that it was being tapped.

Then, he noticed that some of the customers who arrived to see him at the premises of the north London homoeopath, did not appear to be ill and could not describe symptoms. One woman, he was sure, was wearing a microphone. He sensed as well that the atmosphere around AIDS treatment was beginning to change. Alternative practitioners began to discuss break-ins, others had trouble with their phones.

* * *

In October 1988, Sandra Goodman left Britain for America; disillusioned with the continual rebuffs she had received, she went to America with the intention of making contacts there. She returned to Britain for a brief time in May, to keep up the pressure on trials in London. There, she learned that her discussions with the National AIDS Trust had come to nothing. Dr Ian Weller from the Middlesex wrote to the National AIDS Trust, in reply to their letter, saying that there there was insufficient evidence of germanium's immuno-modulating effect to allot trial patients to it.

Sandra Goodman was not happy being punted from one destructively pessimistic doctor to another or between reluctant

---

† Biocare was responsible for making up the vitamin and mineral supplements which Positively Healthy were distributing to their members. In 1991 when Cass Mann was attacked in the *Independent* by Duncan Campbell and accused of selling supplements at a high price to vulnerable AIDS patients, Mann asked Sterling to come to his aid, and vouch for the supplements and their price. Sterling refused. Mann later found that Biocare was controlled in part by Rio-Tinto Zinc, a company at the very centre of the Rockefeller Trilateral Commission and the company which Sir Alastair Frame, then Wellcome Chairman, had previously presided over.

voluntary organisations. Finally, during her short stay in Britain, she contacted a firm of solicitors, who entered into a correspondence about germanium with the DoH. The DoH told the solicitors that germanium was considered a low priority for clinical evaluation and the number of patients available for participation was quite limited. It was, they said, necessary to apply rigorous criteria and there was a lack of *in vitro* clinical work on germanium. It was becoming clear to Sandra Goodman that there was an official 'line' on germanium.

Being the committed scientist she was, Goodman accepted as reasonable many of the things which were said about germanium trials. She had, though, major reservations about the way the answers came to her. Surely, in the circumstances of an epidemic, as many substances as possible should be tested under the authority of the Department of Health? The contrast between the wildly different attitudes to germanium and AZT did not escape her. Hadn't AZT been one amongst hundreds of substances sent to the National Institutes of Health in America, on the off-chance it would have anti-viral qualities? Hadn't AZT been licensed without conclusive trials? Why after AZT was licensed did any systematic testing of new substances suddenly cease?

Back in America, Sandra Goodman met Dr Jariwalla, an eminent virologist, at a conference in Los Angeles. Dr Jariwalla had been working at the Linus Pauling Institute, and had recently tested Vitamin C *in vitro* for its anti-viral qualities, with excellent results.†️ Following the conference, Goodman wrote out protocols for the Linus Pauling Institute, in the hope that she could get *in vitro* tests on germanium off the ground. She described a budget of only $25,000. Even then, in the middle of 1989, she felt that AIDS was such a serious condition that 'even if you are clutching at straws it is worth spending small amounts of money on testing as many things as possible'.

Sandra Goodman returned to Britain in the summer of 1989, still determined to fight her way to a trial for germanium. By this time, however, moves were well ahead, not simply to ensure that she did not carry out trials, but to get rid of germanium completely.

---

† Jariwalla's work was published in 1990 in the *Proceedings of the National Academy of Sciences.* [73]

* * *

In the spring of 1989, Monica Bryant was ready to go on holiday to Greece; it was the first holiday that she had given herself for a long time and she was looking foward to it. She had been in Greece only a few days when she received a phone call from her secretary telling her that a man called Duncan Campbell had phoned her. He had mentioned an article which was coming out. Bryant had never heard of Duncan Campbell. She was exhausted and trying to rest. Soon however, she received more phone calls and now her secretary was panicking. Duncan Campbell was apparently about to go to press with an article about her.

Monica Bryant rang her solicitors from the low-budget Greek hotel she was staying in. It was a difficult call; her solicitor advised her to speak to Campbell. At considerable expense, she rang Campbell at the *New Statesman and Society*. During that phone call Bryant learnt, to her distress and alarm, that Campbell had been in touch with Mike Smith, the man who had worked on and off for three months with her, as part of the Management Extension Programme, the previous year. Despite the fact that it was part of the arrangement under this government scheme that those placed with companies must reveal nothing about them, Smith appeared to have talked at length with Campbell and broken every confidence with which he had been entrusted.

Campbell was later to tell Bryant that he had met Smith after Smith had contacted the Campaign Against Health Fraud. Monica Bryant, however, felt that Smith was not the kind of person to come into contact with such a group. Besides, Smith had no reason at all to feel antagonistic or accusatory towards Monica Bryant; despite not feeling close to him, she had been kind and understanding towards his accumulating problems while he had worked with her. Bryant felt both betrayed and violated by Smith. She was shocked that someone who was supposed to be a business support had given false information to a journalist.

In June, Delatte, who was working in Princes Risborough, received the first phone calls from a person who said that they were a television journalist. He didn't even bother to write Campbell's name down: he wasn't interested. The journalist rang repeatedly, claiming he wanted to make a programme about Delatte and his work. Finally Delatte's partner Michael Dreer convinced Delatte that he should agree to go on television to publicise probiotic treatment for HIV antibody positive men. Delatte rang the journalist. He said that he did not mind being filmed, as long as it was possible to be given a copy of any questions beforehand. He wanted to discuss these questions before the interview: this was agreed.

Delatte was slightly concerned about the television interview and the reporter's persistence. However, in July, he was feeling good about his work. As if to place a seal of approval on his efforts, a letter appeared in the *British Medical Journal* signed by Dr Gazzard, one of the leading AIDS doctors, and four others. The letter included Delta Te in a list of alternative treatments which were being used in London.

Yves Delatte travelled to the LWT headquarters on London's South Bank expecting, as agreed, to first discuss his interview. He went like a lamb to the slaughter. He met the journalist, who was not Duncan Campbell, and he was accompanied into a small, brightly lit room. As Delatte sat down he realised that he was already being filmed. The journalist, now seated on the other side of the desk, began aggressively firing questions at him.

Looking back on this incident, Delatte says that he considered at the time he had two alternatives. He could get up and walk out. On film it would have looked as if he were refusing to answer questions. If he stayed, he could at least answer the questions to the best of his ability. He had done nothing to feel guilty about. With respect to the science of his field he had fifteen years' experience, in respect of the ethics, he was selling a probiotic health supplement, of the kind which was freely available over the counter in Scandinavia. Even the American FDA approved the production and sale of lactic bacteria as a health supplement.

Nigel Townson, an LWT journalist and colleague of Duncan Campbell, asked Delatte the questions, while Campbell, who had entered the room later, sat silently behind Delatte without introducing himself. Townson kept Delatte answering questions in the small hot room, under the glare of bright lights, for nearly two hours, a circumstance which even by the sometimes lax standards of the British police, would be considered 'duress'. The interviewer spoke quickly and aggressively, making it hard for Delatte to translate the questions and then articulate his answers. He knew, even during the interview, that he 'accidentally used a number of wrong words'.

The LWT programme which 'exposed' Yves Delatte, used some one and a half minutes of the extensive interview carried out with Delatte under duress. It was followed a couple of days later by Campbell's article on Delatte in the *New Statesman and Society*, entitled 'Let them eat shit'. [74]

* * *

> A polluting person is always in the wrong. He has developed some wrong condition or simply crossed some line which should not have been crossed and this displacement unleashes danger for someone. [75]

> Sorcerers are supposed to use bodily refuse in pursuing their nefarious desires. [76]

The article in the *New Statesman and Society*, 'Let them eat shit', is a masterstroke of propaganda. It is a tissue of innuendo, unattributed quotes, and simple distortions. More important than any of the obvious untruths, is the psychological power of the article, the way in which it gives voice to basic fears about illness and disease. By entitling the article 'Let them eat shit', Campbell touches upon an internal conflict at least as powerful as the social conflict implicit in the statement's precursor: 'Let them eat cake'. 'Let them eat cake', is a statement of impossible and careless arrogance. Putting the statement 'Let them eat shit' in Delatte's mouth bestows upon him a similar, but more post-modern, cynicism.

Campbell was to use the same, psychological shock tactics to discredit the Ayur-Vedic treatments prescribed by Dr Davis and Dr Chalmers.†

The article dwells upon ideas which undermine commonly held notions of hygiene, pollution and crime. Campbell transposes two images. One is of the orthodox doctor or health worker, who places a 'cordon sanitaire' between sickness and the rest of society. In the extreme, the doctor *is* the cordon sanitaire. Like a lightning conductor

† See this Chapter above.

at grave risk to themselves, doctors place themselves between the sick and society, transforming the evil of illness into the goodness of health. The second image is that of the criminal quack, in this case Delatte, who by virtue of his 'disordered identity' spreads pollution and criminality.

> Delatte's recipe mixes cultivated human intestinal bacteria, including *streptococcus faecalis*, with milk powder or acid whey. [77]

> Delatte has been known to store bacteria and other ingredients for his powder in a domestic freezer, mixing it up in an ordinary kitchen, using normal kitchen scales, and taking no special precautions, such as gloves or overalls, to maintain hygiene or sterility. [78]

> Smith ... described how Delatte had turned up in Brighton a year ago with luggage containing bags of live bacteria ... Smith then watched 'in absolute disgust' as Delatte and Bryant went into Bryant's kitchen and, using kitchen scales, concocted the recipe for Symbion. Several kilograms of the bacteria Delatte had imported were then left in her fridge. The freeze dried bacteria was left loose in the kitchen. Soon afterwards, Smith suffered severe headaches and sinus pains, probably caused by the dried faecal bacteria left floating in the kitchen atmosphere. [79]

By juxtaposing the kitchen, a designated sterile place, with faecal bacteria, Campbell creates the impression of something profoundly polluting. Delatte's health-giving treatments are the very antithesis of scientific medicine or orthodox health treatments because they pollute and contaminate food,† the very thing which we rely upon to keep us healthy.

---

† In June 1989, Monica Bryant published a statement about the two products which she distributed. 'None of the products sold by the Company were manufactured by the Company or Miss Bryant, whether in a kitchen at the Company's offices or elsewhere. Probion was manufactured by a reputable pharmaceutical company in Sweden under strict controls. Probion had been approved for import into the UK for human consumption by the Public Analyst. Symbion and Symbion II were produced by mixing freeze-dried bacteria with a lactose-free food starch. Production was carried out for the Company by a pharmaceuticals manufacturer at its laboratories under strictly controlled conditions. Ecoflorin was purchased by the Company from Whitecliffe Laboratories Limited'.

Delatte is portrayed as a person literally 'between states'. A person in an anarchic and critical condition. This condition is embellished by the idea of Delatte carrying 'luggage'; he is a person with no fixed home. It transpires in the article that not only is Delatte a foreigner, he was also, for a time, an illegal immigrant in Finland. The article carried a photograph of Delatte in a prison cell where he was being held as an illegal immigrant. There is nothing that the orderly bourgeois mind hates more than an illegal immigrant, who offends against all rules of social and national hygiene, introducing a virus into the nation's genetic and cultural stock. Campbell failed to explain that Delatte's illegal immigration entailed nothing more serious than an amorous expedition to Finland, when he was much younger, to see a young woman with whom he had fallen in love. He had overstayed his visa by a day.

As with all of Campbell's articles in this health-fraud series, there is no independent review of any of the witness evidence, some of which is given anonymously. The integrity of witnesses like Mike Smith, who himself brought a great deal of disorder to Monica Bryant's life, is not reviewed, nor are we told anything about his background. Any fair-minded journalist would not have touched Smith with a barge-pole. During his period with Bryant, he was thrown out of his home by his wife, was grieving over his father who died shortly after he arrived, and spoke of needing to appear in court over an unknown matter.

The kernel of the article, however, has nothing to do with Delatte as a health worker, or research scientist, nor with Monica Bryant, nor any of their probiotic preparations. The introduction to the article with its reliance upon the symbolism of pollution, simply sets the stage and leads us into the most important issue – the real consequence of Delatte's disorderly character.

> Delatte has been anxious to deny that he has urged patients to stop taking the conventional anti-AIDS drug AZT, and to buy Delta Te instead. He says he has merely highlighted that AZT can cause anaemia. He also said that, three months ago, 'Susan Jay' (whose real name he told me), a London woman infected by HIV, was given a free supply of Delta Te. After she was given free Delta Te Susan agreed to help debunk AZT, which she had previously tried, in a critical newspaper report on the drug. In consequence of the report about Susan, several other patients

decided to stop taking AZT. [80]

This is evidently the real reason why Delatte was criminalised. Delatte was, like many other people in 1989, guilty of suggesting that AZT, which Campbell considered the 'conventional' treatment for people with AIDS, could have serious side-effects. Yves Delatte was not a criminal nor a 'con-man', but a heretic.

*   *   *

Soon after returning to her home near Brighton from Greece, Monica Bryant found herself the subject of a 'witch hunt'. Someone had faxed copies of the *New Statesman* article, prior to its publication, to all the local papers and radio stations in the Brighton area. The article which appeared in the *Brighton and Hove Leader* [81] was particularly outrageous, and Monica Bryant immediately sued them in the same action which she began against Campbell and the *New Statesman and Society*.

Within days of the *New Statesman* article, Monica Bryant's life changed radically, she found herself boycotted, even by colleagues in the field of alternative medicine. The local fax shop refused to accept faxes without first being paid. She was inundated with calls from confused customers.

Delatte was going through the same trauma: apparently good friends were no longer speaking to him, customers had cancelled cheques which were already lodged in his bank. Five faithful AIDS clients stayed on with him, but fear ran like a fire through the rest of the community and no one was even prepared to listen to his side of the story.

Campbell ensured that the Delatte story was also printed in Finnish newspapers, and as a consequence, after pressure from her parents, Delatte's wife left him, taking their two children into her custody and denying him access. He found himself ostracised by the surrounding society, all of whom seemed to believe that he was an evil crook.

*   *   *

Within two months of 'Let them eat shit', Campbell published a second article in the *New Statesman and Society*.[82] This second article, entitled 'Pretty poison', concentrated entirely upon Monica Bryant and germanium. It was just as inaccurate as the previous article, but because the new article raised a whole tranche of scientific questions, it severely set back Bryant's chances of a successful legal action.

'Pretty poison' is a different order of article from 'Let them eat shit'. It plays upon simpler susceptibilities, more common fears about being duped by quacks. At the start of the article and with breathtaking intellectual dishonesty, Campbell confuses two quite separate forms of germanium. The forms of germanium marketed as a food supplement are germanium sesquioxide and Sanumgerman, both organic forms of germanium. Another form of germanium, manufactured for industrial purposes and called germanium oxide, is inorganic.

Duncan Campbell, while dwelling on anecdotal reports of germanium-induced kidney failure in Japan, deliberately fails to make a distinction between the two forms of germanium until the end of the first page of the article. Having claimed at the beginning that the use of germanium as a food supplement 'is potentially lethal', Campbell describes the 'fad' of using it as leaving death and sickness in its wake. He goes on to link Monica Bryant with the sales in Britain of poisonous germanium, and it is not until the end of the second page that we are told that 'most of the Japanese germanium poisoning reports refer to damage caused by a germanium dioxide'. Apart from the judicious use of 'most', Campbell fails to point out that germanium dioxide is an entirely different substance from the one sold by Monica Bryant.

'Pretty poison' is a mishmash of untruths and half-truths, embellished with expert opinions, particularly from Campbell's HealthWatch crony Vincent Marks. The article is littered with unattributed and unreferenced cases and decorated with airy statements such as the one which runs across the head of the article's second page: *In Japan, a man took a 130mg dose of germanium a day – and died.*

Amongst the anecdotal information about sickness and death caused by germanium generally, and between the intelligence-insulting quotes from Vincent Marks, Campbell manages to make Monica Bryant appear to be a knowing hustler of a poisonous remedy.

From spring 1987 onwards, Bryant and her collaborators
published a series of articles in vitamin and 'health' magazines
intended to draw attention to their new germanium drugs ...
What could be described as a 'vitamin-industrial complex' has
through seemingly expert and well-meaning advice in books,
articles and advertisements encouraged chronically-ill and
therefore vulnerable, people that swallowing germanium
compounds in large doses will strengthen an impaired
immune system, provide oxygen and energy, and relieve
fatigue. [83]

Sandra Goodman was made out to be a mercenary and shady
business associate of Monica Bryant. Campbell even tried to make a
case for Goodman making a part of the profits from Bryant's sale of
'the poison'.

Last year, Sandra Goodman published a book, Germanium –
the health and life enhancer. In the book Goodman ... claims
that she does not 'have an interest in sales, patents or profits from
germanium'. In fact, though Goodman may not have benefited
directly from sales, Bryant admitted three months ago ... 'I've
paid her on a number of occasions, personally and through my
business'. The total sum of money involved was 'of the order of
hundreds of pounds'. (Ms Goodman has now moved to Seattle
Washington and has not responded to a request for comment
made to her publishers) [84]

Campbell purposely avoided mentioning the nature of Goodman's
relationship to Bryant, which was one of a commissioned research
worker. He also avoided mention of Goodman's qualifications. It
would be surprising in the extreme if academic research fees asked by
a highly trained biochemist with a doctorate did not come to
'hundreds of pounds'. As to Campbell's attempt to make it appear that
Goodman was fleeing to America, the suggestion makes even clearer
Campbell's tactical avoidance of serious research.

None of these obvious omissions occur when Campbell writes
about Vincent Marks, the Surrey company director, founding member
of the Wellcome-funded Campaign Against Health Fraud, and a
consultant to the International Sugar Bureau. He is fulsomely
described as 'Professor Vincent Marks, a clinical biochemist at
Surrey University'. Such an appellation however did not improve the

intelligence of his expert opinions:

'germanium is worthless and dangerous poison'.

'Selling germanium as a health cure is thoroughly outrageous quackery'.

'This is exactly what happened with cadmium and some other drugs (sic). *They were killing people by the thousands from kidney failure,* and no one realised the cause'. (italics added)

'On the basis of what we know, tubular kidney damage is exactly what we would expect'.

Although in retrospect it is possible to laugh out loud at the basic silliness of Campbell's writing and the caped crusader type lines spouted by Vincent Marks, what the article was actually saying was that Monica Bryant was willing to kill people in her search for profit. When all the chaff and the baroque disinformation that Campbell indulges in are blown away we are left with the monster Bryant, peddling poison to AIDS patients and other ill and vulnerable people. All of which could not have been further from the truth.

* * *

When Sandra Goodman read 'Pretty poison', she was impressed, 'Had I not known Monica Bryant's operation intimately, I would have thought that what Campbell wrote was true.' Knowing Monica Bryant, and seeing that Campbell's maligning of her was untruthful, Goodman decided to write to Japan to the university researchers who had come up with the 'latest scientific reports', quoted by Campbell in his article. She asked the research workers whether the compound they had studied had been germanium dioxide or germanium sesquioxide.

The reply which she received from Dr Kaoru Onoyama, Assistant Professor, 2nd Department of Internal Medicine, at Kyushu University, was clear:

the label on the bottle indicates that organic germanium (Ge) is contained. At the time, [we wrote our paper] we did not analyse the substance. But after that paper, we found that all the materials, those patients used [the patients who had kidney damage], contained GeO_2 (Germanium Oxide), irrespective of the description of organic Ge on the label. Thereafter, we have studied the difference between GeO_2 (Germanium Oxide) and organic Ge ... toxicity was found to exist only in the former. [85]

But Sandra Goodman had heard something else from Japan. The Japanese government had approached the American government to discuss the possibility of carrying out a trial of germanium on AIDS patients in Japan. The letter from Japan and this new information, helped her to put her own predicament into perspective.

By 1988 when Sandra Goodman's book was published, she was by virtue of that book and of her reading of the extensive research literature on germanium, one of the most knowledgeable people in Britain about the mineral. Regardless of this, she was not approached by anyone to give her opinion about germanium, and when Radio Four broadcast an item on germanium, they called on Vincent Marks. Ignoring the extensive references at the back of Sandra Goodman's book, Vincent Marks claimed that there was not a single piece of scientific evidence to support claims made for germanium.

* * *

Working with the Campaign Against Health Fraud, Campbell passed the information from his articles on to the Department of Health. With improbable speed, the Campaign and its supporters in the Department of Health got an investigation by the Medicines Control Agency into both Yves Delatte and Monica Bryant. At a much higher government level, Campbell's propaganda moved the Department of Health to ban germanium within a month of 'Pretty poison'.

Soon after 'Let them eat shit' appeared, Yves Delatte had a call from an ex-police officer working for the Department of Health, who wanted to question him about his use and prescription of unlicensed medicines. Delatte showed the investigator round his workplace, gave him documents from the FDA and a sample of the lactic acid bacteria which he was using in his formulation. The man left, telling Delatte that there would undoubtedly be a prosecution. They 'needed', the man said officiously, 'a prosecution'.

Proceedings were indeed taken against Delatte and his partner

Michael Dreer. The charges related to the possession and sale of unlicensed medicines, and the supply of those medicines to patients without a licence. Dreer, who had been advised by his solicitor to plead guilty, appeared in court on behalf of the Company which he and Delatte had set up. In fact, there has never been any dispute about the fact that lactic acid bacteria are food supplements and not medicines. Delatte, worried about the court case, had returned to Finland. At a short hearing, Dreer accepted a fine of £4,000 plus costs. Yves Delatte was also charged personally and his plea was entered by his solicitor in his absence; much later in January 1992, he was fined £350 plus costs.

Bryant was prosecuted by the Department of Health for articles she had disseminated on selenium, chromium and germanium. She was accused under the Medicines (Labelling and Advertising to the Public) Regulations of making medical claims for these trace elements. As she had at all times taken the appropriate measures, such as getting stamped approval from MAPAH for all literature and packaging, the Department of Health was finally forced to withdraw its charges. The acquittal hearing was held in July 1991, at Brighton Magistrates Court, where Bryant was awarded nearly £11,000 in costs from central funds.

The real damage to Monica Bryant's life, however, and that of Yves Delatte was not inflicted by the law but by Duncan Campbell. It took over three years for Monica Bryant to become confident enough to trust a limited number of people and to venture out into the world again. Yves Delatte is still fighting to gain access to his children, and prove in a Finnish court that he is not the monster which Campbell claimed. Sandra Goodman was forced into a temporary retirement from scientific research, although her energy is undiminished. In 1992 she had a book on Vitamin C published; it includes a chapter on Vitamin C's anti-viral qualities and its possible use in AIDS cases. [86]

Looking back on the whole affair which has damaged his life and career, Yves Delatte remembered something said by Dr Connolly when they were chatting about the Concorde trials. Affably, he said: 'Of course, if your product became popular, we won't get the people we need on the trials.' Delatte laughed.

A Contemporary Salem: Elizabeth Marsh

The issue was very simple, I had treated a cancer patient. [87]

When Elizabeth Marsh decided to become a therapist and a healer, her decision had nothing to do with any well-ordered course of medical training, or any previous history in the field of health. Until 1981, when she was suddenly deserted by her business partner who left her with an £80,000 debt, Elizabeth Marsh had made reproduction antique dolls. In the middle of this turmoil and having to move out of her house, she suffered the loss of her brother from cancer. Following this period of crisis she set about, in any possible way, outside of orthodox medicine, learning about cancer.

Later in 1981, she travelled to Romania, where she worked and studied at the National Institute of Gerontology, in Bucharest, with Professor Ana Aslan. Professor Aslan, as well as researching degenerative diseases and working on a remedy which she had synthesised called Gerovital (GH²), was also working with mentally handicapped children. Elizabeth Marsh was able to spend a full year observing and studying Aslan's work. Following the year in Romania, from 1986 to 1987, Marsh joined the Bedfont Theological Seminary, a theological college which specialises in healing. She studied theology, homoeopathy and parapsychology. On the conclusion of her training in 1988, she was ordained as a Minister, and also received a PhD, which entitled her to use the title Doctor.

Over the next ten years, the diverse and unusual training which Elizabeth Marsh went through, together with the titles which she used, were to attract the attention of health fraud campaigners. It would indeed have been surprising, if in her journey through the far reaches of alternative therapy, Elizabeth Marsh had not been associated with one or more of the organisations on the lists of the American Council Against Health Fraud. In 1988 she travelled to the United States where she began training with a group called American Biologics (AB), which sells diagnostic microscope equipment for work on live blood cells. The company has become a primary target of the NCHF. Not only does AB treat cancer and AIDS patients in its Mexico-based hospital, it uses, amongst many treatments: laetrile, herbal remedies and megavitamin courses, many of which have been outlawed by the American Medical Association and the FDA.

Other things, as well, have brought American Biologics into direct confrontation with the orthodox pharmaceutical medicine lobby. AB is the primary organisation behind the Committee for Freedom of Choice in Medicine (CFCM) and its publication *The Choice*. CFCM defends and publicises contemporary American struggles for medical choice. AB is also linked to the Bradford Research Institute. Established by one of its leading members, Dr Robert B. Bradford, the Institute carries out research and publishes on subjects as diverse as cancer and nutritional therapies and chelation therapy. In 1989, a leading member of American Biologics, Michael L. Culbert, wrote *AIDS: Hope Hoax and Hoopla*[88], which was published by the Bradford Foundation. The book is an extensive and detailed assault upon orthodox medicine and its response to AIDS; it discusses the many possible origins of AIDS and is scathing about AZT and other pharmaceutical remedies.

When Elizabeth Marsh came back from training in America, she brought with her an American Biologics microscope produced for the diagnostic analysis of live blood cells. AB claims that it is possible to make an early analysis of degenerative illnesses after examining a patient's blood structure. This blood testing, considered by health fraud activists to be quackery, and called on one occasion a 'hoax' by Vincent Marks, is carried out by high resolution video-enhanced visualisation. She became one of the first people in Britain to begin diagnostic work using this equipment.

In September 1988, Elizabeth Marsh set up a therapy centre in Ealing where she began practising homoeopathy, electro-acupuncture and signalysis treatment. The practice took off well, and within months she was seeing between forty and sixty clients a week. From the beginning of her practice, Elizabeth Marsh was always scrupulous about telling patients that she was not a qualified medical doctor and asked people who came to her to sign a form acknowledging that she had told them this. She also told patients that they should inform their general practitioner about the treatment they received from her. Usually she would ask clients if they minded her contacting their GP.

Problems began with her practice in May 1989, the very month that the Campaign Against Health Fraud held its inaugural press conference. In April 1989, a patient had visited Marsh with very general complaints; he claimed that he felt under the weather and was unable to sleep.

A week after the consultation, Marsh was phoned by the patient who revealed that he was a reporter. He asked her a number of questions for a forthcoming article, all of which she answered. She gave him the names of all the people she had worked with and the organisations from which she had received her qualifications. None of these people were contacted.

On May 7th 1989, the *Sunday People* carried an article entitled 'Cancer con doc fleeces victims', by Mark Howard. By any standards the article was a scurrilous piece of journalism. It made no attempt whatsoever to put Elizabeth Marsh's position and contained a number of unsupportable accusations. The article began: 'Fake doctor Elizabeth Marsh cons patients by saying they're dangerously ill and then squeezing them for costly "pre-cancerous" cures. After hooking her victims through newspaper ads, sleazy Mrs Marsh, who has a mail order degree tells them they have "a pre-cancerous condition" '. The short article, sufficient to end Marsh's career, is devoid of evidenced facts and in its penultimate paragraph resorts to personal ridicule: 'Mr Hood reveals: 'She would have looked more at home smoking and drinking pints (sic) of gin in an East London pub" '. As well as Elizabeth Marsh, East London readers of the *People* could have justifiably taken offence.

The references in the article to pre-cancerous conditions and 'cures', relate to a diagnostic technique which Elizabeth Marsh was using at that time. The technique, previously called the Spagyrik system, is now called Signalysis. Blood and urine samples are treated so that they form crystals. It is the contention of those who work with this system that the crystal structure is not only personal to the patient but also can indicate problems in different areas of the body. Results of Signalysis tests come back to the practitioner from the Signalysis laboratory in Gloucestershire, in the form of charts. These charts have one category, amongst many, headed 'pre-cancerous' condition, which is meant to alert the practitioner to sites of high toxicity or degenerative illness.

In the event, Elizabeth Marsh did not consider that the bogus patient Mark Howard needed a Signalysis test. From a variety of tests and from a long consultation, she concluded that he had 'bad eating habits, and an unhealthy lifestyle which created a high level of toxic processes. He had poor elimination processes and possible intestinal Candida.' Following the article, Elizabeth Marsh did not get any new patients and a number of her old patients dropped away. In September 1989, she was forced to close down her clinic.

Determined to continue her work, Marsh began seeing people at her home where she used her study as a consulting room. In October 1989, a woman named Julia Watson, who had seen an advert placed by Elizabeth Marsh in *Here's Health*, contacted her about an appointment. Julia Watson was a writer of romantic novels, under the pen name of Julia Fitzgerald. In May 1989, she had been diagnosed as having ovarian cancer; she was operated on and her ovaries and fallopian tubes removed. Despite an apparent recovery from the cancer, in September 1989 her abdomen began to swell and she became unwell again.

Julia Watson had for years been opposed to orthodox medicine; she was a staunch vegetarian who even treated the family pets homoeopathically. On November 16th when Watson attended Elizabeth Marsh's home for a consultation, she was very distressed. The physical signs that she was seriously ill were obviously apparent: her swollen abdomen, distended with fluid, made her appear pregnant. Elizabeth Marsh carried out basic diagnostic tests during a three-hour consultation. However, realising that Julia probably was suffering a return of her cancer, she advised her in definite terms that she would have to go back to her hospital consultant for treatment.

Three weeks later, Julia Watson phoned Elizabeth Marsh again to tell her that she had been to her hospital and had the fluid drained off, and that she had also been tested for a re-emergence of her cancer. Elizabeth Marsh had made no mention to Julia that in her opinion the cancer had definitely returned, preferring to let Julia's hospital doctor take responsibility for this diagnosis.

A week before Christmas 1989, Julia Watson phoned again, this time, however, she was distraught and crying. She had received a letter from her hospital and consequently phoned her consultant who had told her over the phone that her cancer had re-emerged and she would have to have chemotherapy. Julia Watson was absolutely adamant that she did not want to have chemotherapy and asked Elizabeth Marsh if she would treat her. Realising that this was a most difficult case and considering the responsibility which any treatment would entail, Marsh asked Julia to discuss the matter fully with her family before making any decision.

As Elizabeth Marsh got to know Julia Watson, she found she liked her, she describes her now as 'a beautiful person, a lovely woman'. One of the things which she respected about Julia Watson was her enquiring nature. Julia would not accept any treatment, without first seeking other opinions and reading as much as she was able about the subject.

Julia Watson's first treatment appointment with Elizabeth Marsh was on January 2nd 1990. Arriving with her husband Keith, she explained that seeking alternative treatment enabled her to feel that she was doing something for herself rather than sitting around waiting to die. For her part, despite the distraught state which Julia Watson was in, Elizabeth Marsh made no claims that she could effect any cure but promised to help her as much as she was able. Privately, Marsh saw her treatment of Julia Watson more as a process of preparing Julia for her death, than trying to effect any kind of cure.

Throughout January, Elizabeth Marsh saw Julia Watson almost every day including weekends, usually for a three-hour session, while her husband, Keith Timson, sat in the front room, kept company by Elizabeth's husband. In Marsh's opinion Julia felt a great deal of guilt about her estranged daughter, Juliet Hamilton.

> I knew how serious her cancer was and so did her husband. The only signs of improvement while I treated her was that there was some pain relief and she seemed to feel less guilty about her life than she had when she first came. She was still determined to fight her cancer but I knew that there would be no real improvement. I really saw my task as preparing her for death, without making it clear that she would inevitably die. I wanted more than anything else for her to off-load the guilt she felt and so improve the quality of the last part of her life. [89]

Over that month of treatment, Elizabeth Marsh charged Julia Watson her fee of £45 for a first consultation, and a total of £500 for the remedies and treatments which she gave her and her daughter. Elizabeth Marsh made no charge for her own time, the cost of which, even at the most conservative estimates, would have approached a thousand pounds. Some of Elizabeth Marsh's energy over January was taken up in trying to persuade Julia Watson to see an orthodox doctor with whom she had previously worked. By the end of the month Julia had agreed to see a Harley Street doctor, and an appointment had been made for early February. In the last few days of January, Watson was too ill to see Elizabeth Marsh although they spoke every day on the phone. On the 4th of February, her daughter, Juliet, rang Elizabeth Marsh to say that her mother was very weak and vomiting a great deal, Elizabeth Marsh advised her to call an ambulance. Juliet Hamilton told Elizabeth Marsh that even at that stage, her mother would prefer treatment from her and Julia Watson's son, Cassian, drove over to Marsh's house to get medicine. During this brief meeting with Watson's son, Marsh tried to impress upon him how important it was that his mother saw a medical doctor or went to a hospital.

During Julia Watson's last days, Elizabeth Marsh had the complete trust of her family. On February 5th 1990, while getting ready to travel to London to see the Harley Street doctor, Julia Watson died.

Throughout the whole of the following day, Marsh worked on behalf of Keith Timson, liaising with the Coroner's officer, trying to contact Julia Watson's consultant, so that he could sign the death certificate. The Coroner's officer and Keith Timson both appeared grateful for the help which Elizabeth Marsh gave and she was duly invited to Julia's funeral. A month after the funeral, Keith Timson phoned Elizabeth Marsh to enquire about the medicines which he still had at home.

Three months after Julia Watson's death, in the early morning of Friday April 27th 1990, a small party of police officers and a forensic doctor stood round Julia Watson's grave and watched as her body was exhumed. Following the exhumation, at 6.45 a.m. at High Wycombe General Hospital, Dr Richard Thorley Shepherd of Guy's Hospital performed a post-mortem. The exhumation and the post-mortem had been carried out on the instructions of the Coroner, who in turn had been approached by officers of the Metropolitan Police Fraud Squad. The Fraud Squad, it appeared, had been prompted to act by Keith Timson who some time after Julia's death had become concerned about the treatments given her by Elizabeth Marsh.

By the late morning of April 27th when Dr Thorley Shepherd had finished his post-mortem, the Fraud Squad knew that Julia Watson had died of cancer with no contributory causes and that there could be no basis for any suspicion that Elizabeth Marsh had contributed to her death. Nine days after Shepherd had written his final post-mortem report, however, on May 2nd, the story of the exhumation appeared in the press. In an orchestrated series of articles, Elizabeth Marsh was all but accused of manslaughter.

> The daughter of romantic novelist Julia Fitzgerald told yesterday why she asked police to investigate her mother's death. Juliet Hamilton, 29, was concerned about homoeopathic treatment her 46 year-old mother underwent in her final months as a victim of stomach cancer. [90]

> Juliet, Miss Fitzgerald's daughter from her first marriage, contacted Scotland Yard's Fraud Squad following discussions with her brother Cassian and the writer's third husband Keith Timson. The Yard alerted Thames Valley Police, who are now investigating the death with South Buckinghamshire coroner John Roberts. [91]

Despite the fact that this accusation by innuendo against Elizabeth Marsh was as serious as manslaughter, the *Daily Mail*, like other papers, found no problems in naming her in the story and even adducing other statements which questioned her abilities and legitimacy as a therapist. The use of the unattributed and unevidenced quote from 'an expert' is seen here at its most skilful:

> The British Homoeopathic Society, the Homeopathic Trust and the Society of Homeopaths all confirmed that Mrs Marsh was not registered with them. 'There's been a lot of flak over her work' one expert said. 'Many patients have complained'.

Other more populist papers like the *Mirror* made the story sound like the scenario for a novel by James M. Cain: 'Writer's Body Dug Up By Cops'.

> The body of romantic novelist Julia Fitzgerald has been exhumed as police probe her death after a course of nature treatment. [92]

Although this article was written over a week after the post-mortem statement had been written by the pathologist and despite the fact that there was not one shred of evidence to support an assumption that Julia Watson died of anything other than cancer, Coroner's officer, PC

Cannon felt able to say to the press that 'the suggestion [behind the exhumation] is that the cause of death as recorded was not correct'.

In order to present the story as a news story, and so as to keep going the idea that Elizabeth Marsh was still suspected of having caused Julia Watson's death, the *Mirror*, the *Express* and the *Mail* all intimated that Julia Watson's body had only just been exhumed. Actually two weeks had passed since the exhumation and the post-mortem.

> A post mortem was held yesterday [May 11th 1990] following Thursday's exhumation [the exhumation actually took place on a Friday, fifteen days before the article was published] of Miss Fitzgerald's body. [93]

> Detectives watched as the 46 year old author's body was dug up at Marlow cemetery for tests. [This is true but it wasn't as the story implies, yesterday, it was two weeks previously.] [94]

Why did the newspapers report the story as if it were a news story when it was actually two weeks old? The answer is fairly simple. Had the story been reported logically, the message would have been: 'Post-mortem clears therapist'. This was the only reasonable story consequent upon the exhumation of Julia Watson's body. Julia Watson's family and the Metropolitan Police Fraud Squad, and the Coroner's Office had clearly made serious errors of judgement. In the first instance, the Coroner's Office had failed to advise a post-mortem and an inquest at the time of Julia Watson's death, despite the fact that she had not seen a qualified and registered doctor for some time before she died. The Coroner's officer wasn't entirely to blame for this error, because Keith Timson said at the time of his wife's death that he did not want a post-mortem. The Coroner's Office had also happily accepted the signature of her consultant on the death certificate, despite the fact that he had no recent knowledge of her state of health.

These serious errors were compounded by the Watson family's contact with the media. No doubt feeling emotionally disorientated and grieving at the unordered end to Julia's life, they began to blame Elizabeth Marsh for her death and seem to have had no difficulty in interesting both the police and the media in their new assessment. One gets the feeling, however, that another more powerful hand was at work. Would experienced police officers readily agree to the exhumation of a body, in the case of a woman who had a recorded case of cancer, solely on the word of her distraught family?

From the time of Julia Watson's death, members of the Campaign Against Health Fraud became involved in the case of Elizabeth Marsh. The Spring issue of the *CAHF Newsletter*, contained a short item about Elizabeth Marsh culled from the *Independent* of March 9th 1990. It is evident from this that the CAHF knew of Elizabeth Marsh at least two months before Julia Watson's body was exhumed.

Elizabeth Marsh believes now that the Fraud Squad were most interested in her use of a remedy called Glyoxilide, and it was because she had used this that Julia Watson's body was exhumed. Glyoxylide is a remedy which has been under scrutiny by the FDA in America for a long time, and has been campaigned against by the American National Council Against Health Fraud. It is an oxygen therapy which can be adminstered orally or by injection. It was synthesised by Dr William Koch for use in the treatment of cancer patients. Koch, an American, was persecuted throughout his life by the FDA and the orthodox medical establishment.†

Keith Timson and Juliet Hamilton had apparently informed the police that Julia Watson had been given an injection by Elizabeth Marsh two weeks before her death. But before taking Glyoxilide, Julia Watson, as discerning as ever, had first wanted to read about and understand the background to the treatment. She had taken away Elizabeth Marsh's copy of Koch's own book to read before making a decision. [97]

The police appeared so concerned to find evidence against Elizabeth Marsh, that as well as the post-mortem, they also had a toxicology report made out on all the treatments which Elizabeth Marsh had given Julia Watson, and which still remained at her house, despite Marsh's professional instruction that any unused medication should be destroyed.

At the top of the toxicology report, written two months after the

† Dr William Frederick Koch graduated from the University of Michigan in 1909, and gained his PhD in 1917. He received a medical degree from Detroit College of Medicine and between 1910 and 1913 was a Lecturer at Michigan University. From 1914 to 1919 he was Professor of Physiology at Detroit Medical College. [95,96]

autopsy report, Dr Toseland, of Guy's Hospital, who is not a medical doctor but a PhD, unnecessarily records his own personal and irrelevant opinion about the remedies he examined: '... A number of classical homoeopathic remedies, none of them contain any harmful materials. They are all substances that, in my opinion, act via 'placebo' effect'.

Not long after the death of Julia Watson, the Campaign Against Health Fraud again showed its hand in the case of Elizabeth Marsh. Vincent Marks appeared as an expert in a Sky television programme 'Newsline' which centred upon the first adverse article by Mark Howard in the *Sunday People*. The programme once again attempted to draw an inference about the death of Julia Watson, and her treatment by Elizabeth Marsh. [98]

Presenter :   Successful novelist Julia Fitzgerald was less fortunate, [than one man who had been given a clean bill of health following a pessimistic diagnosis from Elizabeth Marsh] today as her husband completes her final novel, after her death, he rues the day that they put the treatment of her cancer in Marsh's hands.

A month after the exhumation of Julia Watson's body, in June, Elizabeth Marsh was asked by Fraud Squad officers to attend an interview at Holborn police station. She went accompanied by a solicitor; before the interview she was cautioned. It was made clear to her that she was attending the police station voluntarily and could leave at any time. Although the police were pleasant and reasonable, they did not inform Elizabeth Marsh that their exhumation and post-mortem had failed to provide any evidence of a crime.

The first thing which the police showed Elizabeth Marsh was the advert which she had placed in *Here's Health* magazine, through which Julia Watson had come to her. They asked her about invoices which she had given to Julia Watson for the cost of the treatments and asked her to describe the treatments which she had used. Still not having been told that the post-mortem had completely cleared her of any part in Watson's death, Elizabeth Marsh agreed to give the police samples of everything which she had administered to Julia Watson.

In all, Elizabeth Marsh was at Holborn police station for three hours. These enquiries by the Fraud Squad could be seen as perfectly reasonable, were it not for the fact that no suspicious circumstances or reasonable doubt existed to suggest that a crime had been committed. The only evidence which the police had obtained since they began their enquiries was the clear and unequivocal evidence of an independent pathologist that Julia Watson had died of cancer.

Elizabeth Marsh heard nothing more from the police following this interview. In October 1990, however, there was another sign that behind the scenes other forces were guiding the case against her. TV South broadcast a 'Time and Place' programme about healers and alternative practitioners. The programme, which consisted of an audience discussion, introduced and mediated by John Stapleton, would have been reasonably well balanced, had it not been for a disturbing contribution from Juliet Hamilton who stated on the programme that her mother's death was brought about by a quack. Intervening, John Stapleton stopped her from uttering Elizabeth Marsh's name on air. Sitting a few seats in front of Julia Hamilton and giving his opinions, was a Dr Svoboda who was credited on the programme as being a member of the Campaign Against Health Fraud.

* * *

In 1990, Elizabeth Marsh went to Mexico and visited a number of cancer clinics in exile. She spent three weeks at the Hoxsey Clinic where she met a patient who talked to her about a cancer and AIDS treatment called Cancell and its distributors Ed Sopcak (pronounced sob check) and James Sheridan.

Elizabeth Marsh went to meet Ed Sopcak in America and found what she considered a typical American, a man determined in the face of FDA opposition, to pursue his individual right to produce a treatment and distribute it. In another way, though, Sopcak was quite an atypical American, charging nothing for Cancell which he produces with profits from his own unrelated business.

James Sheridan claims to have synthesised Cancell in 1936 after he had seen its chemical formula in a dream. He first called it Entelev. Sheridan, who had worked as a chemist with Dow Chemicals, is now in his seventies. Both he and Sopcak, whom Sheridan gave the Cancell formula to, believe that the creation of Cancell was the work of God, and because of this neither of them should charge for it.

When Elizabeth Marsh acquired her first batch of Cancell, after meeting Sopcak, she was sceptical about its efficacy. She used much of the first batch on her two cats to help with their general health. Thinking more seriously about the claims which were being made for Cancell in the USA, she decided to organise a trial before giving it to any of her clients. In February 1991 she had her own toxicology tests done for Cancell and then began organising a trial for AIDS patients.

Marsh was utterly naive about the politics of AIDS trials. She sent out advertisements for the trial to the Wellcome Foundation, the *New Statesman* magazine and to the Terrence Higgins Trust. A week after posting the advert, she received the inevitable call from Duncan Campbell who asked her questions about her qualifications and the trial. Marsh was completely honest with Campbell, sending him all the information he wanted, by fax to the *New Statesman and Society* offices. The response to the advert was poor, she received only two phone calls, later however, she collected four other subjects from other sources, so making up a complement of six for the trial.

Elizabeth Marsh was determined to carry out her trial in a proper manner. She obtained the help of a qualified medical doctor, who could both examine the trial subjects and oversee their welfare during the trial; she found a central London laboratory which was able to carry out the blood tests and other assays. She wrote a protocol and then, in order to obtain ethical committee approval, she wrote to the Department of Health. After four weeks, the Department of Health had not replied to her letter, so she rang them and was told that she would soon receive the necessary forms. After another three weeks, still not having received a letter, she wrote again. Eventually, having failed to receive any information from the DoH, she decided to go ahead. All six trial subjects were tested for HIV antibodies at Elizabeth Marsh's expense and each filled in a consent form. All the subjects were advised to inform their general practitioners about their participation in the trial. None of the trial subjects were to be charged any money.

The trials began in May 1991, but within a month of them starting, articles heavily critical of Cancell and Elizabeth Marsh appeared in the *Independent on Sunday* and the *Sunday Mirror*. While the *Sunday Mirror* claimed that Cancell was nothing more than a 'worthless mixture of sugar-water, antiseptic and laxative ... at best it will act as a very mild laxative', [99] the *Independent on Sunday*, with a more intellectually stimulating story, while not saying what Cancell was made from, claimed that it 'had to be diluted 1 in 10,000 of the original strength to prevent it killing cells (*in vitro*)'. [100]

Despite being unable to agree on the dangers of Cancell's constituent parts, the two papers concurred on other things. They were in complete agreement, for example, that the Cancell trial was an abomination because it could stop people taking AZT; the *Independent on Sunday* drew on the fair-minded and independent comment of Anthony Pinching in this respect, '... if someone who was benefiting from AZT stopped taking it, they ran the risk of an increased rate of progression of disease; stopping medication might also advance the onset of brain disease'. The *Mirror* quoted one of the Cancell trial subjects: 'Bryan complained: "It's disgraceful for Elizabeth Marsh to give a false sense of security and hope in this way"'.

The other thing on which both papers agreed was that Elizabeth Marsh was a fraud: both papers did their best to extend the public understanding of her criminality. The *Sunday Mirror* claimed, without any supportive evidence, that Elizabeth Marsh was 'exposed in 1989 for selling useless pre-cancer drugs', while the *Independent on Sunday* again in a more restrained manner, regurgitated the matter of Julia Watson's death.

> The Fraud Squad confirmed it had questioned Mrs Marsh after the death of novelist, Julia Fitzgerald ... She was treated by Mrs Marsh ... After her death her family called in the police and her body was exhumed ... The police investigation is continuing. [101]

The police investigation into what? The first two consignments of Cancell which had arrived at Elizabeth Marsh's house had been delivered by United Parcels Services. When the third consignment was due to arrive, in October 1991, Elizabeth Marsh received a phone call from UPS telling her what time the consignment was due to be delivered and checking her address. When the delivery man from UPS arrived, so did Mr Hutchinson, an ex-Metropolitan police investigator from the Department of Health.

Elizabeth Marsh was asked to open her newly-delivered parcels in front of the investigator and their contents were promptly seized. Her house was searched and four bottles of Cancell which were being packed for a doctor in Portugal were also confiscated. In early 1992, Elizabeth Marsh's solicitors received a long letter from the DoH, containing a number of specimen charges which they were considering bringing against her. They ranged from having distributed a medicine without a licence, to distributing a medicine produced in unhygienic conditions.

After a great deal of toing and froing between the solicitors and the DoH, in mid-1992, the DoH settled the charges which it was to bring against Elizabeth Marsh. Two criminal charges were brought against her, and the defence elected to be tried by a jury. The charges were, that in 1990, she supplied Glyoxilide to Julia Watson without a product licence, and secondly, with commercial intent she had issued a misleading advert – a claim that Cancell cured cancer and AIDS – in a booklet which advertised her Cancell trial.

At a preliminary hearing to fix a date for the committal proceedings, held on the 13th August 1992, the prosecuting counsel for the DoH, introducing the charges, told the court that Julia Watson had died after being treated by Elizabeth Marsh. This statement was prejudicial to Marsh's case and although it was true, the inference was misleading. At the committal hearing, the Magistrate threw out the first charge because the prosecution had passed the time limit within which such a charge has to be brought.

The trial at Isleworth Crown Court began on Monday March 29th, 1993. The charge, under the 1968 Medicines Act, was one of the mildest charges in its armoury, that Marsh had issued an advertisement for Cancell which claimed that it could cure cancer and AIDS; she had done this, the charge suggested, with the intention of making commercial gain. The charge related to one line in a booklet which had been sent out in her attempt to attract HIV and AIDS patients to her Cancell trial. The majority of the booklet consisted of a talk by Ed Sopcak. In the talk he claimed that Cancell could cure many forms of cancer and AIDS. It was in relation to this very claim, that Elizabeth Marsh was attempting to hold a trial of Cancell. She had no intention of charging trial subjects for Cancell.

The majority of the prosecution evidence related to AIDS, not surprisingly, as the prosecution had no evidence that Marsh intended to give Cancell to people with cancer. The trial took place in the very week that the *Lancet* published the preliminary results of the Concorde trial, which showed, despite all contrary claims made by the Wellcome Foundation, that AZT was of no practical use in the treatment of HIV. This might have weighed in favour of Elizabeth Marsh if her barrister had made something of it; after all Elizabeth Marsh wanted to do a trial of only six subjects for Cancell. The MRC had overseen a trial of nearly 2,000 subjects, for what turned out to be an ineffective and highly toxic substance.

The prosecution case took place over three days. The three most important prosecution witnesses were Professor Vincent Marks, Professor Donald Jeffries and an AIDS patient calling himself Hugh Fay. Vincent Marks' first statement had to be returned to the Crown Prosecution Service by the defence solicitors, because it consisted not of expert evidence but a half page of subjective remarks. Marks finally testified that Cancell was no good and that Elizabeth Marsh was a quack and a charlatan. Marsh's counsel failed to cross examine him on his financial links with Wellcome or his political links with the Campaign Against Health Fraud.

Professor Donald Jeffries, a Professor of Virology, gave very similar evidence to that which he gave against Doctors Davis and Chalmers. AZT, he said, was the substance against which all treatments had to be tested.

It was, however, the evidence of AIDS patient Hugh Fay, which probably did most damage to Marsh's case. Fay, who was HIV antibody positive, had been employed by the *Independent on Sunday* to visit Elizabeth Marsh posing as a possible trial subject. During his interviews with Marsh he declined to be part of the trial or to take Cancell. What then could his evidence have been? Fay claimed in his statement that Marsh had instructed him to stop taking AZT, a statement which was categorically denied by Marsh. The prosecution had no evidence that Elizabeth Marsh had, over the ten years of practice, and some 6,000 clients, injured or damaged anyone. Fay's evidence was meant to counter this fact and suggest to the jury, that her therapeutic advice was likely to damage patients.

There were, however, more serious problems over Fay's evidence. On the day before he was due to appear as a witness, the prosecution explained to the judge that Fay was dying of AIDS and so could not come to court. There are clear legal guidelines which relate to witnesses who are unable to attend court. These guidelines are there to protect the defendant on the one hand and to ensure that false evidence is not given for the defence or the prosecution, on the other. If a witness has evidence which is contested by the 'other side' then either, the witness has to come to court where he or she can be seen by the jury and cross examined by the opposing counsel, or the court has to be taken to the witness. If neither alternative is possible, then counsel for both the defence and the prosecution have to agree the 'non contentious' substance of the statement which can then be read out in court.

In the case of Elizabeth Marsh, Fay's statement was read to the jury, still containing its most damaging parts, principally that she had instructed Fay to stop taking AZT.

On the substantive matter of whether or not Elizabeth Marsh had issued or caused to be issued an advertisement, claiming a cure for cancer, for her own commercial gain, no material evidence except the receipt of the booklet was offered by the prosecution. The prosecution were unable to prove that Elizabeth Marsh had sent the booklet to its recipient, a barmaid at a gay pub. The fact that Elizabeth Marsh did not give evidence, probably went some way towards persuading the jury that she was responsible for sending out the booklet. There was no evidence that Marsh stood to gain commercially from the claim made by Ed Sopcak that Cancell cured most forms of cancer.

On Tuesday April 6th the jury found Elizabeth Marsh guilty of the charge. The judge delayed sentencing for two weeks. On the night of her conviction, Elizabeth Marsh collapsed and was admitted to hospital. At the end of April Elizabeth Marsh was sentenced to six months imprisonment. The Department of Health had spent thousands of pounds in their pursuit of Marsh, working hand in hand with those within HealthWatch who most definitely had vested interests, both in the cancer industry and the AIDS industry. In the final analysis, the Department of Health and the Medicines Control Agency criminalised Elizabeth Marsh, for no other reason than that she tried to hold a small-scale trial for an HIV management therapy with a non-toxic substance. It was a trial which the DoH knew about, and which the Medicines Control Agency could have discussed with her in a non-prosecutorial manner at any time prior to her embarking upon it.

The unbelievable irony is that Marsh was tried in the same week that the preliminary Concorde trial results were published. This trial had taken four years and had cost the tax payer some £12 million. So serious and so unwarranted had been the claims made by Wellcome for AZT and its benefits to asymptomatic HIV antibody positive patients, that Joan Shenton and Meditel had reported Wellcome to the Medicines Control Agency, who had refused to prosecute.

As for Cancell, no one is ever going to know the truth, which for many reasons suits the pharmaceutical companies and the DoH, down to the ground.

Chapter Thirty Five

The Assault on the Breakspear Hospital

Those whom the Gods wish to destroy, they first cease to insure. [1]

If therapists on the fringes of alternative medicine, who were not qualified doctors, were having a hard time in 1989, the situation was no easier for some fully qualified doctors. This was especially the case, if their life's work involved immunology and they were critical of orthodox pharmaceutical solutions to modern industrial illnesses.

By 1989, Dr Jean Monro was treating patients for a range of conditions, from food allergy and intolerance through to chemical sensitivity and chemical poisoning, at her Breakspear Hospital. She was also treating a variety of illnesses which she believed were related to vitamin and mineral deficiencies, conditions which ranged from migraine to multiple sclerosis and depression.

Since meeting Dr Rea and other doctors like Dr Joseph Miller, in America in the mid-eighties, Dr Monro had become convinced of the benefit of a technique called 'provocation neutralisation', used for the diagnosis and treatment of allergy and chemical sensitivity. The range of tests used by orthodox practitioners for diagnosing allergy is very crude and takes two main forms. In one test, the patient is put on a reduced diet of one or two base foods, such as potato, and then other foods are gradually introduced. Another test involves giving the patient pin-pricks, or scratches of allergens, then waiting to see how the patient responds. As for treatment, orthodox medicine has no solution at all, other than abstention. This is hardly satisfactory, especially when people are increasingly complaining of wide-ranging mutiple allergies and when an increasing number of people exhibit reactions to ambient chemicals which they find impossible to avoid.

Provocation-neutralisation, a treatment pioneered by Dr Joseph

Miller in America, seemed to solve many of the problems of the diagnosis and treatment of allergy, in a specific, effective and non-chemical manner. Initial intradermal injections of very small amounts (0.05 millilitres) of allergens are given to the patient, and the results around the site of the injection are monitored. If the body fails to respond, only a small raised weal appears. If the body does respond, the weal grows slightly, becoming white, hard and raised, with a sharp edge.

The 'neutralisation' treatment involves finding the correct concentration of the same allergen which will neutralise or stop the symptoms. This involves a series of injections, using weaker and weaker dilutions. When a weal is produced which does not grow or become hard, this is considered the neutralising dose. Patients take the solution of allergens, in a series of periodically decreasing subcutaneous injections, or in solution under the tongue, until they no longer show a reaction to the food to which they were previously allergic.

Provocation-neutralisation appears to work on a principle similar to that of homoeopathy, and this is perhaps one of the reasons why it has come so heavily under attack from orthodox medical practitioners. Another reason could be that the treatment depends upon the production of a vaccine, in the form of an allergen solution. By 1989, Dr Monro had established her own laboratory which produced such vaccines.

Although Dr Monro also used conventional pharmaceutical products, in the majority of her work she had cut herself off from the pharmaceutical industry and was successfully treating patients suffering from a wide range of immune deficiency illnesses with vaccines, vitamin and mineral supplements and natural substances already present in the human body.

* * *

Despite increasingly good signs throughout 1989, 1990 was to be a year of almost continous crisis for Dr Monro and the Breakspear Hospital. It began with the publication of a highly critical article, taking the side of the medical insurance companies, in the *Sunday Express*, and it ended with the Campaign Against Health Fraud engineering a 'World in Action' programme which was to close the Hospital.

Doctor Monro's difficulties with the insurance companies began in April 1989, when the firm Private Patients Plan (PPP) withdrew recognition from her. PPP decided that they could no longer recognise Dr Monro, for the purposes of insurance cover, as a doctor whom they would allow to treat their patients. Patients part-way through treatment were suddenly left without cover.

In December 1989, three patients appeared at the Breakspear seeking a consultation with Dr Monro. She saw all three patients. They were, it transpired, bogus patients, who lied about their symptoms. Their stories formed the basis for the *Sunday Express* article published in January 1990. 'Breaking out in a rash of big bills' was a manifesto for the insurance companies and their relationship to complementary medicine.[2] On the surface, the article appeared innocuous enough but between the closely argued financial lines ran a story about Dr Monro, her capability and her determination to overcharge patients.

As the insurance companies began to be affected by the recession, it was inevitable that the axe would fall first on policy-holders who were being treated by alternative and complementary practitioners, especially for such things as allergy. Not only were the insurance companies linked into an industrial and commercial world which was unhappy with the idea of blaming the environment for illness, but, with no real treatment for allergy available on the NHS, recognition of such health problems meant large and ongoing claims for chronic illness.

The *Sunday Express* article articulated the ground plan which the insurance companies had worked out over the two or three years preceding 1990. For Dr Monro and any other doctors in a similar position, the insurance companies argued that, as there was no specialised NHS training for allergists in Britain, those who practised as allergists outside the NHS could not be properly qualified.

> Private health insurers, BUPA and Private Patients Plan, insist that for a patient to qualify for treatment, they must come under the care of a qualified specialist. They define a specialist as someone who holds or has held an NHS consultancy.[3]

Consultants in allergy are thin on the ground in England, and those immunologists who have become consultants and can therefore

suggest that they are allergy consultants (though they are really not),
are in the main tied up with the drug companies and drug company
research. Even if doctors like Dr Monro brought in consultants to
work with them, it is unlikely that they would be qualified in allergy
medicine and therefore able to validate the patients' insurance claims.

In the early days of this attack by the insurance companies on Dr
Monro, the focus was upon her training and qualifications.

> They [the insurance companies] argue that Dr Monro does not
> meet this criterion [that of being a specialised consultant]
> although she has worked in the allergy field for many years. [4]

> There is no recognised training course for allergy specialists in
> Britain, and doctors such as Professor Barry Kay, a consultant at
> London's Brompton Hospital, had to qualify in the US.
> Professor Kay said, 'Allergy is not a speciality in this country
> and we have not even reached the stage of having a home grown
> batch of trained allergists. Allergies are on the increase and there
> should be statutory qualifications and training procedures'. [5]

Although the article did not mention it, Dr Monro also has Board
Examination qualifications from America. This conundrum set by the
insurance companies – no NHS specialisation in allergy, no insurance
cover without a consultant – led Dr Monro into increasing difficulties.
The insurance companies refused to accept each consultant she took
on, making her practice appear increasingly unreliable. The fact that
these hoops put up for Dr Monro to jump through were simply tactical
evasions by the insurance companies and orthodox medical
practitioners, rather than mechanisms to protect patients, was made
clear by the example of Dr William Rea.

Dr Rea, a well-qualified thoracic surgeon and eminent clinical
ecologist in America, had, in the mid-eighties, applied to the General
Medical Council to practise as a doctor in England. Seeing the
developing situation with the insurance companies and desperate to
safeguard treatment for people suffering from environmental illness,
Lady Colfox, the Chairwoman of the Environmental Medicine
Foundation, had taken up his case. The GMC refused to give Dr
Rea a practising certificate. No reasons for the refusal were given. One
reason might have been that enabling Dr Rea to act as a consultant
would have given allergy treatment and environmental medicine a new

authority and in turn this would have affected the insurance companies.

If Dr Monro wanted to treat patients previously covered by PPP, she was forced to find a consultant acceptable to them. In May 1989, she asked Dr David Brooks, who had been the Sub-Dean at St Mary's, Paddington and a consultant cardiologist, to join her at the Breakspear. From the time that Dr Brooks became available, all the patients were seen by him. Because Dr Brooks was highly qualified, PPP had little option but to accept him and provide his patients with insurance cover. They and other insurance companies did, however, still fight over every case, and always took an inordinately long time to pay out.

The insurance companies greeted the advent of the Campaign Against Health Fraud with relief and funds. Here was an organisation made up in the main of professionally qualified individuals, who had the ear of the medical establishment and the pharmaceutical companies. Such an organisation could reinforce the difficult decisions which the insurance companies were having to take. A campaign against 'quackery' would protect the insurance companies from American-style law suits, when they breached their contracts with patients who were undergoing treatment. A whole body of supporting professional opinion could be pushed into the public domain. Company decisions to withdraw cover could be justified as part of common professional practice.

The attitude that PPP took towards its clients who attended the Breakspear was in the beginning random and often illogical. As the Campaign Against Health Fraud established itself, PPP's arguments against cover were confidently honed down to one: that they could not pay-out for chronic conditions. Many allergy patients have chronic conditions, and certainly those patients who had been chemically sensitised by the use, for example, of sheep dip, or were toxically damaged, had chronic illnesses. Even better for the insurance companies was the suggestion adopted by leading CAHF members that there was no such thing as allergy or chemical sensitivity and those who imagined that they suffered it were in fact mentally rather than physically ill.

PPP began advising Dr Monro's patients that there was the possibility of cover, if they sought diagnosis and treatment from another physician, who practised allopathy and used pharmaceuticals, one, in fact, who would not diagnose chemical sensitivity or allergy.

The insurance companies wanted out of the whole area of clinical ecology; if claims were to begin coming in for people badly affected by food additives or ambient chemicals, the insurance companies had somehow to distance themselves from them.

Throughout late 1989 and early 1990, Dr Monro kept hearing on the medical grapevine that in the opinion of some of the medical advisers to insurance companies, her work was fraudulent. Rumours came back to her that she would end up in court, or before the General Medical Council.

* * *

For a number of years, Dr Monro was in correspondence with Dr Ian Bailey, a Director of and a medical adviser to Western Provident Assurance (WPA), a company which covered some of her patients. Unbeknown to her, Dr Bailey was from the beginning a member of the Campaign Against Health Fraud. Dr Bailey had been a general practitioner in Bristol before his retirement in December 1988. It is impossible to know whether Dr Bailey, in his capacity as medical advisor to an insurance company, ever divulged information about the condition of particular patients to the Campaign Against Health Fraud. However, the intimate proximity of a physician who has access to another doctor's records, to an organisation which is campaigning against that doctor, raises serious questions of ethics. There seems little doubt that with regard to the general questions which he raised in correspondence with Dr Monro, Dr Bailey was gathering intelligence.

Dr Bailey had been in correspondence with Dr Monro, not only over individual patients, but also over the general question of allergies. In fact, Dr Bailey took a considerable interest in this matter. On August 7th 1990 Dr Bailey wrote a long letter to Dr Monro containing a review which he had written of the 1990 Conference of the British Society for Allergy and Environmental Medicine, which was held, in association with the American Academy of Environmental Medicine, in Buxton, Derbyshire. [6]

In his cover letter with this review, Dr Bailey expressed 'interested scepticism' about alternative allergy treatments. He was, he said, 'not yet persuaded about provocation-neutralisation', he still looked critically at enzyme potentiated desensitisation and the Alcat Test and he believed that he was in this view, 'at one with some other people in allergy and environmental medicine'.

He told Dr Monro that he had read the debate on the Environmental Medicine Foundation in Hansard. He had, he said, seen 'comments on William Rudd and Cathy Bailey but not, so far as I can see, the Bristol lady who went to Texas and who was said to be allergic to the 20th Century *and I wonder what has happened to her*' (italics added). This last reference is to Sheila Rossall and his question appears to be fishing for information or, at least, provoking comment about her case from Dr Monro. The cases of William Rudd and Sheila Rossall were later to appear as central issues in 'The Allergy Business' produced by Granada Television.

Dr Bailey's report to the WPA on the 1990 Conference on Environmental Medicine was quite damning and made the contributors, particularly Dr Monro, appear rather silly. Dr Monro attended another conference in Bristol in July 1990 and Bailey also refers to this in his review of the Buxton conference.

> I listened to papers on provocation-neutralisation testing and neutralisation therapy and though controlled trials were described I was not impressed by their significance and had difficulty in understanding the underlying mechanism ... I would find the greatest difficulty in justifying to WPA the use of Provocation-neutralisation testing or enzyme potentiated desensitisation ... In conclusion, we should continue to look critically at allergy and environmental medicine.

> It should be noted that Dr Jean Munro (sic) spoke at a conference in Bristol in early July 1990. She believes that millions of people could be suffering from environmentally induced disorders without knowing it; a failure of breast feeding; pollution in the environment; the addition of chemicals to food, air, water; the injudicious use of drugs have all led to weakening of the immune system. She suggests that 30% of the British population could be suffering from environmental ailments. [7]

At no time, during her correspondence with Dr Bailey throughout 1990, did Dr Monro suspect that he was a member of an organisation which had targeted her, and was gathering information which it would use to try to destroy her.

* * *

The most severe blow to Dr Monro's medical practice in 1990, came not from practitioners in Britain, nor from the media, but from a paper published in the *New England Journal of Medicine (NEJM)*. The paper was a report of a double-blind study of symptom provocation to determine food sensitivity. [8] Jewett *et al.* gave injections of provocative allergens to eighteen patients who claimed that they were allergic. The study claimed to find that only 27% of the active injections were identified by the subjects to be allergens from which they experienced symptoms, and 24% of the placebo control injections were identified wrongly as containing allergens. The study concluded, 'When the provocation of symptoms to identify food sensitivities is evaluated under double-blind conditions, this type of testing, as well as the treatments based on 'neutralizing' such reactions, appear to lack scientific validity.'

It was some time before critics of this paper were able to show that it was so flawed that it should not have been published by a journal of the standing of the *New England Journal of Medicine*. Jewett's paper was so bad that it had been consistently rejected for publication, over a five year period, by all other authoritative journals in Britain and America.

An editorial in the same issue of the *NEJM*,† by a British doctor, Anne Ferguson, entitled 'Food Sensitivity or Self-Deception', [9] put Jewett's paper into a medical and social context. Dr Ferguson's evaluation of the paper is far from objective. She describes the diagnostic techniques of food intolerance by unnamed practitioners as 'unusual or frankly bizarre', including 'hair analysis and iridology' as

---

† The *New England Journal of Medicine* has been involved in other 'vested interest' conflicts, most seriously the conflict between Professor Linus Pauling and Dr Ewan Cameron and the Mayo Clinic. The conflict centred on the use of vitamin C in relation to cancer. The *NEJM* sided with the Mayo Clinic against Cameron and Pauling. In her book on this affair, Evelleen Richards describes the *NEJM* in these terms: '*The New England Journal of Medicine* is the oldest and most prestigious and powerful of the medical journals in the United States ... Arnold S. Relman and the journal he edits, therefore endorse ... the standard view, whereby medicine represents itself as a group of responsible professionals trained in scientific, rational, neutral processes, self-regulated by an ethical code. The *NEJM* reflects through its editorial policy the professional view of alternative therapists, as in the main, 'irrational' and 'unscientific'. [10]

well as 'injection provocation tests'. Provocation-neutralisation is a simple and effective diagnostic guide to allergy; it has nothing to do with any 'bizarre' diagnostic techniques such as 'hair analysis and iridology'. No references are given for practitioners who do use such techniques to diagnose food allergy. The introduction of extraneous and prejudicial material into an apparently academic piece of writing is always a sign that health-fraud campaigners and representatives of vested interests are at work.

Dr Ferguson found the 'rigorous evaluation' of the Jewett study confirmation of her own clinical practice when assessing food allergy complainants. 'Unless a clear diagnosis emerges, I tell the patient that food is not causing the symptoms and that he or she can safely return to a completely normal diet ... For those who persist in believing that they have a food intolerance ... I strongly recommend psychiatric consultation.' Which goes to show that you should be very selective about your illnesses and symptoms when visiting your doctor. If you insist you have food allergy, you could end up losing your job on account of being diagnosed mentally ill, losing your home because you cannot pay the mortgage and finally becoming the subject of the present government's non-existent 'care in the community' policy!

To support her view that the presentation of food intolerance often masks a psychiatric disorder, Ferguson quotes the paper written by CAHF member David Pearson [11] which concluded that of twenty-two people referred to an allergy clinic with suspected food intolerance, only four proved to have confirmed allergies to food. Of the eighteen who had unconfirmed allergies, seventeen of them, it was suggested, were psychiatrically ill, ten having depressive neurosis, three neurasthenia, and one each having hysterical neurosis, hypochondriacal neurosis, phobic state, and hysterical personality disorder.

It was interesting that the *New England Journal of Medicine* should have asked a gastroenterologist to review Jewett's paper. Dr Ferguson had also been a member of the Royal College of Physicians' Committee, chaired by Maurice Lessof, which produced *Food Intolerance and Food Aversion*. [12] She has been an advisor to the Dairy Trades Federation and the Milk Marketing Board. [13] It is of course unlikely that Dr Ferguson would have allowed such interests to colour her judgement about food intolerance, which is said by some to be occasionally related to dairy produce.

The Jewett paper and the accompanying editorial in the *NEJM*, were the first clear signs that there was an Anglo-American movement against alternative allergy medicine and provocation neutralisation techniques in particular. In Britain, Dr Jean Monro and the Breakspear Hospital were to bear almost the entire brunt of the coming attack.

* * *

My first short investigation into the Campaign Against Health Fraud (CAHF), carried out over three months at the end of 1989, had alerted me to rudimentary connections between CAHF, Caroline Richmond and Wellcome.

By November 1990, the project was in the past. I was getting on with other work and I wasn't thinking much about the Campaign Against Health Fraud, or its members. Then late one evening I received a phone call from Lorraine Hoskin. In a working-class south London voice, she asked me if I was an investigator; I said I was, sometimes. She said that I had been recommended to her and she would like me to investigate HealthWatch. Her child, she told me, had been a patient of Dr Jean Monro, then Dr Monro had been discredited by HealthWatch and now her child's treatment was in jeopardy. I arranged to meet her in Basildon.

Basildon is a large conurbated shopping centre, overspilled from Essex and east London; you reach it on a train journey through an industrial wasteland which represents the architectural offal of London's more ordered centre. I met Lorraine, accompanied by her second child in a push-chair, outside a shoe shop. We found our way into the Basildon municipal Leisure Centre, where Muzac serenaded unused red plastic chairs and formica-topped tables.

From the moment I met her I trusted Lorraine Hoskin; she gave the appearance of being a tough working-class mother, fighting with determination to protect her children. She seemed, though, an unusual person to be so wound-up about a relatively esoteric organisation like HealthWatch. She was spitting angry about them. It was a while before she was able to settle down and give me the details of how they had intervened in her life.

* * *

Lorraine Hoskin's first child, Samantha, was born by Caesarian section. When she was three months old, she developed sickness and diarrhoea. With this, Lorraine and her husband began a slow descent into horror, the kind of horror it is perhaps only possible to descend into when dealing with large impersonal institutions like the NHS.

The doctors from whom Lorraine first sought advice dismissed Samantha's illness as gastro-enteritis and gave her antibiotics: the sickness and diarrhoea continued. More antibiotics were prescribed but at six months, Samantha wasn't any better. The National Health Service provides no second opinion nor appeals against the pot-luck abilities of general practitioners and hospital consultants. Samantha's condition got worse. Lorraine and her husband became depressed.

When she was a year old, Samantha had scratch tests done, at an NHS hospital, to ascertain whether or not she was allergic. All the tests seemed to come up positive; consequently, the doctor told Lorraine to avoid feeding Samantha all the things for which they had tested. She had responded most seriously to milk and vegetables; so Lorraine took her off these. Her condition did not improve.

After the scratch tests Samantha was prescribed Nalcrom, a food allergy drug produced by Fisons. It is specifically not recommended for children under two years of age. Even for children over two years old, there can be adverse reactions which are listed in *MIMS* as nausea, rashes and joint pain. Fortunately, the pharmacist to whom Lorraine took the prescription knew more about the drug than the doctor who prescribed it. He told Lorraine that she was not to give Nalcrom to Samantha and rang her doctor.

Disappointed with the treatment Samantha had been receiving at the hospital, Lorraine's GP referred her to Great Ormond Street. The consultant Samantha saw there suggested that she tried a number of different diets. Still Samantha didn't get better; now, as well, she was picking up viruses and becoming ill regularly.

Aged two and a half, Samantha collapsed and had an epileptic-like convulsive fit. Lorraine and her husband called an ambulance but by the time they reached hospital the fit had passed: the doctors were unable to diagnose anything. Four weeks later, Samantha had another fit and was taken to hospital again. No diagnosis was made.

Terribly upset by their own impotence and the inability of a variety of doctors to suggest what Samantha's disorder might be, let alone any treatment, Lorraine and her husband went to see a private consultant. The doctor discussed a plausible theory involving the idea that Samantha had a damaged bowel. In terms of treatment, the private sector served Samantha no better than the NHS. The doctor told her parents to simply watch her diet.

Samantha's convulsions became more severe and more frequent; the shaking might last for a day or so, and Samantha could be in a state of collapse for as long as three days. One day, after a complete collapse, in desperation, doctors gave her another course of antibiotics. At the end of the two-week course, Samantha's condition was worse.

Lorraine rang round hospitals in her area trying to see a doctor who would agree to give Samantha a diagnostic examination: she eventually found one. The doctor who saw Samantha that day was dismayed and angered at her condition; Samantha was underweight, her stomach was terribly distended. The doctor rebuked Lorraine who was soon in tears blaming herself for Samantha's condition.

The doctor admitted Samantha to hospital and, during a week-long stay, she carried out a series of tests. Armed with the results of the tests, the doctor came up with a radical suggestion: Samantha should have a colostomy. Lorraine and her husband asked to be referred back to Great Ormond Street for a second opinion. Thankfully, the doctors at Great Ormond Street did not agree with the idea of a colostomy.

Over the following year, Samantha Hoskin was in and out of the Children's Hospital in Hackney, London, and tested by the doctor from Great Ormond Street. On the occasions she collapsed between visits to Hackney, she attended the local hospital. Samantha's life became circumscribed by journeys to hospitals and doctors; she lost more weight and was often in terrible pain. When doctors gave her pain-relieving drugs, they seemed to made her condition worse.

By now, another myriad of symptoms had joined the earlier evidence of illness. Samantha had severe blood pressure problems and had developed a heart murmur. The doctor at Great Ormond Street, unable to make headway with her condition, finally, informally recommended that the Hoskins should take Samantha to see Dr Jean Monro at the private Breakspear Hospital.

Nearly all the doctors whom Samantha had seen understood that her problems were caused by malabsorption of food in the stomach and intestine yet none of them had any idea how this condition might be treated. Lorraine was reluctant to believe that Samantha was suffering from an allergy-related condition. Persuaded by conservative theorising about allergy, passed on to her by the many doctors she had seen, Lorraine felt that Samantha's condition must be the result of some serious internal damage which had occurred at birth. A month or so after Lorraine received the advice from Great Ormond Street, however, Samantha suffered another serious collapse and the GP instructed Lorraine to ring the Breakspear and get an early apppointment.

Dr Monro insisted on seeing Samantha immediately. Lorraine and her husband travelled to the Breakspear, where Dr Monro, concerned about Samantha's condition, admitted the five year old to the hospital.

By October 1990, four months after the first visit to the Breakspear, Samantha Hoskin was fitter than she had ever been during her short life. She was no longer in pain and her weight had risen from two stone to over three. Her blood pressure problems had gone completely and convulsions which had been occurring every two weeks had now only occurred twice in four months.

Both Lorraine and her husband were surprised at the highly specialised treatment Samantha was given at the Breakspear. She was treated for almost everything she might come into contact with, everything which she might eat – some 76 antigens, which were tested under her tongue. Pesticides, artificial colourings, and chemical residues in foods such as pork, chicken and beef, appeared to be a big problem. Lorraine herself took on a commitment to Samantha's treatment, learning as much about it as she was able.

In 1990, with the horror of Samantha's illness slipping into the background, Lorraine was convinced that Samantha's condition was caused by a weakened immune system, unable to cope with problems of food malabsorption. She believes that Samantha's immune system had been further weakened by environmental agents and the drugs she had been prescribed by various doctors.

* * *

Lorraine Hoskin had good reason to be pleased with the work of Dr Jean Monro and the Breakspear Hospital. Unfortunately, Lorraine had been introduced to the benefits of this work at the very time others were setting out to destroy it.

Lorraine had never contemplated private medicine before she went to the Breakspear, but she was, in her own words, 'not so naive that she imagined she would not have to pay for the treatment'. She didn't think that the charges for which Dr Monro billed her were excessive. Initially, Samantha was covered by private medical insurance, with the company Private Patients Plan (PPP). She felt that the treatment she received from Dr Monro was of such a high quality and so comprehensive, that she would, she says, have paid, even if it meant selling their house, something, she adds hastily, she and her husband never had to consider.

Lorraine Hoskin had the first intimation that in attending the Breakspear she had trespassed upon a battlefield, when in February 1990, PPP suddenly withdrew insurance cover from Dr Monro's patients. Lorraine couldn't understand the reasoning behind this. It had occurred in the middle of Samantha's treatment. She had seen children going into the Breakspear with conditions like chronic asthma, hardly able to walk through the doors, and she had seen them a few weeks later, running round the hospital garden. She had spoken to many of the parents, all of whom were in agreement that Dr Monro's treatment had helped their children.

Lorraine Hoskin was soon to learn that the attacks upon Dr Monro had absolutely nothing to do with her abilities as a doctor, nor the effectiveness of her treatments. There was no hint of common sense in the sudden and insistent clamouring to have the Breakspear shut down.

* * *

In the first few months of 1990, Barry Wood, a researcher for the 'World in Action' programme at Granada in Manchester, began discussions with Nick Hayes, an editor who had just moved to Granada from the BBC 'Watchdog' programme, about putting together a programme attacking Clinical Ecology.†

---

† Barry Wood was a colleague of Duncan Campbell, and Nick Hayes had recently worked with Campbell on a BBC 'Watchdog' programme. It was Campbell and Richmond who got 'World in Action' programme interested in Dr Monro and others of the CAHF's targeted practitioners. After Nick Hayes left the 'Watchdog' programme to go to Granada his place as editor was taken by Sara Caplan the partner of Nick Ross, the Chairman of HealthWatch.

Barry Wood was insistent on a number of occasions following the programme, eventually broadcast as 'The Allergy Business', [14] that it had been his idea and that he had convinced Hayes it was worth doing. The truth is probably more complex, because almost a year after the programme had been screened, the Campaign Against Health Fraud, by then called HealthWatch, claimed in the minutes of its Annual General Meeting that the programme had been *its* programme, that it had 'got' it on to television. [15] The programme grew out of the complex relationships which had developed over the previous five years between David Pearson, Duncan Campbell and Caroline Richmond and the introduction of these three people to Ray Fitzwalter, the 'World in Action' producer. Fitzwalter had also come to know the UK Skeptics and James Randi during Randi's visits to Manchester; he was later to produce Randi's series, 'James Randi, Psychic Investigator'.

Confirmation that 'World in Action' had planned for some time to attack Dr Monro, came from a journalist working for the 'Cook Report', who confided to a friend of Dr Monro in March 1989, that 'World in Action' was going to take Jean Monro 'to the cleaners. She charges too much money and then drops patients when the money runs out.' The journalist also hinted darkly that there were unsavoury aspects to Dr Monro's private life. [16]

Throughout the first six months of 1990, Wood researched the programme, approaching a number of people who had been patients of Dr Monro and Dr Monro herself. Because the real programme was being made covertly, Wood never told any of the people he approached that the idea was to refute Clinical Ecology or to attack Dr Monro. In fact, Dr Monro, all too happy to be involved in a television programme she thought was about environmental medicine, gave full co-operation, in the early stages, to Wood and Granada. Most often Wood told patients he approached that he was making a programme about myalgic encephalomyelitis (ME) sufferers and the very real personal trauma which ME caused. In fact most HealthWatch members with whom Wood was working did not even recognise the physical existence of ME.

Initially, Wood had extensive information on Dr Jean Monro, and the Breakspear Hospital, which he had probably been given by Caroline Richmond and Duncan Campbell. This was information garnered by health-fraud activists, pharmaceutical companies and insurance companies, since 1985.

The hundreds of complaints against the programme, following its transmission, included some from people who had been approached by Wood but had refused to be interviewed. He had told these people that he was researching a programme about ME. One woman, who had consistently refused Wood an interview, had after rejecting him, been rung up by members of HealthWatch who tried to convince her that she should take part in the programme.

*   *   *

In April 1990, Maureen Rudd, a patient of Dr Monro, was introduced by Dr Monro to Barry Wood. Maureen Rudd's family had a tragic history of illness; her son William had committed suicide, after serious depression brought on by multiple allergies and ME. William Rudd had been treated by Dr Monro for the five years before his suicide; he had come to her, however, after four years of what Maureen Rudd describes as 'damaging treatment' by NHS doctors. Despite the death of her son, Maureen Rudd was completely committed to the treatments and the practices of Dr Monro.

On the first occasion that Rudd met Barry Wood, he told her that he was researching a programme on environmental medicine. In September, a month before the programme was shown, he rang her to tell her that the programme was about ME. Wood assured Maureen Rudd that the programme he was researching would be sympathetic, and that a number of ME sufferers and doctors would be interviewed.

Following the phone calls, Wood and David Mills, the programme producer, travelled to the Rudds' home and conducted an hour-long interview with her.

William Rudd's suicide came after a nine-year struggle with a debilitating illness, which was finally diagnosed as ME. Until he became ill in 1979, he had been a very fit person: six foot five, a rugby player who was interested in music and played the viola. His academic background was scientific. In 1979, at the age of twenty, he developed glandular fever from which he never properly recovered. The history of his pre-Breakspear treatment is reminiscent of that received by Samantha Hoskin. For four years William traipsed around a variety of

NHS hospitals and doctors, only to be told that in all probability he wasn't really ill.

> NHS specialists and other doctors we saw in the first four years ... would either throw the problem back on the patient and say you're just making it all up, which is very hard because normally one relies on the medical profession and always has ... you hope that they will say well I can't find the cause of your illness, but I will keep looking and in the meantime do what I can to help you ... It's absolutely hearbreaking to be told, 'Oh go away, we don't want to know about you anymore, we can't do anything.' [17]

In her hour-long interview with Wood and Mills, Maureen Rudd was clear about the fact that orthodox medicine had been of no value to her son. From very early on in the interview she talked about Dr Monro, whom William 'found' after four treatment-less years.

> If we had followed up allergies at the time when they were first diagnosed ... we would have done better and we would have found the person who eventually helped us so much, who is Dr Jean Monro. [18]

When William Rudd found Dr Monro, he was so enthusiastic about her treatments, that he suggested the rest of the Rudd family also went to her for consultation. Maureen Rudd had always suspected that she and her family had allergic responses, she was often affected by swellings after eating certain foods and her husband suffered from asthma. Five members of the Rudd family as well as William visited Dr Monro.

> We all went to see Dr Monro ... [the treatment] solved our problems very quickly. [19]

> her treatment did sort out our problems very quickly. [20]

> I had a long list of symptoms which I really can't remember now because they've all gone, but one of the worst was swellings, I used to swell up like a pumpkin, my face ... and sleeplessness ... a long list of migraines and bad headaches. [21]

Under the direction of Dr Monro, William Rudd's condition began to improve. For the first time in five years, he was able to take some exercise without becoming immediately tired. He began gardening.

> He was never so ill once he started treatment with Dr Monro. [22]

> He never did feel as ill again after treatment with Dr Monro, and he was gradually able to take a bit more exercise and do more. [23]

> For four years he'd been able to contribute nothing to the world, and he'd just been a liability, he felt – and a burden, so it was a great blessing when he took up growing vegetables because he was very good at it. [24]

In order to take the strain off William Rudd's immune system, Dr Monro prescribed a regime which involved living away from many of the allergens and toxins which were taking advantage of the virus, still present in William's body. On Dr Monro's instructions, the Rudd family bought and equipped an old caravan, which acted as a controlled environment for William. Living for periods in this caravan also aided his recovery, and up to a year before his death the prognosis for his return to health was good.

In the winter of 1987, however, a number of things happened. William fell and shattered his knee-cap, the operation to repair it necessitated a stay in hospital and a general anaesthetic. Maureen Rudd approached the subject of William's accident in her interview for Granada.

> ... prior to knowing that he had ME [before meeting Dr Monro], he was unfortunately put on a regime of timed exercise, which turned out to be a complete disaster. He gritted his teeth and ran every day for a year in the hopes of being able to get back to Cardiff University, where he had to give up his course, but in fact he was completely ruined by that, his muscles were damaged and he kept falling from then on and had worse and worse falls, until he eventually shattered a knee-cap.

Following the treatment on his knee and throughout the long winter, the Rudd family, who live on a farm in Dorset, were often snowed in. William found it impossible to attend Dr Monro's clinics and was unable to keep strictly to the treatments and check-ups which are a necessary part of those treatments. All these factors precipitated a relapse, which William was emotionally unable to contend with. Finally in February 1988, some time after he suffered a quite separate, emotional set-back, William Rudd committed suicide.

During the unedited Granada interview, Maureen Rudd was asked how much it had cost to have *her whole family*, of six people, treated for their allergies, she replied, 'it probably cost us between £12,000 and £15,000'. She then went on to make clear that she did not consider this cost to have been excessive.

> It is an expensive treatment because it involves one nurse to one patient, and the actual testing at the beginning is time consuming, and we quite understood that.

> It is quite a long-term treatment in that as you are relieved of the symptoms of your allergies, your immune system can begin to recover, and it does begin to recover, and it's very noticeable.

Maureen Rudd found the hour-long interview with 'World In Action', tiring and painful. Wood insisted that she talk about her son's suicide and tried consistently to link the treatment, and especially William's periods in the caravan, with that suicide. Many of Wood's questions dwelt upon the suggestion that William Rudd's illness might have had a psychiatric root, rather than an organic one; on each occasion that it was brought up, Maureen Rudd disputed this idea. In the end, questioned about William's suicide, Maureen Rudd broke down and cried on camera.

* * *

Another woman approached by Barry Wood was Blanche Panton. To some extent Blanche was in a similar position to that of Maureen Rudd. Although she herself was seeing Dr Monro, it was her child, Jade, who was receiving the most focused treatment at the Breakspear. Blanche Panton was, at the time of her interview with Barry Wood, completely committed to the Breakspear and to Dr Monro. In Blanche's case, however, there was a complication: she was separated from her husband, who had taken custody of their child, primarily because Jade was undergoing treatment at the Breakspear. This put Blanche Panton in an impossibly sensitive position, with regard to any television programme critical of Dr Monro.

Blanche Panton had become ill in 1983 after she had Jade. In the following few years she was divorced and her health deteriorated. She developed all the classic symptoms of ME: she experienced chronic fatigue. She had nausea and pains in her abdomen from irritable bowel syndrome, and she had an often continuous cold. At her worst she was unable to walk up and down stairs without getting out of breath and her speech became slurred. She suffered so badly from brain tiredness (known to ME sufferers as brain fag) that on occasions she couldn't string a logical sentence together.

Blanche Panton found no relief from her problems with the NHS doctors she went to. When she finally got to see Dr Monro, in January 1989, both she and Jade were admitted to the Breakspear. Dr Monro diagnosed chronic exhaustion and multiple allergies. Because of the poor state of her immune system, Blanche had become allergic to a wide range of substances. Dr Monro took Blanche and Jade into the Breakspear for a second stay, even though she had no insurance cover and no money at that time to pay for her treatment. During the second stay at the Breakspear it became apparent to Blanche Panton that she was too ill to look after Jade. Her ex-husband, with his parents, who were Christian Scientists, decided that, especially as she was undergoing medical treatment with which they did not agree, they should take Jade away from her.

When Blanche Panton was first approached by Barry Wood at her home in the summer of 1990, he told her that Granada was doing a sympathetic programme about allergies and ME. On that first visit, Wood stayed for an hour or so discussing her condition, and the treatment which she had received from Dr Monro.

Blanche Panton did not hear from Wood for a month after that first meeting, until the early autumn, when he called again. Then, he told her that they were still working on the programme even though it had been delayed. He went over the same ground again with her; she remembers his saying, 'the film is to be an unbiased film about allergy and ME, from the sufferer's points of view and an unbiased review of the treatments available'.

Blanche Panton next received a phone call from Wood to confirm the time and date of a filmed interview. On the day agreed, a film crew arrived at her home with Wood and another man who seemed to be senior to him. While the film crew set up the cameras for the interview, Blanche Panton went into another room with Wood, where they discussed the interview. Blanche stressed the point that in her opinion the things which were being said about Jean Monro were essentially political.

Blanche says that she was calm when the interview was filmed, telling Wood about the treatment which she and Jade had received, and about how that treatment had benefited her. Wood's colleague, who seemed to be in charge, kept interrupting Blanche and asking her to elaborate on her answers. At one point, when she was talking about Jade, he stopped the camera and asked if she could 'answer that question again, but with a bit more emotion'. She told him, 'I can't do that.' She noticed as well that pressure was put on her to stress the fact that Jade had been given injections.

As the interview went on, Blanche began to realise that it was changing direction. Both men were trying to get her to agree that the treatment she received from Dr Monro was cranky. They asked how many vitamin pills she took and how expensive they were, then filmed her going out into the kitchen to take them. The interview lasted about forty minutes.

When they had finished filming, the attitude of both men changed. They made it plain that they thought Dr Monro was making a lot of money, and began to suggest that Blanche was somehow a victim. Blanche felt she had to make a point of saying to Barry Wood, 'I am not a victim.'

On the Sunday before the programme was due to be screened, Blanche Panton was contacted by a friend who had read an advance publicity article in the *Observer*. Up until that Sunday, Blanche was still thinking that the film in which she had participated was in favour of Dr Monro, arguing, as Jean Monro herself did, that such treatment should be available on the NHS. Having spoken to her friend, Blanche was convinced that the programme would be quite different.

Blanche Panton rang Barry Wood throughout the day that the programme was due to be screened. When she did finally speak to him, she asked if the film was going ahead. She made it clear that if the film was, like the *Observer* article, to be an attack upon Dr Monro, then she did not want her interview to be included. Her own secret fear was that if the film was a contentious one, attacking Dr Monro, it would adversely affect her chances of seeing Jade. That conversation took place at about 5.20pm on the Monday evening. Wood told her, 'We don't even know whether it is going out yet.' He would, he said, talk to the director and find out if it was going out, and, if it was, he promised he would have the interview with her edited out.

* * *

Lorraine Hoskin was also approached by Barry Wood in the middle of
August 1990. The call stood out in Lorraine's mind because she had
received it on a Sunday and Wood had apologised. He had rung from
Manchester saying that he had read about Samantha's problems. He
was, he said, interested in doing a programme on allergies and the
effect they had upon individuals' lives.

Lorraine told Wood about Samantha and the treatment which she
had been receiving. Naturally, she was completely supportive of Dr
Monro. The next time Wood rang Lorraine, it was to say that he was
definitely making a programme on allergies; he asked Lorraine if she
would like to participate in the programme. He made arrangements to
visit her and discuss filming with Nick Hayes.

Lorraine Hoskin next heard that the programme had been
scrapped; then in September Wood told Lorraine Hoskin that his
producer had changed the emphasis of the programme. He, Wood
said, had spoken to a number of doctors who were antagonistic to Dr
Monro's treatments. Wood told Lorraine Hoskin that he was angry at
what had happened to *his* programme, because he had intended to
interview a number of doctors who were in favour of Dr Monro's
treatment.

Lorraine Hoskin thought that a programme on allergy and ME was
very important. On hearing that the programme had been scrapped,
she asked Wood if it was possible to re-consider. She did not know, of
course, that Wood was actually going ahead, but now only with
interviews which could be damaging to Dr Monro.

Lorraine Hoskin next saw Wood at the Breakspear ten days before
the programme was screened. He was still at that time saying that he
was doing a programme just about ME. By now, however, although
still being co-operative, Dr Monro had become uneasy about the
programme. Despite this, and as she had nothing to hide, she
continued her co-operation, giving Granada full access to the hospital.

When Lorraine Hoskin met Wood at the Breakspear, Wood
introduced into the conversation the fact that he hadn't yet met any
children who had been taken away from their parents by Social
Services after their parents being treated for allergy. Clearly, Wood
was, by then, looking for notorious cases, in which children had

suffered because of Dr Monro's treatment of their parents.

On that day at the Breakspear, the 'World in Action' camera crew filmed Samantha Hoskin having a bad reaction to an orange. It was a perfect piece of film, giving evidence of the fact that some allergies had serious physical consequences. Because it showed Samantha being successfully treated by Dr Monro, it was also film which to some degree validated her work. Lorraine Hoskin later rang Wood to ask for a video copy of the film. Although Wood told her he would send it, he never did, nor was it included in the programme which was finally screened.

* * *

By October 1990, it was clear to everyone associated with the Breakspear Hospital that the 'World in Action' programme was going to be an attack upon Dr Jean Monro and the Hospital. The two patients who had actually been interviewed by Wood, Maureen Rudd and Blanche Panton, were both people whose stories were shadowed by drama, Maureen because her son had committed suicide and Blanche because her child had been taken from her care. Others who had been approached had turned down interviews, either simply because they were sceptical about the media, were involved in compensation cases, or felt that their health would suffer. There were hundreds of patients and ex-patients who would have given evidence to 'World in Action' about the efficacy of Dr Monro's treatment; one who was eager to do this was Lorraine Hoskin: she, however, despite her appeals, was not interviewed.

When it became evident that the programme was not what Wood had represented it as, a number of people contacted 'World in Action', to try to warn of the serious consequences for patients if, following a damaging programme, the Breakspear was forced to close down. Lorraine Hoskin wrote to Barry Wood, warning him that such a programme could put peoples' lives at risk. She made the point that Wood and his colleagues could not even begin to understand the problems suffered by people with serious multiple allergies. Lady Colfox, who, by 1990, was playing a leading role in the Environmental Medicine Foundation, set up in 1985, also saw the possible consequences. She wrote to Wood,[25] making it clear that, in her opinion, a programme which suggested that there was no hope for allergy sufferers, or those suffering from chemical sensitivity, might lead to people taking their own lives.†

* * *

With a half-hour programme on prime-time television in October 1990, Barry Wood, Nick Hayes, Ray Fitzwalter and the rest of the 'World in Action' team in co-operation with the Campaign Against Health Fraud, a self-appointed campaign group funded by pharmaceutical and private medical insurance companies, almost ended the career of Dr Jean Monro. The programme led to the bankruptcy of the Breakspear Hospital.

Film can have great power and for this reason it should be strictly accountable to, and overseen by, independent people. When a cabal of cynical journalists embark upon a wrecking mission they have the means at their disposal to destroy people and institutions. This they can appear to do in the 'public interest' without once making mention of their own personal ignorances, views or prejudices.

Jean Monro emerged from the 'World in Action' programme depicted as an autocratic crook and empire builder, a charlatan, a greedy, disreputable hole-in-the-wall doctor. Her patients were depicted as self-deluded, irrational people, some of whom had serious psychiatric disorders. Dr Monro's science and hard-won medical practice emerged as witchcraft, an obnoxious trade in damaging injections. Both doctor and patients apparently drifted in a cult-like world of bizarre science fantasy, where television sets gave off noxious gases and people battled paranoically with invisible, and probably non-existent, ambient toxins.

'The Allergy Business' was a classic example of the mass transmission of personal ideological prejudices under the guise of objective reporting. The programme made no attempt at all to put the counterbalancing case for clinical ecology, nor to cite any evidence or references which showed the record of doctors working in that field.

† Following the transmission of the programme, a woman who had previously been a patient of Dr Monro killed herself, principally, it appeared, because she felt that there was now less possibility of her obtaining further treatment.

Not once during the programme were viewers given any background information about those who gave 'evidence' against Jean Monro.

Viewers were not told that Caroline Richmond, who spoke to camera on the programme, has worked at Wellcome's Institute for the History of Medicine since 1985, and that Wellcome made a percentage of its profits from over the counter sales of remedies for such things as hay fever, and flu-like symptoms, the very conditions which Dr Monro treats without drugs. Viewers were given no information about the Campaign Against Health Fraud, about Dr David Pearson or Professor Maurice Lessof, who was actually introduced wrongly as a member of the General Medical Council. While Dr Monro was accused of earning massive amounts of money from her treatments, viewers were not informed about either the salaries of other experts or the profits of the organisations which subsidised them.

The tenor of the unsupported allegations came in the first minute of the programme.

NARRATOR   Sheila Rossall, the pop singer, said to be allergic to the 20th century, deserted and destitute.

Mandy Smith, wife of Rolling Stone guitarist Bill Wyman, dangerously ill.

And Helen Stanford from Bournemouth, dead.

Doctors say all three are victims of the allergy business. And doctors say, despite her Royal support, Britain's leading private allergist, Dr Jean Monro, has misled patients, given needless treatment and, with other allergists, put hundreds at risk ...

Tonight 'World in Action' investigates the allergy business and its leading exponent, Dr Jean Monro ...

Viewers could be forgiven for thinking that Dr Monro had actually treated Sheila Rossall, Mandy Smith and Helen Stanford: she had not. No further mention was made of the 'other allergists who put hundreds at risk', or the circumstances of the death of Helen Stanford. This dramatic introduction, which led people to believe that Dr Monro was responsible for the death and destitution of patients, was followed by four statements which put the case for the prosecution – 'World in Action'.

NARRATOR   This week the General Medical Council will be asked
            to investigate the activities of [the Breakspear and] its
            medical director, Dr Jean Monro.
CAROLINE RICHMOND
            I have three accusations against Dr Monro. That she
            is giving people worthless treatment. That she is
            charging them huge amounts of money for it and that
            she is not giving them the treatment that they need.

It was Caroline Richmond, the trade journalist, who assumed the
position of chief prosecutor, and representing 'The Campaign Against
Health Fraud', put the charges against Dr Monro. Nothing showed
more clearly the malicious intent of the programme than this first
statement by Richmond. That Caroline Richmond should play a
leading journalistic role in an apparently independent investigative
programme was itself a serious criticism of the programme-makers.
Her appearance was an immediate indication of the programme
makers' editorial bias.

    The Campaign Against Health Fraud position on allergy has from
the beginning been conservative. This is inevitable, because those
interests on whose behalf CAHF works – the BMA, National Health
Service doctors, the pharmaceutical and chemical companies, the
insurance companies – find it hard to accept that individuals can be
made ill by chemical and environmental pollutants. If chemical
toxicity, manifested as allergy, does not exist, then, CAHF argues,
those people who suffer symptoms are most likely to be in need of
psychiatric help. The CAHF position was put minutes into the
programme by Fay Evans, a matron who had previously been asked to
leave the Breakspear by Dr Monro.

FAY EVANS   I think that some patients would have been far better
             served consulting psychologists or a psychiatrist.

The principal weakness with such diagnoses is that they tend to fall
apart when put to the patients who suffer the illnesses. This was
something which the 'World in Action' programme had no intention
of doing. It was, however, this accusation which more than any other
insulted and hurt many of the patients who saw the programme or
were filmed in background shots.

David Pearson made a brief contribution to the allergy versus psychiatry argument, when he referred to his own research. Again there were no references given and no review of the research.

NARRATOR NHS experts say while many do not have allergies, they do have other problems which are often ignored. Particularly psychiatric problems, as research at Manchester has shown.

DAVID PEARSON

They [Pearson doesn't state who conducted the research or whether the research was his work] looked here at people who believed they have allergies. With only one exception, all of the patients who had the false belief that they suffered from food allergy would be considered to have a psychiatric illness by a psychiatrist.

Interestingly, Dr Pearson defines the research as being into patients who had 'false beliefs'. Dr Monro's patients, however, were not suffering from 'false beliefs' but from serious organically based illnesses. In this interview Dr Pearson attempts to deny the illnesses of the majority of Dr Monro's patients.

Fay Evans made a number of contributions to the programme, all about the way in which the Breakspear was run. In any fair appraisal of Dr Monro, other members of staff apart from Fay Evans would have been asked their opinion. It was, as well, important that Fay Evans' contributions against Dr Monro were weighed judiciously against her own nursing practice, which one impartial patient described later in a letter to the Independent Broadcasting Authority.

When I first became a patient here [at the Breakspear] I found her [Fay Evans] to be the most unstable and unsettling influence in the Hospital ... I would suggest that this was her problem and not the problem of the Hospital.

When the film approached the career of Dr Jean Monro, one of the country's foremost allergists, it was superficial and trivialising.

NARRATOR Three things that happened help explain her [Dr Monro's] rise to fame. The first was that she came

> across this book on Clinical Ecology ... But the book
> was just the first step.

Dr Jean Monro is not, nor ever has been, famous. To suggest that Dr
Monro's career began when she came across an out-of-date medical
text book is a journalistic absurdity, worthy of a bad biopic. The next
step, according to 'World in Action', was that Dr Monro met Dr Rea,
which is at least a passable truth. The third thing which turned her
into 'today's superstar took one more twist of fate'.

NARRATOR That came in 1980 when she [Dr Monro] came into
              contact with this woman pop singer Sheila Rossall.

Sheila Rossall had been treated by Dr Rea in America: she had not
been treated by Dr Monro. However, when Ms Rossall's expensive
stay in America began to embarrass the government, the Foreign
Office asked Dr Monro to go to America and accompany Rossall back
to Britain. Interestingly, William Waldegrave, later to become
Minister of Health in the Conservative Government, was President
of the 'Save Sheila Rossall Fund'. [26] The 'World in Action' programme
presented this mission undertaken by Dr Monro, in aid of a
controversial case on behalf of the Foreign Office, as if she and Dr
Rea were actually responsible for Rossall's illness.

The introduction of Dr Monro's relationship with Sheila Rossall
was the opportunity for Professor Maurice Lessof to comment on
multiple allergies, as they had been diagnosed in Rossall's case.

MAURICE LESSOF
              Well I think she has seen an awful lot of doctors and
              they all seem to have missed the diagnosis of multiple
              allergy. Now one allergy is usually fairly clear,
              sometimes difficult, but multiple allergies are usually
              a really obvious glaring, er, fierce sort of disease. So,
              er, although it seemed possible, we were rather
              sceptical.

Lessof, who has in the past worked quite closely with Caroline
Richmond, is a classical allergist. He is conservative in the extreme,
and insists that only allergies which are classic in their cause and
prognosis should be referred to as allergy. He did not examine Rossall,

nor were viewers presented with any symptomatic picture of her illness. In a way this was irrelevant because Professor Lessof was speaking a different language from Drs Monro and Rea, both of whom refer to the toxic effect of chemical allergens, and the depletion of the immune system, as precipitating allergic response. Professor Lessof's limited description of allergic responses includes only a few specific causal allergens, like pollen, milk, eggs, wheat, peanuts and an equally restricted number of symptoms, such as hives, running nose, inflammation and at the most extreme, headaches. Professor Lessof does not agree that a chronic debilitating illness, brought on by the accumulation of toxins or by a virus, can in part be manifest by 'allergic' responses.

What the film did not make clear about Sheila Rossall, or the other people mentioned or interviewed, was the fact that the National Health doctors they had attended had all failed to make a plausible diagnosis, or offer effective treatment.

At other points in the programme, Lessof made damning statements about the provocation neutralisation treatment which Dr Monro practises. Presumably making a reference to Jewett's paper in the *New England Journal of Medicine*,† Lessof said:

> There have been some major studies in the United States to try
> to evaluate these tests, totally impartially, and the short answer is
> that they were shown to be of no value whatsoever.

That certainly is a 'short answer'. A slightly longer one would have entailed giving references and discussing the fact that the Jewett paper was criticised and discredited on a wide variety of grounds by a large number of orthodox doctors as well as clinical ecologists, following its publication.

The appraisal of 'provocation neutralisation' treatment was intellectually low-key. Lessof made the point that patients only thought they had been cured because they were ignorant of the fact that science had shown Dr Monro's treatments did not work. He was then asked by the interviewer 'What are the other tests?' Whatever the question meant, *all* meaning was lost on the cutting room floor,

† See this Chapter above.

because Lessof appeared to answer:

> I think that some of it is little more than a racket. I mean large
> sums of money change hands for some of this treatment.

This statement, made in the context of discussing Dr Monro's treatment, was one of the most shocking of the programme because, inevitably, a 'racket' implies a criminal deception, something which was further supported by Lessof's allusion to 'large' but unspecified 'sums of money'. Professor Lessof's salary was not disclosed.

In a concluding remark at the end of the programme, Professor Lessof made a lightly veiled accusation of misconduct against Dr Monro.

> I personally think that the General Medical Council should step
> in far more often than it does. You know, I mean, there are faults
> in the profession and one sees a lot of publicity for people who
> misconduct themselves, and in all kinds of ways, but not in this
> way. Now I think this is far more important to patients than
> some of the other misdemeanours of doctors.

The film was littered with prejudicial and personal innuendo about Dr Monro's lifestyle, none of which was supported by evidence. The film suggested in a derogatory way that Dr Monro had worked as 'an unpaid assistant at London's National Hospital for Nervous Diseases', where she had given 'bizarre experimental treatment to migraine patients'. Because of this, the programme inferred, 'the Hospital refused to renew her contract'.

'Working as an unpaid assistant' makes it appear that Dr Monro's work was menial. In fact she was working as an honorary research doctor, at the National Hospital, while her wage was being paid by Edgware Health Authority. What were the bizarre treatments for migraine? Dr Monro's research showed that migraine was often a consequence of food intolerance and so she treated patients with restricted diets. She was very successful in these treatments. Dr Monro did not have a contract with the National Hospital and she was not sacked, but resigned.

The film consistently accused Dr Monro of earning large amounts of money and having a luxurious lifestyle. At one point her house was shown on screen. If this image was supposed to support this idea of an extravagant lifestyle, it failed miserably. It is ten years since Dr Monro had her house re-decorated. It is five years since she allowed herself a holiday. The Breakspear Hospital was described as 'plush', while it could more reasonably be described as 'spartan'.

By far the most destructive evidence about Dr Monro's practices came unwittingly from the two patients who had thought that they were taking part in a programme which supported Dr Monro's treatment. The 'World in Action' team was highly selective with the two patients. By using Maureen Rudd and Blanche Panton, the film was able to focus on the tragedies which appeared to have accompanied treatment at the Breakspear Hospital.

Thousands of patients have passed through Dr Monro's hands over the last few years prior to the programme, and her success rate is remarkable. While it will always be possible to find people who feel that they have been charged too much, it would be exceptionally hard to find more than a handful of people who are dissatisfied with the medical treatment they have received from Dr Monro. The ultimate and most damning criticism of the 'World in Action' programme, and the fact which points most alarmingly to its involvement with vested interests, is that it did not interview any patients whose successful treatment had been accompanied by a new and healthier life. The programme interviewed only two patients, both of whom had been treated with relative success but whose return to health had been marred by factors unrelated to Dr Monro's treatment.

By way of explanation that only two interviews with patients were shown on the programme, the narrator made the following bizarre statement:

NARRATOR During research for this programme, 'World in Action' spoke to many of Dr Monro's patients. It was felt that the majority were too distressed to be interviewed.

This statement it not only untrue but worse, the insinuation was that Dr Monro had in some way distressed the patients. The truth was that some of Dr Monro's patients were very ill, and a number were further distressed by being contacted by 'World in Action'. Many of those approached refused outright to have anything to do with the programme. This was undoubtedly because Wood selectively approached those patients who appeared to be in tragic circumstances.

The cutting and the editing of small parts of the two interviews, and their presentation out of context, to make it appear that the interviewees were unhappy and sceptical about Monro's treatment, was a masterpiece of propaganda.

The first snip of Blanche Panton's interview was used in the introduction of the programme, as part of the prosecution case.

BLANCHE PANTON

> Financially it has devastated me. I am now £5,000 – over £5,000 – in debt to the Hospital. I need further treatment.

Blanche Panton's worst fears were realised: a ten-second clip from her forty-minute interview was used to suggest that Dr Monro massively overcharged patients. In fact Blanche Panton made only a small payment to the Breakspear and although she was sent accounts for the full bill the Company did not pursue payment.

The programme continually raised the question of treatment cost, while failing to give comparative costs or details of any treatments made available by the NHS. There was a very good reason for this. The NHS does not recognise chemical sensitivity or multiple allergies and therefore has no treatments available.

BLANCHE PANTON

> It seemed to work out at about £150-£180 a day because one is receiving specialised treatment in an environment which is filtered, where there are no pollutants at all.

MAUREEN RUDD

> Well, it is an expensive treatment because it involves one nurse to one patient, and the actual testing at the beginning is time-consuming and we quite understand that, but it probably cost us between £12,000 and £15,000, I should think.

This last remark of Maureen Rudd's was not qualified and the viewer was not given the information that six members of her family had all been treated for allergy-related illnesses. Again and again the question of money was brought up, always as if it were the treatment and financial costs which were causing the damage, rather than the illness itself.

NARRATOR Dr Monro's Breakspear Hospital is only the most successful of about a dozen clinics providing the treatment to thousands of patients. People like Blanche Panton. After two years under Dr Monro she can now no longer afford it. But she still believes in the treatment, even though her situation has deteriorated and her family has broken up.

Blanche Panton and her husband separated before she began receiving treatment from Dr Monro, and Blanche was increasingly unable to afford private medical treatment because of her reduced circumstances. When Blanche stopped having treatment from Dr Monro, her health deteriorated.

BLANCHE PANTON

At first we were given the injection. Then we were shown how to do it. And it was a very frightening, terrifying experience, having to do it, oneself, to oneself, sticking a needle in. But the benefit of doing that far outweighed crossing the initial fear barrier.

As with much else in the film, a perfectly ordinary medical practice was made to appear sinister. The treatment of both William Rudd and Blanche Panton was made to appear bizarre and ritualistic; no chance was given to Dr Monro, or any other specialist, to talk about the damaging effect of ambient chemicals, pharmaceutical treatments or even everyday toxic hazards.

NARRATOR William Rudd was a Breakspear patient. He started Dr Monro's treatment with great hope but he finished it as he was told to, living in this caravan in his parents' garden. It was lined with tinfoil to protect him. The television was enclosed behind glass.

BLANCHE PANTON

At the moment I am semi-fasting most days, and have to be very careful about where I go and what I do, unless I become very ill again. And those times are getting more and more frequent. It means that the bottom line is that I will have to sell the property I am in, which I only own one third of, so I will have to pay back the money I owe to the hospital, plus pay for further treatment, which will leave me with no roof over my head, nowhere to live, and most of all – no money.

The programme left the last words to Maureen Rudd and Blanche Panton, the juxtaposition of their remarks inferring that Dr Jean Monro's treatment had lost Blanche her child, and pushed William Rudd to suicide.

BLANCHE PANTON

The worst thing has meant that I have lost my child. She has been taken away from me and has been made a Ward of Court because the people who are caring for her do not believe that my illness is what is known as 'Total Allergy Syndrome', and also do not believe that Jade has any sensitivity to food or allergy.

MAUREEN RUDD

William did try to keep going, but it was a very great struggle and so he conceded defeat and ... organised his own death very well; he died within about 25 yards of where he was born, and it's still rather hard to talk about.

At this point Maureen Rudd became tearful, leaving the viewer with the lasting impression of the apparent misery which Dr Jean Monro's treatments had caused.

* * *

The Campaign Against Health Fraud used the media extensively to bolster the bias of its 'World in Action' programme. Wood spent time on the phone advertising the programme, so that it would have maximum pre-release publicity. The journalists who talked to Wood had not seen the programme and simply believed that what he told them was backed with detailed evidence. Many of the pre-release newspaper reports in fact contained information which was not in the programme. This extra information was even less objectively presented than the material in the 'World in Action' programme itself.

The principal offender was the *Observer*, which ran an eight column quarter page article entitled, 'Storm over allergy remedies for cancer' [27] by Annabel Ferriman. The article led with a reiteration of the title: 'Dr Jean Monro, the 'total allergy' expert, faces criticism tomorrow for giving unproven remedies to cancer victims and psychiatrically disturbed patients at her alternative medicine hospital'. Some patients at the Breakspear were now definitely categorised, by Annabel Ferriman at least, as 'psychiatrically disturbed'.

The allegation about cancer patients came from a statement made by Fay Evans, during the programme.

NARRATOR   Meanwhile at the Breakspear, allergy treatment was being given to patients with an expanding range of conditions, from ME to even cancer.

FAY EVANS   Our first cancer patient was admitted fairly soon after the Hospital opened. I was very concerned about this, as was the doctor and the other members of the nursing staff, because Breakspear was not equipped to deal with high dependency patients and we didn't have the equipment.

By distorting the truth about the treatment and the patients, the *Observer* tried to make it appear that Dr Monro was *treating cancer*, when she was actually treating *cancer patients*. The maximum period of residence at the Breakspear Hospital at this time was twelve days, during which time, patients were given treatment and therapies which de-toxified their systems, desensitised them to certain allergens and built up their immune system. The cancer patient referred to in the programme stayed only one night at the Breakspear before being transferred to an orthodox hospital for a blood transfusion.

When Dr Monro was asked about the cancer patient in the programme she answered as any immunologist would have answered.

INTERVIEWER

Are you saying that your allergy treatment, desensitisation, has a role in tackling cancer?

JEAN MONRO

I think that it has a role to play in alleviating symptoms because most chronic diseases have problems of a body's immunity.

The problem of living with or overcoming cancer, whether the patient is treated by orthodox or alternative medicine, is clearly linked to the patient's immune system. By resolving problems of allergy and toxicity, the doctor alleviates the pressure on the immune system. In fact, Dr Monro did not treat the patient mentioned by Fay Evans for cancer.

The *Observer* article used interviews with two patients who did not appear on the programme, one 23 year old schizophrenic called 'Tom' and the other a middle-aged teacher called Maureen who suffered from ME. There has been much research done on schizophrenia, diet and food intolerance, especially in the United States. The treatment which Dr Monro gave 'Tom', was a combination of orthodox psychotropic drugs, diet and vaccines for allergy. While Annabel Ferriman says that he 'did not improve', Dr Monro says that after years of being given a poor prognosis by NHS doctors, 'Tom' was at the time of the article 'much better'. As with the programme itself, in the *Observer* article half-truths are not measured against facts.

The *Sunday Mirror*, in its report, toed the health-fraud line, with its purple headline 'Shock probe on "Fergie hospital": Fears over treatment for cancer patients'. [28] Suddenly the one patient who had suffered with cancer when attending the Breakspear became one of many and it appeared as if the hospital was a centre for cancer treatment. A 'Shock probe' is obviously a very serious and weighty tribunal, but its exact nature is not known.

The *Sunday Mirror* article quotes Barry Wood making two generalised statements, which add to the sinister aura presented by the writer Brian Roberts: 'We spoke to patients who parted with large sums of money ... Dr Monro's methods had led to a stream of staff leaving the hospital'. [29]

The *News of the World* also gave Wood the opportunity to air his personal views about the Breakspear, in a short advertisement for the programme entitled, 'Fergie Clinic in TV probe'. [30] The article reports Wood as saying that the Breakspear was 'peddling a questionable treatment'. The 'World in Action' programme would, he claimed, show that patients, 'including cancer sufferers, received treatment that may be irrelevant'.

The *Sunday Telegraph*, the day before the programme, alone of all the papers presented an unbiased and well written account of the treatment given by Dr Monro. [31] The article was accompanied by a large photograph of Linda and Peter Strickland, who had built a pollutant-free bedroom in their north London home. The Stricklands recounted how their lives had been transformed following Dr Monro's treatment.

Immediately following the 'World in Action' programme, Dr Monro began to fight back. With the help of ex-patients, and parents of ex-patients, she began looking for media outlets that would allow her to state her point of view. Lorraine Hoskin was particularly committed to redressing the balance because of the health-giving treatment Dr Monro had given to Samantha. She became one of the two joint secretaries of a newly-formed Breakspear Support Committee and began working strenuously to get publicity. Although, by now, it was apparent to most people that there were covert influences at work behind the 'World in Action' programme, few people knew what those influences were.

During the following month, Lorraine managed to publicise her daughter's case in three influential vehicles, the *Mirror* women's page [32], the (Basildon) *Evening Echo* [33] and in a London Weekend Television 'News Round-up' item. [34]

The *Mirror* article, written by Catherine O'Brien, was the only popular feature article at the time to suggest that there was a struggle going on between orthodox and alternative medicine.

> The war being waged is bitter and bloody, as two hospitals in the alternative field are finding out. The Bristol Cancer Help Centre and Breakspear Hospital are fighting closure following fierce attacks from the medical establishment. [35]

It was this article in the *Mirror* which first gave national exposure to

Samantha Hoskin, who figured prominently in a photograph, surrounded by the foods and chemical sprays – trade names easily visible – which made her allergic. Although the article dealt as well with the Bristol Cancer Help Centre, it focused on Samantha, outlining the nightmare illness she had endured before her mother had found Dr Monro. Following Samantha's story, 'HealthWatch chairman and former scientist Caroline Richmond' was quoted as saying: 'Most people who believe that they are suffering from food allergies are really suffering from *easily treatable* psychiatric disorders.' (italics added) [36]

It was in fact this remark by Caroline Richmond which drove Lorraine Hoskin into a fury. Lorraine was beside herself. What an incredible cheek Richmond had, suggesting that her five year old child, seriously ill from birth, suffered not from some organically based sickness but from mental illness.

Catherine O'Brien also turned to Vincent Marks for a quote. His approach was slightly more sophisticated than Richmond's: 'A lot of so-called alternative medicine is now being recognised as old fashioned folk medicine that became obsolete with advances in science.' The urbane and normally 'sleeping' joint president of HealthWatch, Nick Ross, also gave his opinions in the article. Ross claimed to be 'very much in favour of Bristol', while opposed to those groups who were unwilling to put their treatments to any kind of test. He said that HealthWatch was not against complementary medicine but against alternative medicine: 'What we are against is literally alternative therapy, where practitioners try to persuade a patient against conventional medicine in favour of their own methods. That is outrageous, and can cost lives.' [37] It is not clear how this quote relates to another quote given by Ross in the same article: 'I am all for patient choice.' [38]

The *Mirror* article is also exceptional in quoting Professor Timothy McElwain, one of the authors of the damaging *Lancet* paper on the Bristol Cancer Help Centre.

On Wednesday October 31st the *Evening Echo* carried a quarter page story about Samantha Hoskin, headlined 'Mum defends tot's specialist'. [39] In this article too, Lorraine Hoskin, who had become quickly and intelligently acquainted with the personnel and tactics of HealthWatch, draws them into the limelight: 'Without the Breakspear,

Lorraine claims, Samantha would not be alive today. But she fears a backlash after 'World in Action' visited the Hospital, spoke to a health watch group, nicknamed Quackbusters, and claimed the treatment was often ineffective'. [41] Sandra Hembery who wrote the article in the *Evening Echo*, approached Nick Hayes, Editor of the 'World in Action' programme; he said: 'Our programme was an impartial investigation into the value of the treatment ... we were able to come up with precious few arguments in favour of the treatment.' [42]

Lorraine Hoskin was not content with articles in the newspapers; she quickly became the Secretary of the 'Breakspear Hospital Friends and Supporters Group', and set up a new organisation called the Parents and Children Allergies Sufferers Support Group. Lorraine unleashed a stream of letters, contacted a wide variety of people who she felt might help, and picketed the Granada Television offices in London. With the energy of a mother who saw the health of her daughter jeopardised, Lorraine began banging on doors she did not know existed a year before. She wrote to the General Medical Council and began contacting other parents who were as upset about the programme as she was.

When the *Mirror* article and others, featuring Samantha Hoskin, took on HealthWatch, they precipitated Lorraine and her daughter onto the centre of the stage. Just like the interviewees involved in the Bristol Cancer Help Centre study,† they became civilians caught up in what the *Mirror* journalist had described as a 'bitter and bloody war'.

* * *

Not surprisingly, doctors are not best equipped to deal with politically motivated attacks. First and foremost they are doctors. and it is not easy to begin campaigning when you have sick people waiting to see you. Dr Monro was caught between her commitment to her patients and her 'political' intuition. Her instinct told her to respond immediately.

For advice following the programme, Dr Monro turned to a barrister and to her professional body, the Medical Defence Union

† See Chapter Thirty Six

(MDU). The barrister confirmed her impression that she had a good case against Granada for libel, but suggested that any action could cost as much as £100,000. The Medical Defence Union seemed unwilling to help, although Dr Monro had paid her dues since she first became a doctor.

By the time that the MDU was ready to advise Dr Monro, she had struck her own first blow. With Lorraine Hoskin she went on London Weekend Television. In the short news report, Dr Monro with a certain disregard for semantic accuracy, said that HealthWatch was a group, of 'self-styled doctors'. HealthWatch quickly sent off a solicitor's letter to Dr Monro, demanding an apology. Dr Monro realised that the Medical Defence Union was not going to take her side in the conflict over the 'World in Action' programme when they advised her to urgently apologise to Caroline Richmond for the remark.

* * *

Lorraine Hoskin was deeply hurt by the 'World in Action' programme. Apart from the serious injustice of it, she could see future treatment opportunities for children like Samantha receding. She was also angry with herself, having been taken in by Barry Wood.

The day after the programme, she rang Wood to complain. He rang her back and she had the distinct impression that her conversation was being tape recorded. Lorraine thought it best to reassure him that she didn't blame him, as he was only the programme's research worker. She asked him why someone had decided to make that kind of programme. Wood insisted that it was his producer who was responsible. Lorraine asked him how the Campaign Against Health Fraud had come to be so deeply involved in a Granada programme and asked him whether he knew they were related to the Wellcome Foundation. Faced with awkward questions, and with no desire to be held responsible to Lorraine Hoskin, Wood quickly tired of the conversation.

Lorraine Hoskin, however, is a fighter and she was determined to fight for the continued treatment of Samantha and for the Breakspear. In November, a few weeks after the programme, in concert with other angry parents, she set up the Friends and Supporters of Breakspear (FSB). Within a short time, this group gathered a large membership and Lorraine and others managed to mobilise hundreds of supporters. The group had seven voluntary committee members, and in its first weeks of existence it began a furious media blitz, getting stories on as many programmes and in as many newspapers as possible. Early in November, Lorraine managed to get an item on Thames Television local news. Samantha was filmed, as was Dr Monro. She also managed to get on early morning television, again with Samantha.

Samantha's story was a potent one, and had Lorraine Hoskin been able to keep up the media pressure, it is clear she would have been able to claw back some of Dr Monro's lost credibility. Unfortunately, Lorraine was relatively naive about the kind of battle she was plunging into. She made her first mistake when she put her home address and telephone number at the top of the first FSB bulletin. Nearly three years later, Lorraine was still dealing with the political fall-out of dirty tricks which followed her excursion into medical politics.

Lorraine Hoskin is not given to paranoia but as the Support Group got off the ground, she began to notice the atmosphere of her life changing. The day following her interview with Thames TV, which took place at her home, she started to have problems with her telephone.

The oppressive sense that someone was listening to or monitoring her telephone calls led her, four days after the interview, to ring a special British Telecom number, where she was given advice about possible phone taps. It was three days before BT engineers called at her house to tell her that, although when she had called them someone had been interfering with her line, the line was now clear.

Lorraine would probably have thought little more about her phone, had it not been for an odd incident in January 1991. One morning she received a call from a man whom she did not know but who lived only a few streets away. The conversation was confusing. The man had rung her after getting her telephone number from one of her friends. He had rung her friend, because the friend's telephone number appeared on an itemised telephone bill which he had received but which was not his. Lorraine went to see the man.

The itemised bill which the man had received listed all the outgoing calls made from Lorraine Hoskin's phone from the day of the Thames Television interview until the time that she made the call to the BT phone tapping unit. Appended to the end of the list were a couple of phone calls actually made by the man who had received the bill.

In the list of outgoing numbers called from Lorraine's phone, my number appears, showing the phone call which I received from her asking if I would investigate HealthWatch. When I was shown the list in January 1991, I recalled that I had received a number of odd calls in the days following my conversation with Lorraine. The calls I received were all the same; when I picked up the phone, contrary to the normal procedure, it was I who was asked who I was. Involved in an investigation, as I was then, I am guarded about answering such calls and instead asked the caller who they were; on one occasion I was given the name of a London company which did not exist in the phone book.

When calls are monitored rather than tapped, a task that can be carried out by a BT engineer simply by flicking a switch, the agency which has commissioned the information has to ring all the listed numbers in order to find who subscribes to them. The recipient is then able to build up a 'field' of regular friends and contacts of the person under surveillance. These people in turn can become targets for dirty tricks or rumour information.

When she got hold of the itemised list, Lorraine Hoskin rang a number of the people on the list, only to find that, like me, they had all received similar information-gathering phone calls.

There is nothing you can do in Britain if private parties, such as detective agencies, or government agencies, monitor your calls or even record your conversations. The police respond with quizzical indifference and suggestions of paranoia to such claims. In Lorraine's case, one of the women on the FSB committee was married to a police officer who was deeply perturbed about his private phone number appearing on a list; he consequently made an official complaint to a senior police officer at his station. The complaint pushed the police into a lazy enquiry during which they joked to complainants that 'phone tapping was a bit off their beaten track'.

Campaigns of intimidation and harassment against people who demonstrate opposition to the food and pharmaceutical industries as well as other big businesses follow conventional patterns. They can consist of minor aggravations, such as feeding bad credit-ratings into the system, through to death threats, and grossly intimidating physical attacks. They may also involve burglaries, blackmail, phone-tapping and mail intercepts. None of these activities can be traced back to the vested interests which originate them. Work is passed from industry associations or company middle management to public relations firms and then on to discreet and unprincipled firms of private investigators. Beyond such firms the threads weave out into the criminal communities of large cities and to men who will do most things if the price is right. These men are not familiar with the issues: they are paid, given information about targets, and told how far they can go.

The lexicon of industrial sabotage and dirty tricks is voluminous and, although most basic moves have a history in the work of the intelligence services and other secret organisations, they are often adapted and tailored to fit new circumstances. For nearly three years following her decision to fight back in defence of the Breakspear Hospital, Lorraine Hoskin found herself the subject of a sporadic but identifiable campaign of serious harassment.

In February 1991, Lorraine received a letter from an insurance company. The company was making a substantial claim on behalf of their client against Lorraine for damage to their client's car. Lorraine Hoskin thought little about the letter; she knew that it did not involve her and thought that there must have been some kind of mix-up.

As the months went by, with her own insurance company acting on her behalf, the case took on a bizarre dimension. The claim had been made by a doctor, who said, through his central London solicitors, that on September 6th 1990, Lorraine Hoskin's mini-van – the correct registration number was given – had backed into his car, in the centre of Basildon, causing well over a thousand pounds worth of damage. There were just three problems with the claim. Firstly, Lorraine Hoskin was not in Basildon on the day in question. Secondly, her van is a camper van and not a mini-van and, thirdly, Lorraine knows full well that she did not have any accidents during the stated period.

Despite protestations from Lorraine's insurance company solicitors, the case dragged on until the end of 1992. It became evident to Lorraine's solicitors that a disproportionate amount of energy and money were being poured into the case. In Lorraine's opinion, the case lost any resemblance to an accident claim and began to look more like a campaign against her.

Taken on their own, any of the bizarre and uncomfortable things which have happened to Lorraine could be accidents or coincidences. Placed in context, however, it seems more likely that they were steps in a planned campaign.

In the past, Lorraine Hoskin has bred dogs. She and her husband originally bought a house with a large garden at the back, so that Lorraine could build runs for puppies. She used to specialise in breeding large mountain dogs. She had kept two of the dogs which she bred, one, called Pru, she was particularly fond of. Early in November 1990, on a Sunday afternoon, Lorraine and her husband returned home from a family outing to find Pru dead.

In order to divide their kitchen into an area for cooking, which led onto the back garden, and an area for working, Lorraine's husband had built a pine gate in between two chest-height dividing walls across the kitchen. At the top of the gate the flat upright slats extended a couple of inches above a cross bar. Pru, a very large and powerful dog, appeared to have trapped her two front paws, a foot apart, between the gate's uprights. The vet, who described the death as odd, suggested that the dog must have got her paws caught, then struggling to get out had a heart attack. Lorraine was devastated by the death of Pru and her grief stopped her from putting questions to the vet which might have told her more about the dog's death. Why, for instance, was there blood on the wall near the dog and yet no lacerations anywhere on the dog?

In the autumn of 1991, Lorraine's second dog died, again under mysterious circumstances. Returning home in the early evening after a weekend day out, Lorraine found that, despite the fact that the gates were locked and the surrounding fence was secure, the dog had left the back garden. Later that evening, the dog became ill, retching and vomiting. Over the following three days, the dog's condition worsened to the point where it was feared that it would die. Although over the next few weeks the dog showed some improvement, this was quickly followed by lethargy and a refusal to eat. When it became evident that the dog was still seriously ill and in some pain, the vet recommended that it be put down.

The veterinary surgeon's diagnosis of the dog's illness was quite definite. In his opinion, the dog had died as the result of severe toxic poisoning. The death of both her dogs, and especially Pru, overshadowed two years of Lorraine's life, looming against a consistent backdrop of threats and harassment.

Within a week of appearing on the London Weekend Television

programme, Lorraine Hoskin received her first threatening phone call. Over the following five months, she received three such phone calls, each of which suggested that she would be killed or injured.

The most worrying telephone call, however, came in December 1990. At home alone one evening, Lorraine received a call from a distraught woman, who accused her of having an affair with her husband. Lorraine tried to calm the woman down. Finding out her name, she managed to reassure her that she didn't even know her husband. The woman, whose name was Phyllis Bass, finally told Lorraine that she had rung and accused her because she had come across Lorraine's phone number in a notebook belonging to her husband.

It transpired that it wasn't simply Lorraine's phone number which was noted in Geoffrey Bass's notebook. Phyllis Bass read to Lorraine over the phone other information which she said her husband had written down. Although there were only scraps of information, some of it was quite specific; Lorraine's age was correctly noted as 31 and, despite the fact that Lorraine has no trace of a Scottish accent, her nationality was noted as Scottish, along with her telephone number and address. Other information suggested that Lorraine had a six-year problem with alcoholism and that she had spent time hospitalised and on a life-support system as a consequence. In fact, Lorraine does not have an alcohol problem but a member of her extended family did have a six-year fight with alcoholism and did end up in hospital on a life-support system.

Although Lorraine managed to persuade Phyllis Bass that she did not know her husband, the phone call distressed her. For the first time, Lorraine knew definitely that someone, whom she did not know and had no links with, had information about her: she could only think that the information had been gathered to do her harm.

Lorraine rang to ask my advice; I told her that she must ring Phyllis Bass back and obtain as much information as possible about Geoffrey Bass before she reported the matter to the police. Lorraine did this and then rang the local police. The police involvement in the case from that point onwards is a tale of scepticism and lack of commitment. Lorraine told the police that she had been receiving threatening phone calls and that Phyllis Bass had told her about her husband's notebook. The police, however, refused to call on Phyllis Bass.

In Romford, where the Bass's lived, Geoffrey Bass returned home and, finding what she had done, had an argument with his wife. Furious that she had phoned Lorraine Hoskin, he rang Lorraine to say that his wife had got it all wrong, he neither knew nor had any information about her.

Later still that evening, Phyllis Bass rang Lorraine again saying that she had now destroyed her husband's notebook. Lorraine, realising that good evidence was disappearing, rang Romford police station again and told them she wanted something done immediately about Phyllis and Geoffrey Bass, because in her opinion they might be linked to the threatening phone calls which she had been receiving.

The following day, Lorraine heard again from Phyllis Bass, who seemed to be speaking under instructions from her husband. She sounded tearful and upset. She told Lorraine that she was ringing from the police station where she had gone of her own volition to sort the whole matter out. She told the police that it had all been a mistake, there was no notebook. Phyllis Bass told Romford police that she had suspected her husband of having an affair and that, while looking in the telephone directory she had seen a dot vaguely situated next to the name of Hoskin and had decided to ring that number.

Geoffrey Bass, it transpired, had, until relatively recently, managed an 'animal rendering business'. 'Animal rendering' occurs at the most corrupted end of the processed food chain; it involves using a variety of techniques to force the last bits of meat from bones and use them either in pet foods or human meat products. Rendering also uses all the various aspects of animal carcasses. At the time of the phone calls Bass was working for a mini-cab company. Two police investigations of this incident have concluded that Geoffrey Bass was not involved in any campaign against Lorraine Hoskin.

Because of the relatively serious incidents which were occurring around Lorraine Hoskin and her family, and not knowing whether I was in some way responsible for attracting the incidents to her, I began to restrict my meetings with her. In January 1991, I had occasion to see her to discuss my investigation.

I had not long returned home after meeting Lorraine when I received a phone call from her. After I had left her house, she had gone out to her van which was parked on a quiet, narrow road outside her house. As she was standing in the road, strapping her youngest child into the passenger seat, a car, which she thought started-

up from a stationary position, suddenly drove towards her at speed. She threw herself against the side of the van and the car sped off. Lorraine was sure that the car, containing two men, had driven at her.

The telephone monitoring incident, the matter of Geoffrey Bass and the death of Lorraine's second dog were all reported to the police. Investigations begun by different officers continued lazily and without commitment on and off until the first quarter of 1992. The police came up with no answers, perhaps because from the beginning they refused to ask the right questions. In Britain, industrial and commercial dirty tricks which originate from apparently respectable businesses, are on the whole an invisible statistic, a ghostly occurrence. The fact that profit is the ultimate motive for the harassment of Lorraine Hoskin, makes the crimes committed against her little different from those of any common burglar or street robber. This does not, however, convince the police to adopt new perspectives or champion new victims.

Meanwhile, Lorraine Hoskin has retired from the battlefield of health care. Despite being a strong woman, she found the cost of defending democratic choice in her daughter's treatment too high.

*   *   *

'The Allergy Business' inevitably opened the door to a more general assault upon doctors dealing with allergy and chemical sensitivity, especially those practising 'provocation-neutralisation' treatment. The 'World in Action' programme was seen by many orthodox doctors as a kind of precedent. Really, it was nothing of the kind: the case against environmental medicine was not proven by the programme because the majority of the programme's information was not substantiated.

The strategy of HealthWatch and its members in relation to environmental medicine between 1989 to 1991 involved gathering a quantity of information which appeared to prove its case. In the main, this information was not scientific, and HealthWatch rarely turned to science to validate its arguments. What stands out most about this body of 'information', is the fact that it was self-generated, and little if any of it had been assessed by any peer review process.

In Manchester, the doctors who were campaigning against 'provocation-neutralisation' and other allergy diagnostic techniques and treatments made immediate use of 'The Allergy Business'. Granada Television quickly produced another programme, this time in the 'Up Front' series. Caroline Richmond and David Pearson both worked on the programme. To gather information for it, the producers sent a female researcher, masquerading as a patient, to the Manchester allergy practitioner Dr David Freed.

Dr David Freed

Dr David Freed received a call from a young woman saying that she needed to see him urgently with an allergy problem. As is his practice, Freed told the woman that she must first see her general practitioner and obtain a referral. The woman, however, insisted that she needed to see him urgently and didn't have time to see her GP. Dr Freed was able to fit in an appointment two days later, in his lunch hour.

When the woman arrived, Dr Freed could see straight away that she had no alarming or urgent symptoms. Because he always takes patients seriously, Freed assumed that the woman must have been alarmed about something which to her was real, so he gave her a thorough examination.

The 'patient' gave Dr Freed a list of symptoms; he however was mystified, since neither the alleged symptoms nor the physical findings seemed to justify the urgency she had claimed. He was unable to find anything glaringly wrong with her, and he told her so. During a careful examination he did find an area of soft tissue rheumatism in the woman's neck. Though fairly common, and only rarely turning into an acute condition, such areas can sometimes be the harbingers of rheumatoid disease in later life.

Dr Freed could only think that the 'patient' must be in the very early stages of rheumatoid disease, before the blood tests became positive, and that the stiff neck and fatigue that she had claimed to have must be much worse than it appeared.

He advised the 'patient' that as far as he could see there was no urgency to the problem, which might or might not ever develop into arthritis. He said that if she wanted to ensure that the problem did not develop she could undergo a programme of treatment. As soon as the patient had left he wrote, as he always did, to her general practitioner:

> Miss Jones consulted me on 17th October complaining of a chronic
> fatigue syndrome of a couple of years duration. On examination I
> discovered multiple rheumatic patches in the neck, and I suspect
> that she may be in the early prodromal stage of rheumatoid
> disease. Blood tests are likely to be non-contributory, but I would
> be most grateful if you could let me have a sight of any tests results
> you have had on this young lady in the last two years. [43]

Two days after Dr Freed had seen the patient, he received a phone
call from a programme maker at Granada, who said that they were
about to screen a programme on allergies and asked if he would like to
appear with some of his 'successful patients'. The programme maker
tried to entice Freed onto the programme by claiming that it would be
'good publicity' for him.

Dr Freed would have liked to help correct the imbalance created by
'The Allergy Business', which he had watched with dismay. He had to
refuse the invitation, however, because he is an orthodox Jew and the
programme was scheduled to go out live on a Friday night – the start
of the Jewish Sabbath. Instead, after first checking with the patients, he
offered the programme makers the names of a couple of his patients.
None of Dr Freed's patients were contacted by the programme.

On the day of the programme, Dr Freed was rung and asked again
to go on the programme. He was now told that the female patient he
had seen was actually a programme researcher. The 'patient' was
going to appear on the programme telling the audience that Dr Freed
had claimed she had rheumatoid arthritis.

The programme had apparently sent the 'patient' to a consultant
physician and rheumatologist,† who had told her, after a blood test,
categorically that she did not have rheumatoid arthritis. Freed was told
that he should go on the programme and justify his diagnosis. He was
furious, and especially angry that he had been taken advantage of by a
patient he had only seen out of ordinary hours because he was
concerned about her. Leaving the office that day to pick up his step-
son from school, he was just in time to see a camera crew with the
bogus patient hurrying towards his surgery.

The programme itself was presented as a kind of trial. Although Dr
Freed did not appear, a colleague of his from Manchester, Dr Mumby,

---

† The 'consultant rheumatologist' turned out to be Dr David Pearson.

did do so. Dr Keith Mumby is perhaps slightly more robust that Dr Freed and although he had had previous disputes with Dr Pearson, he felt capable of defending his practice on the programme. The programme began with the bogus patient, who made it clear that she had presented invented symptoms to Dr Freed. She then claimed that Dr Freed had told her that she would have to have a £600 course of treatment and change her diet.

After the bogus patient had provided the news starter for the programme, it moved on to Dr Mumby, whom they had seated alone, in a large black chair in the middle of the studio. Facing him were rows of people who proceeded to examine him. The programme was a typical studio audience confrontation. Sitting in the front row of the inquisitors were Dr David Pearson and Dr Tim David and few rows further back Caroline Richmond. On the other side of the studio, beyond the 'hot seat' and facing the rows of critics, were three of Dr Mumby's patients.

That part of the programme which involved Dr Freed and 'exposed' his diagnosis took less than five minutes but the clear implication was that he was a quack who took money from vulnerable patients. There was nothing libellous said about Dr Freed, but the short exposure wrecked his practice.

> That programme killed off my practice. After that the telephone went completely silent, I didn't get any more referrals for about six months, then it started to build up again very, very slowly. Even a year later, I was still not making a living out of my practice. [44]

A few days after the programme had been broadcast, Dr Freed received a letter from the bogus patient's GP. Perhaps not anticipating that Dr Freed would adhere to GMC rules, and despite giving a false name, the 'patient' had given her GP's correct name and address. The woman's doctor who knew now what had happened apologised for the behaviour of his patient.

In Granada Television, Caroline Richmond and David Pearson had found a corporate mouthpiece for their 'vested interest' assaults upon alternative allergy doctors. After years of trying to destroy such practices by writing articles and making phone calls, Caroline Richmond now had a body of reporters and programme makers who were apparently willing to do her bidding.

If Dr Keith Mumby thought, as he was likely to think, that by appearing on the programme, arguing his case well, he had staved off future attacks upon his practice, he would soon have to think again.

Dr Keith Mumby

> I don't want sympathy and, with at the most a couple of exceptions, no help. But I feel that everyone ought to be warned what is in the wind. What is being attempted here is a serious hi-jacking of a statutory body, the General Medical Council, for the express purpose of suppressing freedom within medicine and eliminating people who practise medicine which is not politically correct. It has started against others, and the abusers of power, emboldened by the current climate ... are now attempting flagrant violations of rights. [45]

In July 1992, Dr Keith Mumby appeared before the GMC facing six substantive charges, and a wide range of subsidiary ones. A number of these charges related to four patients. For clinical ecologists, however, the most worrying stated that he claimed to be a 'specialist' in a treatment which was unsupported and unproven by scientific evidence.

Although Keith Mumby had managed to acquit himself well during the inquisition of 'Up Front', there was a moment when he faltered and didn't seem to know what to say. It was when his inquisitors suddenly produced a letter which he had written to a journalist friend two years before. The importance of the letter to his detractors lay in the fact that it informed the journalist about a successful case and suggested that therein might lie a good story. In the event, no story was written around the case and Dr Mumby's letter was thought to lie undisturbed in the journalist's filing cabinet at his place of work.

It was the appearance of the letter on the programme, rather than its contents, that threw Mumby. Following the programme he rang his journalist friend to ask how the letter had got from his office into the hands of critics. Apparently, one of the Granada researchers had previously worked with the journalist to whom Mumby had written. Not long before the programme, the researcher had approached a member of the paper's office team asking to borrow the office keys for the evening: the request had been turned down. Shortly afterwards there was a break-in at the office. Nothing valuable was stolen, but the letter went missing. This letter was to form the basis of the charge made by the GMC that Dr Mumby had touted for business.

Dr Keith Mumby was one of two doctors besides Dr Monro, who were originally investigated by Granada's 'World in Action' programme. What happened to the information which 'World in Action' gathered on other doctors, but did not use for a programme, is not known. In May 1991, however, a full page article appeared in the *Scotland on Sunday* [46] newspaper attacking Dr Mumby and the surgery which he held regularly in Glasgow. There seems little doubt that the initial information in this article was placed with the paper by people in contact with 'World in Action'.

The highly libellous article was littered with quotes from Dr David Pearson, Dr Tim David and Professor Barry Kay. The tone of the article is little different from the tone of 'The Allergy Business'; Dr Mumby is called a 'crook', his techniques are labelled as 'bogus', and his results put down to 'brainwashing'.

By far the most disturbing aspect of the attack upon Dr Mumby is that the material in the *Scotland on Sunday* article formed the basis for the complaint against Dr Mumby made to the GMC. As in Duncan Campbell's AIDS cases, a small cabal of orthodox doctors began their assault by making unsubstantiated and libellous claims against another doctor through the offices of journalists.

In Dr Mumby's case, the GMC appeared to depart radically from previous practice when it invited patients to tender complaints against him. In this departure the GMC mimicked its American counterparts, the AMA and the FDA, in beginning to act not simply as a professional disciplinary body, but assuming a wide-ranging investigative and prosecutorial function. Such functions should, theoretically, only be fairly assumed by bodies which act with complete independence and whose rules forbid the intervention of interest groups.

Throughout 1991, Dr Mumby heard frequent reports that the GMC was conducting an investigation into his practice, yet this was denied every time he contacted them. While denying its investigation, the GMC kept the media fully informed. It is clearly the case that investigations carried out by professional bodies should involve the subject of those investigations at the earliest occasion. Not to involve the suspect means that there is a presupposition of guilt, a fear that the subject in question, if interviewed, will be forewarned.

Professor Barry Kay, who gave quotes to *Scotland on Sunday* and was to appear as a GMC witness at Dr Mumby's hearing, was far from being a disinterested witness to the work of Dr Mumby. Since the end of 1988, Kay, who worked at the Brompton Hospital where the Concorde trials administration was based, had been heading a Royal College of Physicians (RCP) committee investigating 'alternative' allergy treatments. The RCP had been asked to write this report by the Department of Health. Also sitting on the committee was Dr Anthony Pinching. Dr David Pearson was giving evidence to it and Caroline Richmond was helping to write it up. Many of the public attacks upon allergy doctors working with 'provocation neutralisation' began during the period that this committee was sitting.

When Dr Mumby finally appeared before the GMC, the two witnesses who appeared to give evidence against him, Professor Barry Kay and Dr Anne Ferguson, had previously made clear their position against 'provocation neutralisation'. There are dozens of other British experts who could have been called, some of them equally eminent but with more balanced views: none were. The appearance of Professor Barry Kay at the hearing, showed clearly that the GMC supported the restriction or curtailment of certain non-orthodox specialised practices. It showed as well that as a quasi-legal tribunal, it lacked independence: its case had been built not upon open and above-board information from Dr Mumby's peers, but upon a journalistic smear campaign which a handful of doctors had helped engineer. At the conclusion of the GMC hearing, Dr Mumby was cleared of all the charges which related to his clinical practice. In relation to advertising and the letter which he sent to the journalist, he was 'severely admonished'.

* * *

Following the 'World In Action' programme, a large number of Dr Monro's patients wrote to her offering their sympathy and support. Most were amazed at the bias shown by the programme and some expressed concern that the producers had made no effort to interview any of the many patients whom Dr Monro had successfully treated.

Patients with long-term illnesses were afraid that the programme heralded the end of treatment at the Breakspear. A year after the programme, Dr Monro was forced to put her company into liquidation and close down the Breakspear Hospital. Although the effect of the programme on Dr Monro's practice was serious, and even more so for the staff whom she had to lay off, the most serious consequences were felt by those patients who were in the process of fighting legal actions for damages as a consequence of illnesses caused by chemicals.

In America, collective and individual legal actions against chemical and drugs firms brought by those who used their products or who had been accidentally contaminated, continued to escalate in the nineteen eighties. Base-line negotiation for compensation would often begin in the millions. If that trend crossed the Atlantic and came to Britain, many industrial chemical manufacturers and users, and many government agencies, would become increasingly vulnerable.

The outcome of any legal action for damages involving chemicals depends almost entirely upon the quality of expert witness testimony. In Britain there are few expert witnesses, especially clinicians, able to give testimony to the effects of toxic chemicals upon health. It was inevitable that the conflict between orthodox medicine and environmental medicine would eventually move into the court room where opposing expert witnesses could 'slug it out' usually to the detriment of the patient or claimant.

'The Allergy Business' seriously damaged Dr Monro's reputation and credibility as an expert witness. An analysis of two cases which were before the court after the programme was made shows clearly how it gave the chemical companies and other defendants a head-start in fighting claims made against them.

Liza Ensen†

Until 1985, Liza Ensen worked as a care worker for a Social Services

---

† The essential details and the names of the participants in this account have been changed.

Department in the Midlands. Her job, which was paid on the same scale as that of a home help, involved giving practical and emotional support to 'socially deprived families'.

In mid-1985, Liza was asked by her Department to use an insecticide in one of the houses which had previously been occupied by a client family. Over the next few months, she was increasingly called upon to carry out similar tasks, on occasions fumigating whole houses. The County Council Environmental Health Department, whose job this work had always been, and her own seniors, seemingly took advantage of Liza Ensen's good nature not only to extend her job description but also to give her specialised and possibly health damaging work to carry out. The insecticide which Mrs Ensen used on all occasions was an organophosphate.

In the autumn of 1985, Liza Ensen became ill and after attending a number of doctors who failed to give her a diagnosis, she found Dr Monro. By the time that she saw Dr Monro in January 1988, Mrs Ensen had, after discussion with her solicitors, decided to take an action for damages against her employers, the County Authority.

Liza Ensen underwent a course of treatment with Dr Monro, who also prepared a medical report for her solicitors. Since first meeting Dr Monro, Liza had complete faith in her; she considered her an excellent doctor, the only doctor, in fact, who had been able to help her with her condition.

Liza Ensen next acquired the support of her trade union Health and Safety Officer. He too wrote a sympathetic report for her solicitor. When she began a search for a toxicologist to act as an expert witness, her solicitor suggested that they approach a University department in the north of England; there they found a Dr Jardane. The solicitor made no checks on Dr Jardane to find whom he had previously been funded by, or who funded the department where he worked.

In July 1989, Liza Ensen's solicitors received a first report from Dr Jardane. This report was entirely sympathetic to her case. Then, in 1990, the attacks upon Dr Monro began. The criticisms percolated down to the University where Dr Jardane was employed, more importantly, to the department's funders which, it was later discovered, consisted almost entirely of pharmaceutical and chemical company representatives.

In July 1990, Dr Jardane submitted another report to Liza Ensen's solicitor. This report was supposed to make clear the 'exposure situation', that is, the likely quantity of exposure suffered by Mrs Ensen. This second report was not at all sympathetic to Mrs Ensen's general case. Instead of suggesting that, while working in relatively confined spaces, she had inhaled enough of the insecticide to make her ill, it proposed that she must have been idiosyncratically sensitive to the pesticide prior to her use of it.

Such an argument is *the* defence position of the chemical and pharmaceutical companies whose common argument it is that, used under the proper conditions, respecting the safety regulations and guidelines laid down, the average person can safely use their product. If, however, any of these guidelines are ignored, and if this is combined with use by a *particularly susceptible person* there is then a risk of health damage. With this line of defence the onus of risk is on the user rather than the manufacturer.

Dr Jardane's second report was found, even by Liza Ensen and her husband, to be so obviously flawed as to be of little value. Dr Jardane had based his report upon a model which owed everything to the maker's use-specification, and nothing to the specific conditions of use by Mrs Ensen. Dr Jardane had even contacted the product makers to canvass their opinion.

Perhaps more importantly, Dr Jardane now told Liza Ensen's solicitor that he was 'diametrically' opposed to the views – and treatments – of Dr Monro. As far as he was concerned, neither symptoms of poisoning nor any illness precipitated by exposure to organophosphates would persist as long as Mrs Ensen's. Dr Jardane was not a medical doctor and had no clinical experience; it would seem that he had been tutored in his prejudice against Dr Monro.

The Ensens viewed Jardane's second report as a clumsy attempt by him to withdraw his earlier support and distance his University from the case. There followed a series of 'discordant' letters between Liza Ensen's solicitors and Dr Jardane, in which attempts were made to get him to at least amend the factual errors which now appeared in his report. In the end, the Ensens took the expedient course of instructing their solicitors not to pay Dr Jardane for his report and requested that he no longer be used as an expert witness.

From October 1990, when Granada screened 'The Allergy

Business', Liza Ensen began to feel that her solicitor, far from rebuking Dr Jardane, was beginning to side with him against Dr Monro. Appalled by this possibility, the Ensens asked for a meeting with all the parties concerned.

These matters came to a head in the first half of 1991, when Mr and Mrs Ensen, Dr Jardane, Mrs Ensen's counsel, the solicitor and a trade union representative met for a conference. Liza Ensen's trade union was particularly involved in the case because they had agreed to underwrite her legal costs. During the conference, the solicitor made a number of personal criticisms of his client's principal witness, Dr Monro, while Dr Jardane made the very unprofessional and somewhat crazy suggestion that in order to resolve questions of toxicity, they might conduct live tests on Liza Ensen, spraying the inside of her car with organophosphate insecticide and then getting her to drive round in it.

Perhaps understandably, the barrister made it clear in his advice following the conference, that Dr Jardane could not be used by Mrs Ensen as an expert witness. The barrister also pointed out that as Mrs Ensen's union was now refusing to subsidise the search for another expert witness, it seemed most appropriate to him, that the solicitor should attempt to settle out of court for £2,000 General Damages. At this time, Liza Ensen had been ill and unable to work for five years.

Mr and Mrs Ensen were demoralised by this turn of events, and it was not until they sought independent advice, sacked their solicitor, favourably argued the case for costs with the union, and found a more independent 'expert witness', that they got their case 'on the rails' again.

Lorraine Taylor

In January 1984, Lorraine Taylor, a lone parent with two children, got a job with Airport Transport Warehouse Services (ATWS), a haulage firm based near her home in Hayes. Driving a Mercedes 307 van, Lorraine distributed goods from the ATWS warehouse to firms in the south of England.

ATWS was a non-unionised company. Despite the fact that Lorraine's most usual cargo was chemicals, which she was expected to unload at her destination, she was given no technical information about her loads, no safety clothing or training, nor were there any identifying marks on either the van or the containers she carried.

One day in November 1984, during a routine delivery, Lorraine became aware of a heavy pervasive smell coming from the back of the van. As it was winter, she was driving with the windows almost closed. Soon after becoming aware of the smell, she started to suffer 'flu-like' symptoms – her nose ran, her eyes watered and she began coughing. She did not immediately associate these symptoms with the fumes which now permeated the whole van.

The drum which was leaking was a five gallon tin drum; Lorraine could see where it was split. Unloading it, at her destination, she brought its condition to the attention of the workers who took it from her. These workers asked her whether they should get protective clothing or masks when handling the drum. Not knowing what the drum contained, Lorraine was unable to advise them.

Lorraine returned to the ATWS warehouse with a blinding headache and acute flu-like symptoms; her nose was streaming and her chest constricted. The van she had driven was washed out overnight, then left with its doors open. Returning to work the following morning, Lorraine was told that the van was safe to drive. Within hours of beginning work, however, she again felt ill. At one o'clock she felt so bad that she had to stop the van. She had a blinding headache, her vision was blurred and she could hardly see, her nose was running again, and she was coughing and sneezing. The smell had returned inside the van.

The substance which had leaked from the drum in the back of Lorraine Taylor's van was concentrated Allyl Caproate, a synthetic pineapple essence used in sweets and processed foods. Unable to work, and under the supervision of the hospital, in the weeks following the spillage Lorraine sought advice from a firm of solicitors about suing ATWS.

Lorraine Taylor's most serious oposition was to come not from the company which employed her,† but more covertly from uncommitted solicitors and doctors whose opinions were swayed by industrial

† From the beginning, ATWS accepted short term, limited liability for Lorraine's illness.

interests. Viewed over its duration, the case amply illustrates what can happen when a claimant's solicitors and counsel are swayed by the expert witnesses for the defence.

When Lorraine Taylor went to see her general practitioner, she was unable to persuade him that there was any organic basis to her illness and she was prescribed Valium. Almost a year after the spillage, still suffering from symptoms which stopped her from working, Lorraine Taylor contacted Dr Jean Monro, whom she had seen by chance on a television programme.

Dr Monro had a consultation with Lorraine Taylor in September 1985. She found her to be highly chemically sensitised, now affected by a whole range of chemicals emissions such as traffic fumes, petrol fumes, perfume and spray polish. She found her to be suffering from nausea, bad headaches and attacks of breathlessness. Lorraine Taylor complained of itching and burning skin, abdominal cramps, sore throat, drowsiness, inability to concentrate and forgetfulness. All these symptoms were readily recognisable to Dr Monro as the effects of chemical sensitivity.

One of the problems of measuring chemical sensitivity, or identifying the exact agent involved, is that because of a danger of anaphylactic shock, it is not possible to test the subject with the chemical which caused the initial sensitivity. Dr Monro carried out double blind provocation neutralisation tests on Lorraine, who showed a reaction to terpene, a common basic ingredient of many industrial chemicals.

Dr Monro reviewed her examination of Lorraine Taylor between 1985 and 1990. In 1989, she found her to have raised levels of toluene, xylenes and styrene in her body. Adverse reactions were exhibited to a number of everyday substances such as sugar, food colourings and additives. In Dr Monro's opinion, even in 1989, Lorraine Taylor was not getting better, but was suffering from a 'spreading phenomenon' in which a single large exposure to a chemical 'induces sensitivities to other foods and chemicals'. Dr Monro was of the opinion that contemporary attacks of arthritis-like pain Lorraine was experiencing could also have been the result of the exposure.

Dr Monro recommended a detoxification routine, which combined high doses of vitamins and minerals, saunas, and a course of desensitisation by injection.† Dr Monro told Lorraine Taylor that if she underwent the treatment there was a 60-70% chance of complete recovery. Lorraine Taylor was, however, unable to afford such treatment and, though Dr Monro continued to see her over the next six years, she could only give ameliorating help which did not remove the toxins from her body or desensitise her.

The first solicitor whom Lorraine Taylor consulted about an action against ATWS had little idea of how to proceed with her case, consequently she changed solicitors. Unhappily, she had no more success with her second choice. As in the case of her general practitioner, there seemed to be a reluctance on the part of the solicitors to believe that she was suffering serious long-term chemically induced health damage.

Eventually Lorraine contacted a firm of solicitors who, though they did not normally handle her kind of case, did have some connection with an environmental organisation. In 1988, her new firm of solicitors began in earnest the lengthy process of preparing a civil action for damages against her employers.

In its early stages, the preparation of Lorraine's case went well. The insurance company acting for her employers insisted that she be examined by a psychiatrist, and, inevitably, his report suggested that Lorraine Taylor was imagining her symptoms. Lorraine was also interviewed by a National Health psychiatrist, on her own behalf; he concluded that her mind was healthy and that she did not suffer from delusions of illness.

An osteopath was contacted by Lorraine's solicitor. He was willing to state that, although Lorraine had minimal arthritis, she was caused much joint pain by other illnesses which he was not capable of diagnosing. It was, however, Dr Monro who provided the major part of the evidence in support of Lorraine's case. Dr Monro assembled a good case in support of Lorraine's claim; however, by the time her case was heard, the 'World in Action' programme had been screened and her standing as a professional clinician had been severely damaged.

In October 1991, two weeks before Lorraine's case came to court,

---

† Such regimes are common practice in Europe and America in cases of people who have been accidentally affected by large doses of toxic chemicals.

her solicitors felt fairly confident. Despite it being a difficult case to prove – it was now seven years since the spillage – the symptomatic description of Lorraine's illnesses following the spillage seemed consistent with the recognisable condition of chemical sensitivity. What was perhaps more important, was the fact that the defence, despite a Harley Street psychiatrist and an occupational injuries doctor, were evidently failing to marshall a strong case.

A week before the case was due to be heard, however, Lorraine's solicitor received notice of and evidence from a new witness, Dr David Pearson. The evidence was served late, thus depriving Lorraine's solicitors of the chance to prepare a full answer to it. Although Lorraine's solicitors were annoyed at the lateness of the evidence, they were not willing to ask that the hearing be re-scheduled.

Dr Pearson had not seen Lorraine Taylor, so he could not make a clinical assessment of her condition. His evidence was in two parts; it consisted of a long statement which contested Dr Monro's qualifications, ability, professionalism and understanding of allergy, while attacking the whole notion of environmental illness. Had this been all, and had Dr Monro had time to prepare her rebuttal to this negative evidence, all might still have been well.

Appended to Dr Pearson's statement, however, Lorraine's solicitors found a document entitled: *Allergy – Conventional and Alternative Concepts*. The document was a confidential 'Final Draft' of a report drawn up by a committee of the Royal College of Physicians (RCP). This was the report of the committee which had been sitting for two years under the direction of Professor Barry Kay.

The draft report, which might have appeared to the lay eye to be accurate, argued vehemently and prejudicially against clinical ecology and particularly provocation neutralisation. It transpired later that the report, unfinished as it was, had been tendered to the court by Caroline Richmond in answer to a subpoena, apparently against the express wishes of the RCP representatives. The task of writing up the report had been entrusted to Richmond, although she had no clinical experience and was not a member of the Royal College.

The whole sorry and unprofessional manner in which the report was used in the court case, to support an employer with a poor defence, was made more shocking when it was understood that both Caroline Richmond and David Pearson were members of HealthWatch and had been instrumental in the 'World in Action' programme. By their use of the report, Pearson and Richmond were adding the authority of the Royal College of Physicians to the defence of a large haulage company who were trying to avoid properly compensating a female worker, made ill as a consequence of her work.†

With only a week to go before the hearing, Lorraine's solicitor had little time to trace the information in the document and give it a measured examination. In fact, Lorraine Taylor's solicitor responded to the new evidence in a very conservative manner. Rather than take on Dr Pearson and rebut his evidence, he was heard to complain that he was caught up in a medical war which had nothing to do with his client or his case. This was not true: the medical war being fought by Dr Pearson against Dr Monro and others was entirely germane to Lorraine Taylor's legal case.

Lorraine Taylor's action for damages against ATWS was heard before The Honourable Mr Justice Macpherson, at the High Court in London in October 1991. The case ran for four days. Lorraine Taylor was legally aided.

The plaintiff's case was simple. The chemical spillage in the van Lorraine was driving had had a long-term deleterious effect upon her health and had sensitised her to a number of other substances. Her partner and her son both gave evidence to the fact that Lorraine's health and her disposition had changed following the incident. The psychiatrist and the osteopath also gave evidence on her behalf.

The most important witness for the prosecution was Dr Monro, who gave evidence about chemical sensitivity. In fact, the whole of Lorraine's case rested upon Dr Monro's evidence. If the defence were able, or wanted, to show that there was no long-term deleterious effect from chemical exposure, then they would have to dispute the diagnostic capability and the professional authority of Dr Monro.

The defence counsel kept Dr Monro in the witness box for a whole day. She was asked few questions about the science of immunology,

† For the full account of how this document came to be tendered to the court, and for a complete critique of the report as it was finally published, see Davies S and Downing D. *Allergy: Conventional and Alternative Concepts*. A Critique of the Royal College of Physicians of London's Report. *Journal of Nutritional Medicine* 1992; 3: 331–49. Available from the British Society for Nutritional Medicine, PO Box 3AP, London W1A 3AP, UK.

and was cross examined about the 'World in Action' programme and the devastation it had wrought upon her professional life. The court was not told that the programme had been sponsored by Health-Watch, organised by Caroline Richmond and had starred Dr Pearson. Nor were they told that the programme was the subject of a libel action.

In attempting to cast doubt upon her credibility, the defence's cross examination of Dr Monro became very personal. Her rented surgery space in a private London hospital was brought up, as if such a practice was somehow peculiar. She was cross examined about the role of her son, who worked as an administrator at the Breakspear Hospital, as if this reflected badly upon her professional competence. The defence insisted that Dr Monro, despite her twenty years' experience in allergy and immunology, was not properly trained. Sitting in the well of the court, Lorraine Taylor could see that few, if any, of these issues were relevant to her case.

The essence of Dr Pearson's evidence was firstly that Lorraine Taylor was probably suffering from a psychiatric condition:

> I agree with Dr Bidstrup [a defence expert] that the current pattern of symptoms recorded by her is not indicative of any recognised physical disorder, but is typical of an anxiety state with associated agoraphobia and panic attacks. [47]

Secondly, Dr Pearson did as much as was possible through his evidence to damage Dr Monro's professional character. His critique of environmental medicine was prejudiced and flawed, but because the prosecuting solicitors were not expecting to have to defend Dr Monro's clinical capability they had neither witnesses nor information with which to challenge Pearson.

In his evidence in chief, Dr Pearson suggested that people who believed that they were chemically sensitised had been 'brainwashed' by clinical ecologists and consequently became progressively alienated from 'normal work and social contact'. It was difficult to imagine that this had happened in Lorraine Taylor's case as she had suffered serious symptoms of illness *for a year before she came into contact with a 'clinical ecologist'*.

From a legal point of view, Lorraine Taylor's case was difficult from the beginning. Deposits of toxins which after six years have probably become lodged in fatty tissue, are difficult and expensive to measure. The symptoms of chemical sensitivity, all the aches and pains of a depleted immune system, resemble the symptoms of such problematic illnesses as ME or such everyday illnesses as flu. There is a bitter unwillingness amongst many professionals, legal as well as medical, to explore the organic base of chemical sensitivity. The easy diagnosis of psychiatric disorder is one which has dogged women down the centuries whenever they have complained about damage inflicted upon them by more powerful social individuals or groups.

On the last day of Lorraine's action, her solicitor and counsel decided that they were losing the case and folded their claim, agreeing publicly with the counsel for her employers that her condition was probably the product of an 'egg-shell personality'. Although the chemical spillage might have caused her to be ill, it was only because she was idiosyncratic and vulnerable to such things. Her case, and her illness, were the risks which had to be taken, if we are to live with the benefits of modern chemical science.

The effect which the draft copy of the Royal College of Physicians' Report had upon the case was reflected in the judge's summing up. Evidently believing that Dr Pearson spoke for the general view of orthodox practitioners, he said:

> Dr Monro's ... business seems to be unacceptable to the vast majority of doctors and to the insurance houses, and her methods and treatment have no parallel or place in the National Health Service routines.

The judge awarded minimal costs to Lorraine Taylor for the personal expenses which she had incurred during her search for compensation. These came to half of the amount which her employers had offered her after accepting the immediate liability of the spillage and the short-term effect it had upon her health. In awarding these costs, the judge was at least making it clear that he did not consider the action had been frivolous.

Chapter Thirty Six

Mugging the Cancer Patients

> *You cannot hope to bribe or twist,*
> *Thank God, the British journalist,*
> *For seeing what the man will do*
> *Unbribed, there's no occasion to.* [1]

In the summer of 1989, Penny Brohn, the founder of the Bristol Cancer Help Centre, was invited to appear on a television programme in Birmingham. Arriving at the studio, she found that Michael Baum, whom she was supposed to be in discussion with, had been replaced by another CAHF member, Vincent Marks.† This was Penny Brohn's first encounter with Marks and she was shocked by his aggression and vehemence.

> I'm used to the give and take of argument. I don't mind people
> coming up with their stuff and I counter it, that's what social
> change is all about. But I was shocked at Marks' attitude. [2]

Brohn found reasoned debate impossible with Marks, who threw loaded questions at her which pre-empted logical answer. 'Every question was like being asked '"Have you stopped beating your wife?" Whichever way I answered, I was damned. Marks was utterly unwilling to accept that there was a place for the Bristol Cancer Help Centre in the care of cancer patients. He made allegations about the regime at the Centre, posed as questions.'

Marks began the discussion by identifying Bristol with some stereotypical New Age institution run by crackpot practitioners. These practitioners were, according to him, denying patients proper medical

---

† Penny Brohn was told by a programme researcher, when she arrived at the studio, that Michael Baum was not appearing because, following the CAHF launch, he had received frightening 'hate mail'.

attention, and withholding orthodox medical care from them. Because
Bristol had never done this, Brohn was at a loss as to how to answer
him. The real shock, however, was the aggression.

> I have taken part in some debates in my time, but I realised that
> this was in *another* league. I left that studio gobsmacked. I just
> reeled out. That was the first time that I felt people were really
> angry and vindictive. It was not an intellectual debate. [3]

Penny Brohn had read about the setting up of the Campaign Against
Health Fraud, and a colleague had told her that Bristol was on its
target list. A couple of months after the television interview, a physicist
working at the Bristol Royal Infirmary told Brohn about a talk that
Michael Baum was to give at the Radiotherapy Department. The talk
was about cancer myths, cures, and quackery.

Penny Brohn went to the talk; she was impressed by Baum's
erudition and sophistication, but surprised at his dogmatism and lack
of flexibility in relation to cancer patient care. Any view other than the
orthodox was, according to Baum, not worth considering. 'Baum
labelled alternative practitioners as quacks and made a number of
references to the Bristol Cancer Help Centre being just up the road.'
He was though, Brohn says, fairly careful about what he said.

In the bar after the meeting, Penny Brohn approached Baum and
began a discussion with him. She realised then that Baum was years
out of date with what was happening at the Centre. He did not even
know that one of the founders, Dr Alec Forbes, had left some years
ago. Nor did he know that the Centre was working in close co-
operation with general practitioners and caring, in the main, for
people who had already had orthodox treatment.

Penny Brohn is not a person to miss an opportunity. 'I told him
that it was a great shame that he was so out of touch with what we did
and I extended an invitation for him to visit the Centre.' Baum didn't
take up the invitation. He continued to refer to alternative treatments
on every occasion, and as he was a cancer specialist, he continued to
lambast those institutions which gave alternative cancer care. Like
other CAHF members, he spoke principally from a dogmatically
sceptical position, rather than as someone who had tried to inform
himself about alternative or complementary treatments.

* * *

At the start of 1990 the workers and administrators of the Bristol Cancer Help Centre were on top of the world. From the meagre beginnings of a small self-help group, they had established the most successful complementary cancer care centre in Britain. They had extensive waiting lists and a well-developed therapeutic programme. In the background there was the Imperial Cancer Research Fund (ICRF) funded research begun in 1985, which the staff at Bristol felt confident would show the Centre in a good light.

What Bristol lacked was positive publicity. Penny Brohn had written two books [4] which had publicised what had become known as the Bristol Programme, but the Centre had never quite managed to achieve the level of publicity of the years following its opening in 1980.

In the first months of 1990, at the beginning of the Centre's tenth anniversary year, Penny Brohn began casting round for a film company or a programme maker who would revitalise the debate about the Centre and complementary cancer care. She spoke to producers from Yorkshire Television and the BBC, finally deciding to go with the BBC. It was a decision that she was to regret.

Following the initial discussion with the BBC, it was agreed that there would be two programmes. One would combine and edit the six '40 Minutes' films made in 1983 into a single broadcast. The second programme would chart the growth of the Centre through the eighties and examine its contemporary practices. This second programme would be based on contemporary film of the Centre.

The BBC film unit came to the Centre during the last week of July 1990, finishing filming on the 28th. No one at the Bristol Centre linked the proposed television programmes with the five-year study – now in its second year – which was being funded by the ICRF and carried out by the Institute of Cancer Research. In August, however, the Centre received a summary paper which noted a set of 'interim' results. With another three years to go on the study, no one at the Centre paid much attention to these results.

Around the time that they received the interim results, Penny Brohn began to notice inexplicable changes in the attitude of the film makers who visited the Centre. The earlier friendly co-operation began to give way to an embarrassed secretiveness. Within a short time of filming, the director appeared to come under pressure to change the nature of the film and to present it, not simply as a film, but in tandem with a combative discussion programme. Somehow, without sharing the information with the Centre, the programme makers knew that the 'interim' results of the ICR study were of much greater importance than the Centre imagined.

When the programme producers eventually told Penny Brohn that they had decided to change the format of the programmes, she was concerned. She saw no point in having an unproductive stand up fight on television. After all, these programmes were meant to show the constructive work of the Centre and celebrate its tenth anniversary. Brohn was originally assured that any studio discussion would be more of an informal conversation between people in armchairs and not a structured debate.

> I agreed to allow these programmes to be made on the basis of a
> strict understanding between us all that any discussion
> programme would cover an investigation into where comple-
> mentary medicine had gone and how it had developed during
> the previous ten years. [5]

With one of the doctors from the Centre, Penny Brohn had a meeting with the head of BBC programmes in the Bristol area, Peter Salmon. She was adamant that the Centre would only go ahead with the programmes if there was an agreement on the kind of debate which would follow them. She told Salmon she had seen studio discussions turn into bun fights and made it clear that she would not take part in such an event. It was now evident to Brohn that the programme makers' perception of the films had radically changed from the one which was initially discussed. 'We are going to have to have people on it who don't think much of the movement', said the producer. Brohn told him that this was not a problem, 'provided there was a proper dialogue'.

As August passed and September began, Penny Brohn became increasingly concerned about the focus of the films. The producer seemed to talk to her less and they obviously did not share the same confidence with which they had begun. As the scheduled screening date of the two programmes came nearer, Brohn realised that these dates coincided with the proposed publication of the 'interim' results of the ICR study, which Bristol had been told would be published in the *Lancet* on September 8th. Increasingly, she had the feeling that the Centre was being set up.

When the producer, David Henshaw, visited the Centre one day, Penny Brohn cornered him. She asked him again about the debate. She wanted to know who was going to be in it and how it was going to be staged. Henshaw seemed embarrassed. He blushed, and told her that the debate had been taken out of his hands.† It was now going to be dealt with by the 'Public Eye' programme. Brohn knew this programme had in the past organised debates between antagonistic parties. Not long after that conversation, the 'Public Eye' presenter visited the Centre, and made it clear to Penny Brohn that this debate was going to be just like previous ones.

At some time in the months since the making of the programmes began, the BBC appeared to have been in contact with the ICR researchers, and what had begun as an independent programme about alternative cancer care had been turned into yet another opportunity for vested interests to score ideological points against complementary medicine.

When it was clear that the original agreement had been violated, Brohn and the other administrators at the Centre began to think seriously about trying to pull out. When the programme researcher visited her with the kind of questions which were to be asked, she knew that the debate would be exactly as she had feared. She could also see what would happen if she didn't play ball. The debate would go ahead and the presenter would say that the Centre had declined to appear. Brohn felt that this could seem worse than if she did appear.

* * *

Other alternative practitioners should have the courage to submit their work to this type of stringent assessment. [6]

In 1985, the Bristol Cancer Help Centre had reached an agreement

† Penny Brohn was not to know that David Henshaw, then working for the BBC in Bristol, was a close friend of those in HealthWatch. His picture appeared in one of their Newsletters, showing a selection of apparently false qualifications which he had gathered in his 'quackbusting' work.

with Sir Walter Bodmer, Director of Research at the ICRF, and others, that the ICRF and the Cancer Research Campaign (CRC) would finance two research projects. One would look into the survival of Bristol attenders. The other, more important in Bristol's view, would measure and compare the quality of life experienced by those undergoing orthodox treatment alone and those who attended Bristol either solely or while having orthodox treatment.

The administrators at Bristol were under the impression that both studies were begun in 1986. Apart from administrative matters relating to the research, there was, however, no communication between the ICRF and the body which had been awarded the research, the Institute of Cancer Research,† and the Bristol Centre. It would only become clear four years later, that the quality of life study, a difficult project, demanding extensive creativity, social science research skills and a high financial outlay, had been dumped within months of the work beginning.

The survival research was co-ordinated by Felicity Bagenal, a research assistant at the Institute of Cancer Research, and directed and designed by Professor Clair Chilvers, who was appointed to a Chair at Nottingham University after the work began. Also on the research team were Professor Tim McElwain, a clinician and member of HealthWatch, and Doug Easton, a statistician. At the Bristol Centre, a woman was employed to assemble the sample and to fill out the 'first attendance' questionnaires.

The research was a direct statistical comparison between two groups of patients who had reported first-time breast cancer. One group contained three hundred and thirty four women drawn from the Bristol Cancer Help Centre. The other had four hundred and sixty one drawn from three NHS hospitals in the Surrey area, the Royal

---

† Three members of the Council of the Imperial Cancer Research Fund have a direct link to Wellcome. R.G.Gibbs is chairman of the Wellcome Trust. Professor Sir Stanley Peart, Vice Chairman of the Council, is a Trustee of the Wellcome Trust. Sir John Vane was previously a senior research scientist with the Wellcome Foundation and is a member of HealthWatch. For the links between Sir Walter Bodmer, the ICRF Director of Research, and Caroline Richmond see Chapter Twenty One. For the links between Wellcome and the Institute of Cancer Research see Chapter Twenty Three. For the links between Vincent Marks, HealthWatch member, the ICRF, and Surrey University see Chapter Twenty Eight. For the links between Michael Baum, HealthWatch member, the ICR and Wellcome, see Chapter Thirty.

Marsden, the Royal Surrey County Hospital at Guildford, and Crawley General Hospital.

The research methodology was based upon conventional quantitative survey techniques. Survey schedules were filled in by women who had breast cancer and who were attending the Bristol Centre for the first time between June 1986 and October 1987. Reference was made to case notes made out by these women's consultants and all subjects were to be followed up with a postal questionnaire annually over three years (in this case it was only once before the 'interim' results were published). The women were also asked to fill in a personal postal schedule about alternative treatments and diet which they had followed since attending Bristol. All patients were followed up to June 1988 for a period of only eight months before the interim results were published.

The interim results concluded that 'women with breast cancer attending the Bristol Cancer Help Centre fared worse than those receiving conventional treatment only.'

The paper in which the interim results were published [7] did not state whether or not the control group made any changes in the way that they looked after themselves after being treated with orthodox therapies for breast tumours, whether they changed their diet, or ceased work and had more relaxation, for example. Nor did the paper make clear whether any of the control group had used any forms of alternative medicines following their orthodox treatment

Because randomising the Bristol sample would have entailed turning down attenders, something which Bristol refused to do, those who took part in the study were self-selecting. Area of residence was not used as a sample criterion for the Bristol women and consequently women in the sample came from a number of different areas and had attended a wide range of different hospitals.

Perhaps most importantly, no distinction was drawn in the Bristol sample between those who had stayed for a five-day residential course at the Centre, following their first attendance interview, and those who did not return after that interview. Each first attendance at Bristol was treated as 'treatment'.

On average, women in the Bristol group were younger than the women in the control group. Although it is commonly accepted that tumours develop faster in younger women, this difference in age was not considered significant.

The interim results concluded that women who were, at the time of their attendance at Bristol, free of relapse, were almost three times more likely to relapse than those who did not attend at Bristol (relapse rate ratio 2.85). Amongst those women who relapsed after attending Bristol, the interim results claimed that women were almost twice as likely to die (hazard ratio 1.81) as those who relapsed in the control group.

The paper claimed that, of 334 woman who attended Bristol between June 1986 and October 1987, 104 had died by the end of the follow-up period in June 1988. *The paper did not present a statistic for the number of the 461 control subjects who had died.* With respect to relapse, the paper said that 21 of the Bristol subjects had relapsed, compared with only six of the control sample.

The 'interim' results clearly stated, without any explanation, that there was a causal relationship between attendance at Bristol and developing secondary cancer and then dying. No clear explanatory analysis of the results was given in the conclusion to the paper, although both in the preliminary description of the Bristol Centre, and in the conclusions reference was made to the dietary regime. In both these quotes, there was an unacceptable degree of editorialising which does not fit the presentation of a scientific paper, especially when neither the diets of the Bristol attenders nor those of the control sample had been seriously evaluated in the study.

> The stringent 'Bristol diet' of raw and partly cooked vegetables with proteins from soya and pulses attracted much public interest and a high demand for the services of the Centre – and deep medical scepticism. [8]

> The possibility that some aspect of the BCHC regimen is responsible for their decreased survival must be faced. For example, does radical adherence to a stringent diet shorten life in patients whose survival is already threatened by cancer? Our study certainly shows that patients choosing to attend the BCHC do not gain any substantial survival benefit. [9]

The 'interim' results paper, which came to be called the 'Chilvers report', was published in the *Lancet* after only 18 months of the five-year study. Although what were published were termed 'interim' results, the use of the word 'interim' was a deceptive convenience. In fact, the results were to stand as a premature conclusion to the study. The precipitous publication of the results before adequate follow-up data had been obtained, and the resultant furore, meant that the study had to be aborted.

Anyone experienced in social research would have known that the publication of highly contentious 'interim' results in a sensitive area such as alternative cancer care, would bring a study to grief. The possibility had to be considered that the ICRF and the CRC were actually unwilling to commit either money or resources to a seriously independent five-year study and instead half-heartedly conducted a short-term and inadequate study, the results of which were intended to 'debunk' the Bristol Cancer Help Centre. Was the survey simply a re-run of the many bogus research endeavours carried out by CSICOP-style groups since the late seventies?

* * *

As I mentioned on the telephone last week, we do badge everyone attending our press conferences. [10]

The Bristol Cancer Help Centre was informed about a press conference being held by the ICRF in August, some time after it learned of the 'interim' results. The person who received notification of the press conference did not realise its significance and so did nothing about it for some time. At the end of August, the Centre received a rough draft of a press release to be issued by the Imperial Cancer Research Fund (ICRF). For the first time, in this draft release the 'interim' results were spelt out in words of one syllable.†

Throughout the last weeks of August, the ICRF put Bristol under immense pressure to agree the press release which they intended to send out. Bristol worked hard to try to get the more damaging part of the release altered, especially the statements which suggested that it was primarily the diet at Bristol which was responsible for attenders'

---

† Around this time, there was also a meeting between the Bristol staff and administrators and the authors of the paper. At this meeting Professor McElwain asked the Bristol contingent if they would not now consider closing the Centre down.

deaths. The ICRF, however, seemed to be uncompromising in its position and adamant that the results, though only interim, and without analysis, were going to be put before the press in their most rudimentary form.

In the first days of the preparation of the press statement, the ICRF wanted the BCHC to share in its formulation. Both the press release and the press conference, ICRF Public Relations Officer Janice Wilkins said, would be much more effective as joint ventures.

The ICRF strategy was, from the beginning, to draw Bristol in to support the conclusions of the Chilvers paper and thereby help to cut its own throat. Janice Wilkins enclosed a note with one of the first drafts of the press release: 'I'm very glad we're doing this together – I'm sure it's our best hope of balanced media coverage.' [11] Whether or not the ICRF ever had any intention of trying to bring about balanced media coverage is a moot point. The proposed platform of speakers who would announce the results, listed in the same letter, did not indicate a co-operative venture. The conference was to be chaired by Professor Whitehouse, chairman of the ICRF Committee on Psychological Aspects of Malignant Disease. The rest of the platform was to consist of Clair Chilvers, Felicity Bagenal, Doug Easton and Tim McElwain.

Bristol disagreed most seriously with the suggestion in the press release that diet might be implicated in attenders' quicker demise. Answering its criticism, in a note from the ICRF to accompany their press release, Janice Wilkins paraphrased an answer for the Centre. Perhaps Bristol should say something along these lines:

> We find it difficult to believe that diet is really the problem but, just in case it is, we are now including on diet sheets a warning that patients should go to their family doctors if they experience a weight loss of more than X in Y weeks, while following the diet. We're doing this because we feel it is responsible to play safe until further research uncovers what are the real differences between women with breast cancer who come to us and those who don't. [12]

The suggested statement from the ICRF attempts to formulate the Bristol Centre's policy. It faintly damns the regime at the Centre, even though there was no evidence to merit such conclusions.

The scientists wanted the argument about diet to suit them,

whichever way it was argued. While they gave no credence to a link between a 'bad' diet, processed food, and cancer, they wanted to propose that vegetarianism could have speeded the death of Bristol attenders. The draft statement sent by Wilkins to Bristol was a covert attempt by the ICRF to draw Bristol into making a public admission of guilt and give validity to the ridiculous 'interim' results.

The pressure on Bristol from Janice Wilkins and the ICRF was intense. At one point Wilkins threatened to deny Bristol the right to attend the press conference if it did not reply to one of her faxes by 6 pm that evening. The workers and administrators at the Bristol Centre felt harassed and threatened. When, however, the ICRF consistently rejected alterations to their release, put forward by Bristol, the Centre felt bound to issue its own press release. Having failed to involve Bristol in its own demise, the ICRF was happy to drop all pretence of a co-operative venture. The ICRF issued its own press release, advertising its own press conference at its own headquarters in Lincoln's Inn Fields, on September 5th 1990.

* * *

Those who attended from Bristol approached the room with trepidation. The ICRF had gone to town. As well as the central room for the conference, ancillary rooms had been allocated for TV and radio interviews.

Some time before the conference began, the room was packed, and by the time it started there were people standing at the back. If there was a time when the Bristol people might have understood clearly that they were being 'stitched up', it was then. The press conference had the atmosphere of a circus.

A few days before the conference, Tessa Glynn, one of the staff at Bristol, had received the press list from Janice Wilkins. Tessa felt prompted to ask Wilkins why they had decided to arrange a press conference. 'It would have got out anyway, so we thought we had better do it properly', replied Wilkins – an answer which didn't quite explain arrangements which were on a par with a royal visit to a small African country.

Very few journalists from the British press were not invited to the conference; anyone who was anyone was there, from the *Sun* to *The*

Times, from Reuters to the Press Association. The room was packed
with journalists jotting, film crews filming, and radio reporters
recording.

Penny Brohn and Dr Michael Wetzler, one of the Centre's doctors,
eventually decided that it was in their best interests to sit on the
platform. Even as the conference began, the workers from Bristol still
thought that as the results did not make sense the press would consider
their case with reason. Tessa Glynn did not even think that the press
would be damaging. She thought that everyone would be puzzled
about where the results had gone wrong. 'I was convinced that the
press would question the results of the research.'

There was a point during the press conference when some
journalists did seem intent upon getting to the bottom of the survey.
There was insistent questioning about the number of deaths in the
control group, a figure which the authors of the paper refused to
reveal. It was just as the authors began to feel uncomfortable over this
matter, and the Bristol workers optimistic about the conference, that
Professor Tim McElwain stepped in with his ringing judgement: 'I
would no longer be able to tell my patients that going to Bristol would
do them no harm.' It was, says Tessa Glynn, as if 'there was a distinct
change in the atmosphere, as if that was what the press had come to
hear'. Penny Brohn says that with McElwain's statement, 'it was all
over'. From then on it was evident to Glynn and everyone else from
Bristol that the scientists were going for the jugular. The intimation
was quite specific – the regime at Bristol damaged patients and could
kill them.

* * *

The two BBC television programmes filmed at Bristol in July were
shown [13] a week after the Centre had been plunged into the worst crisis
of its existence.

Penny Brohn felt utterly betrayed by the programme makers and
the 'debate' which followed the second programme, chaired by Peter
Taylor. She found it an extraordinary experience. 'I have never been
treated like that before in my life. I have never been so deceived. It was
the first time that I realised that human beings did that sort of thing to
each other.'

> Karol Sikora† sat with us. It was like the thing with Vincent Marks all over again, though this time there were three of them: Tim McElwain, Jeffrey Tobias – debating with him, is much the same as 'debating' with Vincent Marks – and Lesley Fallowfield.‡

> The programme makers had managed to find someone who had been to Bristol and had felt guilty because she had not stuck to the diet. She was placed on 'the other side' in the debate. They had invited Ros Coward, relying on her to argue against alternative care at Bristol. They didn't know that we were acquaintances and when she arrived she told them that she wanted to sit with me. They said she couldn't because it had all been arranged in terms of opposing sides.

> I could see that it was going to be really bad, much much worse than I had feared. I decided to try and break down their plan, and went and sat with Tim McElwain, but was immediately told to move. From the beginning, there was a very, very bad atmosphere.

The debate allowed Fallowfield, Tobias and McElwain to capitalise on the 'interim' results of the ICR survey, even though, following their publication, these results were quickly disputed. Penny Brohn tried hard to defend Bristol and its ideas, but she was so loudly and vehemently attacked that she left the studio feeling that she had helped in the public humiliation of the Centre. For the next few days, however, Penny Brohn and the Centre were flooded with sympathetic mail. Members of the public expressed shock and disgust at the treatment she and the Centre had received.

Later, when Penny Brohn was able to put things in perspective, she concluded that the hasty publication of the 'interim' results was obviously related to the transmission of the two BBC films, and that there was a common strategy behind them both. 'If', she says, 'the

---

† Karol Sikora is a highly respected oncologist who works at the Hammersmith Hospital in London. Sikora was from the start on the side of Bristol over the Chilvers Report but made few public statements for fear of losing his funding.

‡ Lesley Fallowfield is a psychologist who works in the field of cancer at the London Hospital. Her views appear to be close to those of Dr Tobias and Professor Vincent Marks.

Chilvers report had come out after this programme, then the programme might have been a fairly balanced view about what had happened to BCHC over the last ten years.'

As it was, Brohn had found herself fielding questions from Tobias, Fallowfield and McElwain, not about the work of the Centre, its therapies or its philosophies, but about a diet which they claimed killed people but 'which had not been used at the Centre for nearly ten years'. Penny Brohn kept trying to say, 'It isn't relevant anymore – you are attacking us for a diet which we don't use, and the diet we do now use has been approved by a senior NHS nutritionist.' Again, as was to be the case over the next few months, the critical issue, assaulted time and time again by the activists in, and the associates of, the Campaign Against Health Fraud, was food.

* * *

Rarely, if ever, has a piece of academic work, in an obscure area, merited, or received, so much national publicity. Throughout the second week of September 1990, Britain's national newspapers, television news, and radio current affairs programmes reverberated with what appeared to be a powerful public interest story.

Bizarre is perhaps the only word which really does justice to the sudden wave of press coverage which the Bristol survey provoked. Every newspaper in Britain, whatever its quality, took a sudden and uncritical interest in medical research and the complementary therapies of a small cancer charity.

None of the journalists who reported the research findings over the days following the press conference thought to question them. None attempted, even superficially, to place the so-called 'interim' results or their meaning, within the context of an ongoing debate. It seemed that every journalist who could get there ran from the ICRF press conference, holding pencil and paper shouting 'Bristol Cancer Help Centre kills its patients!'

The wave of coverage over the next week crashed over the Centre like a tidal wave, drowning for days any reasoned assessment of the research. The publicity began with an acceptance of the results. It was followed, weeks later, by a derisory attempt by a few journalists to advertise the fact that the study had been discredited. Then towards the end of the year, the matter caught the eye of the media again with the suicide of Professor Tim McElwain and the resignation of the two staff doctors from Bristol. Early in 1991 there was a series of articles which attempted to reconcile the two conflicting views of the study.

Throughout the whole of this protracted period, not one journalist was willing or brave enough to link the 'interim' results, their publication in the *Lancet* and the ICRF press conference with vested interests, or to place these things in the context of other contemporary attacks upon complementary medicine. None appeared willing to question the integrity of the doctors involved. Even when Professor McElwain cut his throat, thereby hinting at the fact that this could be an issue imbued with enormous conflict, no one was willing to begin attributing blame.

* * *

In the coverage which immediately followed the press conference, the 'quality' newspapers attempted to put a liberal and intellectual gloss on the apparent dangers of Bristol: 'Doctors warn on natural cancer therapy',[14] 'Cancer spread is likelier with holistic therapy',[15] and 'Double risk at cancer unit'.[16] Despite the gloss, however, the 'quality' press still put words into the mouth of the report, insisting, as the *Telegraph* did, for example, that 'Women with breast cancer who undergo alternative therapies including vegetarian diets, healing by touch, and meditation, die sooner than those who rely solely on conventional treatment.'[17] The study did not come to such conclusions: what is more, a number of the sample had not received any treatment at all from the Centre.

The tabloids, on the other hand, splashed thriller headlines across their pages like blood. 'Double death risk at Veg. diet cancer clinic' spluttered *Today*.[18] Inevitably, where they were able, the tabloids drew the Royal Family into the furore. Some made it appear that it was because Prince Charles had backed the Centre, that attenders were more likely to die! 'Danger in a veggie cure for cancer: More victims die at Prince's centre' warned the *Sun*.[19]

The tabloids shared a similarity of literary vision with the medical press, and it was their headlines and articles which most closely resembled the message between the lines in the *Lancet*. The Bristol Cancer Help Centre was depicted as a Hammer Horror institution in which innocent cancer suffers died at the hands of incompetent therapists who forced a terrible regime on their patients: 'Breast cancer patients treated at an alternative health centre backed by Prince Charles are TWICE as likely to die as those receiving standard NHS treatment, it was claimed yesterday'. [20]

One of the most alarming aspects of the post-press conference publicity was that so many of the papers discussed the results of the survey in relation to the diet at Bristol. This is not a direction in which most journalists would naturally have strayed and many reports give readers a clear impression that behind the scenes someone was orchestrating the stories. The study did not present any information about diet despite the fact that the postal questionnaire asked a couple of questions about food intake. In fact, the 'Bristol diet' was not defined by the study and no questions were asked about whether any of the Bristol attenders continued with, or changed to, a certain pattern of nutrition after attending Bristol.

A lack of supportive evidence did not, however, stop newspapers of all shades being suddenly convinced that the 'strict', 'vegan', 'diet', 'regime' at the BCHC probably created secondary cancers and killed people. In a mistitled article in the *Independent*, [21] 'Therapy linked to cancer deaths', Jack O'Sullivan twice referred to the possibility that the diet advocated by Bristol could be the cause of deaths. First in the text of the article, 'However, they [the authors] added that breast cancer patients may need to be warned that the vegan diet advocated at the centre might be damaging.' Secondly, in a quote from Clair Chilvers, 'We could go over [take a look at] the possibility that some people who go there may be carrying the diet to extremes.'

The press conference on the Wednesday had been expertly organised to suit the Sunday papers, enabling journalists to get in two days superficial research, dig up a picture of Prince Charles and manufacture a couple of off-the-cuff quotes. For reasons best known to the journalists involved, none of them appear to have turned to sociologists or statisticians for an analysis of the survey results.

Sharon Kingman and Simon Garfield wrote two stories printed side by side in the *Independent on Sunday*: 'Vegan diet may hold clue to cancer relapses' and 'Five star salad at £605 a week'. [22] Sharon Kingman, a friend of the Campaign Against Health Fraud, a writer for the *New Scientist* and not a lover of alternative therapies, began her piece with this strange paragraph: 'A diet recommended to cancer patients by an alternative treatment centre in Bristol could cause malnutrition according to a leading specialist.' The same tone of unscientific generality and unsupported assertion ran throughout the article. Yet in the seventh paragraph, Professor Tim McElwain is quoted as saying: 'It was difficult to blame the diet without knowing what proportion of the Bristol patients kept to it.'

In her article, Sharon Kingman examines a number of possible hypotheses in an attempt to explain why Bristol attenders died faster than other cancer victims: 'Apart from the food there are several other theories.' Despite her searching enquiry, she failed to examine the possibility that ideology, dirty tricks and poor statistics might have killed off the Bristol patients.

Simon Garfield's article, in terms of objectivity, was hobbled from the outset. Although the headline does not say that attenders at Bristol ate babies, it does claim that the salads cost £605 a week: 'Five-star salad at £605 a week'. Headlines apart, the article turns out to be more honest than most. Garfield did interview at least one Bristol attender who gave the lie to the fact that Bristol was force feeding a vegan diet to its residents; Margaret Swindin said, 'I've eaten some fish here and some chicken, and there's real coffee and tea if you ask for it. There's no regime here, all they do is recommend a certain diet.'

Despite the evidence of this and other on-the-spot interviews, Mary Kenny in the *Sunday Telegraph* [23] knew exactly why the study had come to the conclusions it had: 'Experts may be baffled but I am not. It seems to me that people who go on diets of raw and partly cooked vegetables, beans, pulses and carrot juice can become seriously unwell even if they haven't got cancer: if they have cancer as well, they will – in my view – become seriously worse, quicker.' Is Mary Kenny's view of any consequence? She obviously thinks it is. She used the rest of her column to advertise the meat industry: 'Meat is health; our very bones have been bred on it; we require it. Vegetarianism is, for the most part, unhealthy.' The science is blinding!

It was the journalists, inside and outside the medical press, either members or fellow travellers of the Campaign Against Health Fraud, who really put the boot in. They were at the ideological sharp end of publicising the report, and many of them did nothing at all to make palatable the bitter pill which the report was intended to be. Some, like

James Le Fanu, a member of the Campaign Against Health Fraud, actually revelled in the results, writing an opening paragraph in *The Times*, [24] of which any orthodox doctor could have been proud. 'There is a grim satisfaction in learning that women with breast cancer seeking the help of alternative medicine at the Bristol Centre fare worse – relapse earlier and die sooner – than those who put their trust in conventional medicine.'

Le Fanu went on to express the opinions of which Michael Baum had previously made much. Patients who refuse the advice of their orthodox doctors, he claims, are next seen, following a term with an alternative practitioner, half-digested by tumours: 'All surgeons and cancer specialists have their own stories to tell of patients who disappear after being told of their diagnosis to return a year or two later with serious and usually untreatable disease once the ministrations of an 'alternative' practitioner have failed them. Perhaps this will now happen less frequently.' Such scare stories are not even relevant to the Bristol study because *all* the Bristol attenders had previously undergone orthodox treatment.

Apart from the various specialists and those whose partisan opinions defended vested interests, there were those who commented on the Bristol research from sheer vindictive ignorance. Writing in the *Observer*, [25] Richard Ingrams took the opportunity of his column to support the results of the Bristol survey. This he did without the slightest pretence that he knew anything about the subject. 'Why should everyone find it so "surprising" ' he asked cynically, 'that more cancer patients died when treated at the Bristol Health Centre (sic) than in conventional hospitals?' This article was written a full week after the press conference at the ICRF and when a number of criticisms of the research had already been voiced.

None of the major media reports drew attention to the fact that the big pharmaceutical companies back cancer research and there is a history of internecine struggle between these companies and the proponents of alternative cancer treatments. Nor did any journalists declare their own interests in the pharmaceutical or chemical industry. In the medical press such matters were not in contention because it is known that the majority of the media is subsidised by drug company advertising.

For these reasons, it was hardly surprising to find the real ideological cutting edge of the Bristol study articulated in the medical papers. In a very mild editorial, *GP* magazine [26] suggested that though damaging, the regime at Bristol might be the best of a bad lot. The survey results might, the writer bemoaned, have driven cancer patients into the hands of much greater charlatans. The logic of this editorial is, like the study itself, deeply flawed; the insinuation, however, is clear. Those working at Bristol were charlatans but not extreme ones, '... the latest findings wreck the reputation of complementary cancer care. But they do nothing to inhibit the spread of quackery ... The mildness of the Bristol therapy was and still is attractive to patients with cancer. Now they are asked to believe that a vegan diet, the laying on of hands, relaxation classes and positive thinking are far from benign but indeed dangerous. This gives a golden opportunity to charlatans peddling more aggressive and more harmful "cures".' Presumably by 'more aggressive cures' the writer is referring to orthodox chemotherapy.

Dr Jeffrey Tobias, a consultant radiotherapist, wrote in the *BMJ* [27] on his personal view of the press conference at the ICRF. It was not the results of the survey which angered Tobias nor even the charlatans in alternative medicine, it was the attitude of the Bristol workers. Why had they not immediately conceded defeat and admitted that their work was of no value? 'On the face of it' he blustered, 'they were faced with a serious problem over the credibility of their treatment, though you wouldn't have thought so from the tone of their comments.' In the opinion of Dr Tobias, Bristol just was not playing fair.

Dr Tobias, who had, according to one of the Bristol workers, seemed to be hyperactive at the press conference and harder to control than any of the tabloid journalists, went further than any other commentator in his final comment about Bristol: 'The very fact of the existence of these centres, with their strong message to patients that there really is a reasonable and realistic alternative to conventional medicine, represents a very real threat to the health of a patient with cancer.' The very existence of cancer help centres is a threat to the health of cancer patients! It would be good to see the supportive scientific evidence for that inanity. Such statements contain the classic signs of criminalisation, when even to speak critically of orthodoxy earns punitive condemnation.

In the last part of his full-page article, Dr Tobias claims that conventional doctors have been happily flexible about the treatments they have handed out, willing to change their practices when they do not suit the patient, asserting as Baum frequently does that only orthodox doctors really care about their patients. 'By and large, the medical establishment has ... far from being overtly paternalistic shown itself more flexible and less authoritarian than "holistic" centres.'

The headline to Tessa Richards' review of the *Lancet* paper in the *BMJ*, [28] 'Death from complementary medicine' would have made a good title for a pulp fiction paperback. It was so explicit one wonders why she went to the trouble of writing the article beneath it. This review never once questioned the statistical basis of the *Lancet* paper and used completely inappropriate words to describe the study. It goes without saying that we expect scientific studies to be 'careful', and the use of this word by Tessa Richards in relation to the Chilvers report shows a clear desire to impress upon us the fact that the 'interim' results were correct. Like the headline, the article was an act of semantic bullying.

The writers of the report were asked by different journalists to illustrate and amplify it. This they did with an endless series of quotes which showed they had no doubts at all about their own abilities or the validity of the results.

There was to be much speculation in the coming months as to what part Professor Tim McElwain had actually played in the disaster of the post-press conference publicity. Some newspapers presented him as one of the arch-antagonists of the Bristol Centre: 'There is not a jot of evidence that special diets make any difference'; [29] 'I must now tell my patients that if you go to the Bristol Centre it seems that for some unknown reason, you are likely to relapse and die faster'. [30] Other papers caught him in a more liberal mood.

*   *   *

> When one looks more closely at this report, it turns out to be a pretty rum document. For a start of the 334 so-called breast cancer patients of the Bristol Centre studied, no fewer than 112 attended for one day only. There was no evidence they had actually followed the Bristol 'treatment' in any way. [31]

Although the critical riposte to the publication of the interim results actually began immediately, its effect was slow. The response was unco-ordinated and perhaps more important, it lacked the popularist brevity and media-speak which the results themselves had conjured up. Critical responses were couched with caution in the language of statistics or sociological methodology, some were conservative enough to confound the understanding of lay observers.

In those first few weeks it appeared that the BCHC was unable to come to its own defence. It staggered as if from a knock-out blow, reeled and appeared to have serious doubts about rejoining the fight. It could have been the case that the attack opened up wounds of self-doubt, subconscious uncertainties about the academic standing of the work which was taking place at Bristol. Working on the periphery in any field is hard, working on the periphery in a field where the opposition can accuse you of bringing about the death of cancer patients demands superhuman stoicism.

It is hard to defend unpopular arguments and theories. All the vast resources of the media disappear when people try to propound theories about such things as marginalised religions, fringe politics, animal liberation or alternative medicine. The most effective strategy for Bristol would have been for it to renew its commitment to the original precepts of its work, while at the same time accusing the ICR of dirty tricks.

There was however a great reluctance on Bristol's part to become involved in accusations of foul play, particularly because the Imperial Cancer Research Fund was, like Bristol, a charity. The difficulty is, as Bristol found, that when battle is joined purely on technical issues, rather than ones of principle, part of the opposition's argument has, to some extent, already been conceded

The first critical response to the paper came, as might be expected, from specialists, doctors and oncologists. Within a day of the press conference, Professor Karol Sikora, a long-time friend of Bristol and a leading London oncologist, had marshalled a statement critical of the study and faxed it to Bristol. Karol Sikora's statement was not however couched in terms likely to bring the ringside crowd to their feet.

> Secondly, there seems to be some discrepancy between the Cox
> model coefficient (0.59) + standard error (0.26) given in table VI,
> and the p-value quoted in the text ($p < .001$). [32]

To argue in such terms was, though understandable, to miss the point.

Had the team which presented the 'interim' results been open to democratic scientific debate about the study, they would not have engineered the media circus under the slogans they did. Had there been the intention of serious scientific discussion about the 'interim' results, any real scientist would have submitted them to independent scrutiny by a number of parties: the *Lancet* paper was not even put out to peer review.

For Bristol to have mounted a serious challenge to the validity of the research presented by the ICRF would have required a detailed understanding of the character and motivation of their opponents. While those at the Centre had vague thoughts about the reasons for the attack, they believed implicitly in their opponents' integrity. Given the forces which were ranged against them and the multiplicity of their vested interests, this was a fatal mistake. Their opponents had a history of street fighting, and had set themselves the task of destroying the Bristol Cancer Help Centre. To them, 'science' was never an issue.

The week following the press conference, on September 15th, a letter from Dr Tim Sheard, one of the BCHC doctors, appeared in the *Lancet*. [33] The letter hinted at the basic faults with the research, from a methodological and statistical point of view. Sheard's letter, however, did not analyse the paper in detail, nor provide the reader with much by way of political ammunition to use against the authors.

Sheard did articulate one of the most most fundamental criticisms of the Bristol sample – that it was composed of people who had attended the Centre, but had often stayed no longer than a day and had not returned for treatment. These people had not been the subjects of any therapeutic intervention. The 'interim' results, therefore, implied that women who entered the Bristol building died more quickly than those women who did not enter the building. As Penny Brohn was to say later 'it was a bit like saying that they had been on a number 9 bus'.

Sheard drew attention to the only other comparable study, one by Spiegel *et al.* [34] This study was a randomised ten-year trial which concluded that at 10 years, the intervention group which had used alternative therapy and group support work showed a significant near-doubling in mean survival.†

---

† Interestingly, after only eighteen months of the study, the results were massively in favour of those patients who had accepted only orthodox treatment.

When the *Lancet* published Spiegel's paper in 1989, it also published an editorial, 'Psychosocial intervention and the natural history of cancer', encouraging readers to show a 'healthy scepticism' when considering this 'controversial' field of study. As Sheard pointed out, there was no such similar demand for 'healthy' scepticism when the *Lancet* published the paper from the Institute of Cancer Research.

By September 18th, ten days after the press conference, there was the first glimmer of public criticism of the paper. Dr Jean Monro and *Hospital Doctor* magazine were both being quoted in the national press. Dr Monro, alerted to the damage done by bad research after the paper on 'provocation neutralisation' had appeared in the *New England Journal of Medicine*,† wrote a letter with Dr Mark Payne to the Lancet. This letter appeared in the issue of September 22nd: it fleshed out in some detail the general methodological and statistical errors in the original Chilvers paper.

With her more combative approach, Dr Monro appeared to see something which other experts failed to see. As long as the experts slugged it out in a scientific ghetto, the vested interests would inevitably win because they had already made a massive public exhibition of their results. With this in mind, Dr Monro and Dr Payne contacted the papers when their letter was due to appear in the *Lancet*. Both the *Today* newspaper, [35] 'Cancer clinic damned by quack-buster slurs', and the *Daily Telegraph*, [36] 'Vaccine for skin cancer may be on market in 5 years', carried stories which lifted the issue out of the statistical quagmire. The *Today* story actually mentioned the role of 'quackbusters', the colloquial title for the Campaign Against Health Fraud, in attacking alternative medicine.

Monro and Payne were also the first to make it publicly clear that the Bristol sample had all been treated primarily with orthodox medicine. 'Patients usually attended the BCHC after they had attended a National Health Service hospital. This means that BCHC treatment almost always comes second.' [37] If we add this to Sheard's criticism, that many of the women in the Bristol sample had only attended the Centre for one day, we could see that some proportion of the Bristol sample could just as well have been included randomly in

† See Chapter Thirty Five.

the control sample drawn from the three general hospitals.

Monro and Payne point out in their letter to the *Lancet* that in their opinion the structural faults in the survey were so serious that the paper should have been withdrawn: '85% of patients with breast cancer attending BCHC were under 55 years of age at diagnosis, compared with 73% of controls. Breast cancer before age 55 usually has a worse prognosis, and to ignore the difference in age distribution is not acceptable.' [38] They argued further, that as like was not compared with like, not just in relation to age but also in relation to the severity of the illness, the study 'should have been re-designed or not published'. [39]

In a letter sent to a number of newspapers, [40] the Medical Sociology Group of the British Sociological Association explained that the concluding general inference of the *Lancet* paper could not be drawn from the research presented. Like was not compared with like, and there was a difficulty in attributing the worse outcome of Bristol cases to any aspect of the Bristol therapy. The Bristol cases included those who had not actually taken up any therapy and the paper made no comment on the numbers that had actually continued with the therapy or advice offered by Bristol. The letter concluded with the statement that a meeting of the British Sociological Association regretted that the interim findings had been published when they had.

This damning letter, signed by 54 qualified peers of the authors of the study itself, should have been sufficient for the authors to make a public apology and withdraw the paper. It appeared, however, like the rest of the criticism which was surfacing, to have little effect.

The editorial in the *Hospital Doctor* on 13th September by Stephen Pinn was one of the most ideologically combative statements issued in reponse to the *Lancet* paper. Instead of nit-picking with statistics, Pinn came right out and said it – the paper was a fraud. Entitled 'Slur Figures Don't Add Up' [41], the editorial began 'Whoever first spoke of lies, damned lies and statistics would have found much to commend in a report in the *Lancet* last weekend which has had the effect of single-handedly destroying the reputation of the Bristol Cancer Help Centre and the alternative therapies on which it is based.'

As far as Pinn was concerned, there was no need for uncertain liberal responses to the paper, nor even a refutation of the statistics. He was clear about the strategy and the objective of the paper's authors.

'The damage has been done. The seeds of doubt have been sown – not only in the minds of thousands of supporters of a complementary approach to treating cancer, but in the minds of many NHS doctors who, until now, have been quite happy to refer their patients for such treatment.'

Pinn did also point to some of the larger and more alarming statistical problems in the *Lancet* presentation. 'Of the 334 Bristol patients it was considered pertinent to study, there were 33 relevant relapses (patients developing metastatic cancer three months or more after entry to the study). Of the 461 control patients investigated, 134 relapses occurred. Yet after much 'adjustment', the report arrives at a figure suggesting the relapse figure is three and a half times worse for Bristol than for the control.'

Neville Hodgkinson of the *Sunday Express* was one of the only senior journalists, besides Christopher Booker, to take an independent stand on the Bristol paper. [42] In an article that argued for the Bristol therapy, he laid bare the issues behind the paper. The article began 'It is hardly possible to overstate the harm that doctors are doing patients through the over-prescription of drugs. That includes drugs used to treat cancer, most of which have not been proved to save lives but which sometimes cause terrible side effects.' He ends by drawing the readers' attention to the fact that medical research is not an objective scientific exercise, but 'an ideological battle-ground, in which big money and bruised egos can play as much a part in determining the treatments on offer as genuine concern for the patients'. Neville Hodgkinson also pointed out yet another serious flaw in the statistics of the survey: 'They ignored differences between groups of patients being compared, including the fact that those who visited Bristol – some for only one day – had suffered more extensive [orthodox] surgery'.

Sadly, no other journalists came to the aid of the Centre and its patients. The majority simply followed the ICRF line. On the whole, the administrators of BCHC, and more particularly the patients, were left to fend for themselves, to fight back against one of the most powerful research charities in Britain and against the media.

The media response to the *Lancet* paper showed the press up for what it all too often is, the messenger for vested interests. It would be diplomatic, no doubt, to say that many journalists do not understand that they are writing for vested interests. Diplomatic but not true. A number of the journalists who wrote about the Bristol Cancer Help Centre were not innocents but parties to the attack. Some had previously had contact with the Campaign Against Health Fraud and were active members of the Medical Journalists Association, or had contact with the Media Resources Service at the Ciba Foundation.

* * *

Patients, or survey subjects, do not have recourse to the media in the way that journalists do. Their views are often found expressed eloquently only in the letters columns of newspapers. In these letters it is possible to find a most valuable response to the Chilvers paper.

> Because cancer is so frightening it debilitates the whole person, and the NHS makes no attempt to help in that respect. The methods of the centre were valid and helpful to me and in conjunction with orthodox medicine, have been successful. Do not dismiss it. [43]

> Readers like me, who have benefited from the caring, loving programme which embraces the whole person and who have followed the (near) vegan diet since Feburary 1985 will find both the results of the study, as well as the selective articles that have followed, inconsistent with their experience ... The results are at best inconclusive, at worst fundamentally flawed. There is no evidence to support the theory that diet is the cause of the different results. [44]

> The treatment of the interim results of the BCHC survival study, both by the press and the ICRF, is very worrying. It is irresponsible to pull and attempt to interpret results a mere two years into a five year trial and wrong to call a press conference to publish these findings ... Apart from the moral issue, this is also extremely bad scientific practice. It invalidates the rest of the study, since the women in the sample may well have been frightened by the scare-mongering of the press over the last week. [45]

> The Bristol Centre puts the patient back in control, something that the negative attitudes of doctors and nurses cannot do. [46]

On October 5th an article appeared in the *West Sussex County Times*, written by Deborah Baldwin, who although writing for a local paper, adopts a rigorous attitude to the Bristol study, cleverly putting almost the whole of her article in the words of one cancer sufferer, Jeremy Drake. Mr Drake had terminal cancer, and as well as being a visitor at Bristol, was a member of the Crawley Cancer Support Group. As other sufferers had done, he commented upon the devastating effect which the results of such poor quality research had on patients:

> I was angry, because of the callous way the so-called facts were presented, particularly by television, especially without the background information. I felt incredulity because all eight other patients I spoke to agreed that the things gained from Bristol were generally to do with looking at methods of care and there is no way that can be harmful. [47]

* * *

Heather Goodare, an enterprising and skilled woman, who had attended Bristol and been interviewed for the survey, was more angry than most people about the way in which she had been abused by vested interests wanting to make an ideological point. Her experience of cancer treatment plunged her almost directly into the politics of that treatment. As soon as the results were announced she began a crusade.

In a letter of October 25th which the *Lancet* refused to publish, Goodare says that Dr Vladimir Svoboda from the Campaign Against Health Fraud, appearing on Television South on October 13th†, had said that the Bristol Centre 'refused to subject their patients to the randomised prospective trials'. She points out that though this argument was used frequently by people associated with the *Lancet* paper, it had actually been impossible to randomise the Bristol patients, because it would have meant refusing some people treatment for the sake of a study.

> Your [*Lancet* paper] authors have turned what could have been a plain statement of a regrettable fact into something which suggests that the BCHC was wilfully obstructing a proper investigation. [48]

† See p. 500.

In the months following the *Lancet* paper, Heather Goodare with another survey subject, Isla Burke, and other Bristol attenders infuriated by the research results, gathered together and formed the Bristol Survey Support Group. The group was primarily to support those who felt that they had been abused by the survey. Research subjects are often deliberately reduced by researchers to the most supine of roles. Sucked dry of their life's experience, they are given little in exchange before being cast off.

The subjects of the Bristol study felt more strongly than most survey participants that they had been seriously abused. Not only had they suffered a terrible illness, they had been exploited and misled about the motives of those who were conducting the research into the illness and its treatment. The support group was set up principally because of this, but also because of the effect which the publication of the interim results had upon its subjects. They began the long uphill trek of supporting each other over the emotional crisis which the results had plunged all of them into. They also began to campaign for the truth.

The BSSG was set up in December 1990. The demonstrable need for such a group is itself the strongest and most substantial criticism of the study.† As lay subjects of orthodox medicine's 'great debate' on cancer, patients were not meant to have speaking parts.

* * *

> The [paper's] authors say they regret that their paper created the impression that the Bristol regimen worsened patients' chances and that this had never been stated. 'The media were responsible for this conclusion' Professor Chilvers said. [49]

When the Bristol Centre did finally decide to fight back publicly, it found itself reliant upon the media. Given the unbelievable imbalance of power which was manifest in the reporting of the Chilvers paper, it seemed an impossible task for the Centre to raise itself to its feet again. Whatever was said, the damage had already been done. The name of

† The BSSG demanded that the Charities Commission carry out an investigation of the role of the ICRF and the CRC in the Bristol Survey. Isla Burke and Heather Goodare also made a highly successful film for Channel Four's access programme 'Free for All', entitled 'Cancer positive'.

Bristol Cancer Help Centre was synonymous in the minds of many ordinary people with a regime that killed women with breast cancer.

By early November, the criticism of Chilvers' paper had become public enough for its authors and the backers of the research to know that the issue was not going to go away. Bristol organised its own press conference and the ICRF began reluctantly to plan a strategy of retreat.

Bristol's press conference was due to be held on Thursday November 8th. By then, some journalists were getting the scent of blood and were introducing the BCHC and the *Lancet* authors like boxers at a weigh-in: 'Breast cancer experts today prepared for a new battle between alternative and traditional medical treatments',[50] 'Battle has raged for two months'.[51]

But journalists were still pretending that the opponents were evenly matched and most cleverly side-stepping their own involvement in the whole issue. If it had not been for the original uncritical reports following the ICRF press conference, there would have been no need for a rematch.

The Centre's press conference coincided with the publication of further letters to the *Lancet*: from the authors of the Chilvers paper, from Sir Walter Bodmer and from Dr Tim Sheard at Bristol. As far as the authors of the paper were concerned, their letter of explanation and retraction meant the end of any public debate: 'Everything that we wanted to say has been said in the letter to the *Lancet*', said Professor McElwain.[52]

The *Lancet* letter, signed by the authors of the original paper, made two statements clearly expressing the view that the original paper had not meant to suggest that it was the therapy at Bristol that hastened death. 'We did not claim that our findings constituted strong evidence that some aspect of the BCHC management was the direct cause of the observed difference in outcome.' And more specifically, 'We regret that our paper has created the widespread impression that the BCHC regimen directly caused the difference that we observed in recurrence and survival. This was never stated.'[53]

Coming two months after the press conference this 'retraction', if that is indeed what it was, was worthless and appeared ingenuous. There can be little doubt that at the press conference, the ICR survey team and their sponsors at the ICRF had done nothing to dissuade the media that the regime at Bristol could bring about the earlier death of its attenders. Why was it left two months before this serious misinterpretation of the paper was corrected? If the paper's authors did not suggest that it was the regime at Bristol that accounted for the difference in survival rates, who did suggest this to reporters who led with the story that it was the diet which was responsible? If the paper's authors did not suggest that it was the regime at Bristol that accounted for differences in survival rates, then what did they suggest was responsible? The authors of the paper had unleashed a monster which they were unable to control. When they realised that their project on behalf of vested interests might cast a shadow over their own integrity, they tried to run for the cover of a half-hearted apology.

Two months after the original publication, the authors of the paper were willing to agree with their critics and principally with Dr Tim Sheard of the BCHC that the study contained a number of methodological flaws which invalidated any possible conclusions. In November it was evident to them 'that the difference [between the BCHC and the controls] could be explained by increased severity of disease in BCHC attenders.' Furthermore, it is clear from the letter of Sir Walter Bodmer to the *Lancet* (November 10th 1990) that the authors and the ICRF had conferred on their position. It was the case, Bodmer wrote, that 'the study's results can be explained by the fact that women going to Bristol had more severe disease than control women'. [54] If this was the case, why was it not stated clearly in the paper, and why was the paper published with methodological errors of such gravity?

The retraction, however, earned little in the way of publicity, especially when compared with the original paper. A few desultory articles with bland headlines didn't really do much to clear the air. The *Daily Telegraph* reported the partial retraction most accurately, with its headline 'Doctors' attack on holistic cure is toned down', [55] while *Today* introduced a completely new note into the debate, presumably because they did not have room for big words like 'alternative': 'Herbal cancer clinic cleared.' [56] Neither the sober reports nor the stupid ones did anything to right the balance. 'Flawed' and 'challenged' were the strongest words used to describe the original paper.

The press conference held by the Bristol Cancer Help Centre, where it was reported at all, was covered in five or six lines, often with

Dr Sheard asking that the paper should be 'unreservedly retracted'. Unfortunately to most lay readers, the grounds for this retraction were still obscure.

In the light of the anodyne and half-baked retraction, most people could be forgiven for wondering what all the fuss was about in the first place. Bristol administrators and patients knew because they were still suffering the destructive effects of the 'error'. The publication of the original paper and the surrounding publicity destroyed all confidence in the BCHC and its waiting list quickly dissolved. In early November, it appeared that the major authors of the paper, Drs Chilvers, Easton and McElwain, had managed to extricate themselves from the exercise without a scratch. This was not to be.

* * *

On November 26th, only two weeks after he had put his name to the 'retraction' in the *Lancet*, Professor McElwain, one of the founder members of the Campaign Against Health Fraud and one of the country's leading oncologists, cut his throat in the bathroom of his home in Clapham. Following the letters in the *Lancet*, the *Guardian* had canvassed the opinion of McElwain, who had said with revealing honesty: 'The study was not as good as it could have been.' When asked about his earlier statement that he would now warn patients about the survey results if they wanted to go to Bristol, he said: 'It seems unlikely if you go to Bristol it will do you harm.' [57]

There seems little doubt that McElwain's depression, his admission to hospital on November 23rd and his subsequent suicide were related to the row that had blown up over the Chilvers paper. A man of some integrity, and one who appeared to care for his patients, McElwain seemed to have been dealt a devastating psychological blow when he saw the damage which the Chilvers paper had done. Who knows what pressures were put upon him by the more zealous of his scientific colleagues?

* * *

Within weeks of the devastating attack upon the BCHC, some of the major actors were writing conciliatory letters to the Centre apparently with the intention of 'making-up'. The fact that there was little left of the Centre did not appear to concern them, nor the fact that what the Bristol Centre really needed was a proper public repudiation of the research.

Dr Lesley Fallowfield, a senior lecturer in Health Psychology at the London Hospital Medical College, and a colleague of Professor McElwain, wrote to the Centre following a viewing of 'The Cancer Question', the BBC film made in the summer and shown on September 13th. Fallowfield had been a participant in the programme and appeared to be a vehement critic of the Bristol Centre.

> I have just watched the video of the Cancer Question. I think that it turned out to be a little more confrontational than was probably necessary. We are all after all trying to achieve the same thing, which is to help patients with cancer through one of the most emotionally traumatic experiences of their lives. [58]

In November, following a visit to the Centre, Professor Michael Baum wrote a letter which some might have considered hypocritical. Baum, who had just taken up a senior post at the Institute of Cancer Research, had always spoken against alternative or complementary cancer treatment; he had coincidentally been on the International Advisory Board of the *Lancet* which published the Chilvers paper.

> I would like to reiterate my proposal to join you in some descriptive research so that we can start to identify the personality traits of the patients who favour your support and investigate their attitudes to orthodox and alternative medicine, to be compared with a random sample of patients with cancer who have not sought out your advice.

Apart from suggesting possible new research, Baum was quite cavalier in his agreement with Bristol that there were serious errors in the Chilvers paper.

> [the new information] confirms my own prejudice that there was a very powerful selection bias in the type of patient coming to Bristol, compared with the controls ... It is also plausible that the higher rate of mastectomy for the younger women might indirectly reflect that these had a greater tumour burden at the time of diagnosis ... I am sure if you make these data available to the ICR team, they will recalculate the data, which may then get

> rid of the majority of the difference in outcome between the two
> groups. [59]

Baum gave the impression of not understanding the immense damage which had by that time been done to the Centre. Moreover, while he made it privately clear that there were most serious faults in the Chilvers paper, he took no steps to make any public statement at the time of its publication.† And what are we to make of the naive supposition that if Bristol were to contact the Institute of Cancer Research and tell them where they had gone wrong, the ICR would re-work the statistics? Was this naiveté, or veiled sarcasm? By November 1990, the workers and managers at Bristol were not engaged in any meaningful dialogue with the ICR, the organisation which had all but destroyed their charity.

The fact is that the hard-core critics of Bristol who had organised under cover of the Chilvers report and who had a covert interest in destroying the Centre were utterly unrepentant. Not only were they unrepentant, but they continued to pursue the spurious arguments put forward in the Chilvers report as if there had been no criticism and no retraction. Michael Baum was still writing in concord with the interim results as long as six months after the press conference. Clair Chilvers herself was still sending out the discredited paper as part of her contemporary work and publications without any explanation, six months after the press conference.

Vincent Marks wrote to Bristol within a month of the *Lancet* publication, showing absolutely no regard for the criticisms which had been levelled against the interim results.

> I cannot say that I am altogether surprised since ... I believe that
> the diet that has been advocated or at least recommended by
> you and your colleagues for the past ten years cannot do any
> good, and might conceivably do harm.
>
> I agreed to help you give sound dietary advice to people
> attending the Bristol Cancer Help Centre, and that offer remains
> open. It will, however, require you to stop defending your

† Baum was the co-signatory of a letter to the *Lancet* (with Jeffrey Tobias) published after the Chilvers paper, which took a very critical and superior attitude to the Bristol Centre.

previous practices; indeed possibly to *admit publicly* that it was ill-advised, though not ill-intentioned ... [60]

Such an admission would of course be tantamount to publicly stating support for the 'interim' results – an agreement that it was the diet at Bristol which was responsible for damaging the survival of its patients.†

Following Professor McElwain's death, it was as if his colleagues wanted to gloss over the fateful results of the study. In fact, such results could be seen as the logical culmination of the 'prankster' approach much advocated by CSICOP and UK Skeptics. Dr Ian Smith of the Royal Marsden was quoted in the *Evening Standard* using McElwain's life and death to make yet more ideological mileage on behalf of the health-fraud movement.

> He was a great debunker. Professor McElwain's involvement in the Bristol report reflected a desire to build bridges with the Bristol people and to establish a dialogue. He believed in the truth coming out. That's the basic thing of a scientist. The problem with much alternative medicine is that its claims are just claims, like the claims of an astrologer. He was anxious to test them. But there were problems with the statistical side of the report, not with his side of things. [61]

This same *Evening Standard* article also quoted Dr Lesley Fallowfield. Months after the study, and despite her personal letter to the Centre, she was still publicly endorsing the Chilvers report.

> You could always tell a Bristol patient because they were orange skinned and very thin. They became seriously weight depleted because of the lack of protein in the diet and their skin had an orange tinge because of the vast quantities of carrot juice they drank.

----

† Penny Brohn did take Vincent Marks up on his 'offer to help'. He had told her that a chapter in 'The Bristol Programme' on nutrition was hopelessly wrong and full of mistakes. When, however, she tried to pin him down, he was evasive, telling her he didn't want to give specific examples. When the book was to be re-printed, Brohn told Marks that she was now in a position to start the nutrition chapter all over again, from scratch, so this was his chance to direct her along the right lines. He offered no help and Brohn concluded that he had absolutely no intention of collaborating with her, and had boxed himself into a tight corner.

Fallowfield also said in relation to Bristol:

> The 'healers' smack of quackery to me, it's the equivalent of the
> old travelling shows and snake venom potions.† [62]

* * *

As has been the case with many of the other 'debunking' projects that
scientists have been involved in, there was a pattern to the attack on
the Bristol Cancer Help Centre which identifies it as the work of those
associated with CSICOP, UK Skeptics and HealthWatch. The first
clue is the unscientific nature of the study. This was followed (before its
subjects had time to realise that the project had been terribly
corrupted), by a massive press conference which gave immediate
authority to its results and its methodology. Finally, one of the big give-
aways was the blatant and continued use of the study results, long after
a public retraction had been made.

This comprehensive strategy was just that, a strategy, and no part
of it was the result of simple human error or unhappy mistake. Had
this in fact been the case, those who carried out the study were
powerful enough to have publicly rectified their error. No real attempt
at a retraction or apology was made and there can be no doubt that
the fraudulent results of the study had the desired effect: they almost
destroyed the Bristol Cancer Help Centre.

The unprincipled nature of the continued onslaught against Bristol
is exemplified by a peculiar article which appeared in the *Independent on
Sunday* on May 5th. [63] The article was written by Duncan Campbell,
confederate of Vincent Marks and HealthWatch fellow traveller, and
Alex Holmes, Campbell's aide-de-camp at the *New Statesman*. The
article, published eight months after the Chilvers report had been
roundly condemned, begins by drawing attention to this report: 'The
Bristol Cancer Help Centre, whose methods of treatment were

---

† The quotes from Fallowfield and Smith both use key symbolic words and
concepts frequently used by CSICOP and UK Skeptics, as well as the American
National Council Against Health Fraud. The words 'debunk, 'astrologer',
'quackery', and 'snake venom' are all well-worn words from the health-fraud
lexicon.

criticised last year'. It goes on to suggest a conspiracy in which patients at Bristol are 'encouraged' to buy large quantities of expensive vitamin supplements, made up by 'Nature's Own'. Campbell claimed there was a common link between some members of the Centre, 'Nature's Own', and a spiritualist society.

The story referred to events which had taken place almost ten years previously and was written with Campbell's usual innuendo combined with a cynical lack of explanation. In two seminal paragraphs towards the end, he quotes Dr Lesley Fallowfield. This is the same Dr Fallowfield who wrote a conciliatory letter to Penny Brohn on October 17th, suggesting that 'We are all, after all, trying to achieve the same things.'

> Dr Lesley Fallowfield, a psychiatrist at the London Hospital who has studied the effects of the Bristol treatment on patients, said last week that the programme had caused patients psychological distress. 'They have modified it greatly in recent years, but originally patients were given the impression that unless they followed the diet, and took the supplements, they would compromise their chances of surviving.' [64]

Here again, is evidence of the shadow which from the time of the study was to follow Bristol. The assumption clearly indicated by the quote is that it was the diet and the supplements together with the rigorous enforcement of the regime which led to 'compromised chances of survival'. That is not all: in the next quote from Fallowfield, another scenario is generated, that Bristol is fleecing people of their money.

> Dr Fallowfield added: 'The cost can be extortionate, particularly in some of these institutions where they are prescribed [vitamin supplements]. This in itself can cause further problems for many people with severe or acute illnesses, particularly those in financial difficulties. This is often the case if they have been out of work for some time.' [65]

So, it is not only the diet which reduces survival rates amongst patients at Bristol, it is also the stress created by being forced to buy expensive supplements, especially coming on top of unemployment!

From articles such as this, it appears clear that apparently sympathetic letters written to Bristol after the publication of the 'interim' results, contained nothing but crocodile tears. The attack mounted by the friends of HealthWatch continues years later to exert a ghostly power despite it having been disclosed to the world as a sham.

Chapter Thirty Seven

Attacking Healthy Nutrition

Generally speaking, the physician today has an interest in seeing the sick get well, but not that people be healthy and not become ill. [1]

Patrick Holford

Early in 1989, Patrick Holford, the founder of the Institute for Optimum Nutrition (ION), travelled to America; there, he met Professor Linus Pauling and for a short time investigated alternative approaches to AIDS. Back in London, he wrote an article about AIDS for the journal *Optimum Nutrition*, entitled 'AIDS can be cured'. [2] As its title suggests, 'AIDS can be cured' is a very positive article about the HIV antibody positive condition. It discusses in case detail a number of different ways in which HIV antibody positive people can treat their immune system. The article pays scant attention to AZT.

Treatments which the article's subjects considered useful are those which raised their T cell count: a measure of the health of the immune system. The dietary regimes the article discusses are those which abstain from coffee and tea and forego all chemical drugs. Diets consist principally of raw vegetables and raw fruit with vitamin and mineral supplements. The article is about surviving, and between the lines it argues strongly against the medical myth that a diagnosis of HIV antibody positive means death.

By the time Campbell's article against Yves Delatte and Monica Bryant appeared in the *New Statesman* in 1989, Patrick Holford had come to know and respect Monica Bryant, who had lectured on bacteria and probiotics at ION. After the articles were published, people approached ION to ask whether Campbell was right about probiotic preparations. Wishing to be sure that his support for Bryant was not misguided, Holford sent off Bryant's preparations to be analysed at two laboratories. Both labs returned reports stating that there was no faecal matter in the preparations.

Holford's interest in Monica Bryant's therapies and his defence of her, led him to the Campaign Against Health Fraud. When he found that Vincent Marks was a founder member of the organisation, he began to understand what was going on. He wrote an editorial in the summer 1989 edition of *Optimum Nutrition*.

> The most vicious attack on natural remedies appeared recently in the *New Statesman*, written by Duncan Campbell, involved in the Campaign Against Health Fraud, slamming the use of beneficial human strain bacteria in relation to AIDS and ME as 'selling extract of excrement to sick and dying people.' The article entitled 'Let them eat shit', basically three pages of abuse, claimed that Probiotic supplements including Symbion, a combination of three beneficial bacteria, were 'extract of excrement' and were made 'in an ordinary kitchen'. To test these claims we obtained two independent analyses of the product from Brighton Polytechnic, and a private laboratory. Each analysis confirmed that there were no pathogenic organisms or faecal matter present. Monica Bryant director of the International Institute of Symbiotic Studies, told us, 'There is no truth to the claim that these products contain pathogenic substances or faecal matter. These products are produced by a reputable pharmaceuticals manufacturer and its laboratories under strictly controlled conditions'. [3]

When the next attack on Monica Bryant, 'Pretty poison', appeared, Patrick Holford again went to her defence. He did not think that germanium was an essential nutrient, but he saw no evidence to suggest that germanium sesquioxide was toxic.

Patrick Holford's defence of Monica Bryant, his article about HIV, together with a personal altercation which he had with Duncan Campbell at the 1989 Here's Health exhibition, were adequate reason for Campbell to begin a crusade against both ION and Holford. There was also the fact that Patrick Holford had been involved for the last two years in an ongoing battle with Vincent Marks at Surrey University. As Campbell had joined up with Marks, they now had an enemy in common.

Larkhall

> We have never said that supplementation can increase innate
> IQ; merely that supplements can make children healthier and
> their performance better so that when they are given an IQ test
> they can make a better job of it. [4]

In 1985, the science master at Darland High School in Wales began
trials to compare two groups of school children, some taking vitamin
supplements and the others not. This first trial of the effect of vitamins
on concentration and learning – termed IQ – showed that children
who took the vitamin supplements had an IQ on average six points
higher than those who did not. It was also noted that children given
the supplements had better behaviour scores.

Larkhall Natural Health became involved in the Welsh school trials
when they were approached to make up the vitamin supplemen.s for
them. The Welsh trials followed similar work carried out in America.
Both Dr Robert Woodward and Rita Greer, who worked at Larkhall,
were keen to be involved in the trials, the results of which were likely to
show what they had always felt, that the 'average diet' – which at one
extreme might be woefully inadequate – did not always provide a full
spectrum of nutrients, and so impaired some children's ability to
concentrate, learn, and solve problems.

The first Darland study passed with little publicity. A second trial,
this time lasting for nine months, was carried out between 1986 and
June 1987. In January 1988, after Tandem IQ had been on the
market for a year, the results of the second trial were reported in the
Lancet. [5] These results attracted favourable articles in a number of
papers and BBC 'QED' broadcast a programme about them.

The one exception to the generally constructive interest shown in
the second Darland High School trial was a short piece in the *Observer* [6]
by Caroline Richmond, entitled 'Vitamins for thought'. Richmond
claimed that critics of the study were ignored, she criticised the
methodology and the statistical protocols of the study and finally
suggested that it should be run again to a higher standard.

In July 1989, Professor Donald Naismith published the results of a
study which had been proposed by a group of industry-orientated
nutritionists. Professor Naismith is a colleague of a number of 'old
school' nutritionists who belonged to the Campaign Against Health

Fraud; in the past he has been funded by the food industry. The intention of the study was to replicate and refute the Darland High School trial. Naismith's study was rushed out with a tremendous amount of publicity, but like all similar projects, it was more con than convincing. Naismith's study had been conducted over the period of a month, while the Darland study had been carried out over nine months. The vitamin supplements for the Darland study had been carefully made up by Robert Woodward at Larkhall. Naismith's study used different pills made to different specifications. Inevitably, the Naismith study showed that vitamin supplements *did not* raise IQ levels.

The findings of the Naismith study were published in the *British Journal of Nutrition*. There was one interesting conclusion which crept in almost by accident and was dismissed by Naismith. The study showed that children who had been taking vitamin supplements regularly prior to the trial got a higher IQ score than those who had not taken vitamins.

Robert Woodward and Rita Greer saw the results of the second Darland High School study as a useful contribution to the ongoing debate about nutrition and mental states. They could never have guessed that the 'QED' programme and the publication of their results were to be the beginning of a long period of harassment. From the middle of 1989 onwards, Larkhall became a primary target of both HealthWatch and Duncan Campbell.

On August 17th, Larkhall had the first burglary in a series which was going to continue for over a year and a half.

* * *

Some time after Patrick Holford had argued with Duncan Campbell at the Here's Health show in the autumn of 1989, he received a phone call from him. Campbell wanted to know about Holford's contacts with vitamin companies. Holford was polite but not particularly forthcoming: he also recorded the conversation.

It was clear to Patrick Holford from the phone call that Campbell had got some of his information wrong. In order to clarify the situation, Holford sent a statement to Campbell and told him that if he wanted to ask any more questions, he should put them in writing and they would be answered.

Duncan Campbell, however, began to apply the same pressure to Holford that he had maintained on others he had targeted. He began ringing Holford's place of work frequently, sometimes being very rude to the staff. He then began to say that Holford was refusing to speak to him and finally began to threaten the publication of a story about Holford in an unnamed publication.

Angered by Campbell's tactics, Patrick Holford wrote directly to the *New Statesman*, informing them that Campbell was sending out faxes on *New Statesman* headed paper and asking the editor to tell him if they intended to publish an article about him. He finally found out that Campbell was about to publish a piece in the *Sunday Correspondent*.

Patrick Holford wrote to the *Sunday Correspondent* informing them that if they or Duncan Campbell had any more queries, they should contact him personally. He soon got a reply from the editor suggesting a meeting between Holford and Campbell at his offices. Holford took a lawyer and sat for almost two hours answering questions put by Campbell before the editor and his assistant. At the end of this interrogation, in Holford's opinion, everything had been cleared up. The meeting ended on a friendly note, with Campbell suggesting that he and Holford should have a drink together sometime.

Following that meeting, Patrick Holford's lawyer drafted a letter to the *Correspondent* making it clear that as Holford had been open and honest and hidden nothing, they would not hesitate to sue were the *Correspondent* to publish anything libellous.

About two weeks after this meeting, when Patrick Holford was working late at the Institute for Optimum Nutrition, there was a ring on the door. Opening the door, he was confronted by a large man who asked: 'Are you Mr Holford ... Patrick Holford?'. When he replied that he was, the man produced an automatic camera from behind his back and began taking pictures while walking into the Institute. Holford struggled to close the door and keep the man out. Even at the last minute, as the door was closing, the man was able to hold his camera round the door. When the door was shut, Holford's heart was pounding. Nothing like that had ever happened to him. He was annoyed that he had let the man get pictures of him looking furtive while struggling to shut the door.

The next day Patrick Holford set off in his car to give a lecture on nutrition at a teaching hospital in south London. When he was stopped at a set of traffic lights, the driving side door of his car was suddenly thrown open and the same man with a camera began taking photographs of him. Holford reported both incidents to the police and the Press Council.

* * *

Phoney health information services and Institutes like Holford's ION abound, most of them scarcely disguised sales fronts. [7]

In December 1989, Duncan Campbell's article entitled 'The Rise of the New Age Pill Pushers' appeared in the *Sunday Correspondent Magazine*. [8] The introduction consists of horror stories and unattributable case histories of people apparently seriously damaged by vitamin and food supplements. Following these horror stories come profiles of the targeted professionals involved in what Campbell claims to be nutritional fraud. Such people *appear* to be implicated somehow in the previously described horror stories, and more specifically are only involved in health care issues for mercenary motives.

In the last six months, horrible new frauds have come to light, aimed particularly at AIDS patients. The 'treatments' sold are dangerous. One is a powder called Ecoflorin or Delta Te, whose key, advertised ingredient is food poisoning bacteria. Many patients with ME, allergies, AIDS and other conditions have also been enticed to pay for extremely expensive but nutritionally worthless 'organic germanium' pills. [9]

The horror stories in this article are mainly about those who took a substance called Protexin B. We are told only that Protexin B consists of laboratory cultivated bacteria. A Mrs Harvey from Thetford in Norfolk took it, and testifies that it gave her a real turn. Amongst other things, when she took Protexin B she turned 'yellow like a buttercup. My liver swole (sic) up and my spleen hurt'. Dr Charles Shepherd,

medical adviser to the ME Association and, though not stated, a
Campaign Against Health Fraud member, who had previously helped
Campbell in his campaign against germanium, says of Protexin: 'it's
an immoral, worthless hoax'.

Having set a scene which has no relevance to Patrick Holford,
Campbell launches into a description of Holford, his work and his
Institute. Holford is made out to be a scheming quack: 'The sales
methods of the vitamin-pill trade are often subtle. Patrick Holford who
runs the Institute for Optimum Nutrition in Fulham, is one of Britain's
most articulate new pill pushers'.

The description of Holford's life and work, and his professional
position, is meanly reduced to that of a salesman, a person whose
raison d'être is the making of money out of vulnerable and sick people.
Campbell does not even attempt to engage in a reasoned debate about
vitamins and in common with his other articles, 'The Rise of the New
Age Pill Pushers' is devoid of intellectual nuances.

> Magazines, books, lectures and training courses provided by the
> Institute for Optimum Nutrition (ION) can all be shown to be
> vehicles for promoting and selling Health Plus products. [10]

Holford's entire learning experience and expertise are reduced and
described in terms of self-publicity.

> Holford describes himself as a 'nutritional counsellor', credited
> with the 'Diploma of the Institute for Optimum Nutrition'. But
> Holford awarded the 'diploma' to himself. [11]

It is of course fairly easy to write this kind of cynical junk about
anyone, it is much harder actually to get to the social and personal
heart of the matter and understand people's attitudes within their
social and inter-personal context. Campbell uses the article to make
sweeping value judgements about the worth of people's lives. Having
reduced Holford to criminal rubble, he quotes Dr Andrew Taylor,
friend and colleague of Vincent Marks.

> Dr Andrew Taylor ... runs a genuine trace-element laboratory in
> Guildford as part of the National Health Service. Hair analysis
> test salesmen, says Dr Taylor, make extravagant claims for their
> methods. But patients who are told that they suffer from 'trace
> element imbalance' can be left 'anxious [and] frightened'. [12]

Again, while there is an apparent reality to the life and comment of someone who 'runs a genuine trace-element laboratory', there is no such reality to Patrick Holford's opinions. This is despite the fact that Holford would most probably use a 'genuine trace-element laboratory' if he wanted to obtain an analysis, and despite the fact that Patrick Holford does not generally give diagnostic counselling, and so is unlikely to leave anyone anxious and frightened.

Later in the article, Campbell draws on the erudition of CAHF member Vincent Marks and even manages to regurgitate his case against Cass Mann. The article ends with an advertisement for the Campaign Against Health Fraud, and a quote from Caroline Richmond. There is no mention of who funds CAHF, or where Caroline Richmond was working at that time.

In many of Duncan Campbell's articles, it is possible to glimpse the hard cynicism of CSICOP and HealthWatch. His arguments speak on behalf of a society peopled by pre-packed uniform units which aid production, marketing and consumption. Its inhabitants ask no questions, and forego their personal search for truth because it has all been done for them by the State and its scientists. It is a futuristic world managed by professionals, in which high-technology is the power.

* * *

Three months prior to the publication of the *Sunday Correspondent* article, in September 1989, Robert Woodward appeared on a BSB television programme. Dr Woodward and David Benton, who had worked on the first and second Darland studies, confronted Miriam Stoppard and Professor Naismith.†

Miriam Stoppard was one of the first women to be Managing

---

† Naismith himself was not above championing the cause of vitamins, as long as he was working for the right party; in a promotional piece for Vitalert products, Naismith wrote 'The regular use of specific multi-vitamin, multi-mineral supplements therefore makes sense. They ensure that the body's needs are met even when ideal dietary practices cannot be followed and, for many, will result in a noticeable improvement in physical and mental well being'.

Director of a multi-national drug company when she worked for Syntex in the 1970s.† During the short programme which Stoppard hosted, Robert Woodward didn't get much opportunity to speak. Afterwards he was approached by Stoppard who made it quite clear which side she was on: 'I think your pack [Tandem IQ] is a disgrace' she said.

In 1989 Duncan Campbell began working with the 'Food and Drink Programme'. These programmes are made on a freelance basis by Bazal Productions Ltd. They are accompanied by a magazine published by the BBC, which contains advertising for some of the largest processed food companies.

In the first programme of the 1990 series, on the 30th October, the 'Food and Drink Programme' looked at vitamins. It was a terribly one-sided programme, with one journalist looking at the vitamin supplement said to increase IQ and Duncan Campbell looking at the 'vitamin conspiracy', the British Society for Nutritional Medicine and the doctors who worked within it.

The programme took evidence from Naismith's discredited study and rounded off the item by telling viewers that they had sent three packets of IQ-boosting vitamin supplements to Shropshire Trading Standards Office.‡ Shropshire was known by the 'Food and Drink Programme' to be a prosecution-oriented authority and the programme had a personal contact in Shropshire with one of their trading standards officers who had appeared on a previous edition.

Between August 1989 and October 1990, and later for further specific programmes, Duncan Campbell worked for Bazal Productions gathering 'evidence' against Larkhall and their products. Campbell

---

† Syntex produce allergy drugs; hormones, contraceptive pills and anti-viral drugs.

‡ There is a general principle in trading standards which entails complaints about products most usually being referred to the 'home Authority' (HA). The HA is the trading standards office covering the area where the product is produced and packaged. The reason for this is that if a producer is prosecuted, the cost of that prosecution is borne by the prosecuting authority. The BBC by-passed the HA in the Larkhall case, which meant that the council tax payers of Shropshire shouldered the entire cost of a 'political' prosecution against a London-based firm. The BBC knew that they would have a better prosecutorial chance in Shropshire than in London where Larkhall's local HA had already given them a clean bill of health.

passed his information on to the Campaign Against Health Fraud, which was able to put the 'evidence' before government agencies such as MAFF which CAHF hoped would prosecute.

In October 1990, the burglaries and attempted break-ins at Larkhall began in earnest.

> On the 17th October, in the evening when only the cleaners were present, a man rang the goods entrance bell so persistently that the cleaners felt obliged to answer it. The man said that he was delivering stationery. He wasn't; he was merely trying to gain access. [13]

> The following night at around the same time, a man tried to break down the gate to the yard at the rear of the premises. When he saw that the cleaners had noticed him, he made off in a Jaguar car. [14]

> The same night at 9.10pm, the burglar alarms went off in the factory. The police came and the building was searched. They found nothing and the bells were reset. A few minutes later, they went off again – there was an intruder in the building. The video surveillance camera showed a man trying to open the door inside the front of the building. [15]

For weeks either side of these attempts to enter the premises, completely coincidentally, Larkhall received phone calls from journalists.

> There then followed a string of accusations, much on the lines of the previous phone calls; they were all about how dreadful we were to even think of marketing a product such as Tandem IQ. We were conning people, it was a fraud – all the usual ... [16]

In 1990, a production manager at Larkhall, Paul Hamill, left to join Wellcome. Hamill had been trained by Larkhall and had been with them for three years. He went to work for Wellcome as a machine operator.

By the end of 1990, the number of break-ins and attempted break-ins had become extreme and, to Rita Greer, frightening. Greer, who was handling the burglaries for Larkhall, had been given a special phone number, by her local CID who had assigned two officers to the Larkhall premises. Unable to solve the break-ins, and despite their usual reluctance to proffer other than 'normal' motives for burglaries, officers discussed with Greer the possibility that another company was trying to ruin Larkhall.

On the instructions of the local police, Rita Greer had staff report to her any disquieting circumstances. Throughout the last months of 1990, it was found that the factory was frequently under surveillance. In December there were a number of attempted break-ins, the situation was so bad, that parts of the roof became unsafe and had to be rebuilt. Staff were followed, and occupied cars were often seen parked close to the premises for long periods.

Robert Woodward thinks that the burglaries at Larkhall had, as their objective, information about the Darland High School trial. He believes that someone was trying to gain evidence that Larkhall had paid for the research and so biased the results. Both Woodward and Greer also think that the burglaries were a way of getting information about packaging or contents of supplements which might in some way contravene Department of Health or MAFF regulations. On two occasions, they found products which had been taken off the shelves had been planted in the shop adjacent to the factory. Coincidentally unknown callers asked at the shop for those very items.

On the 21st December, Woodward received another interrogatory phone call from Campbell, which was followed by a lengthy letter sent to Larkhall and by courier to the Greers' home in Hampshire. Campbell tried to get Woodward to appear on the 'Food and Drink Programme'. Woodward told Campbell and Bazal Productions, that he would go on the programme, if four simple conditions were met – including a live interview. Peter Bazalgette, the producer of the 'Food and Drink Programme' wrote to Woodward refusing all four conditions.

By Christmas 1990, the constant attacks upon Larkhall and the invasion of Greer and Woodward's privacy, manifested by endless phone calls at all hours of the day and night from Campbell and Hinks, had become so bad that Greer was near to a nervous breakdown. Her husband, who had multiple sclerosis, was very ill. Over Christmas, the Greers were forced to move home so that they could have at least a short period of peace.

On January 2nd 1991, Campbell arrived at the Larkhall factory with a film crew and tried to force his way into the building. Greer used the special phone number she had been given and the police arrived at the premises in an exemplary one and a half minutes. Campbell's attempts to get in at the front of the factory, through the shop and at the back of the premises, failed and several squad cars of police waited until Campbell and his crew departed. By this time, Robert Woodward knew that he wasn't dealing with normal journalistic practice, but with a concerted campaign to try to discredit him.

> It first struck me that this was a concerted campaign, on the 21st December when Duncan Campbell rang me. In December, he asked me about germanium and Immunomega, he accused me of advertising True-Free foods, (which as prescription items should not be promoted to consumers).† I talked to him about niacin and tryptophan. It was then that he boasted about having access to our computer systems.‡ [17]

Stephen Davies

In the summer of 1989, the British Society for Nutritional Medicine (BSNM) held one of its bi-annual conferences. The subject of the conference was nutrition and AIDS and it was held at St Bartholomew's Hospital. The BSNM had little to say about AZT at their conference, and much more to say about anti-viral and immune system enhancing nutritional therapies.

---

† Rita Greer wrote to and telephoned Campbell regarding his accusation that Larkhall was advertising True-Free flours. The 'advertisement' turned out to be merely a listing of True-Free in a trade price list, which is permissable under the regulations.

‡ The substances which Campbell was asking about, germanium, niacin and tryptophan, are all substances which were banned by the DoH after CAHF had campaigned on them. Campbell reported Larkhall to the Pharmaceutical Society, claiming to have bought niacin by 'self-selection' (as in a supermarket) in the Larkhall shop. This was not true: customers do not have access to products in the shop. An investigation of the sale was carried out by a representative of the Pharmaceutical Society, who found Campbell's accusation to be without foundation.

It came as no surprise to some AIDS activists that the BSNM became, from the time of the conference, a target for Duncan Campbell and the Campaign Against Health Fraud. Campbell attacked all the doctors who were central to the Society – Stephen Davies, Alan Stewart, Damien Downing, Belinda Dawes and Patrick Kingsley – between the time of the conference and the summer of 1992.

Prior to the October 30th 1990 'Food and Drink Programme', Duncan Campbell rang all the doctors involved in the BSNM and asked them a list of questions about their relationship with the companies which produce vitamins. Most of the doctors were willing to give details of this relationship, making it clear to Campbell whether or not they took 'commissions' on the particular company's vitamins which they prescribed to patients, or whether they received a royalty from a company for whom they had designed a vitamin complex.

Although Dr Patrick Kingsley, the Treasurer of the Society, had given Campbell all the information he needed on the phone, Campbell still insisted – for effect – on forcing his way into Kingsley's surgery while he had a waiting-room full of patients. The footage from this invasion was shown on the 'Food and Drink Programme'.

Campbell had to stand on the steps outside Stephen Davies' surgery to be filmed. He intoned with bumptious solemnity that Stephen Davies was the centre of a nutritional conspiracy:

> For all of the five BSNM doctors admit that they, or the clinics they run, have received money from Lamberts either as consultancy fees or commission payments. Biolab, in plush premises near Harley Street, is the centre of the BSNM network. Its Chairman is Doctor Stephen Davies, who said he was too busy to see us. [18]

The taking of commission on vitamin supplements, and doctor – vitamin company relations, are relatively insignificant matters in comparison with the kind of bribery and corruption which takes place between doctors and pharmaceutical companies. Campbell, however, did have a small point, if, that is, his information was correct. It was not.

Stephen Davies had never taken commission nor royalties from

Lamberts on any of the vitamin preparations he handled. Campbell knew this, because following the article about Patrick Holford in the *Sunday Correspondent*, Davies had written to Campbell and the *Independent on Sunday*, making it clear that he did not take commission.

> I never ever had taken any kind of commission. It has been strict policy from the word go, not to accept any royalties, to which I am perfectly entitled within the mores of the medical profession. Certainly I do not take any commission. Although both Alan Stewart and Patrick Kingsley did take commissions from Lamberts, they both used this money to have diagnostic tests done for patients who could not afford to pay. [19]

* * *

Besides the burglaries at Larkhall, other odd things began happening. In December 1990, Rita Greer began assembling the artwork for Larkhall's brochure which was to come out in February 1991. When she finished the artwork, it was sent to a print finishing firm in Diss. In the last days of December, the material was sent to Putney by the firm in Diss so that Rita Greer could check it. Having checked it, she sent it back to Diss, and from there it was sent on to the printers in Leicester.

When the material was finally sent to the printers, the package contained the colour separations for 16 pages (four positive films for each page) and 16 colour chromalins (colour proofs which give the printers a guide for colour printing). The complete value of the art work was in the region of £4,000. The Managing Director of the firm in Diss packed the artwork herself, and, as is common practice, taped everything down to the bottom of the box.

On arrival in Leicester, the package was opened by the printers and, despite the box showing no signs of having previously been opened, only one chromalin remained in the box. The printers rang Greer who contacted the firm in Diss, and both companies complained to British Rail. Despite a thorough investigation, no one was able to find out when the material had gone missing or who had been responsible for taking it. Three days later, however, the remaining 79 negatives and chromalins turned up at a police station in Leicester, slightly scratched but otherwise undamaged. They had been found in a ditch and handed in by a member of the public.

* * *

In 1989, when Duncan Campbell, the Campaign Against Health Fraud and their contacts in the Department of Health managed to get germanium banned, few people outside Sandra Goodman's immediate circle knew that the substance might have been used in trials for HIV management or AIDS. Few people also knew that the ban on germanium was not to be statutorily enforced but was a voluntary ban. Dr Woodward continued to market germanium overseas quite legally.

Natural substances, which can be manufactured by different companies without breach of any patent or licence, are a serious problem to the pharmaceutical companies. While competitors within the same industry are kept in check with a series of cartel arrangements, no such industry pressure can be brought to bear on the producers of food supplements or the distributing agents for 'natural' substances.

In quick succession following the banning of germanium, two other food supplements were suddenly banned, tryptophan and niacin. Both these were naturally-occurring substances. Tryptophan, an effective natural tranquillizer and an anti-depressant, had been used by millions of people for over thirty years, in preference to addictive sleeping pills. In 1989, however, a Japanese chemical company, Shawa-Denko, distributed a batch of contaminated L-Tryptophan. Rumours ran riot and within a short space of time, the story was abroad that tryptophan was a deadly poison. In July 1990, it was banned in Britain; it had already been banned in America. Initially, for nine months, the ban on tryptophan was in the form of a voluntary withdrawal. Then suddenly on September 12th 1991, the Department of Health issued a statement giving retail and wholesale pharmacists and manufacturers fourteen days to clear all stock before it was officially banned.

A number of practitioners who used tryptophan could not help but comment on the coincidence of the ban with the marketing of Prozac, a new chemical anti-depressant from Eli Lilly. Prozac has had the highest marketing profile of any new drug for many years, much of its advertising publicity appearing in news media.†

Within a short time of the ban, more sober minds voiced the opinion that it had only been one batch of tryptophan which had been contaminated and tryptophan itself was not harmful.‡

The ban, however, stayed. The banning of niacin was even more irregular than that of germanium or tryptophan. Again it is a naturally-occurring substance, again it has been used for years by natural medical practitioners, most recently to lower cholesterol levels.†† Research appeared in 1990 showing that huge doses of niacin could damage the kidneys. A voluntary ban on sustained release forms of niacin was introduced by the health trade in agreement with the DoH. The ban was limited and voluntary, for good reason: niacin is put into a large number of processed foods such as some breakfast cereals, and an across the board ban would have stirred up resentment in industry as well as being impracticable. In America, where the problem over niacin had first arisen, all forms of the substance continued to be sold legally everywhere.

On January 15th 1990, the BBC screened an item in the 'Food and Drink Programme', containing all the information which Campbell had managed to collect on Larkhall. It centred on two preparations which, the programme said, contained substances banned by the

---

† In America a number of people are suing Eli Lilly, following claims that their consumption of Prozac triggered off violent neurotic episodes, driving them, in some cases, to kill or mutilate people. In Britain, following a television programme looking at the dangers of Prozac, Michael O'Donnell, the Chairman of HealthWatch, wrote a full-page article in the *BMJ*, making out a case for the drug and ridiculing the programme makers and the attorney who was helping people take actions in the States.

‡ There are obvious parallels here with the banning of germanium: not only were the contaminated batches produced in Japan, but this one apparent safety failure led to an immediate and complete ban. This should be compared with the events which follow the finding that any pharmaceutical product has serious side-effects, consumers are lucky if they can get a pharmaceutical product withdrawn by the regulating authorities within five years.

†† Natural medical practitioners lower cholesterol and break up fatty deposits by 'chelation therapy'. Orthodox medicine, the pharmaceutical companies and particularly groups like the American National Council Against Health Fraud, have waged war against this therapy because it competes with invasive surgery and high tech treatment as well as chemical pharmaceutical therapy.

DoH: sustained-release niacin in Sustaniacin, and germanium in Immunomega.

In relation to germanium, Duncan Campbell repeated all the misleading things which he had previously stated in his 'Pretty poison' article.

> The pills are labelled misleadingly, 'organic germanium', as though they were natural. Seriously ill people, including those suffering from cancer, multiple sclerosis, even AIDS were encouraged to buy and take the pills as though they were the cure they were so desperately looking for.† [20]

> In the late 1980's, Japanese medical reports began to reveal that germanium consumption could lead to kidney failure and even death. I published the results of an investigation ... A government health warning followed. [21]

The essence of Campbell's report was that he had found the Immunomega vitamin complex pills, produced by Larkhall, still contained germanium although it had been deleted from the list of ingredients on the packet. Unless this evidence was manufactured by someone, Dr Woodward believes that it was a simple error that had occurred within the Larkhall packing department; Campbell made it into the crime of the century, insisting that Woodward was ignoring the DoH ban and selling people a poisonous substance.

Campbell claimed on the programme that he had been 'tipped off by confidential sources inside the health pill trade' that Larkhall was still selling supplements containing germanium. He hurried along to Surrey University with the Immunomega he had bought and gave it to his friend Dr Andrew Taylor to analyse. 'Was there germanium in it?'. 'Yes' proclaimed Dr Taylor with emphasis, 'We actually found that there were quite large amounts of germanium present in these samples'. No mention was made of the fact that as a naturally-occurring substance, germanium is present in both baked beans and

---

† The words, 'organic' and 'inorganic', used in relation to germanium are scientific terms, and not 'health-food' terms. An 'organic' compound is one comprising a complex molecular structure involving carbon, hydrogen and/or oxygen and/or nitrogen. 'Inorganic' is a term which describes simple salts such as sodium chloride, potassium bicarbonate, etc. In the scientific tradition the two words represent very real differences.

garlic. In fact, the amount of germanium in the tablets was less than would be obtained in the average daily diet and a thousand times less than the toxic dose of the other quite separate form of toxic, inorganic, germanium. At the end of the item, another 'Food and Drink' presenter told viewers, as if to apologise for Campbell, that Holland and Barrett, the shop from which Campbell had bought his Immunomega, had taken in their stock a year ago, in January 1990.

The second vitamin supplement which Campbell had found on sale inside the Larkhall shop in Putney was sustained-release niacin. On this matter, Dr Robert Woodward was unrepentant: he was not going to collude with the voluntary ban because niacin caused no adverse effects, nor had there ever been any scientifically validated evidence that it had. Woodward maintained that the administration of niacin was the safest and cheapest way to reduce blood cholesterol quickly.

* * *

Considering that the January 15th 'Food and Drink Programme' was Campbell's best shot at criminalising Larkhall, it was a dismal failure. Despite the fact that Campbell again used his contact with Vincent Marks and Dr Andrew Taylor and Surrey University, and despite the fact that the item and the attack upon Larkhall were obviously linked to the Campaign Against Health Fraud, no mention of vested interests was made on the programme.

Many who saw the January item on the 'Food and Drink Programme' were confused, as they were about other items, as to how it got on the programme. Many felt that Campbell's style of presentation was unprofessional and his tone unworthy of the BBC generally and the 'Food and Drink Programme' in particular. A.N. Wilson, writing in the *Sunday Telegraph*, for example, was scathing:

> ... the idea of 'trial by television' is spreading everywhere, even into the trivial shows such as the 'Food and Drink Programme' (Tuesday BBC 2). Last week, they were 'exposing' firms who sold food supplement pills and other quackery of the kind, with the help of veteran whinger and exposer of things which aren't actually very shocking, Duncan Campbell – he of the *New Statesman* and Official Secrets Act case.

Campbell has the self-satisfied, humourless fanaticism of the Scots moralist. He had found some pills which were supposed to make you feel better but which contained a substance, in his view bad for the kidneys, called germanium. We saw an absurd shot of a boffin in a white coat testing this substance at the University of Surrey (didn't know there was one). Yes, as we expected, there's germanium in the pill, and, would you believe it, the manufacturers had not recorded the fact on the packet.

Campbell also found some supposedly illegal potion called niacin, which, we were told, 'in some cases' can cause 'liver failure' ... Viewers were encouraged to sneak on any mountebank or quack selling germanium or niacin. That's just the way Stalin liked us all to behave, spying and telling tales on our neighbours. [22]

On the night of January 15th Larkhall's packing factory in Oxford was broken into again.

*   *   *

In February, Larkhall received a call from their local Trading Standards Office in Wandsworth; the office had received a letter from MAFF enclosing copies of two other letters. The letter from MAFF asked the Trading Standards Officers in Wandsworth to take action against Larkhall for their production and sale of tryptophan, as shown in a copy of an advertisement enclosed with the letter. The first of the two letters enclosed with the MAFF letter was from HealthWatch to MAFF signed by Caroline Richmond, enclosing a copy of the advertisement sent her by a member of the public. The second letter was from the member of the public, Mr Duncan Campbell, to Caroline Richmond, drawing her attention to an advert put out by Larkhall for tryptophan. This last letter was dated January 8th 1991. The advert referred to by Campbell, was a new advert not used by Larkhall prior to the publication of their 16 page magazine, which had gone astray in transit and was not finally published until February 13th 1991.

On the issue of all three natural substances banned in Britain and America in 1989 and 1990, tryptophan, germanium and niacin, Duncan Campbell's erratic investigations, where they did not directly bring about bans, did more to obscure the real issues than to enlighten the public.

* * *

As a consequence of the 'Food and Drink Programme' reporting Larkhall's product Tandem IQ to Shropshire County Council Trading Standards Department in October 1990, Robert Woodward, Rita Greer and the factory managers were interviewed by telephone and in person by Shropshire Trading Standards Officers on different occasions during 1991. These interviews were carried out with the full rigmarole of the law, cautions being given first. One of the interviews was, however, more oppressive than would have been the case had the police been investigating a serious crime. During a long telephone call, Woodward was threatened with arrest and imprisonment. Rita Greer was told to 'get a good lawyer' because she was 'going to need one'.

The investigations were free-ranging; they did not stop at Tandem IQ, but veered off into an examination of the contents of a wide range of preparations produced at Larkhall. Shropshire Trading Standards Authority was to haunt Larkhall for the next two years.

At the centre of the charges was the basic contention that vitamin supplements could not aid mental alertness or add more to fitness than a balanced diet. The charges themselves, however, were phrased in various ways which related to the food labelling regulations, and at the centre of these was the contention that Larkhall had *knowingly* made untruthful claims for their vitamin supplements. Shropshire looked in all the right places for their prosecution witnesses, turning up the very people, like Professor Naismith, who had previously supported HealthWatch's argument.

The first case over Tandem IQ came to court in March 1991, and when it became evident that Woodward had no intention of settling or pleading guilty, Shropshire withdrew from the prosecution, resting their case *sine die*. Robert Woodward and Rita Greer considered this a partial success. It was short-lived: within two months, Shropshire had resurrected the case bringing a whole battery of new charges.†

*   *   *

By the spring of 1991, the Greers could no longer tolerate the harassment at Larkhall and the police advised them to stay away from the factory. In April, Rita Greer's office at Larkhall was broken into and ransacked. The only items stolen were three files containing the notes and text of a book she had been at work on for two years.

A year later, in the spring of 1992, the harassment appeared to have stopped and Rita Greer began to run her business again from Larkhall. Three weeks after she moved back, however, the harassment began again. The shop next to the factory was broken into for a second time. Nothing was stolen but stock was disturbed on the shelves as if the intruder had been looking for something.

A few days later someone deliberately cut through the main telephone, fax and computer cables into the factory. The police recorded it as 'malicious and criminal damage'. Reconnecting the wires took BT several hours. Fortunately, Larkhall was prepared for such an emergency and nothing was lost from the computer records. The clean cut through large cables was in itself very sinister and obviously made by someone with expert skill and knowledge of communications.

*   *   *

In July 1990, following the start of his libel action against Duncan Campbell for the article 'New Age Pill Pushers' in the *Sunday Correspondent*, Patrick Holford began a fight back on a number of fronts. In particular, he launched the Campaign For Health Through Food (CHTF). One of the objectives of CHTF was to begin a fund for those who had to fight libel actions. As far as Patrick Holford was concerned, there was no distinction between the struggle against the vested interests in the processed food industry, the struggle to make people aware of optimum nutrition, and the

† In September 1992, before a Stipendiary Magistrate in Shrewsbury, Larkhall was found guilty on three counts relating to claims made on the packaging of Tandem IQ. The case went to appeal.

raising of a legal fund which, amongst other things, would help the Institute for Optimum Nutrition (ION) fight its action against Campboll

The process of fighting a libel action is complex and protracted. Holford issued his writ in January 1990, as soon as possible after Campbell's article had appeared. The lawyers for the other side delayed presenting their defence to the point where Patrick Holford's lawyer had to obtain an injunction against them, forcing them to do so. The defence turned out to be a 50 page document, which was itself highly misleading and scientifically inaccurate. By July 1990, Patrick Holford had served ION's reply to the defence case.

The Campaign For Health Through Food was set up to focus concern upon a number of damaging developments affecting health foods and natural medicine. Holford was worried both about the attacks upon members of the nutritional community, and particularly concerned about the impending set of new rules and regulations governing vitamin supplements, which were being pushed through the European Parliament by pharmaceutical vested interests.

At the launch of CHTF, Holford put great emphasis on the idea that the campaign would make use of journalists to bring important food and health issues to the attention of the public. He proposed a network of campaign advisers. These advisers were high-ranking experts, including: Professor Linus Pauling, Dr Philip Barlow, Alexander Schauss and Professor Michael Crawford.

Holford stressed that this network of scientists, journalists and doctors and its capacity to raise money for a legal fund, would act as a deterrent against attacks by those representing the processed food industry. The interests of such eminent scientists would ensure that those who mounted attacks while choosing to ignore research material about nutrition could be countered. Holford also discussed Campbell's attack upon him and the grounds upon which he had taken his legal action.

> The Institute has been accused by inference of promoting worthless and sometimes dangerous supplements. On the basis of worthless tests, based upon a worthless philosophy of nutrition, for reasons of financial gain ... These untruthful and unsubstantiated accusations could, we fear, by made against many reputable practitioners who recommend supplements. We

> are therefore glad that ION have chosen to take this issue to court
> and establish that optimum nutrition and supplementation is not
> quackery. We hope that this action will deter future unfounded
> attacks and thereby protect others for many years to come. [23]

Duncan Campbell attended the Campaign launch uninvited, and
inappropriately intervened to make long, rambling and aggressive
statements.

> I think it's important that it is made clear to everybody that this
> campaign is an organisation established by Patrick for purposes
> which include paying his legal costs.

> I am going to ask you to make clear to this meeting that the
> claims you have made in your literature and letter are extremely
> misleading.

> The libel case which you are involved in is purely concerned
> with your reputation, and not with these wider issues. [24]

Campbell finally managed to bog down the launch with questions
about Holford's libel action and the proximity of the proposed legal
fund to Holford's own case.† Campbell also asked questions about
Patrick Holford's links with vitamin companies. Once again,
Campbell's tactics reflected the influence of the American National
Council Against Health Fraud and activists like Victor Herbert.

In October 1991, the *Sunday Correspondent* closed down and,
concerned to settle any pending action before going into liquidation,
they settled their case with Patrick Holford. In the last half of 1992,
Campbell, deserted by the *Sunday Correspondent*'s solicitors, was still
determined to defend the case brought against him. He was, though,
complaining that Patrick Holford had not given him an opportunity to
settle.

† In fact none of the money raised by the Campaign For Health Through Food
was used to fund Patrick Holford's libel action.

Belinda Barnes and Foresight

> I have noticed argument of orthodox doctors and researchers
> that treatments be tested by double blind placebo controlled
> trials. When it comes to pregnant mothers, this is not a
> particularly good suggestion. There will be no placebos from
> Foresight doctors. [25]

Birthright and Foresight are two apparently similar organizations with comparable aims and objectives – to give all prospective parents access to healthy conception and women access to healthy birth. Both are charities, but there the similarities end. Birthright and Foresight have different positions in the world. Birthright is a nationally organised high tech, high finance, high society charity, while Foresight, which struggles along under the administration of Belinda Barnes, is a grass roots advice and help organisation, which also funds non-pharmaceutical university research into health and pregnancy. Birthright is a member of Wellcome's medical research charities conglomerate, the Association of Medical Research Charities; it charges £250 and over for a single ticket to a charity event and in 1991 raised £2 million. Money it raises goes to pharmaceutically-based research scientists to research birth and pregnancy.

The comparison between these two organisations is illustrative of the way in which business, social class and scientific funding are all involved in promoting the most financially competitive medical and scientific research projects. While Professor Michael Crawford struggles away in the Hackney Hospital keeping afloat his work on nutrition, brain size and birth weight with minimal funds, and Foresight struggles to help hundreds of individual cases of people who are unable to conceive or have a history of birth defects, Birthright pours money from the wealthy into 'big science'- orientated projects which research developments in the field of genetics. Such projects will make profits for big business as well as possibly helping individuals.

Birthright's money and the social class of its donors entitle it to something else, which both Foresight and Professor Michael Crawford lack: protection. Birthright is the 'darling' of the society charities, tapping into social connection as diverse as royalty, pop music and the world of theatre. These contacts, especially those within the food and pharmaceutical industries, assure the charity of its continuing existence. Foresight, on the other hand, has no such security, because it gives nutritional advice and finds itself in conflict with the food, chemical and pharmaceutical industries. It is also, therefore, vulnerable to attacks from scavenger organisations like HealthWatch which these industries support.

In 1991, members of HealthWatch, which was by then a charity, were involved in an attack upon Foresight, also a charity. Belinda Barnes picked up the phone one day to find herself talking to a truculent and aggressive Thames Television research worker called Cillian de Boutlier. He was, he said, going to 'expose' Foresight. He asked for an interview, saying that the programme would be done anyway and it would be better for her if she did an interview. Faced with that, Mrs Barnes felt that she did not have much option, and so Cillian de Boutlier came to Belinda Barnes' house with an interviewer, a producer and a camera team. In the pre-interview discussion, the first question that the interviewer asked her reflected the crew's view of the subject: didn't Mrs Barnes think the world would be a terrible place if all babies were healthy? On this level of Darwinian erudition the interview began.

Belinda Barnes found it impossible to voice her opinions in response to the kind of questions which she was asked. Predictably, the programme was an attempt to destroy Foresight and to malign Belinda Barnes and the committed, energetic and sound advice which she and the doctors who work with Foresight had given to thousands of parents and would-be parents over the last fifteen years. Foresight was attacked because it advocated the use of vitamins and food supplements and because its view of pre-conceptional care was in conflict with the views of the multi-national chemical and pharmaceutical companies.

Following the interview, the programme came as no surprise to Belinda Barnes: a number of the thirty four doctors who work with Foresight giving nutritional treatment and advice had already been attacked by HealthWatch. Also, not long before Belinda Barnes was contacted by Cillian de Boutlier, HealthWatch had begun an odd diversionary tactic to try to discredit Foresight.

* * *

In 1989, Foresight received a letter from Professor John Garrow, one of the original members of the Campaign Against Health Fraud; having committed his life to the processed food industry, Garrow now works for Rank. His letter suggested that Foresight's results were not as well documented as they might be. He would be prepared to help with a double blind trial, if Foresight were to fund it. The request was bizarre. As well as having spent his working life in the food industry, Garrow did research for a major multi-national company, whilst Foresight was a small voluntary charity.

Belinda Barnes found Garrow's offer repugnant, mainly on ethical grounds. People who turn to Foresight are often suffering great anxiety and unhappiness because they are unable to conceive. In many cases, Foresight doctors are able to resolve these problems through the clinical application of nutritional medicine and other interventions. A double blind trial would have involved refusing treatment to half of those who turned to Foresight for help.† Anyway, who in their right mind would accept help with scientific research from a member of the Campaign Against Health Fraud?

Belinda Barnes dealt carefully and diplomatically with the letter, discussing the problems and politely but firmly declining the offer which disclosed a not-so-hidden agenda. She was somewhat surprised, therefore, to see her private correspondence with Garrow published in the fourth CAHF newsletter in April 1990, under the heading, 'The Foresight Saga'. The article poured scorn on Foresight and tried lamentably to find criticisms of its aims and methods, drawing mainly upon the letters exchanged with Garrow. Although Belinda Barnes did not know it at the time, she had fallen for one of the Campaign's classic con-tricks. Having drawn an individual or an organisation into a dialogue, they then distort and manipulate the information they gain, and then place it in the public domain.

* * *

---

† The criticism which was levelled against the Bristol Cancer Help Centre by Health-Fraudsters was that it had objected to a double blind trial. Bristol's reasons for turning down such a trial were the same as those given by Belinda Barnes.

> The programme was unfair in that it did not give Foresight a
> proper opportunity to explain to viewers that there was
> substantial scientific backing, in the form of earlier research,
> for their approach to pre-conceptual care. [26]

Early in the new year of 1991, a Thames Television journalist,
Margaret Hendricks, visited three of the doctors who work with
Foresight. Hendricks gave a false name and address to two of the three
doctors, and presented all of them with a set of widely differing
medical family histories. As in other 'bogus patient' cases, the starting
assumption for the three consultations was that the doctors were doing
something wrong.

The 'Thames Action' programme on Foresight was broadcast on
February 15th 1991. The programme made a number of allegations
against Belinda Barnes and Foresight. However, the programme was
most critical of the three doctors whose time the journalist had wasted.
Each doctor, the programme claimed, had given the patient different
regimes. This wasn't true.

Margaret Hendricks had given a different medical history to each
doctor and then because of her subterfuge had been unable to go back
to the doctors for a follow-up appointment. Much to the programme-
makers' chagrin, all three doctors had written in their notes for the
bogus patient: 'This is a basically healthy young woman'. Given this,
Hendricks was forced to try to bully one of the doctors into prescribing
her vitamins; she was offered only a multivitamin supplement.

The programme gave the impression that Belinda Barnes
personally was advising clients on ill-founded and unproven
'alternative' treatments, when in fact Foresight refers people to
doctors. None of the doctors who acted for Foresight were
interviewed, despite this being specifically recommended to the
producer.

The programme did, however, discuss three doctors, who were
cited as 'carrying out unproven medical treatments' on patients. The
programme implied an improper relationship between Foresight and
these doctors, intimating that Foresight got some kind of financial 'kick
back' by sending the patients to doctors. This suggestion was totally
without foundation.

The doctors upon whom the programme dwelt were the same ones
whom HealthWatch and Duncan Campbell had already harassed:

Dr Stephen Davies, Dr Damien Downing and Dr Belinda Dawes, all doctors active in the British Society for Nutritional Medicine.

'Thames Action' refused to examine the results of Foresight's work, although they were available for them to see. They determined that nutritional medicine was unproven and, as usual with HealthWatch associated projects, they weren't interested in the patients, nor in reviewing the abstracted clinical information about the patients. Ideology alone motivated the programme and not health care or care for health.

Not once during the pre-programme discussion with Belinda Barnes, nor in the programme itself, did the programme-makers make clear their links with HealthWatch. In fact, Cillian de Boutlier claimed to Belinda Barnes that he had never heard of HealthWatch. It transpired later that he had been in touch with Duncan Campbell over the programme.

The overall view given by the programme was that Foresight was a sinister and disreputable organisation which was charging people who were at their most vulnerable, large amounts of money for experimental and ineffective treatments. None of the doctors nor the research director of Foresight had been approached by the programme to give a medical view. Later, before the Broadcasting Complaints Commission, the programme-makers claimed that it was not a programme for experts, but one for lay people and they had therefore interviewed Mrs Barnes. However, to dispute her lay views, the programme presented two qualified 'experts', a gynaecologist and Dr Andrew Taylor, Professor Vincent Marks' colleague from Surrey University.†

Andrew Taylor's office on the Surrey University complex is, coincidentally, just a hundred yards from the office in the Chemistry Department of Foresight's research director, Dr Neil Ward PhD. Dr Ward is an ebullient, well-qualified and populist lecturer, a man eminently suited to talk to a lay audience. Mrs Barnes had suggested that Dr Ward be asked to appear on the programme from the onset.

In her later criticism of the programme to the Broadcasting

---

† The BCC was later to say that those consulted by 'Thames Action', were not 'known for their strong beliefs either for or against!'

Complaints Commission (BCC),† Belinda Barnes makes the point that if the programme-makers wanted to accuse Foresight doctors of unethical practice by prescribing and charging for vitamin and mineral supplements, then they should have made a complaint to the General Medical Council. As it was, this 'slur by television', which did not even allow the doctors a right of reply, made the common practice of both the doctors and the charity which they worked for appear to be sinister and crooked.

* * *

The attack on Stephen Davies and the British Society for Nutritional Medicine on the 'Thames Action' programme, was not the last attack. In February 1992, Duncan Campbell produced another item for the 'Food and Drink Programme'. This time the subject of the attack was Dr Damien Downing, Stephen Davies' colleague and co-founder of the British Society for Nutritional Medicine.

More worrying than the item on the programme, however, was a coincidental and completely unrelated incident which occurred at Biolab ten days before the programme.

When Biolab's computer technologist came into work one Monday morning the main computer would not work. When all the connections were checked and the casing taken off, it was found that somebody had opened the computer, disconnected various 'cards', removed the hard disc and only partially rescrewed the screws that fixed it.

The computer was taken to the supplier's maintenance and repair workshop; later that day Stephen Davies was told that the laboratory and research data on 49,500 patients, collected over the previous

---

† The BCC, finding partially in favour of the programme, and partially in favour of Foresight, said in part: 'In the Commission's view, the overall tone of the programme was, however, unfairly derogatory to Foresight, particularly in the section relating to the prescription by Foresight doctors of vitamin and mineral supplements and of the charges made by doctors for them. An impression was given – by the showing of bank notes changing hands and the accompanying commentary – that the doctors, and perhaps Foresight, were benefiting unjustly at the expense of their patients. The Commission understand that the charging by doctors in private practice for prescriptions of this sort is, in fact, sanctioned by the BMA.

seven and a half years, had been completely wiped out. Fortunately, Davies had a back-up copy. If he had not, the sabotage could have closed down his practice. The police officer, a former computer programmer, who attended Biolab when the crime was reported, told Stephen Davies that the damage was clearly the work of a professional.

Chapter Thirty Eight

Conclusions

The AIDS epidemic is an epidemic of lies, through which hundreds of thousands of people have died and are dying unnecessarily, billions of dollars have gone down the drain, the public Health Service has disgraced itself, and science has plunged into whoredom. [1]

In some ways this book does not need conclusions. How the campaign against natural medicine is organised, has grown, and how it has acted, is laid out in some detail in the book. Generally speaking it is evident who has profited from the campaign. This being the case, I would like to take the opportunity of the conclusions to broach some of the broader issues raised by the book.

It is clear that for some time there has been an organised campaign against alternative and complementary medicine. This campaign has become more aggressive as the 'green' movement has grown. Even as this book is being finished, in America, the FDA is involved in yet another attempt to regulate the free availability of vitamins and food supplements. In Europe, the pharmaceutical companies through the European parliament are pressing constantly to control nutritional health products.

If we are not vigilant, there is a possibility that we may lose our access to the history and the future of natural health care. Such a loss would entail another less visible loss. Those who have control of the diagnosis and treatment of human illness, control our bodies. This control of the productive and reproductive human being is at the centre of this struggle. While industrialists desire to maximise profits, scientists want to control the well-spring of human life. Scientific medicine in the contemporary world is introducing new moral and legal paradigms which are radically reshaping society's ethical basis.

When we move from the everyday language of health care and begin to ponder these greater moral and economic issues about power, we immediately open ourselves to accusations of conspiracy theory. It is worth looking briefly at the idea of conspiracy in relation to this book.

Before the industrial revolution our perception of the world was constricted. When anyone did anything of consequence within our community, it usually became known to the population. The place of individuals in the world was seen and understood. Today we inhabit a world of immense size, physically and intellectually the individual is overshadowed by the frenetic activities of global human groups. Despite the pandemic of media information – which some claim makes the world smaller – we understand acts which occur in our world with less precision than we did two hundred years ago.

Individual responsibility is lost in the enormous chaos of the cities. The infinite vortex of information which follows an event, communicated in varying degrees to different individuals, means that no collective, comprehensive or consensus view of the event is ever likely to be articulated. We live in a world of exact communications which relay only broken messages – unquantifiable amounts of information but only partial understanding. The revolution in information technology can also bring us misinformation.

It is this lack of comprehension in the modern world, of which conspirators take advantage. This is as true of scientists and industrialists as it is of fraudsters. In such a world those who spread misleading or damaging information can often get away without being made accountable. This is more true of academics and industrialists, who are not 'policed', than it is of 'criminals'. The modern world is one in which 'wrongdoing' flourishes because the sea of information within which we exist grants the wrongdoer the sacrament of anonymity and takes from us the civilising influences of intimate knowledge and accountability.

In part the themes and the evidence in this book do suggest a number of conspiracies. These have been acted out in secret by groups of people on behalf of vested interests. More profoundly, though, the evidence suggests a cultural concordance, an invisible mix of minute and everyday contracts of cultural, political and economic orthodoxy. To be a party to such hegemony, people do not have to conspire, they need not even be in contact with each other.

The predominant culture of any society is not a conspiracy, it is a taken-for-granted acceptance of many spoken and unspoken precepts. Such a prevailing cultural orthodoxy is more powerful than any conspiracy. A conspiracy can be tracked down, found out, divided, exposed and broken; it is often a material reality. The deep weave of cultural orthodoxy is difficult to unpick, no single individual or group of individuals can be brought to book or held responsible for its collective representation. No single statement or set of statements outlines the code. Orthodoxy does not have a beginning or an end, it simply is; engrained within the consciousness of each individual it goes on largely unquestioned, however bizarre its consequences.

The guiding principles of orthodoxy however are vested in the language and actions of individuals and it is only through these individuals that any 'investigator' can begin to explain the expression of orthodoxy. Rather than it being about conspiracies, I should like to think that this book puts individuals in a context which shows how orthodoxy maintains its substantial power through common assumptions.

* * *

One of the central concerns left at the end of this book might be phrased as a question. Is it the ideology and culture of scientific medicine, or simply considerations of profit which motivate health fraud activists to disempower sick people and leave them bereft of a choice in treatment alternatives?

With such abundant examples of fraud outside alternative or complementary medicine, why do the health-fraudsters alight upon 'quackery'? The underlying structure of the National Health Service is still intact and most people when they are sick go to their general practitioners. Until recently the health sector was highly regulated, and though the Conservative government's creeping privatisation has inevitably opened up the sector to deregulation it is just as likely that dubious or fraudulent practices will appear from allopathic practitioners as from eclectic practitioners. There is also the question of pharmaceutical company malpractice and drug-related iatrogenic damage which demands enquiries and campaigns.

Why do health fraud campaigners pick on one particular type of health care or nutritional advice to campaign against? Except where such campaigns protect science, orthodox medicine and the pharmaceutical industry, their motives appear as irrational as some of the 'cults' which they claim to debunk.

The late twentieth century is a time of many polarities. While the robotization of human culture is one central theme of post industrial society, the search for an experiential end to alienation is another conflicting theme. The end of collective labour and the mass means of industrial production have imposed new demands upon the State and the industry which supports it. The rules of order in this society are new rules, formulated to deal with an ever increasing conflict between the old rationalist paradigm and a new paradigm of individual experience. A range of choices lies between the poles of a global brave new world based upon genetic engineering and a more heterogeneous 'old world' of small communities based upon sensory experience and internal understanding.

Although they never chose themselves to be part of the battle, eclectic medical practitioners are in the front line of these post-industrial struggles. In the field of medicine at least, such people are expressing their 'legitimate difference'. They are eroding the mystique which presently defends the professional monopoly of allopathic medicine. Many of them are also developing a medical approach which will both treat the individual and do battle with the damaging effects of industrial society. With their holistic approaches, they are charting a course for a type of medicine which is more likely than allopathic medicine to nurture an understanding of the inner experiential being.

* * *

The Campaign Against Health Fraud has from the beginning been a rearguard action. Canute-like, it claimed to want to turn back the tide of history. It is a movement which protects the status quo, defending chemical pollutants against natural substances and expensive high tech medicine against age-old preventative treatments. It was in the beginning, and is now, part of a movement which is bound to run headlong into conflict, for it pits the facts of science against the more personally meaningful internal belief systems of individuals. Steeped in the cynical materialism of the American science campaigners, the campaigners are convinced that this conflict is one which they have a realistic chance of changing, not winning. They actually believe that the essence of the human experience can be explained by the biology of the body's parts. Both the paradigm and the social mood, however, are changing, not only against industrial and pharmaceutically based medicine which the Campaign has championed, but also towards a more experiential understanding of the human condition and against expensive 'hard' sciences.

Health-fraud campaigners have consistently refused to take into account the feelings of individuals, especially the feelings and beliefs of those who have sought treatment from 'alternative' practitioners. This peculiar avoidance of subjective considerations by campaigners reflects in their judgements. On the whole, they cling desperately to a purely objective and ideological description of the world. Where such views are confounded by subjective and even scientific experience, as with homoeopathy, they bluntly deny the experience or patronisingly put it down to either a 'placebo effect' or the therapeutic effect of the longer and more relaxed patient interviews.

The truth is, that the health-fraud campaign is not simply a campaign against practitioners, it is also a campaign against patients. If the practitioners are charlatans who give out expensive but worthless remedies, it stands to reason that they or others – usually the media – have convinced the gullible patient of such non-existent illnesses.

So defensive are health-fraud campaigners, about the 'reality' of treatment by alternative practitioners, and so profoundly unserious about their research, that in order to get 'evidence' they do not follow real patients through diagnosis, treatment and after care. Instead they send a bogus patient to a practitioner. This patient presents symptoms, for an illness which he or she does not have, and demands an instant diagnosis. Such a ploy can only confirm in the mind of the investigator that the doctor is a charlatan: it is a deception and we rarely learn anything from deception, except confirmation of our prejudices.

Campaigners also set up bogus research projects which are purposefully carried out with a complete disregard for scientific practice. Again, such projects have little to do with a search for the truth and a great deal to do with the confirmation of prejudice.

* * *

Many of the arguments in the book are concerned as much with science as they are with medicine. Medical science particularly is an orthodox bastion. The medical science professional and the doctor increasingly share a growing power. This power comes first as a consequence of the doctor's knowledge of the human body and is later extended by medical scientists and biologists, who claim to know not only about the human body but about the whole of life.

It is because of the power which medical scientists hold and the undemocratic nature of their work that medical science actually represents a considerable threat to individual liberty. Increasingly medical scientists claim the right and the power to make decisions affecting the circumstances of life and death. In questioning the consequences of professional science, its authority and its undemocratic nature, the dissident is taking on, not only the mystique of the profession, but also the government, which has a hand in determining science policy, the industries which utilise science for production and profit and, finally, all those huge institutions of society which have science as their cornerstone.

The self-exploration of preventative medicine and health is an issue at the very core of the debate about creating an alternative social structure. Somehow we have to turn away from the totalitarianism of medical science and the pharmaceutical industry, its fixation with glittering prizes and magic bullets and return to a more preventative community-orientated approach to medicine, health care and health education.

Nowhere is this conflict more clear than in everything which has happened around that group of illnesses called AIDS. From the beginning, and in relation to all important developments, it appears that the scientists and the doctors got it wrong. This is not in itself unforgivable. The real tragedy is, however, that because of the power and esteem which society has vested in our scientists and doctors, both we and they have been unable to accept that mistakes had been made. Scientific competition and the profit-orientated rules of orthodoxy dictated that there could only be one licensed medicine for AIDS and HIV management for the whole of the first ten years of the epidemic. Furthermore the production of this one medicine was probably based upon wrong hypotheses and its prescription upon a wrong diagnosis.

It is easy to see how all this happened. Science and medicine have become detached from the subjects of illness. Scientists now examine illnesses as if they were abstract phenomena unrelated to the bodies which host them. In the case of AIDS, a virus was found; it became *the* virus, it was studied *in vitro*, a search was made for a substance which could kill it *in vitro*. Nothing could be simpler, it was a text book investigation, *if* the virus were the cause of the illness. Once the virus had been isolated, however, questions about its interactive processes within the human body all but ceased.

The majority of orthodox doctors and scientists were in agreement: the HIV virus attacked the immune system cells, depleting them and leaving the body open to the depredations of opportunist infections. The power and the prevalence, even the peculiarly idiosyncratic history of the virus, which can apparently lie dormant for decades, even the exact mechanism by which this virus caused to be produced twenty five separate illnesses, came to be questioned less and less. Was this scientific method? Surely correct scientific method should have demanded, as it would have demanded in cancer research, that the investigators looked in detail at those individuals who developed the illness in the context of the human society within which they lived and looked at the illness within the context of its individual host.

Despite the fact that the HIV virus appeared to be wholly atypical in its actions, its history and its life cycle, it wasn't until the early nineties that the idea of co-factors was begrudgingly accepted amongst some professionals on the fringes of the scientific debate about AIDS. For those scientists at the critical core of orthodoxy, even now there is a cult-like refusal to admit that it is possible HIV is not the sole cause of AIDS and, more importantly, that the presence of HIV antibodies is not an indication that a person will develop any of the now twenty five designated illnesses which constitute AIDS. The absurdity of refusing to test hypotheses against the clinical evidence reached its zenith in 1992 when the American Centers for Disease Control reclassified a growing number of AIDS cases in which HIV was not present as 'Idiopathic CD-4 lymphocytopenia'.

Much orthodox thinking was from the beginning predicated, consciously or subconsciously, upon the fact that in 1985 the Wellcome Foundation claimed to have found a treatment for AIDS, a drug which killed quantities of the HIV virus and so delayed what orthodoxy determined was an inevitable death. Implicit in this apparent discovery was an end to the AIDS epidemic, for if HIV were the virus solely responsible for the complex of AIDS illnesses and if a start had been made with a drug which could kill some quantities of the virus, then control of the epidemic was assured.

For those who came from within the affected gay community or were drawn in from the scientific or medical periphery and began to question the logic of the HIV theory, there awaited only condemnation, criminalisation and the constant accusation that by refuting the HIV theory they were abetting the deaths of those with AIDS. They were accused as well, without logic or truth, of undermining the 'safe sex' message of the orthodox theorists, and so aiding the spread of the disease.

The argument between the heroes of the medical-industrial complex who stood for rationality and scientific method and those who were truly sceptical, was not, in the end, about science but almost entirely about power. So it was that the medical-industrial complex retained its hegemony, by imposing a powerful censorship and then a moratorium upon legitimate differences of opinion. The investigation of AIDS and the search for its cure demonstrates pre-eminently the totalitarian nature of medical science and pharmaceutical production. The way in which orthodoxy propounded its authority had much in common not just as some have noted, with McCarthyism , but also with the Stalinism which gave rise to it.

AIDS may yet prove to be a Waterloo for many in the medical profession, young gay men particularly will turn to the therapies and the philosophies which keep them alive longest, caring little whether or not they are scientifically or politically correct. At the moment, such therapies appear to be ones which do not include a pharmaceutical component. The unseemly farrago over HIV, AIDS and AZT could mean that the medical profession loses the confidence of a generation of young men whom orthodoxy has threatened with the crucifix of scientific reason yet who have refused to return to their coffins. The scientific dissembling which has taken place around AIDS is infinite and, for many, the integrity of medical science will never recover.

* * *

By 1993 and the end of the Concorde trials, the campaign run by HealthWatch had in the main come to a spluttering end. Looking back upon the whole phenomenon, there seems little doubt that the campaign was primarily intended as a defence of AZT and its clinical trials. If this is the case, the role of HealthWatch members raises many other questions. Not least amongst these is how many HealthWatch members were aware that by aiding the campaign they were actually aiding the Wellcome Foundation in the marketing of AZT?

Other questions might also be asked about whether HealthWatch members were at any time briefed by Wellcome, the Department of Health or the MRC, all of which seem in one way or another to have tacitly supported and benefited from the actions of the campaign.

The summary results of the Concorde trials were announced in April 1993: they showed that individuals who tested HIV antibody positive but were asymptomatic died more quickly and in greater numbers if they were given AZT.

It is of course possible to see the results of the Concorde trials as a vindication of the medical research establishment. Such an argument is put in this way: the results show clearly that it is far better to have large scale long-term trials for drugs like AZT, because we can thereby ensure that toxic drugs or ones with serious side effects do not get licensed. With AZT, however, not only had immense damage already been done, but prescription of the drug continued after Concorde's summary results.

The blanket acceptance of the need for such trials does not anyway answer a series of intricate questions which lie hidden behind the ballyhoo of clinical research and which the public cannot ask because they have no access to intervention. A first set of questions relates to the continuous use of AZT in ARC and AIDS cases between its licensing in 1987 and 1993. This use was granted on the basis of the aborted Phase II trial which ended in 1986. Even though there have been substantial questions raised about the integrity of this trial, the medical research establishment has since cooperated with Wellcome in frequently moving the goal-posts and re-defining AIDS so as to enlarge the potential market for the drug. In America the goalposts were moved so far that AZT was anyway being prescribed for asymptomatics.

Another equally important issue which has to be addressed relates to the moral, ethical and financial obligation which medical research workers owe to the public. Between 1989 and 1993, the British government gave £68 million to the Medical Research Council for AIDS research. Almost all this research was on anti-viral solutions to AIDS; a great deal of it centred upon AZT and benefited the Wellcome Foundation. With so much money from the public purse being used, it is, to say the least, surprising that no public statement has been made in Britain about the outcome of the Concorde trials.

As for the results themselves, it appears that no legal or ethical consequences follow from the fact that the medical research workers who organised Concorde precipitated or perhaps even caused the death of trial subjects to whom they gave AZT. In the cases of Gaston Naessens and Josef Issels, we saw equally sincere medical scientists brought before the criminal courts charged with bringing about the death of patients by failing to provide orthodox treatments.

The Wellcome Foundation negotiated within the Concorde protocols a clause which gave it control of the trial results especially where they were to be used for licence applications. So, despite the fact that the trials were conducted at public expense, in public institutions by investigators and others employed in the public sector, the trial results data appear to have remained private. Wellcome will obviously ensure that such results are not used in licence applications such as the European asymptomatics licence in which it is apparently still interested.

Reading the sub-text of the Concorde trial results, certain unhealthy matters come to light. Investigators, whom Wellcome had chosen because of their commitment to the company, were, when the results became evident, put under immense pressure by the company to change, distort or delay these results. Small cabals of research workers and Wellcome employees were given notice of the results in sufficient time for them to dump their Wellcome shares. Finally and perhaps most damaging, the Department of Health which had an observer present in every committee relating to the trials, remains adamantly tight-lipped about the results. The DoH had entered into a relationship with the Wellcome Foundation over the Concorde trials. It had spent large amounts of the taxpayers' money supporting organisations which promoted AZT and which had provided trial subjects. It had bought the premise, stated in the trial protocols, that the researchers expected to see a 50% increase in length of survival times for asymptomatics given AZT. Why, when this premise turned out to be massively wrong, and when AZT turned out to be not only of no medical consequence but actually damaging to patients, did the Department of Health not make a statement distancing itself from the drug? Why was there no emergency joint meeting of the Department of Health and the MRC and no statement issued about the continued use and prescription of AZT? Why, months after the summary results of Concorde show that AZT hastens death in asymptomatics, is the drug still being given to HIV antibody positive asymptomatic babies in the European-wide PENTA trials?

Medical research and health generally are the most unacceptable aspects of state secrecy. The role played in medical research by government sponsored organisations, and the amount of taxpayers' money spent upon it, are matters of which the public are almost entirely ignorant. One of the consequences of this lack of public debate is that the whole of the government's policy around AIDS, and for that matter HIV, has been governed by its relationship with the company which produces AZT. AIDS was a clear case for an independent clearing-house for public information about the course of the illness and the scientific work which developed around its investigation. Such a clearing-house, which should have been set up immediately AIDS was 'discovered' should have had *absolutely no links* with the pharmaceutical companies.

* * *

There is increasing evidence that competition in some industries and especially within science, now involves a kind of warfare in which the truth in the first casualty. Objective reporting on technical or industrial matters is giving way to disinformation campaigns and propaganda, the point of which is to market a product or destroy a competitor. Increasingly the media are becoming a battleground of conflicting commercial interests.

The treatment of the scientific issues around AIDS, HIV, AZT and the Wellcome Foundation, has exemplified this new mercenary style of journalism. Reporting on these issues has shown clearly that it is difficult to correct misinformation upon such subjects, or make journalists accountable for the inaccuracy of their reports. Although over the last two years there have been a number of ongoing libel actions, and despite hearings before the Broadcasting Complaints Commission and even though journalists themselves were harassed, not one single independent investigation has been held into the objectivity of Duncan Campbell's work around medical fraud. Campbell charged like a mad cow through the fine balance which exists between individual freedom, media powers and fair trading practices and yet not one of his professional colleagues questioned his perspicacity, his motives or his allegiances. Had Campbell been a dissident who chose for his targets powerful people and organisations – as he has done in the past – there would have been never-ending criticism and discussion about his approach.

Throughout the investigation I came across many people, especially within the gay community, who had become fixated with the question of why Campbell had done what he had. Although this question concerned me for a while, it is a fruitless question, to which the easy answers can be ruled out. Campbell is not, for example, the kind of person who would under any circumstances accept money from a vested interest, nor is he a person who would work directly for a vested interest.

The individual is a complex phenomenon and an analysis which suggests purely mechanistic responses will rarely be correct. If an individual moves in two apparently different, even conflicting, intellectual or political directions within a short space of time, the psychological or social roots of this schism could possibly have been there for years. The very conflict might be a seminal aspect of the individual's psychology. Bearing this in mind, it is often pointless to look for *the specific* incident or reason which motivates a change in an individual's thinking or actions.

It is possible to see Campbell's campaign simply as the result of an enthusiasm for science mixed with a particular mental frame which stops him from understanding the feelings or point of view of others. In terms of social justice, however, it is Campbell's supportive milieu which must be most seriously criticised. Without his admiring court of cynical hacks, flattering friends, and frightened fellow-travellers, Campbell would not have got away with what he did.

I finished this book with a heavy feeling of injustices which have not been righted. Individuals whose cases are represented here are people who were subjected to a co-ordinated assault spearheaded by HealthWatch members. Organisations which have been criminalised and publicly traduced have been all but destroyed. The only individual remedy has been for those maligned to take civil actions of one kind or another against their detractors. This is an expensive and time-consuming business.

I firmly believe that there should be some kind of public, judicial tribunal or independent judicial review of all the cases of those whose names and reputations were damaged by HealthWatch, or by those associated with the organisation. The State should pay for such a review because it appears highly probable that the attacks took place with the connivance of the Department of Health and in the context of the Department's refusal to take an independent stand on HIV and AIDS information. These victims of medical orthodoxy should be allowed a forum within which to put their case, without fear of repercussions, even at this late date. Such a tribunal or review should also examine the marketing of AZT. The rules and regulations which cover business practices in the marketing of pharmaceuticals have to be reconsidered and endorsed with serious penalties.

With respect to HealthWatch itself, it seems impossible that the organisation should be allowed to retain its present charitable status. Not only is it a radical campaigning organisation, it has supported covert attacks upon doctors and even other charities.

* * *

This book and the investigation which preceded it have forced me to rethink my view of the National Health Service. I began my work with what I thought was a clear understanding of the difference between public and private medicine. I ended it with an even clearer understanding that the major differences between public and private medicine had next to nothing to do with costs, charges, or affordable treatments. It now seems to me that often there is only one stable criterion which separates public and private medicine. Public medicine is almost always orthodox medicine which leans heavily towards the pharmaceutical treatment of illness. Beyond the strictly patrolled boundaries of orthodoxy, all treatments are in the main forced to be part of the private sector. I was some way into my research before I realised that all the 'private' practitioners I was talking to would desperately have liked to contribute to the National Health Service.

As a socialist I have always had complete faith in the founding principles of the NHS. Research in most fields, however, reveals secret histories and covert agendas. In relation to medicine I now recognise at least three areas of analysis of which I was previously ignorant.

Firstly, there is the ongoing tragedy of the mistakes which doctors make, sometimes on a national scale and often involving large numbers of patients. This iatrogenic plague, which damages through wrong diagnosis, and quack or badly administered orthodox treatments, is uncovered in greater proportion each day.

Secondly, there is the professional defence mounted by doctors against non-orthodox medicine. Treatments and techniques, which might cut the health budget by millions of pounds and benefit the health of the nation, are ignored because they challenge the professional mystique and monopoly of doctors or threaten the profits of pharmaceutical companies.

Finally, there is the whole problematic paradigm of a pharmaceutical company-led health service with its drug-orientated diagnosis and treatment. I used to believe not only in the fundamental principle of socialised health care, but also that such a system inevitably involved a more philanthropic and caring approach than that provided by a private service. Medical professionals, I believed, inhabited a higher moral ground serving the public good within the National Health Service. In fact, I was to learn that many doctors are just as influenced by the biases of class and education and prone to the same mercenary financial inducements as other professionals, whether they work inside or outside a socialised system.

The National Health Service in Britain is presently going through major changes. The driving force behind these changes is the Conservative government's desire to cut public spending and develop a new market-led economy in health care. While most socialists argue the case against market-organised health care as they argue against all other cases of market economics, they consistently fail to address the issue of the drug company monopolies and cartels, an issue which makes the health provision market different from other markets.

As long as health care is overshadowed by the drugs monopolies and cartels and medical practice dominated by the closed shop of professional medical training, the idea of market economics is as fallacious as the socialist idea of a socialised dispersion of care within a need-led system. The power of the drug companies to dictate treatment and cost is immense. Of all the industries, apart perhaps from defence, pharmaceutical production is the only one allowed to support the monopoly practices which presently determine the price and availability of its products. Such monopoly practices have disastrous consequences for the public purse and the health of the consumer.

The drugs bill makes up a substantial part of the costs of health care. The case of AIDS shows how one company can achieve almost monopoly control of a range of drugs used in its treatment. Is it morally or ethically right that a private company make profits of £200 million a year from a drug which has patently failed to cure anyone? Health care costs in Britain could be cut considerably by either statutarily restricting the price of pharmaceutical products or nationalising drug production, while maintaining a mixed economy in all types of medical research. In such circumstances, both the private and public sector research organisations would be working for the government. At the present time, by subsidising research rather than production, the government actually subsidises the private sector with public money. Money given by the government to the MRC, and then granted by them to medical research, first profits the private sector.

The resolve of the present government to cut public spending further will eventually result in the whole of medical research, production, marketing and prescription being controlled by a few enormous corporations. These corporations are presently regulated and made accountable by only the most feeble and incestuously enforced guidelines. Seriously independent controls have to be introduced into pharmaceutical production and marketing.

The dominance of powerful monopolies in health, and the influence of these companies in the teaching of medicine, their predominance in the professional bodies of doctors and ancillary health care workers mean that small community-generated systems of socialised health care do not develop. Many of the self-help groups for particular illnesses, which have previously survived the blandishments of the drug companies, are now being undermined by professional-help groups set up by the very companies which produce the pharmaceutical treatments for the particular illnesses. Professional drugs marketing is eroding the last vestiges of self-help and continuing a trend of de-skilling doctors by selling drugs directly to the vulnerable sick.

Health care costs could be cut by breaking the monopoly which doctors and drug companies have over professional training. There is clearly a need within the NHS for an integrated inter-disciplinary health care system which gives equal authority to both eclectic and allopathic medicine. This should not be, as it is at the moment, a dickering on the margins of the National Health Service, an endless and irrelevant discussion about whether or not cancer hospitals should introduce aromatherapy on one evening a week for women who have had surgery. It should entail fundamental change in the way that doctors are trained.

Chapter References

AUTHOR'S PREFACE

1. Report from a journalist of a conversation with Duncan Campbell.
2. Lauritsen, John. Dunky the litigious journalist. *New Y rk Native*, 20 May 1991.
3. Citizens for Health. *Urgent update for immediate release.* 8 May 1992. See also, FDA's strange raid. *Seattle Post-Intelligencer*, 11 May 1992. *FDA vs. the people of the United States; five years of assault on 'self care'.* The Jonathan Wright Legal Defence and Victory Fund.
4. Bird, Christopher. *The persecution and trial of Gaston Naessens.* Tiburon, Calif: H. J. Kramer, 1991.

PART ONE

CHAPTER ONE. The American Origins of Scientific Medicine.

1. Illich, Ivan. *Limits to medicine, medical nemesis: the exploration of health.* London: Marion Boyars, 1976.
2. Brown, E. Richard. *Rockefeller medicine man: medicine and capitalism in America.* Berkeley, Calif: University of California Press, 1979.
3. Coulter, Harris L. *Divided legacy: the conflict between homoeopathy and the American Medical Association.* Berkeley, Calif: North Atlantic Press, 1982.
4. Ibid.
5. Brown, op. cit.
6. Ibid.
7. Ibid.
8. Coulter, op. cit.
9. Ibid.
10. Flexner, Abraham. *Medical education in the United States and Canada.* New York, Carnegie Foundation for the Advancement of Teaching, 1910. (Bulletin 4).
11. Mullins, Eustace. *Murder by injection. the story of the medical conspiracy against America.* Staunton, Va: National Council for Medical Research, 1988.
12. Ibid.
13. Ibid.
14. Brown, op. cit.
15. Ibid.
16. Griffin, G. Edward. *World without cancer: the story of Vitamin B17.*

Thousand Oaks, Calif: American Media, 1974.
17. Ibid.
18. Lundberg, Ferdinand. *The rich and the super rich: a study in the power of money today.* New York: Lyle Stuart, 1968.
19. Yoxen, Edward. Life as a productive force: capitalising the science and technology of molecular biology. In: Levidow, Les and Young, Bob eds. *Science, technology and the labour process.* London: Free Association Books, 1985.
20. Ibid.

CHAPTER TWO. The Beginning of the Health-Fraud Movement.

1. Wilhelm Reich, following prosecution by the FDA. Quoted in Sharaf, Myron. *Fury on earth: a biography of Wilhelm Reich.* London: André Deutsch, 1983.
2. Carter, James P. *Racketeering in medicine: the suppression of alternatives.* Norfolk, Va: Hampton Roads, 1992.
3. Mintz, Morton. *By prescription only.* Boston, Mass: Beacon Press, 1967. (originally published as *The therapeutic nightmare.* Boston, Mass: Houghton Mifflin, 1965).
   See also: Braithwaite, John. *Corporate crime in the pharmaceutical industry.* London: Routledge & Kegan Paul, 1984.
4. Quirk, Paul J. Food and Drug Administration. In: Wilson, James Q., ed. *The politics of regulation.* New York: Basic Books, 1980.
5. Garrison, Omar V. *The dictocrats' attack on health foods and vitamins.* New York: ARC Books, 1970.
   See also: Mintz, op. cit.; Quirk, op. cit. and Braithwaite, op. cit.
6. Kefauver, Estes. *In a few hands; monopoly power in America.* Harmondsworth: Pelican, 1966.
7. Sjöström, Henning and Nilsson, Robert. *Thalidomide and the power of the drug companies.* Harmondsworth: Penguin, 1972.
8. Garrison, op. cit.
9. Grigg, William. Protests flood FDA over dietary code. *Evening Star,* Washington D.C., 11 October 1962.
   The FDA fights the vitamin craze. Editorial. *Business Week,* 15 July 1972.
   Lobbyist charges 'Tyranny': health food, vitamin bans by FDA rapped. *Pittsburgh Post-Gazette,* 11 June 1973.
10. Senator Edward V. Long, giving evidence before the Senate Subcommittee on Administrative Practice and Procedure (Invasions of Privacy) 1965. Quoted in Garrison, op. cit.
11. Lelord Kordel. Quoted in Garrison, op. cit.
12. Ibid.
13. Garrison, op. cit.
14. Ibid.
15. Ibid. See also Lisa, P.J. *The great medical monopoly wars.* Huntington

Beach, Calif: International Institute of Natural Health Sciences, 1986.

16. Garrison, op. cit.
17. Ibid.
18. Levinson, Charles. *Vodka-Cola*. Tiptree, Essex: Gordon and Cremonesi, 1979.
19. Lyons, Richard D. Disputed health lobby is pressing for a Bill to overturn any limits on sales of vitamins. *New York Times*, 14 May 1973.
20. Garrison, op. cit.
21. Lisa, op. cit. See also: Mullins, Eustace. *Murder by injection: the story of the medical conspiracy against America*. Staunton, Va: National Council for Medical Research, 1988.
22. Lisa, op. cit.
23. Mullins, op. cit.
24. Ibid.
25. Ibid.
26. Lisa, op. cit.
27. Mullins, op. cit.
28. Ibid.
29. Ibid.
30. *Journal of Alternative and Complementary Medicine*, December 1988.

CHAPTER THREE. The American National Council Against
Health Fraud.

1. Horkheimer, Max. *Dawn and decline: notes 1926–31 and 1950–69*. New York: Seabury Press, 1978.
2. Lisa, P.J. *The great medical monopoly wars*. Huntington Beach, Calif: International Institute of Natural Health Sciences, 1986.
3. Ibid.
4. Bavley, A. AIDS activists fight for choice of treatments. *Kansas City Star*, 16 September 1990.
5. Ibid.
6. Ibid.
7. Lisa, op. cit.
8. Ibid.
9. Clinical ecologist MD loses license; Insight into the macrobiotic diet sham. *National Council Against Health Fraud Newsletter: Quality in the Health Market Place*, 14 (1), January/February 1991.
10. Society to be plagued by crank ecology books. *National Council Against Health Fraud Newsletter: Quality in the Health Market Place*, 13 (6), November/December 1990.
11. Herbert, Victor. *Nutrition cultism: facts and fiction*. Philadelphia, Penn: George F.Stickley, 1980.
12. Ibid.

13. Bavley, op. cit.
14. Warren M. Levin, interview with the author.
15. Warren Levin's tape-recorded account of the prosecution mounted against him, entitled PANIC, citing the transcript of the hearing.
16. Jeffery Wiersum M.D. in a letter to the *Townsend Letter for Doctors: an Informal Newsletter for Doctors Communicating to Doctors*, September 1987.
17. Jeffries, T. and Plank, S. *The Daily Iowan.* reprinted in the *Townsend Letter for Doctors: an Informal Newsletter for Doctors Communicating to Doctors*, September 1987.
18. Marshall, Eliot. Academy sued on 'plagiarized' diet report. *Science* 1990; 247: 1022.
19. Warren Levin, op. cit.

CHAPTER FOUR. Selling Science and Industry in America.

1. Dickson, David and Noble, David. By force of reason: the politics of science and technology policy. In: Ferguson, Thomas and Rogers, Joel, eds. *The hidden election.* New York: Pantheon, 1981.
2. Moss, Robert. *The collapse of democracy.* London: Temple Smith, 1975.
3. Dickson and Noble, op. cit.
4. Ibid.
5. Ibid.
6. Ibid.
7. Kurtz, Howard. Dr Whelan's media operation. *Columbia Journalism Review*, March/April 1990.
8. Harnik, P. *Voodoo science, twisted consumerism.* Washington D.C.: Center for Science in the Public Interest, 1982.
9. Ibid.
10. *Introducing American Council on Science and Health, Inc.* ACSH publicity literature, undated.
11. Ibid. See also: Harnik, op. cit.
12. Kurtz, op. cit.
13. *Fort Worth Star Telegram*, 25 September 1980, quoted in Harnik, op. cit.
14. Kurtz, op. cit.
15. Ibid.
16. Ibid.
17. Ibid.
18. Ibid.
19. Garrison, op. cit.
20. Cannon, G. *The politics of food.* London: Century Hutchinson, 1987.
21. Knowles, James C. *The Rockefeller Financial Group.* University of

Southern California: Modular Publications (Module 343), 1973.

22. Harnik, op. cit.
23. Ibid.
24. Ibid.
25. Hodgkinson L. Truth, myth and a load of sweet talk. *Daily Telegraph*, 25 April 1986.

CHAPTER FIVE. The Rational Idea in a Materialist World

1. Dickens, Charles. *Hard times.*
2. Melton, J. Gordon, Clark, Jerome and Kelly, Aidan A. *The New Age Almanac.* East Hiles, New York: Visible Ink Press, 1991.
3. Kurtz, Paul, ed. *Sidney Hook and the contemporary world: essays on the pragmatic intelligence.* New York: John Day, 1968.
   Kurtz, Paul, Hook, Sidney, eds. *The university and the state: what role for government in higher education?* Buffalo, New York: Prometheus Books, 1978.
4. Coleman, Peter. *The Liberal conspiracy: The Congress for Cultural Freedom and the struggle for the mind of Europe.* New York: The Free Press. 1989.
   See also Lasch, Christopher. *The agony of the American Left.* New York: Alfred A. Knopf, 1969.
5. Walter, N. *New Humanist,* June 1979.
6. Ibid.
7. Scientists against astrology. *Humanist,* 35 (5), September/October 1975.
8. Inglis, Brian. *The hidden power.* London: Jonathan Cape, 1986.
9. Melton et al., op. cit.
10. Inglis, op. cit.
11. From 'Starbaby', *Fate,* cited in Inglis, op. cit.
12. Bowart, W. *Operation Mind Control and America's secret power.* London: Fontana, 1978.
13. Hoagland, Hudson. Cited in Gardner, Martin, *Science, good bad and bogus.* Buffalo, New York: Prometheus Books, 1990.
14. Sugar, B. R., cited in Gardner, op. cit.
15. Inglis, op. cit.
16. Kurtz, Paul, cited in Melton et al., op. cit.
17. Melton et al., op. cit.
18. Hofstadter, Douglas R. About two kinds of Enquiry, 'National Enquirer' and 'Skeptical Inquirer'. *Scientific American,* 246, February 1982, 14–9.
19. Hansel, Charles E.M. *ESP a scientific evaluation.* New York: Scribner, 1966; and *ESP and parapsychology: a critical re-evaluation.* Buffalo, New York: Prometheus Books, 1980.
20. Collins, Harry. *Times Higher Education Supplement,* 21 October 1988.
21. Melton et al., op. cit.

22. Carrington, Michael. Raider of the New Age. *Sunday Telegraph*, 16 June 1991.

23. Dr Philip H. Abelson, cited in Nelson, William R., ed. *The politics of science*. New York: Oxford University Press, 1968.

24. The John D. and Catherine T. MacArthur Foundation. *Report on Activities*. Chicago, Ill: The Foundation, 1990.
    Also personal enquiries to the Foundation.

25. Ibid.

26. *Skeptical Inquirer*, 15, Winter 1990 (page actually headed Winter 1991).

27. Ibid.

28. Ibid.

29. Ibid.

30. Fulder, Stephen, Monro, Robin. *The status of complementary medicine in the United Kingdom*. London: Threshold Foundation, 1981.
    Taylor Reilly, David. Young doctors' views on alternative medicine. *BMJ*, 1983; 287: 337-9.

31. Press release issued by Paul Kurtz through Reuters, 2 September 1990.

32. *Skeptical Inquirer*, 13, Summer 1989.

33. Ibid.

PART TWO

CHAPTER SIX. The Case of the Missing Energy.

1. Jacques Benveniste, an interview with the author.

2. Ibid.

3. Benveniste, Jacques et al. Human basophil degranulation triggered by very dilute antiserum against IgE. *Nature*, 30 June 1988.

4. Maddox, John. When to believe the unbelievable. Editorial. *Nature*, 30 June 1988.

5. Benveniste, Jacques et al. *In vitro* immunological degranulation of human basophils is modulated by lung histamine and Apis mellifica. *British Journal of Clinical Pharmacology* 1988; 25: 439-44.
   Benveniste, Jacques et al. Effect upon mouse peritoneal macrophages of orally administered very high dilutions of silica. *European Journal of Pharmacology* 1987; 135: 313-9.

6. MacEoin, Denis. The Benveniste affair and ... the denaturing of science. *Journal of Alternative and Complementary Medicine*, September 1988.
   Sheldrake, Rupert. *A new science of life*. London: Blond and Briggs, 1982.

7. Randi, James. *James Randi psychic investigator: in search of the paranormal*. London: Boxtree in association with Granada

Television, 1991.
8. Maddox, John. Randi, James and Stewart, Walter W. 'High-dilution' experiments a delusion. *Nature*, 28 July 1988.
9. Ibid.
10. Cited in MacEoin, op. cit.
11. Maddox, John et al. Dr Jacques Benveniste replies. *Nature*, 28 July 1988.
12. Ibid.
13. MacEoin, op. cit.
14. 'James Randi: Psychic Investigator'. Granada; a series of programmes beginning Wednesday 17 July 1991, produced by Open Media Productions, London.
15. Randi, op. cit.
16. Ibid.

CHAPTER SEVEN. Clinical Ecology.

1. Charles Dickens. *Hard Times*.
2. Magendie, François. *Phénomènes physiques de la vie*. Paris: Baillière, 1837 - 42.
3. Eagle, Robert. *Eating and allergy*. London: Futura, 1979.
4. Ibid.
5. Ibid.
6. Pulay, Erwin. *Allergic man: susceptibility and hypersensitivity*. London: Muller, 1942.
7. Ibid.
8. Hare, Francis. *The food factor in disease*. London: Longmans, 1905. Cited in Eagle, op. cit.
9. Laroche, Guy. Richet, Charles and Saint-Girons, François. *[L'Anaphylaxis alimentaire]*. Translated by Mildred P. Rowe and Albert H. Rowe. Berkeley, Calif: University of California Press, 1930. Cited in Eagle, op. cit.
10. Bray, George W. *Recent advances in allergy*. London: T. & A. Churchill. 1934. Cited in Eagle, op. cit.
11. Coca, Arthur. *Familial non-reaginic food-allergy*. Springfield, Ill: C.C. Thomas, 1943. Cited in Eagle, op. cit.
12. Carson, Rachel. *Silent spring*. London: Hamish Hamilton, 1963.
13. Lucas, Jack. *Our polluted food*. London: Charles Knight, 1975.
14. Carson, op. cit.
15. Ibid.
16. Dr. Malcolm Hargraves of the Mayo Clinic, cited in Carson, op. cit.
17. Lucas, op. cit.
18. Whiteside, Thomas. *The pendulum and the toxic cloud: the course of dioxin contamination*. New Haven, Conn: Yale University Press, 1977.

19. *Farmers Weekly*, 14 December 1990.
20. 2,500 producers suffer OP dip side-effects, Enfys Chapman cited in *Farmers Weekly*, 14 December 1990.
21. Mr Green, who farms at Bridgnorth, Shropshire, in *Farmers Weekly*, 14 December 1990.
22. Unreferenced study cited in: *Pesticides, chemicals and health*. London: British Medical Association, 1990.
23. *Pesticides, chemicals and health*. London: British Medical Association, 1990.
24 *Assessment of mortality and morbidity due to unintentional pesticide poisonings*. WHO, 1986. (WHO/VB9 86 929). Cited in BMA Report October 1990, op. cit.
25. Goldsmith E. and Hildyard, N. *Green Britain or industrial wasteland*. 1986. Cited in BMA Report, op. cit.
26. BMA Report 1990, op. cit.
27. *Chemistry and Industry*, 21 August 1989.
28. Ibid.
29. Maclean, David, cited in *Chemistry and Industry*, 1 January 1990.
30. Eckholm, Erik. *Down to earth*. London: Pluto Press, 1982.

CHAPTER EIGHT. Dr William Rea: Clinical Ecologist.

1. Capra, Fritjof. *The turning point: science, society and the rising culture*. London: Fontana, 1990.
2. Rowe, A. *Food allergy*. Springfield, Ill: C. C. Thomas, 1972.
   Rinkel, H. J., Randolph, T.G. and Zeller, M. *Food allergy*. Springfield, Ill: C.C. Thomas, 1951.
3. Mackarness, Richard. *Chemical allergies*. Previously published as *Chemical victims*. London: Pan Books, 1990.
4. Rea, cited in Mackarness.
5. Interview with the author.

CHAPTER NINE. Dr Jean Monro: Clinical Ecologist.

1. Tom Lehrer.
2. Private communication with Ivor Harold of Oxford.
3. Gillie, Oliver. The twentieth century claims a new victim - Amanda Strang. *Sunday Times*, 24 January 1982.
4. Ibid.
5. Monro, Jean A. Food families and rotation diets. In: Brostoff, Jonathan, Challacombe, Stephen J. *Food allergy and intolerance*. London: Baillière Tindall, 1987: 303-43.
   Monro, Jean A. Food-induced migraine. Ibid. 633-65.
   Mansfield, Peter, Monro, Jean A. *Chemical children: how to protect your family from harmful pollutants*. London: Century, 1987.
6. Interview with the author.
7. Jean Monro, quoting the work of the Environmental Health

Center, Dallas, in *Detoxification programme.*

8. Hobbs, J. R., White, T. R., Sheldon, J., Mowbray, J. A. and Monro, J.A. CD8 deficiency in patients with muscle fatigue following suspected enteroviral infections [myalgia encephalitica]. In: Poulik, M.D., ed. *Protides of the biological fluids.* Oxford: Pergamon Press, 1990: 391-8.

9. Fried, Rivka. Poison in the air. *Sunday Times,* 7 September 1986.

CHAPTER TEN. Bristol Cancer Help Centre.

1. Halstead, Bruce. William Jarvis' conspiratorial 'innocence' and related matters, Part II. *Townsend Letter for Doctors.*

2. Sharaf, Myron. *Fury on earth: a biography of Wilhelm Reich.* London: André Deutsch, 1983.

3. Haught, S. J. *Censured for curing cancers: the American experience of Dr Max Gerson.* Barrytown, New York: Station Hill Press, 1991. Gerson, M. *A cancer therapy.* Del Mar, Calif: Totality Books, 1958.

4. Issels, Josef. *Cancer: a second opinion.* London: Hodder and Stoughton, 1975.

5. Cancer Research Campaign. *Breast cancer,* 1991. (Factsheet 6.2). Mortality statistics. OPCS. Series DH2. 17, 1990.

6. Interview with the author.

7. Hart-Davis, Duff. *Sunday Telegraph,* August 1973.

8. Newton-Fenbow, Peter D. *A time to heal.* London: Souvenir Press, 1971.

9. Quoted in Newton-Fenbow, op. cit.

10. Quoted in Newton-Fenbow, op. cit.

11. Haught, op. cit.

12. Brohn, Penny. *Gentle giants.* London: Century, 1986.

13. Ibid.

14. Ibid.

15. Ibid.

16. Ibid.

17. Ibid.

18. Doyle, Christine. Cancer remission film is shelved. *Observer,* 7 July 1970.

19. Miller, Henry. *Listener,* 12 November 1970.

20. *Observer,* 22 November 1970.

21. Dobson, Christopher. *Sunday Express,* 28 May 1972.

22. Margach, James and Humphry, Derek. British cancer men attack Issels. *Sunday Times,* March 1971.

23. Report on the Treatment of Cancer at the Ringberg-Clinic Rottach Egern, Bavaria. London: HMSO, 1971.

24. Ibid.

25. Ibid.

26. Ibid.

27. Ibid.
28. Parselle, C.B.B. Letter to the *Daily Telegraph*, 9 March 1971.
29. *Guardian*, 3 March 1971.
30. *Daily Telegraph*, 29 September 1973.
31. *Daily Express*, 4 April 1972
32. *Daily Telegraph*, 8 June 1973
33. Thomas, Gordon. *Issels: the biography of a doctor*. London: Hodder and Stoughton, 1975.
34. *Sunday Telegraph*, 5 August 1973.
35. *The Times*, 21 July 1973.
36. *Daily Telegraph*, 23 July 1973.
37. *Sunday Times*, 29 July 1973.
38. Mills, Roger. A cautious approach to 'holistic' treatment. *Listener*, 14 April 1983.
39. Kidman, Brenda. *A gentle way with cancer*. London: Century, 1985.
40. Richards, Dick. *The topic of cancer: when the killing has to stop*. Oxford: Pergamon, 1982.

CHAPTER ELEVEN. Industrial Food and Nutritional Medicine.

1. Pulay, Erwin. *Allergic man: susceptibility and hypersensitivity*. London: Muller, 1942.
2. Griggs, Barbara. *The food factor*. London: Viking, 1986.
3. Somogyl, John. *International Journal for Vitamin and Nutrition Research*, February 1976.
   Goulart, Frances S. *Nutritional self-defence: protecting yourself from yourself*. Lenham, Maryland: Madison Books, 1990.
4. Goulart, op. cit.
5. Ibid.

CHAPTER TWELVE. Dr Stephen Davies: Nutritional Doctor.

1. Stephen Davies, interview with the author.
2. Ibid.
3. Marks, Vincent. Low sugar confusion. *Doctor*, 30 April 1981.
4. Ferriman, Annabel. The great minerals gold mine. *Observer*, 22 May 1988.
5. Ibid.
6. Ibid.
7. Ibid.
8. Ibid.
9. Ibid.

CHAPTER THIRTEEN. Patrick Holford: ION.

1. Patrick Holford, interview with the author.
2. Holford, Patrick. *The whole health manual*. Wellingborough:

Thorsons, 1983.
3. Patrick Holford, interview with the author.
4. Hoffer, Abram. *Orthomolecular nutrition.* New Haven, Conn: Keats, 1978.
5. Hoffer, Abram and Osmond, Humphry. *How to live with schizophrenia,* London: Johnson, 1966.
6. Pfeiffer, Carl. *Mental and elemental nutrients.* New Haven, Conn: Keats, 1975.
7. Cannon, Geoffrey. *The politics of food.* London: Century, 1987.

CHAPTER FOURTEEN. Belinda Barnes: Foresight.

1. Belinda Barnes, interview with the author.
2. *Prevention of brain disorder associated with low birth weight in City and Hackney.* London: Institute of Brain Chemistry and Human Nutrition, 5 September 1991.
3. Mathews, Robert. Putting bounce back into baby. *Daily Telegraph,* 2 September 1991
4. Davies, Stephen and Stewart, Alan. *Nutritional medicine.* London: Avon Books, 1987.
5. Interview with the author.
6. Barnes, Belinda and Bradley, Susan. *Planning for a healthy baby.* London: Ebury, 1990.
7. Price, Weston. *Nutrition and physical degeneration.* New York: Hoeber, 1939.
8. Williams, Roger. *Nutrition against disease.* Toronto: Bantam, 1971.
9. Shute, Wilfred. *The complete updated vitamin E book.* New Haven, Conn: Keats, 1975.
    See also, Shute, Evan. *The heart and vitamin E.* New Haven, Conn: Keats, 1975.
10. Pauling, Linus. *How to live longer and feel better.* New York: Freeman, 1986.
    See also, Pauling, Linus. *Vitamin C, the common cold and flu.* New York: Berkley, 1970.
11. Pfeiffer, Carl C. *Nutritional and mental illness: an orthomolecular approach to balancing body chemistry.* Rochester, Vt: Healing Arts Press, 1987.
12. Davies, Adelle. *Let's eat right to keep fit.* London: Unwin, 1979.
13. Oberleas, D., Caldwell, D. F. Trace minerals in pregnancy. *Int J Envir Stud* 1981; 17: 85-98.
14. Horrobin, David, ed. *Clinical uses of essential fatty acids.* Montreal: Eden Press, 1982.
15. Hurley, Lucille. *Developmental nutrition.* Englewood Cliffs, N.J.: Prentice-Hall, 1980.
16. Grant, Ellen. *The bitter pill.* London: Hamish Hamilton, 1985.
17. *Foresight index number decoder.* Godalming: Foresight, 1986.
18. Jervis, Norman, Jervis, Ruth. *The Foresight wholefood cookbook.*

London: Aurum Press, 1986.

19. Barnes, Belinda, Colquhoun, Irene. *The hyperactive child*. Wellingborough: Thorsons, 1984.

CHAPTER FIFTEEN. Larkhall.

1. Robert Woodward.
2. Greer, Rita. *Gluten-free cooking*. Wellingborough: Thorsons, 1978.
   Greer, Rita. *Diets to help coeliacs*. Wellingborough: Thorsons, 1982.
   Greer, Rita. *Diets to help multiple sclerosis*. Wellingborough: Thorsons, 1982.
3. Robert Woodward, interview with the author.
4. Pascoe-Watson, George. Addicted to sugar; Mary eats 2lb bag a day for 10 years. *Sun*, 10 June 1991.
5. Robert Woodward, interview with the author.
6. Ibid.
7. Benton, David, Roberts, Gwilym. The effect of vitamin and mineral supplementation on intelligence of a sample of school children. *Lancet* 1988; i: 140-3.
8. Benton, David, Cook, R. Vitamin and mineral supplements improve the intelligence scores and concentration of six-year-old children. *J Pers Indiv Diff* 1991; 12: 1151-8.
   See also Benton, David. The impact of vitamin/mineral supplementation on the intelligence scores of children - a summary and discussion of the scientific evidence. Published by Benton, D. University College, Swansea.
   Schoenthaler, S.J., Amos, S.P., Eysenck, H.J., Peritz, E. and Yudkin, J. Controlled trial of vitamin-mineral supplementation; effect on intelligence and performance. *J Pers Indiv Diff* 1991; 12: 351-62.

CHAPTER SIXTEEN: AIDS.

1. Levi-Strauss, Claude. *Tristes tropiques*. Harmondsworth: Penguin, 1973.
2. Nussbaum, Bruce. *Good intentions; how big business and the medical establishment are corrupting the fight against AIDS*. New York: Atlantic Monthly Press, 1991.
3. Lehrman, Nathaniel S. Is AIDS non-infectious? the possibility and its CBW implications. *Covert Action Bulletin*, 28, Summer 1987.
4. Duesberg, Peter. AIDS epidemiology, *Proc Natl Acad Sci* 1991; 88: 1575-9.
5. Cass Mann, interview with the author.
6. Ibid.
7. Coulter, Harris L. *AIDS and syphilis: the hidden link*. Berkeley, Calif: North Atlantic Books, 1987.
8. Chaitow, Leon and Martin, Simon. *A world without AIDS*.

Wellingborough: Thorsons, 1988.
9. Stuart Marshall, interview with the author.
10. Ibid.
11. Alan Beck, interview with the author.
12. Jarman, Derek. *Modern nature: the journals of Derek Jarman*. London: Century, 1991.

PART THREE

CHAPTER SEVENTEEN. The Rationalist Press Association.

1. Jung, C.G. *Memories, dreams, reflections*. New York: Random House, 1961.
2. *New Humanist*, 1976.
3. Taylor, John G. *Superminds*. London: Viking, 1975.
4. *Nature*, 4 September 1975.
5. Inglis, Brian. *The hidden power*. London: Jonathan Cape, 1986.
6. Ibid.
7. *New Humanist* 1975; 91: 177-8.
8. *New Humanist* 1980; 96: 29-30

CHAPTER EIGHTEEN. British and Irish Skeptics.

1. Russell, Bertrand. *History of Western philosophy*.
2. *British and Irish Skeptic*, January/February 1988.
3. Ibid.
4. Grossman, Wendy. Crimewatch. *What Micro*, January 1992.
5. *British and Irish Skepic*, January/February 1988.
6. Ibid.
7. *Skeptical Inquirer*, 12(1), Fall 1987.
8. *Lancet* 1986; i: 960-1.
9. *Skeptical Inquirer*, 12(1), Fall 1987.
10. Ibid.

CHAPTER NINETEEN. The British Nutrition Foundation.

1. Sutherland, Edwin H. *White collar crime*. New Haven, Conn: Yale University Press, 1983.
2. Lacey, Richard. *Unfit for human consumption*. London: Grafton, 1992.
3. Yudkin, John. *Pure, white and deadly*. Harmondsworth: Penguin, 1988.
4. Cannon, op. cit.
5. Ibid.
6. David M. Conning [Director General of the BNF], cited in the Foundation Annual Report 1989-1990.
7. *The BNF, what it is and what it does*. London: British Nutrition

Foundation.
8. Erlichman, James. *Gluttons for punishment*. Harmondsworth:
    Penguin, 1986.
9. Cannon, op. cit.
10. *Alternative Therapy Report*. London: BMA, 1987.
11. *Food Intolerance and Food Aversion*. London: RCP, 1984.
12. Cannon, op. cit.
13. Ibid.
14. All quotes are taken from the paperback version of the report,
    Food Intolerance: Fact and Fiction, London: Grafton Books, 1986.
15. Ibid.
16. Ibid.
17. Ibid.
18. *Food Intolerance and Food Aversion*, op. cit.
19. *Food Intolerance: Fact and Fiction*, op. cit.
20. Cited in Cannon, op. cit.
21. Ibid.
22. *Food Intolerance: Fact and Fiction*, op. cit.
23. Ibid.
24. Ibid.
25. Yudkin, op. cit.
26. Cited in Cannon, op. cit.
27. Ibid.
28. Ibid.

CHAPTER TWENTY. Wellcome, Part One.

1. Deuteronomy 16:19.
2. Flexner, Abraham. *Medical education in Europe*. New York: Carnegie
    Foundation for the Advancement of Teaching, 1912. (Bulletin
    VI).
    Also: Flexner, Abraham. *Medical education: a comparative study*. New
    York: Macmillan, 1925.
3. Fisher, Donald. The Rockefeller Foundation and the develop-
    ment of scientific medicine in Great Britain. *Minerva* 1978; 16: 20-
    4.
4. Ibid.
5. Ibid.
6. Ibid.
7. Wellcome Annual Report and Accounts, 1992.
8. Ibid.
9. Ibid.
10. Ibid.
11. Ibid.
12. Klass, Alan. *There's gold in them there pills*. Harmondsworth:
    Penguin, 1975.

CHAPTER TWENTY ONE. The Pollution of Science.

1. Margaret Thatcher, speaking at the 50th Anniversary Lecture of the Parliamentary and Scientific Committee, 6 December 1989.
2. Research Defence Association. Annual Report, October 1990.
3. *Science in Parliament*, Vol 47 (1).
4. Dr John H. Gibbons, Director, Office of Technological Assessment, Congress of the United States of America. Annual Luncheon speech; Parliamentary and Scientific Committee, 26 April 1991.
5. Aims and Objectives. PSC Annual Report, 1991, as amended by the 1991 AGM.
6. POST. Annual Report. *Science in Parliament*, 47 (3), 1989–1990.
7. POST. Annual Report, 1989 - 1989 and PSC. Annual Report, 1988.
8. Research and the NHS - current issues. POST, April 1991.
9. POST. Annual Report. 1989–1990.
10. Ibid.
11. PSC. Annual Report, 1991.
12. Tom Wilkie talks to William Waldegrave. *Independent*, 22 May 1992.

PART FOUR

CHAPTER TWENTY TWO. Wellcome, Part Two.

1. Wellcome Pharmaceuticals plc. Annual Report, 1985.
2. Sneader, Walter. *Drug development: from laboratory to clinic.* Chichester: John Wiley. 1986.
3. Lauritsen, John. *New York Native*, March 30 1992.
4. Ibid.
5. Wellcome Journal, June 1987.
6. Ibid.
7. Ibid.
8. Ibid.
9. Ibid., November 1987.
10. Veterans' Administration Cooperative Study 298, February 1991.
11. *Wellcome Journal*, March 1991.
12. Ibid., June 1990.

CHAPTER TWENTY THREE. Wellcome, Part Three.

1. Illich, Ivan. *Limits to medicine, medical nemesis: the exploration of health.* London: Marion Boyars, 1976.
2. *Parliamentary Aids Digest*, 1 November 1988.
3. Report of Bastyr College: Healing AIDS/ARC research project. Research Director, Leanna J. Standish. Undated.

4. Erlichman, James. Wellcoming some nice, easy profits from Aids monopoly. *Guardian*, 23 October 1987.
5. *Lancet*, 339; 27 June 1992.
6. *Wellcome Foundation News*, November 1985.
7. *Guardian*, 25 March 1992.
8. *The Association of Medical Research Charities Handbook*, 1990-1991. AMRC, Tavistock House South, Tavistock Square, London.
9. *Wellcome Journal*, May 1988.
10. Letter to the author from the BMA Foundation for AIDS.
11. Remarks on R & D made 12 November 1987 by Howard Schaeffer and Dr Trevor Jones at the announcement of Wellcome's preliminary results for the year ended 29 August 1987. Background Note, issued by Wellcome.
12. MRC/INSERM trial of Zidovudine in HIV Infection: Concorde 1. Detailed Protocol, August 1988.
13. Ibid.
14. Ibid.
15. Ibid.
16. Tate and Lyle. Annual Report, 1990.
17. Westminster Communications Group Limited. Company Returns, 1991.
18. *Current Research in Britain*, 1985 & 1991.
19. The Wellcome Trust. 18th Annual Report, 1988-89.
20. Ibid. See also, *BMJ*; 298, 20 May 1989.
21. *Current Research in Britain*, 1985 & 1991.
22. The Wellcome Trust. 18th Annual Report, 1988-89.
23. *Current Research in Britain*, 1989 - 1991.
24. The Wellcome Trust. 18th Annual Report, 1988-89.

CHAPTER TWENTY FOUR. Caroline Richmond, Part One.

1. Cannon, Geoffrey. The politics of food. London: Century, 1987.
2. *Medical Laboratory World*, December 1978
3. The Wellcome Trust. 18th Annual Report, 1988-89.
4. Lawrence, Felicity, ed. *Additives - your complete survival guide*. London: Century Hutchinson, 1986.
5. Richmond, Caroline. Medicine and Media. *BMJ* 1986; 292: 754. See also Richmond, Caroline. Food additives? No problem. *New Scientist*, 13 February 1986.
6. *BMJ* 1986; 292: 754.
7. Richmond, Caroline. A newly discovered class of allergens: textile dyes? *BMJ* 1987; 295: 1600-1.
8. Ibid.
9. *Company*, March 1986.
10. Ibid., July 1986.
11. Ibid.

12. Ibid., November 1987.
13. Marks, Vincent. *Observer*, 4 October 1992. See also, *Daily Mirror*, 23 March 1993.

CHAPTER TWENTY FIVE. Caroline Richmond, Part Two.

1. Davies, Stephen. *J Nutr Med* 1990; 1: 167-70.
2. Richmond, Caroline. Feed into the databank for foods free of allergens. *GP*, 2 October 1987.
3. Ibid.
4. Ibid.
5. Ibid.
6. Richmond, Caroline. Can vitamin pills really boost our IQ? *GP*, 26 February 1988.
7. QED. BBC1, 20 January 1988.
8. Benton, David, Roberts, Gwilym. Effect of vitamin and mineral supplementation on intelligence of a sample of schoolchildren. *Lancet* 1988; i: 140-3.
9. *GP*, 26 February 1988.
10. Ibid.
11. Ibid.
12. Ibid.
13. Richmond, Caroline. Are milk hormones safe? *GP*, 17 June 1988.
14. Richmond, Caroline. IQ study seems unscientific. *GP*, 7 October 1988.
15. Ibid.
16. Ibid.
17. Richmond, Caroline. It's all in the mind or in the media. *GP*, 4 November 1988.
18. Ibid.
19. Ibid.
20. Richmond, Caroline. Myalgic encephalomyelitis, Princess Aurora, and the wandering womb. *BMJ* 1989; 298: 1295-6.
21. Ibid.
22. Hartnell, L. Letter. *BMJ* 1989; 298: 1577-8.
23. Wookey, Celia. Letter. Ibid., 1578.
24. Richmond, Caroline. Causes of adverse reactions to milk. *Pulse*, 25 November 1989.
25. Bender, Arnold. *Health or hoax? The truth about health food and diets*. Reading: Elvendon Press. 1985.

CHAPTER TWENTY SIX. The Campaign Against Health Fraud, Part One.

1. Illich, Ivan. *Limits to medicine, medical nemesis: the exploration of health*. London: Marion Boyars, 1976.
2. Griffin, Edward G. *World without cancer: the story of vitamin B17*.

Westlake Village, Calif: American Media, 1974.
3. Happold, F.H. *Medicine at risk: the high price of cheap drugs*. London: Queen Anne Press, 1967.
4. Ibid.
5. Inglis, Brian. *Fringe medicine*. London: Faber, 1964.
    Inglis, Brian. *Drugs, doctors & disease*. London: André Deutsch, 1965.
6. Happold, op. cit.
7. Ibid.
8. Ibid.
9. Ibid.
10. Fulder, Stephen, Monro, Robin. *The status of complementary medicine in the United Kingdom*. London: Threshold Foundation, 1981.
11. Ibid.
12. Smith, Tony. Alternative medicine. Editorial. *BMJ* 1983; 287: 307.
13. British Medical Association. *Alternative therapy*. 1986.
14. Ibid.
15. Ibid.
16. Ibid.

CHAPTER TWENTY SEVEN. The Campaign Against Health Fraud, Part Two.

1. Illich, Ivan. *Limits to medicine, medical nemesis: the exploration of health*. London: Marion Boyars, 1976.
2. Pearson, David J., Rix, Keith J.B., Bentley, Stephen J. Food allergy: how much in the mind? *Lancet* 1983; i: 1259 - 61.
3. Hodgkinson, Neville. Doctors against the allergy quacks. *Sunday Times*, 31 August 1986.
4. Dobbing, J., ed. *Food intolerance*. London: Baillière Tindall, London: 1987.
5. David Freed, interview with the author.
6. Letterhead in possession of the author.
7. *CAHF Newsletter*, Autumn 1989, quoting a letter sent by Campbell to *Hospital Doctor*. Campaign Against Health Fraud, London.
8. *CAHF Newsletter* and Minutes of CAHF Annual General Meetings 1989 and 1990.
9. *Newsletter* of the National Council Against Health Fraud throughout 1990.
10. Four-paragraph article sent to media by Caroline Richmond headed Council Against Health Fraud.
11. Ciba Foundation. Report and Handbook, 1990.
12. Beard, Nick. The Committee Against Health Fraud. *U.K. Skeptic*, 3 (3).
13. *UK Skeptic*, February 1989.

14. Maddox, John. The case against PSI. *B&IS*. January/February 1990.
15. Campaign Against Health Fraud. Invitation to Press Conference, May 8 1989, at the Royal Society of Medicine.
16. Prentice, Thomson. AIDS research. *The Times*, 8 May 1989.
17. Prentice, Thomson. Quacks risk women's lives. *The Times*, 9 May 1989.
18. *Journal of Alternative and Complementary Medicine*, May 1989.
19. Ciba Foundation. Report and Handbook, 1990.

CHAPTER TWENTY EIGHT. Dr Vincent Marks.

1. Marks, Vincent. Quoted in *The Times*, 2 June 1986.
2. British Association of Clinical Biochemists. Annual Report, 1990.
3. *University of Surrey Gazette*, 1985 -1990.
4. Ibid., November 1986.
5. Ibid., February 1986.
6. Ibid., July 1987.
7. Ibid., July 1990.
8. Ibid., March 1989/November 1990.
9. Cancer Research Campaign. Annual Report, 1987, with Handbook, 1988.
10. Cancer Research Campaign. Annual Report, 1988, with Handbook, 1989.
11. Food and Drink Programme. BBC 2, 15 January 1991.
12. *University of Surrey Gazette*, 18 July 1985.
13. The Food and Veterinary Laboratory Limited. Directors' Reports, 1987/1988/1989.
14. Ibid.
15. Ibid.
16. Ibid.
17. Ibid.
18. Ibid.
19. Cannon, Geoffrey. *The politics of food*. London: Century Hutchinson, 1987.
20. Yudkin, John. *Pure, white and deadly*. Harmondsworth: Penguin, 1988.
21. *C-H-O*, June 1990. Advisa Medica on behalf of the Sugar Bureau.
22. Marks, Vincent. *Is British food bad for you?* London: Health and Welfare Unit, Institute of Economic Affairs, 1991.
23. Ibid.

CHAPTER TWENTY NINE. Duncan Campbell.

1. *Sunday Times*, 1 February 1987.
2. Hosenball, Mark and Campbell, Duncan. The eavesdroppers. *Time Out*, 11 February 1987.

3. Campbell, Duncan, quoted in Fraser, Laura. Blows against the Empire. *San Francisco Bay Guardian*, 11 November 1987.

4. *Guardian*, 6 January 1988.

5. Campbell, Duncan. The amazing AIDS scam. *New Statesman and Society*, 24 June 1988.

6. Ibid.

7. Harriman, Ed. Watch out Fergie. *New Statesman and Society*, 23 September 1988.

8. *New Statesman and Society*, 24 June 1988.

9. Ibid.

10. Ibid.

11. Ibid.

12. Ibid.

13. Nussbaum, Bruce. *Good intentions: how big business and the medical establishment are corrupting the fight against AIDS*. New York: Atlantic Monthly Press, 1990.

14. *New Statesman and Society*, 24 June 1988.

15. Ibid.

16. Campbell, Duncan. The amazing AIDS scam. *New Statesman and Society*, 24 June 1988.

17. Horton, Meurig. Bugs, drugs and placebos. In: Carter, Erica and Watney, Simon, eds. *Taking liberties; AIDS and cultural politics*. London: Serpent's Tail, 1989.

18. Ibid.

19. Campbell, Duncan. Aids: patient power puts research on trial. *New Scientist*, 12 November 1988.

20. Ibid.

21. Ibid.

22. Ibid., 6 January 1989.

23. Ibid.

24. Ibid.

25. Ibid.

26. *Inter Action: the Journal of ME Action*, 4, Spring 1990.

CHAPTER THIRTY. Professor Michael Baum.

1. Evelyn Thomas.

2. Evelyn Thomas, cited in the *Observer*, 2 October 1988.

3. Clayton, Paul. *Evening Standard Magazine*, January 1992.
Raphael, Adam. Wanted: human guinea pigs. *Observer*, 2 October 1988.

4. Ibid.

5. Ibid.

6. From unpublished writings of Evelyn Thomas.

7. *Observer*, 9 October 1988.

8. *Observer*, 16 October 1988.

9. Brahams, Diana. Informed consent and randomised controlled trials. *Law Society Gazette*, 25, 28 June 1989.
10. *Observer*, 16 October 1988.
11. Ibid.
12. *Daily Mail*, 29 June 1992.
13. Brahams, Diana. Death of a patient who was unwitting subject of randomised controlled trial of cancer treatment. *Lancet* 1982; i: 1028–9.
14. Brahams, Diana. *Lancet* 1984; i: 1083–4.
15. Correspondence between Michael Baum and Carolyn Faulder.
16. Faulder, Carolyn. A conspiracy of silence. *Good Housekeeping*, February 1984.
17. Minutes of the Working Party on Breast Conservation, October 1984.
18. Faulder, Carolyn. *Whose body is it? The troubling issue of informed consent.* London: Virago, 1985.

CHAPTER THIRTY ONE. The Campaign Against Health Fraud, Part Three.

1. Mintz, Morton. *By prescription only*. Boston: Beacon Press, 1967.
2. Centre aims for breast cancer breakthrough. *Wellcome Journal*, December 1991.
    Wellcome Foundation supports "Breakthrough Breast Cancer" Initiative. News release, Wellcome Foundation Ltd, 1991.
3. National Perinatal Epidemiology Unit. Report 1989–90.
4. AMRC. Handbook 1990 - 91.
5   Personal communication with the author.
6. *University of Surrey Gazette*, 1985 - 90.
7. Cannon, Geoffrey. *The politics of food*. London: Century Hutchinson, 1987.
8. *NCHF Newsletter*. National Council Against Health Fraud Inc.
9. *CAHF Newsletter*, 1, 1989.
10. Ibid.
11. Baum, Michael. Why I will bust quacks. *Journal of Alternative and Complementary Medicine*, June 1989.
12. Ibid.
13. *CAHF Newsletter*, 2, 1989.
14. Wiltsher, Anne. Faith and doubt. *New Statesman and Society*, 7 July 1989.
15. Ibid.
16. Ibid.
17. Shepherd, Charles. Natural health pills can be lethal. *GP*, 18 January 1991.
18. Ibid.
19. Ibid.

20. Derek Jameson. BBC Radio 2, 7 January 1991.
21. Ibid., Professor John Garrow.
22. Ibid.
23. Vitamin supplements. Thames Action. ITV, 23 November 1990.
24. Ibid.
25. Ibid.
26 Ibid.
27. Ibid.
28. Ibid.
29. Prentice, Thomson. Cures for chronic fatigue disorders may be dangerous. *The Times*, 18 September 1990.
30. Ibid.
31. McKenna, Andrew. Food for thought: health food is more popular than ever - but 'natural' isn't always safe. *Bella*, 14 April 1990.
32. Ibid.
33. Ibid.
34. Ibid.
35. Ibid.
36. Ibid.

PART FIVE

CHAPTER THIRTY TWO. Wellcome, Part Four.

1. Kennedy, Ian. *The unmasking of medicine*. Sutton, Surrey: Paladin, 1983.
2. Barclays de Zoete Wedd. Research report: UK Health and Household. Wellcome, Retrovir, Current Assessment, 21st March 1990, by Jonathan de Pass, Steve M. Plag and John Falkenberg.
3. Ibid.
4. Ibid.
5. *Wellcome Journal*, November 1987.
6. Gupta, Susil. *Analysis*, November 1991.
7. *Wellcome Journal*, January 1991.
8. Stuart Marshall, interview with the author.
9. *Wellcome Journal*, April 1990.
10. Prabhudas, Yasmin and Stubbs, Lucy. *The AIDS funding manual: resourcing the HIV-AIDS voluntary sector in London 1991 - 1992*. London: Directory of Social Change, 1992.
11. *Wellcome Journal*, January 1991.
12. *AZT or Zidovudine*. Crewe, Cheshire: Wellcome Foundation Limited, September 1991.
13. *Wellcome Journal*, December 1991.
14. *THT Newsletter*, March 1993.

CHAPTER THIRTY THREE. Fighting the invisible agenda.

1. Dr Charles Farthing.
2. Adams, Jad. *AIDS: the HIV myth*. London: Macmillan, 1989.
3. AIDS myth and money. *New Scientist*, 29 April 1989.
4. Duncan Campbell speaking at the LSE, 13 April 1989.
5. Ibid.
6. Ibid.
7. Campbell, Duncan. Sharp practice. *New Statesman and Society*, 7 April 1989.
8. Duncan Campbell speaking at the LSE, 13 April 1989.
9. Ibid.
10 Ibid.
11. *Pink Paper*, 22 April 1989.
12. *Parliamentary Aids Digest*, Summer 1989.
13. Statement made by Jad Adams, 1992.
14. Campbell, Duncan. End of crisis comes into sight. *New Statesman and Society*, 1989.
15. Deer, Brian. Revealed: fatal flaws of drug that gave hope. *Sunday Times*, 16 April 1989.
16. Ibid.
17. Ibid.
18. Deer, Brian. Under pressure in an AIDS trial. *Sunday Times*, 30 April 1989.
19. Anonymous. Discord over plans to 'wreck' drug study. *New Statesman and Society*, 29 April 1989.
20. Ibid.
21. Campbell, Duncan. Positively Unhealthy. *New Statesman and Society*, 29 September 1989.
22. *Wellcome Trust Report*, 1989-1990.
23. Stuart Marshall, speaking at the OXAIDS Conference 1989.
24. The trials of AZT. *Positively Healthy News*, March 1989.
25. Dournon, E. et al. Effects of Zidovudine in 365 consecutive patients with AIDS or AIDS-related complex. *Lancet* 1988; ii: 1297.
26. Mir, N. and Costello, C. Zidovudine and bone cancer. *Lancet* 1988; ii: 1195–6.
27. Campbell, Duncan and Townson, Nigel. Positively Unhealthy: Duncan Campbell and Nigel Townson uncover an intense and damaging campaign against orthodox treatments for AIDS. *New Statesman and Society*, 29 September 1989.
28. Cass Mann, interview with the author.
29. *Pink Paper*, 7 October 1989.
30. Letter from David Pearson, dated 26 April 1989, to Ms C Rosson.
31. Ibid.
32. Ibid.

33. Ibid.
34. *New Statesman and Society*, 29 September 1989.
35. Witch hunt. *Pink Paper*, 16 September 1989.
36. Ibid.
37. *New Statesman and Society*, 29 September 1989.
38. Veterans' Administration Cooperative Study 298, February 1991.
39. Campbell, Duncan. The Mann affair. *Capital Gay*, 15 October 1989.
40. Confidential document to the Press Council: PART II, Complaint No. AA 17937/D800 - Positively Healthy against New Statesman and Society, undated but referring to Stuart Weir's correspondence of 28 August 1990.
41. Letter 'To Whom it May Concern' from solicitors Moss, Beachley and Mullem, 24 October 1990.
42. Cass Mann, interview with the author.
43. Alan Beck, interview with the author.
44. Minutes of early *Pink Paper* meetings, September to November 1987.
45. Witch hunt. *Pink Paper*, 16 September 1989.
46. Sick Statesman. Ibid., 7 October 1989.
47. Ibid.
48. Derek Jarman, quoted in the *Pink Paper*, 23 June 1989.
49. Unsigned lettter from the *New Statesman and Society* to Mr A. D. Linfoot, The Registrar, University of Kent at Canterbury, dated 1989 and headed 'Private and Confidential'.
50. Alan Beck, interview with the author.
51. ACT-UP London, letter sent to the *New Statesman and Society*, 21 May 1990.
52. Duncan Campbell's letter from *New Statesman and Society*, to ACT-UP, 25 May 1990.
53. Briscoe, Ivan. A professional outsider. *Cherwell*, 18 May 1990.
54. de Jongh, Nicholas. A darker shade of pink. *Guardian*, 11 June 1989.
55. Campbell, Duncan. Taking on the quacks. *New Statesman and Society*, 22 May 1992.

CHAPTER THIRTY FOUR. Trials of strength.

MEDITEL

1. Beveridge, W. I. B. *The art of scientific investigation*. London: Heinemann, 1950.
2. *New Scientist*, 13 July 1991.
3. AIDS: the unheard voices. Dispatches, Channel 4, November 1987.
4. The AIDS catch. Dispatches, Channel 4, 13 June 1990.

5. AIDS and Africa. Dispatches, Channel 4, 24 March 1993.
6. Complaint to the Broadcasting Complaints Commission from The Terrence Higgins Trust, Frontliners Ltd and Positively Women - Adjudication.
7. Complaint to the Broadcasting Complaints Commission from the Wellcome Foundation - Adjudication.

TRIALS BY PINCHING AND GAZZARD

8. Concar, David. Patients abandon AIDS drug after TV show. *New Scientist*, 13 July 1991.
9. Peters, Barry S. et al. Ineffectiveness of AL721 in HIV disease. (Letter). *Lancet* 1990; i: 545-6.
10. Nussbaum, Robert. *Good intentions: how big business, politics, and medicine are corrupting the fight against AIDS*. New York: Atlantic Monthly Press, 1990.

DR GREENSPAN

11. Kingston, Tim. The Brits aren't buying: selling Dr Roka's 'secret' herbal AIDS treatment. *San Francisco Bay Times*, 30 January 1992.
12. Ibid.

SHARP, SULTAN AND BARKER

13. Campbell, Duncan. Sharp practice. *New Statesman and Society*, 7 April 1989.
    Duncan Campbell. Watchdog, BBC 1, 3 April 1989.
14. *New Statesman and Society*, 7 April 1989.
15. Rosenberg, Steven A. et al. Observations on the systemic administration of autologous lymphokine-activated killer cells and recombinant interleukin-2 to patients with metastatic cancer. *N Engl J Med* 1985; 313: 1485-92.
    See also: Rosenberg, Steven A. et al. A progress report on the treatment of 157 patients with advanced cancer using lymphokine-activated killer cells and interleukin-2 or high dose interleukin-2 alone. *N Engl J Med* 1987; 316: 889-97.
16. Sultan, A.J.A. et al. Immunotherapy in rheumatoid arthritis by T-suppressor lymphocytes: experimental model *in vitro*. *Clin Rheum* 1986; 5: 450-8.
17. Jabar Sultan, interview with the author.
18. Davis, Kathleen C. et. al. Lymphocyte transfusion in case of Acquired Immunodeficiency Syndrome. *Lancet* 1983; i: 599–600.
19. Campbell, Duncan. Sharp practice. *New Statesman and Society*, 7 April 1989.
20. Ibid.
21. Sultan, A.J.A. 4th International Conference on Immunopharmacology, Osaka, May 1989. *Int J Immunopharm* 10 (Suppl 1), 1988.

22. Carpenter, Rosemary. Doctors new hope on AIDS. *Daily Express*, 14 December 1987. See also: Carpenter, Rosemary. Year of hope for AIDS sufferers. *Daily Express*, 14 January 1988.
23. *BMJ* 1989; 298: 1519-20.
24. Affidavit dated 24 August 1989, made out for the purposes of evidence at the GMC hearing of Dr James Sharp.
25. Jabar Sultan, interview with the author.
26. Campbell, Duncan. Sharp practice. *New Statesman and Society*, 7 April 1989.
27. Campbell, Duncan. *Capital Gay*, 7 April 1989.
28. Philip Barker, interview with the author.
29. Campbell, Duncan. *Capital Gay*, 7 April 1989.
30. Dr Pinching's affidavit to the General Medical Council.
31. Transcript of Campbell's secret tape recording.
32. Ibid.
33. Hospital for Sick Children, Great Ormond Street. Annual Report, 1992.
    Royal College of Physicians. *Allergy: conventional and alternative concepts.* 1992.

DR LESLIE DAVIS AND DR ROGER CHALMERS

34. Dr Roger Chalmers. Points regarding the letter from the GMC 19th December 1990 [ADH/TM/PDI/9741].
35. Leslie Davis, interview with the author.
36. Dr Roger Chalmers. Points regarding the letter from the GMC 19th December 1990. [ADH/TM/PDI/9741].
37. Campbell, Duncan. Heaven on earth. *New Statesman and Society*, 28 September 1990.
38. Leslie Davis, interview with the author.
39. Ibid.
40. Ibid.
41. Ibid.
42. Bolle, Dietmar. *Body Positive Newsletter*, 10 January 1989. Published by Body Positive, PO Box 493, London W14 OTF.
43. Harley, Gill. Aids victims recover the strength to fight through meditation. *Sunday Times*, 26 March 1989.
44. Campbell, Duncan. *Independent on Sunday*, 19 August 1990.
45. Campbell, Duncan. Heaven on earth. *New Statesman and Society*, 28 September 1990.
46. Leslie Davis, interview with the author.
47. Dr Pinching's affidavit to the GMC in the case of Davis and Chalmers.
48. Harley, op. cit.
49. Transcript of the GMC hearing in the case of Davis and Chalmers.

50. Ibid.
51. Ibid.
52. Ibid.
53. Letter from Dr Pinching to Dr Davis, read into transcript of the GMC hearing.
54. Leslie Davis, interview with the author.
55. From the transcript of the hearing.
56. Ibid.
57. Doctors 'peddled treatment for AIDS'. *The Times*, 16 July 1991. AIDS doctors accused of misconduct. *Daily Telegraph*, 16 July 1991 'Maharishi treatment' AIDS claim disputed. *Independent*, 17 July 1991.
58. CBS Radio transcript, 17 May 1992.
59. Kahn, Ric. Exploiting people with AIDS. *San Francisco Bay Guardian*, 18 December 1991.
60. Sinister forces behind that Maharishi manifesto. *Evening Standard*, 27 March 1992.

DELATTE, GOODMAN AND BRYANT

61. Goodman, Sandra. *Germanium: the health and life enhancer*. Wellingborough: Thorsons, 1988.
62. Campbell, Duncan. Let them eat shit. *New Statesman and Society*, 16 June 1989.
Campbell, Duncan. Pretty poison. *New Statesman and Society*, 8 September 1989.
63. Goodman, Sandra, op. cit.
64. Bryant, Monica. A shift to probiotics. Journal of Alternative and Complementary Medicine, February 1986.
65. Goodman, Sandra. op. cit.
66. Letter from Dr Anthony Pinching, Department of Immunology, St Mary's Hospital, to Sandra Goodman, dated 23 April 1987.
67. Research Proposal: Investigation of Germanium's potential anti-HIV properties, Research Department, Bastyr College, Seattle. Laboratory research to be conducted at the Linus Pauling Institute of Science and Medicine. 1989.
68. Goodman, Sandra. Therapeutic effects of organic germanium. *Medical Hypotheses* 1988; 26: 207-15.
69. Sandra Goodman PhD. 'Application Form for Research and Project Grants'. 1988.
70. Coulter, Harris L. *Aids and syphilis: the hidden link*. Provo, Ut: North American Books, 1988.
Martin, Simon. Review of *Aids and syphilis. Journal of Alternative and Complementary Medicine*, February 1988.
Chaitow, Leon. Is Aids a form of syphilis? Ibid.
The confusing case of African AIDS. *New Scientist*, 18 February

1988.

Levy, E.M., Beldekas, J.C., Black, P.H. & Kushi, L.H. Patients with Kaposi's sarcoma who opt for alternative therapy. Manuscript, 1987. And, Patients with Kaposi's sarcoma who opt for no treatment. *Lancet* 1985; ii: 223.

Badgley, L.E. *Healing AIDS naturally.* Foster City, Calif: Human Energy Press, 1986.

Walker, C.M., Moody, D.J., Stites, D.P. and Levy, J.A. CD8 lymphocytes can control HIV infection *in vitro* by suppressing virus replication. *Science* 1986; 234: 1563-6.

Myss, C. Experience in counselling AIDS victims. Ibid.

71. Letter from Yves Delatte to Dr G. Connolly at the Kobler Centre, St Stephen's Hospital, dated 14 February 1989.

72. Ibid.

73. Harakeh, Steve. Jariwalla, Raxit J. and Pauling, Linus. Suppression of human immunodeficiency virus replication by ascorbate in chronically and acutely infected cells. *Proc Natl Acad Sc* 1990; 87: 7245-9.

74. Campbell, Duncan. Let them eat shit. *New Statesman and Society*, 16 June 1989.

75. Douglas, Mary. *Purity and danger: an analysis of concepts of pollution and taboo.* London: Routledge, 1966.

76. Ibid.

77. Campbell, Duncan. Let them eat shit, *New Statesman and Society*, 16 June 1989.

78. Ibid.

79. Ibid.

80. Ibid.

81. 'Miracle' AIDS cure probed. *Brighton and Hove Leader*, 15 June 1989.

82. Campbell, Duncan. Pretty poison. *New Statesman and Society*, 8 September 1989.

83. Ibid.

84. Ibid.

85. Letter from Dr Kaoru Onoyama, Assistant Professor, 2nd Department of Internal Medicine, Kyushu University, to Sandra Goodman, 24 November 1989.

86. Goodman, Sandra. *Vitamin C: the master nutrient.* New Haven, Conn: Keats, 1991.

ELIZABETH MARSH

87. Elizabeth Marsh, interview with the author.

88. Culbert, Michael L. *AIDS: hope, hoax and hoopla.* Chula Vista, Calif: Bradford Foundation, 1989.

89. Elizabeth Marsh, interview with the author.

90. *Daily Mail*, 12 May 1990.
91. Ibid.
92. *Daily Mirror*, 12 May 1990.
93. *Daily Mail*, 12 May 1990.
94. *Daily Mirror*, 12 May 1990.
95. See: Report of the Government of British Columbia, Canada, 1945/1946, on the treatment of dairy cows with Koch remedy, a study conducted between November 1944 and September 1945.
96. See: Congressional Record, 7 June 1948.
97. Koch, William Frederick. *The survival factor in neo-plastic and viral diseases*. Detroit, Mi: published by the author, 1961.
98. Sky Television, 11 June 1991.
99. AIDS wonder cure is just a 20p laxative. *Sunday Mirror*, 21 April 1991.
100. Toxic 'Aids Cure' drug used on volunteers. *Independent on Sunday*, 21 April 1991.
101. Ibid.

CHAPTER THIRTY FIVE. The Assault on the Breakspear.

1. Anon.
2. Blackman, Oonagh. Breaking out in a rash of big bills. *Sunday Express*, 28 January 1990.
3. Ibid.
4. Ibid.
5. Ibid.
6. Review of 1990 Conference of the British Society for Allergy and Environmental Medicine, cited in a letter from Dr Bailey to Dr Monro, 7 August 1990.
7. Ibid.
8. Jewett Don L., Fein, George, and Greenberg, Martin H. A double-blind study of symptom provocation to determine food sensitivity. *N Engl J Med* 1990; 323: 429-33.
9. Ferguson, Anne. Food sensitivity or self-deception? (Editorial). *N Engl J Med* 1990; 323: 476-8.
10. Richards, Evelleen. *Vitamin C and cancer: medicine or politics?* London: Macmillan Professional and Academic, 1991.
11. Pearson, D.J., Rix, K.J.B. and Bentley, S.J. Food allergy: how much in the mind? A clinical and psychiatric study of suspected food hypersensitivity. *Lancet* 1983; i: 1259-61.
12. Royal College of Physicians. *Food intolerance and food aversion*. 1984.
13. Cannon, Geoffrey. *The politics of food*. London: Century Hutchinson, 1987.
14. The Allergy Business. World in Action, Granada Television, 15 October 1990.
15. Minutes of the Annual General Meeting of HealthWatch 1991.

16. Enfys Chapman, the co-ordinator of Pesticide Exposure Group of Sufferers (PEGS), conversation with Graham Thompson, a reporter then working for the Cook Report.
17. From the transcript of the complete recorded interview obtained from Granada by Maureen Rudd after 'The Allergy Business' had been screened.
18. Ibid.
19. Ibid.
20. Ibid.
21. Ibid.
22. Ibid.
23. Ibid.
24. Ibid.
25. Letter from Frederica Colfox suggesting that allergy sufferers might take their own lives.
26. Sheila Rossall Fund leaflet.
27. *Observer*, 14 October 1990.
28. *Sunday Mirror*, 14 October 1990.
29. Ibid.
30. *News of the World*, 14 October 1990.
31. Private Allergy Clinic may face treatment inquiry. *Sunday Telegraph*, 14 October 1990.
32. Is there an alternative? *Daily Mirror*, 21 November 1990.
33. Mum defends tot's specialist. (Basildon) *Evening Echo*, 31 October 1990.
34. LWT News, 10 November 1990.
35. *Daily Mirror*, 21 November 1990.
36. Ibid.
37. Ibid.
38 Ibid.
39. *Evening Echo*, 31 October 1990.
40. Ibid.
41. Ibid.

DR DAVID FREED

43. Letter from Dr David Freed to general practitioner. October 1990.
44. David Freed, interview with the author.

DR KEITH MUMBY

45. Keith Mumby - Urgent and Confidential: a communication from Dr Keith Mumby to supporters.
46. *Scotland on Sunday*, 9 December 1990.

LORRAINE TAYLOR

47. Transcript of Dr Pearson's evidence.

CHAPTER THIRTY SIX. Mugging the cancer patients.

1. Anon.
2. Penny Brohn, interview with the author.
3. Ibid.
4. Brohn, Penny. *Gentle giants*. London: Century, 1987.
   Brohn, Penny. *The Bristol Programme*. London: Century, 1987.
5. Penny Brohn, interview with the author.
6. Chilvers, Clair et al. Survival of patients with breast cancer attending Bristol Cancer Help Centre. *Lancet* 1990; ii: 606-10.
7. Ibid.
8. Ibid.
9. Ibid.
10. Janice Wilkins, Public Relations Department, Imperial Cancer Research Fund, 4 September 1990.
11. Letter sent by Janice Wilkins to Bristol Cancer Help Centre, 29 August 1990.
12. Ibid. Note attached.
13. Public Eye debate: The cancer question. BBC 2, 13 September 1990.
    Public Eye debate: The cancer question. BBC 2, 14 September 1990.
14. *Daily Express*, 5 September 1990.
15. *Daily Telegraph*, 6 September 1990.
16. *Guardian*, 6 September 1990.
17. *Daily Telegraph*, 6 September 1990.
18. *Today*, 6 September 1990.
19. *Sun*, 6 September 1990.
20. Ibid.
21. *Independent*, 6 September 1990.
22. *Independent on Sunday*, 9 September 1990.
23. Kenny, Mary. *Sunday Telegraph*, 9 September 1990.
24. Le Fanu, James. Nature's way to bad medicine. *The Times*, 7 September 1990.
25. *Observer*, 9 September 1990.
26. *GP*, 14 September 1990. (Leading article).
27. Tobias, J. Surely a natural cancer remedy can't be dangerous - can it? *BMJ* 1990; 301: 613.
28. Richards, Tessa. Death from complementary medicine. *BMJ* 1990; 301: 510-1.
29. *Guardian*, 15 September 1990.
30. *Guardian*, 6 September 1990.

31. Booker, Christopher. *Sunday Telegraph*, 16 September 1990.
32. Statement sent by Karol Sikora to the Bristol Cancer Help Centre.
33. Sheard, T.A.B. Letter. *Lancet*, 15 September 1990.
34. Spiegel, David et al. Effect of psychosocial treatment on survival of patients with metastatic breast cancer. *Lancet* 1989; ii: 888–91.
35. *Today*, 18 September 1990.
36. *Daily Telegraph*, 18 September 1990.
37. Monro, Jean and Payne, Mark. *Lancet* 1990; ii: 743-4.
38. Ibid.
39. Ibid.
40. Letter from Margaret Stacy and 54 other signatories, Department of Sociology at University of Warwick. *Independent*, 21 September 1990.
41. *Hospital Doctor*, 13 September 1990 (Editorial).
42. Hodgkinson, Neville. The case for a gentle strategy. *Sunday Express*, 11 November 1990.
43. Flatt, Malcolm. *Sunday Times*, 16 September 1990.
44. Hayes, Anita. *Independent on Sunday*, 16 September 1990.
45. Thomson, Rosy. *The Times*, 15 September 1990.
46. Harris, Vicki. *Evening Standard*, 10 September 1990.
47. Baldwin, Debrah. *West Sussex County Times*, 5 October 1990.
48. Goodare, Heather. *Hospital Doctor*, 25 October 1990. (Letter, sent originally to *Lancet*)
49. Hunt, Liz. *Independent*, 9 November 1990.
50. New row over alternative cancer cure. *Evening Standard*, 6 November 1990.
51. Cancer study 'gave false impression'. *Evening Standard*, 8 November 1990.
52. *Independent on Sunday*, 11 November 1990.
53. Letter from Chilvers, Clair et al. *Lancet* 1990; ii: 1187-8.
54. Letter from Bodmer, Sir Walter. *Lancet* 1990; ii: 1188.
55. Doctors' attack on holistic cure is toned down. *Daily Telegraph*, 9 November 1990.
56. *Today*, 9 November 1990.
57. McElwain, Timothy, quoted in *Guardian*, 9 November 1990.
58. Correspondence between Dr Lesley Fallowfield and the Bristol Cancer Help Centre, 17 September 1990.
59. Correspondence between Baum and BCHC, November 1990.
60. Correspondence between Vincent Marks and Penny Brohn, 8 October 1990.
61. McAfee, Annalena. *Evening Standard*, 14 January 1991.
62. Ibid.
63. Campbell, Duncan and Holmes, Alex. Cancer Centre linked to vitamin row firm. *Independent on Sunday*, 5 May 1991.

64. Ibid.
65. Ibid.

CHAPTER THIRTY SEVEN. Attacking healthy nutrition.

1. Horkheimer, Max. *Dawn and decline: notes 1926–31 and 1950–69*. New York: Seabury Press, 1978.
2. AIDS can be cured. *Journal of Optimum Nutrition*, Spring 1989.
3. Ibid. Summer 1989.
4. Robert Woodward in an interview with the author.
5. Benton, David and Roberts, Gwilym. Effect of vitamin and mineral supplementation on intelligence of a sample of schoolchildren. *Lancet* 1988; i: 140-3.
6. Richmond, Caroline. Reactions: Vitamins for thought. *Observer*, 20 March 1988.
7. Campbell, Duncan. The rise of the New Age pill pushers. *Sunday Correspondent*, 3 December 1989.
8. Ibid.
9. Ibid.
10. Ibid.
11. Ibid.
12. Ibid.
13. *Health Standard*, Winter 1990.
14. Ibid.
15. Ibid.
16. Ibid.
17. Robert Woodward, interview with the author.
18. Transcript of the Food and Drink Programme. BBC 2, 30 October 1990.
19. Stephen Davies, interview with the author.
20. Transcript of the Food and Drink Programme. BBC 2, 30 October 1990.
21. Ibid.
22. Wilson, A.N. *Sunday Telegraph*, 20 January 1991.
23. Transcript of tape recording of the launch of the Campaign for Health Through Food.
24. Ibid.
25. Belinda Barnes, interview with the author.
26. The Broadcasting Complaints Commission adjudication on the complaint from Foresight, September 1991.

CHAPTER THIRTY EIGHT. Conclusions.

1. Lauritsen, John. *The AIDS Wars*. New York: Asklepios, 1993.

Bibliography

Part One

Anderson, Jack. Yes, psychic warfare is part of the game. *Washington Post*, 5 February 1981.

Arnove, Robert F. *Philanthropy and cultural imperialism*. Pelican, 1979.

Bellant, Russ. *The Coors connection: how Coors family philanthropy undermines democratic pluralism*. South End Press, 1991.

Berliner, Howard S. The holistic alternative to scientific medicine: history and analysis. *International Journal of Health Services*, 10(2), 1980.

Berliner, Howard S. & Salmon, J.Warren. The holistic health movement and scientific medicine: the naked and the dead. *Socialist Review*, 43, pp 31-32, 1979.

Berliner, Howard S. Scientific medicine since Flexner. In Salmon, J. Warren (ed). *Alternative medicines: popular and policy perspectives*. Tavistock, 1985.

Berliner, Howard S. *Philanthropic foundations and scientific medicine*. Unpublished doctoral thesis, Baltimore: Johns Hopkins University, 1977.

Bloyd-Peshkin, Sharon. The health-fraud cops: are the quack busters consumer advocates or medical McCarthyites? *Vegetarian Times*, August 1991.

Brown, E. Richard. He who pays the piper: foundations, the medical profession and medical education. In Leverby, R. & Rosner, D. (eds.) *Health in America: essays in social history*. Temple University Press, 1979.

Collier, Peter & Horowitz, David. *The Rockefellers: an American dynasty*. Simon & Schuster, 1976.

Coulter, Harris L. Homoeopathy. In Salmon, J. Warren (ed). *Alternative medicines: popular and policy perspectives*. Tavistock, 1985.

Dalrymple, James. Geller's legal battle of wills. *Sunday Times*, 20 October 1991.

Dickson, David. *The new politics of science*. University of Chicago Press, 1984.

Doyle, R.P. *The medical wars*. William Morrow, 1983.

Fishbein, Morris. *Fads and quackery in healing: an analysis of the healing cults, with essays on various other peculiar notions in the health field*. New York: Blue Ribbon Books, 1932.

Fishbein, Morris. *The medical follies: an analysis of the foibles of some leading cults, including osteopathy, homoeopathy, chiropractic*. New York: Boni and Liveright, 1925.

Fisher, Donald. American philanthropy and the social sciences in Great Britain 1919-1939: the reproduction of a conservative ideology. *Sociological Review*, 28(2), 1980.

Fried, J. *Vitamin politics*. Prometheus Books, Buffalo, New York, 1984.

Gardner, Martin. *Order and surprise*. Oxford University Press, 1984.

Geller, Uri & Playfair, Guy Lyon. *The Geller effect*. Jonathan Cape, 1986.

Harnik, Peter. What, me worry? Defending corporate 'progress' is Elizabeth Whelan's most important product. *Nutrition Action*, February 1982.

Harrington, Michael. Raiders of the New Age. *Sunday Telegraph*, 16 June1991.

The John D. and Catherine T. MacArthur Foundation. *Programme and Policies*. Chicago, Ill.: The Foundation, 1989.

Johnson, Loch K. *America's secret power: the CIA in a democratic society*. Oxford University Press, 1989.

Joint Hearing before the Select Committee on Intelligence and the Subcommittee on Health and Scientific Research of the Committee on Human Resources, United States Senate. *Project MUKLTRA, the CIA's program of research in behavior modification*. US Government Printing Office, Washington, 1977.

Kevles, Daniel J. *The physicists: the history of a scientific community in modern America*. Vintage Books, 1979.

Kuhn, T.S. *The structure of scientific revolutions*. University of Chicago Press, 1962.

Lee Caplan, Ronald. Chiropractic. In Salmon, J.Warren (ed). *Alternative medicines: popular and policy perspectives*. Tavistock, 1985.

Lithgow, Tony. Jailed for trying to heal. *Journal of Alternative and Complementary Medicine*, December 1988.

Lithgow, Tony. The patients revolt. *Journal of Alternative and Complementary Medicine*, March1989.

Lithgow, Tony. Exposed: the twenty-five year conspiracy. *Journal of Alternative and Complementary Medicine*, January 1989.

McRae, Ronald M. *Mind wars: the true story of Government research into the military potential of psychic weapons*. St. Martins Press, 1984.

Nelson, William R. (ed). *The politics of science*. Oxford University Press, 1968.

Quigley, Carroll. *Tragedy and hope: a history of the world in our time*. Macmillan, 1966.

Rawlins, Dennis. Remus Extremus. *Skeptical Inquirer*, Winter 1981-1982.

Rothmyer, Karen. Citizen Scaife. In *Raising hell: how the Center for Investigative Reporting gets the story*. Addison-Wesley, 1983.

Schlesinger, Arthur M. Jr. *The age of Roosevelt: the coming of the New Deal*. Vol. II. Heinemann, 1957.

The Sunday Times Insight Team. *Suffer the children: the story of thalidomide*. André Deutsch, 1979.

Walters, Robert S. & Blake, David H. *The politics of global economic relations*. Prentice Hall, 1992.

Whitaker, Ben. *The foundations: an anatomy of philanthropy and society*. Eyre Methuen, 1974.

Part Two

American Cancer Society. *Unproven methods of cancer management*. The Society, 1976.

Ashford, Nicholas & Miller, Claudia. *Chemical exposures: low levels and high stakes*. Van Nostrand Reinhold, 1991.

Bartle, Hazel. Quiet sufferers of the silent spring. *New Scientist*, 18 May 1991.

Bartlett, Gerald. Allergy girl dies after eating nuts. *Daily Telegraph*, 4 February 1992.

Bircher, Ruth Kunz. *The Bircher-Benner health guide*. Unwin Paperbacks, 1983.

Bishop, Beate. *A time to heal: triumph over cancer, the therapy of the future*. Severn House, 1985.

Bland, Jeffrey. *Your health under siege*. Stephen Greene Press, 1981.

Boly, W. Cancer Inc. *Hippocrates Magazine*, January/February 1989.

Braverman, Eric R. & Pfeiffer, Carl. *The healing nutrients within*. Keats, 1987.

Brostoff, Jonathan & Gamlin, Linda. *The complete guide to food allergy and intolerance*. Bloomsbury Publishing, 1989.

Brown, Phylidda. Monkey tests force rethink on AIDS vaccine. *New Scientist*, 21 September 1991.

Buist, Robert. *Food intolerance: what it is and how to cope with it*. Harper & Row, 1984.

Capra, F. *The turning point: science, society and the rising culture*. Bantam Books, 1982.

Carr, Simon. Doctors, the enemies of hope. *Independent*, 18 March 1992.

Chamberlain, Geoffrey. *The safety of the unborn child*. Penguin, 1969.

Cheraskin, E., Ringsdorf, W.M. & Sisley, E.L. *The vitamin C connection*. Harper & Row, 1983.

Chowka, P.B. The cancer charity ripoff. *East-West Journal*, 23(9), July 1978.

Cook, Judith & Kaufman, Chris. *Portrait of a poison: the 2,4,5-T story*. Pluto Press, 1982.

Cunningham, Alastair J. *Understanding immunology*. Academic Press, 1978.

Davis, Adelle. *Let's get well*. Allen &Unwin, 1979.

Deadly dip. *Chemistry and Industry*, 1 October 1990.

De Vries, Jan. *Viruses, allergies and the immune system*. Mainstream Publishing, 1988.

Duesberg, Peter. AIDS: non-infectious deficiences acquired by drug consumption and other risk factors. *Research in Immunology*, 1990.

Duesberg, Peter & Schwartz, Jody. Latent viruses and mutated oncogenes: no evidence for pathogenicity. *Progress in Nucleic Acid Research and Molecular Biology*, 43, 1992.

Eisenberg, Arlene, Murkoff, Heidi & Hathaway, Sondee. *What to eat when you're expecting*. Thorsons, 1989.

Epstein, Samuel S. *The politics of cancer*. Anchor Press, 1979.

Epstein, Samuel S. Profiting from cancer: vested interests and the cancer epidemic. *Ecologist*, 22(5), September-October 1992.

Epstein, Samuel S. *Testimony on Agent Orange and H.R.6377 before the House Subcommittee on Medical Facilities and Benefits of the Committee on Veterans' Affairs*. July 1980.

Feingold, B.F. *Why your child is hyperactive*. Random House, 1974.

Fotherby, Linda. *2,4,5-T and 2,4-D: the case against phenoxy herbicides*. Friends of the Earth, 1980.

Freed, David. The provocation-neutralization technique. In Dobbing, John (ed). *Food intolerance*. Baillière Tindall, 1987.

Gerson, Max. *A cancer therapy*. Dura Books, 1958.

Graham, Frank. *Since the silent spring*. Hamish Hamilton, 1970.

Greden, J.F. Coffee, tea and you. *Science*, January 1979.

Greer, Rita. *The right way to cook*. Dent, 1985.

Greer, Rita & Woodward, Robert. *The good nutrients guide: a practical handbook on vitamins and other health food supplements*. Dent, 1985.

Grmek, Mirko D. *History of AIDS: emergence and origin of a modern pandemic*. Princeton University Press.

Hadji, L., Arnoux, B. & Benveniste, J. Effect of dilute histamine on coronary flow of guinea-pig isolated heart. Inhibition by a magnetic field. INSERM, U200, 1991.

Hanssen, Maurice. *E for additives: supermarket shopping guide*. Thorsons, 1986.

Haught, S.J. *Cancer: think curable! The Gerson therapy*. The Gerson Institute, 1983.

Hay, A. *The chemical scythe: lessons of 2,4,5-T and dioxin*. Plenum.

Henshaw, David. Body or soul. *Listener*, 13 September 1990.

Hills, Hilda Cherry. *Good food, gluten free*. Roberts Publications, 1976.

Ho, David D. et al. Quantitation of human immunodeficiency virus type 1 in the blood of infected persons. *New England Journal of Medicine*, 14 December 1989.

Hodgkinson, Neville. When humility is healthy. *Sunday Times*, 14 April 1989.

Hughes, R. & Brewin, R. *The tranquilizing of America*. Harcourt Brace Jovanovich, 1979.

Hunt, Jeremy. 2,500 producers suffer OP dip side-effects. *Farmers' Weekly*, 14 December 1990.

In the beginning: was there a link between polio vaccines and HIV? *Economist*, 14 March 1992.

Iver, David F. & Anderson, Kenneth A. *Industrial medicine*. Chapman Hall, 1986.

Jungk, Robert. *The new tyranny: how nuclear power enslaves us*. Warner, 1979.

Kamen, Betty & Kamen, Si. *Total nutrition during pregnancy*. Appleton-Century-Crofts, 1981.

Kaufman, Chris. *Not one minute longer! The 2,4,5-T dossier*. (National Union of Agricultural and Allied Workers submission to the Minister of Agriculture.) NUAAW, Headland House, 308 Gray's Inn Road, London WC1, March 1980.

Kent, Ann. Suffer in the city. *The Times*, 26 June 1992.

Kollerstrom, Nick. *Lead on the brain: a plain guide to Britain's number one pollutant*. Wildwood House, 1982.

L'affaire de la "mémoire de l'eau". *Le Monde*, 1 March 1991.

Lawrence, Felicity (ed). *Additives: your complete survival guide*. Century, 1986.

Lederer, Robert S. Origin and spread of AIDS: is the West responsible? *Covert Action*, 28, Summer 1987.

Lehrman, Nathaniel S. Is AIDS non-infectious? - the possibility and its C.B.W. implications. *Covert Action*, 28, Summer 1987.

Lewith, George, Kenyon, Julian & Dowson, David. *Allergy and intolerance: a complete guide to environmental medicine*. Green Print, 1992.

The London Food Commission. *Food adulteration and how to beat it*. Unwin, 1988.

Lucas, Jack. *Our polluted food: a survey of the risks*. Charles Knight, 1975.

Lynes, Barry & Crane, John. *The cancer cure that worked! Fifty years of suppression*. Marcus Books, 1987.

Lynn, Richard. The role of nutrition in secular increases in intelligence. *Person. Individ. Diff.*, 11(3), 1990.

McCarrison, Robert. *Nutrition and health*. The McCarrison Society, 1982.

McCarrison, Robert. *Studies in deficiency disease*. Oxford Medical Publications, 1921.

Mackarness, Richard. *Chemical victims*. Pan, 1980.

Mackarness, Richard. *Not all in the mind*. Pan, 1981.

Maddox, John. Rage and confusion hide role of HIV. *Nature*, 357, 21 May 1992.

Mansfield, Peter & Monro, Jean. *Chemical children: how to protect your family from harmful pollutants*. Century, 1987.

Melville, Arabella & Johnson, Colin. *Immunity plus: how to be healthy in an age of new infections*. Penguin, 1988.

Mills, Roger. A gentle way with cancer? Cancer: a cautious approach to 'holistic' treatment. *Listener*, 14 April 1983.

Millstone, Erik. *Food additives: taking the lid off what we really eat*. Penguin, 1986.

Pauling, Linus. *Vitamin C, the common cold and the flu*. Berkeley, 1981.

Pevera, Judith. Crippled by tending his flock. *Independent*, 30 June 1992.

Pfeiffer, Carl C. *Zinc and other micronutrients*. Keats, 1978.

Positively Healthy News, Issues 1 to 5, January - September 1989.

Price, Weston A. *Nutrition and physical degeneration*. Price-Pottinger Nutrition Foundation, 1945.

Purdey, Mark. Mad cows and warble flies: a link between BSE and organophosphates? *Ecologist*, 22(2), March-April 1992.

Quillin, Patrick. *Healing nutrients: a guide to using everyday food to prevent disease and promote wellbeing.* Penguin, 1989.

Randolph, Theron G. & Moss, Ralph W. *An alternative approach to allergies: the new field of clinical ecology unravels the environmental causes of mental and physical ills.* Harper & Row, 1990.

Rapp, Doris J. *Allergies and the hyperactive child.* Simon & Schuster, 1979.

Rapp, Doris J. *Allergies and your family.* Sterling, 1980.

Rapp, Doris J. *Is this your child? Discovering and treating unrecognised allergies.* William Morrow, 1991.

Rea, William J. *Chemical sensitivity.* Volume 1. Lewis Publishers, Boca Raton, USA, 1992.

Rickard, Bob. Science friction. *Fortean Times*, 52, Summer 1989.

Schauss, Alexander. *Diet, crime and delinquency.* Parker House, 1981.

Schroeder, H.A. *The poisons around us.* Indiana University Press, 1970.

Simonton, O. Carl et al. *Getting well again.* Torcher, Los Angeles, 1978.

Simonton, O. Carl & Simonton, Stephanie. Belief systems and management of the emotional aspects of malignancy. *Journal of Transpersonal Psychology*, 7, 1975.

Strange bedfellows sing together. *Chemistry and Industry*, 21 August 1989.

Turner, James S. *The chemical feast: the Ralph Nader Study Group report on food protection and the Food and Drug Administration.* New York, 1970.

Verrett, Jacqueline & Carper, Jean. *Eating may be hazardous to your health.* Simon & Schuster, 1974.

Walker, Caroline & Cannon, Geoffrey. *The food scandal.* Century, 1985.

Watterson, Andrew. *Pesticide users' health and safety handbook.* Aldershot: Gower, 1988.

Williams, Roger J. *Nutrition against disease: environmental prevention.* Pitman Publishing, New York, 1971.

Wilson, Des. *The lead scandal: the fight to save children from damage by lead in petrol.* Heinemann, 1983.

Woodward, Robert. *A practical guide to some nutritional and alternative approaches.* Roberts Publications, 1988.

Wynn, M. & Wynn, A. *The prevention of handicap of perinatal origin.* Foundation for Education and Research in Child Bearing, 1976.

Zamm, A.V. & Gannon, R. *Why your house may endanger your health.* Simon & Schuster, 1980.

Part Three

Bender, Arnold E. Dietary supplements. *BNF Nutritional Bulletin*, May 1988.

British Nutrition Foundation. *Annual Reports* 1985-90.

Clark, C.M. & Mackintosh, J.M. *The School* [of Tropical Medicine] *and the site: an historical memoir to celebrate the 25th anniversary of the School.* H.K. Lewis, 1954.

Cookson, Clive. Wellcome to Robb's school of business. *Financial Times,* 3 May 1991.

Fisher, Donald. The Rockefeller Foundation and the development of scientific medicine in Great Britain. *Minerva,* 16, 1978.

Frieden, Jeff. The Trilateral Commission: economics and politics in the 1970s. *Monthly Review,* 29(7), December 1977.

Greene, Mary. How Nike got a run for no money at the Science Museum: does commerce taint academic integrity? *Independent,* 7 May 1991.

Hale, N. & North, J. *The world of UCL 1928-1990.* UCL, 1991.

Jackson, Tony. Discarding an image of other-worldliness: the Wellcome Foundation. *Financial Times,* 19 July 1985.

Jones, Thomas. *A diary with letters 1931-1950.* Oxford University Press, London, 1954.

Jones, Thomas. *Whitehall diary.* Vol. II. 1926-1930. Keith Middlemas (ed). Oxford University Press, 1954.

London School of Hygiene and Tropical Medicine. *Annual Reports 1985-1990.*

Manson-Bahr, Patrick. *History of the School of Tropical Medicine in London.* H.K. Lewis, 1956.

Middlemass, Keith. Lord Franks. Obituary. *Independent,* 17 October 1992.

Richmond, Caroline. Chronic fatigue syndrome. *Scientific and Public Affairs,* 5(3), 1990.

Ross, Nick. What hope is there for a nation of innumerates? *Daily Telegraph,* 12 April 1993; also *Scientific and Public Affairs,* Spring Issue, 1993.

Science groups aid threatened. *Daily Telegraph,* 27 February 1992.

University College, London. *Annual Reports, 1985-1990.*

Vincent, Lindsay. Wellcome's Guardian: Sir Roger Gibbs. *Observer,* 8 March 1992.

Walters, Robert S. & Blake, David H. *The politics of global economic relations.* Prentice Hall, 1992.

Part Four

Abrahams, Paul. A marketing prescription for Wellcome. *Financial Times,* 1 June 1992.

Adams, Stanley. *Roche versus Adams.* Jonathan Cape, 1984.

Braithwaite, John. *Corporate crime in the pharmaceutical industry.* Routledge & Kegan Paul, 1984.

Brown, Phylidda. A Wellcome injection of cash. *New Scientist,* 1 August 1992.

Burnell, Liza. *The role of science and economics in producing therapies for AIDS: with specific reference to the development of AZT.* Unpublished BSc thesis, University of Manchester, 1989.

Chetley, A. *A healthy business.* Zed Press, 1990.

Clayton, Paul. Kill or cure: how medicine exploits human drug tests. *Evening Standard Magazine,* January 1992.

Coleman, Vernon. *The medicine men.* Temple Smith, 1975.

Coleman, Vernon. *The health scandal: your health in crisis.* Sidgwick & Jackson, 1988.

Coleman, Vernon. Paper doctors: a critical assessment of medical research. Temple Smith, 1977.

Collier, Joe. *The health conspiracy: how doctors, the drug industry and government undermine our health.* Century Hutchinson, 1989.

Cooper, M.H. *Prices and profits in the pharmaceutical industry.* Pergamon Press, 1966.

Deitch, R. Dr. Griffin's departure from the department. *Lancet,* 21 July 1984.

Doyal, Lesley. *The political economy of health.* Pluto, 1983.

Dyer, Clare. Wellcome sues New Statesman and Society. *British Medical Journal,* 26 November 1988.

Erlichman, James. Coma goes against the grain. *Guardian,* 20 July 1991.

Erlichman, James. Food watchdog denies conflict of interest. *Guardian,* 20 July 1987.

Erlichman, James. HIV test kits banned over despair fears. *Guardian,* 25 March 1992.

Farber, Celia. Fatal distraction. *Spin,* June 1992.

Farber, Celia. Sins of omission: the AZT scandal. *Spin,* November 1989.

Ferriman, Annabel. Mr Cube's research sweetener outrages dentists. *Observer,* 1 March 1992.

Gould, Donald. *The medical mafia: how doctors serve and fail their customers.* Sphere, 1985.

Griffith, Ben et al. *Banking on sickness.* Lawrence & Wishart, 1987.

Gupta, Susil. The AIDS fraud. *Analysis,* January 1992.

Hansen, Ole. *Inside Ciba-Geigy.* International Organisation of Consumers' Unions, 1989.

Heimoff, Steve & Sommer, Julia. Is the HIV AIDS theory all wrong? *CalReport,* Newspaper of the University of California at Berkeley, Fall 1991.

Herxheimer, A. & Collier, J. Promotion by the British pharmaceutical industry, 1983-8: a critical analysis of self-regulation. *British Medical Journal,* 3 February 1990.

Hughes, Sylvia. France investigates ethics of AIDS test. *New Scientist,* 23 March 1991.

Karpf, Anne. *Doctoring the media: the reporting of health and medicine.* Routledge, 1988.

Kennedy, I. *The unmasking of medicine.* Paladin, 1983.

Lang, R.W. *The politics of drugs.* Saxon House, 1974.

Lauritsen, K. et al. Withholding unfavourable results in drug company-sponsored clinical trials. *Lancet,* 1, 1987, 109.

Lazarides, Linda. Letter. *Independent on Sunday,* 12 August 1990.

Lumley, J.A. The British pharmaceutical industry 1868-1968. *Practitioner,* 201, July 1968.

Mansfield, Peter. Letter. *Independent on Sunday,* 5 May 1991.

Marsh, Peter. Prescribing all the way to the bank: hard science and high capitalism meet in the pharmaceutical industry. *New Scientist,* 18 November 1989.

Marshall, E. Quick release of AIDS drugs. *Science,* 245, 1989.

Medawar, Charles. *Drug disinformation.* Social Audit, 1980.

Medawar, Charles. *Insult or injury? An enquiry into the promotion of British food and drug products in the third world.* Social Audit, 1979.

Medawar, Charles. *The wrong kind of medicine.* Consumers' Association and Social Audit, London, 1984.

Melville, Arabella & Johnson, Colin. *Cured to death: the effects of prescription drugs.* New English Library, 1982.

Report of the Committee of Enquiry into the relationship of the pharmaceutical industry with the National Health Service, 1965-67. Chairman: Lord Sainsbury. HMSO, 1967.

Silverman, M. & Lee, P.R. *Pills, profits and politics.* University of California Press, 1974.

Sonnabend, Joseph A. Review of AZT multi-center trial data obtained under the Freedom of Information Act by Project Inform and ACT-UP. *AIDS Forum,* January 1988.

Swann, J.P. *Academic scientists and the pharmaceutical industry.* Johns Hopkins University Press, 1988.

Veitch, Andrew. Three members of drugs body paid by firms. *Guardian,* 16 August 1985.

Wellcome: one hundred years (1880-1980) in pursuit of excellence. Wellcome, 1980.

Winfield, M. *Minding your own business: self regulation and whistleblowing in British companies.* Social Audit, 1991.

The Campaign Against Health Fraud

Baum, Michael. Bridging the gulf. *Complementary Medical Research,* 5(3), October 1991.

Baum, Michael. Letter on homoeopathy. *British Medical Journal,* 2 March 1991.

Baum, Michael. Quack cancer cures or scientific remedies? *Clinical Oncology,* 9, 1983.

Baum, Michael. Science versus non-science in medicine: fact or fiction? *Journal of the Royal Society of Medicine*, 80, June 1987.

Beard, Nick. Quackbusters: the official launch of the Campaign Against Health Fraud. *British and Irish Skeptic*, May/June 1989.

Campbell, Duncan. 1,227 - and counting: the politics of AIDS. *New Statesman & Society*, 22 January

Campbell, Duncan. AIDS: the race against time (early intervention AZT). *New Statesman & Society*, 6 January 1989.

Campbell, Duncan. BBC embarrassed by link to 'IQ pill' sales. IQ trials on QED. *Independent on Sunday*, 24 February 1991.

Campbell, Duncan. Cult doctors investigated over herbal anti-AIDS pills. *Independent on Sunday*, 19 August 1990.

Campbell, Duncan. Doctors paid commission by drug firms. *Independent on Sunday*, 5 August 1990.

Campbell, Duncan. Downgrading the danger of AIDS. *New Statesman & Society*, 30 November 1990.

Campbell, Duncan. GMC is asked to look at doctors' 'sleep treatment'. *Independent on Sunday*, 18 August 1991.

Campbell, Duncan. An investigative journalist looks at medical ethics. *British Medical Journal*, 29 April 1989.

Campbell, Duncan. Media standards: science and nonsense. *New Statesman & Society*, 29 June 1990.

Campbell, Duncan. The parliamentary bypass operation. *New Statesman & Society*, 23 January 1987.

Campbell, Duncan. Pill firm break kickback pledge. *Independent*, 28 October 1990.

Campbell, Duncan. Taking on the quacks. *New Statesman & Society*, 22 May 1992.

Campbell, Duncan. Vitamin pills withdrawn from sale. *Independent*, 1 October 1990.

Campbell, Duncan. VOD's up doc? Reviewing the hazards to your health from the computer 'radiation shield' manufacturers. *Personal Computer World* December 1989.

Campbell, Duncan. Why I am quackbusting. *Interaction: the Journal of ME Action*, 4, Spring 1990.

Chalmers, Iain. Letter. *British Medical Journal*, 28 January 1989.

Chalmers, Iain. Letter. *British Medical Journal*, 16 February 1991.

Chalmers, Iain. Proposal to outlaw the term 'negative trial'. *British Medical Journal*, 30 March 1985.

Hodgkinson, Neville. Allergy hoaxer stirs up a fuss. *Sunday Times*, 3 January 1988.

Le Fanu, James. Setting a hack to catch the quack. *Sunday Telegraph*, 1 March 1992.

Marks, Vincent. Putting sugar in perspective. Supplement to *The Grocer*, 9 February 1985.

Martin, Simon. Letter. *Guardian*, 10 January 1990.

O'Donnell, Michael. Looking sideways. *Medical Monitor*, 8 March 1991.

O'Donnell, Michael. One man's burden. *British Medical Journal*, 7 December 1985.

O'Donnell, Michael. Trial by anecdote. *British Medical Journal*, 5 January 1991.

Orvice, Vikki. Surgeon threatened with assault charge over hysterectomy. *Daily Mail*, 29 June 1992.

Quack cures that baffle biochemists. Association of Chemical Biochemists. *Medical Laboratory News*, 28 May 1990.

Richmond, Caroline. The Campaign Against Health Fraud. *Practitioner*, 233, 8 October 1989.

Richmond, Caroline. Cases involving '20th-century diseases' start landing in British courts. *Canadian Medical Association Journal*, 146(4), February 1992.

Richmond, Caroline. Keeping calm amid the allergy craze. *Doctor*, 12 March 1992.

Richmond, Caroline. Letter. *British Medical Journal*, 6 December 1986.

Richmond, Caroline. Letter. *Journal of Alternative and Complementary Medicine*, October 1990.

Richmond, Caroline. A vade mecum for hypochondriacs. *British Medical Journal*, 26 August 1989.

Richmond, Caroline. Natural and swashbuckling healers. *British Medical Journal*, 17 February 1990.

Richmond, Caroline. Poem. *Lancet*, 1 December 1990.

Richmond, Caroline. Protecting patients against quacks: what are the possible problems? *MIMS*, 15 February 1991.

Richmond, Caroline. They call themselves human canaries. *Independent*, 14 January 1992.

Richmond, Caroline. When allergy fear becomes craze. *Hospital Doctor*, 12 March 1992.

Secrets case private eye guilty. *Basingstoke and North Hampshire Gazette*, 3 February 1989.

Shepherd, Charles. Magnesium injections. *Perspectives - ME Association Newsletter*, Summer 1991.

Shepherd, Charles. Natural health pills can be lethal. *G.P.*, 18 January 1991.

Sill, Lindsey. Inciting secrets charge private eye. *Basingstoke and North Hampshire Gazette*, 5 January 1989.

Sill, Lindsey. Private eye's secrets boast. *Basingstoke and North Hampshire Gazette*, 6

January 1989.

Who's protecting who - and from what? *Journal of Alternative and Complementary Medicine*, August 1989.

Part Five and General

AIDS programme complaint dismissed as witch hunt. *The Times*, 23 February 1991.

"ALERT" Health freedom - where has it gone? National Council for Improved Health. December 1990.

Badgley, Laurence. *Healing AIDS naturally*. Human Energy Press.

Bauhoffer, U., Davis, L., Van Den Berg, W.P. and Janssen, G.W.H.M. *Application of Maharishi Ayur-Veda in infection with the Human Immune Deficiency Virus (HIV) - case reports*. Presented at the fourth International Conference on AIDS, Stockholm, Sweden. 1988.

Booth, W.S. Chicago anti-trust trial. A.C.A. *Journal of Chiropractic*, 18(3), 1981.

Brown, Phylidda. French 'ban' facts to deter AIDS pioneer. *New Scientist*, 22 June 1991.

Burroughs Wellcome Fund. *Annual Report*. 1990.

Chirimuuta, Richard and Chirimuuta, Rosalind. *AIDS, Africa and racism*. Free Association Books, 1989.

Chopra, Deepak. *Perfect Health - the complete mind/body guide*. Bantam Books, 1990.

Chopra, Deepak. *Quantum Healing: exploring the frontiers of mind/body medicine*. Bantam New Age Books, USA, 1989.

Collected Papers, scientific research on Maharishi's Transcendental Meditation and TM-Sidhi programme, Vols. 1-5. MVU Press. Holland, 1977-1989.

Cook, Judith. *Whose health is it anyway?: the consumer and the National Health Service*. New English Library, 1987.

Cowe, Roger. Effects of wonder drug wear off. *Guardian*, 3 May 1991.

Cowley, Geoffrey et al. PROZAC: a promising new weapon against depression. *Newsweek*, 26 March 1990.

Dillner, Luisa. BMA gets tough with fraudulent doctors. *British Medical Journal*, 14 December 1991.

Doctors peddled AIDS treatment. *The Times*, 16 July 1991.

Downing, Damien & Davies, Stephen. Allergy: conventional and alternative concepts. *Journal of Nutritional Medicine*, 3, 1992.

Duesberg, Peter H. AIDS epidemiology: inconsistencies with human immunodeficiency virus and with infectious disease. *Proceedings of the National Academy of Sciences*, 88, February 1991.

Duesberg, Peter H. A giant hole in the HIV-AIDS hypothesis. *Sunday Times*, 31

May 1992.

Duesberg, Peter H. Human immunodeficiency virus and acquired immuno-deficiency syndrome: correlation but not causation. *Proceedings of the National Academy of Sciences*, 86, February 1989.

Duesberg, Peter H. Retroviruses as carcinogens and pathogens: expectations and reality. *Cancer Research*, 1 March 1987.

Duesberg, Peter H. The role of drugs in the origins of AIDS. *Biomed. and Pharmacother*, 46, 1992.

Farber, Celia. Out of Africa. *Spin*, March 1993.

Germanium-containing dietary supplements. Department of Health circular, 10 October 1989.

Germanium dangers. *Lancet*, 23 September 1989.

Gillie, Oliver. AIDS Trust undermined by internal strife. *Independent*, 31 August 1990.

Goodman, Sandra. *Germanium: the health and life enhancer*. Thorsons, 1988.

Goodman, Sandra. Therapeutic effects of organic germanium. *Medical Hypotheses*, 1987.

Goodman, Sandra. *Vitamin C: the master nutrient*. Keats, 1991.

Hamilton, Nick. A revolution in medicine. *Observer*, 7 April 1991.

Haynes, Jo. Scathing college report on alternative therapy withdrawn. *Pulse*, 14 March 1992.

Hencke, David. Millions in AIDS cash unspent or diverted. *Guardian*, 23 October 1991.

Hodgkinson, Neville. AIDS 'rebel' blames scientists for deaths. *Sunday Times*, 17 May 1992.

Hodgkinson, Neville. Epidemic of AIDS in Africa 'a myth'. *Sunday Times*, 21 March 1993.

Hodgkinson, Neville. Experts mount startling challenge to AIDS orthodoxy. *Sunday Times*, 26 April 1992.

Hodgkinson, Neville. The truth is, we don't know what causes this disease. *Sunday Times*, 26 July 1992.

Horrobin, David F. The philosophical basis of peer review and the suppression of innovation. *Journal of the American Medical Association*, 263(10), 9 March 1990.

Kennedy, Ian. *The unmasking of medicine*. Allen & Unwin, 1981.

Klein, R. *The politics of the National Health Service*. Longman, 1983.

Kolata, Gina. After five years of use, doubts still cloud leading AIDS drug. *New York Times*, 2 June 1992.

Kolata, Gina. Imminent marketing of AZT raises problems. *Science*, 20 March 1987.

Lambert, E.C. *Modern medical mistakes*. Indiana University Press, 1978.

Lauritsen, John. AIDS criticism in Europe. *New York Native*, 15 June 1992.

Lauritsen, John. The AIDS war: censorship and propaganda dominate media coverage of the epidemic. *New York Native*, 12 August 1991.

Lauritsen, John. FDA documents show fraud in AZT trials. *New York Native*, 30 March 1992.

Lauritsen, John. Something rotten in the British AIDS establishment. *New York Native*, 10 February 1992.

Lock, S. Misconduct in medical research: does it exist in Britain? *British Medical Journal*, 10 December 1988.

Maharishi Ayur-Veda: documents, scientific research, bibliographies, letters. MVU Press. Holland, 1990.

Mangold, Tom. AIDS: the debate intensifies. *Sunday Times*, 26 July 1992.

Matsusaka, T, et al. Germanium-induced nephropathy: report of two cases and review of the literature. *Clinical Nephrology*, 30(6), 1988.

Morgenthaler, John & Fowkes, Steven William (eds). *Stop the FDA: save your health freedom.* Health Freedom Publications, California, 1992.

Pharmaceuticals: a consumer prescription. A discussion paper on the structure and regulation of the pharmaceutical industry. National Consumer Council, London, 1991.

Preparations containing germanium - advice to consumers. Department of Health press release, 6 October 1989.

Pritchard, B.N.C. Collaborating with the pharmaceutical industry. *British Medical Journal*, 17 March 1979.

Root-Bernstein, Robert. Rethinking AIDS. *Wall Street Journal*, Europe, 19-20 March 1993.

Scheinberg, I.H. & Walshe, J.M. *Orphan diseases and orphan drugs.* Manchester University Press, 1986.

Sharma, H. *Freedom from disease.* Veda Publications, Canada, 1993.

Stallibrass, Alison. The Bristol Cancer Help Centre: surviving and growing through our crisis. *Holistic Health*, Summer 1991.

Stewart, Gordon. Conspiracy of humbug hides the truth on AIDS. *Sunday Times*, 7 June 1992.

Supplementary benefit. *Evening Standard*, 23 February 1990.

Thallon, Cheryl. Germanium update. *Natural Food Trade*, circulation update 5,439.

Thorne, Frank. Bid to ban Di's pills. *Daily Mirror*, 8 September 1989.

Tryptophan and germanium. *Chemist and Druggist Supplement*, 17 March 1990.

Watson, Jeremy. Medical Council to investigate allergy doctor. *Scotland on Sunday*, 25 August 1991.

Wood, Barry. Keep taking the tabloids. *New Statesman & Society*, 1 July 1992.

Zidovudine and other drugs against HIV. *Drug and Therapeutics Bulletin*, 28 December 1988.

Epilogue

The business of AIDS. Editorial. *Independent*, 3 April 1993.

Connor, Steve & Counsell, Gail. Shares tumble after trial of AIDS drug. *Independent*, 3 April 1993.

Cookson, Clive & Abrahams, Paul. AIDS drug effectiveness in question. *Financial Times*, 2 April 1993.

Day, Timon & Woolcock, Keith. Wellcome in price crash riddle. *Mail on Sunday*, 4 April 1993.

Fairbairn, Sarah. £½bn AIDS hit at Wellcome. Business Day. *Evening Standard*, 2 April 1993.

Fairbairn, Sarah. Wellcome fails to stop the damage. Business Day. *Evening Standard*, 7 April 1993.

Hodgkinson, Neville. AIDS truth falls victim to virus of ignorance. *Sunday Times*, 14 March 1993.

Hodgkinson, Neville. The cure that failed. *Sunday Times*, 4 April 1993.

International Educational Development Inc. and Project AIDS, International. *An urgent appeal for action: regarding AIDS, HIV and human rights*. Presented to the U.N. Commission on Human Rights. Geneva, 1993.

Mihill, Chris. Firm disputes test failure of AIDS drug. *Guardian*, 8 April 1993.

Naylor, Sara. Consultant dismisses AIDS epidemic theory. *Independent*, 17 April 1993.

Wellcome's AZT sales threatened. *Financial Times*, 2 April 1993.

SELF-HELP, CAMPAIGN AND PRESSURE GROUPS IN HEALTH AND MEDICINE

Many of the following organisations rely entirely on donations and membership fees. Please enclose an SAE when requesting information. The list is by no means exhaustive, but will provide a good starting point.

GROUPS IN THE UK AND EUROPE

FOOD ADDITIVES

- Food Additives Campaign Team

c/o Dr Eric Millstone
Science Policy Research Unit
Mantell Building
Sussex University
Brighton BN1 9RF
Tel: 0273 686758

A coalition of additive-aware & campaigning bodies.

- Parents for Safe Food

5-11 Worship Street
London EC2A 2BH
Tel: 071 628 2442

Campaigns & info. on improvement, safety & quality of food.

- The Food Commission

5-11 Worship Street
London EC2A 2BH
Tel: 071 628 7774

Independent consumer watchdog on food issues.

- Hyperactive Children's Support Group

71 Whyke Lane
Chichester
West Sussex PO19 2LD
Tel: 0903 725182 (10am-3.30pm Mon-Fri)

Info., support, research. For info. send SAE 9"x4".

AGRICULTURE/FOOD/ENVIRONMENT

- Communities Against Toxins

31 Station Road
Little Sutton
South Wirral L66 1NU
Tel: 051 339 5473

- Environmental Medicine Foundation

Symondsbury House
Bridport
Dorset DT6 6HB
Tel: 0308 422956

- Friends of the Earth

26-28 Underwood Street
London N1 7JQ
Tel: 071 490 1555

- Genetics Forum

258 Pentonville Road
London N1 9JY
Tel: 071 278 6578
Fax: 071 278 0955

**National public interest/
pressure group in field of
biotech & genetic engineering.**

**- GRAIN: Genetic Resources
Action International**

Jonqueras 16-6-D
E-08003 Barcelona
Spain

**Campaigning for traditional
farming practices.**

- Green Alliance

Tel: 071 836 0341

**Monitors/lobbies gov. policy
on the environment.**

- Green Network

9 Clairemont Road
Lexden
Colchester
Essex CO3 5BE
Tel: 0206 46902

**Non-party political federa-
tion of local groups.**

**- Greenpeace
Environmental Trust**

30 Islington Green
London N1 2PN
Tel: 071 354 5100

**- Greenpeace Libertarian
Environmental Group
(London)**

5 Caledonian Road
London N1 9DX
Tel: 071 837 7557

**London branch of anarchist
environmentalist group.**

- The National Food Alliance

same address as Food Com-
mission.

**Alliance of organisations, to
develop and improve food
and agriculture policy.**

- SAFE Alliance

Sustainable Agriculture, Food
and Environment
21 Tower Street
London WC2H 9NS
Tel: 071 240 1811
Fax: 071 240 1899

**Umbrella of organisations
lobbying for agricultural re-
forms.**

- The Soil Association

86 Colston Street
Bristol BS1 5BB
Tel: 0272 290661

**Organic farming/reduction
in use of pesticides.**

**- Women's Environmental
Network**

Aberdeen Studios
22 Highbury Grove
London N5 2EA
Tel: 071 354 8823

**Campaigning, lobbying, re-
searching.**

ANIMAL WELFARE

- Animal Liberation Front

BCM 9240
London WC1N 3XX

**Publishes newsletter
Arkangel, available from
above address.**

- **British Anti-Vivisection Association**

P O Box 82
Kingswood
Bristol BS15 1YF

- **Campaign to End Fraudulent Medical Research**

P O Box 302
London N8 9HD
Tel: 081 340 9813

- **CIVIS**

POB 152
Via Motta 51
CH 6900, Massagno/Lugano
Switzerland

- **Compassion in World Farming**

20 Lavant Street
Petersfield
Hampshire GU32 3EW
Tel: 0730 268070

Campaigns for animal welfare in farming.

- **Doctors in Britain Against Animal Experiments**

P O Box 302
London N8 9HD
Tel: 081 340 9813

Campaigns on scientific grounds against using animals in medical research.

GENERAL HEALTH INFORMATION

- **Help for Health**

c/o Wessex Area Health Authority
Highcroft
Romsey Road
Winchester
Hampshire SO22 5DH

Database of 3000+ voluntary/self-help groups in health and disability.

The Bulletin of the Nutritional Health Foundation

23 Clarence Road
East Cowes
Isle of Wight
Hampshire PO32 6EP

Periodic worldwide review of current key literature in nutritional science, aimed at the lay reading public.

- **What Doctors Don't Tell You**

4 Wallace Road
London N1 2PG
Tel: 071 354 4592
Fax: 071 354 8907

Monthly compilation, researches drugs, medical & surgical procedures.

INFORMATION ABOUT
PHARMACEUTICAL
COMPANIES AND
PRODUCTS

- **Health Action
  International**

  HAI-Europe
  Jacob van Lennepkade 334T
  1053 NJ Amsterdam
  The Netherlands

  **Produces international in-
  formation and reports on
  drug companies, their advertising and profits.**

- **Social Audit Ltd**

  Freepost
  P O Box 111
  London NW1 0YW
  Tel: 071 586 7771

  **Has carried out a number of
  studies of businesses, particularly the pharmaceutical
  industry.**

INFORMATION ABOUT
COMPLEMENTARY
MEDICINE

- **British Dental Society for
  Clinical Nutrition**

  1 Welbeck House
  62 Welbeck Street
  London W1M 7HB
  Tel: 071 486 3127

  **Practitioners of natural, hol-
  istic dentistry.**

- **British Society for Allergy
  & Environmental
  Medicine**

  Acorns
  Romsey Road
  Cadnam
  Southampton SO4 2NN
  Tel: 0703 812124

- **British Society for
  Nutritional Medicine**

  P O Box 3AP
  London W1A 3AP
  Tel: 071 436 8532
  Fax: 071 580 3910

- **The Council for
  Complementary and
  Alternative Medicine**

  179 Gloucester Place
  London NW1 6DX
  Tel: 071 724 9103

  **Association of professional
  organisations; can refer to
  reliable training courses/
  practitioners.**

- **The Centre for the Study of
  Complementary
  Medicine**

  51 Bedford Place
  Southampton
  Hampshire SO1 2DG
  Tel: 0703 334752

- **Institute for
  Complementary
  Medicine**

  P O Box 194
  London SE 16 1QZ
  Tel: 071 237 5165

  **Can refer to reliable practi-
  tioners in complementary
  therapies; list of support
  groups.**

COMPLEMENTARY TECHNIQUES AND APPROACHES

ACUPUNCTURE

- Acupuncture & Chinese Herbal Practitioners Association

1037b Finchley Road
London NW11 7ES
Tel: 081 455 5508

- British Acupuncture Association & Register

34 Alderney Street
London SW1V 4EU
Tel: 071 834 1012

AROMATHERAPY

- International Federation of Aromatherapists

The Royal Masonic Hospital
Department of Continuing
Education
Ravenscourt Park
London W6 0TN
Tel: 081 846 8066

CHIROPRACTIC

- British Chiropractic Association

29 Whitley Street
Reading
Berkshire RG2 0EG
Tel: 0734 757557

HEALING

- The Confederation of Healing Organisations

Suite J
The Red and White House
113 High Street
Berkhamsted
Hertfordshire HP4 2DJ
Tel: 0442 870660
Fax: 0442 870667

Umbrella for about 16 different healing organisations. In addition, see The Seekers Guide - A New Age Resource Book, Button and Bloom (eds), Harper Collins/Aquarian.

HOMOEOPATHY

- The Society of Homoeopaths

2 Artizan Road
Northampton NN1 4HU
Tel: 0604 21400

MASSAGE

- British Massage Therapy Council

9 Elm Road
Worthing
West Sussex BN11 1PG
Tel: 0293 775467

MEDICAL HERBALISM

- National Institute of Medical Herbalists

9 Palace Gate
Exeter EX1 1JA
Tel: 0392 426022

NATUROPATHY/
  OSTEOPATHY

**- British College of
    Naturopathy &
    Osteopathy**

Frazer House
6 Netherhall Gardens
London NW3 5RR
Tel: 071 794 3106

**- British School of
    Osteopathy**

1-4 Suffolk Street
London SW1Y 4HG
Tel: 071 930 9254

**- Incorporated Society of
    Registered Naturopaths**

328 Harrogate Road
Moortown
Leeds LS17 6PE
Tel: 0532 685992

TRADITIONAL MEDICINE

**- Association of Ayurvedic
    Physicians in the UK**

12 Agar Street
Leicester LE4 6ND
Tel: 0533 666746

**SPECIFIC HEALTH
PROBLEMS**

ADDICTION TO
  PHARMACEUTICAL
  PRODUCTS

**- Riverside Mental
    Health Trust**

Dr C Hallstrom
Charing Cross Hospital
London W6 8RF
Tel: 081 846 1511

**Must be referred by GP;
info., advice, support, counselling on use of benzoes &
withdrawal.**

**- CITA: Council for
    Involuntary
    Tranquilliser Addiction**

Cavendish House
Brighton Road
Waterloo
Liverpool L22 5NG
Tel: 051 949 0102

**The only national helpline;
can refer to local groups.**

AIDS

- Positively Healthy

P O Box 71
Richmond
Surrey TW9 3DJ
Tel: 081 878 6443

**Probably the only non-Well-
come-infiltrated HIV+/AIDS
advisory group in the UK.**

**- Lavender Hill
    Homoeopathic Centre**

33 Ilminster Gardens,
London SW11 1PJ
Tel: 071 978 4519

**Homoeopathic care of HIV+
infiltrated and AIDS patients.**

ALLERGY

- AAA: Action Against Allergy

24-26 High Street
Hampton Hill
Middlesex
TW12 1PD
Tel: 081 943 4244

**Info., advice, members'
helpline.**

- Allergy-Induced Autism

3 Palmera Avenue
Calcot
Reading RG3 7DZ
Tel: 0734 419460

Support and self-help.

- Food & Chemical Allergy Association

27 Ferringham Lane
Ferring
West Sussex
Tel: 0903 241178

- National Society for Research into Allergies

P O Box 45
Hinkley
Leicester LE10 1JY
Tel: 0455 851546

ASTHMA

- The National Asthma Campaign

Providence House
Providence Place
London N1 0NT
Tel: 071 226 2260

Helpline; in touch with local sufferer groups.

CANCER

- Aspect (The Jeannie Campbell Breast Cancer Radiotherapy Appeal)

29 St Luke's Avenue
Ramsgate
Kent CT11 7JZ
Tel: 0843 596732
Fax: 0843 853184

Nationwide distribution of free info. regarding fighting breast cancer *without* radical surgery.

- BACUP: British Association of Cancer United Patients

3 Bath Place
Rivington Street
London EC2A 3JR
Tel: 071 696 9003
Fax: 071 696 9002

Umbrella organisation; can put in touch with specific sufferer groups. Cancer Information Service: 071 613 2121; Freeline (from outside 071/081 areas): 0800 181199; Counselling Service: 071 696 9000.

- Bristol Cancer Help Centre

Grove House
Cornwallis Grove
Clifton
Bristol BS8 4PG
Tel: 0272 743216
Fax: 0272 239184

Holistic approach to therapies. Nationwide support groups.

- CALL: Childhood Cancer & Leukaemia Link

30 Knowles Avenue
Crowthorne
Berkshire RG11 6DU
Tel: 0344 750319

Nationwide individual, mutual support network for parents.

- **Cancerlink**

  17 Britannia Street
  London WC1X 9JN
  Tel: 071 833 2451

  9 Castle Terrace
  Edinburgh EH1 2DP
  Tel: 031 228 5557

  Provides info. on treatments, help with setting up support groups.

- **Contact-a-Family**

  170 Tottenham Court Road
  London W1P 0HA
  Tel: 071 383 3555

  Publishes: The CaF Directory of Specific Conditions & Rare Syndromes in Children, with their Family Support Networks.

- **Gerson Therapy**

  Pat Faulkner
  57 Bridge Street
  Pershore
  Worcestershire WR10 1AL
  Tel: 0386 556922

- **The Deborah Stappard Trust**

  c/o Sheila and Colin Compton
  Chapel Farm
  Westhumble
  Dorking
  Surrey RH5 6AY
  Tel: 0306 882865

  Raises funds for special needs of Gerson therapy.

- **The Springhill Centre**

  Cuddington Road
  Dinton
  Aylesbury
  Buckinghamshire HP18 0AD
  Tel: 0296 748278

  Rehabilitation, respite and terminal care centre.

- **Women's National Cancer Control Campaign**

  128 Curtain Road
  London EC2A 3AR
  Tel: 071 729 1735

  Helpline, info.

EATING DISORDERS

- **Eating Disorders Association**

  Sackville Place
  44 Magdalen Street
  Norwich
  Norfolk NR3 1JU
  Tel: 0603 621414

ENDOMETRIOSIS

- **Endometriosis Society**

  Unit F8a
  Shakespeare Business Centre
  245a Coldharbour Lane
  London SW9 8RR
  Tel: 071 737 0380

  Support group for sufferers of problematic/painful menstruation and infertility.

HYPERACTIVITY

- Hyperactive Children's Support Group

71 Whyke Lane
Chichester
West Sussex PO19 2LD
Tel: 0903 725182 (10am-3.30pm Mon-Fri)

Info., support, research. For info. send SAE 9"x4".

ME

- ME Action Campaign

P O Box 1302
Wells BA5 2WE

MIGRAINE

- British Migraine Association

178a High Road
Byfleet
West Byfleet
Surrey KT14 7ED
Tel: 09323 52468

Sufferer-run support group; helpline.

- Energy Medicine Developments Ltd.

17 Owen Road
Diss
Norfolk IP22 3ER
Tel: 0379 644234

MS

- Federation of Multiple Sclerosis Therapy Centres

Unit 4
Murdoch Road
Bedford MK41 7PD
Tel: 0234 325781

INFORMATION ON INDIVIDUAL RIGHTS

- Bulletin of Medical Ethics

(Editor: Dr Richard Nicholson)
Professional and Scientific Publications Ltd
BMA House
Tavistock House East
Tavistock Square
London WC1H 9JR
Tel: 071 387 4499

Publishes in the field of health care ethics.

- CERES: Consumers for Ethics in Research

P O Box 1365
London N16 0BW

Campaigning for informed consent.

- VDU Workers Rights Campaign

City Centre
32-35 Featherstone Street
London EC1
Tel: 071 608 1338

NUTRITIONAL ADVICE

- Complementary Medicine Centre (Allergy Care)

9 Corporation Street
Taunton
Somerset TA1 4AJ
Tel: 0823 325022
Fax: 0823 325024

Mail order foods, remedies and dietary aids for those with special needs. Previously FoodWatch International.

- **The McCarrison Society**
  24 Paddington Street
  London W1M 4DR
  Tel: 071 935 3924
  **Info., research & advice on
  nutrition and health.**

- **The Society for the
  Promotion of
  Nutritional Therapy**
  1st Floor
  The Enterprise Centre
  Station Parade
  Eastbourne BN21 1BE
  Tel: 0323 430203
  **Independent info., lobbying,
  and directory of practi-
  tioners.**

- **The Vegetarian Society**
  Parkdale
  Dunham Road
  Altrincham
  Cheshire WA14 4QG
  Tel: 061 928 0793

PESTICIDE EXPOSURE

- **NAG: National Action
  Group**
  c/o Orchard House
  Porlock
  Minehead
  Somerset TA24 8QE
  **Small, sufferer-run cam-
  paign against use of organo-
  phosphate sheep dip.**

- **PEGS: Pesticide Exposure
  Group of Sufferers**
  4 Lloyds House
  Regent Terrace
  Cambridge CB2 1AA
  Tel: 0223 64707
       (9am–9pm)
  **Takes up cases of chemical
  exposure.**

- **The Pesticides Trust**
  23 Beehive Place
  London SW9 7QR
  Tel: 071 274 8895
  Fax: 071 274 9084
  **Independent forum for
  monitoring, informing, re-
  search.**

- **South West Environmental
  Protection Agency**
  Heathfield Farmhouse
  Callington
  Cornwall PL17 7HP
  Tel: 0579 84492
  **Campaigns and advises
  about organo-phosphates
  and agrichemicals.**

- **Unicorn Ataxia Group**
  33 Victoria Avenue
  Widley
  Waterlooville
  Hampshire PO7 5BN
  Tel: 0705 386050
  **Sufferers' support/advice
  group for cerebellar ataxia
  following chemical exposure.**

PRE-CONCEPTIONAL CARE

- **CHILD**
  P O Box 154
  Hounslow
  Middlesex TW5 0EZ
  Tel: 081 571 4367
  **Self-help support group for
  childless/infertile people.**

- **Foresight: The Association
  for the Promotion of
  Pre-conceptual Care**
  Mrs Barnes
  28 The Paddock
  Godalming
  Surrey GU7 1XD
  Tel: 0483 427839

- **ISSUE: The National
  Fertility Association**
  St George's Rectory
  Tower Street
  Birmingham B19 3UY
  Tel: 021 359 4887
  **Self-help charity providing
  general advice on infertility.**

- **Maternity Alliance**
  15 Britannia Street
  London WC1X 9JP
  Tel: 071 837 1265
  **National charity, advises on
  pregnancy and parenting for
  women and men.**

RADIATION

- **CIRCUIT**
  c/o 153 Trevelyan Drive
  Westerhope
  Newcastle upon Tyne
  NE3 4BY
  **A support group for people
  sensitive to electro-magnetic
  radiation.**

- **CORE: Cumbrians
  Opposed to Radiation
  in the Environment**
  98 Church Street
  Barrow-in-Furness
  Cumbria LA14 2HT
  Tel: 0229 833851
  **Local campaigning group
  with national contacts.**

- **Greenpeace Nuclear
  Campaigns**
  30 Islington Green
  London N1 2PN
  Tel: 071 359 7396

- **Friends of the Earth**
  26-28 Underwood Street
  London N1 7JQ
  Tel: 071 490 1555

VICTIMS OF SPECIFIC
TREATMENTS/DRUGS

- **Association of Parents of
  Vaccine-Damaged
  Children**
  2 Church Street
  Shipston-on-Stour
  CV36 4AP
  Tel: 0608 61595

- **DES (diethyl stilboestrol)
  Action Group**
  c/o 52-54 Featherstone Street
  London EC1Y 8RT
  Tel: 071 251 6580

- **Human Growth Hormone**
  Institute of Child Health
  University of London
  30 Guilford Street
  London WC1N 1EH
  Helpline: 071 404 0536

- **Human Insulin**
  National Diabetic Federation
  36 St David's Crescent
  Aspull
  Wigan
  Lancashire

- **Myodil Support Group**
  8 Thornley Close
  Rotton
  Oldham
  Lancashire
  please enclose an SAE.

- **Radiation Action Exposure Group (RAGE)**

  North West Group
  c/o Vicky Parker
  24 Lockett Gardens
  Trinity
  Salford M3 6BJ

  Southern Group
  c/o Jan Millington
  5 Bramble Croft
  Millbrook Road
  Crowborough
  East Sussex TN9 2RF

  For people suffering damage through radiotherapy treatment.

- **Steroid Aid Group**

  The Honorary Secretary
  P O Box 220
  London E17 3JR

- **Toxic Shock Syndrome**

  c/o Women's Environmental
      Network
  Aberdeen Studios
  22 Highbury Grove
  London N5 2EA
  Tel: 071 354 8823

- **Tranquilliser Action Group**

  82 Windsor Avenue
  Grays
  Essex RM16 2UA

LEGAL ADVICE IN DRUG/
   MEDICAL/
   ENVIRONMENTAL CASES

- **Action for Victims of Medical Accidents**

  Bank Chambers
  1 London Road
  Forest Hill
  London SE23 3TP
  Tel: 081 291 2793

  Provides advice and help with investigation into claims.

- **Association of Personal Injury Lawyers**

  10A Byard Lane
  Nottingham NG1 2GJ
  Tel: 0602 580585

- **Julian Bobak, Solicitor**

  George Ide, Phillips
  Lion House
  79 St Pancras
  Chichester
  West Sussex PO19 4NL
  Tel: 0243 786668

  Specialises in drug/medical negligence cases.

- **The Law Society**

  Legal Practice Directorate
  50 Chancery Lane
  London WC2A 1SX
  Tel: 071 242 1222
  Fax: 071 831 0057

  Keeps a register of lawyers specialising in medical negligence cases, and in cases involving particular drugs (e.g. human insulin, benzodiazepines, Myodil).

- Leigh Day & Co

Solicitors
37 Gray's Inn Road
London WC1X 8PP
Tel: 071 242 1775

Specialise in environmental cases (e.g. Sellafield, Docklands).

- ELF:

Environmental Law Foundation
Lincoln's Inn House
42 Kingsway
London WC2E 6EX
Tel: 071 404 1030

Lawyers, medical, scientific, technical experts providing redress for people suffering damage with environmental cause.

WATER

- ACOPS:

Advisory Committee on Pollution of the Sea
57 Duke Street
London W1M 5DH
Tel: 071 499 0704

Research & policy formulation & education.

- Camelford Victims

c/o Doreen Scudder
The Moorings
Trefew Road
Camelford
PL32 9TP
Tel: 0840 212817

Local campaign. Can provide info. on Camelford incident.

- Marine Conservation Society

9 Gloucester Road
Ross-on-Wye
Herefordshire HR9 5BU
Tel: 0989 66017

Research & lobbying for protection of marine environment.

- National Anti-Fluoridation Campaign

36 Station Road
Thames Ditton
Surrey KT7 0NS
Tel: 081 398 2117

- National Pure Water Association

Meridan
Cae Goody Lane
Ellesmere
Shropshire SY12 9DW
Tel: 0691 623015

WOMEN'S HEALTH

- King's Cross Women's Centre

71 Tonbridge Street
London WC1H 9DZ
Tel: 071 837 7509

Advises on complementary & orthodox therapies; campaigns, reports.

- Women's Health

52 Featherstone Street
London EC1Y 8RT
Tel: 071 251 6580

Reference library on women's health issues.

- Women's Liberation Lesbian Line

BM Box 1514
London WC1
Tel: 071 837 8602

- **Women's Nutritional
    Advisory Service**
  P O Box 268
  Hove
  East Sussex BN3 1RW
  Tel: 0273 771367
  Fax: 0273 820576
  Specialist advice on conventional and complementary approaches to health.

GROUPS IN AMERICA

It has not been possible to research the many campaigning and advisory groups which exist in America. However, the following groups are all campaigning for freedom of choice in health, and would be a good starting point for further information.

- **American Academy of
    Environmental
    Medicine**
  P O Box 16106
  Denver
  CO 80216
  Tel: 303 622 9755

- **American Holistic Medical
    Association**
  2727 Fairview East
  Seattle
  WA 98102
  Tel: 206 322 6842

- **American Preventive
    Medical Association**
  PO Box 2111
  Tacoma
  WA 98401
  Tel: 206 926 0551
  Fax: 206 922 7583

- **The Center for Science in
    the Public Interest
    (CSPI)**
  1755 S Street NW
  Washington DC 20009
  **Produces magazine called
  'Nutrition in Action'.**

- **The Choice Newsletter**
  Committee for Freedom of
    Choice in Medicine, Inc.
  1180 Walnut Avenue
  Chula Vista
  CA 92011

- **Citizens Alliance for
    Progressive Health
    Awareness**
  P O Box 394
  Wayne
  PA 19087
  Tel: 215 640 2788
  Grass-roots organisation.

- **Citizens for Health**
  PO Box 368
  Tacoma
  WA 98401
  Tel: 206 922 2457
  Fax: 206 922 7583
  Non profit-making citizens' organisation.

- **The Civil Abolitionist**
  PO Box 26
  Swain
  NY 14884–0026

- **Council for Responsible Nutrition**
  1300 19th Street NW
  Washington DC 20036
  Fax: 202 872 9594
  Researching nutrients.

- **Foundation for the Advancement of Innovative Medicine**
  2 Executive Blvd, Suite 201
  Sussern
  NY 10901
  Tel: 914 368 9797

- **Fur N Feathers**
  PO Box 2011
  Burbank
  California 91102

- **HEAL**
  16 East 16th Street
  New York
  NY 1003
  Alternative therapeutic approaches to HIV antibody positive and AIDS.

- **Health Forum**
  PO Box 1973
  Provo
  UT 84603
  Tel: 801 224 2987
  Fax: 801 221 0663
  Grass-roots lobbying organisation.

- **National Council for Improved Health**
  1555 West Seminole
  San Marcos
  CA 92069
  Tel: 619 471 5090
  Grass-roots organisation of manufacturers, retailers and health professionals.

- **National Nutritional Food Association**
  150 Paularino, Suite 285
  Costa Mesa
  CA 92626
  Tel: 714 966 6632
  Fax: 714 641 7005
  Manufacturers' and retailers' lobby group.

- **Nutritional Health Alliance**
  P O Box 267
  Farmingdale
  NY 11735
  Tel: 800 226 4642
  Open to health professionals, manufacturers and retailers.

- **PRISM: People for Reason in Science and Medicine**
  P O Box 1305
  Woodland Hills
  CA 91365
  Tel: 818 345 9654
  Non profit-making organisation.

- Supress
PO Box 10400
Glendale
California 91209-3400

**- The Townsend Letter for
    Doctors**
911 Tyler Street
Port Townsend
WA 98368-6541

Index

ABC trial, 308, 376.
ABS *see* Advanced Biological Systems
Acquired Immunity Deficiency Syndrome *see* AIDS
ACSH *see* American Council on Science and Health
ACT-UP, 24, 403.
Adams, Jad, 313, 370-7, 379-80, 382, 389, 399, 406-7
additives *see* food, additives
Adler, Michael, 365
adoptive immunotherapy, 417-40
Adoptive Immunotherapy Unit, London Bridge Hospital,*see* Sharp
Advanced Biological Systems, 412-4
Advertising Standards Authority, 339, 341
Advisory Committee on Pesticides, 86-7
Advisory Council on Science and Technology, 234-5
Agricultural and Food Research Council, 206
AIDS, xvi, 23-4, 35, 100, 166-82, 239-42, 286, 312-23, 354-68, 369-506, 608-9, 622, 638, 643, 644, 645, 646, 647, 748, 650
see also AZT
see also HIV
AIDS Therapeutic Trials Committee, Medical Research Council Committee on AIDS, 261-3, 410
AL721, 313, 316-7, 365, 387, 410-1
Alar, 44
All Party Parliamentary Group on AIDS, 248-50, 259, 367
allergies, 99-109
see also clinical ecology
The Allergy Business, 520-70
Allergy - Conventional and Alternative Concepts, *see* Royal College of Physicians.
allopathy, 3-4
allyl caproate, 564

Alternative Therapy, British Medical Association report, 199, 284-6
AMA *see* American Medical Association
American Academy of Allergy, 93
American Association for the Advancement of Science, 54, 225-6
American Cancer Society, 20-1
American College of Allergy, 93
American Council Against Health Fraud *see* National Council Against Health Fraud
American Council on Science and Health, 27-8, 41-8, 206, 210, 214, 275, 303
  Scientific Advisory Board, 26
American Dietetic Association, 14
American Humanist Association, 48-50, 190-2
American Medical Association, 4-8, 13-21, 24, 26, 87, 95, 199-200, 338
  Committee on Quackery, 19-20
American Nutrition Foundation, 14
American Pharmaceutical Association, 20
Anderson, John, 117
Anderson, Roy, 235
APGOA *see* All Party Parliamentary Group on AIDS
Aronson, Jeffrey Kenneth K, 262
Arthritis Foundation, 20
Ashwell, Margaret, 205
Association of British Science Writers, 292
Association of Medical Research Charities, 229, 253, 292, 335, 631
Ayur-Vedic medicine, 413, 441-65
AZT, xvi, 23, 181, 219, 235, 355-68, 369-506, 645, 646, 647, 648, 650, 652
  clinical trials, 241, 244
  Concorde trials, 248, 250, 256-8, 262-3, 295, 318-23, 359, 372,

374, 377-80, 387, 390-2, 406,
409, 424, 447, 489, 504, 608-9,
619, 646, 647, 648
marketing, 239-47, 249-63

BAAS *see* British Association for the
Advancement of Science
Bailey, Ian, 512-3
Baldwin, Deborah, 596
Banton, Nick, 250
Barker, Philip, 415-41
Barlow, Philip, 629
Barnes, Belinda, 152-9, 338, 631-6
Barrett, Stephen, 25-7, 32, 59
Bass, Christopher, 334
Bass, Geoffrey and Phyllis,
Baum, Harold, 229, 324, 334
Baum, Michael, 290, 294-6,324-33,
335, 338, 439, 572, 588, 602-3
BBC, 220
television programmes, 164, 193,
274
cancer, 116-8, 123-4, 126-8
'Public Eye', Bristol Cancer Help
Centre, 575, 583
Vitamin and food supplements
'Food and Drink Programme',
616-20, 623-5
QED, 610-1
BCC *see* Broadcasting Complaints
Commission
BCHC *see* Bristol Cancer Help
Centre
Beard, Nick, 199, 290-1, 293-4, 334,
336-7, 404
Beck, Alan, 180-2, 394, 397-403,
406
Bender, Arnold, 229, 269, 274, 336,
342, 345-6
Benton, David, 164, 615
Benveniste, Jacques, 63-74
BHA *see* British Humanist Associa-
tion
Bide, Austin, Sir, 260
Biocare, 477
Biochemical Society, 229
Biolab Medical Unit, 142-4, 146,
159, 338, 636-7
Bircher-Benner, Max, 133-4

Birthright, 631
Black, Douglas, Sir, 206-7, 227, 284
Blakemore, Colin, 228
BMA *see* British Medical Association
BNF *see* British Nutrition Foundation
Bodmer, Walter, Sir, 127, 226-9,
292, 576, 599-600
Body Positive, 319, 364, 386, 451
Bolle, Dietmar, 176, 449-50
Bondi, Hermann, Sir, 190, 192, 229,
292
Booker, Christopher, 595
Boots, 226, 233, 264
Bottomley, Virginia, Secretary of
State for Health, 367
Bounds, Walli, 340
bovine somatotropin *see* BST
Bovine spongiform encephalopathy
see BSE
Bradford Research Institute, 491
Brahams, Diana, 329, 334
Breakspear Hospital, 101, 106, 507-
70
Breast Cancer Biology Group, 298
breast cancer, 326-33
see also Chilvers report
see also Bristol Cancer Help Centre
Bridle, David, 399-400
Bristol Cancer Help Centre, 112,
125-31, 331, 448, 452, 544-5,
572-607, 633
Bristol Survey Support Group, 598
British Association for the Advance-
ment of Science, 205, 226-9, 232,
234, 265, 292, 334
British Association of Clinical Bio-
chemists, 299
British Association of Science Wri-
ters, 265
British Dietetic Association, 229, 452
British Humanist Association, 189-
90, 192, 229, 292
British and Irish Skeptic see Skeptic
British Medical Association, 85, 87,
118-200, 206, 253-4, 297, 344
Board of Science, 122, 206
Foundation for AIDS, 253-4
British Nutrition Foundation, 164,
203-14, 229, 272

British Society for Allergy and Environmental Medicine, 141
British Society for Nutritional Medicine, 141, 143, 616, 619-20, 636-7
British Sociological Association, Medical Sociology Group, 594
British Sugar, 205
Broadcasting Complaints Commission, 408-9, 635-6
Brohn, Penny, 112, 125-31, 571-3, 575, 582-4, 592, 604, 606
Brooks, David, 511
Brownings Clinical Laboratories, 417-39
Bryant, Monica, 388, 416, 472-3, 477-9, 484-9, 608-9
Bryce Smith, Derek, 150, 156
BSE, 303, 306
BST, 275
Burke, Isla, 598
Burn, Steven, 398, 402
Burroughs Wellcome, 222, 240, 317, 377
Burroughs Wellcome Fund, 40, 43
Burton, Lawrence, 33
Burton, Stephen, 398, 402

Caffeine, 45-7, 136
CAHF *see* Campaign Against Health Fraud
Campaign Against Health Fraud, xv, 196, 198-200, 209-10, 225, 249, 252, 254, 272-4, 280-96 297, 299, 301, 303, 314-5, 318, 323-4, 329-31, 334-47, 374, 383-6, 403-4, 424, 463, 486, 491, 498-9, 504, 508, 511-2, 515-6, 521, 531-2, 540, 571-2, 586-8, 593, 596-7, 609-10, 615, 617, 620, 625, 633, 641, 642
(*later called HealthWatch, q.v.*)
Campaign for Health Through Food, 628-30
Campbell, Duncan, 291, 307-23, 406-89, 520-1, 558, 649
and Adams, Jad, 370-7
Beck, Alan, 180-2
Deer, Brian, 377-81
Mann, Cass, 381-405

Amazing AIDS scam (article), 313-4
BBC Secret Society programmes 390-3
Bristol Cancer Help Centre, 605-7
British Society for Nutritional Medicine, 635-6
Campaign Against Health Fraud, 291, 334
'Food and Drink Programme' (BBC Television programme), 616-20, 623-5
and Larkhall Natural Health Ltd, 617
'Let them eat shit/Pretty Poison' (articles), 481-7, 624
and vitamin and food supplements, 622-6
Holford, Patrick, 608-9, 611-5
Woodward, Robert, 610-1, 615-9, 624-5
Greer, Rita, 610-1, 615-9
Davies, Stephen, 619-21
Barnes, Belinda, 635
Larkhall Natural Health, 625-6
and 'Positively Unhealthy' (article), 390-3
'Rise of the new age pill pushers' (article), 613-5
'Sharp practice' (article), 415-40
and Zircon, 309-10
Cancell, 500-4
cancer,*see* Bristol Cancer Help Centre
see television programmes, BBC,
see breast cancer
Cancer Act, 118
Cancer Research Campaign, 576, 579
Working Party on Breast Conservation, 331
Cannon, Geoffrey, 148, 212, 267-9, 302, 304

Cardiac Society, 17
Carnegie Foundation, 7-8, 38, 55
Carson, Rachel, 82
CCHI *see* Coordinating Conference on Health Information
Center for Science in the Public Interest, 45-6
Chalmers, Iain, 334-5, 340
Chalmers, Roger, 413, 441-65, 476
Channel 4 Television 'Dispatches Programme',
  'AIDS: the Unheard Voices', 375, 407
  'The AIDS Catch', 407
  'AIDS and Africa', 407
  'AZT – Cause for Concern', 409-10
Chilvers report, 571-607
Chilvers, Clair, 576, 580, 603
Chopra, Deepak, 450
CIA, 38, 49, 52, 56, 190, 308
Ciba Foundation, 334
  Media Resources Service, 292, 341, 596
  Ciba Geigy, 43, 291, 298, 398
Clifmar Associates, 299
Clinical ecology, 74-109, 521, 534
Co-ordinating Committee for Cancer Research, 119-23
Coca, Arthur, 79
Coca-Cola, 43-5, 204
Coeliac Association, 102
Coeliac Society, 164
Coeliac Trust, 162
Colfox, Lady, 510, 529
Committee on the Public Understanding of Science, 227, 232
Committee on the Safety of Medicines, 242-3, 359
Committee for Scientific Investigation of Claims of the Paranormal, 48-59, 192-201, 266, 269, 292-4, 338, 579, 604-5, 615
Commonwealth Fund, 8
Community Research Organisation, 175
Concorde trials (AZT), 248-50, 256-8, 262-3, 314, 359, 372, 374, 377-80, 387, 390-2, 406, 409, 424,

447, 489, 504, 646, 647, 648
Congress for Cultural Freedom, 49, 56
Conning, David, 205, 229
Connolly, Michael, 475-6, 489
Consumers' Association, 145, 341, 346
Coordinating Conference on Health Information, 19-20, 22-3
Coors, Joseph, 37-8
COPUS *see* Committee on the Public Understanding of Science
Council Against Health Fraud *see* Campaign Against Health Fraud
Council for Better Business Bureau, 20
Council for Democratic and Secular Humanism, 193
Council on Medical Education, 7
Crawford, Michael, 153, 629, 631
Crouch, David, Sir, 260-1
CRUSAID, 249, 363, 365, 386, 412, 444, 446
CSICOP *see* Committee for Scientific Investigation of Claims of the Paranormal
CSICP *see* Committee for Scientific Investigation of Claims of the Paranormal
Culbert, Michael L, 491
cyclophosphamide, 327

Dalgliesh, Angus, 252
David, Tim, 108, 273, 287, 556, 558
Davies, Stephen, 138-46, 159, 338, 619-21, 635, 636-7
Davis, Leslie, 413, 441-65, 476
Davis, Nathan Smith, 4
Dawes, Belinda, 620, 635
de Boutlier, Cillian, 632, 635
Deer, Brian, 377-82, 387, 393-4, 402, 406-7
Delatte, Yves, 249, 416, 438, 457, 465, 469-72, 474-7, 479-84, 488-9, 608
Delta Te, 469-72, 474-7, 479-84, 488-9
Delves, Trevor, 151
Department of Health, 240, 252, 256, 299, 360, 478, 488-9, 501,

503, 505, 618, 622
and British Nutrition Foundation, 206
and Campaign Against Health Fraud, 339
and Drug and Therapeutics Bulletin, 145
Medicines Commission, 242-3, 339
Dickerson, John, 150, 158
Disease Free Society Trust, 442, 450
Ditchley Foundation, 221, 231
Dixon, Bernard, 192, 266, 292, 336
Donsbach, Kurt, 25
Dow Chemicals, 42-3
Downing, Damien, 620, 635, 636
Drake, Jeremy, 597
Drug trials, informed consent, 324-33
Duesberg, Peter, 371, 407, 410
Durovic, Stevan, 17

Easton, Douglas, 576, 580, 601
Eaton, Cyrus S, 191
Eli Lilly, 261, 298, 304, 622-3
Ensen, Liza, 560-3
Environmental medicine,
  see clinical ecology;
Environmental Medicine Foundation, 90, 105, 510, 513, 529
Environmental Protection Agency, 41, 86, 98

FACT see Food Additives Campaign Team
FAIR see Family Action Information and Rescue
Fallowfield, Lesley, 331, 584, 602, 604-6
Family Action Information and Rescue, 285
Farthing, Charles, 245, 358, 372, 411
Faulder, Carolyn, 330-3
FDA see Food and Drug Administration
Federal Trade Commission, 14, 16, 20, 22
Ferguson, Anne, 279, 514-5, 559
Ferriman, Annabel, 143, 541
Fischl, Margaret, 246

Fishbein, Morris, 4
Fitzgerald, Julia see Watson, Julia
Fitzwalter, Ray, 521, 530
Flew, Anthony G N, 190-1, 194
Flexner Report, 7-8
Flexner, Abraham, 7, 215
Food Additives Campaign Team, 267-8
'Food and Drink Programme', BBC Television, 616-20, 623-5
Food and Drug Administration, 11-9, 24-6, 96, 111, 244, 257, 271, 498, 638
Food Intolerance Data Bank, 212-3
Food Intolerance and Food Aversion (report), 207-13, 272-3, 279, 284, 515
Food and Veterinary Laboratory Ltd, 301, 306
Forbes, Alex, 125-7, 129, 572
Ford Foundation, 8, 38
Foresight (The Association for the Promotion of Preconceptual Care), 152-9, 631-6
Foster, Anna, 288-90
Foundation for Science and Technology, 234
Frame, Alistair, Sir 221, 477
Franks, Oliver, Sir, 220
Frazer, Alastair, 211
Fredericks, Carlton, 15
Freed, David, 288-90, 554-7
Frontliners, 386, 391, 408, 444, 446, 449

Gallo, Robert, 168, 259
Garfield, Simon, 596-7
Garrison, Omar V, 14-5
Garrow, John, 144-5, 294, 336, 340, 342, 633
Gates, Frederick, 6-7
Gauquelin, Michel, 51-2
Gay Medical Association see Lesbian and Gay Medical Association
Gazzard, Brian, 246, 254, 409-14, 423, 426, 433, 445, 454-5, 461, 476, 480
Geller, Uri, 193, 199
General Foods Corporation, 45
General Medical Council, 108, 418,

422, 427, 441-2, 445, 448, 452-65, 510, 512, 531-2, 536, 545, 558-9, 636

Germanium, 249, 304, 339, 388, 394, 465-9, 472-3, 477-9, 484-9, 619, 624, 627

Gerson, Max, 110-1, 113-4, 130-1, 133

Gibney, Michael, 302-3

Glaxo, 226, 260

Glynn, Tessa, 581-2

Glyoxilide, 498, 503

Godfrey, David, 361

Goodare, Heather, 597-8

Goodman, Sandra, 445, 472-3, 477-9, 484-9

Granada Television, 72, 107-8

'World in Action', 508, 520-70

Grant, Ellen, 157

Gray, Juliet, 207-11, 298

Greenspan, Howard, 412-4, 464

Greer, Rita, 161-5, 610-1, 615-9, 621-8

Griffin, G E, 626

Griffin, J, 299

Griffiths, P, 246

Grossman, Wendy, 197, 201

Guildhay Anti-Sera, 300

Guildhay Laboratory Services, 299-300

Hamilton-Fairley, Gordon, 118-9

Happold, F.H, 281-3

Hare, Francis, 78

HARP see Healing AIDS/ARC Research Project

Harriman, Ed, 314

Hawkins, P, 246

Hayes, Nick, 520-1, 528, 530, 545

Healing AIDS/ARC Research Project, 250

Health foods, 160-5, 340-7

see also Larkhall Natural Health Ltd

HealthWatch, 199, 270, 299, 340, 342, 369, 383, 391, 452, 522, 544, 546, 548, 553, 567, 575-6, 605, 611, 623, 626-7, 632, 634-5, 646, 650

(formerly Campaign Against Health Fraud, q.v.)

Heap, Michael, 201-2

Heinz, 43, 205, 346

Helbert, Matthew, 431-2

Hendricks, Margaret, 634

Henning, Geoff, 412-3

Hennings, Rosemary, 356, 363

Henshaw, David, 575

Herbalife, 25

Herbert, Victor, 26-7, 31-9, 98, 214, 203

Herxheimer, Andrew, 336

Hinks, Tim, 617

HIV, 24, 104, 166-82, 241-58, 356-506, 608-9, 622, 643, 644, 645, 648, 650

see also AIDS; AZT

'The HIV Myth' (book), 313, 370-7

Hodgkinson, Neville, 595

Hoffmann-LaRoche, 25-6

Holford, Patrick, 147-51, 608-9, 611-3, 613-5, 621, 628-30

Homoeopathy, 3-6, 23, 57-8, 63-74

Hook, Sidney, 49-50

Hoskin, Lorraine and Samantha, 517-20, 522, 528-9, 543-53

Howard, Mark, 492, 499

Howard, Toby, 197-8

Hoxsey, H, 110

ICI, 205, 219, 232, 234, 299, 324, 335

ICR see Institute of Cancer Research

ICRF see Imperial Cancer Research Fund

I G Farben, 9, 280

Immuno-augmentative therapy, 33

Imperial Cancer Research Fund, 119, 127, 229, 298, 324

and Bristol Cancer Help Centre, 571-607

and Wellcome Foundation, 576

Inglis, Brian, 281

Ingrams, Richard, 588

INSERM, 63-74, 258, 263

Institute of Cancer Research, 127, 251-2, 335, 445, 448

and The Wellcome Foundation, 251-2, 263, 335, 445-6, 576

Chilvers report, 571-607

Institute of Economic Affairs, 303
Institute of Food Research, Norwich, 298
Institute of Food Technology, 229
Institute for Optimum Nutrition, 148, 150-1, 274-5, 608, 612, 614, 629
International Humanist and Ethical Union, 189-90, 193
Issels, Josef, 110-25

Jariwalla, R, 478
Jarvis, William T, 25-6, 28, 59, 464
Jay, Margaret, Baroness, 364
Jeffries, Donald, 411, 447, 504
Jellicoe, Lord, 229, 234, 259
Johnson, Anne, 246
Jones, Trevor M, 243, 264

Kansas City Committee on Health and Nutrition Fraud and Abuse, 25
Kay, Barry, 510, 558-9, 567
Keel, Aileen, 427, 431, 436-7
Kefauver hearings, 12, 281
Kellogg, 43, 45, 205, 346
Kellogg Foundation, 8
Kennet, Lord, 229, 231
Kenny, Mary, 587
Kidman, Brenda, 127
King, Edward, 386-90
Kingman, Sharon, 586-7
Kingsley, Patrick, 620
Kingsway Public Relations, 261, 356
Kingsway Rowland, 261, 356
Koch, William, 498
Kordel, Lelord, 13, 18
Kurtz, Paul, 48-51, 191-3, 198, 338

laetrile, 18, 21, 27
Lant, Ariel, 345
Larkhall Natural Health Ltd, 160-5, 274, 338, 610-1, 615-9, 621-8
Tandem IQ, 610-1, 615-6
Lawrence, Felicity, 267
Le Fanu, James, 336, 370, 588
Leatherhead Food Research Association, 213
Lederle, 25
Lesbian and Gay Medical Association, 366

Lessof, Maurice, 208, 273, 531, 534-6
Levin, Warren M, 29-37
Lisa, P J, 25
Lissauer, T, 246
Lloyd, Ian, Sir, 231
Lodge-Rees, Elizabeth, 155-6
London Bridge Hospital, see Sharp
London University,
    School of Hygiene and Tropical Medicine, 215, 229, 254, 260-1
    teaching hospitals, funding, 215-6

MacArthur Foundation, 55
McColl, Ian, Lord, 127-8
Macdonald, Ian, 212
McDonalds, 32, 205
McElwain, Timothy, 118, 128, 330, 544
    and Bristol Cancer Help Centre, 576, 579-80, 582-5, 587, 590, 599, 601
McKenna, Andrew, 345-6
Macevoy, Ron, 443-4
Maddox, John, 66, 69-73, 293
MAFF, 84, 86, 204-6, 240, 267-8, 275, 297, 301, 618, 626
    and Campaign Against Health Fraud, 339
Maharishi Ayur-Ved see Ayur-Ved
Mainliners, 364
Mann, Cass, 170-82, 373, 379-406, 615
Mann, Jonathan, 245-6
Mansfield, Peter, 268
Marks, John, 254, 297
Marks, Vincent, 142-3, 150-1, 207, 252, 254, 263, 271, 296, 297-306, 324, 335, 344, 391, 485, 488, 499, 504, 544, 571, 635
    and Bristol Cancer Help Centre, 583, 603-4, 609
    Campaign Against Health Fraud, 290, 334, 340, 346
    and Holford, Patrick, 614-5
Marshall, Stuart, 175-6, 373, 381-3, 385, 389, 392
Marsh, Elizabeth, 490-506
Martin, Simon, 176

MAV (Maharishi Ayur-Ved) *see*
  Ayur-Vedic medicine
MCA *see* Medicines Control Agency
ME *see* myalgic encephalomyelitis
Medical Defence Union, 545-6
Medical Journalists Association, 266,
  291, 596
Medical Research Council, 119-20,
  206, 216, 232, 255-8, 259-63,
  264, 292, 297, 300, 302, 318-24,
  356, 379, 391, 423, 427, 447, 473,
  504, 646, 648, 652
  Committee on AIDS
  Aids Therapeutic Trials Commit-
    tee, 261-3, 410.
Medicines Act, 339, 342, 503
Medicines Commission, 242-3, 339
Medicines Control Agency, 242-3,
  408, 488, 505
Meditel, 407-10
  'AIDS: the Unheard Voices', 375,
    407
  'The AIDS Catch', 407
  'AIDS and Africa', 407
  'AZT – Cause for Concern', 409-
    10
Merck, Sharp, Dohme, 198, 232
Middlesex Hospital, 320
Miller, Joseph, 103, 288, 507
Miller, Melanie, 267
Mills, Roger, 126
Ministry of Agriculture Fisheries and
  Food *see* MAFF
Monoclonal antibodies, HIV, 300
Monro, Jean, 99-109, 155, 157, 507-
  70, 593
MRC *see* Medical Research Council
Mumby, Keith, 288, 555-9
Myalgic encephalomyelitis, 227, 277-
  8, 305, 521, 526, 542, 570

Nader, Ralph, 26
Naessens, Gaston, xiii
Naismith, Donald, 610-1, 615-6, 627
National Aids Trust, 364, 382, 386,
  409, 445, 473, 477
National Council Against Health
  Fraud, xv, 22-9, 47, 98, 198-9,
  213, 335, 630

and AIDS issues, 464
and American Council on Science
  and Health, 26, 41
and Campaign Against Health
  Fraud, 291
and CSICOP, 48, 59
Special Task Forces, 26
National Health Federation, 13, 18
National Health Fraud Conference,
  23
National Health Service, 100-2, 130,
  162, 232, 254-7, 273, 282, 315,
  319, 336, 360, 428, 441, 447, 517-
  8, 522-3, 527, 538, 542, 595, 646,
  647, 648, 650, 651, 653
National Institutes of Health, 9, 69,
  168, 240, 251, 298, 317, 326, 414
National Rivers Authority, 84-5
NCHF *see* National Council Against
  Health Fraud
Neil, Andrew, 380
New Right, 37-41
Newton-Fenbow, Peter, 115-7
Niacin, 619, 622, 624, 627
Nussbaum, Robert, 411
NutraSweet, 205
Nutrition Foundation, 204

O'Donnell, Michael, 334, 336, 456,
  623
Office of Public Service and Science,
  233
Office of Science and Technology,
  225
Office of Technology Assessment,
  230-4, 248
Official Secrets Act, 308-12
Olson, Robert, 45-6
Onoyama, Kaoru, 487-8
Optimum Nutrition, Institute for,
  147-51
O'Sullivan, Jack, 586
OTA *see* Office of Technology
  Assessment
OXAIDS, 182, 385-90

P&SC *see* Parliamentary and Scientific Committee
Panton, Blanche and Jade, 525-7,
  529, 537-40

Parapsychological Association, 54
Parliamentary Office of Science and
    Technology, 229-33, 248
Parliamentary Science and Tech-
    nology Information Foundation,
    231-2
Parliamentary and Scientific Com-
    mittee, 228-34
Partridge, Nick, 366-7, 398, 413-4,
    457-8, 463-4
Pauling, Linus, 30, 35-7, 147, 478,
    629
Payne, Mark, 593
Pearl, Susan, 363, 365
Pearson, David, 107, 272, 287-90,
    337, 383-4, 391-2, 515, 521, 531,
    533, 554-6, 558-9, 567-70
    Campaign Against Health Fraud,
Peart, Stanley, Sir, 227, 229, 250
Pepper hearings, 22, 31
Pepper, Claude, 22-3, 200, 213
Pesticides, toxic effects, 81-8
    see also Alar; 2,4,5-T
Pfeiffer, Carl, 147, 149
Pfizer, 44, 260
Pharmaceutical Advertising Council,
    25
Pilkington, Alastair, Sir, 234, 292
Pilkington, Pat, 125-6
Pinching, Anthony, 262-3, 381, 410-
    3, 419-20, 423, 431, 433, 439,
    444-5, 454-5, 460, 473, 476, 502,
    559
Pink Paper, 179-82, 375-6, 379, 389,
    397-405, 406
Pinn, Stephen, 594
Positively Healthy, 176, 178-81, 373,
    381-97, 411, 449, 477
Positively Women, 364, 367, 408
POST see Parliamentary Office of
    Science and Technology
Powell-Tuck, Jeremy, 336, 340
Pownall, Mark, 334, 339
Prentice, Thompson, 344
Private Patients Plan, 109, 509, 511,
    520
Probiotics, 468, 472-3, 477-9, 484-9
Probus Biomedical, 299-301
Proctor and Gamble, 205
provocation neutralisation, 507-8,

514-5
    see also Monro, Jean, and Mumby,
    Keith
Proxmire, William, 16-7
Prozac, 304, 622-3
PSTIF see Parliamentary Science and
    Technology Information Founda-
    tion

Quatro Biosystems, 301

Radio Immunoassay, 299
Rand vaccine, 18
Randi, James, 50, 52-3, 55, 58, 69-
    73, 195, 198, 293, 521
Randolph, Theron G, 79-80, 89, 104
Raphael, Adam, 324, 330, 333
Rapp, Doris, 104
Rationalist Press Association, 190-6
Rawlins, Dennis, 52
RCP see Royal College of Physicians
RDA see Research Defence Associa-
    tion
Rea, William, 100-1, 109, 159, 507,
    510, 535
Reese, C, 299
Reich, Wilhelm, 110-1
Renner, John, 24-5, 464
Research Defence Association, 227-
    8, 265
Retrovir see AZT
Revell, Andrew, 365, 366-7
Richards, Dick, 127-8
Richards, Tessa, 590
Richmond, Caroline, 198, 264-79,
    287-96, 305, 314, 329-30, 335-8,
    345, 379-80, 404, 462, 516, 521,
    531-2, 534, 544, 554, 556, 559,
    567-9.
Rinkel, Herbert, 79-80
Robb, John, 220
Robens Institute, Surrey University,
    109, 299, 391
Roberts, Gwilym, 164
Rockefeller, 45, 260, 269
Rockefeller, David, 221
Rockefeller Foundation, 8-10, 16-8,
    37-8, 55, 215-6, 220, 262, 266
Rockefeller, John D, 5-6
Rockefeller, John Jnr, 6-8

Rockefeller, Nelson, 96
Rooke, Denis, Sir, 228
Rosenberg, S, 418
Rossall, Sheila, 99-101, 513, 531, 534-5
Ross, Nick, 294, 334, 336-7, 339, 520, 544
Rowe, Albert, 78-9
Rowland Worldwide, 261, 356
Royal College of Physicians, 206-7, 272, 289, 326, 455, 515, 559, 567-8, 570
Royal College of Surgeons, 229, 442-3
Royal Pharmaceutical Society of Great Britain, 229, 231, 456
Royal Society, 226-7
RPA see Rationalist Press Association
Rudd, Maureen and William, 513, 522-5, 529, 537-40

Saatchi and Saatchi, 261, 356
Sabbagh, Karl, 198
saccharin, 44, 46
Sandoz Pharmaceuticals, 298
Sara Scaife Foundation, 42
Scaife, Richard, 37-8
Schauss, Alexander, 468, 629
Science Research Councils, 228
scientology, 53, 201
Septrin, 222
Sever, Peter, 250
Sharp, James, 373, 379, 415-41, 476
Shawa-Denko, 622
Shawcross, Lord, 122
Sheard, Tim, 592-3, 599-600
Shenton, Joan, 375, 407-10
Shepherd, Charles, 277, 341-2, 613
Shepperd, Alfred, Sir, 234-5
Sheridan, James, 500
Sherwood, Martin, 361, 365, 378
Sikora, Karol, 583, 591
Simonton, Carl and Stephanie, 110
The Skeptic, 198-201
Sloan Foundation, 9
Smith, Ian, 604-5
Smith, Joseph W G, 261
Smith, Mike, 483
Smithers, David, Sir, 118-9, 122-3, 125
Sopcak, Ed, 500, 505

Sollis, Kelvin, 181, 398-400
Sonnabend, Joseph, 168, 377
Speas Foundation, 25
Spiegel breast cancer study, 592-3
Stare, Frederick, 43, 45
Sterling, John, 477
Stewart, Alan, 620
Stewart, Walter, 69-70
Stoppard, Miriam, 108, 615-6
Sugar Association, 45
Sugar Bureau, 47, 259, 302
Sultan, Jabar, 415-41, 448, 476
Sutton, Ron, 361
Svoboda, Vladimir, 500, 597
Swann, Lord, 220
Syntex, 25-6, 616

T cell function, 169
Tamoxifen, 324, 327, 329, 335
Tandem IQ, 610-1, 615-6, 627
Tate and Lyle, 259
Taylor, Andrew, 299, 391, 614, 624-5, 635
Taylor, H Doyle, 19-20
Taylor, John, 193-5
Taylor, Lorraine, 563 - 70
television programmes, 'Thames Action', 632-6
  see also BBC; Granada; Channel 4,
Terrence Higgins Trust, 319, 364-6, 386, 394, 406, 408, 411-2, 414, 442, 449, 451, 453, 455, 457, 463, 465, 473, 501
Thalidomide, 377
Therapeutic Antibody Centre, 300
Thomas, Evelyn, 324, 326-30
Thomas, Gordon, 117, 123
Threshold Foundation, 283-4
Tobias, Jeffrey, 331-2, 583-4, 589, 603
transcendental meditation, 442-3, 447
Trilateral Commission, 96, 221-2
tryptophan, 304, 619, 622-3, 627
Turner, Paul, 459-60
2,4,5-T pesticide, 240

UK Skeptics, 198-202, 287, 521, 604-5
Unilever, 298

Uniroyal Chemical Company, 44

vaccines, whooping cough, 222-3
Vane, John, Sir, 227, 336, 340
Vaughan, Gerard, Sir, 229, 231-2
vitamins, 17-8, 340-7
  and IQ, 164, 346
  and nutrition, 132-7
  vitamin B1, 136
  vitamin C, 478,489
  see also health foods; Larkhall
    Natural Health Ltd; Stephen
    Davies and British Society for
    Nutritional Medicine

Waldegrave, William, 99, 233, 534
Walford, John, 334-5
Walker, Caroline, 267, 269
Ward, Neil, 151, 158, 635
Warrell, D A, 262
Watney, Simon, 367, 400
Watson, Julia (Julia Fitzgerald), 493-500
Weir, William, 447
Weissenberg, Sidney, 18-9
Weiss, Robin, Dr, 251-2, 263, 335, 445-6
Wellcome Foundation, 215-23, 226, 233, 239-63, 266-7, 314, 319-20, 324, 335, 355-68, 374, 377, 385, 404, 406, 408-9, 424, 435, 443-5, 449, 462, 472, 501, 506, 631, 644, 646, 647, 648
  Association of Medical Research Charities, 229, 253, 292, 335, 631
  and Campaign Against Health Fraud, 339
  Corporate Donations Executive, 361
  and Parliamentary Office of Science and Technology, 229-33, 248
  see also AZT; Burroughs Wellcome

Wellcome Institute for the History of Medicine, 253, 450, 462, 531
  Unit of the History of Medicine, London University, 266-7
Wellcome Trust, 216-7, 226, 229, 232, 235, 254, 262, 267, 335,462
Weller, Ian, 262-3, 320-2, 372, 378, 380, 473, 477
Wessely, Simon, 334
Westminster Communications Group, 261, 357
Wetzler, Michael, 582
Whelan, Elizabeth, 28, 32, 42-5, 214, 275
Whitehead, Tony, 365, 394
whooping cough vaccine, 222
Wiewel, Frank, 33
Wilkins, Janice, 580-1
Wilson, A N, 625
Wiltsher, Anne, 241
Wolpert, Lewis, 227
Wood, Barry, 520-2, 524-30, 540, 542-3
Woodward, Robert, 161-5, 610-1, 615-8, 621-8
'World in Action', see Granada
World Sugar Research Organisation, 212, 229
Wright, Jonathan, xiii
Wujastyk, Dominik, 450, 462

Zidovudine see AZT
Zovirax, 219, 356

The Chemical Empire
Chemicals, pollution, biohazard and human illness

The following is an outline of Martin Walker's current project: if you feel that you would like to contribute to it, by sending references, books, papers, articles, research materials, offering personal case history material, or funding, please write to Martin Walker, c/o Slingshot Publications, BM Box 8314, London WC1N 3XX, England.

This book is an attempt to draw together present knowledge about a wide range of pollutants and human health. The book will be in three parts: chemicals, pollution and biohazard.

Each health-damaging pollution will be looked at historically and analytically and each illustrated by in-depth case histories. Each section of the book will focus, in part, upon the effects of pollution upon the human reproductive system, the embryonic and small child.

Although this may appear to be a 'depressing' and 'negative' book, its primary purpose is to document, in a popular way, a 'field' of twentieth century health damage. This is an essential prerequisite to the acceptance and development of new and more progressive forms of preventative, natural health practice.

In order to ensure that the book does not become a text book, the in-depth case histories will deal with a variety of ways in which people and groups have campaigned for compensation and changes in regulations. This will make the book a valuable resource for anyone who wants to campaign against environmental health damage.

PART I
Chemicals

A history of the chemical industry : Concentrating on the growth of the industry between 1900 and 1945, the development of chemical warfare and the extensive use of pesticides following the second world war.

Food and chemicals : The addition of non-nutritive substances to food has become increasingly common since the start of the industrial revolution. Today the public is largely ignorant of the array and type of chemical additives in food, principally because, despite labelling, manufacturers have fought long and hard to mystify the subject.

Animal husbandry and food : Looks at the way animals bred for food are affected and treated by chemicals and pharmaceuticals.

Pesticides, herbicides and insecticides : This chapter will pay specific attention to the use of pesticides throughout the Commonwealth countries and British colonies after the second world war and to their contemporary use in developing countries, which are increasingly supplying cheap food for the developed world.

Pharmaceuticals : The major iatrogenic illness-precipitating drugs will be looked at, as well as those widely used drugs and treatments which have a deleterious effect on human health in a less noticeable way.

Working with chemicals : It has long been recognised that workers in certain industries suffer specific work-related illnesses: in the last twenty years sensitivity to some old work-related illnesses has increased; at the same time, new ones have developed. This section will look at such subjects as the recent campaign against some industrial paints.

Domestic chemicals : Thousands of new chemicals are developed every week and many of these end up in the home. The health effects of such chemicals are sometimes not revealed for many years.

PART II
Pollution

A history of pollution : A historical overview of pollution, concentrating firstly on the period following the industrial revolution in Britain and then upon the present situation in the developed world, paying particular attention to eastern Europe.

Air pollution : Serious cases of asthma and other respiratory illnesses have trebled over the last ten years. A number of experts have suggested that the causes of this increase can be found in a general weakening of the immune system and the poor quality of air.

Sea pollution : Britain deposits large quantities of raw sewage straight into the sea. Some of Britain's sea-side resorts are now so polluted that swimming can lead to illness. The British coast is also a haven for off-shore chemical dumping which is beginning to have an effect upon the health of fish and other sea creatures.

Freshwater pollution : Many of the chemicals used on land eventually find their way into the water table; our fresh water is poisoned by effluents from factories, residues from pesticides and even de-icing chemicals from the wings of aeroplanes.

Land pollution : Land dumping, in-fills and the burial of toxic waste are increasingly serious problems in a de-regulated society. Apart from the obvious despoiling of the countryside, no one knows what the long-term effects of this waste dumping will be.

Electro-magnetic pollution : There is growing evidence that different frequencies of electro-magnetism have a degenerative effect upon the human body. As society depends more and more upon 'hidden energy', there is increasingly a need to understand its health status implications.

PART III

Biohazard

A history of biotoxicity : Although this field might appear to be relatively new, humans have always suffered illnesses following the consumption of ill-prepared or unfit biological substances. The difference between the past and the present is that while in the past illnesses might result from accidents, the introduction of biohazardous material into the food chain now takes place on an organised mass scale in relative secrecy.

The preparation of animals for human consumption : Apart from the matters to do with 'animal welfare' discussed in Part I, the preparation and processing of food which is of animal origin are continual threats to human health: from eggs which spread salmonella, to offal which might harbour viral illnesses and pathogenic organisms.

Vaccines : The introduction into young children's bodies of relatively lethal viral material has been of concern throughout the last century to a small but vociferous group of campaigners. Ignored by the orthodox medical world and the pharmaceutical companies, these organisations claim that vaccines decisively weaken the immune system and can bring to the subject the very illnesses against which they are meant to be protecting.

Medicines : Some medicines are prepared using biological material from humans or animals. Recent publicity has been given to the use of human growth hormone treatment, a constituent part of which preparation was taken from the pituitary glands of dead bodies. It was later suspected that the remedy had introduced Creutzfeld-Jakob disease to the patients.

Allergy and the immune system : Serious allergic responses have had growing publicity over the last five years. The death of a number of young people from anaphylactic shock has provoked campaigning groups to demand more exact food labelling. Many orthodox medical practitioners, however, still fail to recognise allergic conditions.

Nutrient deficiency illnesses : While many orthodox doctors claim that there are no nutrient deficiency illnesses in the modern developed world, others claim that processed and denatured food has lead to a new series of illnesses brought about by lack of certain vitamins and minerals.